THE INSTITUTION FOR

SOCIAL AND POLICY STUDIES

AT YALE UNIVERSITY

THE YALE ISPS SERIES

DOUGLAS W. RAE

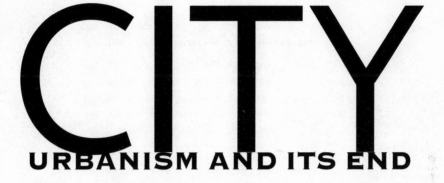

CITY

URBANISM AND ITS END

YALE UNIVERSITY PRESS · NEW HAVEN AND LONDON

Designed by Nancy Ovedovitz and set in Scala type by The Composing Room of Michigan, Inc. Printed in the United States of America by R. R. Donnelley, Harrisonburg, Virginia.

Library of Congress Cataloging-in-Publication Data

Rae, Douglas W.
City : urbanism and its end / Douglas W. Rae.
p. cm. — (Yale ISPS series)
Includes bibliographical references and index.
ISBN 0-300-09577-5 (cloth : alk. paper)
1. New Haven (Conn.)—Politics and government—20th century.
2. New Haven (Conn.)—Economic conditions—20th century.
3. New Haven (Conn.)—Social conditions—20th century.   4. City and town life—Connecticut—New Haven—History—20th century.
5. Industrialization—Social aspects—Connecticut—New Haven—History—20th century.   6. Urban renewal—Connecticut—New Haven—History—20th century.   I. Title.   II. Series.
F104.N657R34 2003
974.6'8043—dc21   2003009974

A catalogue record for this book is available from the British Library.

The paper in this book meets the guidelines for permanence and durability of the Committee on Production Guidelines for Book Longevity of the Council on Library Resources.

10 9 8 7 6 5 4 3 2 1

For my favorite citizens of New Haven:
Ellen, Hugh, Katie, Kim, and their families,
even as they stray to the canyons of Manhattan and Colorado, and
even into the swamplands of New Jersey and Cambridge

The trust of a city street is formed over time from many, many little public sidewalk contacts. It grows out of people stopping by at the bar for a beer, getting advice from the grocer and giving advice to the newsstand man, comparing opinions with other customers at the bakery and nodding hello to the two boys drinking pop on the stoop, eyeing the girls while waiting to be called for dinner, admonishing the children, hearing about a job from the hardware man and borrowing a dollar from the druggist, admiring the new babies and sympathizing over the way a coat faded. Customs vary: in some neighborhoods people compare notes on their dogs; in others they compare notes on their landlords. Most of it is ostensibly utterly trivial but the sum is not trivial at all. The sum of such casual, public contact at a local level—most of it fortuitous, most of it associated with errands, all of it metered by the person concerned and not thrust upon him by anyone—is a feeling for the public identity of people, a web of public respect and trust, and a resource in time of personal or neighborhood need. The absence of this trust is a disaster to a city street. Its cultivation cannot be institutionalized.

Jane Jacobs, 1961

CONTENTS

CONTENTS

PREFACE

City: Urbanism and Its End pursues the course of urban history across the boundaries that separate political science from sociology, geography, economics, and history itself. The book's origin, however, goes back to a collision between academic political science and the actual politics of one city. In January 1990, I left the chairmanship of the Yale political science department to become chief administrative officer (CAO) of the city of New Haven, Connecticut, under its first African-American mayor, John Daniels. Over the eighteen months spent in that job, I came to see the city in a more complicated way than before. I was often, in fact, puzzled by the oddness of fit between my thoughts on urban politics and power, and the things I found myself doing from day to day. Dazed by the rush of work, I had no time to theorize about the city while I was working for it. On my return to Yale in the fall of 1991, I began trying to make sense of my experience in City Hall.

I had spent two decades as a colleague of Robert Dahl, whose *Who Governs?* was the best known-work on the subject. In that justly famous book, Dahl had focused on the control of city government decisions. He had concluded that power, understood as control over those decisions, was widely shared among different groups. Moreover, he elegantly described a historical "transition from the old pattern of oligarchy based on cumulative inequalities to a new pattern based upon dispersed inequalities." Raymond Wolfinger's *Politics of Progress*, based on direct observation during the administration of Mayor Richard C. Lee, deepened and (mostly) confirmed Dahl's analysis. Along with Nelson Polsby's book on community power studies, *Community Power and Political Theory,* this body of work came to be known as pluralism, or the pluralist school. I was familiar with the elaborate methodological and often ideological debate surrounding this work, and I had contributed modestly to the confusion with one paper of my own.[1]

The irresistible fact, which came into focus very slowly for me, was that city government is *itself* a weak player in a larger system of power.[2] The problems faced by city officials have to do with making the most of the city's small (and fragile) power base in dealing with players as varied as airline schedulers, street-corner entrepreneurs, union leaders, neighborhood potentates, racial spokesmen, bond rating agencies, bankers, public housing tenant leaders, criminal gangs, real estate developers, insurance underwriters, and government agencies at state and federal levels. Even "forces" as ineffable as popular culture—from its veneration of green lawns on quiet streets to its hypnotic fascination with firearms—form part of the power environment in which city government must operate. City decisions that work effectively in any but the most trivial cases are explicitly or implicitly complemented and supported by decisions taken outside City Hall.[3] The interesting questions in local government all therefore turn on chains of decisions *outside* the confines of City Hall.

If ever there was a moment to reinforce the weakness of city government, it occurred in the early months of 1990 in New Haven. The city had elected its first black mayor precisely when it was experiencing its worst fiscal crisis since the 1930s. By the time John Daniels was sworn in, something like a $20 million hole had appeared in the city budget, helping to explain the decision by incumbent Biagio DiLieto not to seek reelection the previous fall. A regional recession was also in progress, making it even more difficult to make ends meet in city government. Crime, and the fear of crime, were two problems, not just one problem—and both were out of control. By my third week as CAO it was clear that several hundred city workers would have to be laid off unless we could obtain remarkable concessions from at least four distinct unions that represented parts of our four-thousand-person workforce. Several top union spokesmen were intransigent, and many of the leaders showed considerable indifference to the fates of (very junior, often black or Hispanic) people who would lose their jobs in a layoff under the unions' seniority rules. Layoffs were no threat to senior leadership, and we thus had to carry some of them out. Meanwhile, overtime spending was running hundreds of thousands of dollars above budget. Restricting overtime spending was made difficult by an accumulation of work rules designed to protect opportunities for overtime: many workers had home mortgages based on incomes with thousands of dollars in overtime built in. My responsibilities included operations in mainline departments—police, fire, public works, parks, libraries—and budgetary control for those, plus education. With a record high rate of violent crime, and an administration committed to improved (and labor-intensive) community-based police services, it was hard to press down on that large budget. In the case of education, where enrollment-driven state mandates for spending were a fact of life, we failed at first even to cut the rate of increase in spending. When I hinted at the idea of diminished fire facilities, a former mayor called the next day at 6 A.M., quoted the local paper's account of my idea, and advised bluntly: "Don't fuck with my firehouses, Doug, my boy." For related reasons, spending on parks and public works was almost as hard to cut deeply. The work was better than any diet for my corpulent midsection: in the first six months of the job I lost forty pounds, yet the city achieved only a modest reduction in its spending.

We were in deeper trouble on the income side. The wholly inadequate cash flow that lay behind our fiscal crisis was generated in large measure by local property taxes. Those taxes were already high enough to accelerate a continued flight to the suburbs—a flight that had begun in the 1920s and generated a net decline in population after 1950. Businesspeople looked on in horror at a city government, already charging higher taxes than any of its nearby suburban rivals, announcing diminished service delivery due to layoffs. Paying more for less sounded to them like a bad idea. Vast portions of the city were tax-exempt—Yale, the hospitals, the churches, a remarkably extensive public housing stock—and the city received only partial compensation from the state government's PILOT program (payment in lieu of taxes). A majority of the city government's own workers, including several of the union leaders, were living outside the city, paying taxes to our suburban competitors with their central city salaries. Tax delinquencies were climbing beyond 6 percent, and it was easy to envision a death spiral: lower revenues forcing increased tax rates, these in turn causing still lower collection rates and forcing still higher rates, and so on. Ever-vigilant functionaries in the New York bond-rating agencies sensed our trouble and acted to protect investors by downgrading the city's credit rating, thereby increasing our borrowing costs and threatening to accelerate our death spiral.

In the middle of all that, power over the decisions of city government seemed less valuable than power over economic and social outcomes. It was one thing to control the outputs of city government (putting qualified and well-paid teachers in classrooms, for example) and a very different thing to achieve the intended result (students learning what they need to learn). Years later, back in my Yale study, I would formalize a distinction between powers of govern*ment* and powers of govern*ance*, giving two very different meanings to Dahl's question "Who Governs?": "Who controls the policy decisions of city government?" or "Who governs those changes which matter most critically to the people and institutions located within that city?" Only if city government itself was a very strong power player were these two questions at all close to being one and the same. And, most emphatically, city government didn't seem to be a strong player when looked at from my City Hall desk in 1990 and 1991.

Try a real example. "How best to deploy each eight-hour police patrol shift?" is a question of government. How you make that precious shift as effective as possible as part of a process that actually protects citizens against violent crime is a governance issue. As city officials, we were driven over and over again to focus on tactical questions of government such as "Do you have cops walk beats which will maximize their visibility to citizens and potential criminals, or do you have them walk beats where they are most likely to detect and intervene in actual crimes?" On reflection, that is a harder question than it at first seems, and we often opted to maximize visibility at the expense of intervention.[4] Whichever tactical choice you make, your power to achieve the best result in crime prevention *depends largely on decisions taken by thousands of people not directly connected to city government.* Signaling to those thousands of others, in the hope of influencing their decisions, becomes a vital objective. In 1990 and 1991, I was wholly preoccupied with practical particulars, scores of them in each working day, and far too busy to reflect on the government-governance gap.

I have spent much of my time since leaving city government in July 1991 trying to understand the maelstrom of urban governance. Only when I began to press far into the urban past, into an era when the gap between government and governance was narrower, did I begin to see what had happened to put the city where it was in 1990. The long, slow process of urban development had begun with a series of large capital investments made in the late 1840s and had accelerated up through World War I. Over that period New Haven and other similar cities were on the leading edge of capitalist development. What we were dealing with in the 1990s had begun to take shape in about 1910–17, during the last period of centered urban growth the city would experience. For this reason I ended up devoting roughly half of this book to a case study of conditions when the city was at its peak, during the mayoral administration of one Frank Rice, who was sworn in on January 1, 1910, and served almost until his death on January 18, 1917.

Part I is a reconstruction of New Haven as it was at the height of its urbanism.

For the moment, let "urbanism" stand for patterns of private conduct and decision-making that by and large make the successful governance of cities possible even when City Hall is a fairly weak institution. I have selected the years 1910–17 as my window on urbanism. Might, say, 1905–15, or 1908–17, have served just as well? I am sure they would have. But I found in Mayor Rice an interesting and sympathetic companion whose efforts to manage the city's government provide a revealing and sensible narrative background for the work. Chapter 2 is the story of centering industrial development in New Haven from the 1840s, when American capitalism began to take on its eventual shape, up to 1910, when Mayor Rice's little period begins. Chapter 3 sets out a sort of social geography of business in the city during the Rice years, beginning with the evening of August 24, 1910, when many business notables and their spouses (mostly wives, but some husbands) gathered for a festive evening in celebration of one couple's twenty-fifth wedding anniversary. I pay special attention to the thick fabric of tiny stores that spread across the city's neighborhoods with a density that seems remarkable in retrospect. These stores were, I argue, only partly in the business of selling groceries: they were also governing sidewalks and the people who walked them. In Chapter 4, I set forth a geographic analysis of residential life: Where did factory operatives, laborers, professor, clerks, CEOs, and schoolteachers live? How did neighborhood boundaries take shape around economic classes in the city of that era? How might these habits of residence have influenced the leadership structure of the city? Chapter 5 surveys the thick layer of organizations that lay between the business firms or other employers and strictly private life. From the Washington Glees football club to the Colored Masons, from Bikur Cholim B'nai Abraham temple to St. Donato's parish, from Società Marineria Italiana di Mutuo Soccorso to the Friendly Sons of St. Patrick—hundreds of organizations provided vast opportunities for civic participation, for the formation of social capital, and for good fun in its striking variety. The "civic fauna" of such organizations turns out to have been more open-textured and democratic than I at first expected, and this seems to have been important in the governance of New Haven. In Chapter 6, about politics and government, I sketch a portrait of Frank Rice's "sidewalk republic." This was an honest, well-intentioned government, but not a particularly farsighted or nimble one, to say the least. But it was, so far as we can tell, adequate to the felt needs of the period—a period in which riches of industrial development, retail trade, residential life, and civic activity supplied a kind of urbanism that considerably reduced the demand for governmental intervention in ordinary life.

Urbanism of the kind that did so much to support City Hall in Frank Rice's time would come to an end over the course of the twentieth century, and this is the subject of Part II. In Chapters 7 and 8, I chronicle and analyze the shifting dynamic of city life from roughly 1917 to the 1950s. This is a complex story—far too complex to sum up here. But a few major themes can be listed:

- the shift of control over key manufacturing plants from locally grounded firms to national corporations;
- the "urban thrombosis" brought on by massive reliance on automobile transport in the absence of necessary parking and arterial thoroughfares in the city;
- the accelerating development of residential suburbs;
- the erosion of neighborhood retailing, particularly with the arrival of major chain stores;
- the privatization of leisure with the broadening range of broadcast entertainment and recorded music;
- the continued stability of certain key civic institutions, such as the Catholic parishes;
- the growth of Yale University and its increasing detachment from local loyalties;
- the accelerating die-off among fraternal and sororal organizations in the city;
- the replacement of amateur-led organizations with professionally staffed service providers;
- the arrival of African-Americans in large numbers, synchronized with the decline in industrial employment, which had been the major magnet;
- a 1937 New Deal study of New Haven which classified most of its neighborhoods as grade C and grade D for mortgage purposes, and set the stage for the redlining of central city neighborhoods;
- the early development of large-scale low-income housing projects in New Haven;
- the emergence of a regional hierarchy with old-fashioned urban neighborhoods on the bottom rung.

As these two chapters make clear, the city was by 1950 a very different place from what it had been in 1917—and a much harder one to make work. The last part of Chapter 8, written by the late Honorable Richard C. Lee (mayor, 1954–70), chronicles life in a working-class ward during the late Depression years, when Lee was first elected to the Board of Aldermen. This story, titled "Snow Tickets," evokes the older habits of urbanism that came under so much pressure at mid-century, and it introduces the politician who would dramatically attempt to renew the city when he was elected mayor.

Chapters 9 and 10 are about the Dick Lee era, urban renewal, and the realization that the city was not going to return to its former glory even with massive federally funded intervention. The first of these chapters tells the story of a growing rivalry between Irish and Italian groups in city politics, and of Lee's eventual uneasy marriage of the two groups in the Democratic Party. It also tells how Lee came to be an advocate of urban renewal, and how the idea of the "slumless city" emerged from his early career. Chapter 10 tells the story of Lee as mayor. In this period Lee overcame many of the limitations of city government by creating parallel institutions, funded externally and managed by technocrats whose aims and loyalties had nothing to do with city politics. His urban renewal effort was run from what he called the Kremlin, dominated by Ed Logue and other brilliant, often Yale-educated figures who were able to operate almost entirely outside normal political constraints. Here the brave strokes of physical renewal, their social costs, and some of their unintended consequences are set forth.

Urban renewal failed to forestall the end of urbanism. Population (especially affluent white population) and real estate investments and taxable assets flew faster and faster toward suburbs, and surplus housing stock was left behind in the central city. Poverty, concentrated public housing, educational failures, and crime came to dominate New Haven in the 1970s and early 1980s. Civic disengagement—especially in volunteer-led organizations—announced itself. Small-scale neighborhood retailing, once so vital, fell off sharply in the years after Lee. No longer is central place economically privileged against the regional periphery. No longer is City Hall able to rely on the governing functions of a fine-grained civic fauna, or of neighborhood retailing. No longer is the office of mayor an object of intense political competition. No longer is it possible to chart the city's best future without thinking about a far larger regional context, reaching at least as far as Manhattan and the surrounding boroughs of New York City. And, yet, for all that, there is a future for New Haven and cities like it. These are the subjects of Chapters 11 and 12. The former provides massive evidence for the end of urbanism as it accumulated in the 1960s, 1970s, and early 1980s, and the latter tells the story of the central city left to cope with the end of urbanism.

In the years from about 1910 to about 1980 New Haven illustrates the broad course of urban change shared by many American cities. Most of the urban centers east of St. Louis appear to have gone through many of the events I chart in New Haven. Some—Chicago, Cleveland, New Orleans, Indianapolis, Pittsburgh, Minneapolis–St.Paul, Detroit, Boston, Philadelphia, Buffalo, and even the outer boroughs of New York—paint fairly similar pictures on far larger canvases. Others—Providence, Syracuse, Rochester, Camden, Newark, Wilming-ton, Dayton, South Bend, Hartford, Bridgeport, Worcester, Springfield, and Al-bany—represent variants of the same story on about the same scale as New Haven. Each of course has thousands of entirely local turns and twists, but all, broadly speaking, have faced the end of urbanism in much the same sense that New Haven has. This book therefore invites comparison with these and many other American places. It is not in the main a comparative study, because I have devoted so much of my research to movements within the local region.

Since about 1980, New Haven has found itself on a course of adaptation rare among American cities. Its only important large export "industry" was by then a university, and Yale haltingly is beginning to understand itself as the dominant economic and civic institution in New Haven. Five Yale presidents have moved the institution away from its insular habits—Kingman Brewster (1963–77), A. Bartlett Giamatti (1977–86), Benno Schmidt (1986–92), Howard Lamar (acting 1992–93), and Richard C. Levin (1993–present). Five mayors have jousted and negotiated with them: Bartholomew Guida (1970–76), Frank Logue (1976–80), Biagio DiLieto (1980–90), John Daniels (1990–94), and John DeStefano (1994–present). There are a few partly parallel stories, but each has a major point of difference. For example, Providence is like New Haven in being a post-industrial city, yet it has state government along with Brown University, Rhode Island School of Design, and Providence College (to say nothing of its felonious former mayor Buddy Cianci). Ann Arbor is dominated by the University of Michigan but never was an industrial city. Austin never was an industrial town, and it has a great deal going on in advanced technology outside the University of Texas. Universities in cities like Pittsburgh, Philadelphia, Syracuse, South Bend, Durham, and Rochester inhabit formerly industrial cities, but none occupies anything like the central role that Yale has in New Haven today. The closest par-allel to New Haven in recent decades is perhaps Oxford, England. Both were in-dustrial cities, both are now dominated by world-famous universities. The emer-gence of a sort of "blue republic" in New Haven is a fascinating story, but it is a story for the next book. This book is about urbanism and its demise, told with the specificity and particularity of the city I know best, but told with a thought to the other places that have written broadly similar histories of their own.

Urbanism charts a time-bound story, one in which it is possible to understand later episodes only if you first have some inkling about earlier ones. Thus, history became the first of four disciplines to which I would begin accumulating debt. I have tried to respect the historians' craft, even after a lifetime squandered on social science. I have focused on some periods—the 1840s, 1910–17, the late Depression years, the Lee years, and the aftermath of urban redevelopment—at the expense of others. For this I can simply ask the reader to judge whether I have chosen episodes that explain and illuminate. The other three disciplines from which I have borrowed heavily are economics, sociology, and geography. The central thread of the story is the jolting path of change in capitalist economies. This process of "creative destruction" is particularly interesting to the least mobile, least agile organizations in a capitalist democracy. Most American cities are sitting ducks, unable to move out of the way when change comes roaring at them. Consequently, the story of capital organizing and reorganizing itself lies at the core of urban history, especially in the bare-knuckles environment of twentieth-century American capitalism. Social organization, never easily detached in practice from the economy, turns out to be important, too. The city's governability is to a considerable extent dependent on its civic life—on events out in the neighborhoods, in clubs, churches, temples, sporting fields, saloons, ethnic groups, mutual aid societies. What keeps streets safe and civilized—even more than good police work—is out in the civic fauna, far from city government. Changes in civic life therefore turn out to be more than a little important to the governability of any city. So I have made extensive use of sociology, especially of the work being done by Robert Putnam, Theda Skocpol, Peter Dobkin Hall, Gerald Gamm, and others affiliated with Harvard University's "civic engagement" project.

Finally, geography turns out to be important. Its importance runs from very gross, macro patterns to the very smallest, finest-textured spatial differences. Thus, for example, New Haven is one of several dozen U.S. cities that have experienced broadly similar arcs of growth and decline. Examples include St. Louis, Baltimore, Hartford, Providence, Philadelphia, Syracuse, and Detroit. All are lowland, slow-water cities, which capital favored in one era and not in a later one. That story is partly economic history, partly geography. At a much finer level, I remember noticing in my days in city government that crime and other key features of urban life showed remarkable respect for invisible boundaries. Thus, for example, violent crime was a daily event on one side of Prospect Street, yet a single incident on the other side was a startling phenomenon. Similarly, economic development followed geographic grooves at sidewalk level—strings of thriving shops along one street, row upon row of failure and marginality on others. For these reasons the reader will find dozens of maps, some of them down to the level of individual households, to illustrate the changing spatial organization of the city and its neighborhoods.

The concept of "urbanism and its end" arose first from my slow discovery of my most fundamental discontent with the old community power debate in political science. Both the advocates of pluralism and most of their critics were concerned primarily with the power-wielders, who controlled decisions *in* city government. The limitation of this analysis is fundamental if city government itself is a weak player in a larger system. As urbanism waned, the institutions of city government became weaker arenas of power. Focused on the city of 1990, at first, then, the end of urbanism meant the end of thinking about city government as a pivotal and more or less autonomous power system.

The second and more important meaning of the phrase has to do with a historical story of urban centering, and its ending. In what I'll call an "urbanist" setting, even very weak, quite rigid city government is consistent with the well-governed city—because other sectors of local society accomplish so many tasks of governance so well. People crowd toward the city core in looking for places to locate manufacturing plants, housing, stores, churches and temples. Jobs are plentiful, dollars flow. The organizations that plant themselves in city soil encourage structured cooperation on city streets, monitor behavior on sidewalks which are beyond the direct vigilance of police officers, and in countless ways nurture "social capital" in city life. As the research progressed, I concluded that the urbanist era in New Haven reached something of a peak around the time of World War I and announced its own end emphatically in the Vietnam War era. When, for all the heroic exertions of urban renewal under the leadership of Dick Lee, the city suffered the summer riots of 1967, Lee surrendered his office in 1969, and the city and Yale set upon one another in the early 1970s, the urbanist era was nearly done. By the fall of 1979, when the dreadful strike at Winchester Repeating Arms more or less ended the city's role as a mass-manufacturing center, the end of urbanism was at hand. I carry the narrative up to the 1979 strike and the decision of Mayor Frank Logue to seize the plant in the name of public safety. This dramatic assertion of City Hall's authority met with summary rejection in court, and the strike precipitated the loss of the city's major remaining industrial base. I carry a few major strands of economic and social and political change right up to the present in order to show what is meant by urbanism's ending.

The third and last resonance of the term "urbanism" attaches to the vibrant recent movement that announced itself as the New Urbanism. Centering especially on the Miami design studio of Andres Duany and Elizabeth Plater-Zyberk, this movement seeks to recapture the look, feel, and function of a more humane era. New Urbanist design encourages front porches, carefully rendered sidewalks, and scores of other details that evoke what this movement means by "urbanism." The movement presents the intriguing hope that some of the strengths I find in the old urbanism may live again. I am, of course, less confident about the central functions of urban design than are some New Urbanist thinkers, but the challenge is an interesting one, and the shared objectives are inspiring.

I apologize to colleagues in these fields—history, economics, geography, sociology, even architecture and planning—for whatever sins of ignorance I have committed in using their work and the work of their predecessors. And I am grateful for the quality of work on which they allowed me to rely. I apologize to my colleagues in the Daniels administration both for the numerous deficiencies in my performance on the field of battle in 1990–91 and for the timing of my analysis of the city's problems nearly a decade after they left office in 1994. With that, I will not further delay the reader.

CHAPTER 1

CREATIVE DESTRUCTION AND THE AGE OF URBANISM

Industrial mutation . . . incessantly revolutionizes the economic structure from within, incessantly destroying the old, incessantly creating a new one. This process of Creative Destruction is the essential fact about capitalism. It is what capitalism consists in and what every capitalist concern has got to live in.—JOSEPH SCHUMPETER, 1946

All fixed, fast-frozen relations, with their train of ancient and venerable prejudices and opinions, are swept away, all new formed ones become antiquated before they can ossify. All that is solid melts into air. . . . During its rule of scarce one hundred years, [capitalism] has created more massive and more colossal productive forces than have all preceding generations together. —KARL MARX AND FRIEDRICH ENGELS, 1847

The old nations of the earth creep on at a snail's pace; the Republic thunders past with the rush of the express. The United States, the growth of a single century, has already reached the foremost rank among nations, and is destined soon to out-distance all others in the race. In population, in wealth, in annual savings, and in public credit; in freedom from debt, in agriculture, and in manufactures, America already leads the civilized world.—ANDREW CARNEGIE, 1886

An old customer ambles into a downtown New Haven shop looking for a small roll of tape, yet leaves with two larger rolls and a heavy-duty dispenser: "Seven dollars' worth, I give it to you for six." Joseph Perfetto is still a businessman after seven decades on the job. He needs to be good, because New England Typewriter & Stationery is under water. As we talk, rain drips into a large coffee can on the table between us, the last of a storm ended the night before. Rust on the can's rim suggests this isn't its first tour of emergency duty catching water. Rain has made its way layer-by-layer through the remnants of four stories above the shop—those floors currently constitute the abandoned corpse of the old National Hotel.

During the worst of yesterday's storm, whole buckets filled with rainwater in an hour's time. I had called the store, one of the longest-surviving small shops in downtown New Haven, hoping to speak with the owner, only to hear: "No, I don't want to talk about business, there isn't hardly any business, and the rain's falling into the store by the bucket." The conversation was over. A few hours later I drove downtown to Crown Street, thinking I might help mop up and make enough of a friend to earn a conversation. The door was locked, the goods covered in plastic, buckets placed strategically throughout the store. The next day I stopped by unannounced and found the proprietor in a better frame of mind. He introduced himself as Joseph Perfetto—Italian for perfect, he says—age eighty-eight. Energetic, witty, urbane in a gruff fashion. Much as he hates the idea of retirement, Perfetto is looking for someone to buy his stock of office supplies, his aging display racks, and his printing equipment.

Perfetto must close his shop not because of his own age, not because of his store's decrepitude, and not because his building has lost some of its roof. The man remains strong enough to sell transparent tape and typewriter ribbons all day long (two years later I found him climbing a ladder to clean windows at his home). The store could be refurbished and the roof repaired in weeks if there were still a market niche robust enough to justify the investments. Perfetto has to close his doors because the city in which his business is designed to operate is *gone*—having disappeared little by little in fits and starts for decades, beginning even *before* New England Typewriter & Stationery had begun making serious money in the 1950s. To be sure, the older city has been replaced by one that uses many of the same bricks and much of the same asphalt, along with nearly all of the old names for streets and neighborhoods. These material and cultural fossils invite an illusion of continuity: these same streets were here a century ago. But only in the most superficial sense is that so, for the streets have changed utterly—in their daily functions, their social meaning, even their moral standing—for those who use them, and for those too timid or prideful to come near

Figure 1.1. Hope Carpentieri and Joseph Perfetto in their downtown store, c. 1948.
Photo courtesy Mr. and Mrs. Joseph Perfetto.

them. The old streets belong to a place whose scent is everywhere inside New England Stationery & Typewriter, and whose ghosts are just across the street as I take my leave (figure 1.1).

From Perfetto's shop window I look across Crown Street and confront an expanse of undulating asphalt forming a cheaply engineered parking lot, along with some nondescript commercial buildings, now largely empty. What stood here, and what life occurred within, at the crest of urbanism? Later, in the crowded stacks at Yale's Sterling Memorial Library, I learn what was arrayed, east to west on the north side of Crown Street, in 1913.[1]

• Theodore Martus residence, also home to Bertram Martus, who is a toolmaker, 101 Crown.
• Emil Scheuerman's Saloon, 103 Crown.

3

- Hugo J. Simon & Sons Delicatessen, 105 Crown.
- The Charlton Hotel, 107 Crown, also the home of Lorin Benson, perhaps the hotel's manager.
- Oscar G. Billiau, caged bird retailer, 111 Crown.
- Christian J. Berg, barber, 113 Crown.
- J. C. Heinrich's Restaurant, 115 Crown.
- John C. Heinrich residence, 117 Crown.
- Gray's Club, the residence of Gertrude Carter, and the residence of Ernest Koelbl, all at 119 Crown.
- Adam Ziegler Saloon and Camp Gray, Inc., both at 121 Crown.

This mixing of uses—a little commercial hotel, people's homes, a club, a deli, a restaurant, booze, birds, and a barber—has been reduced to the single purpose of parking cars. The place seems to have been full of urban vitality—crowding enterprise next to enterprise, irregularly textured, scaled to the unsystematic and varied needs of ordinary humans. Just to the left of the parking lot, facing Church Street, I see what was once the Connecticut Savings Bank. Its Crown Street facade is decorated by six mammoth Greek Revival columns, the building's birth year MCMVII (1907), and the motto "Thrift, Industry, Enterprise." In the time of urbanism, such a bank was directed by New Haven citizens and channeled money mostly to local borrowers—perhaps to people like Oscar Billiau for his bird store or Emil Scheuerman for his saloon. Today, renamed First Union, this structure houses a minor branch outlet buried four layers deep in a large financial corporation (Wachovia) headquartered six hundred miles south of New Haven.[2] The bank building remains, still an imposing stack of Proctor white marble, even as the bank itself is lost to its former city. Scarcely discernable in these few artifacts is a city in its era of urbanism.

That city was a crowded place filled with people, their money sunk into the ground as tenements and machine shops and saloons. Economic energy and ingenuity flowed inward because high-value manufactured goods flowed outward. Investors and skilled workers came to town in pursuit of the dollars they could earn at Winchester Repeating Arms, Sargent Hardware, New Haven Clock, Osterweis Cigars, and scores of other firms that exported goods to national and world markets. These exporters fed cash to thousands of wage-earners and to a multitude of smaller specialty manufacturers and machine tool shops that in turn furnished them with supplies and expert services. All the while, this inward-flowing torrent of money was creating opportunities for smaller entrepreneurs to sell groceries, clothes, furniture, movie tickets, beer, souvenir photographs, religious statues, and a hundred other things to those who brought home a weekly paycheck. Such a check conveyed revenue from consumers across a continent who saw fit to purchase hardware, wristwatches, guns, bird cages, and rubber boots made in New Haven. Every such dollar raced through a thick web of transactions in the city, running from corner grocer to her whole-saler to the wages of a delivery man to his tenement landlord to a Saturday night at the neighborhood saloon then perhaps to the Sunday morning collection plate. Deep down in this web of economic relationships were typewriter ribbons and the scores of other products that Joe Perfetto sold in downtown New Haven during his seven-decade career. The way Joe Perfetto got into a business of his own tells us a lot about his vitality and the vitality of the city he recalls:

By the time I was seven, I had a little business lighting stoves and turning switches for the religious Jews who lived around the old synagogue on Rose Street. I was also in charge of delivering magazines to students over at Yale while still in grade school. In 1924 I started out working for Barnes Type-writer at the age of fourteen. Barnes would take off for Florida, leave the place in the charge of his daughter, and she was never there, always out with some guy.[3] So I ran the place, more or less. Took my first typewriter apart the first day there and put it together. Mechanically inclined, I suppose. Worked for him five, six years until the Depression started in.

One morning I was home, supposedly on vacation, which most of the time I never got—got paid for it but worked anyway. I got a letter saying that he was gonna reduce my pay from $27 a week to $20 a week, on account of the Depression. Everybody was cutting—the telephone company, Winches-ter. They weren't paying anything, $13 a week. So I asked how come he had to cut mine. He said, "We're not making any money, everybody's doing it, we have to do it." I said, "Mr. Barnes, I'm making about $400 a month for you, all your work, all your guarantee work, any deliveries not included, just what I tell you to charge customers for my work. Think about all that work for the *Register*. You're only givin' me $100 a month, taking in $400, think about it." [Barnes responds:] "You don't know what you're talking about." "Yes, I do, every time I give you a slip, I keep a duplicate." [Barnes retorts:] "You're not supposed to do that. Anyway, I treat you like a son, I'm like a fa-ther to you." I says I'll go to work for Blakeslee with a pick and shovel but I still gotta have that $27. He wouldn't do it so I said I'm gonna have to quit. I emptied out my tool bag, all the spare parts, and put 'em in the drawer, left 'em there. I said, "How about a letter of recommendation?" He said, "You won't need it, you'll be back next week." I said, no, I'd like to have a letter. He wrote one about how I was honest and trustworthy, nothing about how good I worked. Not that I was the errand boy, the shoeshine boy or what: I was just honest and trustworthy.

So I went out, that was on a Saturday. I went down to a friend of mine used to help out at Dorer's Music Shop; he was quite famous there. I told him, and he said, "What are you worried about?" He took me over to Commerce Street, to a print shop there, and we had some name cards made up. Monday morning I went out, passed out some of those cards, telling people I was working for myself now, and if they could use me I'd appreciate it. Would you believe I made $113 the first week working for myself? I didn't have anything but a tool bag, not a ribbon to sell, not anything. So I made the $113 that first week, and I've been at it ever since.

Even as the Depression set in, the city churned out enough demand that a smart kid could find his way into the money stream on a weekend's notice.

Later, bored with the asphalt parking lot, I turn left (west) down Crown Street, toward the city center, where I immediately confront an edifice radically alien to the texture of urbanism. The building's surface consists almost entirely of bricks, many of them glassy white, others forming unglazed dung-brown rectangles. No windows interfere with the aridity of design, and the few remaining doors are boarded shut. This great box—about 300 by 200 by 40 feet high—appears big enough to swallow up several hundred shops like Joe Perfetto's New England Stationery & Typewriter. The big box—for about thirty years home to a Macy's department store—dates to the era of urban renewal (1954–70), and to the demolition of several city blocks constituting the core of the central business district. It was created in an attempt to *restore* the lost city of urbanist New Haven, although it gives every appearance of hostility to the smallness, the unevenness, the very humanity of a place that could harbor saloons, delis, hotels, and a caged bird store along one little stretch of sidewalk. Walking around the block, to the far side of the big box, I see that a massive parking garage, crafted by Paul Rudolph in what architects call brutalist style, abuts the Macy's box and extends south well beyond it to a zone formerly occupied by a very similar department store building (Malley's), recently demolished.

Glancing down George Street, south of the garage, I survey two additional Jurassic structures—the War Memorial Coliseum (slated for demolition in 2003) and the world headquarters of the Knights of Columbus—arising from the same mid-century era and expressing the same urgent desire to create something grand in the central city. These buildings, along with the wavy asphalt parking lot on Crown Street, are material artifacts from the end of urbanism.

CREATIVE DESTRUCTION

In the course of a single generation, capitalism creates new wealth and new demands for its consumption scarcely imaginable at the outset. In the generation between 1880 and 1910, for example, the real value of the U.S. gross domestic product per person rose from $3,835 to $5,905—a spurt of better than 50 percent (all figures are inflation-adjusted to year 2002 dollars). In the years separating 1940 from 1970, GDP per capita leapt from $7,909 to $19,070— about 240 percent. As the generations pass generations, growth compounds growth: an average American living in the year 2002 is eight to ten times as well off as she would have been in 1880.[4] Anyone who has walked the streets of an American city or driven those of its suburbs in recent decades knows that the fruits of this abundance are deposited very unevenly: economic growth and economic equality are very different things, but the brute fact of relentless long-term growth is beyond dispute, and it stands at the very core of American urban history.[5]

Capitalism drives growth by remorselessly refusing to preserve the past (even when it markets the sentiment of a remembered past in film, fashion, and architecture). No manufacturing plant is permanently secure against novel competition, no system of transportation permanently withstands disruptive change, no corporation is immune to takeover or bankruptcy. No store can be insured against the disappearance of its customers or the obsolescence of its merchandise. No profitable line of business—from hotels to stores specializing in caged birds, from stationery stores to saloons—will stand for long undisturbed by the curiosity of would-be competitors. No place—city, suburb, hamlet, or farmstead—is secure against the emergence of a new economic geography that drains vital populations and investments in the space of a few decades. In seeking ever fresh forms of production, ever larger markets, ever higher returns on investment, capitalism routinely destroys older ways of doing business, older technologies, older plants—and in so doing profoundly transforms the communities that have formed around them.

Downward-sloping change in a city typically unfolds without a big bang, without an eruption that makes headlines, but instead by the rapid accumulation of small changes. A familiar little store goes dark, displaced by a larger, brighter one, miles away. Soon enough, the new retailer also displaces a dozen other small-fry scattered across the same city. A novel product, made an ocean away, begins to succeed in local markets—including the same bright new store—at the expense of an established item produced in town. Yet another product, lacking all novelty save its low price, appears in the region and begins to drive one made locally at a higher price from store shelves (locally and nationally). Still a third novelty (think of early radios or, later, television sets, for example) becomes a substitute for seemingly unrelated products (caged birds or saloons, perhaps) and begins to cut away customers from stores that still try to trade in the now less compelling goods. Facing falling demand, a manufacturing plant cuts down on its night shift, then prunes away part of the day shift, then becomes part of a firm headquartered a day's travel away. Eventually, top management of the new firm shifts capital investment elsewhere, and the old plant becomes a brown-field site. Rents on apartments near the old plant fall, yet vacancy rates still rise little by little from year to year. Seen a day or a year at a time, and a neighborhood at a time, the changes seem increasingly *normal*—as unworthy of discussion as, say, the sharpening cold of morning while the calendar pages for October and November fall away. Only as changes shingle up—one over another and another—does the cumulative effect of creative destruction emerge for all to know.[6]

Classic Phases of Creative Destruction At any given moment, there will be zones where creation rises and other places where the lengthening shadows of destruction fall. In one such moment, cities of a given type may create themselves and grow larger, only to be eroded with the passage of time. None of this follows a tidy plan; all of it unfolds with the complex interaction of capital, technology, and the gifts of nature or intellect available to each place. In, say, 1820, American capital attached itself to downward-rushing water, so that hydropowered mills could loom raw cotton into cheap textiles never before available at prices working people could afford. Upland New England cities like Holyoke, Lowell, and Norwich, straddling rivers at their fastest lines of fall, grew and prospered in this era.[7] Their growth occurred at the expense of hand labor and cottage industry, which once produced competing textiles at greater cost and in much smaller quantities. Fabrics produced cottage-style in western Massachusetts or southern Vermont no longer could command their old customers as cheaper machine-made stuff flooded into New York, Boston, and Portland, eventually reaching even the rural counties of Vermont and Massachusetts. Even so, factories of as many as one hundred workers remained relatively rare in this era, and capital was for the most part invested in smallish plants. Manufacturing centers of this era were consequently much smaller than industrial cities of a later generation.

Even in the most profitable years of water-driven manufacturing, rival technology gathered steam, and soon enough its promise was touted everywhere, as for example in the May 12, 1849, issue of *Scientific American:*

A water-mill is necessarily located in the country afar from the cities, the markets, and the magazines of labor, upon which it must be dependent. Water appears to run very cheaply, but it always rents for a pretty high price, and the [capital] cost of dams, races, water wheels etc is on the average quite as great as that of a steam engine and equipage. . . . A man sets down his steam-engine where he pleases—that is, where it is most to his interest to plant it, in the midst of the industry and markets, both for supply and consumption of a great city—where he is sure of always having hands near him, without loss of time in seeking for them, and where he can buy his raw materials and sell his goods, without adding the expense of double transportation.[8]

By 1870, the creative edge of capital had moved into steam-driven plants producing consumer goods—clocks, doorknobs, hammers, rubber boots—faster and cheaper than ever before. Flat water in lowland cities like Boston, New Haven, New York, Newark, Philadelphia, Baltimore, Pittsburgh, Chicago, Cleveland, and Cincinnati offered a decided advantage in the inbound transport of coal and the outbound distribution of products made using its fossil heat. These cities burned cheap coal in ever greater quantities, attracted eager labor from the agricultural hinterlands of Europe, and built factories on a scale unmatched in previous history. By 1873, U.S. immigration reached 459,803, mostly from Germany and Great Britain, many settling in these lowland manufacturing cities. A generation later, between 1905 and 1915, immigration approached a million souls each year, most commonly from Italy and Russia, still crowding into the burgeoning lowland cities.[9] The old fall-line cities gradually lost competitive traction as steam replaced stream in textiles, paper-making, grain-milling, and a host of other activities. Where once a hundred-horsepower water mill had been a magnet for investors and workers alike, a thousand horses of exploding steam now carried the day. Factories of greater size, and capital investments of unprecedented scale, became commonplace in major cities, even in middling ones like New Haven.

When (in 1847) Marx and Engels generalized that capitalism had "created more massive and more colossal productive forces than [had] all preceding generations together" they were seeing only the earliest—*least* massive, farthest from colossal—prototypes of the urban factory system. These small beginnings would soon be dwarfed by the rise of cities based on the massive consumption of coal and the resulting power of steam-driven machinery To find this looming colossus, these Europeans were looking on the wrong side of the Atlantic. As Andrew Carnegie would write in 1886: "The old nations of the earth creep on at a snail's pace; the Republic thunders past with the rush of the express. The United States, the growth of a single century, has already reached the foremost rank among nations, and is destined soon to out-distance all others in the race. In population, in wealth, in annual savings, and in public credit; in freedom from debt, in agriculture, and in manufactures, America already leads the civilized world."[10]

Carnegie's metaphor of the rushing express is no accident. By about 1900, capital's leading edge was an increasingly efficient national network of railroads which allowed the formation of integrated joint stock corporations serving markets larger than ever before imagined.[11] Oil refining, meat packing, and the cigarette, textile, chemical, and steel industries were dominated by large corporations binding together producers, processors, distributors, and consumers in vast webs of activity woven through the railways, which are themselves operated by increasingly complex corporations. The vast network of financial relations, which today converge on Wall Street, began to emerge and become the central nervous system of American capitalism in financing the railroad system over the course of the nineteenth century. This in turn allowed the development of corporations capable of bundling together equity investments from thousands of families and organizations across the land and across oceans. The increasing accumulation of capital in large corporations led many to imagine a Darwinian process favoring big business. Carnegie was one of these: "How far the concentration of capital is destined to go, no one can foretell. The survival of the fittest means here the survival of the most economical; and that large establishments are more economical than small ones is proved by the non-survival of the latter. It is probable that the only limit to the concentration of labor is that imposed by the capacity of the directing mind which presides over it."[12]

Big capital worked to the further advantage of lowland cities, as rail reinforced water in the efficient movement of fuels, raw materials, and manufactured products across continental markets. People deciding where to build manufacturing plants were attracted by large pools of labor and clusters of other firms capable of providing needed supplies and services. Moreover, these amenities tended to constitute large markets for finished goods, so that a "cumulative causation" drew firms to places where firms are drawn, where firms are drawn ad infinitum.[13] Economies of scale in the storage and distribution of coal, oil, chemicals, steel, and other staples of manufacturing added further advantage to these cities. And the development of what will eventually be known as suburban sprawl was limited—less by taste or preference than by the absence of fast, flexible transportation capable of linking peripheral locations to the central city. This limitation would of course disappear as automotive transport generated a fresh maelstrom of creative destruction after about 1920.

ACCIDENTS OF URBAN CREATION

Beginning in about 1840, a concatenation of four events and two nonevents began to emerge in the United States; they would constitute what I'll call accidents of urban creation. All of these outcomes are wrapped within the evolution of American capitalism, with its sharply increasing capacity to create and to destroy, and to influence the course of government policy. These developments were: the rising dominance of steam-driven manufacturing, already noted; an agricultural revolution allowing the nation to support more and larger urban centers; the emergence, largely as a result of integrated railroad systems, of national markets accessible from central-city manufacturing plants; a critical timing gap between the maturation of that rail system (which centralized cities) and the coming automotive and truck transportation (which decentralized them); a sustained period of relatively open immigration allowing accelerated growth in the supply of urban labor; and a delayed and uneven spreading out and implementation of distance-compressing technologies such as alternating current (AC) electricity. The two nonevents (late motor vehicle development and delayed electrical grid implementation) are no less important than the four affirmative events (steam, farming, rail, immigration). The coincidence of these six features is critical to the story. Nobody planned this concatenation of events, and very few saw it unfold with the lucidity afforded by a century of hindsight.

Once cities approach truly urban densities, biological necessity makes them bulk importers of food and drink, to fill people's stomachs, and of fibers, to cover their backs. Only as the hinterlands generate big surpluses does it become possible to sustain large cities in large numbers—but in late nineteenth-century America just that occurred. As agriculture relentlessly substituted capital—formed up as John Deere's steel plow, Cyrus McCormick's mechanical reaper, Haber-Bosch ammonia-based fertilizer—for the sweat of strong backs, more and more goods could be produced by fewer and fewer people. One way to track this trend is by adding up the hours of direct labor required to produce a standardized bushel basket of wheat.[14] In 1840, the required labor was roughly 2 hours and 20 minutes (down from 3 hours and 45 minutes a generation earlier). In 1900, 1 hour and 5 minutes. In 1950, 16 minutes. In 1970, less than 6 minutes.[15] Just as impressive is the amount of harvested-and-baled cotton produced by one hour of direct labor: in 1840, 1.1 pounds, and in 1970 18.4 pounds.[16] This sort of development—repeated in more or less similar ways for potatoes, poultry, and a hundred other commodities—forever changed the vital biology of place. In 1840, the full-time labor of a farmworker could sustain the needs of perhaps four human stomachs, one of which was his own. By 1910, the ratio reached seven stomachs to one farmworker—by 1950, fifteen to one, by 1970, forty-seven to one.[17] Of course, these agricultural surpluses did not directly *cause* the emergence of more and larger cities, but human decision-makers could hardly have created them absent the new abundance.

There had always been a tiny number of great cities, but only as this changing biology of place unfolded could relatively large cities become numerous—and thus repetitive units of social organization. In 1840, only three American cities—New York, Baltimore, and New Orleans—exceeded 100,000 inhabitants (two others, Boston and Philadelphia, were just under that figure, and no others exceeded 50,000). By 1880, twenty U.S. cities had breached the 100,000 mark—including New York, Philadelphia, Brooklyn (a municipality in its own right until 1897), and Chicago, at better than a half million each. A whole middle tier of industrial cities was pushing its way up, including Cleveland, Pittsburgh, Buffalo, Newark, Jersey City, Detroit, and Milwaukee. By 1910, fifty cities had passed 100,000 population, now including New Haven at 133,605 (thirty-fifth largest at the time). By this early stage of the twentieth century, substantial cities had become an organizing unit of American life.[18] This development, opened by the swift rise in farm productivity, would have been impossible only half a century earlier.

Agricultural production was further amplified by the development of rail transport during the decades bracketing the Civil War. Total U.S. track mileage climbed from 9,021 in 1850 to 52,922 in 1870 and would go on to surpass 100,000 by the early 1880s.[19] Indeed, after the war's end in 1865, sixty consecutive years would each see the addition of 1,000 miles or more of new railroads somewhere in the country.[20] By 1876, with 340,000 rail cars in active service, this ever-denser rail network made it profitable to ship grains and meat products from the flatlands of Iowa, Illinois, Nebraska, and Oklahoma to the great eastern centers of population—thus shifting agricultural production to areas where the application of machinery was cheapest and most effective.[21] As William Cronon has amply demonstrated, Chicago and its stockyards transformed the western grasslands by creating wholesale markets for meat and grain, gathered and processed there, then shipped further east to city markets.[22] The incoming tide of western food products, moreover, accelerated the decline of agriculture in New England, and compelled many rural families to seek work in industrial cities.

Even more fundamentally, the integrated railway systems that matured in the closing decades of the nineteenth century—the Baltimore & Ohio, New York Central, Pennsylvania, and Union Pacific, most strikingly—pushed steel tentacles into wider and wider markets. Supplemented by regional systems like the New York, New Haven & Hartford Railroad, these carriers linked every major city to markets fast approaching 100 million increasingly well-funded consumers. And Connecticut was well served by its 1,000-mile network. In 1911, the state had nearly 35,000 railroad workers, and more passenger cars, than Amtrak today has nationally.

Not only did rail cheapen and enhance inward-bound supplies of food, coal, and raw materials, it also rushed outward-bound manufactured goods to continental markets. This permitted, and handsomely rewarded, the sinking of great sums into city-centered plants built on plots of land where coal and steam and labor could be brought together more efficiently than anywhere else.[23] Manufacturers swarmed over urban railheads much as ants swarm over a dollop of jelly on a summer afternoon, crowding one another for each sweet particle of economic sugar. Where rail *and* heavy shipping came together in one city—Boston, New York, Chicago, St. Louis, Cleveland, Buffalo—the inward-rushing pressure of manufacturers on urban land reached fever pitch, and leaps of population growth followed immediately. New Haven became exactly such a case in the decades following the arrival of rail service in the late 1840s.

As Colin Clark writes, the broad contours of urban economic history in the nineteenth and twentieth centuries were to a very large extent determined by rail and road.[24] And one particular phase turns out to be critical to our analysis of cities like New Haven—namely, the interval during which rail was in full operation and effective highway transportation was still in the future. As Clark has it, "Railway transport overthrew, for the first time in history, the natural barriers which had hitherto prevented too great a concentration of industry in any urban center. The great cities of the world up to that date indeed had been still built up primarily for political, military, or religious importance rather than their commercial or industrial functions; from 1830 onwards the latter were to predominate."[25] One may of course quibble: Amsterdam, Genoa, and Venice were more than anything else commercial trading centers long before rail.[26] With rail, nevertheless, urban businesses could reach far larger markets in shorter times: the pace of central-place development quickened as a result. But the development of densely centered cities depended also on the *absence* of highway transport: "The railways immeasurably cheapened long-distance transport. But once the goods had been unloaded from the train or ship on to a horse-dray their costs of transport were very high. The inevitable consequence of this was that industry was concentrated in compact and densely populated industrial towns, or directly along the waterfront in sea ports."[27]

This rail-before-trucks-and-cars period is the great centralizing era for cities like New Haven, Bridgeport, Buffalo, Cleveland, Minneapolis, Detroit, Pittsburgh, and Trenton.[28] The interval's critical feature is the *contrast* between the cheapness and reliability of *fixed-path* transport via rail (and sea), on the one hand, and the expensive, unreliable nature of *variable-path* transport (horse vehicles in the main) once goods and people reach a railhead destination. Rail focused manufacturing plants in central locations, and the poverty of local transportation compelled people to live nearby, retailers to locate nearby, and a whole train of other centralizing effects to occur.[29] As Clark continues, "Motor vehicles unfroze this concentration. Costs are incurred inevitably, in getting goods off ship or rail on to a motor truck; but once this has been done, unlike a horse vehicle, it makes little difference whether you carry them two or twenty miles."[30] A great expansion of railroading dominated the half-century beginning in the 1870s and ending in the 1920s.[31] The number of rail cars in operation nationally expanded from 340,000 in 1876 to an all-time crest of 2,483,179 in 1919—after which time no further net expansion would occur in the national railroad car inventory. This period of railroad expansion was the principal era of urban centralization. By its end, New Haven had more or less completed its population growth and was deep into its era of economic prosperity.

The coming of motor transport accelerated rapidly by the 1920s, reaching 10,493,600 vehicles, accounting for 55,027,000,000 passenger miles in 1921, the year the federal government passed its first full-blown Highway Act (figure 1.2). No exact beginning and end can be assigned to the era of rail-dominant urbanization, but an educated guess is quite easy: from about 1870 until about 1920, rail was dominant.[32] Over the remaining eight decades of the twentieth century, automotive transport became ever more dominant, surpassing 100 million vehicles by 1970 and greatly exceeding 200 million today. The intoxicating liberty provided by the automobile would become the single most corrosive factor in American urban life by the late 1920s and would persist in the twenty-first

Figure 1.2. Miss Boroughs at the wheel of her roadster near
the New Haven Green, 1910. Photo by T. S. Bronson. NHCHS.

century.[33] But here our emphasis falls on the *absence* of automotive pressure during the fifty years during which centralized urban development reigned.

Over those same years, booming immigration supplied eager labor to the expanding urban factories, and talent of every kind to the cities around them.[34]
While the Chinese Exclusion Act of 1882 and similar laws restricted the immigration of Asian peoples, Europe provided an abundance of immigrants. Between 1871 and 1920, 26.3 million people (23.1 million of them Europeans) arrived in the United States as immigrants.[35] Their yearly numbers averaged more
than 500,000 for the five decades, rising to nearly a million (994,000) each year
from 1904 through 1914. During this critical period the leading sources of immigrants were Italy, Russia, and certain parts of Eastern Europe. Immigrants
were, very sensibly, attracted in large numbers by industrial and commercial opportunities in precisely the same increasingly crowded central cities we have
been tracing here. New Haven was one such case: its "foreign born white" population rose from 3,697 in 1850 to 45,686 in 1920.[36] One of these families was Joe
Perfetto's: "My father came from Italy—[Province of] Benevento, from a little
town there. The whole town my father came from, *everybody's* Perfetto. My
brother went there looking for Perfettos: Which one?—the mayor, the priest, the

whole town! Here in the city, my father worked for Cowles & Company. He was their top locksmith. He spent over fifty years there. All the locks, all the repairs. In fact I think he invented most of their locks. He worked for the company, never got anything for it, just steady work for fifty years."[37]

During the early 1920s political reaction against immigration, especially against newcomers from southern and eastern Europe, reached the boiling point. Congress passed the so-called Emergency Quota Act in 1921, capping legal immigration at a total of 357,802 per year, and limiting any nationality group to 3 percent of its representation in the 1910 census. The Immigration Act of 1924 shifted the base year from 1910 to 1890 (making the mix "whiter" and less Catholic) and at the same time reducing quotas from 3 percent to 2 percent. Fully implemented by 1929, this more restrictive quota system effectively reduced immigration to a relatively minor element of urban growth in the succeeding generation.

CLOSING THE ERA

The early 1920s repeatedly appear as a terminus for the era of centered urban development—the tapering of railroad expansion, the age of the automobile's beginning as symbolized and affirmed in the Highway Act of 1921, the sharp restriction of immigration in the 1921 and 1924 acts. In the world of letters, Sinclair Lewis brings George Babbitt—self-serving hypocrite in love with the automobile and with the suburban tract houses it helps him market—to the best-seller list in 1922.[39] The emergence of General Motors—king of integrated corporations with its "family of cars" from Chevrolet to Cadillac—as a dominant force in American life is all but complete by about 1927.[38] As will be seen later in the book, the decentralization of urban regions would begin in earnest in the 1920s, a fact due only in part to the availability of automobile commuting. Also at work were a whole series of technologies for energy distribution, broadcasting (radio, television) and "narrowcasting" (telephone). In succeeding chapters I will analyze these developments in greater detail. Here, allow me to focus on electricity alone.

In the closing decades of the nineteenth century, two systems of electricity competed fiercely—Thomas Edison's direct current (DC) and George Westinghouse's alternating current (AC). DC had many advantages of safety, and Edison went so far as to promote the electric chair, based on Westinghouse's AC system, as a demonstration of its hazards.[40] But DC had the economic defect of wasting power as lines of distribution extended across space. Only within a mile or so of the central generator was DC practical. Precisely because of its superiority in dispersing energy over great distances, AC won out—a fact that became more or less obvious as early as 1891, when the first industrial use of alternating current occurred in the United States.[41] Thousands of other electric factories would eventually follow, opening up the countryside to industrial, commercial, and residential use. Once the AC grid reached across any urban region, the incentive for central-place location of industry based on energy costs disappeared: copper wire could, in effect, move steam across miles and miles, leaving the coal and soot behind near river and rail as the energy departed central-city generators. But, as is so often true of major technologies, the actual implementation of the AC grid proceeded slowly. As late as 1917 the nation's electric utilities were turning out just over 25 billion kilowatt-hours per year. By 1929 this output would more than triple, reaching 92 billion.[42] By 1950, 629 billion kilowatt-hours were feeding homes and stores and plants spreading across regions from Connecticut to California. Even more important for our purposes, the AC grid grew, first, as central-city infrastructure, then edged its way into the countryside.[43] In New Haven's case this was certainly true, as data for 1921 reveal that 82 percent of electric utility customers remained within the city itself.[44] Within a few years, the balance would shift perceptibly toward a dispersion of residential population, work activities, and commerce—and toward what I will call the end of urbanism.

The national forces that lined up between about 1870 and the 1920s helped to shape the city that became home to Joe Perfetto's store. During this time, two of these forces were important by their absence: motor vehicles with the highway system on which they relied, and a well-developed electrical grid spanning urban regions. The other forces were made important by their presence: the (temporary) dominance of steam-powered manufacturing, the agricultural revolution needed to sustain more and larger urban centers, the maturation of a well-integrated railroad system, and, finally, the willingness of government to permit a great wave of immigration during the same decades. There was nothing inevitable or even predictable about this temporary historical alignment: if God, or nature, should elect to run the same history a thousand times, there is no particularly good reason to expect that the same alignment would recur very often, or at all. And if the people living in New Haven (or any other similarly situated lowland city) in 1840 were asked to predict the future, it seems likely that the events of 1870–1920 would escape their prevision altogether—much as the very different course of later events escaped twentieth-century observers. The particularities of capitalist development are, in these ways, notoriously inscrutable. I use the term "urbanism" to denote five general features of the city as it emerged between the 1870s and the 1920s and, as it continued, with increasing attenuation, into the later decades of the twentieth century. Namely:

1. *Industrial convergence,* creating large outward flows of products beyond the city and its region, creating the basis for a powerful stream of wages and investment capital to energize the city. These wages were the juice that nurtured a richly variegated community of retail business, a robust housing market, a textured civic life. Most of all, industrial convergence creates a bountiful supply of relatively attractive jobs luring workers and their families to the city and keeping them there (Chapter 2 outlines this process in New Haven's case). Not insignificantly, from the view at City Hall, industrial convergence largely underwrites the tax base as manifested in plant and equipment, as well as in employee housing and retail space supported by employee wages.

2. A *dense fabric of enterprise,* illustrated by the many hundreds of tiny grocery stores that carpeted the city's neighborhoods, provides a potent source of social cohesion, a localized network of relationships, and an important stream of income to proprietors. Other forms of neighborhood retailing—hardware stores, bakeries, even saloons—reinforce the fabric. At a somewhat larger scale of enterprise, downtown establishments—department stores, specialty retailers (like Joe Perfetto), restaurants, theaters, and hotels—further reinforce the business fabric of the city. These many thousands of firms constitute a form of social capital helping to govern city life (see Chapter 3).

3. A *centralized clustering of housing* concentrating families of all classes and ethnicities in a relatively compact central city. This was driven less by taste than by economic and technological forces that compelled those engaged in either industrial work and management, or in the operation of other enterprises, to live fairly close to the job. While, as shown in Chapter 4, distinctive working-class neighborhoods emerged within this concentration, all groups of every level lived in close proximity to others from very different economic strata. This in turn compelled a certain frequency of contact with strangers having different manners of expression, dress, and consumption—perhaps encouraging a certain urbanity in the course of a lifetime lived in the city.[45]

4. A *dense civic fauna* of organizations outside the business sector provided another layer of cohesion and governance. Included here were a vast array of religious congregations, mutual benefit societies, fraternal and sororal clubs, athletic clubs and leagues, schools and academies, and the like. As the inven-

tory established in Chapter 5 suggests, this was—by modern standards—a remarkable fauna indeed. Moreover, most of its components were not just *for* the benefit of city residents, they were also run *by* those residents. And, importantly for city governance, we will see that the leaders of many such organizations were drawn from lower tiers of the economy, and from working-class neighborhoods.

5. An important *pattern of political integration* was made possible by the concentration of leaders from business and civic organizations inside the city on a more or less full-time basis. Absentee management of local banks, manufacturing plants, schools, civic clubs, and congregations was the exception rather than the rule. Economic citizenship, expressed as the ownership and active management of enterprise, generally coincided with political citizenship, expressed as local residence and electoral participation—even as candidacy for City Hall offices. City government was admittedly a rigid and less than athletic feature of the urban setting, but its handicaps were greatly ameliorated by the presence of in-town leadership from all sectors. City government could afford its foibles because it controlled land use in a place offering all the advantages of industrial convergence, retail density, a large residential population, and a rich array of civic opportunities (see Chapter 6).

These features imply no golden age. At the very height of urbanism, the city was redolent of garbage, its streets littered with manure. The squeal and bang of heavy equipment rang out, interrupted by the screech of trolley brakes. Housing standards for working-class families would shock most twenty-first-century Americans, including residents of present-day low-income public housing. Many of the entertainments on offer would seem dull to a generation raised on cinematic sexuality, televised warfare (the NFL, *The Sopranos*, CNN's version of Operation Desert Storm, or the taking of Baghdad in 2003), and vacation travel at 600 mph to places beyond the wildest dreams of most city dwellers in, say, 1910. Bigotry was routine, barring Jews and Catholics alike from all the old Yankee clubs. Even within faiths, Italian and Irish Catholic congregations required separation, as did German and Russian Jews in some cases. Ethnic slurs—"nigger," "mick," "yid," "dago," and the rest—were for many urbanites the ordinary barking noises of social distance. Industrial and human waste ran unprocessed into the Quinnipiac River and Long Island Sound. Death among children and young adults came all too often, and polio victims, with their stunted limbs, were everywhere to be seen. There is no going back to this, and I intend no sentimentality in writing of it.

AMBIVALENCE TOWARD URBANISM

Urbanism was not altogether popular, even in its heyday.[46] From the time of Jefferson, Americans have been encouraged to admire rural independence and to mistrust cities. Even at the height of urbanism, popular journalism eagerly dissected its seamy features—its rotten tenements, its failed sanitation, its vulnerability to epidemic, its corrupt building inspectors, its clattering factories, its sulphurous chimneys, its manure-strewn avenues, the rudeness of its poor, and the avarice of kleptocratic party bosses.[47] Adults came to be urbanites less as an explicit choice than as a necessary byproduct of other choices: pick a job, pick a flat tolerably near the job, seek stores tolerably near the flat, and Presto, you've chosen a city life. Freedom seemed for many to lie in escape to open space beyond city limits. This was so even for Joe Perfetto: "I live in Hamden [a first-ring suburb north of the city], been there almost 50 years. . . . Right at the beginning of Hamden, Davis Street. Last house on the block in those days. Out the front door, you got [East Rock] park; out the back door, you go hunting. That was 1950, June or July."[48]

As problems arose in the city, most Americans had a historically rooted script for leaving those cities behind. What John Stilgoe calls the "American come-outer" tradition begins with the memory of immigration: "All Americans, except those of direct African ancestry, descend from people who more or less willingly deserted homelands, who ventured forth for a hundred reasons out of England, Ireland, Russia, Poland, Italy, China. Americans teach their children that the come-outers sought religious freedom, safety from tyranny, refuge from military conscription, and above all opportunity to better themselves and their children economically, usually, but not invariably, by owning land." Stilgoe continues: "If the Irish were right to desert an island struck by famine and misrule . . . why should they not have begun deserting eastern American cities in the 1920s when a number of complex issues seemingly defied solution?"[49]

By the time New Haven had become a mature industrial city, around 1910, the suburban idea was embedded in the American scene and fit admirably with Stilgoe's come-outer ideology. The fit, of course, required a judgment against cities—that is, an evil from which to come out. This was readily supplied in a nation that had from Jefferson's time identified its soul with the countryside and with the independence of rural life. On the one hand, the muckraking tradition that attacked the corruption of central city life—as in Lincoln Steffens' *Shame of Our Cities*—worked to stigmatize the core municipalities. On the other, the squalor of tenement life would provoke outrage, as in Jacob Riis' turn-of-the-century documentary. In the same era, at the height of the centered city, it was possible to link emerging technology with social criticism, as Adna Weber did: "We have learned that the packing of human beings into tenement barracks devoid of light and air is not due to the necessity of any natural law, but to the greed of man. The city, even the largest city, can now be made as healthful as the country, because cheap rapid transit enables city workers to live many miles away from their work-places."[50]

THE SHOCK OF MOBILITY

Two economic events—the advent of the AC electric grid and of automotive transport—ended the urbanism-friendly age of centered development. Together these events created the deep technological basis for almost limitless mass mobility—people moving, and living where they please, across virtually every region of a continental nation. The earlier of the two great events was the triumph of AC electricity, in the development of a power grid that could distribute energy almost anywhere, without respect to the advantages of central-place locations. Electric power would undermine on-site steam manufacturing and would allow the development of horizontally extensive factories powered by tiny motors directly linked to each element of the production process—each lathe, each drill press, each stamping machine with its own power. It would also, of course, enable real estate developers to churn cornfields and cow pastures into housing tracts on an unprecedented scale.

The other critical event is not the mere emergence of cars, but the emergence of *very cheap* cars backed up by a political and economic coalition capable of imprinting their tire tracks on society at large. Automobiles had been available to the rich for a generation when the pivotal democratizing development occurred at the Ford Motor Company's plants in Detroit. Radically improved assembly techniques in this single city allowed management to reduce the retail price of a Model T from $850 to $360 in seven years after 1910—while at the same time increasing real wages and profit margins.[51] The world-bending efficiency was achieved in labor hours per car, which fell from 1,260 in 1912 to 533 in 1915 (and to 228 hours by 1923). Instead of building cars standing in place, Ford began to build them as they rolled (or were carried mechanically) from work station to work station in an assembly line. The stupendous economies in assembly cost yielded lower retail prices and a vast increase in unit sales. The yearly totals shot up from about 14,000 Model T's in 1909–10 to 785,000 of them in 1916–17.[52] This in turn provided an incentive for the rapid expansion of oil drilling and refining, created a national constituency for the Highway Act of 1921, and kick-started scores of car-related industries ranging from rubber manufacturing to automotive glass production. As a principal consumer of heavy industrial products—steel, oil, rubber—the automobile industry made itself essential to every decision about the American economy, so central that a cabinet member in Dwight Eisenhower's mid-century administration could dare to assert that what was good for General Motors was good for the country. It also energized the evolution of perhaps the two most powerful of American labor unions, the United Auto Workers and the Teamsters. By the mid-twentieth century, capital's great lever of change was no longer the railroads but the automobile industry and its innumerable paved tentacles across the landscape—a landscape now incidentally laced over by a nearly endless grid of AC wires ready to emit energy anywhere on a few days' notice. This era is notoriously hard on the older lowland cities, as highways tilt competitive advantage toward cheap land in open spaces, with agglomerations such as greater Los Angeles, Atlanta, Denver, Dallas–Fort Worth, and Houston emerging nationally and suburban halos of prosperity forming around older central cities. Not only were open spaces once useful only for farming accessible to the automobile and truck; they could also be reached by the AC grid, inviting manufacturing, commerce, and habitation as never before.

All this set in motion an avalanche of spatial reorganization across North America that would determine more about the future of cities than the sum total of decisions taken by all the mayors and all the city councils known to that period. Its shockwaves would travel across space and through time, and they are still in motion nearly a century later, roaring through cities like São Paolo, Cape Town, Shanghai, and Manila. And it is still backed up by a more or less indefeasible coalition of economic and political interests—running from Portland cement to synthetic rubber, from oil refiners to real estate developers, from auto workers to big-box retailers, from suburban congressmen to state governors elected by green-lawn majorities. The regimes of "automobility" and electrification now spread across the wide world, defining a dramatic turn toward modernity in places as different from the United States and each other as Brazil, Zimbabwe, Egypt, China, and Russia.

CITY HALL AND ITS FRAILTIES

Just as Henry Ford's industrial managers were rolling out the Model T, Frank Rice (mayor of New Haven from 1910–17; figure 1.3) busied himself with more pedestrian issues: "There should be uniformity in the construction of our side-

Figure 1.3. Mayor Frank Rice, c. 1910. NHCHS.

walks. Absolute uniformity of materials should prevail in the construction of the walks in a single block, and strong efforts should be made to effect the construction of uniform walks the entire length of the streets of the city. The day of the brick sidewalk has passed, and I shall endeavor to stop the repairing of our brick walks within the city limits."[53]

This passage from his 1910 inaugural address is unfair as a sample of Mayor Rice's intellect, but, as will be seen later, not wholly unrepresentative of his vision. His Board of Aldermen would preoccupy itself, quite understandably, with the quality of trolley service, milk inspections, and the efficient removal of manure from the streets.[54] His peers in places like Baltimore, Newark, Camden, St. Louis, and even Detroit itself were preoccupied with similar issues—and wholly powerless to change the train of events set in motion at Ford's Highland Park assembly plant and in the ranks of George Westinghouse's corporate empire. It is not, of course, as if this train of events hinged unilaterally on Ford's reconfiguration of one assembly plant or on Westinghouse having beaten an insatiable thirst for AC electricity into the American economy: other paths of industrial innovation would have led to the same general future. But Ford and his production engineers determined more about New Haven and hundreds of other cities than did anyone living in those places at the time—certainly more than any elected city officials of the period. Among all the theaters of creative destruction that defined twentieth-century history, none was more fateful for the governance of cities than the rise of mass-produced, popularly priced cars, rolling across an electrified landscape. The resulting regime of mass mobility, as we may call it, created power for car dealers, corporate executives, and plain citizens that mayors and aldermen could scarcely dream of resisting with the mere power of City Hall. Now cities could of course make smarter or dumber adaptive moves as the technological landscape shifted beneath their streets, but they would make those moves at a disadvantage.

Cities are among the least agile creatures in America's system of capitalist democracy—they move slowly, reactively, and awkwardly in response to change initiated by more athletic organizations. It is consequently possible to be a powerful and politically secure mayor without being able to govern crucial aspects of a city's future. It may likewise be impossible for *any* person or coalition within such a city to govern these features of the community's future. If we ask who governs such a city, we may mean either of two main things: Who controls the policy decisions of city government? Or who governs those changes which matter most to the people and institutions within that city? An answer to the first question would entail looking at power relations in setting city government's agenda, in deciding what to do about the issues included, and in implementing the resulting decisions.[55] An answer to the second would require much broader analysis, a review of all the arenas which impinge on outcomes in that city—even where corporations in other states, or governments on other continents, make the plays. In actual cities, confronting the mobility of people and capital, the mutability of economic resources, and the unpredictable course of technological change, an answer to the first question (about local government) may provide limited illumination of the second question (about governance of what matters most to a city and its people).

Governance may be thought of as the entire stream of decision-making which determines the future welfare of a city, its firms, its institutions, and its people. Maximally effective governance will preserve existing economic opportunities and open new ones. It will allow entrepreneurs to develop firms in endless variety and to quickly respond to emerging consumer needs. It will protect residents and visitors alike against crime, disease, and risk of fire. Almost as important, it will protect city people against the debilitating *fear* of crime, epidemic, and fire. It will generate and maintain an appropriate housing stock, and infrastructure to support it. It will provide for the education and civilizing of children, and it will provide relevant indoctrination for newcomers. It will find ways to protect the weak and helpless, although it may very well resist making this service to humanity the special and unique role of one municipality in an entire region.

In any capitalist society, where vast authority is delegated to private decision, City Hall will invariably be just one of many places where decisions contributing (for either good or ill) to the city's governance are being made. Sometimes, indeed, City Hall will be a relatively marginal locus of power over issues of great importance.[56] A free society grants wide autonomy to individuals, families, religious congregations, creators and performers of popular culture. In any such society, governance decisions will be made hour by hour in every nook and cranny of the city, without so much as a nod toward City Hall.[57] Business decisions, sometimes taken in meeting rooms beyond the horizon, may dramatically affect the governance of any city. In a benign environment—to which I will give the title urbanism—the forces of governance outside City Hall will carry forward decisions that tend to support the city's interests. When, on the other hand, these forces of governance turn ugly, city government's weakness may be exposed for all to see. That weakness has three key facets.

First, all local governments have limited legal autonomy within the U.S. federal system. As Gerald Frug observes, "A city is the only collective body in America that cannot do something simply because it decides to do it. Instead, under American law, cities have power only if state governments authorize them to act."[58] By 1909, the subordination of cities to state legislatures was a matter of textbook recitation: "The real seat of authority is not in the city, but in the state legislature. The legal validity of an act by the city, e.g. issuing its bonds, contracting for water-works, for a sewer or a pavement, regulating the use of its streets, is not determined by the will or expressed desires of its citizens, but by the will of the legislature as set forth in some statute. The city is not merely the creature of the legislative will, it may be and often is the helpless victim of legislative caprice."[59]

This view had been inscribed on federal doctrine as early as 1907 by the U.S. Supreme Court in *Hunter v. Pittsburgh:* "The State . . . at its pleasure may modify or withdraw all [city] powers, may take without compensation [city] property, hold it itself, or vest it in other agencies, expand or contract the territorial area, unite the whole or a part of it with another municipality, repeal the charter and destroy the corporation. All this may be done, conditionally or unconditionally, with or without the consent of the citizens, or even against their protest. In all these respects the State is supreme."[60]

To mention but one important example, legislatures can require cities to subsist largely on revenue from property taxes, *and,* at the same time, declare tax-exempt property belonging to universities, hospitals, religious organizations, and other public charities. Like any other corporation, cities can lobby in state capitols for more favorable treatment, but they have no power of their own to set these basic policies, even as they apply within municipal limits.

Second, cities are by and large confined by rigid territorial limits. Comparing a municipal corporation to a business corporation is instructive on this point: one must stick with its initial territory while the other can move and flex and bend, seeking lucrative transactions wherever they are to be found. "If Saab automobiles sell poorly in Virginia, let's concentrate on New York, Vermont, and New Hampshire instead"—or so might we imagine a marketer reasoning about that company. No such option is available to cities: "If New Haven's policies aren't working out in New Haven, let's try San Francisco" makes no sense. More specifically, many cities, particularly in the northeastern United States, suffer from fixed, or, as David Rusk would say, "inelastic" boundaries.[61] As once-open land turns into suburban sprawl, the legal weakness of cities is compounded by the mobility of capital and of skilled workers. Even when state government permits a city to impose a particular tax on its residents or property owners, the extent of any exaction must be carefully limited—lest those most able to pay depart, leaving behind only those least able to do so.[62] Or consider school integration. If a central city rigorously integrates its schools, and white middle-class families move to suburban systems, the city is powerless to overcome the resulting segregation.[63] It follows that cities must simultaneously function like firms competing in a market system and as units of government—a pair of tasks far easier to combine in eras of centered growth than in eras of decentering and decline.

Third, city governments are often organized as cumbersome systems of checks and balances, broadly analogous to governments of states or nations. In an era when the outward mobility of labor and capital was less important, because suburbs were marginal to central cities, the institutions of city government developed as if such competitive pressure would never come. City charters called for multiple legislative checks on any alteration of policy; boards and commissions multiplied like rabbits. The federal Constitution, with its multiple veto points, often served as an inspiration for the little republics that governed cities. Given the Yankee mistrust of newcomers from Ireland, Italy, and Poland, slowing down the course of city policy doubtless seemed a good idea in most state legislatures. Moreover, as machine politics became an object of bourgeois outrage, it seemed quite sensible to put as many fetters as possible on the rascals in fedora hats—whomever they might be at a given moment. The result was to make the cost of adaptation in city policy very high, and to further limit the agility of city government as it faced a more and more challenging environment over the decades of the twentieth century. In Part I we will see a modest City Hall succeed despite itself. In Part II we will see a far more impressive City Hall, led by the brilliant Richard C. Lee, fail in most of its goals. Urbanism, and its passing, defines most of the difference.

FEDERAL ADVENTURES IN URBAN GOVERNMENT

The immense powers of the U.S. federal government have only on occasion been directed explicitly to urban policy, and this for good reason. As one notable 1967 study of urban problems says of the United States:

In the management of its [domestic] affairs, its potential resources are greater, and its uses of them more inhibited than anywhere else in the world. Its policies are set to run a legislative obstacle race that leaves most reforms sprawling helplessly in a scrum of competing interests. Those which limp into law may then collapse exhausted, too enfeebled to struggle through the administrative tangle which now confronts them, and too damaged to attack the problems for which they were designed. This humiliation of the will of government is popularly reckoned not a bad thing. Both the abundance of resources, and the hamstringing of their exploitation, expresses the triumph of democracy.[64]

The authors are certainly right about much of American policy-making, particularly as it relates to helping either poor people or poor neighborhoods. Only on points of near-perfect national unanimity does the federal government act with concerted force. Foreign policy and national defense to one side, such points of consensus are apt to be ones on which massive consumer interests and major producer interests converge. One of these is the hegemony of the automobile, and another is the sanctity of the detached single-family home—neither of which has been friendly to our cities, both of which have been backed and sustained by governmental initiatives of stupendous proportions.[65] When policy runs *with* the grain of capitalism—as it does with the automobile industry and the building trades and once did with the railroads—the full powers of a continental state can be mobilized. When policy or ideology runs *against* the grain of capitalism, as any major redistribution of property would, it is dead from the start. When policy runs *across* the grain of capitalism—as with urban policy in all its phases except the construction of new housing and highways—laws passed in aid of our cities do indeed tend to limp across the finish line too feeble to make much of a difference. And when national urban policies do make a difference, it is sometimes not at all the intended difference.

In New Haven's case, three episodes of deliberate federal intervention stand out—in scale, in drama, and in impact on the governance of the city. The first, dating to Franklin D. Roosevelt's New Deal, was the Home Owners' Loan Corporation (HOLC). This agency, intended to reduce mortgage failure rates nationally, conducted detailed housing market studies across the country, especially in and around important cities. The effect was to send a powerful signal to bankers that the city's historical neighborhoods were high-risk places—places from which a prudent investor would withhold credit for the purchase, repair, or renovation of housing. The second episode began in the late 1930s and hit stride during the 1940s and 1950s. This was the massively subsidized construction of low-income housing projects under what eventually became the Department of Housing and Urban Development (HUD). While the intent was in part altruistic—yet also in considerable part the outcome of pressure from developers, unions, and the building trades—the eventual effect worked in concert with the HOLC studies to expand and make permanent zones of poverty and racial segregation that came to define the most difficult problems faced by New Haven in the late twentieth and early twenty-first centuries. No attempt to hinder school performance, or to encourage unemployment and even criminality, could have been much better designed than the piling up of subsidized low-income housing in exactly the places jobs were (or would become) hardest to find.

Third, and most central to the end of urbanism, comes urban renewal as first authorized under Title I of the Housing Act of 1949, and expanded under the Housing Act of 1954. Richard C. Lee, who served as mayor from 1954–70, quickly became the most visible leader in urban renewal nationally, being credited in one instance with having created in New Haven the nation's first "slumless city." New Haven pursued urban renewal more vigorously, more ingeniously, and more expensively (per capita) than any other city in the country.[66] One whole neighborhood, doubtless meeting the common man's definition of a slum, was razed. The very core of the central business district, showing strong signs of decline by the 1950s, was bulldozed and replaced with large-scale commercial facilities better suited to a suburban than to an urban setting. Other parts of the city were taken apart and put back together, in some instances with considerable success, in others not. Lee and his administration were everything that

28

Frank Rice was not—visionary, innovative, bold, technically sophisticated, infused by the confidence and intellectual resources of a great university. And yet, in attempting to restore the city to its former vitality, the Lee administration would in the main fail. It would fail not because of its own errors (of which there were some), but in spite of its (more than occasional) brilliance. It would fail not because it lacked resources or power, but in spite of its resources. It would fail because it was up against the end of urbanism.

URBANISM OLD AND NEW

I have portrayed urbanism as concretely as possible, largely to facilitate your journey into my historical research. But in so doing I have slighted some less tangible features. Urbanism accumulated a legacy of habits and expectations for conduct in daily life. In Fernand Braudel's wonderful description, such routines "control us without our even being aware of them . . . [eliciting] those thousands of acts that flower and reach fruition without anyone's having made a decision, acts of which we are not even fully aware." These encouraged every household, and nearly every individual, to be an active agent in society, and to do so within the relatively public setting of city life. There were immense differences of wealth and income, yet virtually everyone was an agent of market society—earning, selling, buying, exchanging, producing, consuming. As Braudel says of a much earlier era, "The market economy served as a link, the driving force, the restricted but vital area from which flowed encouragement, energy, innovation, enterprise, new awareness, growth, even progress."[67] Moreover large numbers of people took on complex identities, with job, nationality, ethnicity, and roles in civil organizations crisscrossing one another. In this age, every household was to some extent engaged by the shared enterprise of making a living within the context of a city that, itself, constituted a shared enterprise. There was competition and conflict aplenty, but framed more often than not by the habits of civil society. Vulgarity and bigotry were commonplaces, and yet neighborhood life had enough social glue that most days passed in civil peace. It is difficult or impossible to verify and test these intangible features of urbanism across the decades: they are "soft tissue," which seldom records itself in the fossil record. They are no less important for being harder to see through time, and I will keep them in mind throughout the analysis.

Why might you join me in this exploration? For three good reasons. First, many of the problems faced by city government today arise from the historical adaptation of its institutions to a far more supportive environment—an environment where control over urban land use represented real power, where law enforcement was carried out substantially by civilian agents operating as storekeepers, as school principals, and simply as engaged neighbors helping one another to cope with the behavior of fifteen-year-old miscreants. Such an urbanist environment tended, without much explicit effort, to support trust and cooperation among civilians, and thus to reduce the strain on public sector responsibility for the keeping of good order and civil respect. As Jane Jacobs wrote:

> The first thing to understand is that the public peace—the sidewalk and street peace—of cities is not kept primarily by the police, necessary as the police are. It is kept primarily by an intricate, almost unconscious, network of voluntary controls and standards among the people themselves, and enforced by the people themselves. In some city areas . . . the keeping of public sidewalk law and order is left almost entirely to the police and special guards. Such places are jungles. No amount of police can enforce civilization where the normal, casual enforcement has broken down.[68]

We have lost some of that supporting function. David Nye suggests the following important historical progression: "Whereas the steamboat and the train had been used to create central arteries, nodes of intersection, and dense zones of public interaction (such as railroad stations and theatre districts), Americans combined automobiles and electrification to invent privatized spaces: suburban tracts, shopping malls, gated communities, pastoral corporate estates, and 'edge cities' beyond the urban core."[69] If I am able to *evade* differences, and conflicts, by seeking private escape, is it not possible that I will lose some of the skills once so useful in negotiating those differences and resolving those conflicts? Is it not likely that I will leave behind empty spaces which will, in Jacobs' term, become jungles? This conjecture, supported by historical crime statistics, is a major reason to keep an eye on urbanism even after its passing.

Second, urbanism embodies some important ideals of a democratic society—one in which people are engaged with one another, where an individual who is a drill press operator by day may be a civic potentate by evening, where trust is earned through lifelong engagement. These ideals, bundled today under the flag of social capital, can be explored to good effect in the age of urbanism.[70] Central to the democratic experience is contact with difference—other races, other nationalities, other economic classes, other language groups. And, too often, the end of urbanism has undermined that experience by promoting social homogeneity within municipalities, leading to the evolution of regional hierarchies in which "purified communities" (Richard Sennett's term) bring likes together, safe from contact with persons different from themselves.[71] In such regional hierarchies, or ladders, the bottom rung more often than not lies in the formerly working-class neighborhoods of central cities, where opportunity is scarce, danger is commonplace, and democracy in any plausible sense seems out of reach. The notion of urbanism provides a useful perspective for critical study of such hierarchies.

Third, the New Urbanism school of design is among the most important movements afoot in our current debate on the future of American city life.[72] This movement harks back to design patterns from what I am calling the urbanist era (in truth, that is, the *old* urbanism), and does so for reasons having everything to do with the desire to recapture urbanism's power to order and govern social space humanely and well. New Urbanist designs encourage public interaction, engagement, and grounded living through features such as open porches, which look very like features found in abundance in houses from about 1910.

But design alone is apt not to suffice in isolation from other features. The extent to which the New Urbanism's design strategy can be integrated with cultural, economic, and governmental requirements for success in real city neighborhoods remains largely for the future to decide. In pressing toward that future, urbanism becomes an idea around which a fresh vision may be formed. The old urbanism—the city of steam and manure—cannot be recaptured, and it would not suit our needs if it could be. But certain critical details of that older urbanism—the magic of small commitments to place, the value of strangers in ordinary life, the humanity of well-ordered sidewalks—must be among the principal guideposts to a new era of urbanism in the twenty-first century.

URBANISM

CHAPTER 2

INDUSTRIAL CONVERGENCE
ON A NEW ENGLAND TOWN

When I first saw this city in 1812, its population was less than five thousand, and it looked to me like a country town. I wandered about the streets early one morning with a bundle of clothes and some bread and cheese in my hands, little dreaming that I should live to see so great a change or that it would ever be my home. I remember seeing the loads of wood and chips for family use lying in front of the houses, and acres of land then in cornfields and valued at a small sum, are now covered with fine buildings and stores and factories in about the heart of the city.—NEW HAVEN MANUFACTURER CHAUNCEY JEROME, 1860

Untouched by coal and steam during the first few decades of the nineteenth century, New Haven remained a town of fenced gardens and uncrowded squares.[1] These genteel features are exactly the ones that least anticipate the coming of industrial capitalism. What they did anticipate was the late twentieth-century suburb, or rather the fantasy such a suburb's promoters sought to depict for potential buyers. Amos Doolittle's 1824 "Plan of New Haven" emphasizes the area—a pre-industrial core organized around a seventeenth-century common—that would five decades later become the administrative and commercial center of an industrial city.[2] Doolittle's description reads in part as follows:

The original or Old Town was laid out in Nine squares, each 52 rods and separated by streets 4 rods in breadth. . . . The center Square is called the Public Square and is set all round with two rows of trees enclosed by a handsome railing, and is allowed to be the handsomest piece of ground in the United States. The surrounding squares, by an act of the Corporation, have been divided into four squares each, with suitable streets running parallel to the original streets. . . . The Houses are in general two stories high and built of wood, in a neat and handsome style but not expensive; however, there are several built of brick and stone three stories high. Most of the buildings stand on the street forming the squares, but not in a direct line; many are indented, so as to form handsome courtyards in front of which the owners spare no pains in having neatly fenced and ornamented with ever-greens & flowering shrubs. Almost every house is furnished with a piece of ground sufficiently large for a good garden; many are large enough to contain most kinds of valuable fruit-trees suited to our climate. The inhabitants of New Haven pride themselves very much on the cultivation of their gardens. On the whole it may be said, that there are few places better supplied than New Haven with every thing calculated to render life comfortable & agreeable.[3]

Doolittle is selling a city with an early specimen of boosterism—a genre that would grow more prevalent, more overdrawn (and often more risible) over the course of the nineteenth century and into the twentieth.[4] Unlike many later writings of its ilk, Doolittle's advertisement for New Haven exudes a *pre*-industrial sensibility. It is, one might even say in hindsight, an anti-urban advertisement for the city that would become New Haven. His enthusiasm runs toward the convenience of quiet streets, the beauty of natural sights, the cultivation of gardens and fruit trees at the town center. He directs attention to trees, gardens, courtyards, neat houses of modest design. Doolittle describes a pleasant town little different from the 1812 "country town" remembered by Chauncey Jerome in his 1860 memoir. The city's image in these works is far closer to that of suburb or borderland than to anything truly urban.[5]

Just two decades after Doolittle published his account, Jerome would begin operating the most efficient clock factory then known to the world. It would be a factory so ruthlessly well conceived and cleverly managed as to drive the products of older methods of manufacture from shop windows in New York, London, and Chicago. And Jerome would do all this within walking distance of the old pre-industrial town center. Looking back on the half-century between 1812 and the appearance of his 1860 memoir, Jerome would conclude that "I cannot now believe that there will ever be in the space of future time so many improvements and inventions as those of the past half century—one of the most important in the history of the world. Every day things with us now would have appeared to our fore-fathers incredible."[6]

New Haven itself would reflect those changes dramatically, but the new built city would emerge as an overlay on a long and very slow history of centered development.[7] Unlike central cities that began to attract industry without having developed anything much in their histories (Chicago, for example), New Haven would deposit its industrial capital—made visible in brick and steel and audible as clang and clatter—over and around a quieter grid created before an industrial city could even have been envisioned. New Haven before industrial capitalism was, to be sure, part of a market society, but it was a market of small things moving slowly, and New Haven's only large organizations—Yale College and the established Protestant churches—stood ostentatiously apart from the world of capitalism that would assert itself so forcefully in just a few short decades.

PRE-INDUSTRIAL CENTERING

New Haven in the 1820s was already an old town, approaching its two-hundredth anniversary. The near-perfect symmetry of the Old Township's central nine squares—2,840 feet (or 172 rods) on each side, enclosing about 175 acres of land—stands at the core of Doolittle's map and is already (in the 1820s) a central landmark and symbol of the town's antiquity.[8] The three-by-three structure was created in 1637–38 by the original European settlers and actually completed by 1640 (figure 2.1). This grid is sometimes imagined as a wilderness interpretation of Marcus Pollio Vitruvius' first-century Roman town plan; more commonly it is understood as an attempt to dig an idealized biblical city into wilderness stone and clay.[9] Whatever dream inspired the central squares, their symbolic importance is beyond dispute: New Haven's central district has organized the city's mental map of itself for 360 years. It has become more complicated, going from nine to twenty-nine squares between 1784 and 1802 as each original square was bisected by a new end-of-century street (as recounted by Doolittle, among others).[10] Streets are cut through old blocks, buildings erected and eventually razed. In the twentieth century whole neighborhoods were mercilessly "renewed" with federal grants, but the main design of nested squares endures through the centuries. The effect has been to provide a legible center for the city. As Kevin Lynch tells us, "legibility" refers to the "apparent clarity . . . of the city setting. By this we mean the ease with which its parts can be organized into a coherent pattern. Just as this printed page, if it is legible, can be visually grasped as a related pattern of

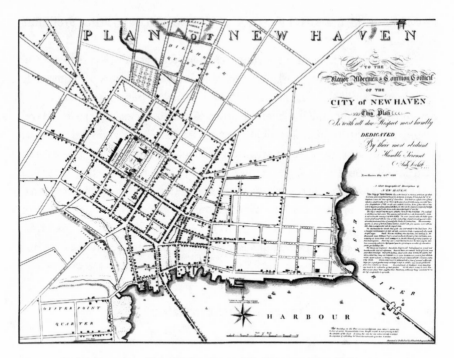

Figure 2.1. Plan of New Haven (1824) by Amos Doolittle.

recognizable symbols, so a legible city would be one whose districts or land-marks or pathways are easily identifiable and are easily grouped into an over-all pattern."[11]

This square of squares—with the old Public Square, now called the New Haven Green, in its center—defines the most salient and most central landmark now, just as it did in 1824 and even as it did in 1640. Almost alone among the man-made features of New Haven, the same squares would serve as perceptual anchors in 1863 when Union troops rallied there on the way to war, in 1910 when Frank Rice took over City Hall, in 1960 when Dick Lee erected his "Progress Pavilion" across from the Green at Church and Chapel, and in 2003 when the New Haven Festival of Arts and Ideas enlivened the Green with music and dance. In figure 2.2, the Green stands behind its iron fence to the right along Church Street, with City Hall on the left. Anyone familiar with the city immediately recognizes the legible center in this location.

The central squares were more than a merely perceptual core of the city: they were the focus of a pre-industrial activity and investment. In figure 2.1, we see

Figure 2.2. Church Street with City Hall, trolley tracks, and New Haven Green, c. 1900. NHCHS.

the original three-by-three grid anchoring the middle of the town as it stood in 1824. What was then the Public Square stands in the middle of that arrangement with one major square on each side of it (three churches identify this area in figure 2.1). The streets that were added later intensified development by creating a finer grid (these are shown in finer lines inside the nine large blocks in figure 2.1). The original nine-square arrangement created nearly four miles of street frontage on which houses, churches, and other structures might be constructed. The added streets increased this street by nearly 2.3 miles, yielding a more than 50 percent boost of potential central square locations (if all twenty-nine resulting squares can still count as central). These constituted perhaps half the city's total street frontage in Doolittle's time, but vastly more than half of the activity and investment.

The major centering institutions of this pre-industrial town—church, commerce, government, education—were all located inside the grid. The original New Haven Colony, an independent state with legal pretensions rivaling those of a great nation, endured only briefly (1637–65) before being absorbed as a town by Connecticut Colony. That colony's home very nearly *was* the nine squares, even as it laid claim to territory in places that have become Long Island and even Delaware. The "Semi-Capitols" of Connecticut were until 1871 located in both Hartford and New Haven, with the local capitol located on New Haven's Public

39

Square or Green from 1715 until that date. After 1784, when New Haven was in-corporated as a Connecticut city (within the freshly invented United States), the headquarters of city and county government, along with the remnants of the old town government, were all located centrally in the nine squares. The court sys-tem and jail were there as well, as were two fire companies. Religious institutions had played a dominant role in early New Haven history, and they continued to be important through the nineteenth century. The three major Protestant houses of worship—United Church, Center Church, and Trinity Church—stood in a row on the central Green, flanking the Statehouse. Yale College was also within the grid, a block west of the churches. Two schools also adorned the city center. Com-mercial activity was centrally focused, with a public market, two banks, a coffee-house, a tavern, and many small workshops located within the nine squares.

The salt water of Long Island Sound has been pushed away from the city cen-ter, but in 1640 the sea came within a one-minute walk of the original grid. What became nineteenth-century Fleet Street ran about 150 yards from the intersec-tion of State and George to the base of the city's major ocean shipping facility—Union or Long Wharf (State and George meet at the southern corner of the grid in figure 2.1). This major pier supported more than two dozen commercial houses, literally and economically. After having been lengthened the previous decade, Long Wharf was about 3,500 feet long in 1824.[12] Water Street ran east-west the length of the harbor and gave access to three other wharves (Tomlin-son's, Peck's, and Prescott's) as well as the shipyard that stood near the foot of Olive Street, just east of Fleet.

This seaport infrastructure functioned as an umbilicus through which the central squares sucked up commercial opportunity from afar. Ground transport was slow, uncertain, and costly. Access to markets, and to society in all its forms, was therefore concentrated almost entirely in the nine squares and the saltwater piers nearby. At the very beginning of the nineteenth century, as historian Rollin G. Osterweis observes, "New Haven was a thriving seaport with as many as a hundred foreign-bound ships leaving its wharves each year. Duties on imports averaged $150,000. The Long Wharf was lined with commercial houses, and the life of most of the citizens bore some relationship to the busy harbor. Much of the trade involved the British and French West Indies, to which went cargoes of grain, butter, meat, vegetables, cattle, horses, and lumber, and from which the vessels returned, carrying sugar and molasses to be made into rum."[13] After Jefferson's 1807 embargo—known locally as a "Damnbargo"—New Haven's oceanic commerce would never be quite what it had been before. The closely linked core and seaport would nevertheless together remain important—indeed, they would grow increasingly important in coming decades as industrial technology and capitalist investment found in them a new point of focus.

Here is one indication of the joint pulling power exerted by the two closely linked areas in pre-industrial times. Doolittle's 1824 map depicts about 1,100 buildings. Of that total, 560 lie within the nine squares, and an additional 232 are clustered in the waterfront district, making a total of nearly 800. Something close to three-quarters of the city's buildings were thus centered in these places. If we take construction cost and size into account, the proportion is doubtless far larger, perhaps on the order of 95 percent of cost and square feet of floor space. For every purpose but farming—for commerce, artisanship, administration, instruction, worship, eating, drinking, and even secure and convenient sleep—central locations trumped peripheral ones. With time, some noxious activities, like tanning, would be forced to the periphery, but in nearly all matters this was a centered pattern of economy and society.

Moreover, central investments in buildings and infrastructure in any year increased the value of central investment in subsequent years. Once there was a considerable heap of capital invested irrevocably in this one place by many different households, congregations, agencies of government, firms, and other organizations, the place was transformed and rendered valuable as never before. Particularly given the poverty of ground transport, being close to others, their organizations and facilities, came to be worth a premium for each newcomer to the region. It is perhaps helpful to think of this capital—sunk into streets and roads, docks and stage houses, houses and churches, schools and a college—as creating a "second nature" that bends the inherited "first nature" of a site to serve human needs.[14] The construction of a house, however modest, creates a second nature when it occupies a piece of ground. The double row of elms and iron railings, which later defined the Public Square, transformed it from first nature to second nature.

City formation occurs as the result of innumerable decisions to invest labor and materials in a place and in so doing to transform it from first nature to second nature. This shingles up a cluster of commitments to place, grounding the interests of those who build and pay for building all the houses and public structures, who create and maintain the streets and square, who sustain the churches and schools from year to year with their money and their effort. So the built city is, in that way, to be understood as a geographic cluster of commitments by first hundreds and then thousands of investors. True enough, planks are planks, nails are nails, and stones are stones, but they are also—just as important for the purpose of understanding cities—little signs of commitment to a place. Some are placed by investors of large capital, others by small-timers, some by those who seek to accumulate great wealth by planting small wealth in the ground, others by those who seek nothing more than shelter and a place to make ends meet. All these commitments are made permanent, or at least enduring, by the institutions of real property—the rights associated with continued ownership of places and things.[15] As commitments accumulate over generations—and as demand for central-place land-use opportunities rises—densities increase, and the centering of place becomes increasingly pronounced. Thus did a strongly focused central city develop around the original nine squares, within profound limitations set by moss-back technology, limited markets, and geographic isolation.

THE LOWLAND CITY

People and institutions make commitments to places not at random, but on the basis of promise. In the eighteenth and early nineteenth centuries, the dominant form of urban promise was the harbor city. The top fifty American cities in 1820 were virtually all harbor towns—either coastal port cities or cities abutting one or more large navigable rivers.[16] The biggest cities of the era were mostly coastal ports, topped by New York (1st in rank, with about 123,000 people), Baltimore (3rd), Boston (4th), New Orleans (5th), and Charleston, South Carolina (6th). New Haven belonged to a second tier of Atlantic ports that included Providence and Newport, Rhode Island; Portland, Maine; Norfolk, Virginia; Portsmouth, New Hampshire; Nantucket, Newburyport, Gloucester, Marblehead, Plymouth, Beverly, and New Bedford, Massachusetts; Elizabeth, New Jersey; New London, Connecticut; Wilmington, Delaware; and Brooklyn. New Haven ranked 25th in size among U.S. cities in 1820 (with just over 7,000 souls), and 23rd in 1830 (with 10,180 folks)—a mid-major, one might say. The other important category of lowland cities was located on slow-moving rivers, the largest being second-ranked Philadelphia, on the meeting of the Schuylkill and the Delaware Rivers. Other riparian port cities included Albany (11th), Richmond (12th), Cincinnati (14th), Pittsburgh (23rd), and Hartford (36th). Only a handful of 1820s cities were located in upland places away from major navigational opportunity, even though much of the nation's still-tiny manufacturing base was located in upland towns like Lowell and Holyoke, Massachusetts, at the time. The great efficiency that would combine steam power with lowland transport remained a generation in the future.

The lowland harbor city of course prospered in proportion to the quality of its water transport, which was in this era the only economically viable form of transport for heavy goods to national and world markets. As one authoritative economic history of the period concludes, "Roads were virtually useless as avenues of commerce."[17] The best highways constructed by the ancient Romans were superior to those being used in New England during the early nineteenth century. Indeed, Braudel informs us that, from Roman times until the age of rail, "with horses, coaches, ships, and runners, it was the general rule to cover at most 100 kilometers (about 62 miles) in 24 hours."[18] This limitation, imposing very high labor costs for transportation of bulk products, limited markets for most products to tiny regions, and hence removed the incentive for investment in large-scale production. Only very compact, high-value items (clothing, luxury foods, jewelry, machinery, fine instruments) could in most instances reward overland transport to distant markets.

Many of the coastal cities—Gloucester, New Bedford, and even New Haven—derived a further competitive advantage in their access to the still-vast fisheries and whaling resources of the North Atlantic. Water was also a privileged form of passenger transport. Although ships of the day traveled mostly by sail, and sailed at some peril, land travel was even less certain and slower. Here is an instance, referring to New York–Boston travel in a somewhat earlier period, 1787: "In those days there were two ways of getting to Boston: one was a clumsy stage that travels about forty miles a day, with the same horses the whole day; so that by rising at 3 or 4 o'clock and prolonging the day's ride into night, one made out to reach Boston in six days; the other route was by packet sloops up the sound to Providence and thence by land to Boston. This was full of uncertainty, sometimes being traveled in three and sometimes in nine days."[19] By 1813, something called the New York and Boston New Line Diligence Stage shortened the trip considerably: leaving New York at 2 A.M. on the first day would let you reach Boston on the second night of the journey.[20]

Access to river and ocean shipping, with all the deficiencies of the era, was a sufficient incentive for the growth of most major American cities in the era that ended in the mid-nineteenth century. By 1824, steam-powered vessels had improved these travel times, with New York now being within a half-day's voyage from New Haven's Long Wharf. Even so, most vessels coming and going from New Haven's harbor in 1824 were powered solely by the wind, and steamships often relied on auxiliary sails.

Nineteenth-century New Haven was a port of middling quality. Its harbor was fairly well sheltered from all points of the compass, although it was heavily silted along the shore. The resolution of this problem took the form of repeated dredging and recourse to longer and longer piers, sometimes reaching outlandish lengths.

This is doubtless why Long Wharf had been extended to nearly three-quarters of a mile by 1811.[21] Such a wharf, seen with twenty-first-century eyes, would be not just a transportation node but also a wholesaling district, a rough-and-tumble shopping mall, a crowded street, and the best place to pick up fresh news of the larger world. It was, moreover, a splendid jumping-off place for maritime adventure. Perhaps the most important maritime success story concerned the New Haven seal-hunting fleet of the early nineteenth century. With ten ships of up to 350 tons' displacement each, the fleet worked the South Atlantic, with enough success that one stretch of beach used to dry furs on the coast of Patagonia was known as the New Haven Green. Pelts were taken as far as Canton for sale, and some considerable fraction of New Haven's wealth in the period was accumulated by this fleet.[22] While there were occasional spikes of prominence in world commerce, New Haven never enjoyed an enduring competitive edge over larger coastal ports to its north and south.

Most of the city, and all of its areas that developed before about 1900, stand just above sea level on a coastal plain, deposited as glacial fill and as the alluvia of three rivers known today as the Quinnipiac, the Mill, and the West. These are short-haul rivers covering a combined total of roughly two hundred square miles in drainage basins.[23] They are both too shallow and too irregular to sustain commercial navigation, and they fall so gently that they provide only modest hydraulic force for generating energy once they have reached New Haven's coastal plain. The Quinnipiac, largest of the three, happened to issue in a wide mouth that formed a useful harbor—without which no substantial city would have developed on the site before the age of rail.

SHIFTING ECONOMIES OF ENERGY

New Haven and other cities in the early nineteenth century were trapped between two eras of world technology. The older "technic"[24]—based primarily on the power of falling water, supplemented by wind and the muscle power of animals, including men and women—had been in practical use for centuries and even millennia. All of its features, including mills driven by waterwheels and turbines, were known to the ancients. Even the structural use of iron was practiced by the ancient Greeks—they stabilized their great stone columns with a poured central core of metal. The newer technic was based on burning coal, to heat steam boilers that generated mechanical force transmitted to an endless variety of machines and vehicles, and on the associated advances in the metallurgy of iron and steel. This newer technology—constituting the intellectual capital of the first Industrial Revolution—centered on the steam boiler, which turned heat into motion through the expansion of steam in pistons. These machines and their accessories were already well known to businesspeople in New England by the early 1800s, with firms and individuals offering expert knowledge to be found in New Haven, just as in Boston, Providence, and Portland. Applying this knowledge at an industrial scale nevertheless took generations to unfold, and it was not until after the Civil War that the dominance of steam was beyond argument. The coal-steam-steel technology offered a differential advantage to lowland cities—cities that lacked the power of falling water could now overcome that deficiency, and at lower cost than their upland competitors, who lacked the transport infrastructure required to move coal efficiently. Moreover, the flat water that made it cheap to bring in coal also made it easy to ship out products—an amenity the upland fall-line technology could seldom if ever match economically.

In the technology of energy, as in so many other fields of human endeavor, a long lag invariably comes between a paper scheme and a piece of machinery that actually works. And after that there is a great leap between one or a few practical machines and the effective deployment of such machines on a scale large enough to change the development of whole cities and regions. A mature technological system capable of shaping cities requires capital investments in plant and equipment to produce the new device, a system of distribution, a way of financing the cost of new units, and the sustained ingenuity to make machines work under unforeseen conditions. If several such changes are being made in parallel, it further requires the integration of one ingenious adaptation with another. When all this is accomplished, it is time for workers on the plant floor to invent ways of getting around troubles introduced by novel equipment and unexpected requirements for supply and repair. Added up, this chain of requirements can take many decades, as in the case of major innovations like the coal-steam-steel complex in question. For comparison: How long is it taking now to fully implement the fruits of electronic information technologies begun in the 1940s? And when will the promised gains in productivity be fully or even mainly realized?

In the case of steam, a particularly dramatic early implementation occurred in commercial navigation, commencing with Robert Fulton's string of successes leading up to the scowlike *Clermont*'s demonstration voyage on the Hudson in 1807.[25] More advanced models, with hulls capable of handling ocean water, emerged after 1813 with the launching of the beamy *Fulton*. This very ship reached New Haven by late March 1815 in a fashion fairly typical of early development:

The Steam Boat Fulton commenced her trip to New Haven on Tuesday last. She left New York a little after five in the morning and arrived at New Haven [Long Wharf] at half after four in the afternoon, having completed her passage in a little better than eleven hours. From the performance of the boat at this time, it may be concluded that she will not often, if ever again be so long on her route. The machinery had not been tried out since last season and she was not in perfect order. Some alteration had to be made in the boiler which rendered it in some measure imperfect. She having been obliged to supply herself with such wood as the New York market afforded at the opening of spring, it was the worst kind and the least calculated to afford the necessary supply of steam. The force of steam which she ordinarily carries is four to six inches on an average [2–3 pounds] but on this voyage she seldom had more than one inch, often less. . . . Yet under all these disadvantages the boat completed her voyage . . . without any aid from sail.[26]

This voyage was part of a slow-starting transformation, a century after the first working steam engine in 1712 and half a century after James Watts' demonstration of a well-regulated steam engine in 1765.

So long as the transition to coal-steam energy generation remained immature, cities faced the ancient trade-off between access to transport and access to energy. As David Nye writes,

Early American cities were located either at tidewater or along broad, navigable streams that could not be used to produce much water power. As a result, cities were the sites of trade and skilled artisanal labor, but they contained few mills or factories. Mills and factories were dispersed across the countryside. Providence, Rhode Island, had no textile mills, but there were more than 120 in the surrounding hills. Mill communities were clustered among hollows in the steeper valleys, where water fell sharply. They were almost never adjacent to navigable streams. Indeed, an 1843 congressional report declared: "Water power and good navigable streams are as incompatible as any two things in nature."[27]

This was assuredly true of New Haven. In its thirty-five-mile course, the Quinnipiac falls a total of 140.9 feet—almost exactly 4 feet per mile. This gradual rate of fall, moreover, declines as the river approaches sea level and is regularly reversed by tidal action in the last few miles. In data for 1880, this river was used to generate a total of 735 horsepower in upstream sections of New Haven County.[28] Its course through the city emerges slowly from wide marshes and offers negligible power potential—scarcely worth mentioning except on an outgoing tide. The West River offered a little more force during periods of high volume but provided at best minor economic contribution to industry. Only the Mill River offered commercially competitive waterpower as far downstream as New Haven, and that on a distinctly minor scale.[29] Eli Whitney himself failed in his largest contract for the production of firearms, due in part to the difficulty of building and maintaining an efficient water turbine at this site.[30] New Haven in 1824 was, as a result, mostly a city of trade and artisanship: removed from waterpower by river space, and from steam power by the time it took to make it practical on the factory floor.

The water-wind-animal technology that still governed most of New Haven's economy up to about the 1850s carried with it a cluster of decentering forces, which acted to limit the advantage of central-place locations in an urban region— at least in the case of a lowland city. The most fundamental of these decentering forces is of course access to waterpower. As one anti-urban commentator generalized in 1832, "Steam aggregates workers and promotes vice while water power disperses them with benefit to their morals."[31] The economic importance of decentering waterpower may be observed as late as the 1840s if we look at the manufacture of cotton cloth in Connecticut by county. Table 2.1 compares New Haven County with upland, largely rural Windham County, in northeastern Connecticut.[32] The ratios run about 35:1 in favor of the less populous place. The key to Windham County's success in the cotton milling business is not far to find in its many fast-falling streams—French River, Brandy Brook, Leland Brook, and the like. The location of Norwich (then a top-sixty city nationally), just south of Windham County at the top of the Thames River's navigable portion, created a nice combination by linking those upland mills with water transport and access to world markets.

Partly for reasons of energy, and partly for reasons of economic organization, most of New Haven's manufacturing up through the 1840s was carried out in small shops. As Ira Katznelson writes of the national pattern, "Until the 1840s manufacturing clearly had a subsidiary role in the older port cities. Local markets were too small and the national transportation system too primitive to support large-scale manufacturing independent of mercantile imperatives. Rather, the urban economy was characterized by highly diversified industrial production in small handicraft and unmechanized firms that had relatively low output."[33]

Of the firms listed in table 2.2, the average number of employees is about fourteen, and this would be far lower save for the influence of a few large industries, such as clockmaking (then in its infancy with fewer than a hundred hands).[34] Notice also that the bulk of New Haven's employment and production is com-

Table 2.1. Cotton Textile Production, 1845

Variable	New Haven County	Windham County
Cotton spindles in use	3,968	100,083
Pounds of cotton consumed	271,020	4,810,166
Yards of cotton cloth produced	500,000	17,500,471
Value of cotton cloth	$30,000	$1,237,944

Source: Tyler, 1846.

fortably adapted to the older technologies. Carriages and related production (springs, castings, tanning) account for just over half the jobs and about 60 percent of the capital in table 2.2.[35] In contrast, steam and brass together account for just ten jobs and $3,000 in capitalization. The old technology kept the firms small by making it very difficult to organize large plants around intensive energy consumption—and kept upriver energy consumption at a distance from easy and cheap means of distribution. Moreover, the going pattern of economic organization made it difficult to amass capital in quantities required by large-scale factories. The standard forms of ownership were sole proprietorship and partnership, both of which typically required that the direct operators of a firm also be its equity investors.[36] The coming dominance of the joint stock company in the years after 1840 would change that irrevocably.

Agriculture also limited centralization. Agricultural energy could beat either of two principal paths into the economy—either as work done by animal muscle or as vegetable foodstuffs consumed by those animals whose muscle-power would perform work. Neither could be generated without access to wide open spaces and good soil, either for grazing or for cultivation. Access to extensive land—hence to the dispersed benefits of solar energy transmitted by photosynthesis—was by its nature decentering. A century before the mechanization of agriculture became feasible, population needed to be stationed across broad reaches of the landscape to do the necessary work. This is true in some degree even today, but it held far greater importance in the nineteenth century, when agricultural production remained labor-intensive in the extreme. From 1640 onward, New Haven had generated smaller towns—usually on the explicit basis of religious schisms, but also one suspects that economics and ecology exerted steady pressure toward decentralizing population.[37] The result was an irregular ring of smaller towns surrounding New Haven.

Each member of the inner ring of nineteenth-century satellite towns—Branford, Hamden, North Haven, East Haven, Orange, and Woodbridge—was an

Table 2.2. Selected Manufacturing Firms in New Haven, 1845

Industry, by product	Firms	Total capital	Total employment	Mean employment
Coaches, wagons, sleighs	24	$287,600	460	19.2
Latches, locks, handles	3	$ 74,500	115	38.3
Indian rubber suspenders	1	$ 14,000	100	100.0
Clocks	1	$ 40,000	90	90.0
Carriage springs, etc.	4	$ 38,500	74	18.5
Castings (metal)	4	$ 64,900	71	17.8
Chairs, cabinets	9	$ 26,050	71	7.9
Worsted fabric	4	$ 8,000	37	9.3
Tin and sheet iron	8	$ 24,400	35	4.4
Sashes, blinds	3	$ 14,800	32	10.7
Paper	1	$ 50,000	30	30.0
Leather	6	$ 29,600	27	4.5
Soap, candles	4	$ 12,200	16	4.0
Hats, caps	3	$ 3,500	15	5.0
Files	2	$ 3,500	10	5.0
Cordage	2	$ 4,700	8	4.0
Steam engines, boilers	2	$ 2,000	6	3.0
Brass foundries	2	$ 1,000	4	2.0
Musical instruments	2	$ 2,000	3	1.5
Total of samples	85	$ 701,250	1,204	14.2

Source: Tyler, 1846.

agricultural village organized around a Congregational church. In 1820, these six towns together had (for the last time before 1970) more residents than the central city. This reflects three historical facts: that the considerable decentering power of agricultural production (croplands are of necessity space-intensive) limited the population density, that the poverty of transportation limited the importation of basic foodstuffs, and that the industrial take-off of the central city was just coming into sight in 1820. The city's growth would, starting in about 1840, dominate its region for more than a century. Only as the era of urban renewal drew to a close in 1970 would these towns overtake the city in total population, long after the economic disappearance of large-scale agriculture in the region.

By the nineteenth century a spatial division of labor had emerged, with most agricultural production being carried out in perimeter towns. Using Daniel Tyler's 1845 survey of production as a rough measure, New Haven's share of most standard farm products is seen to vary between about 3 and 13 percent of the total for these seven towns.[38] In no agricultural product did New Haven come close to being a regional leader. Some differences of specialization had emerged among the rural towns so that, for instance, East Haven and Branford led in the potato business, and dairy farming seems to have been most intensive in Orange, Woodbridge, and Hamden. In the larger context of New England agriculture, the New Haven region seems to have been altogether ordinary, contributing 1–3 percent of Connecticut's output in most cereal and dairy commodities in the period.

It is sometimes supposed that the late twentieth- and early twenty-first-century decentralization of manufacturing to Greenfield sites constitutes a novel phenomenon, but this is not entirely so. As already suggested, access to fast-falling water often pulled shop floors far from central cities and their rich markets. New Haven's slow-moving rivers were a competitive hindrance compared with the bigger, stronger Housatonic and Naugatuck Rivers—which ran toward Long Island Sound through western sections of New Haven County and attracted major facilities to westerly towns like Derby, Naugatuck, Waterbury, and Oxford. In 1845, for instance, Derby produced 500,000 yards of cotton and 15,000 yards of woolen fabrics. Naugatuck produced 150,000 yards of woolen "satinet" cloth valued at $110,000 the same year. Even the inner-ring villages had manufactories of their own. Paper and tin products were being fabricated in East Haven. Hamden was home to a brass foundry, a firearms plant, and several producers of carriage springs. North Haven manufactured metal castings, door latches and handles, locks, chairs, cabinets, shoes, screw augers and drill bits, carriage bolts, and the like. Branford had a modest output of agricultural equipment. Even tiny Woodbridge produced friction matches, candlesticks, and carriage wheels.[39] The central city did enjoy some advantages in transport, especially after the Farmington Canal opened in 1829 to supplement New Haven's transportation system over the course of its very short lifespan (it was converted to rail in less than twenty years).[40] And some of those advantages would prove important in years to come.

CHEAP ENERGY AND LOCATION OF STEAM MECHANIZATION

An early hint of things to come is hidden in the 1845 economic data for New Haven and other towns in the surrounding county.[41] Anthracite coal (known in the period as "stone coal") began arriving in the area by about 1827.[42] In 1845, the burning of anthracite coal was recorded for New Haven and nine other nearby places, with tonnage and its value or cost recorded for each (table 2.3). Notice, of

Table 2.3. Coal Consumption, New Haven
and Area, 1845

Town	Anthracite tonnage	Anthracite cost or value in dollars
Branford	60	360
Derby	2,636	13,640
Meriden	920	5,980
Middlebury	30	240
Naugatuck	314	2,349
New Haven	3,552	17,310
North Haven	100	670
Oxford	36	216
Wallingford	67	469
Waterbury	834	7,146

Source: Tyler, 1846.

course, that there is considerable variation in the total tonnage burned: New Haven and Derby leap off the page for sheer quantity. But the interesting datum concerns cost per ton (estimated as value/tonnage). Waterbury anthracite is the costliest, at $8.57 per ton. Middlebury, Naugatuck, Wallingford, North Haven, Oxford, and Meriden also confront higher than average prices.[43] They are too far away from cheap, fixed-path transportation as was provided by coastal shipping and would soon be provided by the coming of rail. New Haven's cost was $4.88 per ton, and Derby's was only a little higher, at $5.17. These economies of transport and scale accruing to lowland towns foretold a growing force in the economic and social history of New Haven over the next seventy years: a premium would be attached to central city locations for manufacturing, and with it an implicit penalty would be imposed on peripheral locations. Transport costs would favor lowland locations like New Haven. Economies of scale would favor central locations like New Haven. Between the two convergent factors, a lasting competitive advantage would be created. Half a century later, in 1892, a style of booster very different from Doolittle would contend that:

Among the conditions which have for many years aided in promoting the growth of the city is the cheapness of fuel for domestic use and the supply of our manufacturing industries. No town in New England has been able to obtain their fuel at rates as low as have been afforded our customers. . . . The right place to manufacture successfully is evidently at a point where raw materials accumulate naturally, is contiguous to and easy of access from the original sources of supply, and where, at the same time, there is cheap power, cheap fuel, and advanced and ample facilities for marketing the products. New Haven has always furnished these conditions in preeminent degree. Situated at a focal point of six lines of railroads, connecting the city with the markets of the East and West, the lumber regions of the North, and the coal fields of the South, and bordered by the water of the Sound, with a harbor and channel that accommodate ships of the largest size, material necessarily accumulates here, and cheap power is amply provided and assured for all time.[44]

Doolittle's vision of fenced gardens has been replaced by a vision of efficient smokestacks, a bustling harbor, and the noisy poetry of freight yards. While the forecast of cheap power "for all time" turns out to have been badly mistaken, the basic story told here is correct and powerfully so for the years leading to 1910. Capital would flow into the core city and build itself into Strouse-Adler, Cowles, Sargent, Fitch, Candee Rubber, Bigelow, National Pipe Bending, Winchester, and all the others. Joseph Sargent's 1863 decision to move his manufacturing plant from New Britain to New Haven was made for exactly these reasons: "Costs of shipment to and from New Haven were lower than to and from New Britain. Goods can be shipped from New Haven to Bellows Falls cheaper than from New Britain. Coal, iron, and other materials can be delivered on the New Haven wharf as low as at New York."[45] The cost advantages achieved in New Haven figured heavily in Chauncey Jerome's 1860 account of the decision to move his clock factory into the city in 1844:

When I moved my . . . business to New Haven, the project was ridiculed by other clock-makers, of going to a city to manufacture by steam power, and yet it seems to have been the commencement of manufacturers in the country, coming to New Haven to carry out their business. Numbers came to me to get my opinion and learn the advantages it had over manufacturing in the country, which I always informed them in a heavy business was very great, the item of transportation alone over-balancing the [cost] difference between water and steam power. . . . There is no place on earth where [clock manufacturing] can be started and compete with New Haven, there are no other factories where it can possibly be made so cheap. I have heard men ask the question "why can't clocks be made in Europe on such a scale, where labor is so cheap?" If a company could in any part of the old world get their labor ten years for nothing, I do not believe they could compete with the

Yankees in this business. They can be made in New Haven and sent into any part of the world for more than a hundred years to come for less than one half of what they could be made for in any part of the old world.[46]

Here, as in the previous quotation, the author combines a modest overstatement of what was true as he wrote with a groundless forecast that it would continue so into another century. From the 1840s onward, Jerome had used steam and skilled labor to stamp out the metal gears for clocks previously made singly as castings, thereby precipitously driving down the world price of shelf clocks. Jerome Manufacturing sent its products into markets across the globe and sold them in the hundreds of thousands on the basis of value for money. Here is a telling story about his pricing policy and its relation to British markets:

> Around 1840 Chauncey Jerome, a Connecticut clock maker, used inter-changeable parts to produce a one-day brass clock for less than fifty cents. He exported some to England in 1842. English customs reserves the right to confiscate goods at their invoice valuations to protect themselves against undervaluation. The clocks were clearly undervalued by English standards, and they were confiscated. This was fine with Jerome; he had sold his ship-ment at full price quickly and easily. He sent another, larger load, which was duly confiscated. But when he sent a third, still larger load, the customs au-thorities acknowledged their earlier errors and allowed it in.[47]

New Haven was then a cost-competitive environment for manufacturing as it had never been in previous history—and would cease to be a few generations hence. New Haven and other manufacturing cities in the northeastern United States had by the 1850s become objects of considerable interest to outsiders. An 1854 British parliamentary "Report on the Machinery of the United States of America" notes Eli Whitney's famed armory, by then more than half a century old, but attends in detail to three other New Haven plants:

> Jerome's Clock Manufactory. In this establishment clocks are made in im-mense quantities for home use and exportation; 600 per diem being the yield, with 250 men employed.
>
> Machinery is most extensively used in all parts of the manufacture, and the clocks at a very low price, the movements of some costing only $1.
>
> Mssrs. Davenport and Mallory's Works. This [is] a manufactory of pad-locks and locks; and the same system of special machinery is applied to every particular part; and all . . . can be interchanged.
>
> Mssrs. Candie [sic] and Company's Factory. This is a manufactory of india

rubber shoes, in which machinery is applied as far as practicable, and with 175 hands 2,000 pair are daily produced.[48]

The authors were seeing characteristic Yankee ingenuity applied to complex manufacturing under conditions of cheap energy and expensive labor—with the substitution of machine force for hand craft at every turn, and with increasing reliance on the so-called American system of interchangeable parts. For New Haven, as for many cities sharing its strategic position, this was only the beginning of economic expansion.

RAILROAD DEVELOPMENT AND CASCADING CENTRAL CITY INVESTMENT

Trains became pivotal at this stage. Steam-powered rail transport appears to have had several birthdays between 1803 and 1812 in the United Kingdom, but the first commercially useful U.S. railroad was evidently the Mauch Chunk Railroad, which carried Pennsylvania coal, as early as 1826. By the summer of 1830, Peter Cooper's one-horsepower Tom Thumb was able to carry three dozen passengers on a short run through Baltimore. By the early 1830s, short-haul railways were springing up in Philadelphia, New York, and several smaller places. Construction of track expanded more or less exponentially in the earliest years: 40 miles in 1830, 99 miles in 1831, 199 miles in 1832.[49] Service between Hartford and New Haven began in 1839, and the critical New York & New Haven line was opened a decade later (although freight equipment would be added only in 1851). The Farmington Canal became the New Haven & Northampton, leading north and west from Long Wharf in 1847. Eastward service to New London, and thence Boston, opened in 1852.[50] By 1869, a dozen companies saw fit to buy advertising space in a New Haven directory under the heading of "Steam Railways," even when they were steamship or horse rail companies by name.[51] By the mid-nineteenth century a new technic, driving people and resources toward the centers of lowland cities across America, was thus in full operation.

A cascade of investment and innovation in New Haven would occur in the late 1840s and succeeding years, whose dynamism may perhaps be grasped by looking at a highly selected chronology:

1843   L. Candee Rubber Co. is founded
1844   Chauncey Jerome moves his main manufacturing operations to New Haven
        New York & New Haven Railroad incorporated

1847 American National Life and Trust Co. formed, with Yale Prof. Benjamin Silliman Sr. as president

  New Haven Gas Company organized

  New York & New Haven Railroad laid out

  Oliver Winchester brings the city's first shirt factory, hires 800 workers

  New Haven Gas Company chartered, builds plant on St. John Street

1848 New York & New Haven Railroad opens for service as far as Williamsburgh, New York, on December 29, 1848

  New Haven & New London Railroad chartered

  New Haven & Northampton Railroad completed using much of the Farmington Canal line

1849 Gas lighting of New Haven streets begun

  New Haven–New York rail opens passenger service

  New Haven Water Company chartered

1850 Shoninger Organ founded in New Haven

  Jerome Manufacturing becomes a joint stock corporation

1851 George Newhall opens carriage plant in New Haven based on steam power

  Merchants Bank opens

1852 New Haven & New London Railroad opens

  Railroad service to New London begins

  Candee Rubber becomes a corporation, with $200,000 capital

  Philip Fresenius establishes his brewery in New Haven

  Edward Malley forms dry goods business, which shortly becomes a major department store

1853 Eli Whitney Blake, nephew of the great man, invents the "Blake stone breaker" for crushing rock for road-making, using pressure up to 27,000 pounds per inch. It becomes a standard for road-building technology well into the twentieth century.

  Quinnipiac Bank opens

1854 New Haven Steam Saw Mill opens with 250 hp and $50,000 in capital

  Tradesmen's Bank founded. Elm City Bank also founded, later to be Second National

  Seneca Oil founded in New Haven by James M. Townsend (later drills first well ever in Pennsylvania)

1855 Tradesmen's Bank opens

  Gas lighting of New Haven Green begun

1857   New Haven Clock formed out of wreckage of Jerome firm, led by Hiram Camp, James English, James Hillhouse, and one Marmanus Welch

This listing greatly understates the number and complexity of investments but perhaps captures something of their variety and tempo. Not just manufacturing but retailing and infrastructure are emerging on an altogether novel scale. Rail is spreading across whole regions. By the Civil War's beginning, New Haven has become a spider strategically placed at the center of her own steel web, with branches reaching out to New York, Boston, Hartford, Northampton, Bridgeport, and all the hundreds of other market towns reachable from those places. And capital is being organized and reorganized in a manner that will become increasingly familiar (note the case of Jerome manufacturing's arrival, failure, and reorganization in a very short period—a period during which its production reached 200,000 per year and world markets responded very favorably). Capital in its many forms is growing in density within the central city of New Haven and will continue to do so well into the twentieth century.

CENTERING TECHNOLOGIES IN ENERGY AND TRANSPORTATION

The complex of centering technologies can for present purposes be boiled down to four features.[52] First, it depends on the development of low-cost, high-reliability fixed-path transport. This is transport designed to carry high volumes of materials, goods, or people to a relatively small number of predetermined destinations along a set route. Low cost is achieved by high volume and rigid targeting—one did not move 10,000 tons of coal, or a train-load of immigrants, nimbly and flexibly from door to door, village to village. The most important terminal points of fixed-path transportation were, or fast became, central-place locations.[53] As we have seen, coastal shipping was well developed in New Haven before 1800; canal shipping served the city from 1829 to 1846; as just noted, rail would come full-blown in 1851 with the first freight operations of the New York & New Haven (later New York, New Haven & Hartford) Railroad. The railroads of course formed the supreme instance of fixed-path transport, with all its essential features: "Although railroads could be extended almost anywhere, a good one was costly to build, rigidly fixed in place, and efficient only for routine mass movement of standardized commodities (including passengers) in a limited variety of uniform vehicles."[54] Table 2.4 sums up the rapid deployment of this technology.

Table 2.4. Horsepower in Fixed-Path Transport, 1850–1910

Year	Railroad locomotives	Powered merchant ships	Ships under sail	Total fixed-path	Percentage growth
1850	586[a]	325	400	1,311	
1860	2,156	515	597	3,268	149.3
1870	4,462	632	314	5,408	65.5
1880	8,592	741	314	9,647	78.4
1890	16,980	1,124	280	18,384	90.6
1900	24,501	1,663	251	26,415	43.7
1910	51,308	3,098	220	54,626	106.8

[a]Horsepower is × 1,000.

Source: U.S. Department of Commerce.

Second, centering development depends on *an energy technology attaching a penalty to consumption at long distances from the point of generation.* The burning of coal to make steam is a classic case. Putting aside the mine itself, coal in great quantity is economically delivered only close to rail and shipping heads, hence New Haven's price advantage. Unlike alternating current electricity (which travels well across long distances), old-fashioned steam is a localizing energy technology: its distribution—by mechanical belts and pulleys—is economical only over very short distances.[55] The productive force—in looming textiles or grinding metal, say—must therefore be consumed close to the point of its generation as steam.[56] This feature, shared by steam and water power alike, accounts in considerable measure for the compact, multifloor design of most nineteenth-century factories—since such designs (by approaching cubic form) minimize average distances from generation to deployment. Steam, moreover, must be generated close to fixed-path transport if it is to be competitive. This creates a high premium for central-place industrial development. The positioning of Sargent & Company at New Haven's confluence of rail and shipping is exactly what this technology rewards and in the long run requires of manufacturers.

A massive *concentration of labor at the site of manufacturing* is both cause and consequence of centering development. The Industrial Revolution—still in progress during the twenty-first century—repeatedly substitutes capital for labor, machinery for muscle. But the early version of industrialism, which led to the centered city, demanded a great deal of direct human labor at the plant. Many operations were done by brute force—for example, the shoveling and loading of materials, the packing and loading of finished product, the removal of waste materials from shop floors. Even where great mechanical leverage was achieved it typically required the continuous intervention of operators who controlled and fed each piece of equipment. Nothing that would strike us as a case of "automation" was achieved in this period. Moreover, machinery required continuous service and repair. Even, for instance, in an activity as refined as clock-making, Jerome Manufacturing would have need of nearly a thousand workers. Sargent hardware would need many more. And a truly heavy manufacturing operation, such as the Winchester Repeating Arms plant in New Haven, would use more than 10,000 workers. The effect was to concentrate population, and with it to draw in housing, retailing, worship, and all the rest of daily life.

A fourth and last feature of centered development is the absence of high quality variable-path transportation. Variable-path transportation allows the traveler to pick his route, and to revise it, during the course of a journey. In 1824, horses and shoe leather were dominant methods of going to destinations not scheduled by rail and ship—to the store, church, home, school, and work. These were very nimble yet very slow methods of getting around—practical only over short distances, thus limiting to the development of peripheral locations for house, school, church, and the like. In the coming decades, the horse trolley and eventually the trolley itself would offer a compromise between fixed and variable-path transportation, making possible the partial diffusion of population over the cityscape.[57] But the preautomotive poverty of variable-path transportation would keep people close to the urban core right through the mayoral days of Frank Rice, 1910–17. Even as late as 1900, New Haven had fewer than fifty miles of paved streets in its total inventory. Even these were littered with horse manure in quantities difficult for the twenty-first-century reader to imagine. Horses probably deposited at least fifty acre-feet of excrement yearly—enough to fill the Yale Bowl (constructed in 1913) up to about the tenth row above the playing field in one year, and enough to fill it totally in a decade.[58] In figure 2.3, we see Congress Avenue in the Hill neighborhood, dense with stores and pedestrians using very old techniques for getting around. The woman, left foreground, seems to be using a baby carriage to haul lumber![59]

New Haven's great period of centered development, running from about 1850 to 1920, was sustained by the historical coincidence of all four features. Together with a national revolution in agricultural productivity, and an era of open immigration, these features constitute New Haven's version of what I have been calling the "accidents of urban creation." There was nothing fated about the matter, just the peculiar sequence of technological success stories and failures, put in place by the compulsions of capitalist organization. Fixed-path transportation,

Figure 2.3. Mixed retail and residential use of Congress Avenue, c. 1890. Note woman in left foreground using baby carriage to transport lumber. NHCHS.

materializing in rail and ocean shipping, was abundant, cheap, and fairly reliable. Accidents were common, and the casualties among railroad men ran in the thousands some years. But, for all that, rail was an overwhelming economic force in this period. It ran, moreover, in all directions from New Haven. The dominant (nontransport) energy technology was steam transmitted by belt and shaft, an arrangement that all but compelled central-place location for heavy manufacturing. The associated manufacturing required massive labor; and the working-class neighborhoods, which developed around the old plants, are testimony to a last feature. Variable-path transportation—in the form of cars—got good enough to let workers escape the shadow of the plant only toward the end of the era. For all these reasons, steam boilers and steam fitters, factories and operatives in the thousands, sweatshops and seamstresses, tenements and families crowded into the center of New Haven and learned to live with one another at close range. This was a fragile coincidence that came apart over the course of the years 1920–70.

HORSEPOWER REVOLUTION

The New Haven story is embedded in a deep transformation in the American economy over the last half of the nineteenth century. A useful way of capturing this larger story line is to estimate the grand total of all the mechanical energy at the disposal of firms and other organizations in the U.S. economy in any given year.[60] The estimates consider only "prime movers" to avoid double-counting: If a turbine generates energy from falling water or pressurized steam (prime mover), we count that power and do not go on to also count the power exerted by the machines, vehicles, or appliances its energy in turn drives. Thus, electricity never counts in the total since it is always derived from a generating source, such as falling water, rushing steam, or the fossil heat of coal, gas, and oil. As table 2.5 indicates, the total horsepower in the economy increased sixteenfold over a six-decade span ending in 1910. The great leap upward in total energy was related as both cause and effect to the concentration of capital investments in high-energy commitments to transportation and manufacturing. Because industrial energy could do so much, and could allow the relatively efficient employment of large workforces, corporate organization grew rapidly in such fields as railroads, oil, coal, steel, and heavy manufacturing. The ability of corporations to assemble large concentrations of capital made continuous change in energy technology possible on a scale never before contemplated by practical people. Investments in horsepower were, from the view of almost any one firm, compulsory: the threat of competition (and substitution of wholly new products) by others using massive energy again and again compelled increasing reliance on power machinery, high-temperature distilling, and fast transportation of bulk loads. Between 1860 and 1910, the horsepower economy thus grew at a rate equivalent to a steady 4.7 percent each year.

This infusion of fossil power revolutionized fixed-path transportation, which worked to the very decided advantage of the lowland cities. As table 2.4 suggests, ships and trains—mostly trains—came to command mechanical energy on a scale unmatched in human history. The lowland harbor cities—New Haven, Baltimore, Brooklyn, New York, Philadelphia, Pittsburgh, Chicago, Cleveland, Buffalo, and all the rest—gained a major and long-lasting competitive advantage with the arrival of freight and passenger rail. Not only were lowland cities natural rail terminals because of their harbors, they were also attractive because less costly rail routes almost invariably ran at low (and relatively constant) elevations. The result was a powerful set of incentives for investment in urban industry: rail to deliver coal at the cheapest rate, coal to produce steam at competitive cost, steam to drive manufacturing at costs below competition, labor gathered in increasing throngs to feed and tend the machines, housing for working families, retail near the housing. And, wherever people were congregated in great density came the institutions of daily life—schools, saloons, clubs, singing groups, the-

Table 2.5. Total Horsepower in the U.S. Economy,
1850–1910

Year	Total horsepower (× 1,000)	Percentage growth
1850	8,495	
1860	13,763	62
1870	16,931	23
1880	26,314	55
1890	44,086	68
1900	63,952	45
1910	138,810	117

Source: U.S. Department of Commerce.

aters, athletic teams, mutual benefit societies, ethnic organizations, and all the rest. Thus came the centered industrial city.

Even in the face of these mechanical eruptions, the absolute total animal horsepower in the U.S. national economy *grew* in every decade between 1850 and 1920, starting at an estimated 5,960,000 horsepower in 1850 and ending up at 22,430,000 horsepower by 1920. In Connecticut, no comparable data are available, but it is quite probable that the total began falling after about 1890 as the competitive force of western agriculture made itself felt. But nationally its *relative* importance declined in every decade from 1850 onward. Animals accounted for roughly 70 percent of the national horsepower pool in 1850, rivaled distantly by steam and water. By 1880 their share was down to 45 percent, to 29 percent in 1900, and to less than 5 percent by 1920 (scarcely 0.01 percent today). The really important trend is in the *total* horsepower of the U.S. economy. Between 1850 and 1920 total horsepower expanded more than fiftyfold. *By the 1920s horsepower equivalent to the national total in 1850 was being added to the economy every ninety days.* And a very high fraction of the total added between 1850 and 1920 was devoted to centering technologies: rail, heavy shipping, and steam-powered factories producing goods for export beyond the city and even beyond its region.

REVOLUTIONARY CAPITALISM

These technological developments are generally thought to be the most innovative products of the late nineteenth century. While immense ingenuity, particularly at the shop-floor level, was to be found everywhere, this view is misleading in two respects. First, most of the technologies were already well defined before this period—steam boilers of a sort went back centuries, and the Manchester of the early 1800s looked like a pretty good confirmation of their practicality. As early as 1801 Philadelphia was using steam to pump the public water supply.[61] It was in the implementation, financing, and management of the technology that the era's most remarkable and lasting innovations occurred. Second, institutional invention by and for capitalist enterprise was the most fundamental and world-shaping event of the period. In 1840, proprietorships and partnerships dominated the economic landscape. No firm of that period had the organizational capacity to manage a workforce of 50,000 of a production process designed to reach national (even world) markets on a massive scale. By 1910, direct ownership had been displaced at the center of the American economy by the joint stock corporation and its associated institutions—equity markets integrated across wide geographies, professional management, vertical integration, penetration of immense markets, and aggressive accumulation of capital. These changes were, however, linked to the prevailing technologies of the era. As Alfred Chandler, the great historian of American business, writes:

> The modern corporation had its beginnings in the eighteen fifties with the swift spread of the railroad network and the factory system during that decade. The railroads, as the nation's first big business, came to provide the only available model for financing and administering the giant industrial enterprises. The railroads played this role because their promoters, financiers, and managers were the first to build, finance, and operate business enterprises requiring massive capital investment and calling for complex administrative arrangements. The financing of the railroads required such large amounts of money that it brought into being modern Wall Street and its specialized investment bankers. . . . An individual or partnership simply could not supply enough capital to build even a small railroad. The sale of corporate stocks and bonds was essential. . . . But the railroad was only the model. The parent of the large corporation was the factory. The modern factory with its power-driven machinery and its permanent working force, whose tasks were subdivided and specialized, appeared in the United States as early as 1814. Yet until the swift spread of an all-weather transportation network, including the railroad, the ocean-going steamship, and the telegraph, relatively few factories existed in the United States outside of the textile and related industries. Then in the late eighteen forties and fifties factory production began for the first time to be significant in

the making of sewing machines, clocks, watches, ploughs, reapers, shoes, suits, and other ready-made clothing, and rifles and pistols for commercial use. The same years saw the spread of large integrated iron works.[62]

These capitalist firms provided compelling motivation for the implementation of industrial technologies, and consequently the drive toward centralized urban development. The giants of the period—U.S. Steel, Standard Oil, American Tobacco, International Harvester, American Can, Pullman, U.S. Rubber, Armour and Company—all occupied major central city locations in places like Chicago, Pittsburgh, Cleveland, and Baltimore. But literally thousands of lesser firms were competing for competitive advantage in every way available to them—and one of the best was to capture and develop space in central cities enjoying access to heavy transportation, large labor pools, and tightly woven commercial webs for supply and distribution. Cities of this sort did not, by and large, have to beg these companies to invest. And New Haven became such a city in the last half of the nineteenth century. This development required nothing more than passive competence from City Hall.

REGIONAL GROWTH, CENTERED ON THE CITY

In her 1930 history of New Haven County, Mary Mitchell quotes an 1890 observer of the New Haven hinterlands as follows:

> Formerly there were many small manufactories in the country and many country mechanics: wagons, shoes, clothes, harness, and all the various articles used in the country were largely made in the country. As the country blacksmith, wagon-maker, shoe-maker and tailor have gone to the cities and now do their work there, the country lawyer and store-keeper have followed. As the rural population has declined from these causes, and the farmer, who saw his farm decreasing in value, his capital shrinking, his crops no longer paying fairly because of Western competition, has turned his thoughts also to other fields of enterprise, and thus farming in some towns has actually declined.[63]

The remedies proposed for Connecticut farming were numerous, and Mitchell quotes one expert as suggesting "raising sheep, veal, horses, poultry, eggs, squabs, trout, carp, honey, mushrooms, beef" but "not all of course on the same farm." While population in New Haven's first-ring satellites had fallen by 15 percent in the 1880s, the general picture was one of static to slow-growing communities. While Woodbridge had lost nearly half its population over the nineteenth century, other towns—East Haven, Branford, Orange, Hamden, North Haven—were growing slowly.[64] But, compared to the central city, now stoked with cheap energy and a corresponding competitive advantage, the hinterlands seemed to shrink in comparison. The city's population was driven forward with increasing velocity by the explosion of economic activity. Between 1850 and 1920 the place experienced an eight-fold growth in population. Roughly speaking, New Haven added its full 1850 population of twenty-odd thousand souls to its population every ten years for the next sixty years. In 1820, New Haven and its six most immediate suburbs stand at parity in total population. By 1850 the ratio approached 3:1 (20,345 to 7,524). By 1870, nearly 5:1 at 50,840 to 10,831. By 1910, the ratio was 8:1 (133,605 to 16,820). This is a classic story of centering growth.[65]

It is, moreover, a critical piece in our understanding of twenty-first-century New Haven. In the whole history of the place since Europeans arrived to stay in 1637, one short period accounts for the vast majority of all population growth. This is the era of centered industrial development running from 1840 to 1920. Even if we concentrate on just the last fifty years, starting in 1870, the point makes itself. In this half-century, 111,727 new citizens were added to the city's total—net of death and departure. This short period produced *more than two-thirds of the total net growth achieved across all the centuries,* and it is exactly the period sketched in Chapter 1 as the "accident of urban creation." The housing stock of present-day New Haven owes more to this period than to any other. And so too does nearly every other aspect of city life reach back to this era of accelerating growth. The eventual failures of mid-twentieth-century New Haven were set up by this great rush of central city growth, and by its abrupt end.

If we look at the whole of New Haven County, a more complex picture emerges. New Haven's growth is of course still remarkable, but it must be set against the growth of other industrial nodes located in towns such as Waterbury, Derby, Ansonia, Naugatuck, Milford, and Meriden. By 1910, Waterbury was a city nearly rivaling New Haven, with about 90,000 people and a booming industrial core, now well served by rail. The Housatonic River's "valley towns" of Derby, Naugatuck, and Ansonia shared a major boom in metals manufacturing, particularly in brass. Meriden had become a national center for the making of flatware. And the resulting story was one of growth within growth. As New Haven boomed between 1850 and 1910, so did its county.[66] The boom in manufacturing output in New Haven was widely shared in other municipalities in the county. In 1900, for instance, New Haven ranked first in Connecticut for total manufacturing output. Here are some other New Haven County rankings for the same year: Waterbury third, Ansonia fifth, Meriden sixth, Naugatuck ninth, Wallingford fifteenth, Derby twenty-first, Seymour twenty-fourth, Orange twenty-ninth.[67] As the city grew from about 20,000 to about 133,000, the county grew from about 63,000 to nearly 356,000. Thus what looks like a marginal percentage gain for the city (from 32 percent to 37 percent of the county) corresponds to a vast expansion occurring *both* in the city and in the county at large. This in no way contradicts the narrower story about first-ring towns but is instead a reflection of the satellite nodes of industrial growth that were following New Haven's upward curve. This win-win pattern of growth was not to be repeated in the late twentieth century, and we have no good reason to anticipate its recurrence early in the twenty-first.

In the high summer of New Haven's industrial growth, the city was a focal point in a still larger statewide development. By 1909, Connecticut ranked first nationally in production for brass and bronze products (44.6 percent of the national output), clocks and watches (21 percent), corsets (38.5 percent), firearms and ammunition (58.5 percent), refining of precious metals, machine screws, silverware, needles, pins, and hooks (63.3 percent). It was top three in many other lines, including sewing machines and their accessories, typewriters, wood screws, nails, linseed oil, pens, and rulers.[68] In many of these, New Haven and the smaller towns within the county were leading centers of production. Here again, the theme is growth within growth, expansion within expansion.

SPECIAL PLACE OF THE NEW YORK REGION

New Haven started out very close to New York and grew much closer as a result of railroad transport. Throughout the period of centered development in New Haven, New York had a towering importance in virtually every line of industrial production and in the increasingly important capital markets centered in lower Manhattan. In 1909, New York's 25,938 manufacturers produced more than $2 billion in value, nearly half of it added value rather than cost of materials. These represent well over 10 percent of the corresponding totals for the United States as a whole. New York ranked among the nation's top producers in fields as diverse as printing and lumber products, tobacco manufacturing and meat-packing, women's apparel and steel-making. New Haven, just seventy-five miles up the coast, was producing about $51 million in total value, $26 million in value added—something like 1 part in 45 when compared to the City of New York. The seventy-five-mile radius around New York City defined the densest industrial and commercial region in the world as of 1909–10, and New Haven's part in it was surely less than 1 percent. New York was also the largest, most efficient capital market in the country and quite probably in the world—a critical element in industrial development and in the emergence of well-financed joint stock corporations of the sorts that came to lead New Haven's economy. Much of New Haven's success in the industrial summer derived from its integration into the New York region, both as a source of capital and labor, and as a marketplace for both consumer products and capital goods produced in the smaller place.

As the railroads created continental markets for manufactured goods, they did not create continentwide opportunities for the establishment of manufacturing cities. In the early twentieth century, immense quantities of capital had been invested in places like Chicago, Milwaukee, St. Louis, Detroit, Pittsburgh, Youngstown, Philadelphia, Boston, New York, Buffalo, Syracuse, Cleveland, Baltimore, Bridgeport, Hartford, and New Haven. Seen on a continental scale, these cities were a closely woven network of railroad hubs, each a market for all the others, each a producer for each of the rest—and all, taken together, producers for the rest of North America. As historical geographer D. W. Meinig writes:

> A great majority of the nation's industrial capacity and diversity was concentrated in only a portion of the northeastern quadrant, occupying less than 10 percent of its continental expanse. Furthermore, despite the longings and fervent promotions for industrial growth in every other part of the country there were many indications that this fundamental economic pattern, this gross imbalance in regional development, was essentially complete and stabilized. Such persistence was based not just on the enormous investment in physical plant and systems of operation (for capital was ever seeking new areas of promise) but on the unprecedented efficiency of procurement and marketing on a continental scale. Once the railroad network neared completion, this specialized region, itself complexly laced together with the most modern trunk lines, could bind the rest of the nation into its orbit for "no transportation technology in history has been more centralizing than the railroad."[69]

Thus did New Haven come to occupy a privileged position within a privileged region in early twentieth-century America. New York was the tarantula at the center of the manufacturing and financial web that was American capitalism, and New Haven was one of the smaller spiders situated nearby. Mayor Frank Rice did not plan, propose, cause, or control this development, but his city was immensely advantaged by it nevertheless.

IMMIGRATION POLITICS AND POPULATION GROWTH

New Haven's growth surge was of course part of the nation's great spike of European immigration—2.2 million in the 1870s, 4.7 million in the 1880s, nearly 3.6 million in the 1890s, and a whopping 8 million between 1901 and 1910. As these decades rolled by, the regional composition of the newcomers shifted toward the southern and eastern edges of Europe—from Germany, Ireland, and the United Kingdom toward Italy, Russia, and Hungary. Indeed, by the time Rice was mayor, New Haven would boast its own elegant Italian Consulate looking out on Wooster Square. These nationalities—always speaking in unfamiliar languages, violating old-native customs of dress and manner—were threatening to many existing groups, and all manner of resistance to continued expansion of immigration developed. Much of the labor movement sought tighter controls on immigration, and many leading figures in the Progressive movement sought to tighten controls, often buttressing their views with social-scientific research purporting to demonstrate the inferiority of specific nationalities. The Immigration Restriction League sought to create wide coalitions for the imposition of tighter and tighter restrictions. Interestingly enough, these efforts met with limited political success in the U.S. Congress until just after the Rice era in New Haven. As early as 1882, a Chinese Exclusion Act had been adopted, and in 1907–10, Senator William Dillingham of Vermont chaired a special commission bearing his name. As one leading account of these proceedings reports,

The Dillingham Commission held no public hearings. Instead, its staff compiled an extensive body of empirical research that purported to demonstrate the perils that new European immigrants posed to the nation. The recurrent theme of its forty-two reports was the vast contrast between immigrants from traditional European source countries and those from southern and eastern Europe. Whereas old immigration brought the skilled and industrious who were well acquainted with republican institutions, newer arrivals represented an invasion of "unskilled laboring men" from "less progressive countries of Europe." Individual reports underscored the close association of new immigrants with a host of vexing social problems.[70]

As it happens, only in 1917, with an Immigration Act imposing a self-consciously arbitrary literacy test, did the doors begin to close. The National Quota Laws of 1921, 1924, and 1929 served to more or less permanently restrict opportunity for Italian, Russian, and other nationalities that were not heavily represented in the U.S. population prior to 1890. With quicker restriction, the story of urban growth in New Haven—as in New York, Boston, Pittsburgh, Cleveland, Chicago, and scores of other cities—would have been a smaller and poorer story.

BUILDING TOWARD 1910

Centered growth caused, and was caused by, a long, high-crested wave of money washing over the built environment. In 1850, New Haven encompassed 5,353 dwellings. By 1910 it held 17,466 dwelling structures housing 29,271 families—almost twelve thousand too many for a single-family housing stock to accommodate.[71] These multiunit homes are mostly the two-deckers and three-deckers that so clearly define New Haven's neighborhood fabric today. They were also tenements, some of them built fast to shoddy standards. But none of this can be understood apart from the immense investment in streets and sewers, rail and water lines that made possible the emergence of a centered industrial city. Figure 2.4 shows the streets that existed in 1910 but not in 1824—a dense filigree of urban blocks which would form the matrix for housing and factories, schools and stores in the industrial city.[72] The seventeenth-century three-by-three grid is included for reference, and the open spaces near the city center are streets appearing in Doolittle's 1824 map, thus omitted from this account of newer additions.

The rail lines form a radial geometry around the old nine squares, more exactly around the waterfront section south and east of those squares (these are the thicker lines in figure 2.4). These pulsing arteries of industrial supply and distribution were all essentially completed by the end of the Civil War, and they exerted a dramatic influence on industrial location from that period forward. Joseph Sargent, quoted earlier about his 1863 move to New Haven, picked a location where rail and water transport met, and where lighter variable-path transport was handy as well. His plant location is indicated in figure 2.4, just west of the rail spur in the center of town. The rail and harbor infrastructure would induce a cascade of centralizing decisions as manufacturers sought cheap transport by locating in Sargent's fashion, which in turn would induce construction of worker housing nearby, which would in its turn shape retailing, school siting, the layout of Roman Catholic parishes, fire companies and police precincts, saloons, clubhouses, sporting facilities, and theaters—all the stuff of the emerging industrial city. And all that stuff would make the place home for working families, who would in turn staff newly arrived capitalist enterprises as the paydays rolled by.

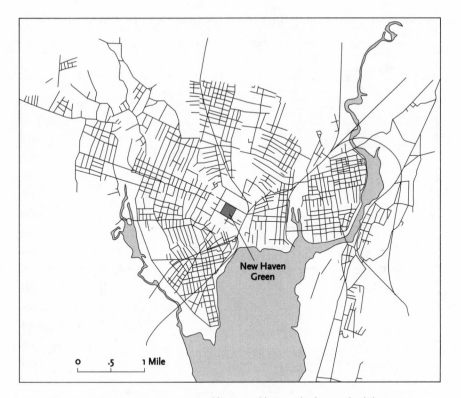

New Haven
Green

0   .5   1 Mile

Figure 2.4. New Haven streets, and heavy rail lines, which were built between 1824 and 1910.

THE GROWTH ASSUMPTION AND THE CIVIL IMPROVEMENT REPORT OF 1910

In the same year Rice assumed office, a three-year study of the city's future was completed and issued its "Report of the Civic Improvement Committee."[73] With Frederick Law Olmsted as its lead consultant, the handsomely produced and copiously researched report laid out an ambitious City Beautiful plan for New Haven.[74] The report expressed concern for newcomers, especially for those of distinctly non-WASP identity, but its tone was above all optimistic. New Haven was a great city, growing greater by the day. It would need new avenues aping Haussmann's Paris, new parks on Olmsted's standard in New York, new and far better rail facilities, public constructions modeled after those of Washington, Budapest, and Baltimore. Caught up in this expansive spirit, the report projected more and more growth for New Haven in the decades after 1910 (figure 2.5 is taken directly from the 1910 document).

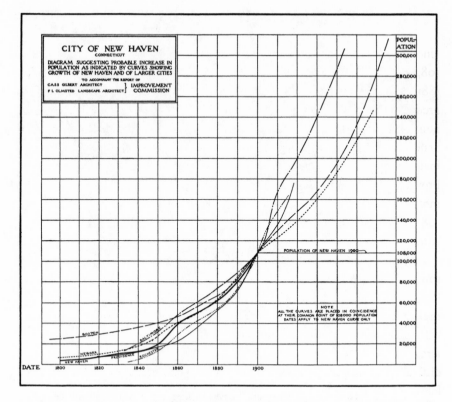

Figure 2.5. Projected growth of New Haven's population after 1910, based on rates of growth in other cities as they passed 108,000 persons. From "Report of the New Haven Civic Improvement Committee" (1910).

The report offers the following interpretation for this somewhat eccentric projection of population growth in New Haven and a few other industrial cities up to 1910:

> The matter of first importance is the population. The accompanying diagram shows the five-fold growth of New Haven since 1850. It also shows for comparison the growth curves of certain larger cities so placed upon the diagram that the point in each curve representing a population of 108,000 is made to coincide with the point in the New Haven curve representing the census of 1900 when its population was 108,027.... A comparison of these curves before and after having passed the 108,000 mark suggests the probable doubling of the present population of New Haven in about the next twenty-five years, and a population of some 400,000 by the year 1950."[75]

Aided by hindsight, we know with certainty that this extrapolation was erroneous. But the reason for the error is far more instructive than its mere existence. Here are the approximate dates at which the other cities would have hit the 108,000 mark: Baltimore in 1841, Boston in 1843, Newark in 1871, Providence in 1881, Rochester in 1886.[76] All these dates are within or before the period that produced the accident of urban creation—when technological, social, and economic forces were engorging central cities as never before or since in the United States. Thus, in the diagram, Baltimore's curve is retarded by fifty-nine years to match New Haven's, Boston's by fifty-seven years, Newark's by twenty-nine, Providence's by nineteen, Rochester's by fourteen. Each of the cities in question more or less doubled its population in the twenty-five years after reaching 108,000, which provides the basis for the projection that New Haven would do so as well.

This analysis won't stand scrutiny, and this is for a historically interesting reason. A first suspicion would be that the 1910 authors "cooked" their data by selecting in advance cities that happened to meet their required rate of growth in the years after hitting 108,000. This would be a sad curiosity—these were people with national reputations for competence and integrity—but historically uninteresting. The truth is more interesting. The authors could have chosen a quite different group of cities—Chicago, New Orleans, Cincinnati, Pittsburgh, Buffalo, Cleveland, Indianapolis, or Syracuse, say—and reached broadly similar extrapolations. They could indeed have picked New Haven at some earlier stage if they were willing to accept a lower threshold than 108,000. The authors were apparently supposing that there is something about cities at the given size level (e.g., about 100,000) which would let you predict their future growth regardless of historical timing. They were willing to ignore the date at which this level was reached, as if some trans-historical mechanism were at work in 1841, 1881, and 1910, and would continue to determine rates of urban expansion for 1930, 1950, and on into the indefinite future. Thus, the authors go on to reason that: "In the absence of radical and unexpected changes in economic and social conditions, such as to interrupt the worldwide phenomenon of steady urban development, it is more likely than not that the end of the twentieth century will find New Haven Green at the center of a metropolitan population of about a million and a half, substantially the situation of Boston Common today."[77]

As already seen in Chapter 1, the decades leading up to 1910 were remarkable for their encouragement of central city development. And the future was not remarkably encouraging of central city development. A turning point lay just about ten years in the future as the 1910 authors made their calculations, and its technological basis was already in progress in Ford's production plants as they wrote. In the years after 1920, these cities grew not exponentially but by very modest addition: In the two decades after 1920, only Baltimore achieved double-digit gains, and all six of these cities were finished with their periods of rapid development (Baltimore would decline very sharply after 1950). All six lost population in the late twentieth century, and only Boston shows much sign of new growth in the early twenty-first century. New Haven itself actually lost a little population in this period, when, according to the Gilbert and Olmsted calculation, the city should nearly have doubled in size.[78] The error, easy to spot with the advantage of hindsight, is that the authors carried their extrapolation across a great historical divide. They were living near the end of a great centering era, and reasoned as if capitalist development would, somehow, continue to promote change in unchanging ways—drawing people and investment inexorably into now-aging city centers. What they overlooked was the coincidental and temporary phase of technological development, which explained a period of rapid centering development. And, in the bargain, the reinforcing impact of capitalist institutional development in the same years—hardly a repeatable or cyclic event—appears to have altogether escaped attention in setting assumptions about growth in the 1910 study. They were living not at the beginning, but near the end of centering development—a period in which the fabric of enterprise would be gathered in unprecedented density at the city center.

CHAPTER 3

FABRIC OF ENTERPRISE

He enlarged the store after the living quarters were dismantled and added many lines of merchandise. Originally, these included candy—much of it sold by the penny's worth, cigarettes, cigars, and chewing tobacco; as well as a line of family dry goods. . . . When a freezer was added, so that ice cream could be sold, it was a big event, as was also the addition of a peanut vending machine from which hot peanuts could be dispensed. That machine was kept on the sidewalk in front of the store, because of the danger from the live charcoal which it burned.—RUTH GINSBERG CAPLAN, 1993

In the era of urbanism, one could very nearly describe the city as a vast network of implicit conspiracies between businesses and their customers. City life was sustained by a layered fabric of business relationships—large firms and small, wholesale and retail, engaged in manufacturing or distribution, providing transportation or accommodation, creating housing or health services or entertainment or any of a hundred other things people will pay for. Businesses which survived for any length of time, came to know their best customers and learned to accommodate their needs. Perhaps the accommodation was nothing more than a cheerful greeting; perhaps it came to knowing that the customer wanted his shirts starched. Perhaps the accommodation provided a retail grocer with the freshest green goods at a slight price premium. Perhaps, more substantially, it was an agreement on a better price in return for a standing order. Being a citizen of the city meant, among other things, being wrapped up in this web of relationships, being "a somebody" as one produced, sold, bought, and consumed the stuff of everyday life.

In the peak years of its urbanist era, New Haven's fabric of enterprise was rich and multilayered, centered and grounded. Its richness lay in the number and variety of enterprise—including thousands of small retail stores, services of every imaginable variety, major industrial firms of world stature. It was centered in that the firms were very tightly clustered in the central city—around its industrial nodes, where working-class housing grew up in abundance, and in its downtown business district. It was grounded in having an abundance of business organizations led and managed by people living in the city, and reliant on the city for success—reliant on city customers, reliant on city workers, reliant on city suppliers. And it was integrated through mixed-use locations, long before zoning came along to regulate and homogenize land use.[1] These features—far from universal to urban history—probably seemed commonplace and unremarkable (though not quite inevitable[2]) in the high summer of industrial urbanism over which Frank Rice presided as mayor. Seen in the rear-view mirror, these features are far from commonplace, and in many respects inspiring to urban patriots who seek the best futures for their twenty-first-century cities.

THE POLIS' ANNIVERSARY DINNER

Mayor Frank Rice and his wife went to dinner on a Thursday evening in August 1910 at a home just north of Oak Street. The invitation for an evening at 10 Howe Street came from Sylvester Zefferino Poli and his wife, Rosa Leverone Poli (figures 3.1 and 3.2). Poli was born on New Year's Eve 1859 at Piano Di Coreglia in

Figure 3.1. Sylvester Poli, entertainment entrepreneur and leading Italian-American citizen of New Haven, c. 1910. NHCHS.

Figure 3.2. Rosa Leverone Poli, at the time of her twenty-fifth wedding anniversary, 1910.
NHCHS.

Tuscany. He was sent off to Paris in 1872 as an apprentice in wax sculpture and immigrated to the United States in 1881.[3] He met his wife in Chicago, where he was busy fashioning wax figures of the "anarchists" condemned for their roles in the Haymarket Riots of 1886.[4] He built his initial capital operating "dime museums," consisting mostly of macabre wax figures, including the hanged Chicago anarchists. His first large success came with something called Poli's Wonderland in downtown New Haven—evidently a hybrid of vaudeville and the dime museum, featuring acts like "Missouri Giantess" Ella Ewing, "who would stride through the audience holding aloft a five dollar bill which patrons could try to snatch."[5] Poli also ran vaudeville and movie houses in Waterbury, Bridgeport, Hartford, Springfield, and Worcester. By 1906 he was operating as a joint stock corporation with a newspaper-announced capitalization of $5 million (perhaps a theatrical overstatement, although his New Haven tax bills of a few years later would suggest some real wealth). Whatever his financial standing, Sylvester Poli was running an important business, and its largest house came to occupy a conspicuous place in the life and times of New Haven in coming years (figure 3.3).

The *New Haven Evening Register* reported on the anniversary dinner of August 25:

At their residence in Howe Street this evening, Mr. and Mrs. Sylvester Poli will celebrate their 25th anniversary with one of the handsomest entertainments ever given in this city. Every detail of this interesting silver wedding has been carried out on an elaborate scale, and no pains have been spared by the host and hostess, both masters of detail, to make the event as perfect as it is possible for a house entertainment to be.

For several days the house and grounds have been in the hands of the dec-

Figure 3.3. Poli's Bijou theater, Church Street, downtown New Haven, c. 1930. NHCHS.

orators, and the rooms are now abloom with flowers, dahlias, palms and ferns . . . the colors of the blossoms harmonizing with the color schemes of the various rooms. . . .

The lawn has been turned into enchanted gardens with hundreds of Japanese lanterns through which softly gleam incandescent lights. The big 100-foot marquee created at the back of the house is decorated with dahlias and palms and ferns, and illuminated by handsomely shaded lamps and lanterns. The marquee is to be used for the dinner to which 400 have been asked. . . .

Immediately after the guests are seated at dinner Senator McGovern will introduce the three younger daughters of the house, and then will come the most charming feature of the celebration, when they crown their mother in honor of the day, with a wreath of lilies of the valley. During the dinner, the orchestra in charge of Mr. Menges from the New Haven theater will be stationed in the summer house, and among the numbers played will be two wedding marches composed for the event. One is by Enrico Batelli of this city, which is named "Poli Silver Wedding March."[6]

The Poli house and its elegant lawn now lie buried under North Frontage Road—the westbound part of the Oak Street Connector created in 1956–59 by urban renewal—the razing of 694 dwellings that housed about 4,000 residents.[7] The home's location is interesting both for its eventual fate and for its closeness to the unmistakably working-class Oak Street neighborhood: it is characteristic of the period that people of considerable wealth often lived close to people with very little. The Weibel Brewery stood a few blocks west on Oak Street, and most of the housing between it and the Polis' home was occupied by working people, often overcrowded in shoddy tenements. St. John's Roman Catholic Church stood just three hundred yards away, a fact that probably had some bearing on the Polis' choice of residence. St. John's served a big flock, and Father John Coyle reported as many as 2,500 worshipers on Easter 1913.[8] The good father noted further in his year-end report to the Diocese of Hartford that all but perhaps four of his families were in command of the English language (two "national parishes" had been set aside in New Haven for the Italians, and one apiece had been provided for those arriving from several other countries).

The Polis' guests that evening included members of about a hundred New Haven households. Father Coyle was there, as was Theresa Weibel, longtime widow of brewer Joseph (she was running the Weibel Brewery by 1894 and had recently turned the job over to Charles Nicklas, also present at the Poli dinner). The Nathaniel Kendalls—Kendall was CEO of the rival Yale Brewing Company—were there as well. Henry Fresenius (head of a third brewery and city treasurer) and saloon-keeper Cornelius Shanley made clear the limited role of an increasingly shrill temperance movement in picking the guests. A gaggle of physicians with Italian surnames—Verdi, LaGambina, Mariani, Limauro, Gianmarino—spent the evening with the Polis. Other guests might be thought of as Italian-American by profession and name: Paul Russo, a lawyer and owner of the *Stella D'Italia* newspaper, along with Joseph Santella, editor and proprietor of the rival *Corriere Del Connecticut*. About a dozen other families joining the festival were Italian by name and not by profession: Joe Callegari worked for Poli as a theater manager; Emidio Balsamo was a coal dealer; David Lorenzi was a sculptor; Rocco Ierardi was an assistant city attorney; Joe Leverone was stage manager at Poli's Bijou theater; Peter Trenchi was a trolley conductor for the Connecticut Company, which ran the main trolley services in town (he later became Sylvester Poli's personal secretary).

Yet this *serrata da principe* was not an occasion for Italian chauvinism.[9] If Russo and Santella were in the Italian-language news business, Phillip Troup was with the *Union*, which claimed the largest circulation of all the city's English-language papers. The Ullman brothers—Isaac and Louis—were German Jews who worked for the corset-maker Strouse-Adler and ran the local Republican Party. Names like McCarthy, Sullivan, Callihan, Kelly, and McHugh suggested anything but an Italian heritage. Names like Kannegiesser, Moegling, Goetz, and Konold confirmed an impression of democracy across nationality lines. Only the old-line Yankees are missing.

Neither was this a snobbish or plutocratic occasion. Frank Lorenzi was a bartender. Frank Strong was a carpenter. Ed Bean ran a garage. Charlie McFeeters was a carpenter and builder. Mark Ryder sold insurance. Tommy Sullivan and George White managed hotels. Mario Petrucelli was a clerk. And it was not in any conventional sense a socially exclusive evening: not a single family belonging to the all-WASP New Haven Lawn Club appears to have made the guest list—not the Sargents, not the Whitneys, not the Dana clan, not the English family, not the DeForests, not the Farnams, the Hotchkiss tribe, not the Watrouses or the Welches.[10] Some of these families might have seen fit to join the Polis for their anniversary if asked; some were perhaps unwilling to rub shoulders with these relative newcomers. Most of the Polis' guests were from late nineteenth-century immigrant families, and a good many of them were Catholics or Jews who would have been ineligible for membership in the Lawn Club.

This gala evening—like the careers of those who joined to celebrate it—symbolized a growing industrial city, with new people, new talent, and new ways of doing things. New Haven was an industrial town by 1910, with 590 manufacturing firms ranging in size from tiny specialty shops with a half-dozen workers to vast factories with acres of shop floor and up to six thousand workers. The Census reports 26,874 New Haven manufacturing jobs in 1909, up about 10 percent from five years earlier.[11] These were hard jobs with long hours, mostly between forty-eight and sixty hours weekly. The plants were noisy with the grinding and stamping of metal parts, the roar of steam-driven machinery, the incessant hum of whirring belts. Factories smelled of oil and coal, paint and chemical solvents—some of which doubtless threatened the health of workers. And they were low-wage jobs when compared with the best managerial and professional posts available in a town like New Haven. But they were, on a world scale, trophy jobs in an economic system that offered opportunity out of all proportion to the old country—whatever country that may have been. A steady hand could earn $2 per day, six days a week, four-plus weeks a month—grossing $50 per month. That was what you could make with ordinary talent and no special luck. Some did considerably better. And $50 was enough to live well by the standards of the period, and perhaps even to save little by little toward a house.[12]

These firms, especially the big ones, required labor well beyond the local supply and for decades had been drawing people looking for factory jobs from across the Atlantic. Fully 92,218 of the city's 133,605 residents were either foreign-born or had at least one foreign-born parent. With another 3,561 blacks and a handful of Asians, the Yankees—"native born whites of native stock"—amounted to less than 30 percent of the city's people. Of the foreign born, 13,159 were Italian, 9,004 Irish, 7,980 "Russian" (most of these were Jewish families in flight from that region's anti-Semitic tyranny), 4,114 from Germany, about 1,800 from England, roughly 1,000 apiece from Austria, Scotland, and Canada. Even Mayor Rice was an immigrant of sorts, his family having moved from Vermont to rural Massachusetts to nearby Cheshire and thence (during his childhood) to New Haven.

These immigrants—along with thousands more arriving from the American hinterlands—captured both manufacturing jobs and spin-off entrepreneurial niches created by the former. At the center of the urban economy were 143 fairly large manufacturing concerns organized as joint stock companies. These incorporated firms stood in sharp contrast to sole proprietorships and partnerships because many of them were *capable of raising capital in increasing quantities and of operating large plants sending products to markets on a national and even international scale.* The largest—Sargent Hardware, Winchester Repeating Arms, and New Haven Clock—operated almost as cities unto themselves. The 143 corporations—perhaps a quarter of the city's total manufacturing establishments—commanded 86 percent of the capital investment, 82 percent of the wage-earners, 83 percent of the payroll, and 82 percent of the value added in New Haven's industrial sector.[13] These were the big export producers which brought capital and cash and talent from the rest of the world to fuel the growth of industrial New Haven.[14] Their employees, with their $50 monthly incomes multiplied by thousands of individuals, were the theatergoers who made possible Sylvester Poli's original empire, the worshipers who filled Father Coyle's pews, the drinkers who consumed Theresa Weibel's beer, and the people who in a hundred other ways made possible the careers represented at the Polis' party.

To keep this very local corporate dominance in perspective nationally, it should be noted that the really large corporations of the era were springing up all across the continent. Between 1880 and 1900, giants like Coca-Cola, Westinghouse, Sears Roebuck, General Electric, Pepsi, and Goodyear were founded. In the 1900–20 interval came U.S. Steel, Ford, 3M, General Motors, Black and Decker, and IBM (under its earlier name, Computing-Tabulating-Recording Company).[15] Corporate New Haven never developed on quite that scale, although the New York, New Haven & Hartford Railroad was assuredly part of the big time in American business, even when its directors were under criminal investigation. While some New Haven brands had national recognition (Winchester rifles and Sargent hardware), the city's manufacturing firms were still local, embedded in the place. A generation later, and in some cases even sooner, many would be sucked up by larger national corporations, losing their relationship to the New Haven community.

SYLVESTER POLI AND THE CIVIC IMPROVEMENT COMMITTEE

In June 1907, Yale instructor George Dudley Seymour wrote an open letter of roughly 11,000 words to urge the adoption of a city plan for New Haven.[16] Various versions were carried in the local press—including the *Register,* and the *Union.* The "letter" is an impressive document, detailing dozens of proposals and invoking the experience of cities as varied as Washington, D.C., Cleveland, Buffalo, Paris, and London. One feature of Seymour's pitch is important: he seeks to lift principle and planning ideals above commercial self-interest and politics of the ordinary sort. "In the case of each city," he wrote, "experts from outside have been invited. Local prejudices are thus eliminated."[17] The abstractly *best* ideas were to wash away the particular city's accumulated idiosyncrasies. Seymour maintained that master ideas should trump the interplay of self-seeking interests: "The laying out of every street and the placing of every public building should proceed on a definite and controlling idea, there should be a dominant principle of design, an adaptation to an end clearly seen, an effort to weld all together into one balanced composition. To these requirements should be added courage—a certain audacity. To timidity, to 'the weak hand of uncertain purpose' to obstinacy and selfishness, as well as to the absence of a principle, do cities owe the insignificance of many of their streets and thoroughfares."[18]

This was a root-and-branch rejection of the political regime that Frank Rice and Isaac Ullman were running, a fact which would limit the practical impact of Seymour's initiative on the city's future. Seymour's view was derivative of the City Beautiful movement then at high tide, and this vision harked back to the pre-industrial (or by 1910 *anti*-industrial) vision that will be recalled from Amos Doolittle's account of New Haven in 1824 (Chapter 2). Thus did architect Cass Gilbert congratulate New Haveners on having inherited something as beautiful as the original Green, and warn them about the old city having been "encroached upon in recent years by so-called 'modern improvements' and buildings ... erected regardless of the environment and without harmony of style."[19]

At a public meeting, called in response by then-mayor John P. Studley, the assembled populace had voted to create something called the New Haven Civic Improvement Committee. Its membership roster appears at the front of its official report in December 1910—exactly as follows:

THE NEW HAVEN CIVIC IMPROVEMENT COMMITTEE

Hon. ROLLIN S. WOODRUFF	MAX ADLER
Hon. JOHN P. STUDLEY	JAMES T. MORAN
GEORGE DUDLEY SEYMOUR	FREDERICK F. BREWSTER
GEORGE D. WATROUS	HARRY G. DAY
WILLIAM W. FARNAM	Rev. ANSON PHELPS STOKES, Jr.
FREDERICK D. GRAVE	HENRY H. TOWNSHEND

SYLVESTER Z. POLI.

OFFICERS.

Hon. ROLLIN S. WOODRUFF, Chairman.
GEORGE DUDLEY SEYMOUR, Secretary.
HENRY H. TOWNSHEND, Assistant Secretary and Treasurer.

Why, one asks almost involuntarily, is Poli alone on the seventh row? Perhaps the point was to balance the page left-to-right despite the odd total of names. Fair enough, but why Poli instead of, say, Watrous or Woodruff? Alphabetical order is no help by way of explanation.[20] An answer is given in the text of the 1910 report: "Mayor Studley within a few days [of the mass meeting] appointed the above New Haven Civic Improvement Committee, barring Mr. Poli, whose name was added by the Committee at a meeting held October 7, 1907, in order that our Italo-American citizens might be represented."[21]

This is suggestive of the learning process by which established groups adjust their previously unchallenged presuppositions in responding to rapid change. Possibly there were street-corner barbs about why a WASP establishment amounting to perhaps a quarter of the city should command eleven of twelve appointments on a committee charged to consider the whole city's future (Max Adler, a well-established German Jew, had been included from the beginning).[22] The rest seem to have been pretty conventional Protestant members of the local business and educational establishments.[23] Neither women nor blacks nor any number of other groups made the list. But it was growing obvious that in matters political, and even more patent in matters economic, the time had come to take notice of people like Sylvester Poli. For all that, Poli remained alone on the seventh line in a document printed thirty-eight months after the initial appointment of a committee.

Both the initial exclusion of Poli, and his symbolic marginality later on, make a certain kind of sense. First, Poli had come up through the rough-and-tumble of vaudeville entertainment, a path doubtless scorned by some of the Yankee families, even in light of the claim forwarded in 1907 that he "had learned many years ago that vaudeville as a form of entertainment could please without offending even the most fastidious taste, and he has always insisted that a Poli performance shall include no word or action that might not be used in his own or any other man's parlor in the presence of his wife and children."[24] At a deeper level, Poli was above all a man of market society. His investments were doubtless attentive to the prospects of real sales, real income streams, real lines of paying customers. While the Poli residence was rather grand, and became still grander late in his life, Poli was a practical guy.[25] Such a person, even when honored by inclusion in a group regarded by its own members and many others as high company, might look askance at the construction of a grand boulevard from the train station to the Green, without an obvious economic return. He might also be inclined to doubt the wisdom of displacing people—customers—in the construction of grand public buildings. And he might be expected to identify with the self-interested lives of people like those who joined him and Rosa to celebrate their twenty-fifth anniversary—brewers and saloon-keepers, contractors and hoteliers, ward leaders and real estate men.

The actual report, drafted by architect Cass Gilbert and famed planner Frederick Law Olmsted, takes note of the city's shifting demography: "It is clearly evident that the percentage of old New England stock in the population is progressively diminishing. People of the old New England stock still to a large extent control the city, and if they want New Haven to be a fit and worthy place for their descendants it behooves them to establish conditions about the lives of all the people that will make the best fellow-citizens of them and of their children. The racial habits and traditions, the personal experience and family training, the economic conditions and outlook, of the newer elements of the population, are such that a laissez faire policy applicable to New England Yankees is not going to suffice for them."[26]

The Gilbert-Olmsted report, printed generously on fine paper with a fold-out color map, remains a landmark document of City Beautiful planning.[27] The authors advocate better fixed-path transport in the form of stronger rail lines and (what would probably have been very wise) public control of harbor development. They advocate wider sidewalks, stronger arterial streets, and a solution to the immense congestion then building up near the New Haven Green, where something like 20 million trolley rides began or ended in their base year, 1907 (the city's trolley system sold 31.6 million rides in total for that year). They advocate a central boulevard linking the rail station to the Green, modeled after thoroughfares of the sort constructed by Baron Georges Haussmann in Paris a generation earlier.[28] Most of all, they advocate urban parks, and some of their ideas are visible in New Haven today, notably Edgewood Park, which is built to an Olmsted design. Many of these planning ideas were good ones, and the city might profitably have adopted more of them than it did, but they were not ideas likely to elicit great enthusiasm from New Haven's city government.

The reference to "racial habits and traditions" is a detached and sterilized version of the jingoism abroad in New Haven and other American cities at the time.[29] Here, for instance, is a headline from the *Register* published the same month (June 1907) the Improvement Committee was established: "New Haven Road to Get Rid of Italian Help."[30] The subtitle asserted "Excitable Temperaments Make Much Trouble." The context was a strike, and the tenor of the sentiment is clear enough in the views attributed to an unidentified official of the New York, New Haven & Hartford: "We have had about enough of these excitable Italians. They have caused more trouble, not only during the past month or so, but for years past, than the men in other branches of service and we don't want them. We will get rid of this lot of disturbers as soon as possible and hope that they will all strike to save us the time and trouble of discharging them. This does not relate to the track repairers and common laborers. They have their little strike now but it includes the Italian foremen on road work. They are paid $2.40 a day and they want this raised anywhere from 10 cents to 25 cents a day. We have decided to get rid of the whole outfit and are going to do it, but of course it will take time."[31]

It would be another long generation before an Italian-American captured the office of mayor in New Haven (William Celentano, elected in 1945).[32] But in 1910, all the immigrant nationalities, and a great many old-liners of "native stock," were already busily at work building a commercial and industrial city whose principles of operation were utterly different from those contemplated by City Beautiful and its advocates in New Haven. In 1940, Seymour would recall the 1910 episode: "I cannot forbear calling attention to the Report, dated 1910, of Mr. Cass Gilbert, Architect, and Mr. Frederick Law Olmsted, Landscape Architect, to the New Haven Civic Improvement Committee. I am free to say that, *although this Report by two of the best known men in the country received little attention here in New Haven*, it received much in other places."[33]

The commercial and political institutions with which City Beautiful planning principles were so obviously at odds were at work in City Hall under the leadership of Frank Rice, in corporate industry under the Sargents and their peers, in entrepreneurial practice under Sylvester Poli—and some thousands of less visible figures to whose efforts we now turn. At the end of 1910, the Gilbert-Olmsted document in hand, Rice would reflect as follows on his first year in office:

> It would appear ill-timed on my part to take unto myself any credit for the work that has been done. The fact is we don't boast that we have done any great work. We have worked to the best end with the limited money at hand. The appropriations have been none too large and our endeavor has been to make the best showing with the money at hand. We have attempted no radical improvements, but we have tried to make a steady improvement in all conditions. As to stating what has been the most important event of the administration, I don't believe there has been any. If I had to make an answer to that question I should say that the *best work, in my opinion, has been in the improvement of the city sidewalks.* The good labor begun on the walks has been continued, and as the perfection of that endeavor has been my particular hobby this year, I am pleased at the results obtained.[34]

Such a man, operating in such a political regime, was unlikely to embrace the City Beautiful as proposed by Gilbert, Olmsted, Seymour, and a thousand others. He was, both by temperament and by office, wholly unable to cope with the scale of the Gilbert-Olmsted proposal. Instead, with heavily passive-aggressive irony, Rice kept to the good-sidewalks theme of his inaugural address 364 days earlier. A start toward understanding that response—and the nature of a mayoral regime in this era—may be made by looking at the humble neighborhood store. Most of the mayor's constituents relied on tiny groceries and other neighborhood stores for their daily food, for their livelihood, or both.

MICRO-RETAILING: GROCERIES, BAKERIES, SALOONS

The families represented at the Polis' silver anniversary dinner were, with just a few exceptions, living in and through local business. Even the professionals—doctors, lawyers, musicians—would quickly have recognized themselves as being "in business." With the likely exception of Father Coyle, all would have understood themselves as running a business or working for someone who did—and Coyle, for that matter, was used to doing annual balance sheets for the Diocese in Hartford. Even Mayor Rice was fond of likening the city to an industrial enterprise. The city in 1910 was filled with the spirit of enterprise, and a thick, multilayered economy of firms defined the city for Rice, for Poli, and for those who would follow them. At the top was a layer of manufacturing corporations that brought great energy to the local economy, but at the other end of the food chain were the least well capitalized and smallest firms of all.

Lacking any personal link to the family, Harris Ginsberg was perhaps too small time to mingle with Sylvester Poli and his guests. In 1913 he was operating a combination confectionery and dry goods business in the 700 block of State Street:

> Several months prior to his marriage, my father bought a retail store on State Street, for the total sum of one hundred dollars. The purchase included the stock and fixtures—and of course its good will—as well as the meager furnishings of two large rooms in the rear, separated by a wall, which were used as living quarters—a kitchen and a bedroom. . . . During the earliest years, my mother tended the store, while my father, with a pack of merchandise on his back, made calls on his select clientele, often walking as far as Branford. The sale of two sheets and two pillow slips, with a towel or two to a future bride, was considered a "big" sale. Many times the sale was consummated on credit, making any number of subsequent trips necessary to collect the balance. Later he discontinued this activity and devoted all of his time to the business in the store. He enlarged the store after the living quarters were dismantled and added many lines of merchandise.[35]

Ginsberg was competing from the bottom, with people like Anna Veloci, Elias Ratner, James Mulvey, Fanny Sachs, Antonio Cervero, or the Bechel brothers. The Beschels later owned three of the fifty-nine grocery stores located within a one-third-mile crow's flight radius of the Poli residence in 1913 (near the middle of figure 3.4). The stores are so close together in some places that the names must be left out in the illustration. There are roughly two stores for each four-sided city block, and the density of enterprise is greatly understated in this map, which leaves out bakeries, barbershops, fishmongers, dressmakers, merchant tailors, saloons, cigar stores, confectioners, stationers, shoemakers and sellers, restaurants, music studios, and medical practices. To an extent unimaginable today, the city was enveloped by a dense fabric of small enterprises, each focused on a tiny territorial market in which it held a precarious competitive edge. The business edge, when it existed, had everything to do with local ties, personal loyalties, neighborly connectedness. Today, in places like midtown Manhattan—where vertical construction compresses residential space at ratios of 50:1 or even 100:1 by stacking people hundreds of feet above sidewalk height—we witness far

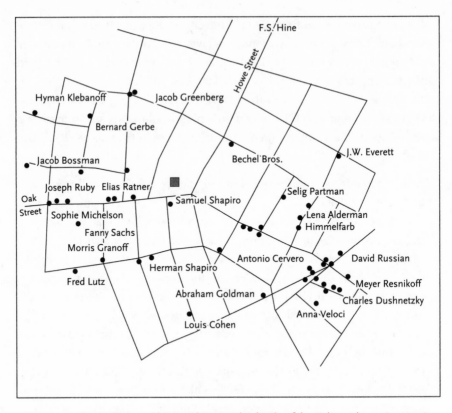

Figure 3.4. Grocery stores (dots) within one-third mile of the Poli residence (square in center), 1913.

higher commercial densities on a per-block or per-acre basis, but not on a per household or per capita basis.

In 1913, New Haven had 628 retail grocers, with about 50 more located in its first-ring suburbs (notably the borough of West Haven and the town of Hamden). These stores formed a dense network across the city's industrial neighborhoods (figure 3.5). With perhaps 135,000 people, this meant that the average store could count on a customer base of less than 220 people—at most 65 or 70 households. The most extravagant estimate would yield no more than 100 households per store. These were places where neighbors met and shared a little conversation. They were also places where a numbers game might transact its retail business, or a place where one couple might compare notes with another about the dubious behavior of neighborhood kids. They are part of a larger fabric—church, school, barbershop, bakery, hardware store, precinct house—woven by a neighborhood. These stores evidently were repelled by the central space around the original nine squares, and at the convergence of the trolleys in that same place. This is not difficult to understand: (1) rents were far too high for ordinary food retailing in the central area, and (2) groceries were bought by people highly conscious of perishability and transport costs. With the ice box standard of refrigeration, and shoe leather for transportation, this would gave a considerable premium to stores within a block or so of home. Grocers of the era located so as to provide themselves with a spatial advantage in a small sub-market—and by the same decision they gave up on large markets.

But how could this work out financially? First of all, notice that a customer base consisting of many modest incomes would do more for retailers selling life's necessities than would a cash base of the same magnitude but with large incomes going to just a few households. Let us suppose that each of the 60 or 70

Figure 3.5. Grocery stores projected over trolley lines and nine-square central grid, 1913. Numbers indicate neighborhoods: 1. Hill, 2. Wooster Square, 3. Fair Haven, 4. Dixwell-Newhallville, 5. Westville.

households has an industrial worker as its head, and that such a head—directly or by delegation to another family member—spends 20 percent of the family's income on food, and suppose, for simplicity, that he or she spends it all at one store. If each customer spends $10 (20 percent of $50) per month, the gross receipt per store is perhaps $650. With a 20 percent gross profit margin, that makes $130 per month per store. This perhaps translates to something like $60 per month in net profits—enough to make the grocery business stand up against most forms of manufacturing employment so long as business remains this good. If the store is family-operated—most were—it is quite possible that this income stream is combined with another job, perhaps a factory job. Of the 628, 97 were run under women's names, and the number actually operated by women was probably higher. The labor of children and adolescents would be folded into such an operation on a daily basis, appearing nowhere in the formal accounts of the operation.

The rewards are modest, the risks large. If a family netted $60 a month, that was a nice working-class income. But the hours were long, perhaps eighty per week, and the risks considerable. The essential business problem for these groceries is obvious: If this works for you, why not for me? The capital costs of starting up such a store were low, and access to wholesalers—located in a string along State Street—was relatively convenient. This risk of competitive entry is the classic bane of small retail everywhere, and it was at work in New Haven in 1910. If a store's current base of customers is sixty households, and a new store moves in to pare away twenty of these, operating costs stay about the same, but net profits fall by much more than a third. If the storekeeper attempts to make up the difference by raising prices, her market share will probably fall further, perhaps to the point of extinction. As we will see in the survivorship analysis, this is exactly what happened to hundreds of these small operations.

While they lasted, these were supremely grounded institutions—committed irrevocably to places and the people living in them (figure 3.6). Is it in the interest of John Grillo that his block of Broad Street be a safe and peaceful place to live and do business? Is Sam Lear motivated to look out for the families living near his store on Arch Street? Would Mary Gilhuly go out of her way to keep up the sidewalk on her patch of Franklin Street? Do such people have a reason to care about the common good of their neighborhoods? Yes, because neighborhood decline implies business extinction. Do they have an incentive to function as centers of communication and cooperation for their customers? Yes on both counts. The value of these enterprises lay almost entirely in their relation to place and its people, and the resulting effect was to ground the interests of these grocers and their families in very specific spots. This in turn would contribute importantly to the maintenance of peace and civility in each such neighborhood or sub-neighborhood.[36]

It is of course necessary to understand these little stores and their implicit functions in the larger context of a centered industrial city. The stores are concentrated not around the central grid of nine squares but in the major industrial working-class neighborhoods of the city. In figure 3.5 I have inserted five numerals to indicate these districts:

1. The Hill, an area of industrial development along the shoreline south of downtown.
2. Wooster Square, the neighborhood located at the confluence of the city's major rail and shipping facilities and hosting the large manufacturing facilities of Sargent Company, New Haven Clock, and Cowles Manufacturing, among others.
3. Fair Haven, a neighborhood of lighter manufacturing, combined with marine activities.
4. Dixwell-Newhallville, home of Winchester Repeating Arms and a host of its suppliers.
5. Westville, a very small manufacturing node surrounding Diamond Match, Greist Manufacturing, and other early factories located there in pursuit of the West River's waterpower.

We will see these areas in greater detail shortly, but I mention them here to suggest the obvious link between manufacturing plants, worker housing, and the density of retail groceries. Notice, in passing, that most of the groceries are located off the trolley lines by a block or two, presumably because rents are lower and business is supremely local.

A little less local in customer base were the bakeries, 78 of them in 1913. These more specialized firms needed more customers each because they could hope to attract only a very small fraction of each customer's monthly income stream. Groceries ran on just over 210 customers each on average at this time. The bakeries (figure 3.7) required an average of about 1,700 persons each—perhaps 400 to 450 households. Despite the commonsense similarity, the spatial ecology of bakeries is utterly different from that of groceries. Here, location is keyed to the trolley lines and their potential access to more extensive markets. Side-street locations are found in just a dozen cases. The bakeries are differentiated by nationality and ethnic factors, and they appeal in part to neighborhood clienteles. Some, like the Mohican Company, with its two downtown sites, or Connecticut

Figure 3.6. New Haven grocery store with female staff (center) and neighborhood children (right), c. 1895. Yale University Manuscripts and Archives, from the collection donated by Thomas Sieniewicz.

Pie Company of Chapel Street, sought citywide markets. But many sought niche markets. It is difficult to imagine that Vinny Cacase of Wallace Street or Sal Rascatti of Hill Street expected to attract crosstown customers. Similarly, Jacob Hyman of Oak Street was probably focused on his neighborhood and a few blocks beyond.

There were more places to drink your carbohydrates than places to buy them dry, since the neighborhood saloon was far more pervasive than the bakery. About 400 were up and running in 1913. These watering holes were, more often than not, holes—small bucket shops serving Weibel's or Yale or Frersenius or some other local brand of beer at cheap prices for a very local clientele. A few saloons, particularly those attached to hotels, were quite grand. But most were not larger than the first floor of a very modest home—say twenty feet by thirty feet. As figure 3.8 suggests, the Hill neighborhood, south of the nine squares, was especially dense with saloons in 1913. Washington Avenue had more than its share, as did Oak Street, Meadow Street, Crown Street, and, of course, Chapel Street, running just south of the Green. True to stereotype, a high fraction of the saloon-keepers had Irish surnames: Patrick McGushin, Frank Quinn, Patrick Toohey, Francis Kiernan, Cornelius Connors. German and German-Jewish names were almost as common: Ignatz Adler, Anna Beisler, Leopold Braun, John Weis. Ital-

ians were in the bar business by 1913, but in relatively small numbers (not surprising, because most were quite recent arrivals). Missing, by and large, were the
classic WASP names. It seems probable that drinking in saloons and saloon-
keeping were working-class activities practiced with greater gusto by the foreign-
born than by old Yankees. While drunkenness was a common police complaint
during these years, it is also probable that a certain amount of social connectedness was created and sustained in these little spigots of beer.

This layer of urban society would be damaged seriously in January 1920, when
the Eighteenth Amendment to the U.S. Constitution imposed prohibition. With
enforcement through the Volstead Act, prohibition would drive all the saloons
out of open commerce, and most entirely out of business. Some, especially those
in urban settings like New Haven, managed to carry on sub rosa, and criminal activity came to focus heavily on the new opportunity to sell booze at inflated prices

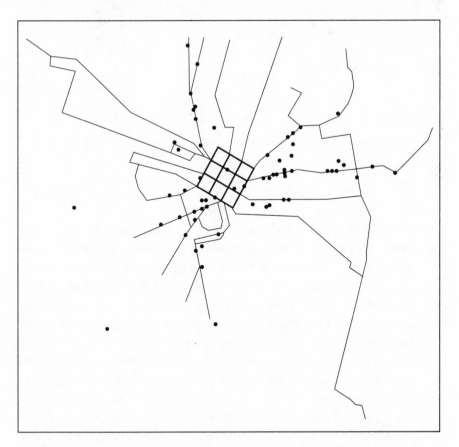

Figure 3.7. Retail bakeries projected over trolley lines and nine-square grid, 1913.

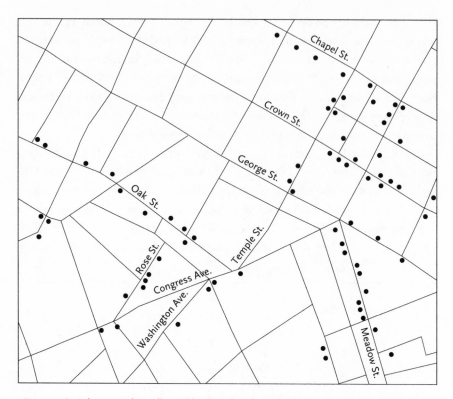

Figure 3.8. Saloons in the Hill neighborhood and central business district (CBD), 1913.

created by the "noble experiment." Thirteen years later, deep in the Depression, the Twenty-First Amendment would restore sanity.

The big fact of neighborhood retailing was very small enterprise. Proprietors operated under pressure from large numbers of similarly tiny competitors in each line of merchandise or service. One contemporary observer later reported that "competition among the merchants was ferocious as indeed it was a buyer's market. Shoppers had many choices of stores, 3–4 bakeries, 6–7 meat markets, 5–6 groceries, etc. 'The customer is always right' was the keyword of the merchants—after all, there was always another shop next door or across the street."[37]

Quite apart from general groceries were about 200 butchers and meat dealers, 45 dairy and milk dealers, 23 fish markets, 70 druggists, 230 confectioners, 200 shoe stores, more than 350 dressmakers, 60 furniture dealers, 170 music teachers working out of their homes, 45 coal dealers, 65 cigar stores, and 62 laundries (true to stereotype, about half operated by people with Chinese names). These were precarious and difficult ways to earn a living, and they would prove themselves mortal in the course of generational time. But they were grounded institutions, gluing a commercial fabric to life in the neighborhoods.

In present-day debate about cities, we often wish it were possible to re-create the rich texture of neighborhood retailing. It did a great deal to stabilize street life and to enliven connections between people as they passed from butcher to grocer, seamstress to shoe store. It was also no doubt valuable to have thousands of petit bourgeois families spread across the city, acting first as part of an owning class, then as customer and consumer. It is important to remember that the richness of this arrangement cannot easily be reproduced in the very different milieu we now inhabit. Three factors work against neighborhood retailing, any one of which would be more or less lethal to the commercial fauna of 1913 as just described:

1. Retailing depends on *export industries* that feed the cycle of exchange. If export industries—companies with paying customers outside the city and its immediate region—bring home dollars, then a retail fabric can recirculate them. As exports decline, the richness of retail circulation is curtailed.
2. Small, very decentralized retail operations are *vulnerable to competition from larger operations* that can achieve economies of scale and undercut prices. As early as 1913 chain stores were beginning to encroach upon New Haven streets and those of other similar cities. By the 1950s, pressure from big operators would prove lethal to many forms of neighborhood retailing.
3. The richness of the fabric depended on a *permissive treatment of mixed-use neighborhoods by government.* But already in 1916, with New York City's zoning ordinance in place, the country would set out to homogenize land uses and, in particular, to drive a wedge between residential and commercial areas. Neighborhood retailing would be seen as a failure of that effort almost everywhere, including New Haven, which adopted zoning in 1926.

With these three pincers advancing quietly against small shops, it would seem unlikely that fine-grained retail fabric could survive in later decades. With notable and precious exceptions, the trend turned sharply downward after about 1940, when all three of these threats had begun to take a toll.

BANKERS AND BROKERS

Before the Glass-Steagall Act of 1933, banking and investment brokering were permissibly combined in a single organization. Indeed, banking could be combined with virtually any other line of business. In 1910, New Haven's banks were for that reason much more diverse than they were later to become. In central square locations, chartered banks—First National, Connecticut Savings, City Bank of New Haven, National New Haven, People's, Yale National, and New Haven County National—plied their wares, including, quite often, investment and brokerage services. But so could Pasquale Fusco, Antonio Pepe, Frank DeLucia, and others, who conducted banking in conjunction with real estate and stock brokerage operations. A free-lance banker like Fusco could be counted on to develop a mortgage market among his conationals, and this form of banking may well help to account for the remarkable rate at which immigrant New Haveners had acquired property by the 1930s.[38] Notice (figure 3.9) that all the Italo-American independents are located outside the nine squares, either in the Hill to the south or in the Wooster Square neighborhood to the east. Rents were doubtless far lower in these locations than in the more central ones occupied by chartered banks. These were exactly the areas settled most densely by Italian immigrants in this period, and they were areas in which these families owned their homes decades later.

So, too, at the same time could established brokerage houses set themselves up in banking—Butterworth, Lomas & Nettleton, Hayden, Stone, Inc. Even a major local department store—Edward Malley Company—could go into the banking trade. The chartered banks with bankish names remained inside the central grid, with offices on Chapel, Orange, Church, and State, for the most part. Only Broadway Bank and Trust strayed from the box to locate on the street by the same name (west of the grid).

These were truly local banks, grounded in the city and its web of business relationships. National debt markets were less efficient than they are now, and transactions tended to be made locally if not face-to-face. While the bankers' interests were in many respects contrary to the interests of their depositors and loan-seekers, these institutions were run locally by people living in New Haven—often living within blocks of the people with whom they were doing business. While three of the banks were quite new (People's was founded in 1905, Union and New Haven Trust was formed in 1910, Broadway Bank and Trust in 1911), most of the chartered banks were old by 1913: Mechanics' Bank dated to 1824, City Bank to 1831, National Savings to 1838, Tradesmen's to 1855, First National to 1863, Yale National to 1865.[39] Unlike bankers in the late twentieth century, these people were generally content to run safe, moderate-profit loan portfolios, and they felt no compulsion to seek the highest returns available nationally. Neither was it their habit to resell mortgages on secondary markets hav-

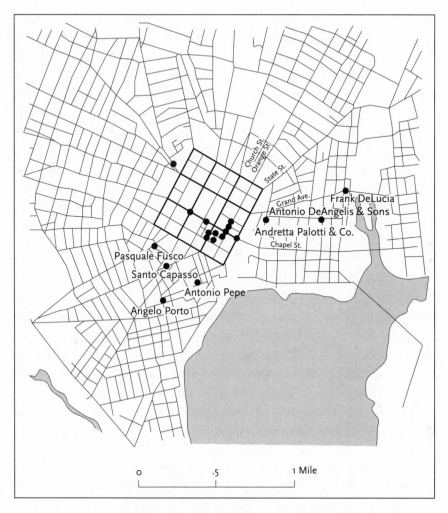

Figure 3.9. Bank locations, 1913. Chartered banks shown without labels. Individual banking operations shown with names of principals.

ing national reach, as is routinely done today. They were, in short, local banks, living mainly from local transactions.

A generation later, the Yale Institute of Human Relations would conduct a family survey in New Haven, gathering a remarkably rich portrait of the city in early Depression years. In Thelma Dries' summary of the findings lies the following observation: "The foreign born owned their homes to a greater extent than did the native white groups. Specifically, 37 percent of the foreign born owned their homes in contrast to about 27 percent of the native white groups."[40] Put another way, 6,692 foreign-born heads of household owned their places while just 2,641 "native whites of native parentage" could say the same. These are interesting observations, coming as they do before any massive suburbanization could be invoked to explain the lower rate of native-stock homeownership. It is therefore difficult to resist the temptation to speculate that the banking offered by a Pasquale Fusco or an Antonio Pepe may have formed part of an informal network through which Italian working-class families became depositors in the early years and over time were lent the money required to buy their homes. Quite apart from these personal banks, the very local character of banking in these decades opened opportunities for recent arrivals that might not appear generations later, after managerial control of local banking had been largely detached from city residents.

DOWNTOWN COMMERCIAL AND CORPORATE CORE

The chartered banks are part of a more diverse but no less concentrated core of business organizations. These organizations—many of them joint stock corporations—are concentrated in the southwestern part of the original eight-square perimeter of the New Haven Green. In figure 3.10 I show a single block, directly south of the Green, in which the commercial vitality of the central business district is palpable. The "100 Percent Corner" of New Haven commercial real estate is at Church and Chapel, on the southeast corner of the Green, at the lower right in figure 3.10. From this corner, as from no other, the city's trolley system gathered customers in the millions each month.

Most visible in the daily life of the city were the major department stores: Gamble-Desmond, Edward Malley, and Shartenberg-Robinson (the first two shown, and the last a block east of the zone shown in figure 3.10). These were the high-volume, broadband marketers of this era, and their dominance had everything to do with locational advantage. Many of the region's best-paid workers—bankers, lawyers, brokers, professional managers of corporations whose physical capital was elsewhere—worked in these blocks, including the lesser cross streets, such as Crown and Orange, and often walked to work from their homes. Thousands of homemakers relied on department stores both for ordinary purchases and for special occasions—gifts for holidays, weddings, and birthdays. On average in this era, each of the city's 130,000 people took well over 200 trolley trips per year. The trolley system was organized starfish style, with each arm anchored to the downtown hub. This meant that of the roughly 90,000 adults, each averaged over 300 rides, and almost all found themselves passing through downtown often enough to spend a considerable fraction of their income nearby. Riders often

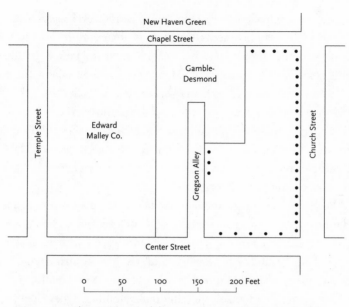

Figure 3.10. The city's central department store block, south of the New Haven Green, before urban renewal.

arrived downtown in anticipation of a visit to one of the big department stores, which was an exciting experience:

> The downtown department store probably represents the climax of downtown retailing. Aside from providing opportunities for people to purchase a wide range of goods, these stores also, with a touch of theater provided by displays and window decorations, imbued shopping with drama and romance and offered people a chance to escape the mundane world and to dream—and have fun. The downtown department store embodied urban excitement. Its well-trained, courteous staff, its many amenities—from doorman to luxurious bathrooms—and its pleasant tearooms and restaurants made the shopping experience not only exciting but pleasant and enticing. As the customers were coddled with service, clerks and staff were made to feel part of a big and happy family.[41]

The big department stores like Gamble-Desmond worked as "anchors" in close association with an endless variety of small enterprise. The block in question held well over a hundred other firms. Gregson Alley, cleaving the department store block, contained a saloon, a club, a restaurant, a clothier, a shoe store, and a home for the restaurant's owner, one Harry Goldberg. The Church Street side of the block was a warren of enterprise, housing on street level or upstairs no fewer than seventy-eight establishments—including, for example, a gaggle each of law offices, insurance brokerages, real estate offices, and tailors. In one stretch measuring scarcely fifty feet stood the Mooney & Kennedy Saloon, the Williams Saloon, and the Toole-Maginn Saloon (96, 100, and 104 Chapel). Other lines of commerce included architecture, stenography, marine brokerage, construction, sign painting, photography, lightbulbs, shoes, badges, gaskets, and a boot-black stand operated by a Mr. Gus Pardajis. All in all, this block, bounded by Church, Chapel, Temple, and Crown, accounted for roughly 150 business locations, two-thirds of them engaged in retailing.

The other large downtown retailers include three piano dealerships, Rembert's stationery store, two haberdasheries, Platt's seed and plant store—all of them joint stock corporations. They are commingled with several hundred smaller retail organizations, generally specialty stores requiring large customer bases due to their relatively limited capacity to attract income from each customer. These stores sold furniture, children's clothing, typewriters, sporting goods, books and magazines, hats, and countless other specialized lines. The central business district stood south and east of the Green, encompassing perhaps a dozen city blocks. In these sixty-odd acres we find not fewer than 80 major joint stock corporations among the 185 operating in New Haven, with at least $50,000 in announced capitalization.[42] Some of these are retailers and banks already considered. Fifteen were the administrative headquarters of wholesalers. Wholesale coal, for example, was being brokered out by Benedict & Pardee, Benedict & Downs, and All Rail Coal, Inc.—all within a few hundred feet of one another. Wholesale lumber also drew several firms to the commercial core. Bulk groceries and food goods were concentrated here, with Imperial Granum, L. C. Bates & Company, and Russell Brothers offering wholesale prices to local retailers (figure 3.11). The McKay Company was wholesaling oysters on Church Street. Two companies were offering wholesale electrical equipment. Butler & Tyler were selling wholesale shoes, and the Sheehan Company was selling wholesale liquor.

All the major utilities were clustered here. The United Illuminating Company was on George Street. Southern Connecticut Telephone, New Haven Water, and two other water utilities were on Crown Street, along with New Haven Gas Light Company. All of these firms of course located their major plants in cheaper areas, but they clustered their administrative offices in this small district.

Many of the firms in this zone were conducting construction and real estate transactions. Among these were Federal Realty Corporation, the Day Estate Cor-

Figure 3.11. L. C. Bates wholesale
groceries, c. 1880–90. State Street,
New Haven. NHCHS.

poration, Connecticut Railway & Lighting (a holding company), Lathrop & Shea,
the Bank Building Company, New Haven Mortgage, the Weeks Land Company,
New Haven Real Estate Title, Lenox Realty, and the Mason Company. Few represented manufacturing concerns, which tended in this period to be administered
from major plant sites. There were exceptions, such as Twin Safety Razor.
Chicago-based Armour meats found itself represented by a shipping facility bor-
dering State Street with access to a rail spur.

This downtown core was in a sense the center of centered development. Business administration, and commerce at several levels (from specialty retailing
up), were concentrated in a tiny area. They were located in the same area as city
government, and close to the court system. Interestingly, business leaned heavily toward the eastern and southern portions of the nine-square grid, away from
the zone influenced most by Yale and by the major Protestant congregations to
the west and north. Perhaps this was a historical follow-on from the influence of
maritime commerce, which had for centuries been concentrated around Long
Wharf, also to the southeast of the nine squares. But the ultimate muscle behind
the city's economy lay elsewhere, out in the manufacturing districts where land
values were lower, where transport facilities dominated the landscape, and
where working-class housing grew up around the plant gate.

Figure 3.12. Chapel Street traffic jam, c. 1930. NHCHS.

But the downtown core was also problematic, even early in the twentieth century, with an immense burden of traffic and conflicting priorities for its passage. Figure 3.12 suggests this difficulty as it looked during a 1930 traffic jam. The pedestrians crowd one another; the trolley and the cars scarcely avoid contact in the street. This was fine for CBD commerce at the time: there was no other game in or near town. But within a few decades, central-district shopping would no longer enjoy that considerable advantage.

GROWTH OF INDUSTRY AND ACCESS TO HEAVY TRANSPORT

New Haven's industrial summer was fueled by cheap energy in the form of coal, which drew investments in plant and equipment close to rail and ocean shipping facilities. This in practice meant that land within something like 500 yards of rail or shipping facilities was best suited for manufacturing plants. In figure 3.13, the original nine squares are shown in gray for reference. The remaining streets shown in figure 3.13 have in common the key feature of proximity to rail or heavy shipping facilities (500 yards or less). These streets constituted the prime industrial area of New Haven in 1910, and for many decades after that. These were the places Sargent, Winchester, New Haven Clock, and most of the other major manufacturers elected to position their production and shipping facilities. And because major manufacturers located here, so did their suppliers— machine tool shops, foundries, engineering firms, and others. The nearby streets in nearly every case developed as working-class housing. Some plants were located outside this zone, and some working-class housing developed beyond its limits, most notably the Oak Street neighborhood, west and south of the nine squares. So, too, did some elegant and expensive housing from an earlier period find itself in the midst of an industrial neighborhood (Wooster Square, for instance). But no similarly profound division of the city's streets is to be found since the original nine squares were laid down in the late 1630s. The subsequent development of the city, right into the dawning of the twenty-first century, would again and again repeat the same broad outline of streets. One might almost say that the historical tune of twentieth-century New Haven is one reprise after another of this boundary structure.

The industrial areas stand in sharp contrast to the remaining streets, which lacked this critical feature. These transport-poor areas were eventually privileged as residential areas. The large block east of the harbor was in 1911 a thinly populated area with an abundance of shoreline summer houses and resort hotels, such as the Shoreham, the Lighthouse Point Hotel, and the Morris Cove Hotel. This East Shore area is today a distinctive neighborhood, and its present features—its social homogeneity, its lack of industrial scars—owe a great deal to its isolation in 1913. The large block north of the nine squares is the Whitney Avenue corridor, also highly distinctive today. As we shall see in Chapter 4, it was already something of a place apart even in 1913. City Point stands directly south of the nine squares, jutting into the harbor. Westville is at the far left in figure 3.14, and the West Rock neighborhood (then utterly rural, save for the Springside poor farm) stands at the extreme upper-left corner of the map. All of these nonindustrial areas stand out in later history because of their early isolation—one as a sort of isolation zone for public housing residents (West Rock), the rest as desirable middle-class neighborhoods.

The fundamental energy behind this spatial division, and behind the febrile growth of New Haven's economy in the Frank Rice era, lay in a handful of major manufacturing firms that had discovered how to exploit the city's competitive advantage. One of these, which stands above most of the rest, provides a good entrée to this group of firms.

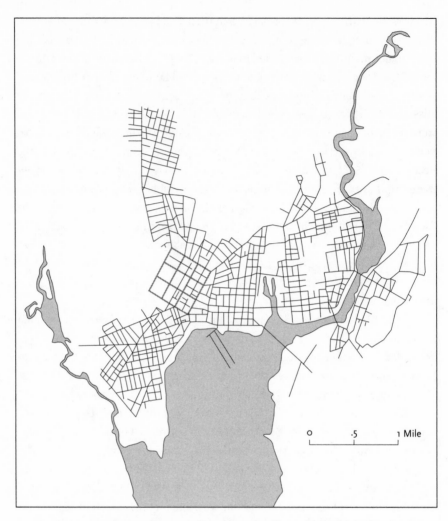

Figure 3.13. New Haven Streets within 500 yards of heavy shipping facilities, 1911.

Sargent and Company The Sargent Company hardware plant is a model for New Haven manufacturing at its height (figure 3.15). While much smaller than the era's giant (Winchester Repeating Arms), Sargent is a fine example of muscular development in central-city locations. Both rail and water transport reach the plant via the harbor and Belle Dock railyards. Shipping by both steam and sail commingle in their service to Sargent. In this picture the ships are met, at Wallace and Water Streets, by horse-drawn vehicles, although in 1910 cars were becoming important in city streets. The plant burned 15,000 tons of coal and coke annually for heat and mechanical energy. Two 60-horsepower coal-burning steam engines had been brought to New Haven in 1864 when the plant opened, and they were improved upon over the years. By 1916, nine engines produced a total of 2,000 horsepower. Power was distributed to the plant floor by eight miles of shafting and seventy-five miles of belting.[43] At the payoff end of that transmission system, 4,700 powered machines stood ready for each shift of operators on twenty-one acres of interior space (under seven acres of roof). In an average week, 560,000 iron castings were produced. The place was illuminated by 7,000 electric lights and protected by 11,929 sprinkler heads. The docks were set up to receive coal in great quantities, and to receive heavy materials. Product left the

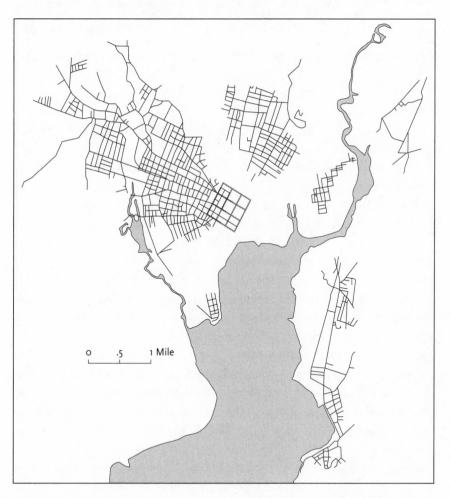

Figure 3.14. New Haven Streets not within 500 yards of heavy shipping facilities, 1911.

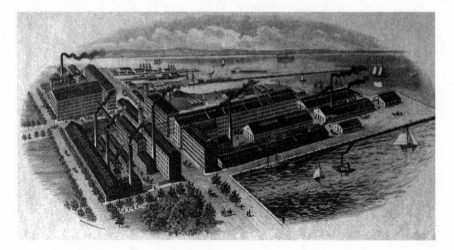

Figure 3.15. Sargent Hardware plant, near Long Wharf, c. 1890. Courtesy Sargent Company and Assa Abloy, Inc.

plant mostly by rail, at an average rate of thirty tons a day. The Sargent plant grew outward from Water Street by filling tidal flats with rubble and muck, so that a whole series of letter-designated buildings stretched from A to V and accommodated production runs reaching from screws to doorknobs, from power hammers to string dispensers.

The company's 1910 catalogue weighs over twelve pounds and has more than 1,300 pages of pictures, specifications, and prices. More than 50,000 distinct product types were for sale, and some could be customized for major purchasers. Thus, for instance, doorknobs are shown with the crests of the University of Iowa or the St. Paul, Minnesota, school system inscribed three-dimensionally in the castings. This anticipates the "mass customization" movement in U.S. manufacturing by about eighty years, and it indicates a high degree of sophistication in corporate management at Sargent. The catalogue suggests a firm bent on forward integration toward its markets, with a keen eye even for relatively limited market niches. The company produced, for example, hammers specialized for work on cornices, saws for horticulturists, butchers, and cooks, as well as for carpenters, and screws for carriages. The main market lay in architectural hardware—locks, hinges, handles, plates, closers, and other materials required for the construction of a door. These elements are offered in immense variety, with left-handed and right-handed versions, and with almost endless variety in metal finishes and decorative detail. In the language of business Sargent was an aggressive competitor, extracting great economies of scale (many units being cheaper at the margin than a few) and economies of scope (it being economical to produce many related items using the same basic capital—plant, administration, marketing, and distribution channels).[44] Combining New Haven's cost advantages with its growing workforce, Sargent could address national and world markets as a low-cost producer of goods with immense markets at distant points.

This was a family-controlled joint stock corporation with intimate connections to New York markets—which is to say, world markets. Joseph Bradford Sargent (1822–1907) had created a sales organization in the 1850s, representing a variety of hardware manufacturers on 5 percent commission in New England. This experience would be invaluable to the company once it emerged as a major manufacturer. Sargent and his brothers were also modestly engaged in manufacturing in New London, Connecticut, before coming to New Haven but met with tight labor markets and difficult transport logistics. By 1864, Sargent and his brothers had moved their main plant to the New Haven harbor, capturing access to both rail and shipping terminals in a single stroke. In making this move, J.B., as he was called by familiars, made a major commitment to the city of New Haven: "As we view the magnitude of the undertaking, it is clear that here in the city of New Haven Joseph Bradford Sargent intended to make his mark. Here he would build the factory of his dreams which would stand as a monument to his energy, enterprise and imagination."[45]

The New Haven investment was so large that the firm could succeed nationally or worldwide only if it succeeded in New Haven. This in some important degree aligned the interests of the Sargent Company with those of the New Haven community. It also constituted what economists call a credible commitment to a place, giving confidence to others that this was a trustworthy location to make commitments of their own. This was true of suppliers and of workers, even though Sargent was quite capable of swallowing the former and discharging the latter. The Sargent plant—ever growing seaward in the forty-six years leading up to 1910—was a source of confidence to other investors, who could count on it to share tax burdens, and to builders, who could count on it as a money pump for nearby flats and tenements.

The firm had access to national markets, with a main sales operation located at 94 Centre Street in New York. This followed an earlier manufacturing and marketing firm, Sargent and Boggs, located in New York. Sargent also had branch offices in Boston, Philadelphia, and Chicago—covering the major regional markets of a country still heavily centered in the northeast. Sales and promotional efforts reached Britain, France, Italy, Australia, China, Mexico, and a dozen other countries, often in the person of Sargent himself.[46]

The J. B. Sargent family—twelve children and two wives over the course of a half-century stay in the city—first lived on Wooster Street near the plant, and later in a mansion on the northeast corner of the New Haven Green (corner of Elm and Church Streets.) Most of the children attended public schools, and Sargent was deeply involved in the community and its governance. He was a Lincoln Republican until the 1870s, when his opposition to protective tariffs would lead him to the Democratic Party. Running as an activist Democrat for mayor in 1890, Sargent was an advocate of strong city government and a booster of the city as a manufacturing center. Here are some passages from his booster-style inaugural address of January 1, 1892:

> When the use of coal as a means of producing steam power became common, the peculiarly good location of New Haven for manufacturing became more known, and has to a great extent been taken advantage of. It is mainly by manufacturing industries, aided by [such] capital as can be induced to come here, or accumulate here, and guided by some knowledge of the sciences as comes from modernized Yale university, that New Haven must grow to be a large city in the early future. New Haven is located at the head of a deep-water harbor on the north side of Long Island Sound, and open to the south with its cooling breezes of summer from over the salt water. It is protected by high hills from the cold land winds of winter. . . . It is only five hours distant from New York by water and two hours hourly by railroad trains. It connects in New York harbor with the great sources of supply of metals, coal, lumber and other materials, both foreign and domestic for the manufacturer's use. It is on the railroad highways between New York and Boston. It has railroad connections with the whole continent, unsurpassed by any other locality, and its vessels enter all Atlantic and gulf ports. . . . At the right, at the left, and behind the city are the demands of the whole continent for manufactured goods.[47]

Mayor Sargent was a Democrat by party affiliation, a manufacturer by conviction, and a progressive by ideology. He sought public ownership of the New Haven Water Company, United Illuminating, and the street railroads. He was capable of real bombast against the monopolies and their political allies: "The price of the product delivered in the cities should be regulated within righteous limits by the authority of law. But in the case of the private monopolies the truly just rate is never known to the authorities and the private monopoly fattens on the hypocritical cupidity of partisan leaders."[48] He sought to use public resources in aid of health, education, and recreation among the poor. He could also be colorful about the local press, once calling the *New Haven Register* the "meanest, lowest copperhead newspaper in New England except the *Hartford Times* which is just even with it."[49]

Until his death in 1907, J. B. Sargent was the epitome of a locally grounded business leader whose firm employed thousands of people and pumped money from across the world into New Haven's streets. This is not to suggest that he gladly pumped more of it than necessary into the streets. Once, when Sargent attempted to cut the wage of iron molders by 10 percent, a work stoppage erupted. Sargent at once restored molders' pay to its original level but then sent directives on consecutive days reading "Business very dull. Discharge 20 molders," and "Business duller. Discharge twelve or fifteen molders." The tactic of keeping some parts of a workforce long term, and speaking of them as members of the family was, as we will later see, mixed with a tendency to employ other workers on a revolving-door basis to fit short-run needs.

New York, New Haven & Hartford Railroad If the Sargent Company was grounded in New Haven, the system of transportation that linked it to world markets was not. True enough, six major divisions of the NYNH&H railroad—the New York, the Berkshire, the Northampton, the Hartford, the Air Line, and the Shore Line—converged in New Haven. Just as the trolleys formed a radial feeder system for the central grid, the "New Haven Road" formed a similar radial system around the city itself. But the company was anything but an instance of grounded enterprise. It was a financial structure that sought to monopolize all forms of fixed-path transportation in New England; it stood as part of a larger attempt to control commercial transportation nationally. J. P. Morgan was at the apex of that effort, and the railroad board consisted entirely of men he could control. Here is a suggestive observation about differences of opinion in NYNH&H board meetings, noted by Charles Mellen, president of the company: "It was Mr. Morgan's way, when he wished to cut opposition and discussion short, to fling his box of matches from him, bring his fist down, and say 'Call a vote. Let's see where these gentlemen stand.' And we always stood where he expected us to stand. That is to say, we stood in awe of him."[50]

If J. B. Sargent thought he saw the evil of monopoly in local utility companies in 1890, the New Haven in 1910 was on an entirely different order of magnitude. Composed in the first place of many smaller, shorter railroads merged to make up its 501 miles of track, the New Haven was a limiting case of what the business world calls horizontal integration. Horizontal integration consists of controlling as many of your competitors as possible, and as many of the firms offering substitutes for your product as possible. Competitors meant other railroads. Substitutes mostly meant steamships and trolley lines. The New Haven had in the years between 1890 and 1910 come to attain majority ownership of the following railroads: Stamford & New Canaan (1890), Hartford & Connecticut Valley (1892), New York, Providence, & Boston (1893), Shore Line Railway (1897), the Housatonic Rail Road (1898), seven small railroads in 1905 alone, and six more by 1908. It was thus essentially without direct competition in southern New England. It had by the early 1900s become possible to travel between towns and cities on trolleys, and the New Haven sought to snuff out this potential substitute for heavy rail by controlling seven major trolley companies in its area of operation, including the Connecticut Company, which was dominant in New Haven itself. These subsidiaries in turn owned and controlled many lesser trolley lines. Thus, for instance, the Connecticut Company acquired twenty other lines and leased fifteen more. Since trolleys required electric power in this era, the New Haven also acquired the Housatonic Power Company, which in turn acquired or leased nine other power companies. Since each of these firms and each of the trolley companies controlled a local monopoly on its own service, the New Haven was a monopoly of monopolies. For good measure, the New Haven acquired New England Navigation, the Hartford & New Haven Transportation Company, the Maine Steamship Company, and the various subsidiaries of these steamship companies. Thus did the New Haven come to control all forms of fixed-path transport in southern New England.[51]

Other Major Companies New Haven had an abundance of manufacturing firms in this era (590 in all), of which many were centered in New Haven (like Sargent, unlike the railroad). Here are some leading instances:

Winchester Repeating Arms Company, founded by Oliver Winchester, absorbed Eli Whitney's Whitney Arms Company in 1858. Established in 1870 at its permanent site just north and west of the Yale campus, this was a worldwide brand name with large markets in military and sporting weaponry. In 1916 it occupied 81 outdoor acres for production and another 23 acres for shipping and storage. Its steam boilers produced 7,650 horsepower, and its steam turbines added 11,175 more. It consumed 75,000 tons of coal, 3.4 billion cubic feet of combustible gas, 10,000 tons of steel, and 13,500 tons of lead, and occupied 3.25 million feet of interior plant floor.[52] It was the largest manufacturing employer in New Haven and one of the largest in the world, reaching 12,000 workers by 1916 under the impetus of World War I.

New Haven Clock Company, founded in the 1850s, built on the stamped-brass technology of Chauncey Jerome's clockworks to become a low-cost producer on a world scale. The plant occupied two city blocks along the rail spur that also served Sargent Hardware, Cowles, and National Paper Box. The firm, which employed roughly 1,000 wage-earners, had introduced electric clocks by 1910.

L. Candee & Company was organized in 1842 and had become a well-capitalized joint stock corporation as early as 1850. The company distributed its rubber boots and galoshes worldwide, and was a major element of the New Haven economy. Using twenty-one steam boilers and five large Corliss engines for power, Candee's four-acre plant was a classic instance of central-place manufacturing. Its buildings were up to five stories tall, defining the vertical style of manufacturing facility so often associated with steam power. President Henry Hotchkiss lived in a Hillhouse Avenue mansion, about a mile from the plant.[53]

Strouse-Adler & Company, founded in 1861 as I. Strouse & Company, was a national leader in women's foundation garments and associated accessories. This was a labor-intensive cutting and sewing operation with roughly 1,000 wage-earners in a single large plant. President Max Adler lived just two blocks from the plant gate and was a major figure in the city's life.

Andrew B. Hendryx Company claimed to be the world's largest manufacturer of birdcages and related hardware—indeed, he said he produced more than half the world's total supply. The plant employed about 500 hands.

Bigelow Company was a joint stock corporation producing steam boilers for national markets. The Bigelow family was living in New Haven in 1910.

Sperry & Barnes was a meat-packing firm handling about 200,000 hogs per year. The firm was, by 1910, controlled by Armour & Company of Chicago.

Peck Brothers & Company manufactured plumbers' materials and fittings for the distribution of water, steam, and gas. Like Sargent, Peck Brothers operated sales offices in Chicago, New York, and Boston. This joint stock company had reached $720,000 in capitalization by 1897.

A lesser number of major manufacturing operations were in fact branches of companies grounded in other cities. These were exceptions to the New Haven pattern of 1910–16: the plants were owned by corporations with no grounded connection with the city. Their top management was located elsewhere, and their ownership was generally outside Connecticut. Of these, the most important were:

Diamond Match Company, incorporated in 1881 at $11 million, was a national consolidation of local producers, one of which had been A. B. Beecher & Sons of New Haven (Westville). The company was operated from headquarters in Chicago and was not in any sense a grounded enterprise in New Haven.

American Steel & Wire Company, a steel fabrication plant capitalized at $9 million, was a major New Haven employer operated out of Cleveland.

National Folding Box, Inc., was a maker of kraft and other cardboard box materials. NFB operated out of New Jersey.

A. C. Gilbert Company was the manufacturer of the once-dominant Erector Set construction toy. The company was founded by Yale alum Alfred Gilbert a few years after he won the pole vault in the 1908 Olympics. It won world markets for its product, peaking at about 2,500 workers at the New Haven plant in the 1950s, declining abruptly in the 1960s.

Seamless Rubber Company was a specialist in the early manufacture of automobile tires and inner tubes, managed from Detroit.

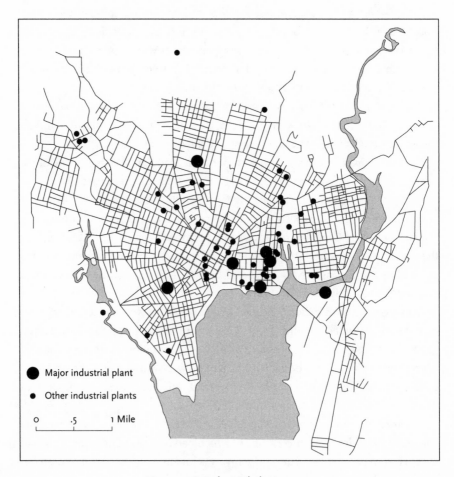

Figure 3.16. Industrial plants, 1913.

Although these plants have no real connection with the city, they elected to invest in centered development in New Haven. If we take these and a few dozen other larger manufacturing firms into consideration, we find New Haven's principal sources of economic energy heavily concentrated in the industrial neighborhoods singled out in figure 3.16. Forty-three of the fifty-five plants shown, including all the major ones, are located in manufacturing neighborhoods. Something like 85 percent of the jobs offered by these fifty-five plants are in industrial neighborhoods, and there is a clear area of focus near the city's heart. Sargent, New Haven Clock, Candee, and Strouse-Adler form a tight cluster just west of the nine squares, with close access to both rail and ocean shipping facilities. Winchester, Seamless Rubber, and American Steel & Wire occupy more distant positions, all well served by fixed-path transportation, and all well within reach of working-class streets with their thousands of wage-earning families.[54]

FABRIC OF ENTERPRISE

The industrial neighborhoods of this era are forever different from the rest of the city, for it is primarily in these areas that the fabric of enterprise grew rich and thick with the production of manufactured goods for the rest of the country and the world. These neighborhoods, close to rail tracks and shipping wharves, were the center of life in the era of Frank Rice, Sylvester Poli, and industrial New Haven. It is in these areas that the architectural hardware installed in growing cities of the western United States rolled off the Sargent production lines at thirty tons per day. It is here that the Winchester rifle, famed for its reliability, was readied for shipment to every state in the Union, and to every continent of the world. It is in these neighborhoods that clocks cheap enough and good enough for ordinary families to own and live by were rolling off the loading docks and heading overland by rail to hundreds of retail distributors in towns like Atlanta and Birmingham, Chicago and Des Moines, Los Angeles and Portland. It is here that the utilitarian infrastructure of daily life across a continent—rubber boots and cardboard boxes, sewing machine bobbins and adding machines—were prepared for the growing markets of an industrial society.

The nine-square grid in New Haven's center was likewise important in this era—as a center of governance and adjudication, as a center for department-store retailing, as a hotbed for specialty retailing, as a core banking area, as a zone filled with brokerage and financial administration of capital enterprise. While the nine squares were planned on purpose, as assertions of earthly order by a Puritan elite, the equally important industrial neighborhoods were not planned in any such way. They emerged from planning and engineering decisions taken by railroad developers, shippers, and, of course, manufacturers. But the boundaries created by these industrial neighborhoods would again and again turn out to be deeply consequential in the long, slow politics of urban history. They would never eclipse the symbolic and logistical importance of the old three-by-three grid—but they would prove themselves every bit as important as the decades rolled by.

Both the central squares and the industrial neighborhoods were in Rice's era focal points of centered development. Manufacturers competed for the privilege of locating their plants in the industrial neighborhoods, and for the advantages that went with such sites—cheap energy, close access to incoming materials, efficient channels through which finished product could be dispersed to distant markets. They also benefited from access to more and more abundant supplies of working men and women, living close by, eager to obtain the best possible wage in return for their hard work. While the logic is different in the central grid, with the trolley system playing a pivotal role, the phenomenon of centered development is no less vigorous. Retailers large and small competed for the chance to open their doors on the noisy, crowded, and lucrative streets of the central district. So did bankers and brokers, along with many others, who sought office space near the New Haven Green.

CHAPTER 4

LIVING LOCAL

A city is not an extended family. That is a tribe or clan. A city is a collection of disparate families who agree to a fiction: They agree to live as if they were as close in blood or ties of kinship as in fact they are in physical proximity. . . . A city is a place where ties of proximity, activity, and self-interest assume the role of family ties. If a family is an expression of continuity through biology, a city is an expression of continuity through will and imagination—through mental choices making artifice, not through physical reproduction.
—A. BARTLETT GIAMATTI, 1989

The urbanist city was full of citizens who were committed to it—by choice, by chance of birth, by economic necessity, or by some combination of these. A salesman or theatrical performer who passes through a city is not its citizen; he is uncommitted, ungrounded—a mere visitor, from whom no particular loyalty should be expected. Here is a test: Does the city he visits have anything to say about who he is? Probably not. A suburban commuter is perhaps considerably more committed, but for her, life and work are things apart. Her identity is perhaps tied to the city, but only in part. A fully grounded city citizen would work full time within her city, would live her nights and evenings there, would educate her children there, would routinely shop in stores there, would worship there if anywhere, would live in a social network pinned down on the city. Its streets, saloons, restaurants, corner stores, plant gates, ballparks, and many more very particular and localized features would organize her life. It would be hard to say who she is without reference to her city.

Such a citizen might not *like* all these organizing features of her life, but they would play a defining role in daily activity regardless. To a certain extent, the person's sense of well-being and her sense of the place's well-being would be intertwined: it would be hard for her to think all was well with her personally, or with her family, if the neighborhood was going to hell. Such a citizen might moreover be expected to routinely encounter others who shared the city as an identity, despite significant differences of race, class, or ethnicity. Again, she might or might not like these others, and her own identity might be defined in part by her differences from them, but she would learn to deal with differences as a routine part of urban life. When most of those who occupied such a city each day were thus part of its local networks—more exactly, its network of networks—we might speak of a grounded community. The urbanist industrial city of Frank Rice's era was substantially thus.

Such a city is, among many other things, a sort of school for urbanity—learning the skills and insights required for getting along with differences, for moving in a crowd not consisting of your own landsmen, for adjusting to people richer or poorer, more or less pious than oneself. Bart Giamatti wrote in praise of those skills under the flag of urbanity:

> Over millennia, this refinement of negotiation—of balancing private need and public obligation, personal desire and public duty, into a common, shared set of agreements—becomes a civilization. This is the public version of what binds us. That state is achieved because city dwellers as individuals or families or as groups have smoothed the edges of private desire so as to fit, or at least to work in with all the other city dwellers, without undue abrasion, without sharp edges forever nicking and wounding, each refining an individual capacity for those thousands of daily, instantaneous negotiations that keep crowded city life from being a constant brawl or ceaseless shoving match. When a city dweller has achieved that truly heightened sensitivity to others that allows easy access, for self and others, through the clogged thoroughfares of urban existence, we call that smoothness urbane. We admire the capacity to proceed, neither impeded nor impeding. If our origins or sentiments are rural in orientation, we may not trust that urbanity, for it may seem too smooth, too slick, but we cannot help but recognize in it a political gift in the deepest sense. . . . Throughout the several millennia of our Western culture, to be urbane has been a term of high praise precisely because cities are such difficult environments to make work.[1]

Not every city is a school for urbanity, and it is easy to picture a city organized so as to minimize contact with differences. One might suppose that the link between work and home would be close only for people near the bottom of the economy, low wages and long hours forcing them to cut transportation time and costs to a minimum. Insofar as this were so, we might envision a cluster of entirely proletarian neighborhoods close to the plant gates filled with the least well paid industrial workers and other low-income families, living in the noisome shadow of the factory. Within those precincts there might be further segregation by nationality, religion, or skin. Then we might envision a ring of somewhat better paid industrial and clerical workers just a bit farther from the plants, with still another ring of middle-class professionals living outside the city altogether. This spatial hierarchy would isolate income classes, encouraging upper-income people to detach their interests and experiences and identities almost entirely from those of inner-ring workers. This pattern of organized isolation would make urban coping skills—dealing with differences in the people you meet daily—less essential for higher groups and would greatly diminish the rate at which working-class people were exposed to those on higher rungs of the ladder. It would also deprive the city of a leadership cadre that would otherwise find its members deeply involved in the daily routines of the city and identified with the interests of the municipality itself. The city's population would be best grounded near the bottom of its economy and worst grounded near the top—a pattern familiar at the dawn of a new century for most American cities.[2] Urbanity, so far as any evolved, would be left mostly to the poor, who would be incapable of buying its substitute in spatial homogeneity.

New Haven in the Frank Rice era around 1910 was nothing of the sort. People at the bottom *and* at the top of the workforce usually lived in town, close to their places of work, and therefore fairly close to one another. There were significant neighborhood differences, with the emergence of class boundaries which would remain significant to the present day. It is possible that the centering of politics and society around neighborhoods rather than on the shop floor served to blunt class differences.[3] But the general pattern was to live in the central city in a way that is localized around the place of work. That is, for example, people working in Wooster Square tended to live in that neighborhood or in others nearby. This was true, with some variations, at all levels of the city economy and social structure, not just among the most marginal workers.

It will become apparent that the neighborhood structure of twenty-first-century New Haven can be understood in large part by reference to the dwelling and working habits of the centered industrial town. The class mixtures and developmental sequences evident in 1910–17 foretell a great deal about the city's organization today. The lines of fracture evident in 1913 were opened up by the explosive changes that unfolded in the decades which separate us from that period. As the boundary between corporate managers and workers formed in the centered city, so would the lines between classes emerge in our own time. And as the density of use in working-class neighborhoods justified by centered industrial development fell away, arrangements that had made pragmatic sense in 1890, 1900, and 1910 would seem increasingly troublesome in 1990, 2000, and very likely 2010. Features of the city that worked pretty well when a high fraction of the citizens were grounded to its neighborhoods would work less well when more and more became part-time New Haveners.

WORKING-CLASS LOCALISM AND THE SARGENT COMPANY

Between January and June 1910, the Sargent Company hired more than five hundred new workers for its Water Street hardware plant (suggesting, by the by, both a robust business and a high rate of turnover among workers).[4] On being picked for work in one of more than twenty production centers, each newcomer signed an employment ledger. When I handled those ledger books recently, their pages were still smudged with the oil of working hands, somehow giving the impression that they had been inscribed nine minutes, and not nine decades, earlier.[5] Many signatures are unpracticed, some letters slanted forward and others tilted backward in a single name, some strokes strong and straight, others meandering as the author makes tiny mid-stroke corrections. Some signers offered only two initials, others provided full names in elegant script. The ledgers allowed nearly an inch of vertical room per signature, and many of the signers used it all—"Edward Bailey, age 14, 19 Garden St, New Haven" occupies nearly an inch of altitude and most of the eight inches allowed side to side.

These signings are the microscopic record of centered industrialism. For some, the resulting contract would foretell a lifetime of work on a Sargent production line stamping out doorplates or machining lock tumblers. For others, this was the first and very temporary job in a new country. For an unlucky few, this would be a last stop before the trench warfare of World War I. Whatever the length of the contract, it was at once a commitment to a company and a commitment to a place—to a particular manufacturing town, and to a more or less definite part of that town. Work to a considerable degree determined place of residence—or, more exactly, they determined each other. Today we are inclined to see work and life as worlds apart, but residents of the centered industrial city

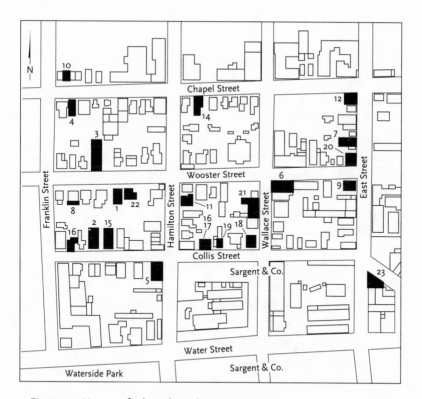

Figure 4.1. Homes of selected new hires, Sargent Hardware, just north of the plant, spring months of 1910.

needed to fit them together. Moreover, once the person fits work and home to a neighborhood, she is committed to similarly localized choices for schooling, grocery shopping, religion, and so forth. The centered industrial city was for this reason a closely integrated network of residential neighborhoods, all of them dependent directly or indirectly on the manufacturing core of the city.[6] And the centering was, to use a twenty-first-century term, broad band—encompassing a high fraction of all life's parts.

There are obvious intimations of localism in Sargent employment ledgers. Wallace, Wooster, East, Franklin, Hamilton, and Chapel Streets all ran near the plant's site on Water Street. Collis Street also was close to the Sargent plant but is now buried under Interstate 91:

1. M. Acamfora, 64 Wooster Street
2. Frank Cammira, 47 Collis Street
3. N. Constantinope, 71 Wooster Street

4. James Egan, 486 Chapel Street

5. S. Esposito, 28 Collis Street

6. Lawrence Floyd, 29 Wallace Street

7. A. Gaspino, 174 East Street

8. Antonio Gambarde, 51 Collis Street

9. M. Gradioso, 156 East Street

10. Michael Garlly, 487 Chapel Street

11. Anthony Imperatore, 20 Hamilton Street

12. Joseph Juknit, 180 East Street

13. Angelo Lura, 51 Collis Street

14. F. Ligori, 436 Chapel Street

15. F. Luibello, 45 Collis Street

16. D. Monaco, 29 Collis Street

17. Vincenzo Natale, 29 Collis Street

18. Anthony Piscitelli, 16 Wallace Street

19. Dom Pantero, 25 Collis Street

20. Michael Sleany, 164 East Street

21. Viccent Spinello, 24 Wallace Street

22. A. Vissiccio, 62 Wooster Street

23. E. Vaccino, 19 East Street

As will quickly be seen from figure 4.1, these workers were living close enough to hear the nearest production centers of the Sargent plant as they slept at night—and doubtless to smell the coal being burned to generate steam at the plant (the numbers in the map match those preceding each name). Densities were very high in comparison with the rest of New Haven—and by comparison to the regions of Europe (mostly central and southern Italy) from which these people were coming. Thus, for instance, the block of Collis Street between Hamilton and Franklin was home to 71 adult workers or widows in 1913 (roughly, one person for every seven feet of street, not counting the children). A little north of the area covered by figure 4.1, a block of Franklin Street only about 650 feet long housed 164 adult workers or widows—roughly, one for every four feet of street. They were living largely in tenements, many of them constructed quickly in the decades before their signing on with Sargent.[7] It was an untidy, cluttered, noisy neighborhood that had the singular advantage of immediate shoe-leather access to the plant gate—combined, doubtless, with very little private living space and few hours of tranquility in the daily cycle.

The map tells us little about the overall distribution of homes among the new

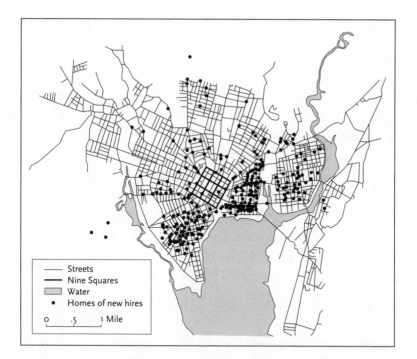

Figure 4.2. Homes of Sargent Company new hires, citywide, spring months of 1910. Each dot may represent several homes at one address or homes at two or more closely bunched addresses.

hires of early 1910. (I picked my list of workers to fit onto the map.) As we look further into the ledger books, we find workers living farther from the plant—a Sobolewski of Silver Street, an O'Neill of Grafton Street, a Pedden of Dixwell Avenue, a Palmieri of Oak Street. We discover innumerable particulars, as well. Sobolewski shared his digs at 41 Silver Street—about a mile from the plant but near the train station—with three other recent hires at Sargent, all evidently his countrymen (Mssrs. Pussick, Wedelski, and Booyzouski).[8] More is revealed when we "geocode" the address file of all the 1910 new hires, using an electronic street grid reconstructed block-by-block from a 1911 atlas.[9] The process is imperfect, but locations were found for 474 out of 499 legible addresses with enough specificity to be used (an address defined simply by the name of a long street is less than helpful). The result is shown in figure 4.2, with the Sargent plant indicated just below the densest concentration of worker homes.[10] The main concentration of fresh recruits—nearly 150 workers—was in the Wooster Square neighborhood, where the plant was located. The second greatest concentration

119

was in the Hill neighborhood, south of the nine squares, where 74 new hires were living in early 1910. Fair Haven, east of Sargent, accounted for 52, and the Oak Street area, running west from the nine squares, housed 24 (these neighborhoods are delineated in figure 4.7). Thus 299 of the 474 workers for whom adequate data are in hand—nearly two-thirds of the total—were bunched together in these four working-class neighborhoods. This is centered industrialism expressed by local living.[11]

A slightly more exact (if less human) way of parsing the same information is to measure the crow's flight distance between worker homes and the plant. The results are:

- 162 new hires (34 percent) lived within half a mile of the Sargent plant
- 138 (29 percent) lived in the next ring, between a half and a whole mile away
- 102 (22 percent) lived between 1 and 1.5 miles away
- 72 (15 percent) lived more than 1.5 miles distant

Thus, 85 percent lived within 1.5 miles of the plant where they were employed, and the vast majority dwelt within the city of New Haven. Indeed, the ledger records only a handful of new hires living beyond city limits: three in Branford, three in Hamden, four in West Haven (then a borough and postal address, not a town), one in Stamford, four in New Britain, and a couple farther away. For those recording distant addresses, like New Britain, one can only guess that they had signed on for just a day or two's work, or that they planned to move closer to the workplace.

WORKING-CLASS GEOGRAPHY

Sargent's new hires were just one of many groups of workers evincing centered localism in their choices of homes.[12] Since similarly complete employment rolls are unavailable for other employers, I have drawn a quasi-random sample of 5,500 persons listed in the 1913 Price and Lee New Haven City Directory.[13] This represents somewhat less than a 10 percent sample of total households at the time. If we then select people by occupational criteria—What did she do? Who did he work for?—we have a rough-and-ready basis on which to chart living patterns within the city and its immediate suburbs (addresses in the suburbs are less reliable in this data set than in others).

Winchester Workers Winchester Repeating Arms was an even bigger industrial employer than Sargent, with several thousand employees at one large campus located a couple of miles west and a little north of Sargent. This was a colossus,

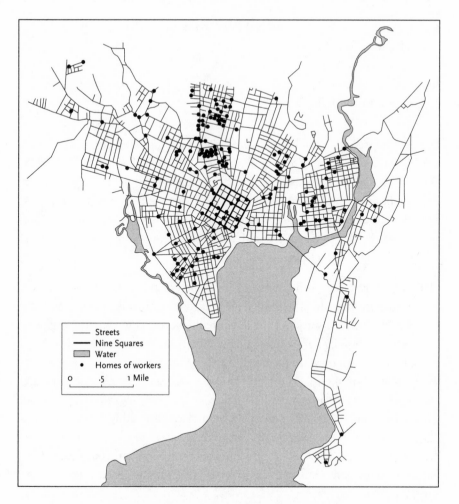

Figure 4.3. Homes of Winchester employees, 1913.

reaching peaks in the range of 21,000 full-time workers during world wars.[14] We turn up 305 Winchester workers in our sample; 278 survive the hazards of electronic mapping to appear as dots in figure 4.3. The Winchester plant itself was located in the open space (above the nine squares, between the clusters of dots). These workers were much like the Sargent new hires in their overall pattern of centered localism, with a distinct bias toward the immediate vicinity of the plant. Whereas the Sargent people clustered in Wooster Square near one plant, the Winchester people clustered in the Dixwell-Newhallville corridor near another. But they were slightly less densely clustered around the plant gate. Here is a comparison with the Sargent new hires:

Distances from Plant	Winchester Workers, 1913	Sargent New Hires, 1910
Less than ½ mile	32%	34%
Less than 1 mile	45%	63%
Less than 1 ½ miles	63%	85%
Farther than that	27%	15%

The less-dense clustering in the immediate neighborhood corresponds to a somewhat lower overall housing density in the Dixwell-Newhallville corridor than in Wooster Square—a difference attributable mostly to the nearly complete absence of tenement housing near the Winchester site.[15] As it happens, 85 percent of the Winchester people lived within two miles, while 85 percent of the Sargent people lived within a mile and a half. Although similar in broad outline, the two distributions differ in this detail.

Railroad Workers Railroading was of course the critical system of cheap, fixed-path transport that gave a locational advantage to companies like Sargent and Winchester. Railroad work—from track maintenance to locomotive engineering—was also a fairly large direct source of employment (although at times a difficult one to pin down in the data).[16] Two hundred fifty-five railroad workers are identifiable in the 1913 sample, of whom 231 are accounted for in figure 4.4. While the major rail yards and the central passenger terminals were fairly well localized just south of the nine squares, it is not possible to tidily define work sites for these workers (the central rail depot, labeled in figure 4.4, is one of many work sites). A tendency to concentrate in southerly neighborhoods near the rail lines is evident in the map, indicating consistency with the general theme of centered localism.

Laborers and Seamstresses Several additional groups of working-class New Haveners from this era are known to us only by what they did, not by the firm or industry for which they did it. Of these, laborers are among the most important and numerous. Some were employed by large firms like Sargent or Winchester or New Haven Clock, reporting to a fixed point each shift, but this was somewhat exceptional. Most worked in construction doing heavy lifting for the building trades—carrying hod, moving brick, digging footings, and other tasks for which carpenters, masons, and other skilled tradesmen were overqualified. Their work sites were scattered and ever-changing, so proximity to any one site was irrelevant in the long run. Living near the bottom of the economic scale, and facing a moving target for each week's job site, laborers could be expected to seek out the lowest rents available in the most centered locations. This appears to be exactly

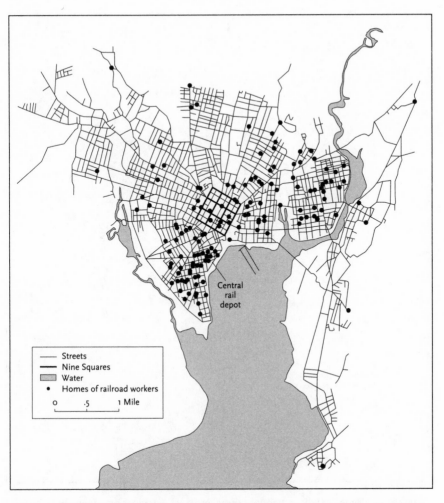

Figure 4.4. Homes of railroad workers, 1913. Each dot may represent several homes at one address or homes at two or more closely bunched addresses.

what they were doing in 1913. Figure 4.5 shows the homes of exactly 300 laborers from the 1913 sample.[17] The largest concentration of laborers (112 of 300) lived in Wooster Square, and another 66 laborers were living in the Hill and Oak Street neighborhoods. Fair Haven accounted for 50 more, Dixwell-Newhallville for 19. To extrapolate actual density from this small sample: 112 may suggest 1,000 in Wooster Square, 66 in the Hill and Oak Street perhaps 600, 19 may indicate a couple hundred in Dixwell-Newhallville. Like the Sargent new hires, these families were definitively working class, and so were the neighborhoods in which they were concentrated. Their centered residential choices are, if anything, more pronounced than those of the other groups considered so far.

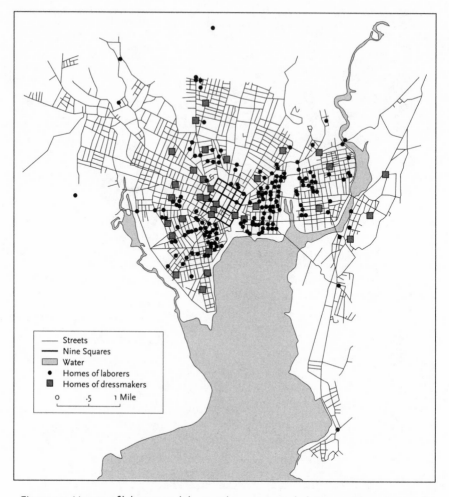

Figure 4.5. Homes of laborers and dressmakers, 1913. Each dot may represent several homes at one address or homes at two or more closely bunched addresses.

Dressmaking appears to have been a cottage industry in 1913 New Haven (see figure 4.5). Nearly all the dressmakers were women, a good many doubtless married to working men. Their residential choices are broadly consistent with those of the laborers and likewise suggest the pattern of centered localism. One guesses that their customers were often their neighbors, or at least their neighbor's neighbors, and that habits of patronage tended to be reciprocal. A grocer's dressmaker is quite apt also to have been her customer when it came time to buy supper.

Clerical Workers Clerical occupations were a large and rapidly expanding fraction of the workforce in early twentieth-century America as larger, more complex
organizations became increasingly common. Paper-handling, recordkeeping,
and transaction-management became central to every urban economy, and New
Haven was no exception. In a 1910 workforce of 57,109 people, clerical occupations accounted for 4,816 jobs on the narrowest definition and 7,460 on a
broader definition.[18] Figure 4.6 shows 413 of the 441 clerical workers' homes
that show up in our 1913 sample—in which a quite strict definition of "clerk"

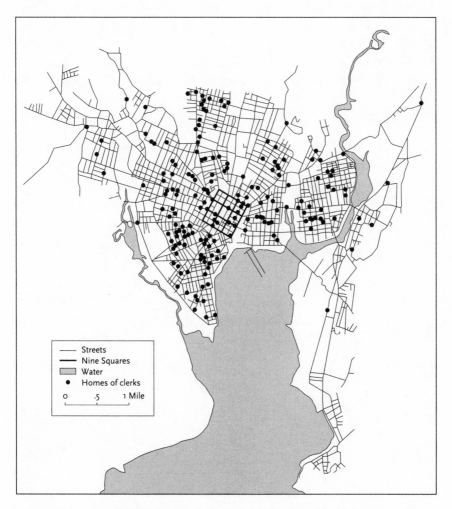

Figure 4.6. Homes of clerks, 1913. Each dot may represent several homes at one address
or homes at two or more closely bunched addresses.

seems to have been applied. A slightly greater number of clerks live apart from the densest working people's neighborhoods than is true for other groups, but the overall pattern of lives grounded in central city neighborhoods holds for this group as for the others considered already.

Working-Class Localism There is a strong convergence among the working groups so far considered, and the great majority of all these groups were living in a compact set of neighborhoods. Seven neighborhoods, most of them quite compact, pretty much defined the residential city for working people in the Frank Rice era. Some were tiny (Dixwell covered about 0.16 square miles, Newhallville about 0.27, Oak Street about 0.41, Wooster Square exactly half a square mile). The Hill was larger (0.73), and Fair Haven still larger (1.02). All six neighborhoods were thickly, not to say exclusively, working class. One additional area, not really a neighborhood, is labeled as the State-Orange corridor in figure 4.7. This

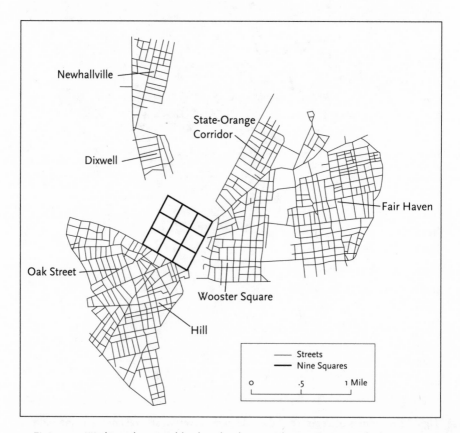

Figure 4.7. Working-class neighborhoods, shown with nine-square grid, about 1913.

is a zone of transition running northeast from downtown, and it contained a mix of working families and families with other status markers. Even counting this area, the total amounted to just 3.4 square miles, which contained about 82 percent of the working-class households tracked above.[19] Among the Sargent new hires of 1910, 91 percent lived in these areas, compared with 87 percent of the laborers, 84 percent of the Winchester employees, 79 percent of the clerical workers, 77 percent of the railroaders, and 75 percent of the dressmakers. These areas will appear again as central points of focus in New Haven a century later.

UPSCALE LOCALISM

In Frank Rice's New Haven, the best-paid and most secure occupational groups lived close to working-class people, sometimes right next door. Like the less privileged workers, most of them lived near their jobs. Yet there were significant boundaries between the neighborhoods deemed suitable for these advantaged groups and the rest of the city. These bourgeois zones run through and between the working people's neighborhoods. In figure 4.8, these streets are shown; labels for the working-class neighborhoods are shown lightface type. At the center are the old nine squares, also known to this era as the First Ward. Just to the west we find the Dwight neighborhood, and then, farther west, the Edgewood neighborhood.[20] To the north is the more elongated Whitney corridor, or East Rock neighborhood. This last area, low in density and high in value, was by any reckoning the most desirable residential neighborhood in the early twentieth-century city. As the Gilbert and Olmsted report of 1910 had it, this was New Haven's "high-class northern residential district."[21] Other parts of the city, notably Westville, were becoming fashionable in this period but had not yet been developed substantially. Taken together, these neighborhoods constitute just under 1.9 square miles of land area—more than half of the working-class total but for far less than half as many people. With roughly 10 percent of the city's total land, these neighborhoods captured perhaps 80 percent of the city's most affluent and influential families.

Corporate Officers Let's begin with senior business management—the top officials of joint stock corporations doing substantial business in New Haven as of 1913. These firms are all capitalized at between $50,000 and $10 million, or are listed as major employers in the 1913 city directory. Of the 175 firms for which a chief executive, typically titled president, could be identified, we have the following breakdown for place of residence:

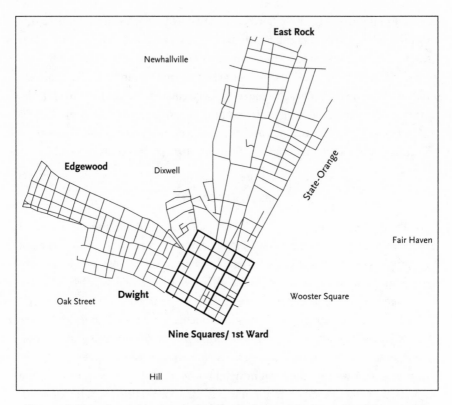

Figure 4.8. Upscale neighborhoods (boldface), shown with nine-square grid and other neighborhoods, about 1913.

• 28 CEOs lived altogether outside the New Haven region
• 26 lived in the region but outside the city
• 121 lived in New Haven itself (figure 4.9)

The twenty-eight living outside the region indicated a growing pattern that would become ever more dominant over the course of the twentieth century. Recall that this is an era of corporate integration, both horizontal and vertical.[22] Horizontal integration—combining competing firms in a single industry across the country—would diminish the grounding of top management in each city. This is because top management of the combined corporation would be located in one city, often distant from the cities in which most of the subsidiaries were located. Vertical integration—combining firms at each step, from raw materials to manufacturing to sales and distribution—would have something of the same effect on grounded leadership in the towns that might otherwise have been home

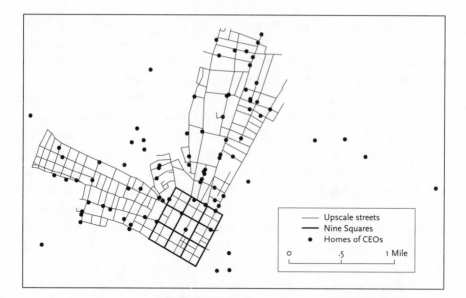

Figure 4.9. Homes of corporate CEOs, projected over upscale neighborhoods, 1913. Each dot may represent several homes at one address or homes at two or more closely bunched addresses.

to the component firms. Thus, what would perhaps appear to the casual observer as a New Haven meatpacking plant might turn out to be a distribution channel owned by a Chicago company that had swallowed up the New Haven outfit for purposes of distribution in New England. In fact, the New Haven meat-distribution firm of Sperry & Barnes listed Edward Swift of Chicago as its president, just such a case. So top management would owe loyalty not to New Haven but to Chicago. Both of these patterns would have major impacts on New Haven and scores of other cities later in the twentieth century.

Most of these out-of-region executives ran integrated corporations, doing business on a more or less continental scale, often with no powerful roots in any one city. Take the case of Henry Flagler, president of the Peninsular & Occidental Steamship Company, which provided logistic service to New Haven harbor.[23] Flagler lived in New York City, and often in Palm Beach, Florida, and the firm in question was but one of many for which he was given responsibility by the interlocking set of holding companies whose interests ran from Standard Oil to the New York, New Haven & Hartford Railroad. He was in no sense grounded to New Haven or any other place. Others like him included W. P. Palmer of American Steel & Wire (Cleveland), D. S. Walton of National Folding Box & Paper (East Orange, New Jersey), Walter Parker of Seamless Rubber (Detroit), and Edward

Wolf of Celluloid Starch (Philadelphia). A similar case is offered by the Brad-
street investment house, run by Henry Dunn of New York, with a retail branch
office in New Haven and in scores of other cities. A different pattern is illustrated
by the paper entities of New Haven Real Estate Title and New Haven Real Estate
& Power, both listing one H. A. Jackson of Boston as president. Yet another instance is the large downtown department store Shartenberg-Robinson, chaired
by Jacob Shartenberg of Providence. A more important case is that of George
Sargent of New York, who came into control of the Sargent Company after the
death of J. B. Sargent in 1907.[24] These are all exceptions to the pattern of centered localism, and to the idea of grounded leadership in the city of New Haven.
These outlanders constituted about 16 percent of the city's major CEOs in 1913.

An additional twenty-six business chieftains were living in the region, but
outside the city itself. Eleven lived in the borough West Haven (it would not
become independent of the city until 1921). Several others lived in other industrial centers nearby. Charles Nettleton of New Haven Gas Light lived in the manufacturing town of Derby, about ten miles west of New Haven; Charles Logan
(Logan Brothers' wholesale groceries) lived in Bridgeport. Cornelius Tracy of
New Haven Investment lived in industrial Waterbury. Only a dozen lived in what
would come to be seen as conventional suburbs of New Haven. Examples include Fuller Manufacturing's Egbert Fuller of Pine Orchard, Branford, Floss
Starch's Adam Sattig of Woodbridge, and E. B. Sheldon's Walter Gracie of Orange. These people are a further exception to the general pattern of centered localism, accounting for between 8 and 15 percent of the total, depending on how
one classifies the West Haven contingent (and a lone East Haven resident).

That leaves 121 New Haven CEOs living in New Haven—roughly 75 percent of
the total firms. Given double-assignments, where one person ran two companies, the total of individuals boils down to just over 100. This is a big concentration of senior business leadership, and it was a formidable crew. Looking only at
those whose firms were heavily capitalized (the dollars shown are in 1913 denominations, about eighteen times more valuable than 2002 dollars) or who
were exceptional in some other respect, we have:

- John Alling of Southern New England Telephone (first of its kind in the world,
  capitalized at $10 million) and Security Insurance ($1 million)
- Eli Whitney III, of New Haven Water, Union & New Haven Trust, Branford Wa-
  ter, and several smaller firms (combined capital over $4 million)
- Winthrop Bushnell of Connecticut Power ($2.25 million capital)
- James English of United Illuminating ($2 million)

- Louis Stoddard of Bingham–New Haven Copper & Gold ($2 million) and the New Haven Hotel Company ($1 million)
- Walter Camp of New Haven Clock, and "inventor" of American football at Yale
- J. E. Hubinger of J. C. Hubinger Starch ($1 million) and Eastern Machine Screw ($100,000)
- Henry Hotchkiss of Candee Rubber ($600,000)
- Rollin Woodruff of C. S. Mersick ($500,000)
- Nathan Kendall of Yale Brewing ($600,000)
- Franklin Homan of American Oyster ($500,000)
- Walter Malley of the Edward Malley Company department store ($300,000)
- Nathan Hendryx of Andrew Hendryx, world's largest manufacturer of bird cages
- Edward Strouse of what would soon become Strouse-Adler corsets
- Louis Cowles of Cowles manufacturing
- Minotte Chatfield of New Haven Pulp and Board and Chatfield Paper
- Frank Bigelow of National Pipe Bending
- C. D. Parmalee of Narragansett Bay Oyster
- Wheeler Beecher of Geometric Tool
- David Gamble of Gamble-Desmond department store
- Luella Shuster of F. B. Shuster, manufacturers of wire processing machinery (and still operating in New Haven as of 2003)
- Frederick Farnsworth of Eastern Machinery
- Charles Nicklas of Weibel Brewery
- William Harmon of Pond Lily dying works
- Jacob Malcon of New Haven Construction and Investment
- Harry Joroff of New England Grocery wholesalers
- Henry Newton of National Engineering
- Frank Frisbie of Mercantile Safe Deposit
- George Converse of McKay Oyster

This is, of course, just a sampling of resident CEOs, who are in turn only part of a larger, localized business leadership class. Putting aside mom-and-pop retailing, it appears that there must have been something like one thousand city residents with senior management and ownership stakes in New Haven's business. But for our purposes, a look at the residential choices made by this more limited group will suffice.

Of the 105 executives for whom I was able to obtain valid addresses, 89 lived in upscale areas (85 percent). Of these, 52 lived in East Rock, 16 in Dwight, 15 in

Edgewood, and 6 in the downtown First Ward. Notice that the outliers fell in de-cidedly working-class neighborhoods, for the most part (Wooster Square is in this respect misleading, having developed a pocket of expensive housing all its own). Dixwell had 5 CEOs, Oak Street 1, Fair Haven 4. Note also that many of these top executives lived on or near streets abutting working-class neighborhoods, which are close by in every direction except Edgewood's western and East Rock's eastern flank. One may say that class had a spatial signature here, but it had blurred edges and very close contact with large numbers of less affluent people.

Yale Professors The Yale professorate in this era was small and tightly tied to an institution which was decades from becoming a full-fledged university. Arthur Twining Hadley was president of Yale in these years, and he was a wonder to all: "To attend a lecture by Hadley was a memorable experience: he twirled; he teetered on the edge of the platform; he twined about any object handy. Mean-while, one arm slashed in his famous pump-handle motion, while the other swung about his head. He had even been known to step into a wastebasket and then struggle to extricate himself, all without interrupting the flow of his lecture. Fortunately, the intellectual content of his material was so absorbing that it never got lost in all his gyrations."[25]

Under Hadley's leadership, Yale introduced increasingly competitive stan-dards for recruiting and promoting its faculty, and the 1913 roster of full profes-sors (131 in all) contained a number of luminaries.[26] Some were public figures. William Howard Taft had just returned to the law school after being the nation's twenth-seventh president and would later go to the Supreme Court; Walter Camp had long since single-handedly codified the rules of American football and placed Yale near the top of the sport's national pecking order; Wilbur Cross would become governor of Connecticut (figure 4.10). Others were renowned for their scholarship: historian Max Farrand, economist Irving Fisher, chemist Frank Austin Gooch, and mineralogist Edward Dana are examples. But the fac-ulty was still largely a teaching staff for what had, in the main, remained a college more than a university, and a rather small, somewhat provincial college at that. It was a closed place in certain critical respects, one of which was a pronounced re-luctance to appoint Jewish faculty or to admit Jewish students in appropriate numbers.[27]

To a degree now difficult to picture, Yale was deeply embedded in the city of New Haven. In figure 4.11 we see the distribution of the homes of full professors in 1913. The striking feature is that nearly all of the professors lived in a very small area. Of the 131, only 8 lived outside city limits, and of these just 2 could be

Figure 4.10. Three New Haven notables:
Republican leader Colonel Isaac Ullman, former
U.S. President William Howard Taft, and Walter
Camp, c. 1915. NHCHS.

said to live in anything resembling a suburb.[28] Of the 114 for whom we can locate specific New Haven addresses, 87 lived in the East Rock corridor, 14 lived near the Green downtown, and 13 lived in the Dwight neighborhood. With three-quarters living in East Rock, this picture of localism outdoes that of the Sargent new hires of 1910, of whom just 34 percent lived in Wooster Square. Of the professors, 81 percent were within a mile of the Yale College campus, and 48 percent were within half a mile. Virtually all lived within a mile and a half. While both faculty and students were recruited from a national catchment area, the dwelling habits of the senior faculty suggest something like a neighborhood college. Certainly—and this is the point—this higher-status group displayed as decided a pattern of centered localism as any less privileged group we have been able to identify in this period.

One additional point: there were micro-neighborhoods, often consisting of a single block face, in which academic and town elites lived together at close quarters. Hillhouse Avenue was dominated by upper-tier business leaders—Hotchkiss, Hooker, Fitch, Farnam, English—living close by with such Yale figures as Timothy Dwight, Edward Dana, Walter Camp, and Horatio Reynolds.[29]

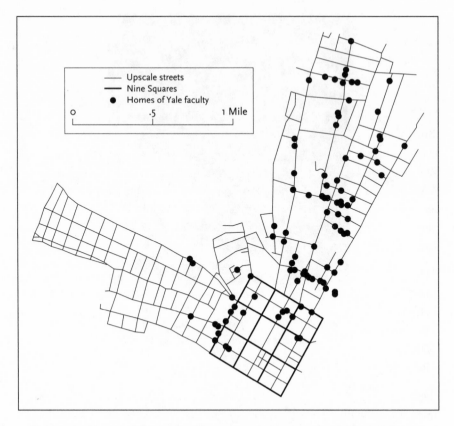

Figure 4.11. Homes of Yale professors, projected over upscale neighborhoods, 1913. Each dot may represent several homes at one address or homes at two or more closely bunched addresses.

Ex-President Taft was around the corner on Prospect Street. Concentrations of similar magnitude could be found on Edgehill Road, Trumbull Street, Edwards Street, and Livingston Street. This does not, of itself, suggest anything specific about the cross-linkage of academic and business elites. But it does suggest a kind of familiarity, and a likely sense of co-membership in the New Haven community. Anecdotal evidence reinforces that suspicion, as we find Walter Camp a little earlier "who simultaneously ran the New Haven Clock Co. and coached the Yale football team and who also served as chairman of the Chamber [of Commerce's] Recreation Committee and its Welfare Committee."[30]

Proprietors There was a tiny civic elite whose members served between 1913 and 1917 as Proprietors of Common and Undivided Lands. This mostly meant acting as owners of the New Haven Green.[31] From the seventeenth century on, the common lands were considered the joint property of the original colonists and their heirs. Until the early nineteenth century, this meant having a large group meet to decide policy for such areas as the New Haven Green. As this became cumbersome and impractical, a Committee of Proprietors of Common and Undivided Lands was created and affirmed by acts of the Connecticut State Assembly in 1810 and 1875.[32] The Proprietors, five in number at any given time, were perhaps as restrictive and homogeneous a group as could be found in the industrial city. Membership had for the better part of two centuries been confined to male WASPs from old New Haven families—typically families of the "Standing Order" left over from colonial and federalist days.[33] Consulting the minutes of the (very infrequent) meetings held in 1913 and 1917, we find this roster of six participants, listed by name, occupation, work address, and home address:

Henry T. Blake, lawyer, 361 Temple Street, 361 Temple Street
Leonard M. Daggett, lawyer, 42 Church Street, 60 Wall Street
Henry F. English, lawyer, 839 Chapel Street, 38 Hillhouse Avenue
W. J. Trowbridge, banker, 170 Orange Street, 221 Church Street
Oliver S. White, lawyer, 69 Church Street, 89 Trumbull Street
Roger S. White II, lawyer, 69 Church Street, 270 Everit Street

These family names were "old" already in 1910, and three had been honored by nineteenth-century street names (Blake, Daggett, White). These men were all working in the nine-square central business district. Indeed, with the exception of Roger White's home to the north on Everit Street, this is by far the most tightly centered group in the entire range covered by this chapter. Blake lived and worked in the same house and wrote with dry wit about the historical Green: "Before [October 1639] . . . the stocks and doubtless the whipping post had been erected on the market place; and thus these emblems of Christian civilization were the earliest tokens of its dedication to free institutions and public enjoyment. Four days later . . . as the record tersely informs us, 'the Indian's head was cut off and pitched upon a pole in the market place,' this being the second step in the improvement of the Green and the first attempt to put a cheerful face upon the public pleasure ground."[34]

Trowbridge had a walk of just four hundred yards to and from work. Daggett had a trip of about six hundred yards to make each day. English and Oliver White lived about 0.6 miles from their offices. Only Roger White had much of a commute to make—1.95 miles between Everit Street and the White Brothers' Church Street offices.[35] All, thus, lived within the heart of upscale New Haven.

Despite their differences from the Sargent new hires, they were just as tightly centered in the city—perhaps even more so. And their homes were either within the old nine squares or north of them, following a pattern similar to that of the CEOs' (included in figure 4.9 for comparison).

All three of these upscale groups—executives, faculty, and Proprietors—were living predominately in local neighborhoods of the central city. With the exception of certain integrated corporations, business and business leadership were bonded to place. The Yale faculty was clustered in its favored neighborhood even more tightly than any of the industrial workforces considered earlier. All of these people led lives locked firmly in the central city: New Haven was their place of work, it was where they lived, it was where they made friends, it was where they married off their children, and in innumerable other respects it was their community. Success of place was bundled together with the success of self, of family, and of enterprise. City decline and more personal failure were implicitly connected for these people as they are now connected for only a very few.

CLOSE QUARTERS, STRANGE VOICES

As suggested in Chapter 1, it would be a mistake to think of the centered industrial city as a golden age of urbanism. First of all, working-class neighborhoods were often very densely populated. The area of Wooster Square just north of the old Sargent plant (Sixth Ward at the time) contained 8,054 people on less than 167 gross acres of land—about 50 people to the acre or, by extrapolation, around 30,000 per square mile. Parts of the Hill neighborhood were almost as dense.[36] These are high densities, although they do not begin to approach national or world highs. Quality of housing was also in many instances deplorable—tenements, crowded close to one another, with shared toilets and only the most rudimentary amenities. Where long land parcels with narrow street frontage existed, "back tenements" were often developed, to the horror of city planners: "Back tenements, unsanitary shacks, crowding, secrecy, and filth are the results of crowding poor and ignorant people into a region where each of the insufficient number of dwellings has a long piece of wasteland tucked in behind it out of sight. The dwellings are terribly needed, are more in demand in such a district than anything else except food, and the back tenement or lodging shack is the natural response. . . . But the ordinary back tenement itself is a frightfully wasteful method of housing, morally and socially as well as economically."[37]

The experience of diversity—of voices utterly different from one's own, of national memories at odds with one's own heritage, of manners and customs that would have been wholly unacceptable in the old country—was a central fact of life. This was true for the Old Yankees and even more emphatically true for the newer arrivals. It was likewise doubtless true for the blacks, who had fallen to less than 3 percent of the city's population with the avalanche of European arrivals. According to the 1910 Census, "native whites of native stock" now made up just 28 percent of the population. "Native whites of foreign or mixed parentage" constituted 37 percent, and "foreign born white" about 32 percent. There were 13,159 Italian born, 9,004 Irish born, 7,890 "Russians," and 4,144 German born, giving a multilingual and multicultural feel to the city in 1910.[38]

One way to get a sense of the contact that each group would have had with all the others is to look at the enrollment figures for elementary schools in this period.[39] Of fifty elementary schools in 1908, not one drew as many as 80 percent of its students from one nationality/racial group. (This would change by 1915, however, as the Wooster Square schools were flooded with Italian children.) Here are some representative examples for 1908:

- Hooker School (East Rock area): 53% "American," 24% Irish, 18% German
- Scranton School (Oak Street neighborhood): 23% "American," 21% German, 13% "Russian," 12% Irish, 11% Italian
- Winchester School (Dixwell area): 26% "American," 22% Negro, 18% Irish, 13% German, 7% Russian, 5% Italian
- Carlisle Street School (Hill section): 78% Italian, 5% Polish, 3% Russian, etc.

This pattern of national integration was neither universal across institutional contexts (the Catholic parishes were quite deliberately as homogeneous as possible), nor would it have seemed to everyone a source of joy. Yet it is important. It compelled people to deal with differences, and to do so in a grounded context, from which escape into the "purity" of one's own identity was impossible. Combined with the prevalence of mixed uses—retail, residential, industrial—this was just the sort of "disorder" to which Richard Sennett's seminal *Uses of Disorder* directs our attention. Writing of an imagined walk down Chicago's Halsted Street in 1910, he tells us that:

> We would be conscious that it was filled with "foreigners," but at every place with different kinds of foreigners, all mixed together. A native might tell us that a certain few blocks were Greek or Polish or Irish, but were one actually to look at particular houses and apartment buildings, one would find the ethnic groups jumbled together. Even on the Chinese blocks of the street— for the Chinese are supposed at this time to have been the most closed of

ethnic societies—there would be numerous families from Ireland or eastern Europe.

The functioning of all these groups on Halsted Street would appear hopelessly tangled to modern observers. For the apartments would be mixed in
with stores, the streets themselves crowded with vendors and brokers of all
kinds; even factories, as we moved to the southern end of Halsted Street,
would be intermixed with bars, brothels, synagogues, churches, and apartment buildings.[40]

Very much the same could have been seen on lower Chapel Street or on Congress Avenue or on Oak Street in New Haven. The result was a complexity, a familiarity with the unfamiliar, and a kind of urbanity that typified the centered industrial city of this period. Residents did not necessarily love, or even like, one
another, but they shared a grounded commitment—for better or for worse—to
the streets and institutions of a particular city that had brought them together
from across the globe. None could say who they were, or sought to become, without reference—implicit or explicit—to their city.

A NOTE ON THE SUBURBS WITHIN

Well over 85 percent of the city's people in 1910–13 lived in the neighborhoods—upscale or downscale—that constituted the core city of that era. My estimates from the 1913 sample show that the working-class precincts claimed about
65 percent of the total population, and upscale areas accounted for perhaps another 22 percent (remember that a considerable fraction of the households thus
included were not themselves upscale). But there were other places to live within
city limits, typically places that had emerged as "trolley car suburbs" in the late
nineteenth century.[41] In figure 4.12, the working-class neighborhoods are shown
in full tone and the upscale areas in halftone. The city outline (as it exists today)
encloses these areas along with five others, which constitute the internal suburbs
of 1911.

Westville had developed in the late nineteenth century under the leadership of
Donald Mitchell and to a considerable extent on the strength of private funding.[42] It had been part of the town of New Haven, and not of the city of New
Haven, until 1897, when the two governmental layers were folded together and
Westville was annexed to the city along with Fair Haven East.[43] These two neighborhoods had been joined—to each other and, more importantly, to the city center, by the Fair Haven and Westville Horse Railroad as early as 1860.[44] Westville

would be home to 3,588 by 1910, while Fair Haven East (now called the Heights) would house 2,386.[45] Further south, in the tenderloin east of New Haven's harbor, was a thinly settled area mixing permanent residences with resort hotels and summer houses along the shore. With about 2,700 residents in 1910, this area was perhaps the most isolated of the interior suburbs. It was also staunchly independent. A major part of it, organized as the Fairmont Association, refused full membership in the city well into the 1950s, providing privately financed services such as fire, police, and public works.

The area labeled Whalley-Goffe in figure 4.12 was distinctly less suburban in this era than the others mentioned above. It was served by several trolley lines in 1910, and is mostly within walking distance of the central city. It was, however, neither working-class nor upscale: none of the upscale groups were found here, and only a minor fraction of the working-class cohorts lived in this area. It did have a great many people with middling occupations and apparently functioned as a middle-class neighborhood.

The Springside Farm area protrudes from the city's northwest corner, in a splendidly rural setting near West Rock. Although it contains ideal land for sub-

Figure 4.12. Internal "suburbs" of New Haven, c. 1913.

urban development—by the standards of 1910 or 2010—this area has a far from typical development history. This three-hundred-acre site had served as a location for poor relief even before the Civil War, and the city had invested $100,000 in a new almshouse there in 1886.[46] A few decades later, Arnold Dana would urge further isolation of the almshouse, combined with upscale development for this area: "The Almshouse (Springside) occupies a choice location for first-class residences. Once again remove this establishment to some low-priced location beyond the crowded city limits, and develop or put on the market the current 300 acres or thereabouts (1,800 lots). As an exceptionally fine situation for the best class of city homes . . . this tract, it would seem, should be gradually marketable by some first-class real estate firm at not less than $3,500 per lot."[47]

Dana's proposal went nowhere. Even in the early years of the twenty-first century, this area—now called West Rock—would contain a surfeit of project-based public housing, occupied almost exclusively by very poor families, mostly African-Americans. It enjoys little in retail shopping, social services, or anything else except its still spectacular landscape.

CHAPTER 5

CIVIC DENSITY

Considering the central importance of voluntary organizations in American history there is no doubt [such groups have] provided the people with their greatest school of self-government. Rubbing minds as well as elbows, they have been trained from youth to take common counsel, choose leaders, harmonize differences, and obey the expressed will of the majority. In mastering the associative way they have mastered the democratic way.
—ARTHUR SCHLESINGER, JR., 1944

In the use of the phrase social capital, I make no reference to the usual [understanding] of the term capital, except in a figurative sense. I do not refer to real estate, or to personal property or to cold cash, but rather to that in life which tends to make these tangible substances count for most in the daily lives of people, namely goodwill, fellowship, mutual sympathy and social intercourse. . . . If [the individual] comes into contact with his neighbors, and they with other neighbors, there will be an accumulation of social capital, which may immediately satisfy his social needs and which may bear a social potentiality sufficient to the substantial improvement of living conditions in the whole community.—LYDA HANIFAN, 1916

In 1882, Michael Campbell, born in Ireland, achieved the position of assistant foreman in Sargent's packing department. Having been educated only to age eleven before joining the labor force, Campbell at age twenty-two was the quintessential "joiner": he took music lessons at the New Haven School of Music, joined the New Haven Gymnasium to "build up his muscles," attended night school at the YMCA to hear lectures by Yale faculty, debated and listened to orations at the New Haven Literary Association, was secretary of a martial drill team, was active in the local Republican Party, was a member of the Ancient Order of Hibernians, was a regular in the St. Aloysius temperance society, and was a parishioner at St. Patrick's Catholic Church in Fair Haven.[1] Many of these organizations were ethnic in character and orientation, but others had nothing to do with being either Irish or Catholic. Campbell's civic life appears to our eyes exceptional in its breadth, and he was doubtless unusual among his contemporaries. But his habit of busy engagement was emblematic of the city as it would be in the Frank Rice era, and Campbell's civic involvement was a rehearsal for Rice's even more remarkable story.

Boom-time life in New Haven was perhaps less busy a generation after young Campbell came along, but it was still very busy. Work typically claimed five and a half days of the week, more for some. And, by twenty-first-century standards, much of the work was pretty demanding—hard physical toil, repetitive motion, soul-numbing routine, noisy machinery, poor lighting, dubious ventilation, and limited opportunity for flexible scheduling. Yet, seeing 1913 with 1913 lenses, life offered new freedom. The workweek was down by half a day from the previous generation, and reliance on mechanical force had greatly reduced wear and tear on strong backs. Working people had access to wider and wider ranges of popularly priced goods and services—entertainment, clothing, housing, education for the kids. Much of the newly available leisure "stayed home" since family was often the central source of meaning in daily life and an enormously time-consuming object of labor. For working families, mostly for their women, housekeeping was still largely done without benefit of mechanical help from vacuum sweepers, dishwashers, or any but the most rudimentary laundry equipment.[2] Cooking demanded time and effort and tolerance for heat. An icebox was just that. And households were generally far bigger than they are today. Yet, for all that, there remained time for places and organizations that involved neither work nor family. These organizations constitute what I call the civic fauna.

THE CIVIC FAUNA

The population of organizations in the stretch of life that lies between work and family was large and richly varied. What these organizations had in common, for our purposes, is that they brought people together as nominal peers in settings that escaped strictures of gainful employment—and did so on a basis far more open-textured than the nuclear family. Here are some organizations belonging to this civic fauna:

- Elks East Rock Lodge No. 193
- Grand Army of the Republic, Von Steinwehr Post No. 76 (German)
- Elm City Free Kindergarten Association
- Colored Masons, Oriental Lodge
- Società Marineria Italiana Di Mutuo Soccorso
- Ladies of the Maccabees, Lilian Hollister Hive
- Washington Glees football team
- Benevolent Society of the U.S. for Propagation of Cremation, New Haven Chapter
- Daughters of Rebekah, New Haven Lodge No. 3
- New Haven Symphony Orchestra
- Bickur Cholim B'nai Abraham
- New England Order of Protection, Mozart Lodge No. 193
- St. Mary's Roman Catholic Church
- Arbeiter Maenner-Chor
- New Haven Lawn Club
- First Swedish Methodist Episcopal Church
- Center Church
- Hopkins Grammar School
- Ezekiel Cheever School
- Friendly Sons of St. Patrick

This is in every respect a mixed bag, with organizations large and small, nationally franchised and locally concocted, sacred or secular, nationality proud or universalistic, prejudice ridden or democratic, fun loving or preachy. The vast majority of these organizations were managed and led by locals, with little or no professional staff on site—although many were linked to national organizations with professional staffs, and an occasional ringer would turn up on a local athletic team (in one instance, the famed baseball player Ty Cobb turned up in a New Haven uniform). Only a relatively small number were run by professionals at the local level (the schools, for example). They were mostly operated, as Peter Dobkin Hall points out, both by and for members of the local community.[3] All or virtually all of the people who were assembled by these organizations—whether for religious worship or a fraternal lodge meeting or a sporting contest—were mem-

Figure 5.1. New Haven Athletic Association, member-runners, 1915. NHCHS.

bers of locally grounded communities (figure 5.1). And the acts of assembly and association almost certainly deepened and enriched participants' sense of loyalty to and identity with place.

While most recent scholarship restricts attention to "voluntary" or "nonproprietary" organizations, I have included some privately controlled and government-funded organizations here as well. My interest in such organizations stems from their function in bringing together members of a community, allowing them to develop shared identities on a local basis, and sometimes to hone political and social skills by rubbing both elbows and minds with people different from themselves. Where there was an abundance of such organizations—where civic density was very high—it localized and enriched the urban experience. Consider the example of spectator sport, admittedly not among the most enlightening of all civic activities but an important one nevertheless. Perhaps it was a Saturday morning spent cheering on the New Haven White Wings or the New Haven Colonials against a baseball opponent from Waterbury or Hartford (or even, on rare occasions, so notable an opponent as the Boston Red Sox). Perhaps the team was owned by a private operator; perhaps it was operated by a membership club. That difference no doubt mattered—it was perhaps more fully my team if my club operated it than if a private citizen owned it for profit. Without minimizing the difference that ownership structure makes, note that the experience was in either case grounded in local community. The team was New Haven's own, and it played its home schedule on New Haven's dirt. Or perhaps it was even more specifically local, down to one neighborhood, as would have been the case with the Annex Athletic Club's football team. When these very local events are compared with events having no link to local community whatsoever there is a distinct and meaningful difference. In cheering on the New York Yankees or the New Jersey Nets, I might as well be thinking of Staten Island or the Hamptons as of New Haven. I might even be in Havana, where Yankees fans abound. I can cheer for the Yankees in New Haven, but I will likely do so alone and not as part of a festive crowd. As Robert Putnam might say, "Cheering alone." Some of the same applies to a local symphony or theater company or jazz band. It may well be that an artistically superior version of *Macbeth* is to be found on public television or in Boston, but the version given outdoors in a New Haven park by the Elm City Shakespeare Company will let Shakespeare bring people into their city, not lead them out of it.

Very little is local all the way through. While a baseball team may be entirely local in its fan base and even in its player roster, it plays in a league that is regional and by a set of rules established nationally. Sargent Company was a New Haven firm, but it would have shriveled and died without its national and international network of distributors and suppliers. St. Mary's Roman Catholic Church was a supremely local and territorially rooted New Haven institution in, say, 1913, but it was governed by a world-spanning hierarchy whose apex rose 4,000 miles from its altar. And while East Rock Elks Lodge No. 193 is local in membership and leadership, it is in effect franchised by a national organization. As Theda Skocpol writes,

> From the very beginning of the American nation, democratic government and political institutions encouraged the proliferation of voluntary groups linked to regional or national social movements. Increasingly, groups were tied into translocal organizational networks that paralleled the local-state-national structure of the U.S. state. Moral-reform movements, farmers' and workers' associations, fraternal brotherhoods and sisterhoods, independent women's associations, veterans' groups, and many ethnic and African American associations all converged on this quintessentially American form of voluntary membership association.[4]

This reliance on state and national organizations is not to be mistaken for an early equivalent of twenty-first-century uprootedness, since these organizations

were self-consciously and systematically rooted to local communities. As Skocpol observes,

> U.S. fraternals and their female partner groups required a potential mem-
> ber to apply to the lodge nearest his or her residence or have its written
> permission to apply elsewhere. Traveling members had to have formal
> documentation from their local and state units to be admitted as visitors
> away from home. Just as Americans had to establish their voting rights in
> their local communities and states, so too did they have to establish their
> membership in translocal associations through their home communities.
> American associations may have encouraged outward ties, but no rootless
> cosmopolitanism was allowed. The national and state jurisdictions of fra-
> ternals maintained elaborate zoning rules. New local lodges were required
> to have the endorsement of previously chartered units in their vicinity, as
> well as the approval of the relevant state jurisdiction. The point of these
> rules was to embed members in local groups and—perhaps even more
> significant—to manage the creation of local groups so as to avoid unneces-
> sary fragmentation and duplication.[5]

Beginning with the temples and churches, turning next to the fraternals and
sororals and then to schools, large nonprofits (Yale, the hospitals), and the world
of sport and entertainment, I will sketch the civic fauna in the years just before
and after 1910.

RELIGIOUS ORGANIZATIONS

New Haven began, in 1637–38, as a wholly intolerant Puritan colony, and it remained more or less subject to sectarian hegemony until just about the time capitalist development took off in the 1840s. This history of intolerance is characterized with baleful humor by the Reverend Thomas Duggan's 1930 history of
Connecticut Catholicism: "If Papists' came and remained and ultimately became
part of the body politic, they were not invited. Nor, indeed, were they wanted. . . .
Why were they not wanted? The question is one of psychology. The English settlers of New England had suffered persecution for conscience sake at home.
They had come here to be free, but not to share their hard-earned freedom with
others. Let the others cull out an El Dorado for themselves. They must not so far
presume as to cross the frontier won by our valor and consecrated by our Puritan
blood. Inconsistent? Yes. Inconsistent, but human: and with all their austere
virtues, the first New Englanders were human!"[6]

In the same year that New Haven was formally chartered as a city within Connecticut, the 1784 Toleration Act empowered other Christian sects to worship openly and to collect contributions from members—but members nevertheless had to produce a "certificate" proving membership in order to avoid an otherwise mandatory tithe to the local Congregational Church. As Rollin G. Osterweis notes, this left some room for complaint: "While this was an improvement over the rigid system which preceded it, a 'certificate man' was still treated as a lower order of being socially and a handicapped citizen politically. Another common grievance was the predominance of the established church in education; even the faculty of Yale College limited itself to those who followed the Saybrook Platform variety of Congregationalism."[7]

By 1818, these grievances—and objections to the Congregationalist Standing Order in civil society—produced a state legislative majority favoring deeper change. By August of that year, a new Connecticut constitution was adopted, under which "freedom of worship was extended to all and freedom to organize ecclesiastical societies 'to any Christian sect.'"[8] Only in 1843 did religious liberty go so far as to include Jews, then arriving for the first time in numbers from Germany. The effect was to open religious worship to free competition at just about the time capitalist development began in earnest.

Protestant Congregations By the time New Haven had reached its industrial midsummer's day, around 1910–13, about ninety congregations offered themselves to the community.[9] Well over half were Protestant Christian organizations. Eleven old-line Congregationalist Churches were still in place, including the earliest and most prestigious—Center Church and United Church on the downtown Green. The Church of the Redeemer served fashionable East Rock and ran the Welcome Hall settlement house on Oak Street as a domestic mission. Every neighborhood of the city, and every one of the surrounding towns, had a Congregation of its own, and a plurality of the Protestant middle class remained at least nominally committed to them. The Congregationalists also had adapted in some degree to the city's changing demography. Dixwell Avenue United Church of Christ was a prominent and fairly prosperous black congregation by 1913—as it remains today. An Italian Congregational Church sprang up on Greene Street in the Wooster Square neighborhood, filling up with newly arrived workers. So too were there Danish-Norwegian and Swedish congregations. With sixteen such groups in all, Congregationalism remained the commonest organizational form of religion, and Yale remained nominally Congregationalist even as it adopted an increasingly secular curriculum. This being said, one could no longer think of

New Haven as a one-denomination town—and if one insisted on such a view, neither the Congregationalists nor any other Protestant sect would win the prize.

In New Haven, as elsewhere, Protestantism itself had become more heterogeneous. There were, for instance, nine Baptist churches by 1913, including three broad-based regular congregations (First Baptist, Immanuel, and Howard Avenue), along with several national or racial houses (German, Italian, Swedish, black). Thirteen Methodist congregations dotted the landscape and shared the less upscale reaches of Protestant life with the Baptists. Trinity Church on the Green was high-church, and there were a dozen additional Episcopal congregations in town, of which St. Paul's (near Wooster Square) was perhaps the strongest. With German and Scandinavian arrivals came Lutheranism—three separate instances of "German Evangelical Lutheranism," along with English and Swedish versions. There was just one Presbyterian congregation; a half-dozen others included Seventh-Day Adventist, Unitarian, and Christian Science. While the degree of fervor among congregants may have been far less in 1913 than in, say, 1713, the Protestant canopy had grown thicker and had adapted itself to a more varied urban population.

One church building tells more of the city's religious history in the nineteenth and twentieth centuries than any other. Clock manufacturer Chauncey Jerome had started construction of a Congregationalist church on Wooster Place, facing Wooster Square itself, just before his financial debacle occurred. The building, which experienced fire or structural collapse on five separate occasions, would pass from the Congregationalists to the Second Baptist Church (split off in dispute from the first) to the First Baptist Church, which was in possession of the place until 1897. At that point, the First Baptists elected to follow their congregation northward, to lower Livingston Street, in the East Rock neighborhood. The Archdiocese bought the building and dedicated it as St. Michael's Church. It would experience what may well have been the most meteoric growth of any Roman church in New England.

Catholic Parishes Catholicism had arrived with the construction of Christ's Church in the Hill neighborhood during the winter of 1832–33, but with acute difficulty. On May 8, 1833, when the gothic structure's balcony was first filled with worshipers, it gave way, killing two. After reconstruction, the building burned on June 11, 1849, apparently at the hands of an arsonist. In the next effort, the canny Father James Fitton reportedly "took care to have his church stand between two buildings, both owned by Protestants."[10] The coming of Catholics in numbers corresponded, often literally, with the relative decline of Congregationalism. In 1851, South Church had been constructed by the Congregationalists in the Hill section. By 1871, it had been purchased by the Catholics, and it became Sacred Heart Church in 1874.[11]

The growth of Catholicism, and the growth of New Haven industrialism, were closely intertwined, since a high fraction of the arriving workforce was at least nominally Catholic. As will be recalled, most of the city's net growth over its full history occurred between 1860 and 1920—a city of 36,267 becoming a city of 162,537 in that span. A high proportion of the newcomers, perhaps 70 percent, were Catholics. No case illustrates this better than St. Michael's Church in the Wooster Square neighborhood, to which so many Italians were attracted by Sargent and other employers. The original structure had been built for the Congregationalists, and it was purchased to become an Italian-nationality parish in 1889.[12] In its original authorization, St. Michael's was *the* Italian parish for greater New Haven, and its growth was remarkable. The annual reports sent by priests at St. Michael's to the Archdiocese of Hartford form the following progression: 1905 (13,000), 1910 (18,400), and 1913 (24,470), a near doubling of parishioners in eight years.[13] By late 1915 the hierarchy had intervened to redistribute half of these worshipers to St. Donato's in Fair Haven, also devoted to Italians, and St. Michael's flock was reduced to about 12,500 souls.

The profoundly territorial nature of the Catholic parish is illustrated by a later letter, from the archbishop to the three Italian parish priests of New Haven, emphasizing the lines established in 1915 between St. Donato's and St. Michael's. The letter reads in part, "It is the duty of each pastor to remind people who attend Mass at his church that they really belong to the parish in which they have their domicile. This principle of law applies to national as well as to territorial parishes, since all national parishes in the Archdiocese of Hartford have definite boundaries (statute 94 of the First Synod . . .). When parishioners move away from the parish, they must be told kindly but firmly that they may no longer consider themselves members of the parish."[14]

From the fifteenth century on, the Roman church had defined its parishes territorially. It complicated this idea with nationality parishes in the nineteenth-century America primarily as a political adaptation to the friction between a largely Irish priesthood and other parishioner nationalities—Polish, Italian, and German, in particular.[15] New Haven had three Italian, one Polish (St. Stanislaus), one German (St. Boniface), and one small Lithuanian (St. Casimir). Immigrant families demonstrated a strong proclivity for establishing homes within walking distance of their nationality church, as with the concentration of Poles near St. Stanislaus on State Street in New Haven to this day.

Table 5.1. Catholic Parishes, 1913

Church	Year founded	Neighborhood	Total Catholics in parish, 1913
St. John's RC	1834	Hill	3,429
St. Mary's RC	1851	East Rock, Yale	3,314
St. Patrick's RC	1853	Wooster Square	3,300
St. Francis Church	1867	Fair Haven	4,219
St. Boniface Church (German)	1868	Downtown	1,000
St. Aedan's	1872	Westville	
Church of the Sacred Heart RC	1874	Hill	4,870
St. Louis RC	1889	Wooster Square	1,200
St. Michael's (Italian)	1899	Wooster Square	24,470
St. Joseph's RC	1900	East Rock, State–Orange Corridor	2,828
St. Peter's RC	1902	Hill	1,941
St. Stanislaus (Polish)	1902	State–Orange Corridor	3,000
St. Anthony's RC (Italian)	1903	Hill	1,700
St. Rose's RC	1907	Fair Haven	3,100
St. Casimir (Lithuanian)		Wooster Square	1,500
St. Brendan's RC	1913	Whalley-Dixwell	2,000
Totals			61,871

The Catholic presence in New Haven was strongly rooted in its system of parishes by 1913, and the dates of their founding closely track the surging growth of the city's population. As noted in table 5.1, New Haven Catholicism was a big, well-funded operation, reaching every neighborhood and accounting for about $1.6 million in property value. It was to a large extent a church of recent arrivals, with nationality parishes accounting for 31,270 persons (just over half the total). The churches themselves were by and large very young, eight having been established in the brief span between 1899 and 1913. These eight young parishes accounted for 40,539 Catholics, nearly two-thirds of the city total.

This expansive organization created a powerful layer of civil society, and insofar as it lived up to the billing of Catholic neighborhood life, it was a thick layer indeed: "The Catholic instinct is to wrap a completely Catholic cocoon around the buzz of transactions of daily life—not just weddings and baptisms or Sunday services, but also social clubs, schools, hospitals, charitable organizations, professional societies for Catholic doctors and lawyers, Catholic chapters within trade unions, Catholic veterans organizations. The thick textures of Catholic life were easier to maintain in cities."[16] As the author of this generalization notes, however, there was considerable variation between nationality groups in their willingness to live within the Roman cocoon. The Irish, from whom so high a fraction of clergy were recruited, were especially willing to be wrapped thickly in Catholic life. The Poles likewise appear to have committed deeply to their church in the new country. The Italians, in contrast, were often far less willing to be thus enveloped. Table 5.2 gives illustrative data—by no means proving any large generalization about the nationalities—for four selected New Haven parishes: St. Stanislaus with its Polish congregation, St. Mary's with a largely Irish composition, St. Boniface with its Germans, and St. Michael's with its Italians. Each year's report to the archdiocese includes an estimate by the priests on the number of their parishioners who "made their Easter duty" by attending confession and taking communion during the spring holiday season. The Poles of St. Stan's lead the table at 83 percent, and the Italians of St. Michael's come in at less than half that percentage.[17] It is likely that many among the 24,470 parishioners were unaware of their membership in the church, perhaps being included in the rule of thumb that all Italians arriving in the Wooster Square area were to be considered Catholic. In other cases, we may reasonably guess, churchgoing wives enrolled their families without eliciting what would today be called informed consent from their husbands. Some, indeed, were failing to make Easter duty by worshiping with the Italian Baptists nearby. The considerable anticlerical culture from which many of them came may also have played a role. If we take Easter duty as a signal of voluntary membership in the church, we may then look at contributions to the church for the calendar year 1913 as a rough proxy for intensity of attachment. Here the differences are even more pronounced. The Poles were giving better than $20 per capita, the Germans and Irish nearly as much, and yet even those who made Easter duty among the St. Michael's flock averaged less than $1 for the year. The Irish and Germans, relatively better established in this period, perhaps found it easier to support the church than did other groups. The very low figure for St. Michael's may in some part reflect the poverty of the Wooster Square Italian immigrants, but we have no evidence of special affluence among the Poles. One would guess that the Italians were, on average, less enthusiastic about the parish life than were the Poles and probably than were most Catholics.

The overarching conclusion is that the Catholic parish system created a powerful layer of civil society, with all manner of social, educational, and civic activities for tens of thousands of people in the industrial city. If it wasn't the Holy

Table 5.2. Selected Data on Catholic Participation, 1913

Church	Catholics making Easter duty	Persons making Easter duty as percentage of Catholic population	Receipts per duty maker
St. Stanislaus (Polish)	2,500	83.3	$21.72
St. Mary's (Irish)	2,100	63.4	$15.79
St. Boniface (German)	600	60.0	$15.55
St. Michael's (Italian)	7,704	27.4	$0.84

Name Society on Tuesday evening, perhaps it was the Confraternity of the Rosary or a parish soccer team or a choir or the routine of parochial school—a thicker layer for some than for others, but a participatory blanket of some importance for many of the families included among the sixty-thousand faithful in church estimates. And, as will be seen later in the book, the Catholic parish system, with its intense commitment to place, represents a stabilizing force as the centered, grounded city begins to dissolve. As Gerald Gamm suggests, whole neighborhoods may benefit, even the outsiders: "If Protestants and Jews and Non-believers know that a large community of Catholics are apt to stick with their parish ties while an area declines, then these others may sustain their confidence in the neighborhood's future, and the decline may in that measure be resisted."[18]

Jewish Congregations If the Catholics met with initial hostility, they weren't alone. An editorial in the *New Haven Register* of May 26, 1843, whined as follows: "Whilst we have been busy converting the Jews of other lands, they have outflanked us here, and effected a footing in the very cent[er] of our own fortress. Strange as it may sound, it is nevertheless true that a Jewish synagogue has been established in this city—and their place of worship . . . was dedicated on Friday afternoon. Yale College divinity deserves a court-martial for bad generalship."[19]

The temple in question was Mishkan Israel, located in a succession of rented rooms in downtown New Haven for roughly a decade after its beginning.[20] The first permanent structure was acquired in September 1854, from the Third Congregational Society. Featuring six tall columns and a spire indicating its origin, the first permanent temple of Mishkan Israel was located on Court Street in downtown New Haven. There were divisions over the years—some concerning

Ashkenazi versus Polish ritual, others concerning the place of women in worship, others concerning finances and leadership—but this congregation would grow and prosper over the nineteenth century's remaining decades. By 1897, Mishkan Israel had constructed a large and handsome structure bearing no trace of hand-me-down architecture at the corner of Orange and Audubon, a few blocks east of the Yale campus (figure 5.2). German-Jewish New Haveners were well established by the late nineteenth century, and they had begun to assume positions of leadership in the civic life of New Haven by the early twentieth century.

With the eruption of Russian anti-Semitic pogroms in the 1880s, and the growing employment base in industrial New Haven, a major new wave of Jewish immigration crested between about 1885 and 1910. These newer arrivals were mostly without capital and enjoyed few of the advantages that their German coreligionists had accumulated. As Werner Hirsch writes, "The native tongue of the non-German-speaking Eastern European Jew was Yiddish. To the German, this sounded like a very poor, uncultured speech. The German Jew did not (and

Figure 5.2. Congregation Mishkan Israel, corner Orange and Audubon Streets, c. 1950. NHCHS.

would not) speak Yiddish (although he had his own peculiar 'Juedisch' dialect, very much akin to Yiddish). The German Jew was also more assimilated, as well as more affluent, than the Easterner."[21]

This newer wave of Jewish immigration would lead to the formation of many new congregations, and thus to a diversification of Jewish life in the city's neighborhoods. Here are some instances: B'nai Jacob (1882), Bikur Cholim (1888), B'nai Israel (1892), Sheveth Achim (1900), Mogen David (1903), Keser Israel (1909), Shara Torah (1895), Adas B'nai Jeshurun (1908), and Beth Israel (1914).[22] Bikur Cholim, Sheveth Achim, and Shara Torah were largely Russian congregations with very orthodox customs of worship. On a smaller scale, and with a distinctly less hierarchical organizational structure, this parallels the Catholic expansion of the same era. New Haven grew larger, and far more diverse culturally, over these years, but the fauna of organizational structure expanded more or less apace, creating and preserving an intensely structured community.

Like Catholicism, Jewish life reached far beyond the conventional bounds of religion. Orthodox congregations, intensely territorial, were organizing frameworks for neighborhood life. Less territorial, and more mobile, reform Judaism was nevertheless capable of organizing life in aspects as diverse as athletics, education, culture, and the provision of social services to the indigent. As with the Catholics, external discrimination served to intensify group identity and to prompt organizational innovation outside the conventional limits of religiosity.

The early 1900s and the influx of Eastern European Jews brought on an increase in social anti-Semitism at Yale. Jewish students found themselves unable to join secret senior societies and fraternities; even many of the athletic teams were closed to them. Consequently, the East European boys formed what became known as the Atlas Club. . . . By 1921 the Atlas Club had about 100 members, many of whom were either Yale students or graduates. On Friday nights they would usually have a dance preceded by a basketball game. Although these Jews came from Orthodox families, they had the dance and basketball game on Friday night since Friday drew the largest crowds and therefore was most profitable. In 1922 the Atlas Club played the Yale basketball team and won 42–22. . . . In that same year Yale's varsity basketball team was slumping. A group of Yale alumni prepared a report charging that Jewish athletes were consistently rejected. . . . At the insistence of the new basketball coach, Joe Fogarty, players were selected regardless of whether they were "black or white, Jew or Gentile, so long as they could play basketball."[23]

Seen together, the religious layers of the centered industrial city were thick, diverse, and richly textured. Some congregations—like Center Church, St. Mary's Church, and Mishkan Israel—were organizations of citywide and regional influence, reaching far above the neighborhood level. No less important in their impact on daily life were the scores of humbler congregations rooted to the particularities of a given neighborhood, providing a framework for everyday life in civil society. Whether it was Bikur Cholim on Factory Street or St. Mike's in Wooster Square or the Italian Baptist Church on George Street, each provided a normative community for its members and often also for those with whom they came into contact in daily life.

CLUBS AND FRATERNAL ORGANIZATIONS

The organizations active around 1910 represented a half-century of buildup in the national and local fauna of clubs and fraternities or sororities. These were largely amateur organizations open to local leadership and organized around very local communities. An outfit could be found to meet nearly any imaginable niche, and to get around nearly any pattern of exclusion. Some were downright silly, or so it would seem from their self-descriptions. Thus, for instance, we run across this entry in the 1913 New Haven City Directory: "Haymakers Slammerhassett Association Number 1 1/2. Chief Haymaker, Joseph Carey, Collector of Straws, H. H. Davidson, Keeper of Bundles, Wilfred Tuttle."

Many others are more sober sounding, often based in a cause (temperance, women's suffrage, good government) or a felt need (insurance against unemployment, sickness, or disability). It is impossible to dissect and classify all of the clubs that turn up in my data (464 in all), so I will instead simply give some sense of their variety (local, national), their sharing of common facilities, and the grounding of their elected leadership in local community.[24]

Wholly Local Clubs and Organizations Every neighborhood appears to have had some altogether local clubs, typically focused on shared concerns about services and development or on a sporting activity, or both. Thus, for example, we find on the eastern shore of the harbor the Annex Athletic Club, the New Haven Yacht Club, and the Fairmont Association (which actually provided fire services and the like). The Hill neighborhood had the Washington Glee Club (actually a very broad club, fielding, among other things, a variety of athletic teams), the City Point Yacht Club, the Kimberly Athletic Club, and a variety of Catholic clubs. Fair Haven had the Pequot Club (figure 5.3), the Quinnipiac Canoe Club, the Columbus Social Club, and others. Dixwell had its Nonantum Fish and Game Club along with a range of "colored" clubs, all meeting at 76 Webster Street. Westville had its Village Improvement Association. East Rock had the New Haven Lawn Club.

Perhaps the most eccentric and wholly local club of the era was known as the Inquisitors Club—much too private to be published in a city directory. Judging from the minutes and photographs that remain, this was a dining, debate, and baseball club for affluent gentlemen. It met on a rotating basis in their homes— nearly all of which were in East Rock. On one occasion, the minutes read, "The business of the meeting was entirely alcoholic except for the customary rejection of new members. This time the machine failed to work and Dr. Joseph Marshall Flint slipped through unanimously. James E. Wheeler [was] caught by one button; W. Byrne H. by several. Try again boys." At another Inquisitors meeting, the recording secretary, titled "Coroner," was Victor Tyler, a prominent businessman with an Edwardian sense of jollity: "A meeting of The Inquisitors was held Friday, December 13, 1908. At 55 Hillhouse Avenue . . . Absent Canby and Bingham. Canby's absence made it necessary for the Coroner to [af]flict the meeting by taking the chair. The minutes of the previous meeting were read and made part of the sacred archives. Upon sitting down at the table the sumptuary laws of the club were found to have been broken by the presence of sherry on the table. The club showed its deep-seated disapproval of this by consuming every drop of it amidst savage cries of resentment from the heaviest consumers."[25] The members, all but one a resident in East Rock, were on that occasion gathered in the home of Henry Hotchkiss, whom we met earlier as CEO of Candee Rubber. The others were social and economic peers of his.

A less fatuous but at least equally upscale club was known as the New Haven Social Science Association. This group was composed of senior business leaders and a few Yale faculty. It included J. B. Sargent, who was at once a member and a frequent speaker. At the meeting held in December 1901, Sargent had given his views on the Chinese Exclusion Act. Having traveled China on business, Sargent reported the people "as to morals, industry, and honesty fully the equals of Americans" and argued (not disinterestedly) for a free and abundant flow of immigrant labor. On other occasions, the group debated the pros and cons of piecework pay in manufacturing (showing both remarkable sophistication and fairness toward labor's viewpoint),[26] looked at the growing influence of small towns in Connecticut politics, assayed the operation of street railway monopolies nationally, and addressed a long succession of other topics. The club voted to

Figure 5.3. Cast of *The Mikado* as performed by the Pequot Club, 1902. NHCHS.

abolish itself in 1906 and to distribute its treasury of $55.31 equally among the members.

A small set of exclusive and ethnically exclusionary clubs were also important in the city of this period. The New Haven Country Club (actually in suburban Hamden), the New Haven Lawn Club (East Rock), the downtown Quinnipiac Club and Graduates Club were foremost among these. All were exclusionary toward Jews, Catholics, and, without need for notice, blacks. Social historian Marcia Synnott records one revealing dust-up involving Yale and anti-Semitism in one of these clubs: "Even a faculty appointment did not insure social acceptance. The elite social club for Yale men and faculty in New Haven was the Graduates Club." In 1920, Yale had appointed Milton Winternitz dean of the Medical School, and he applied for membership in the Graduates Club. Yale President Hadley found himself reduced to threats in urging a favorable decision: "While our Club is not nominally connected with Yale more than any other college, it is actually connected with it a great deal, and a belief that the Club allowed itself to ignore the interests of Yale in a serious matter would greatly imperil its prosperity." Winternitz was shortly thereafter elected a member of the Graduates Club.[27]

Another important layer of organizations linked nationality and racial groups

Figure 5.4. Stella d'Italia float, downtown parade, c. 1920. NHCHS.

or held out exclusionary policies that made them ethnic enclaves. The New Haven Lawn Club discriminated against Jews and Catholics and newcomers of all descriptions, making it a WASPs-only organization. The Knights of St. Patrick, the Hibernians, the Swiss Society, the Swedish Republican Club, Ukrainian Sitch, the Viking Sick and Benevolent Society, the Rutherian Greek Catholic Society, the Garibaldi Society, the Sons of Jacob, New Haven Schwaben Verein, the Germania Bicycle Club, the Caledonian Club, Stella d'Italia (figure 5.4), and many other organizations were founded around the very idea of national identity. Others—the German-Jewish Harmonia Club, the Francophile Champlain Club—appear to have formed around nationalities without being entirely defined by them. At least in the case of Harmonia, the principal motive for formation probably had to do with discrimination in other quarters, such as the Graduates Club or the Lawn Club.[28]

Yet another class of local organizations grew up as mutual aid and insurance organizations, defined around a place of employment. The Edward Malley Company Members Protective Association, the New Haven Clock Company Mutual Aid Association, the Winchester Mutual Aid Association, and the Mutual Aid

Association of the New Haven Fire Department illustrate this organizational pattern. In the function of mutual insurance, these small and very local organizations were at some competitive disadvantage, since the larger, nationally organized fraternal and sororal organizations were often carrying out exactly the same business.

In very large firms, like Winchester Repeating Arms, all manner of clubs grew up among employees and were often granted use of company facilities. Winchester employees, for example, had teams representing the firm in basketball as the Winchester Rifles (men) and Winchester Riflettes (women), along with intramural leagues for softball, archery, bowling, and sundry other social amusements. Live theater was also on the company menu, and whites in blackface shared the stage with actual blacks in an oddly posed photo from a later period (figure 5.5). The basketball team so coyly posed in figure 5.6, representing Hull's Brewery in the late 1930s, is one among scores of similar artifacts suggesting the evolution of civil society at the very edges of the industrial plant gate.

Nationally Franchised Fraternals and Sororals As Hall's research reveals, the era of New Haven's centered industrial growth was also an era of exponential growth in fraternal and sororal organizations. In 1850, just one such organization occupied New Haven turf, but then:

1860	16
1870	41

Figure 5.5. Winchester theater troupe, 1947. NHCHS.

Figure 5.6. Hull's Brewery basketball team, 1939. NHCHS.

1880	61
1890	155
1900	204
1910	257[29]

The numbers are, in one way, a trifle misleading. We are talking about far fewer than 257 national organizations in 1910, since, say, the Masons show up as fourteen New Haven chapters, and a further six chapters affiliated nationally with the Colored Masons also turn up in New Haven (to say nothing of the related Scottish Rite organizations). Similarly, there are ten white and three "colored" chapters of the Odd Fellows, plus four Rebekah groups for (white) women. With two notable exceptions—the Knights of Columbus, founded in New Haven during 1882, and the Daughters of Isabella, founded in 1897—New Haven is an external site for the national organizations, not altogether unlike scores of other communities across the land.[30] (Both of these Catholic organizations retain world headquarters in New Haven at this writing.) In table 5.3, I show 22 national organizations that accounted for 3 or more New Haven franchises each, for a total of

164 local lodges and chapters.[31] This suggests a fairly high level of integration into the national movement toward fraternal and sororal organizations, even though several large nationals were wholly absent from New Haven in this period—the Grange (hardly surprising), the Moose, the PTA, and the Shriners. The National Women's Suffrage Association shows no local chapters *by name,* but several Political Equality Clubs and the like occupy its niche.

These organizations—about 270 local chapters in the city of New Haven as of 1913—constituted a large genus within the civic fauna of the period. Every night of the week, every month of the year, was occupied by the regular meetings of fraternals and sororals, with Monday a little less busy than other weeknights and Saturday left open more than other nights. Wednesday and Thursday evenings

Table 5.3. National Organizations With Multiple Chapters in New Haven, 1913

Organization	New Haven chapters, 1913	Membership above 1% nationally in 1900–20
Masons, Colored Masons, and Scottish Rite	23	Yes
Odd Fellows and Daughters of Rebekah	17	Yes
New England Order of Protection	12	No
Knights of Pythias	11	Yes
Ancient Order of United Workmen	10	Yes
Knights of Columbus	10	Yes
Foresters of America	9	No
Fraternal Benefit League	8	No
Grand Army of the Republic	7	Yes
Order of United American Mechanics	7	Yes
Ancient Order of Hibernians	6	No
Eastern Star	6	Yes
Royal Arcanum	6	No
Women's Christian Temperance Union	5	Yes
Eagles	4	Yes
Improved Order of Heptasophs	4	No
Woodmen of the World	4	Yes
Catholic Temperance Societies	3	No
Encampment	3	No
Patriarchs Militant	3	No
Patriotic Order Sons of America	3	No
Red Men	3	Yes

Figure 5.7. Masonic Hall, 87–89 Church Street, 1901 or 1902.
Note "Frater Martyr" memorial to President William
McKinley, recently assassinated. NHCHS.

were jam-packed. Most of these outfits met twice monthly, a few weekly, a few once monthly. In 1913, the 270 such lodges and chapters appear to have held over 6,700 plenary meetings in total. If an average of 50 members turned out for these occasions, that would make a total participation count of 335,000 per year in a city with fewer than 100,000 adults. If we add some reasonable guesses about committee and leadership meetings to these plenary sessions, the total runs well beyond a million.

Although chapter meetings were dispersed widely, several shared facilities were in almost continuous use. The Knights of Pythias Hall (890 Chapel Street) was the regular meeting place for nearly forty organizations, as varied as the Grand Army of the Republic, Ladies of the Maccabees, the Foresters, the United Mechanics, the Retail Butchers Protective Association, the Marine Engineers Beneficial Association, the Sons of St. George, and the St. Michael's Young Men's Club (not to mention the Pythians themselves). Similarly, the Odd Fellows Hall (95 Crown Street, near the store run decades later by Joseph Perfetto) hosted meetings for all manner of other clubs and lodges. The Colored Masons and Colored Odd Fellows shared a building at 76 Webster Street, off Dixwell, which was the hub of endless activity in black New Haven. Yet another Knights of Pythias Hall (400 State) was a hub for the Eagles, Sons of Judah, Caledonians, Order of Israel, and the Letter Carriers Association. The American Order of United Workmen's Hall (25 Grand) was host to the Heptasophs, a Knights of Columbus chapter, the Red Men, and others. While meetings were staggered by time, the intermixing of lodges and sororities across national organizations, and across nationality groups, suggests a certain degree of social cross-pollination. Only race seems to have been a near-absolute basis of separation in meeting space. Club life was of course interwoven with business and politics, a pattern neatly illustrated by figure 5.7, showing 85–89 Church Street in about 1901. The principal building is a Masonic Hall, but it is heavily larded with commercial establishments—Spalding the druggist, Johnson's haberdashery, a coal broker, Louis Burton the lawyer, George Burton the insurance broker, and at least two other back-office commercial operations. In the middle of the frame we find a portrait of President William McKinley, assassinated in September 1901 at Buffalo, New York. Decorated with flag and bunting, the picture is inscribed "Frater . . . Martyr" by his Masonic brothers in New Haven.

CLASS BACKGROUND OF LEADERS

Is Arthur Schlesinger right in supposing that leadership in these voluntary organizations is a school for democracy? "Considering the central importance of voluntary organizations in American history there is no doubt it has provided the people with their greatest school of self-government. Rubbing minds as well as elbows, they have been trained from youth to take common counsel, choose leaders, harmonize differences, and obey the expressed will of the majority. In mastering the associative way they have mastered the democratic way."[32] A contrasting view, advanced by Ira Katznelson, among others, holds that by the end of the nineteenth century, urban class segregation meant that the "membership of lodges, benefit associations, parish churches, gangs, athletic clubs, fire companies, and political clubs no longer cut across class divisions in the social structure."[33] While it is impossible to pin down all the relevant facts, the class distribution of top positions in civic organizations, and the geography of home addresses analyzed below, give substantial support to Schlesinger's optimism.

If the top boss at work is also the top boss at the Odd Fellows—or the Daughters of Rebekah—then the civic learning is, in a sense, misplaced. Those who already have plenty of practice at leadership (or flat-out coercion) simply find another outlet for their bossiness. Of course, leading volunteers may stretch the skills and soften the voice of a company president, but Schlesinger's vision is a more democratic one. Was the world of clubs and nonprofits really a school for democracy? There is limited but suggestive evidence from the 1913 occupations of club potentates, and, while mixed, it supports the notion that club leadership was fairly well spread across the class structure. This is not to say that laborers headed their pro rata share of voluntary organizations along with company presidents, but it is to say that people in blue-collar and modest white-collar jobs very often headed civic organizations.

Captains of industry *do* head a fair number of organizations, as might be expected. In the 1913 data (which include nonprofits other than clubs and churches), we find twenty-eight instances involving twenty-seven heads of companies.[34] With 334 organizations showing complete data, this comes to 9 percent having leaders who were presidents the next morning. Using the residential sample data (Chapter 4) for 1913, we can readily infer that company heads were represented well beyond their numbers. Of the 4,122 people in our sample with clearly identifiable jobs, 24 were presidents of firms (many of which were very small). At 0.58 percent of the workforce, 9 percent is a fifteenfold overrepresentation. This is hardly surprising, especially if we look at the kinds of civic organizations they headed. Some were upscale clubs—Henry Sargent headed the Country Club, William Pardee the Yacht Club, Thomas Farnam the Lawn Club, George Basset the Quinnipiac Club. Others were heavily capitalized public charities—Eli Whitney III headed the New Haven Hospital, Thomas Hooker the New Haven Dispensary, Samuel Hemingway the Home for Aged and Destitute Women. Others were business organizations being run by—who else?—businessmen. Only four ordinary fraternal or sororal organizations have top business leaders at the helm.

Let's augment these observations by adding the learned professions: eleven lawyers, five professors, five clergy, four physicians, two dentists, one architect. These are not by and large business leaders, but they may be counted against the rate of popular participation. By the wildest stretch of the evidence, one could not make a case for members of the business and learned professions heading anything much beyond a fifth of the organizations constituting the civic fauna—leaving about 80 percent in the hands of people who were more likely to take than give orders during the workday.

At least 128 civic organizations were headed by people in working-class jobs—slightly more than a third of the total. Most of these occupations—stretching from coachman to railroad engineer, machinist to waiter, laborer to saloonkeeper—are displayed in table 5.4. Another 58 organizational potentates are

Table 5.4. Working-Class Jobs Yielding Organizational Presidencies
in the Civic Fauna, 1913

Occupation	Number of potentates	Occupation	Number of potentates
Foreman	11	Butcher	1
Printing and related trades	8	Carriage worker	1
Engineer	5	Cigar packer	1
Machinist	4	Coachman	1
Secretary, stenographer	4	Driver	1
Blacksmith, horseshoer	3	Janitor	1
Carpenter	3	Laundress	1
Dressmaker	3	Letter carrier	1
Laborer	3	Saloonkeeper	1
Mason	3	Shoemaker	1
Watchman	3	Tailor	1
Bricklayer	2	Tinner	1
Plumber	2	Waiter	1
Railroad conductor	2	Working-class total	70
Barber	1		

listed in the city directory simply as "employed at . . ." This designation generally indicates being in a subordinate position, and in the vast majority of cases indicates being a factory operative, materials mover, or maintenance staff member. Among these "merely employed" club leaders, sixteen worked for Winchester Repeating Arms, five for the railroad, five for Marlin Fire Arms, three each for Sargent Hardware, Candee Rubber, and New Haven Clock. Two each worked for Peck Brothers (plumbing manufacturer), and National Folding Box. The rest were scattered among other firms, generally manufacturers, plus New Haven Hospital, and one individual who appears to have been a live-in servant.

Another 71 heads of civic organizations held white-collar jobs, as will be seen in table 5.5. These people are sometimes in highly skilled, artisan occupations (a fresco painter, no less!), and they may well have made very good money (a jeweler, five commercial travelers), and a few may have been influential at work (a reporter, three chief clerks). It remains nevertheless clear that most of these are not apt to have been figures of great authority during the workweek. As with the blue-collar potentates, leading a civic organization was an experience that would have honed political and social skills not well served by the routines of working life.

It seems not unreasonable to add thirteen female leaders listed only as "wid-

Table 5.5. White-Collar Jobs Yielding Organizational Presidencies
in the Civic Fauna, 1913

Occupation	Number of potentates	Occupation	Number of potentates
Clerk	21	Librarian	2
Real estate broker and salesman	7	Brewer	1
Salesman	7	Fresco painter	1
Commercial traveler	5	Grocer	1
Secretary and stenographer	4	Hat dealer	1
Chief clerk	4	Jeweler	1
Inspector	3	Matron	1
Nurse	3	Musician	1
Bookkeeper	3	Reporter	1
Draftsman	2	White-collar total	71

ows" to this group of civic potentates who were not workplace chieftains. Adding them to 128 workers and 71 white-collar employees, we arrive at 212 nonelite civic potentates in a total of 334—nearly two-thirds of the available positions.[35] Allowing for the vagaries of the historical data, we can conclude with certainty that a majority of all civic organizations were headed by regular folks for whom high office was not a routine expectation in life. This leads me to conclude that Schlesinger was broadly correct about the operation of civic life, and that this portion of the civic fauna ran deep in the city's class structure.[36] This leaves two further questions:

• Was there a predominant pattern of gender differentiation? Yes, most organizations were defined by gender specialization, and a great many excluded women altogether. No female could head an Odd Fellows lodge or be an Elk. And about two-thirds of all these organizations were for men. But there were a great many "sister" organizations (the Daughters of Rebekah for the Odd Fellows, the Women's Relief Corps for the GAR, and so forth), and there were freestanding organizations run by and for women such as the Women's Christian Temperance Union (after 1907, the Daughters of Isabella was administratively independent of the Knights of Columbus).
• Did leadership roles reach all the way down through the classes? Clearly not. Not a single peddler, porter, or gardener headed a club. The inmates of the almshouse were left out of civic life almost altogether—although we will shortly encounter one possible exception.

This analysis confirms the broad reach of civic life in this period and understates it by ignoring the thousands of less visible tasks being performed by committees, and by lesser officials of civic organizations. There is every reason to think that the thickness of opportunity, and the connectedness of civic engagement, was great indeed. But we may also want to know a little about the microgeography of civic leadership in completing this picture.

DEMOCRATIC GEOGRAPHY OF CIVIC ORGANIZATION POTENTATES

The broadly democratic texture of civic participation indicated by the occupations of organizational heads is strikingly reinforced by a look at their residential geography. In figure 5.8, the homes of top officers from the civic fauna are displayed. Upscale neighborhoods were well represented: of 337 leaders for whom addresses could be located, 26 lived in East Rock, 32 within the original nine squares, 17 in Dwight, and 9 in Edgewood—making a total of 84 (about 25 percent) of the total in upscale settings. This is not to indicate that a quarter of the potentates were patricians—to live within the nine squares, the northeastern edge excepted, was to live in the most cosmopolitan and heterogeneous of neighborhoods, and the same was more or less true of Dwight. Moreover, many of these people were not in very fancy jobs to begin with: the 84 include a voice teacher, a shoemaker, a foreman, and several others who violate any upscale stereotype.

Nearly 200 of these leaders lived in generally working-class neighborhoods. The leading neighborhood for potentate residence was the Hill, south of the nine squares. With 97 civic presidents the Hill was also home to a considerable fraction of the working class (see Chapter 4). The Hill of course included some choice subneighborhoods, and roughly a dozen of these people were living in rather grand houses.[37] But for our purposes, these are not very interesting as exceptions, since those individuals lived within areas filled with working people of modest means. And most of the potentates from the Hill were machinists, foremen, clerks, and the like. The Dixwell neighborhood housed 23 leaders, of whom more than half headed "colored" organizations. Wooster Square, teeming with newcomers, housed 21. Fair Haven[38] housed 52, and Newhallville housed half a dozen. The intriguing 200th individual was a Mr. Michael Murphy, president, Division 3, Ancient Order of Hibernians. No middle initial decorates the name. When we try to check his home address, we find (not surprisingly) the real Michael Murphy and six imposters. As it turns out, six of the seven lived in working-class neighborhoods, and the remaining one roomed in the almshouse at

Figure 5.8. Homes of civic potentates, 1913. Each dot may represent several homes at one address or homes at two or more closely bunched addresses.

Springside Farm. Could the head Hibernian have lived in the almshouse? Probably not, but the thought is tantalizing.

Civic leadership, then, was stitched into all of the city's neighborhoods (table 5.6).[39] On a per capita basis, upscale neighborhoods were mostly overrepresented among potentates, just as one might expect. Tiny Westville held 223 percent of its pro rata share, a finding consistent with our knowledge that a middle-class, substantially Jewish suburb was developing in this period. East Rock was overrepresented, at nearly 180 percent. Dwight, also upscale, was underrepresented, perhaps because of its large student population in this era. But notice that Dixwell had about its expected share, while the Hill was overrepresented by a quarter. Fair Haven was not far short of its proportional share among the city's

Table 5.6. Neighborhood Representation Among Civic Potentates, 1913,
Selected Neighborhoods

Neighborhood	Percentage of population	Percentage of potentates	Actual as percentage pro rata share
Westville and West Rock	2.2	5	227.3
East Rock	4.3	7.7	179.1
Hill	23	28.8	125.2
Dixwell	6.7	6.8	101.5
Fair Haven	18.2	15.4	84.6
Dwight	7.6	5	65.8
Wooster Square	15.1	6.2	41.1

civic potentates. Among the working-class neighborhoods considered here, only Wooster Square, with its thousands of new arrivals, was greatly underrepresented on a pro rata basis. This last observation is consistent with the relatively low level of participation in St. Michael's parish noted above.

Proportionality of representation in civic leadership is a convenient yardstick but is not the central issue. With variations on a theme, it is fair to conclude that the geography of civic leadership was broadly democratic. People stationed well below the brass at work were often themselves the brass in civic life. While many of the civic organizations had national ties, their leadership was grounded in the ordinary neighborhoods of the city. Conversely, the neighborhoods were for the most part linked to the network of civic organizations, so that one would encounter someone with a senior role in civic life almost anywhere in town. Finally, the links between civic life and the commercial city were almost certainly too numerous to count.

YALE AND THE HOSPITALS

In the opening decade of the twenty-first century, Yale University and two major hospitals are strikingly important survivors from the era of centered urbanism. Their significance as employers grew, at almost alarming rates, in the late twentieth century, and they almost certainly must play a strategic role in any good future New Haven may seek for itself. But they are not the same organizations now that they were then.

Let us look, first, at the geography of Yale's entering classes. A particularly revealing set of data concerns the students admitted to the Sheffield Scientific

School within Yale in the early years of the twentieth century.[40] "Shef," as it was known, was decidedly less prominent socially than were other parts of the university, and this may have increased its accessibility to public school graduates. It was in any case a very major part of Yale, and we are fortunate to have the historical record of its admissions decisions. These data indicate some combination of two features not easily imagined in the twenty-first century: 1) that New Haven public schooling included a generous share of the very highest quality academic preparation available in the United States, and 2) that Yale was to some degree a local institution. It is difficult to sort these out, and the answer matters only marginally to our main story.[41] But it is evident that New Haven High School, a.k.a. James Hillhouse High, was indeed a good school, attracting competent college-bound students. And Yale was less cosmopolitan a century ago than it is today.

But the essential fact is less concerned with school quality than with grounding in local community. New Haven High School was sending many of its best students to Yale, and the numbers were actually growing in the period covered by table 5.7. While the city's academic high school topped the world in Sheffield admissions, it was one of four New Haven schools contributing local students (table 5.8). Hopkins Grammar School sent about eight students a year, Booth Prep 3.6, and the University School another few. In this decade, these schools—all located in the city itself—averaged a total of 44 admissions per year. We have already seen the striking degree to which Yale's senior faculty and officers lived locally. To a measurable degree, one could say that this was education by and for members of the local community. Although the great majority of Yale students were from out of town, townies were handsomely represented in the classrooms of this increasingly prestigious college.

This anchoring of the Yale student body in New Haven is one thing; the anchoring of three New Haven student bodies at Yale was another. Across the century, until February 1955, three city high schools stood together on a six-acre patch of what would otherwise have been the Yale campus (figure 5.9). Fronting Broadway was (1) Boardman Trade, serving vocational and technical students. In the middle, suitably locked between Yale's gym (left, looking like a church) and its Hall of Graduate Studies (right, with ivory tower at edge of frame) stood (2) Hillhouse and its high academic standards. To the rear stood what had been (3) Commercial High and what became Wilbur Cross High School, serving business and comprehensive curricula over the decades. This concentration of educational activity must have all but compelled contact between Yale students and the high school kids—and served as a constant reminder that Yale was for better or worse an urban institution. The sale of these buildings by Mayor Richard Lee to Yale

Table 5.7. Admission to Sheffield by Leading
Preparatory and High Schools, 1898–1907

School	Students admitted
New Haven High School	306
Phillips Academy	295
St. Paul's	119
Laurenceville School	102
Hotchkiss School	96
Hill School, Pittstown, Pa.	91
Hopkins Grammar School	71
Taft School	53
University School, Cleveland	42
Cutler School, N.Y.	34
Bridgeport High School	32
University School, Chicago	29
Chicago Latin School	17
Derby High School, Conn.	17
Morgan School, Clinton, Conn.	11
Brooklyn Poly Prep, N.Y.	8
Greenwich High School, Conn.	4

and its president, Whitney Griswold, may have served mutual advantage when it occurred, but it proved to be among Lee's least popular decisions.[42]

This flow of students into Yale, and the adjacency of campuses, is an important fact about the urbanist city as it differs from the present one, but it is not necessarily an indicator of actual good will between town and gown in the period. There were some nasty episodes, including a local headline reading: "Mayor 'Roughed' by Students: Dean Jones to Take Action."[43] According to the report, "Set upon by a dozen Yale students when he attempted to save three women from their indignities during a football mass meeting in front of the Eli gym at Elm and York streets last night, Mayor Frank J. Rice who commanded the arrest of one of the students, appeared as star witness of these cases for general breach of the peace." This suggests caution in imagining an age of good feeling between town and gown, but it in no way contradicts the notion that Yale was closely linked to the city in this period.

The hospitals display even stronger grounding in local community. Start with the simple matter of patient loads. In the year 1909, New Haven Hospital admitted a total of 2,183 patients. Of these, 1,514 were residents of New Haven itself—

Table 5.8. Yearly Sheffield Admissions from New Haven Schools, 1898–1907

Year	New Haven High	Hopkins Grammar	Booth Prep	University School of New Haven	Yearly New Haven total
1898	17	8	0	0	25
1899	16	10	5	0	31
1900	22	5	3	0	30
1901	24	2	7	0	33
1902	18	6	2	0	26
1903	48	6	11	1	66
1904	38	8	3	2	51
1905	55	11	3	4	73
1906	32	11	0	8	51
1907	36	9	2	9	56
Totals	306	76	36	24	442

more than two-thirds. Adding in the rest of New Haven County brings the total to 1,953, or about 90 percent.[44] At the Hospital of St. Raphael, 2,409 were admitted, of whom 1,773 were New Haven residents (73 percent).[45] Both organizations were staffed mostly with New Haven residents, and both were tied into the local civic organizations. New Haven Hospital, a creature of the General Hospital Society of Connecticut, had a governing structure filled with New Haven figures—Eli Whitney III, Simeon Baldwin, William Daggett, Max Adler, Thomas Hooker, Henry Farnam, Henry English, H. G. Day, and John Studley. Sylvester Poli was missing, as were all of his countrymen, along with the East European Jews. But this was a very local, grounded organization serving a mostly local community of physicians and patients. St. Raphael—founded in response to the exclusion of Catholic doctors elsewhere in town—was grounded in its parish supporters, including those at St. Boniface, Sacred Heart, St. Mary, St. Francis, St. John, St. Patrick, St. Joseph, St. Stanislaus, and St. Peter of New Haven, along with St. Lawrence of West Haven. Edward Malley—the department store retailer—was this hospital's largest donor at $5,000, followed by scores of givers of sums down to $2. While a great many of these donors have Irish and Italian names, we also find visible WASPs and German Jews among the supporters (Studley, Trowbridge, Strouse-Adler company). Literally hundreds of small donors are recorded for 1909.

Figure 5.9. Three public high schools located in and near the Yale campus, c. 1950. They are (1) Boardman Trade, (2) Hillhouse, and (3) Commercial. Yale's Payne Whitney Gymnasium is at upper left, and the Hall of Graduate Studies stands at extreme right. NHCHS.

These large, heavily capitalized nonprofits were not regional or national institutions which happened to be located in New Haven. They were in substantial degree grounded in the city of which they were part. While no American hospital can be imagined as a populist institution, these were in notable degree run by and for a local urban community.

SCHOOLS, TEACHERS, AND PUPILS

Written with Stephen Lassonde

The greatest school for self-government in any city—for the rubbing of minds or elbows—was more often than not the neighborhood public school. In Frank Rice's New Haven this school was intensely local: it employed faculty living nearby to teach students living in their own neighborhood. Elementary schools in dense, working-class parts of the city drew their students from a radius of two

Figure 5.10. Graduation portrait, Dwight School, 1917. NHCHS.

or three blocks, on average. This limited school size, which maximized the possibility of familiarity between teachers and neighborhood families. And as we have already seen, by 1913 the majority of these families were immigrants. If it is the habit of immigrants to cling to whatever fragments of the familiar they can husband, then the success of the public schools in weaving people into the fabric of the city's life was due in part to the willingness of immigrants to view the neighborhood elementary school as an inevitable (if sometimes incomprehensible) feature of their new world. The very inescapability of the neighborhood school joined it to the church or temple, the barbershop, the shoe repairman, the baker, and the pushcart peddler as a local institution. Even though the majority of things American were encountered as palpably alien, to immigrant parents the neighborhood school acquired an aspect of intimacy from its daily association with the constricted scope of their transplanted lives. For immigrant children especially, the school was a compass to civic life—a guide to the society of strangers whose city they inhabited. However disdainful, strange, or remote, their teachers and many of their fellow pupils served as exemplars of "American" life. The marvelous formality of the eighth-grade picture at the Dwight School in 1917 sounds a patriotic theme, consistent with the World War I era, and displays a remarkable diversity of faces, about a dozen of them black (figure 5.10).

Living Patterns of Teachers The case of the Zunder School in 1913 is shown by figure 5.11. Here, the school's faculty homes are shown by gray symbols, and the school itself is shown by a black symbol. The nine squares give a point of refer-

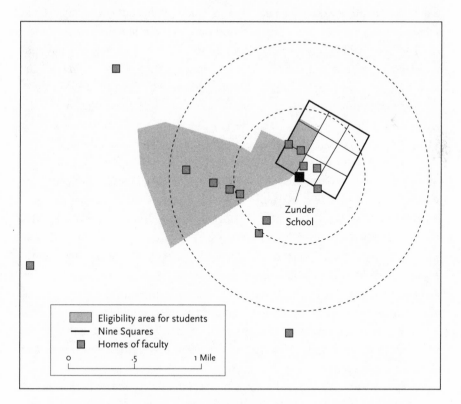

Figure 5.11. Residence patterns of faculty for Zunder School, a neighborhood school, c. 1913.

ence, and the circles indicate half-mile and one-mile radii around the school it-self. Eight faculty members live within a half-mile of the school, eleven of four-teen within a mile, just two well beyond that readily walkable distance.[46] The Zunder pattern is more or less representative for forty-seven schools spaced more or less in proportion to population density across the city (the high schools and trade school had much broader catchments). This would have had the effect of producing a weave of overlapping school faculties and would very probably have contributed to civic density.

The faculty members quite often had been educated in New Haven as well. In the case of Zunder's staff, ten of fourteen came out of the New Haven Normal School—a publicly sponsored teachers' college.[47] Moreover, all of those ten in-structors were graduates of New Haven High School. This is not always the pat-tern, but neither is it exceptional. All the faculty at the Ferry Street School came out of the city's academic high school, and all save one attended the Normal School. Overall, systemwide, a decided majority of teachers had graduated from one or both of these New Haven institutions.[48] I point this out not to suggest that school systems adopt protectionist hiring practices but simply to observe the depth of grounded localism evident in the school system. This may well have en-couraged some limitations of vision, but it also would have encouraged familiar-ity with the city, its people, their traditions, and their material circumstances.[49]

The neighborhood school represents civic density at its thickest. While partic-ipation in voluntary organizations reflects actual choices made by people in their associations, school attendance laws, effectively enforced by 1900, compelled as-sociation with others unlike oneself and all of the conflict and hard-won har-mony that implies. The Zunder School example illustrates the point. In 1913 (about the midpoint of our data on the ethnic composition of New Haven's schools from 1900 to 1930[50]) the Zunder School had one of the two highest concentrations of children of Russian Jews. Two-thirds of its student body was identified as "Russian" by the school census in 1915. While the city's other schools grew increasingly homogeneous between 1900 and 1930, Zunder be-came more diverse, as its pupils were almost equally divided among "American" and "Russian" and Italian immigrant children by the onset of the Great Depres-sion. The common experience throughout the public schools during this period was, then, one of constant exposure to people of other ethnicities, races, and socioeconomic groups.

By reputation, neighborhoods changed from Italian to Jewish to Irish or to Pol-ish within the space of one or two blocks, but even so, the reality was that Italians, Jews, Irish, and Poles routinely lived on top of and next door to one another. As long as schooling occurred at the elementary level in the neighborhoods where children played, and parents, siblings, and kin toiled, all was relatively familiar. The school, then, while foreign and for some even objectionable in content, was not necessarily seen as an irritant or as a source of ineluctable change.

As children grew older they moved to schools outside their own neighborhoods. With the initiation, in the 1910s, of a curriculum more suited to the interests of non-collegebound students, and with the decline of youth jobs that began decisively after World War I, more children from more varied backgrounds were promoted into schools many blocks away from home.

The pyramidal design of city school systems like New Haven's combined with geography to separate older children from their families and communities. By 1930 the city's public school system would consist of fifty-four elementary schools at its base, each with small enrollments, four junior high schools with comparatively large enrollments, and two high schools and a trade school at its apex, each boasting enormous student populations.[51] The four junior high schools were built during the 1920s to accommodate the growing numbers of teens electing to continue their schooling, and these were necessarily at some distance from the neighborhood elementary schools that fed them. The junior high schools were instituted with the aim of creating an easier transition to the city's high schools, and by 1930 a wide majority of young people attended one of the city's high schools.[52]

If schooling created a physical sphere of relations with others from beyond the immediate world of family, teachers and principals were models of "American" or middle-class life that offered proximate alternatives to the worldviews of the children they served. The schools were colonizers, in effect, foreign "hosts" to the communities they inhabited. This relationship was reversed, however, when children completed sixth grade. The remoteness of the high schools from the elementary schools and junior high schools that flowed into them required that most students journey past the businesses and municipal establishments of downtown New Haven. The walk to school visually reinforced the perception of civic authority as something foreign and grounded outside of young people's own neighborhoods. Whether students walked or traveled by streetcar, the city high schools were interwoven into the fabric of New Haven's other grand civic institutions: City Hall, Center Church, the municipal court house, the public library, Chapel Street's department stores, Broadway's retailers, the ancient New Haven Green itself, and, of course, Yale University. New Haven's neighborhoods, in their scaled-down familiarity, stood in shrunken contrast to the granite ambitions of this old Yankee city. And while the sensation of being culturally at sea was deepest and most daunting to the children of immigrants, it was palpable nonetheless to all but the very few whose forebears had been the merchants, industrialists, and civic leaders of Old New Haven. The high schools, then, offered young people both a glimmering prospect of individual success and upward mobility on one hand and the fearsome possibility of failure on the other.

The educational fauna also included more than two dozen independent or proprietary schools. We have already encountered Hopkins Grammar School, Booth Prep, and the University School of New Haven as contributors to Yale's Sheffield Scientific. There were many others, including the fledgling Hamden Hall Country Day, Roxbury Tutoring School, the Rutherford Institute, St. Mary's Academy, and Chapman's. Other organizations provided vocational training— Stebbing Tutorial, Yale Business College, and Connecticut Business University. The New Haven Normal School of Gymnastics and the New Haven School of Music appear to have been aimed at leisure enjoyment.

FUN AND GAMES

The coming of mass broadcast media, like the arrival of massive "automobility," lay in the not too distant future in 1910–17. And this meant that the world of entertainment was (to twenty-first-century eyes and ears) amazingly local. In 1913 New Haven was home to about sixty public halls devoted to meeting, doing good, and being entertained. Here are the names of a few, selected to indicate their variety: Socialist Hall, Republican Hall, Salvation Army Hall, Union Hall, Trades Council Hall, Grand Opera House, Chamber of Commerce Hall, Arbeiter Manner Chor Hall, Germania Hall, Teutonia Hall, Red Men's Hall, Music Hall, and Harmonie Hall. There were thirty-one theaters, most of them showing movies, and every working-class neighborhood had at least one theater of its own: the Arcade, the Life, and the Dewitt in the Hill; Henderson's Bronx Theatre and the Lyric in Dixwell; the Majestic in Oak Street; DeLucia Brothers' Pequot and Pavone's in Fair Haven. There were larger and fancier downtown houses, such as Poli's Wonderland, Poli's Bijou, and the Globe. And there were movie houses like Airdrome and the Orpheum in Savin Rock's White City (a seaside amusement park in West Haven). The movie houses, showing work produced far afield, were exceptional: most of New Haven's entertainment was live and local.

Sports of every sort were the rage, as is suggested by the front page of the *New Haven Evening Register* for November 20, 1909. The top of the page offers,

"Greatest Gridiron Battle Says Captain Coy" of Yale's football game at Harvard five days in the future. Below this, in the right-hand column, is another story, "Court Orders Dissolution of Standard Oil Company." The photo of Standard's John D. Rockefeller is humbled by pictures of Yale and Harvard players. This *was* an exceptional year, at the end of an exceptional period for Yale football. Between 1872 and the game in question, Yale had lost a total of 17 games, winning 100, losing 4 with 5 ties between 1900 and the end of the 1909 season.[53] The Yale 1900 team had been national champion, and the 1909 team was unbeaten, untied, and unscored-upon in ten games. In 1913–14, the team's commercial success would justify construction of the 70,000-seat Yale Bowl. Legendary Yale coach Walter Camp would lead the body that codified the rules of American football, partly in response to a call from Theodore Roosevelt to make the college game safer—since it was killing up to thirty players a season in the first decade of the century. Yale football would inevitably decline, relative to this peak period of national prominence, but it remained a New Haven institution for most of the twentieth century. Football was perhaps the jewel of Yale athletics, but it wasn't anything like the whole story. As sportswriter Bob Barton observes:

> In many sports, Yale was what put New Haven on the map. In track, for instance, Yale was huge. A. C. Gilbert—father of the Erector Set and American Flyer model trains—was heading into his senior year when he won the pole vault in the Olympics at London in 1908. Forrest Smithson, Olympic 110-meter hurdles champion that year, was a Yale Law School dropout. . . . Yale's baseball team was good enough to take on the pros. In April 1901, the Elis beat the New York Giants 5–4, with shortstop Jimmy O'Rourke and second baseman Lloyd Waddell using the hidden ball trick. The losing pitcher was Hall of Famer Christy Matthewson. The same month, the Elis lost 4–3 in 13 innings to Connie Mack's Philadelphia Athletics.[54]

Yale athletics were prominent, attracting national press and often large crowds. Events which now attract little more than a scattering of friends and relatives—collegiate track meets, baseball games—commonly drew thousands of spectators. But neither Yale nor any other educational institution was at the core of New Haven's sporting life in the Frank Rice era. As Barton writes, "Most of the action, whether in football, basketball or baseball, involved teams representing various clubs, such as the Washington Glee Club, and the Annex, Pioneer, Walnut, Williams, and Maple athletic clubs. Companies such as Winchester and Acme Wire had teams, too. Out of town opponents included the All-Wallingfords, and All-Waterburys, the Starlights of Naugatuck, Remington and American Chain of Bridgeport."[55]

In order to capture the texture of this athletic localism, and the mix of club with school and university teams, I have culled a few illustrative passages from the November 1909 *Register* sports pages:

The biggest football game left for this city, the Annex-Glee club contest, for the New Haven championship, will be seen by a crowd which will rank a close second to that which witnessed the Yale-Princeton match.

"Red Hot Race on the Rollers." The five-mile relay race on rollers, which is scheduled to take place this evening at the Quinnipiac skating auditorium in Grand Avenue promises to be hotly contested.

The Montowese A.C. played its last football game of the season and lost to the Emeralds, 10 to 0. The feature of the game was the good sportsmanship.

"Helen Taft One of Prominent Football Guests." Miss Helen Taft, daughter of the President, was one of the prominent and popular visitors to the city Saturday for the [Yale-Princeton] football game. Miss Taft came on from Bryn Mawr, for the event and during her stay here was the guest of Mr. and Mrs. William Farnam.

"Mallory Jumps, Roller Polo War Now in Sight." The Interstate Roller Polo league began its playing season last night. The only National league player to jump to the western organization is Bert Mallory, the Providence goal tender, a New Haven boy.

"Homesteads Beat Monarchs." Since the defeat of the Monarch football team yesterday afternoon by the crack Homestead football eleven near East Rock by a score of 16–0, the many followers of the Homestead team are ready to bet all kinds of money on their aggregation, which lines up against the Elms next Sunday afternoon.

"Abe Alderman a Star End." One of the fastest players on the New Haven High School eleven today is Abe Alderman, who has been playing a remarkable and consistent game at left end for that school and also has jumped into prominence by his wonderful punting and drop kicking. . . . He is fast as streaked lightning down the field after a punt and usually nails the opposition runner in his tracks.

"Our Polo Team in Banquet to Meadow Brooks." The Polo club of this city and the Taconic club of Hartford were represented at a dinner given by the Polo

Association at Delmonico's Saturday night in honor of the victorious Meadow Brook club, which, playing at Hurlingham, England, last summer, defeated a team of picked English players.

"Sarsfields Win From Emeralds." Gaelic football was played yesterday afternoon at Baker's lot between New Haven teams.

"Homesteads Win From Elms, 17–0." A crowd of fully 1,500 people say the Homesteads defeated the Elms yesterday afternoon on the grounds at Baker's field by a score of 17–0. The teams played for a purse of $25, and the 150-pound championship.

"Clintons Put Five on Floor." Manager Herman Trisch has been getting his basketball talent together for enrollment under the colors of the Clintons and he has just made up his five for the season. He said this morning that his lineup would be as follows: Forwards, Saxe, Frankel, and Grant; guards, Alderman, Frisco, and Clancy; center, Andy Parker.

CIVIC DENSITY AND SOCIAL CAPITAL FORMATION?

One good way of thinking about civic density is to consider the institutional mechanisms for the creation and preservation of social capital. Churches, temples, clubs, teams, and all the rest are places where people create social capital with one another. It is a suggestive fact that the *idea* of social capital arises during the period when cities like New Haven still offered very high levels of civic density. In 1916, Lyda Hanifan captured the idea, and seems to have coined the term, admirably:

In the use of the phrase social capital I make no reference to the usual [understanding] of the term capital, except in a figurative sense. I do not refer to real estate, or to personal property or to cold cash, but rather to that in life which tends to make these tangible substances count for most in the daily lives of people, namely goodwill, fellowship, mutual sympathy and social intercourse. . . . If [the individual] comes into contact with his neighbors, and they with other neighbors, there will be an accumulation of social capital, which may immediately satisfy his social needs and which may bear a social potentiality sufficient to the substantial improvement of living conditions in the whole community. The community as a whole will benefit by the cooperation of all its parts, while the individuals will find in his associations advantages of the help, the sympathy, and the fellowship of his neighbors.[56]

Several others, including Jane Jacobs, have since independently discovered this idea, and Robert Putnam has made it a part of speech in American English with his *Bowling Alone*.[57] It is a useful idea, and Hanifan got it right in 1916—in recommending rural policy in conscious *emulation of urban life* built up with civic density of just the sort we have reviewed here. The ideas around which this chapter and the several before it have been organized—centering, groundedness, civic density—are all related to this admittedly inexact concept. But being inexact is sometimes useful, especially when one is wrestling with something as complex as a city. The fabric of enterprise discussed in Chapter 3 is about connectedness as it is created in commerce, down to the neighborhood grocery store. The impact of living locally, in close proximity to others, even to others very different from oneself, is also a way of talking about the creation of trusting connectedness with others in a community—that is to say, social capital. And the organizations considered in this chapter—churches and temples, clubs and associations, locally grounded hospitals and institutions of higher learning, schools, halls, sporting clubs, and even neighborhood movie houses—all are bulwarks of social capital.

Putnam distinguishes between two uses of social capital: (1) bonding similar people together, and (2) bridging groups of different people.[58] The first would be illustrated by the nationality parishes, the ethnic clubs, and many of the smaller organizational units assayed here. The latter, corresponding closely to what Richard Sennett means by *The Uses of Disorder*, would be hinted at by the composition of the basketball roster given a moment ago—bringing together people with names like Clancy, Alderman, Frisco, Frankel, Grant, and Parker. The use of social capital for bonding may be the single greatest preventive mechanism against crime, especially if it occurs at the level of the neighborhood.

The supreme task of urban life in this period was the formation of social capital in bridging differences of the sort that very nearly defined urbanity. This was the work of local athletics, of amateur theater, of the meeting hall, of the school, and in many cases the work of the fraternal and sororal organization. It was the work of crowded streets, jumbling together shops and homes, saloons and houses of worship. It was the work of corners where trolleys stopped, and where neighbors met almost by accident from day to day.

CHAPTER 6

A SIDEWALK REPUBLIC

When Frank Rice emerged as a dark horse among seven GOP hopefuls for the mayoral nomination in September 1909, young John Day Jackson, publisher of the *New Haven Evening Register,* must have burned the midnight oil—or ordered someone else in the paper's Crown Street headquarters to do so. Emerging only on the second ballot of the GOP convention, Rice would appear to have been a total outsider to those who wrote only casually about New Haven politics. When the general election came, Rice squeaked past Democratic incumbent J. B. Martin, 9,707 to 9,301, perhaps aided by 786 votes wasted on Socialism. Lacking both political visibility and an old New Haven name, Rice was a mystery to the local press, and Jackson's nameless reporter would have chewed many pencil stubs trying to figure out how to introduce to his readers a politician whom he described as a "dark horse . . . less known than any man ever nominated for mayor."[1]

Actually, much of the *Register*'s readership knew Rice well. He had spent twenty-five years in town, working in a range of jobs that brought him in close contact with the people of New Haven. After attending an institution disingenuously calling itself the Yale Business School, he started as a bookkeeper for Hoadley Ives, a hardware manufacturer and Republican Party activist; moved on to a store in Hamden; then successively worked as a trolley conductor, ran one of downtown's few grocery stores, and managed the Hutchinson, a private dormitory for Yale. Outside of work, Rice was a champion of civic engagement. The upper echelons of New Haven—business leaders, political bigwigs, and society dons—might have remembered meeting the new mayor at a function of the New Haven Chamber of Commerce or the New England Business Men's Association. Ordinary folks—patriots, pew patrons, and do-gooders—would have regularly seen Rice at meetings of the Methodist Episcopal Church or the YMCA. Rice ran from meeting to luncheon to lecture; he was probably known at least casually to a few thousand New Haven residents by the time he ran for mayor.

On inauguration day, January 1, 1910, County Sheriff Patrick McGuinness escorted the new mayor from still-incumbent Mayor James Martin's office to an aldermanic chamber in City Hall. Standing amid patriotic bunting and floral tributes, Rice revealed his vision for New Haven: "Politics should be eliminated from the departments of police, fire and education as far as possible. The persons employed in these departments should be treated fairly and well paid, and should be promoted according to the quality of service they have rendered. In return, they should give the city the best service in their power."

This was Rice's gesture to progressive business, with its preference for performance over politics, career service over patronage, a good day's pay for a good day's work. Rice's progressivism was carefully short-armed: meritocracy for teachers and cops was one thing, but no such starchy doctrine needed to confound the useful role of patronage in public works, parks, and maintenance functions. Rice was no proponent of large programmatic goals and would probably not have been nominated and elected mayor if he were. He certainly would have been a less successful mayor if he had tried to push through a massive program of change. A generation earlier, in 1890, manufacturer J. B. Sargent had become mayor on an ambitious Democratic Party ticket of reform—including public ownership of the water company—but failed in his agenda. It is probable that Sargent overestimated the flexibility and power of city government, an error of which this new man was constitutionally incapable. Rice was a sincerely modest figure, both in assessing his personal abilities and in estimating the possibilities of city government. His top policy priority, receiving far more follow-up than merit hiring for education and safety services, was truly pedestrian, starting with uniform sidewalks and going toward the promise that his City Hall would be a business-oriented regime, with modest goals and an organizational focus that nobody could mistake for populism:

> There are many other matters which might be taken up at this time and discussed at length, but I think it unwise. It is the aim of this administration to

work in harmony with every agency for the upbuilding of New Haven. It invites the co-operation of the Civic Federation, the Chamber of Commerce, and the Business Men's Association, and every similar organization in the city. I shall be glad to receive suggestions from every source organized or individual, for the betterment of the city. Full of faith for the future, I pledge myself, fellow citizens, to the service of the city. To deserve the confidence you have shown by your suffrage shall be the ambition of my administration.[2]

Could the new mayor's dull vision—seemingly limited to business organizations—govern a complex and dynamic city such as New Haven? In fact, Rice's unadventurous style was well suited to a city government at once rigid and difficult to operate in service of any but the most routine objectives. Throughout his tenure Rice focused on modest programmatic goals; his avoidance of grander visions either reflected shrewd realism about the institutional disabilities of city government or constituted an instance of blind-staggering good luck in the fit between task and temperament.

When Rice came into office, New Haven did not rely on government for the decisions that mattered most. Nongovernment actors—including some of the organizations that Rice joined for social advancement and business contacts—underwrote quality governance. Choices made by businessmen, family heads, civic leaders, churchmen, schoolwomen, and customers in distant places buying New Haven's wares were all implicitly part of the city's governance, and the role of government could remain modest without jeopardizing the interests of the city and its people. New Haven benefited from an active civic sector long after the mayor's death in 1917; urbanism's fundamental difficulty in our own time— the yawning gap between *government* in the narrowest and *governance* in the broadest sense—was a distant threat. In 1910, New Haven was reaching the crest of centered development.

GOOD BUSINESS IS GOOD GOVERNMENT

The democratization of city politics had taken a decisive turn in 1845, near the beginning of serious capitalist development, when the property requirement for voting was repealed. Two distinct versions of urban community were thereby set in perpetual competition with one another.[3] One, the older and less democratic, defined the political community by material stakeholding—by property ownership, by business investment, by the commitment of fixed economic assets to the place and to its tax rolls. The other defined the community by reference to residence—the commitment of one's person, and her family, to the city constituted the defining act of membership. These two conceptions have been in tension since long before 1845, but it was not until then that their rivalry became a palpable fact of routine politics. On the first idea, the city's interest and that of its property holders are more or less the same; on the second, the city's interest and those of all its residents are more or less the same. The challenge of urban politics and policy—and of mayoral leadership—is to find ways to protect and nurture business interests and at the same time protect the shared interests of a democratic city.[4]

What centered development did for New Haven in Frank Rice's era was to limit the conflict between these two communities. To be sure, many city residents were without real estate holdings, but they were almost invariably linked to property holders as residential tenants, or as employees of business, or as both of these. Several thousand were themselves business owners, even if most owned enterprises of very modest scale. Few indeed were those living outside the almshouse who were not somehow linked to property—as its owners, as its tenants, as its labor force. Moreover, since property taxes can be passed on to tenants, nearly everyone was in some sense a taxpayer to city government. And the city of that era knew that even renters had an economic stake in the costs and value of property. A 1909 headline from the *New Haven Evening Register* screams, "Tax Burden Falls on Rent Payers," in which a man is quoted thus: "If the tax rate goes through, I won't pay it. I shall raise my rents enough to make up the difference as will no doubt everyone in the city who has a place to rent."[5] The obverse relationship is perhaps more important: virtually everyone belonging to the community of ownership also belonged to the community of residence. This was true for the vast majority of property holders, and even for the top managers who ran their firms. This meant that property holders had compelling interests in common with residents, since they were residents themselves. Property-based citizenship was in the main a subset of residence-based citizenship, in sharp contrast to New Haven and scores of similar cities just a few decades later.

A second tension endemic to urban politics pitted those who paid taxes against those who lived on salaries generated from tax dollars. Earned incomes in the market economy are usually conceived to be won by voluntary agreement with customers or employers who have themselves won their cash by mutually agreed transactions.[6] The central tenet of neoclassical economics is that any deal voluntarily agreed to by both parties must create value—a view which, when suitably hedged, is surely true.[7] The commonsense version draws a hard line between freedom and coercion in the disposition of one's money. Tax money is involuntary, a necessary evil accepted but usually not agreed upon, or so at least goes the common thought. If the employees of a city are too well rewarded, or appear sluggish and self-seeking in their performance of public duty, this will appear a grave offense against taxpayers who must satisfy customers and bosses for their daily bread. A pro-business ideology derives energy and credibility from this tension. Since government can (in theory) always compel payments from unwilling customers, and (in theory) business can never do so, a businesslike approach to government, attentive to costs, is a diminution of coercion. Thus, in 1911, Rice defends his mayoral record over the first term of office by saying: "In addition to being free from any suggestion of private gain, there have been made advances far beyond those of any previous administration, and throughout the policy has been one of broad economy in which the interests of the taxpayers are guarded."[8]

Though well known and respected enough to be elected mayor, Rice knew that he was a decidedly junior member both of the business and political establishments. He believed in business and put his faith in its institutions, but he realized that New Haven's business elite would not invite him to lunch at the club. When he saluted the Civic Federation, the Chamber and the Business Men's Association in his inaugural address, Rice was playing his symbolic (and as yet tenuous) links to men like Eli Whitney III (descendent of *the* Eli Whitney), bank chairman and water company president three times over; Henry Hotchkiss, president of a large rubber-manufacturing firm; Andrew Hendryx, world's leading manufacturer of bird cages at the time; Henry Rowe, whose oysters were distributed nationally; Morris Tyler, who ran the regional phone company; the Sargent family, major manufacturers of architectural hardware; Max Adler, head of Strouse-Adler corsets; and Wheeler Beecher, manager of the Diamond Match plant. The Republican Party was another link to the people who ran more than two hundred other joint stock corporations doing business out of New Haven; the GOP, its ward leaders, and his network of friendships provided connections to the thousands of people running smaller firms—grocers, dressmakers, painters, plumbers, carters, and saloonkeepers—serving their workforces.

The 1909 election, which brought Rice and the GOP a slender 406-vote plurality, shows increasing Republican control over upscale neighborhoods and internal suburbs. For his first victory, Rice doubled GOP pluralities in advantaged neighborhoods and suburbs and reduced the GOP deficit in other areas by about one-third. This base for Rice's incumbency would be consolidated fully in 1911. In his first election as an incumbent, Rice ran up a 2,564-vote edge in his upscale-suburban base, at the same time cutting the Democratic plurality in other areas by nearly 1,000 votes. The elections of 1913 and 1915 continued the same geography of competition; Rice became New Haven's first-ever four-term mayor, and in 1915 the *Register* pegged him as "the most popular man who ever ran for public office here."⁹ We know in hindsight that it was Rice himself rather than the GOP organization that achieved this result. In 1917, Republican incumbent Samuel Campner was thrashed by Democrat David Fitzgerald. Campner didn't even carry the upscale wards, although he did hang on to two of the internal sub-urbs. The GOP base built around Rice eroded to give the Democrat a 2,500-vote victory. Only three other GOP candidates would win election as mayor of the city in the remaining eighty-two years of the twentieth century.¹⁰

Frank Rice's attention to three specific business organizations in his inau-gural address is more pointed than it at first appears. He could have saluted any number of very different New Haven organizations—he was an active member in many. There was a plethora of clubs, voluntary associations, and benevolent societies organized around diverse ethnic backgrounds, religions, avocations, and professions. But Rice offered no specific greeting or invitation to take part in running the city to the Mechanics League, the Master Carpenters Association, the Brotherhood of Locomotive Engineers, the National Association of Letter Carriers, the Knights of Labor, Brewery Workers Local 37, International Brother-hood of Electrical Workers Local 90, Bartenders Local 217, or the "General Union of Italians" a.k.a Metal Polishers Union Local 205 at Sargent and Com-pany—organizations that many in his constituency could identify with.¹¹

But the Business Men's Association, the Chamber of Commerce, and the Civic Federation—all housed in the Chamber's offices at 185 Church Street—were a trinity of power at the peak of New Haven's business community. Rice's speech was a clear signal of his immediate politics and the way he would go about being mayor.¹² Rice's campaign postures in 1909, 1911, 1913, and 1915 consistently focus on business. Four days after his 1909 victory, Rice told the press:

> I quite realize that the city of New Haven has entered upon a new era of progress and development, in fact, that we are upon an epoch-making pe-riod. The appearance of our buildings, public and private, is being gradually changed for the better, and the prospects are for even more changes in that line, which I foresee will make our town a real city beautiful. . . . I shall heartily co-operate with the Chamber of Commerce in its activities to draw attention to New Haven as a manufacturing center, to attract new indus-tries, and to encourage the expansion of the very important ones we have at

present. Without being parsimonious, I shall try to conduct the public business of the city on an economical basis.[13]

This was a winning formula, and by 1915 the Democratic challenger, Albert W.
Matoon, presented himself almost entirely by reference to business. His October
3, 1915, newspaper ad reads:

A BUSINESS MAN FOR MAYOR

Advocates Adoption of Modern Methods of Handling

This City's Business

Stands for Progress in Municipal Affairs

And the spending of all the money we can afford for beautifying our good
    city

And making it a delightful place to live in—BUT NO MORE

Believes it is possible to stop extravagant methods of running city business
    and thus

Reduce Tax Rate to Normal Percentage

Even after Rice's death the *Register* would endorse his successor (Samuel Campner) by pointing out that Campner "has followed in the footsteps of the late
Mayor Rice, whose unusual success as an honest, broad-minded business head
of the city has been a potent force in the recent up-building of New Haven."[14]

Business institutions were as central to the city in this period as they would
ever be. The Chamber, next door to the seat of New Haven County government
and two doors down from City Hall, completed the triangle of city governance;
the three structures faced the city's Green, looking across at the three ancient
Protestant churches and the Old Campus of Yale University. If the churches had
been dominant institutions one hundred years before, these seats of business
and government were dominant in 1917—as, quite possibly, Yale will be in 2017.

City government in this era was a business regime. As Clarence Stone defines
the term, a regime consists of the "informal arrangements that surround and
complement the formal working of governmental authority. All governmental
authority in the United States is greatly limited—limited by the Constitution,
limited perhaps even more by the nation's political tradition, and limited struc-
turally by the autonomy of privately owned business enterprise. . . . Because local governmental authority is by law and tradition even more limited than authority at the state and national level, informal arrangements assume special
importance in urban politics."[15] Frank Rice would again and again reach out to
business leadership to help him run the difficult apparatus of city government;

he made New Haven government function within its very serious limitations by reliance on the instincts and habits of the business community.

BRITTLE AND RIGID BUT SLOW

Imagine a working day early in the Rice administration. Sitting in his Church Street office, the mayor clutches his head in pain. On his desk lies the City Charter of 1899, possibly the most inconvenient and archaic feature of New Haven city government. Rice came from a business background, where account books were logical and advertisements pithy; the Charter appeared to have been written by lawyers, handsomely paid for each additional word. Rice must have asked himself—looking at the 227 sections spanning 100 printed pages—what the charter-drafters had against anyone who would seek to carry out a far-reaching, coordinated program on behalf of the city or its people. How many sleepless nights would the new mayor have to spend memorizing the procedural duties of New Haven government? Here, for example, are the headings of the charter dealing with police and fire (section number followed by summary of provisions):

46. Police department and its board of six commissioners defined
47. Functions of police elaborated
48. Appointment of police commissioners by the mayor required
49. Appointment of police chief by mayor
50. Pay for chief to be $2,500, commissioners to define other pay grades
51. Rank for retired officers prescribed
52. Police department required to provide voting places in each ward
53. Inspector of Lamps established
54. Fire department and its five-member board defined and described
55. Duties of fire department enumerated
56. Mayoral appointment of fire commissioners prescribed
57. Duties of the fire marshal defined
58. Superintendent of fire alarms established
59. Property and purchasing practices for the departments of police and fire defined
60. Powers of police and fire chiefs further elaborated
61. Transitional provision for application of this charter to existing employees of police and fire departments
62. Transitional provision for ordinances applicable to these departments
63. Commissioners of fire and police forbidden to sell liquor

64. Boards to have power of appointment and promotion
65. Power to fire firemen and policemen given to boards
66. Police Relief Fund and Firemen's Relief Fund established, with six subsections saying how moneys are to be collected and for these funds
67. Lost, abandoned, and impounded property to be added to the relief funds
68. Boards of the departments to be trustees of these funds
69. Retirement of officers and firemen permitted, pensions to be between a quarter and a half of previous salaries
70. Payments to widows of officers and firemen permitted, up to $2,000
71. Regulations applied to retirees
72. Clerk to record doings of boards and trustees

As he read this document, Rice perhaps thought back to the 1907 U.S. Supreme Court decision settling the powers of cities in relation to state governments: "The State . . . at its pleasure may modify or withdraw all [city] powers, may take without compensation [city] property, hold it itself, or vest it in other agencies, expand or contract the territorial area, unite the whole or a part of it with another municipality, repeal the charter and destroy the corporation. All this may be done, conditionally or unconditionally, with or without the consent of the citizens, or even against their protest. In all these respects the State is supreme.[16]

In perfect conformity with this doctrine, the General Assembly of Connecticut created a city government so rigid, so saddled with legislative process, so constrained by boards, bureaus, and commissions as to be a nightmare for any who would lead—or even follow—in a sustained strategy of change.[17] Any action requiring the coordination of multiple departments would need to get past a number of independently elected (and often ornery) executive officers, a cumbersome legislative apparatus, and multiple boards and commissions. The Charter of 1899 encouraged pursuit of the routine and all but forbade transformational leadership. As mayor, Rice could respond to natural disaster and mobilize for war, but he faced extreme difficulty in pursuing a governance vision broader than consistent sidewalks. Rice was not, by nature, a dominant leader; confronted by the forbidding costs of municipal innovation, he was even less bold.

The organizational structure of city government was a seemingly endless proliferation of meetings and groups needing to have them. This is doubtless consistent with the general pattern of "rubbing elbows and minds" with others, as Schlesinger would say.[18] But it made doing the public's business pretty difficult, in New Haven and many other American cities of the period. As Frank Goodnow

Making Sidewalks a Priority

As it happened, city sidewalks were at the top of Frank Rice's agenda. The mayor's very first communication, on January 10, 1910, to the Board of Aldermen—New Haven's one elected legislative body, with the ability to delay whatever its committees thought worthy of delay and the power to override the mayor's veto with a two-thirds majority—called their attention to the "unsatisfactory condition of the sidewalks of the city."

Rice pledged to cooperate with the Department of Public Works and asked for a special committee to take charge of the investigation. Rice was optimistic about the situation: "Although the power of the city in ordering new sidewalks is to some extent limited, I am convinced that the most glaring cases of unfit walks can be speedily eliminated if the present ordinances are enforced and new walks are laid down as soon as those now in use become unsafe."

A month later, the Special Committee on Sidewalks asked the Board of Finance to appropriate short-term funding for work on sidewalks, as "nearly fifty claims [were] entered against the city for injuries to persons resulting from defective and dangerous condition of the sidewalks of our city since the first day of January, 1910." The committee also recommended uniform materials in each block be adopted, as proposed by Mayor Rice, but this issue was tabled and sent to the Committee on Ordinances.

By March 7, the aldermanic *Journal* recorded an exceedingly detailed ordinance on sidewalk construction (for example, "The bottom course of the walk shall consist of crushed stone varying in size from one-half inch to two inches in longest dimension."). The order mandated that "only cement, flag, tar concrete and asphalt mastic sidewalks shall be laid in the city," and it banned tar sidewalks from the downtown area. This responded to the mayor's inaugural denunciation of *brick* sidewalks but failed to respond to his pointed request for uniformity of material within any one block. This objective would be met on a block-at-a-time basis; for instance, on May 2, 1910, the board passed the following ordinance: "ORDERED, That a concrete walk and curb be laid on the westerly side of Livingston street between Edwards and Lawrence streets, beginning at Edwards street and extending northerly about 150 feet to Lawrence street, by the owners of property fronting thereon and to the satisfaction of the Department of Public Works on or before July 2, 1910."   Continued on facing page

> This meant that the city would contract out the sidewalk, and bill the abutters in proportion to their frontage, for a sidewalk of uniform construction in concrete. Of such small, often incomplete victories did political life mostly consist. And yet, at the end of his mayoral career, Frank Rice could claim to have installed about two hundred miles of uniformly cemented sidewalks.
>
> (All quotations from "Journal of the Board of Aldermen of the City of New Haven, 1910.")

wrote at the beginning of the century, "The result of the introduction of [the board] system was completely to disorganize the municipal administration. Each important branch of city government was attended by a board or officer practically independent of any other municipal authority."[19]

The chief of the Department of Police Services, for example, was accountable not simply to the mayor but also to a board of seven commissioners, of whom the mayor was one. The mayor was entitled to appoint two board members to three-year terms each January. Even after packing a board with his own loyalists, a mayor would need to entreat with them, and often to kowtow to them, in the performance of the most routine work. In any attempt at major change, such boards might be expected to act as nearly endless energy sumps.[20] Extrusions of the same general description were attached to every muscular department of city government, including education, health, charities and corrections, libraries, and fire. Others, such as the Lamp Department, had an aldermanic committee ("Lighting"), and still others, such as public works, had special committees on compensation and on engineering. The roll-call of particular departmental boards was rounded out by a civil service commission, a commission on sinking funds, a board of engineering examiners, a board devoted to steam boilers, a special tax committee, a board of assessors, a board of selectmen, a board of relief, some trustees for the almshouse farm, a board of harbor commissioners, a board on teachers' retirements, a board for janitorial retirement, a committee on contagious disease, a building line commission, a commission on public memorials, a commission on municipal records, a committee on the Fourth of July celebration, and a committee to deal with scholarships to Yale.

Faced with this system, Rice took two important steps. First, and most fundamentally, he tailored his ambitions to the modest scale permitted by the government he headed. Second, he took control of all the important boards and commissions through the appointment powers of his office (figure 6.1). He invited

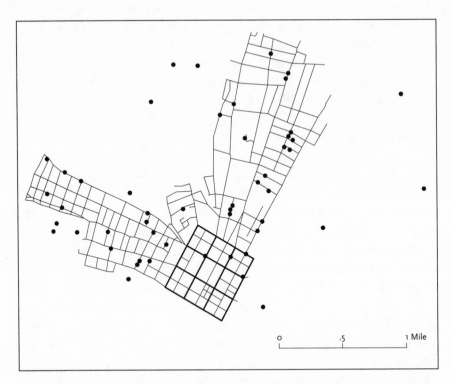

Figure 6.1. Homes of persons appointed to major city boards by Mayor Frank Rice, projected over upscale neighborhoods, 1916.

Table 6.1. Occupations of Those Holding Major
Board Appointments, 1916

Occupation	Number	Percentage of total
Big business	23	35.4%
Small business	10	15.4%
Lawyer	9	13.8%
Yale faculty member	5	7.7%
Superintendent	6	9.2%
Manual worker	5	7.7%
Medical doctor	2	3.1%
Cleric	2	3.1%
Housewife	1	1.5%
Clerk	1	1.5%
Journalist	1	1.5%

> ### Filling the Boards
>
> Rice packed the most strategic boards—those having no controlling rela-
> tionship to one profession (for example, the Board of Health)—with busi-
> nessmen. The Board of Finance consisted of five businessmen and two
> business lawyers (plus the mayor and the controller). The Police Commis-
> sion had five representatives of major business firms in its six seats. Fire
> had a business majority. The Committee on Sinking Funds, playing a cen-
> tral role in debt finance, was all business. The Library Board had just three
> businesspeople, along with a blue-collar worker, a clerk, two clergy, and a
> professor. Parks had two each of workers, professors, and lawyers, leav-
> ened with one businessperson. The Board of Education had the adminis-
> tration's sole female appointment (a Yale faculty wife), a Yale professor, two
> M.D.'s, two businesspeople, and a supervisor in the box department of Sar-
> gent Co.

business, with the learned professions as needed, to participate in governing the
city (table 6.1). This was his central strategy for making the cumbersome system
of boards work tolerably well.

With patience, and continued success at the polls, a mayor could achieve control of the important boards and commissions; but he could not do so without
continuous investment of time and effort in matters that would otherwise be delegated to executive subordinates. If something were complex enough to require
coordinated change across multiple departments, the canopy of boards would
become a considerable deterrent to action. Typically, action would be channeled
into single-department routines, or flow within the established committee structure of the Board of Aldermen. Difficult projects would be abandoned before
they were begun, in rational anticipation of the price mandated by success.

OUTPUTS OF CITY GOVERNMENT

The routine outputs of city government are of three kinds: transactions, ordinances, and services. These are the modest accomplishments of City Hall, and
they are what Frank Rice's administration paid attention to. Given the institutional apparatus at hand, that is hardly surprising.

Transactions, involving in most instances very few players, were the most frequent outputs of city government. They dealt with highly specific and banal is-

Figure 6.2. Construction of the tunnels for the Yale Bowl, 1912. NHCHS.

sues—new sewer lines and retrospective tax abatements—that were of intense personal interest to parties directly involved. Which projects to do when? How to apportion costs? Most transactions were economically trivial; a few were monumental. The construction of the Yale Bowl (figure 6.2) required elaborate permitting and regulation due to its scale and unusual engineering. So large a project required many tiny decisions, but they fell well within the established routine of transactional government. Contracts for service by private vendors constituted a mainstay transaction. Since New Haven was in a growth period, contracts for street paving and sewer construction were numerically dominant. And competitive bidding, with contracts almost always given to the low bidder, was standard procedure under Frank Rice. Here, for instance, are the bids for sewer construction on Highland Street, from Prospect to St. Ronan in 1910:

Joseph Whitby, $2,767.50
Dwyer & Mannix, $2,588.00
Laurence O'Brien, $2,371.50
Thomas F. Maher, $1,696.00[21]

Maher won the job as low bidder. The city was also continuously subject to legal actions over real or alleged harms due to negligence on the part of government. The single most common allegation, as Rice would have been glad to tell you, was defective or ill-kept sidewalks. One of the many 1910 settlements orders "that the City Clerk be and is hereby authorized and directed to draw an order on the City Treasurer for the sum of sixty dollars in favor of Herbert J. Birnley on account of injuries to person caused by fall on icy sidewalk." Other charges ranged from fallen trees to collapsing excavations. These transactions, counted in the thousands over the course of Rice's administration, were at the heart of city government. There was ample opportunity to reward friends and punish enemies in small ways, but the dominant pattern was getting city business done within the routines that made daily action possible. The city that Rice left for future generations was built by these routine transactions; problems were solved incrementally, and urban infrastructure was gradually accumulated. This work was accomplished by ordinary men meeting ordinary challenges.

In Rice's mayoral era, the Board of Aldermen generated roughly one new ordinance, or major amendment to an existing ordinance, each month. The largest cluster of these regulatory interventions concerned construction practices. These were for the most part boilerplate texts that could be found with minor differences across the country in city ordinance books.[22] And most of them were sensible responses to concern for the stability and durability of the built city:

Iron pipes required for sewage waste lines, 1910
Sidewalk construction ordinance, 1910
Foundation walls regulated as to thickness, 1910
Regulation of emergency exits in public places, 1911
Authorization of Board of Aldermen to set property lines for new streets, 1911
Regulation of standards and uses of reinforced concrete, 1911
Plumbing code specified and licensing required, 1912
Requiring fireproof construction for tall buildings open to the public, 1912
Electrical code specified and licensing required, 1912

Regulation of commercial transactions was also routine. A prohibition on the sale of heroin by doctors was part of a national movement. Safety ordinances about retail fireworks and flammable motion picture film were sensible responses to real dangers. Most were a miscellany of regulative adjustments to fairly routine issues of urban life. Smaller sets of ordinances concerned public health: in 1912, the board decreed that manure be kept in covered boxes until removed from the city. The aldermen also responded to the growing traffic congestion in the city by prohibiting passing on the right (1910) and requiring street obstructions to be lighted (1912). Two ordinances dealt with personal conduct: one restricted the hours during which people under fifteen could rollerskate on city sidewalks while forbidding the practice to older skaters except with the permission of all abutting property owners; the other set rules of decorum for persons visiting city parks.

The last group of ordinances were concerned with the governmental process itself:

Oath-taking required in testimony on property values, 1910

Authorization of corporation counsel to bargain over claims on authority of mayor, 1910

Clarification of mayor's appointive powers, 1911

City Clerk to print three hundred copies of aldermanic committees, 1912

These were hardly breathtaking interventions. They were the humdrum routine of institutional adjustment, scarcely worthy of public notice. But this legislative work is not silly, not a waste of time, not a fraud. It just makes no sharp changes of direction, no complex redeployment of the city's resources, no resolution of deep social conflict. And it certainly required little reflection on deep-running changes in the urban environment.

The real business of city government, then as now, was the steady and reliable provision of urban services; in this area Rice's administration mostly implemented past decisions by state and city government. These are even less spectacular than the ordinances. But they often played a vital role in the promotion of public health and safety, and in improving the quality of daily life on the streets of New Haven. Here is a sampler of city services from the Frank Rice era:

Street cleaning and maintenance: The city streets of this era were still mostly unpaved, and those that were paved included a great range of materials. About ten miles of street were being paved each year, although only a part of this was new—much of it simply resurfaced already paved streets. Unpaved streets required frequent sprinkling to keep down dust, and were treated with oil often (most got three treatments per year). Paved streets required almost continuous repair (765 tons of stone went into potholes in 1913). But in a city where horses were still important, the biggest issue was street *cleaning*. Busy downtown paved streets were cleaned by hand nightly. Streets with trolley tracks were hosed down daily. Busy streets serving factories were cleaned up to three times weekly. This was labor-intensive, patronage-sustaining activity of no small importance to the livability of the city.

Bridges: The city maintained scores of bridges, of which thirty-one required major or minor repairs in 1913. Four were drawbridges, requiring continuous staffing. (The Quinnipiac bridge opened nearly 8,000 times in 1913, about half for sailing vessels and half for steamers.)

Garbage collection: Garbage, but not "rubbish," was collected in this era, and the Rice administration went to considerable lengths to improve service. Collections were done twice weekly year-round, and as often as practicable in summer. The city did its own collection in East Rock, the nine squares, Dixwell, and Newhallville ("high-class and middle-class residential" in the argot of the time). This garbage was hauled three miles to Springside Farms for consumption at its piggery. It contracted out the rest of the hauling to private farmers, who were paid partly in cash (about $5,000 yearly) and partly in usable pig food. The 1916 reports indicate trouble keeping help, "owing to the unusual wages paid by close-by factories." Complaints and lapses of service are counted and reported, indicating modest improvement in 1915 and 1916.

Sewers: A simple sewer system led to Long Island Sound, and it required continuous maintenance. For example, in 1916, 3,620 sewer catch basins were cleaned. This arrangement was, of course, better than none at all, but it was wholly inadequate from the perspectives of public health and marine ecology. Rice and his administration appear to have concentrated single-mindedly on operational issues rather than on these larger policy concerns.[23]

Schools: With a total 1916 enrollment of 28,766 (average attendance was 24,255), the school system was bursting at the seams. Elementary education accounted for most of the total, although high schools represented an increasing fraction (up from 2,360 in 1909–10 to 3,806 at the beginning of the 1916–17 school year). Summer schools were operated for children having difficulty or doing exceptionally well, and a variety of commercial courses (salesmanship, plumbing, drafting, electrical work, pattern making, machine shop) were offered. This was then, as now, the largest department of city government, with something on the order of 1,000 total employees. Private and parochial schools handled nearly 4,000 students in 1916.

Trees: A 1916 survey counted 24,679 street trees in the city, of which nearly 8,000 were American elms, which were under attack from Dutch elm disease. The city removed 536 elms that year; sprayed more than 8,000 elms and other trees; and planted several hundred trees.

Public bath: The city operated a year-round public bath service, with a cumulative total of nearly 80,000 users in 1912. By 1916, usage reached 115,000. This was an important supplement to tenement housing in the period, and the city appears to have met the need well.

Table 6.2. Felony Arrests, 1910–16

Crime	1910	1911	1912	1913	1914	1915	1916
Assault	10	17	17	15	21	13	24
Burglary	92	62	111	107	102	101	67
Murder	2	2	2	3	3	3	5
Murder, attempted	1	3	2	NR	0	NR	NR
Manslaughter	1	3	NR	NR	1	NR	3
Non-support	NR	NR	NR	137	139	124	173
Theft	376	219	433	348	448	388	493

Milk inspection: The milk inspectors conducted 7,239 examinations—of stores, farms, dairy processing plants—in 1916. Of 739 farms visited, 54 were given orders to improve sanitation, and 24 were banned from New Haven markets. Licenses to sell milk in New Haven were issued to 968 establishments, 858 of them markets and stores, the rest route men. Six establishments were charged with watering their milk, and all were convicted of the offense.

Police services: The Police Department grew under Frank Rice between 1910 and 1916 from 146 to 208 patrolmen. By the latter year, a majority of this force had been appointed by the Rice administration (106, counting new officers still in probationary status). The law-enforcement responsibilities of the department included a vast array of crimes, but something like the main story can be gleaned from the extracts provided in tables 6.2 and 6.3.

While crime data are notoriously open to manipulation, murder and its close equivalents are not. In a city that starts this period (1910) at about 130,000 population and ends (1916) at about 160,000, the number of murders never exceeds 5 and only once exceeds 3. On a per capita basis, it peaks in 1916 at 3.2 per 100,000. Combining murder with manslaughter and attempted murder, we reach a rate well below 10 per 100,000—a rate that most modern American

Table 6.3. Misdemeanor Arrests, 1910–16

Offense	1910	1911	1912	1913	1914	1915	1916
Begging	57	64	80	55	34	30	56
Breach of peace	811	1,099	885	1,057	1,254	1,577	1,707
Drunkenness	2,536	2,816	3,000	3,798	3,879	4,221	5,620
Idleness	70	63	79	136	166	168	167
Lascivious carriage	84	103	118	114	234	196	269

cities would aspire in vain to reach. Property crimes are also low. Among misdemeanors, the striking figures are for public drunkenness and breach of the peace—offenses that start high and rise markedly over the period. Did drunks get easier to find, or did Methodist layman Rice's police department get more serious about finding them? We will never know.

Fire services: The Fire Department was both a service agency and a regulatory one. In its regulatory function, in 1916, it carried out 39,007 building inspections, of which 12,741 were reportedly done by the fire marshal and his assistant.[24] These revealed 717 code violations, ranging from unsafe chimneys to the use of wooden ash holders. The marshal also granted more than 700 licenses, the commonest of which concerned the sale of kerosene at retail. The department, with about 170 firemen, organized into 17 companies located throughout the city, responded to 811 fires in 1916, with total losses of $586,031.32 (inflating to about $10 million today). The greatest single loss occurred in the rail yard just south of downtown, where on March 26, 1916, a fire inflicted losses of $233,000 (about $4 million).

Weights and measures testing: The commercial health of the city depended, one supposes, on a degree of trust between buyer and seller about fair measurement of weight and volume. The city seems to have been all over this concern, conducting tests and inspections on more than twenty thousand scales and other gauges in 1916 alone.

Springside Farm: This farm-with-dormitories, located far from the residential city, functioned as a site for "indoor relief" to the indigent sick and aged. Its daily census of population ranged from about 350 persons up to about 480, of whom about 60 percent were men and fewer than 10 percent were children. Up to 800 different individuals might spend all or part of a year at Springside. In most years something like 70 people died there, and many others were discharged or transferred to specialized facilities (for tuberculosis, for the insane).

The farm produced no small stream of food products. Its piggery sometimes housed better than 1,000 animals, and the 1912 output included 6,846 pounds of pork (plus $8,117 from the sale of live hogs), 17,800 ears of corn, 6,626 heads of cabbage, 75,252 quarts of milk, more than 400,000 pounds of ice. The farm ran at a small net profit of $6,492.41 in 1912, although only the very direct costs of operation are counted in the ledger.

Outside poor relief: The Department of Charities and Corrections provided a variety of services and highly specific payments to its "outside" clients. In 1912, it handled 450 hospital stays, 511 doctor's visits, 1,873 grocery orders, 1,072 rent checks, 128 orders of coal, 102 burials, 5 pairs of glasses, 5 sets of braces, 12 orders of medicine. The total bill for that year came to $12,264.37. The rent checks averaged about $5.40 each, the burials $8.80 apiece, the grocery orders $1.48, the glasses $1.12. In the ledger, beside all these gross items, appears the line "Care of Fannie Oats" at $104.54—too costly to be a horse, but what? A mystery to history.

Building inspections and permitting: In a period of rapid growth—with an average of more than 1,000 units of housing being started each year of Rice's tenure[25]—the management and regulation of construction was a hot activity for city government. Typically, another 500 permits would go to other forms of construction each year—stores, warehouses, office buildings, garages, factories, laundries, and all the other spaces required to meet market-driven demand for space in the city.

These services, ordinances, and transactions formed the whole product of Frank Rice's Sidewalk Republic. They added up to thousands of tiny actions—a license here, an inspection there, a new pavement or sewer or sidewalk. A new rule for operating movie theaters—this was the major work of city government. Some, like education and health, stand out in their strategic importance; others, like weights and measures, recede to the background. Nearly all the activities catalogued here are routine, simple actions. Rice's approach was to do them well and systematically, and to control costs to the best of his ability. He used the institutions of city government to the best of his ability, and he used them for tasks they could be made to do. Large, transformational endeavors were not included.

In most respects, this very capable execution of routine government was adequate to the city's needs. Much could be relied upon from the business community, from the civic fauna, from the neighborhoods woven through with stores and clubs, churches and temples, and from a tax base that seemed to grow almost of its own accord. There were, to be sure, strains of conflict between labor and ownership in manufacturing, between Yale and the townspeople, between nationalities, and even between regions of origin within a single nationality (for example, north versus south among the Italians). There were, in the view of temperance activists, too damned many saloons (doubtless true) and too many drunks (quite probably true). There were unmet demands for justice, already forcefully articulated with respect to women's suffrage and scarcely yet articulated with respect to racial discrimination. Yet city government was narrow enough, and ran in deep enough ruts, that most of the conflict in the city was outside the agenda of city government. And most of the highest aspirations for dramatic change were beyond the capacity of Frank Rice and his government.

URBANISM AND CITY HALL

In this era, City Hall was marginal to economic life. It provided virtually no housing, it built no malls or office towers, but it maintained infrastructure and improved it modestly. It did articulate rules of commerce and implement modest enforcement services. It exercised police power and maintained public safety. It regulated public health within the limits of its ability. But it relied in overwhelming degree on market forces, which helped to sustain opportunity, to attract and retain taxpaying citizens, and to allocate resources to the highest bidder. This was the era of urbanism. This was, above all, an era in which "self-governance" very often meant just that: urban society regulated or resolved most of its own conflicts, so that formal government needed to enter into only a few of them. The pressures of centered development, with factory jobs abundantly available, was part of the story. The dense fabric of enterprise, with perhaps three thousand retailers holding down street-corner and mid-block sites throughout the working-class neighborhoods and the downtown, was at once a normative force ("eyes on the street," as Jane Jacobs would say) and a major layer of opportunity for each generation of workers and their families. The relatively thick layer of housing, thickest of all near industrial plants, was of very uneven quality, yet its residents appear to have regulated their neighborhoods with admirable success. The *joint* impact of housing and retailing was almost certainly a critical element of self-regulating urbanism. Jacobs explains this intuition admirably:

Stores, bars and restaurants, as the chief examples, work in several different and complex ways to abet sidewalk safety.

First, they give people—both residents and strangers—concrete reasons for using the sidewalks on which these enterprises face.

Second, they draw people along the sidewalks past places which have no attractions to public use in themselves but which become traveled and peopled as routes to somewhere else; this influence does not carry very far geographically, so enterprises must be frequent in a city district if they are to populate with walkers those other stretches of street that lack public places along the sidewalk. Moreover, there should be many different kinds of enterprises, to give people reasons for crisscrossing paths.

Third, storekeepers and other small businessmen are typically strong proponents of peace and order themselves; they hate broken windows and holdups; they hate having customers made nervous about safety. They are great street watchers and sidewalk guardians if present in sufficient numbers.

Fourth, the activity generated by people on errands, or people aiming for food or drink, is itself an attraction to still other people. (*Death and Life of American Cities*, 36–37)

The dense civic fauna doubtless had something to do with self-governance, allowing people to engage with one another, and to build trust across lines of difference. I suspect, based on interviews with people who lived in the city's worst slum (Oak Street) a generation later, that another whole layer of civic life was also very important. Here I have in mind "organizations" too informal—too disorganized one might say—to meet our understanding of the term "organization." These consisted of sustained relationships between clusters of people, often of different national and ethnic identities, in which familiarity and trust would be expressed by nicknames, often humorous ones, or by casual jokes or by gossip. Often, jokes and nicknames would entail glancing reference to nationality stereotypes, or to the physical and linguistic oddities of an individual. Often, too, members of such groups might exchange small gifts and favors—a cigarette, a bus token, almost any inexpensive item of value—and would cooperate in daily tasks. In many if not all cases, these groups based their affinity on neighborhoods and on the daily routines that brought them together on the way to or from work, to or from shopping, to or from the local bar or snack shop.[26]

Table 6.4. Illustrative Property Tax Bills, 1916

Taxpayer	Valuation	Tax owed
Winchester Repeating Arms	$10,000,000.00	$175,000.00
New Haven Gas Light	$ 4,110,710.00	$ 71,937.43
Edward Malley	$ 1,315,636.00	$ 23,023.63
New Haven Water	$ 1,296,960.00	$ 22,696.80
Sargent	$ 1,296,395.00	$ 22,686.91
Sylvester Poli	$ 843,705.00	$ 14,764.84
Candee & Company	$ 769,419.00	$ 13,464.83
Marlin Arms Co.	$ 741,210.00	$ 12,971.18
American Steel & Wire	$ 709,350.00	$ 12,413.63
Sperry & Barnes	$ 507,510.00	$ 8,881.43
Strouse-Adler	$ 222,780.00	$ 3,898.65
Cowles	$ 202,057.00	$ 3,536.00
Eli Whitney	$ 183,315.00	$ 3,208.01
Raphael D'Amico	$ 16,750.00	$ 293.13
Michael and Christina McGovern	$ 3,600.00	$ 63.00
Carlo Toscano	$ 1,040.00	$ 18.20

At the level of political economy—most crassly, money to support city govern-ment—the urbanist era was also favorably disposed to Frank Rice's needs. Indus-trial convergence meant that large firms, subject to full-rate property taxes, were numerous and large (table 6.4). The $10 million valuation of Winchester's New Haven property in 1916 translates to $163 million in 2002 dollars, while the $4.1 for New Haven Gas Light becomes $67 million. These firms, and hundreds more, derived a large enough economic advantage from central-city locations that the threat of movement to low-tax suburban sites was not yet real. Individuals—grand ones like Whitney, ordinary ones like Carlo Toscano—formed the residen-tial portion of the city's grand list. That grand list seemed utterly secure, and the city government's function was largely passive in relation to it. The market signals being transmitted by decision-makers large and small worked in favor of the city's economy, and Rice's relatively modest agenda was rendered effective by those de-cisions—decisions for which His Honor took little credit, and deserved none.

NOT TRANSFORMING THE CITY

Mayor Rice made no attempt to transform the city, or to take a strategic ap-proach to its probable future. No great effort was made to improve the harbor, or to anticipate the increasingly evident pile-up of automobiles in the central busi-ness district, or to gain leverage over state policy. In a period when surrounding towns might have seen a worthwhile benefit in being annexed to the central city, no such effort at expansion was undertaken. When called upon to confront the New York, New Haven & Hartford Railroad over the disgraceful condition of its New Haven station, he ducked the issue. The one clearly defined case study of possibly transformative policy in Rice's reign appeared in the issuance of the re-port on improvements issued at the end of his first year in office.

In December 1910 Cass Gilbert and Frederick Law Olmsted's Report of the Civic Improvement Committee found its way to Rice's desk. This was a self-confident document funded by the most prominent families in the city and backed intellectually by the national City Beautiful movement.[27] The sponsors of the project—contributors of $100 each—were a who's who of the city's business and intellectual elite. The list began with Governor Rollin Woodruff, Eli Whitney III, and Isaac Ullman and ran to multiple representatives of leading families such as the Farnams, Englishes, Pardees, and Trowbridges.

Among ninety-three "specific recommendations and suggestions" on sub-jects large and small, the report proposed the following transformational changes in the city of New Haven:

- Reworking the railroad infrastructure
- Giving city government control of the harbor
- Limiting building heights, so as to even out development of commercial construction
- Creating a grand downtown thoroughfare and a modest subway beneath the nine squares
- Creating a railroad station plaza with something resembling the Washington Mall running from Union Station to the near edge of the commercial core of downtown
- Widening major street rights-of-way between 85 and 100 feet
- Instituting a systematic plan to reduce automotive and trolley congestion in the central business district
- Separating storm and sanitary sewers
- Greatly expanding the park system
- Establishing playgrounds within five minutes' walk of every home
- Eliminating rear tenement housing

The mayor did his best to ignore the document. At the end of the month of the report's publication, a journalist asked Rice about the main achievement of his first year. The response indicated no inclination toward vast undertakings:

> I think it is for the people to say what has been the most telling event in municipal life in the past year. It would appear ill-timed on my part to take any credit for what has been done. The fact is that we don't boast that we have done any great work. We have worked to the best end with the limited money at hand. The appropriations have been none too large and our endeavor has been to make the best showing with the money in hand. We have attempted no radical improvements, but tried to make a steady improvement in all conditions. As to stating what has been the most important event of the administration, I don't believe there has been any.
>
> If I had to make an answer to that? I should say that our best work, in my opinion, has been done in improving the city sidewalks. The good labor begun on the walks has been continued, and as the perfection of that endeavor has been my particular hobby this year, I am pleased at the result obtained.[28]

Rice was probably needling the City Beautiful crowd in his passive-aggressive focus on sidewalks. Of the many Gilbert-Olmsted suggestions, he seems to have willingly pursued only one—the development of neighborhood playgrounds, which doubtless seemed a practical and politically useful activity. By 1915, Rice had set up playgrounds across the city, especially in tenement districts, and claimed that the public cost worked out to just one cent per child per hour of play.[29]

Why not embrace this ambitious and well-articulated plan? One likely possibility is that Rice didn't much like the City Beautiful ideal. He was a man who devoted himself to *excellence in small things,* to serving concrete and practical needs as ordinary women and men understood them. What use would he have for grandiose civic architecture, a majestic boulevard, or a striking plaza? Rice may have supposed that business interests would build grand architecture if they saw a profit in it. He seems not to have had the slightest inclination to undertake the work from City Hall.

Subsequent events reveal the true extent of Rice's enthusiasm. The following May, the Board of Aldermen established a seven-member City Plan Commission, with the mayor as chair. This was, in effect, to be the implementing body for the City Beautiful agenda and other large planning ideas. Here, Rice doubtless thought, is one more accursed commission to be managed. Worse yet, it could be expected to plan the impossible from an administrative and fiscal point of view. The mayor appears also to have identified this ambitious, transformational work as a thing to be stopped dead in its tracks. George Dudley Seymour, who had initiated the Civic Improvement Committee in 1907, was appointed secretary of the commission; he resigned from it after just a year of service. Years later, he wrote the following account of his experience:

> Mayor Rice was not in favor of city planning, notwithstanding the fact that cities and towns, not just in the United States but throughout the world, were engaged in turning to its advantages. He failed rightly to understand the movement, which he seemed to think was based on aesthetics, rather than on fundamental social and economic conditions, transportation, traffic, sanitary engineering, streets and building lines, parks, recreation grounds, etc. In his annual budgets, Mayor Rice never asked for any appropriation for the work of the commission, which obviously could not be done by its members personally, since it involved expert work in the field, the preparation of maps, the compilation of traffic and other statistics, etc. Mayor Rice would not allow the Secretary to call meetings of the commission, nor would he fix upon a plan of stated meetings. The meetings were called by him, largely at least, at his own discretion and pleasure.[30]

Rice stonewalled City Beautiful to death by withholding necessary staff support, controlling the meetings, and demoralizing its most ardent proponent.

There was hostility in the mayor's attitude for the movement, and for some of those who sought to drive it forward. But there was also something more purposeful.

Rice had a measured sense for the capacities of city government, and he must have regarded the building of a City Beautiful as well beyond them. The financial resources might be raised in part from private sources, but the tax shadow of any serious implementation would be a long one. The required coordination of departments across city government would be a nightmare of administration and bureaucratic politics. The tiny and unevenly gifted professional staffs of his Building and Public Works Department and of his comptroller's office could not begin to perform the heroics demanded by such grand projects. So Rice dragged his feet, closed his wallet, and went on with his more mundane work. And the City Beautiful remained a dream—at least until the arrival of Dick Lee nearly half a century later.

REST IN PEACE

On August 23, 1916, a newspaper headline announced, "Mayor Rice is Quite Ill." It read, in part: "The mayor attended a shore dinner last Saturday and was present at the Press club sheep bake on Sunday. He complained of not feeling well when he arrived at the Press club outing, but the feeling apparently wore off. The mayor joined in the sports, especially in the fat man's race and shortly after became ill. It was believed that he had overexerted himself and he went to his home. Dr. Gompertz was called in and at once diagnosed the case as one of ptomaine poisoning."[31]

The following week Rice seems to have broken down physically and emotionally, losing control of himself during a Board of Finance meeting. Shortly after, the mayor was taken to his family's farm in Monroe, Connecticut. While Rice managed to visit City Hall in December 1916, he never again worked a day as mayor. By year's end he was diagnosed with gall-bladder trouble, and an operation was performed. The incision failed to heal, and Rice never recovered. He died on January 17, 1917.

A great outpouring of grief followed, with some twenty thousand citizens filing through the aldermanic chamber to view Rice's body. A massive funeral was held in Yale's Woolsey Hall, with dignitaries from far and wide in attendance, including President William Howard Taft. The day after his death, the *Register* wrote: "New Haven never had a mayor like Frank Rice. Others have come

up to the chief office in the gift of the city by way of politics. He was chosen by reason of an almost spontaneous demand for a man of the people, who would de-
vote himself to honest administration of their affairs, to give every person in the
city, from greatest to least, a square deal. He was given a trial on that ground and
he made good. . . . His return to the office for a third and fourth term, after a
manner unprecedented in the political history of New Haven, was an evidence of
the faith and gratitude of the people of the city."[32]

Frank Rice was a good man and a devoted public servant. Whether by luck or
by wisdom, he chose to use the very limited power of city government to accomplish the thousands of routine tasks for which it was well suited. Clean milk almost always reached the city, and dirty milk usually did not. All the streets were
swept, and some were paved. The schools were filled with students and well-
trained teachers from the area. Playgrounds were established wherever children
lived so they could play with minimal supervision. The city kept its taxes low and
gave contracts to the lowest bidder. Laws were mostly enforced, fires were fought
efficiently, and violent crime was rare. The library lent its books by the thousands, and the parks were by and large well kept. Thousands of trees were
planted, while tens of thousands were pruned and sprayed. The city grew larger
and richer year by year. And, true to his inaugural promise, the city's sidewalks
grew longer, more uniform, and more serviceable as the years passed.

At the same time, the forces of centering development pressed inward on New
Haven, funneling investment toward the city core, and urbanism flourished.
The rail junction and yard facilities in New Haven supported a powerful armory
of manufacturing plants that sent products away and brought back money in
their place. Steam made by coal-generated energy gave further advantage to a
central location, only a little threatened by the growing potential of electrical distribution to distant sites. Great quantities of labor were required wherever manufacturing took place and brought work to local residents. A tightly woven fabric
of enterprise stretched across the city, running from the downtown center of
commerce and urbanity through hundreds of corner stores, saloons, billiard
halls, and laundries. Civic life was filled with energy, with hundreds of clubs
competing for time in the lives of thousands of citizens, with sport and entertainment abundant and spread out across the neighborhoods. Churches and
temples stood in their traditional places, and new ones appeared yearly to organize the lives of congregations living nearby.

The city's economic and social strength was an inherited fortune. Frank Rice
and City Hall did not create all this, and the city fathers did not worry overmuch

about sustaining it. But no benign "invisible hand" would tend this inheritance following Rice's death. Centering forces would press with a lighter touch in every passing month in the decades to come. On August 25, 1916, less than a week after Rice's illness began, a full-page ad ran in the *Register*.[33] It began, in seventy-two-point type, thus:

300 Lots Have Been Sold in New Haven's Beautiful New Suburb in Six Days.
Racebrook Estates
Plenty of Good Locations Still to be Had—if you buy at once
6 Month's Subscription to the New Haven Register Secures One of these Lots for
$59
(Choice and Corner Lots Slightly Higher)
Terms: $5.00 Down, $1.00 Weekly

The ad goes on in smaller type to foretell the future:

Every block will be divided into building lots. Streets are being cut through, graded; shade trees planted and other improvements. Property restricted to desirable people. There will be a warranty deed given to every lot. The title will be perfect, and even the taxes will be paid. You can build upon it, you can sell it, you can do what you please with it. You can go in in family groups, or get as much as ten thousand square feet of it together. Different families can go in together and own a whole block if they wish, so long as no more than four lots go to one family.

On the following Sunday, the *Register* ran another big ad offering "free motor cars" leaving the corner of Church and Chapel by the downtown Green every hour from 10 A.M. to 4 P.M. to visit Racebrook Estates, boldly described as "New Haven's Next Big Restricted Suburb."[34]

As John Stilgoe asks, "If the Irish were right to desert an island struck by famine and misrule rather than rebelling against the English, why should they not have begun deserting eastern American cities in the 1920s, when a number of complex issues seemingly defied solution?"[35] At just about the same moment, one might have asked rhetorically whether Henry Ford might be expected to limit production of his Model T, once sales passed 700,000 per year, so as not to pose intractable problems for those very cities. Or whether Westinghouse Electric should forgo the opportunity to wrap the continent in a grid of alternating current that would change the economics of energy distribution, and of land development, irrevocably. Or whether there would be anything to do about the coming of large retailers who would tear out a city's fabric of enterprise. Or just how great a hierarchy of residential inequality could be built on the "restricted" marketing principles that were at work in Racebrook and a thousand other developments like it. Without answers for these, and for a great many equally hard questions, Frank Rice sleeps on even now beneath a maple tree in Evergreen Cemetery.

PART TWO

END OF URBANISM

CHAPTER 7

BUSINESS AND CIVIC EROSION,

1917–1950

The simple and ingenious pleasure of being in the center of so much power, so much speed. We are a part of it. We are part of that race whose dawn is just awakening. We have confidence in this new society which will in the end arrive at a magnificent expression of its power. We believe in it. Its power is like a torrent swollen by storms; a destructive fury. The city is crumbling, it cannot last much longer; its time is past. It is too old. The torrent can no longer keep to its bed. It is a kind of cataclysm. It is something utterly abnormal, and the disequilibrium grows day by day.—LE CORBUSIER, 1929

Henry Ford is supposed to have said that history is just one damn thing after another. Maybe so, but explanations of economic location are almost always historical, and the history does tend to have a "one damn thing after another" character.—PAUL R. KRUGMAN, 2000

In nearly all we know of precapitalist history, the powers of culture, superstition, authority, and organized violence have been marshaled against the threat of innovation. Capitalism, uniquely among historical economic systems, tilts the battle toward the forces of change: from its European beginnings, "liquid capital proved to be a chemical solvent: it cut through the cracked varnish of the medieval town and ate down to the raw wood, showing itself even more ruthless in its clearance of historic institutions and their buildings than the most reckless absolute rulers."[1] The great urbanizing technologies of the nineteenth century—coal, steam, rail, steel—had built cities and dimmed the already limited economies of hinterlands. The very organizations that financed and managed these urban technologies in America were, moreover, themselves largely creatures of the great cities—of New York, Pittsburgh, Cleveland, Chicago, Boston, and St. Louis. Urban firms had recruited the best (and cheapest) available people from local hinterlands and from the distant agricultural districts of Europe alike.[2] Marketing finished goods across continental distances, they had accumulated capital in the central city and its financial institutions. In so doing, they created vast central-place investments and great concentrations of workers in the cities that resulted.

The economic and technological conditions that formed the "accident of urban creation" in nineteenth-century America had run their course by the time of Frank Rice's death. No longer was power directly generated by steam hegemonic in the manufacturing economy. Rail transport remained important, yet it was soon to be challenged by trucking. Immigration, which had flooded cities with eager workers for decades past, was about to be constricted radically by Congress. The AC electric grid was approaching effectiveness across most urban regions, and would within half a generation dominate virtually all of them—scattering manufacturing, commerce, and housing across once undeveloped plains and valleys. And, of course, the car was revving its political and economic engine, preparing to claim its privileged position in American culture and commerce. As these features shifted, the underlying link between the capitalist forces of change and the needs of cities became less and less positive. The process took something like three decades, but its impact would be felt by 1950 with great force.

Between 1917 and 1950, New Haven would, little by little, grow less favored by the forces of change. It would be more exposed to economic erosion and to the loss of local control over locally sited plants and facilities, and it would begin to see itself needing help in defense against economic change with the coming of urban renewal in the Federal Housing Act of 1949. This is no tale of sudden collapse. Despite the predations of the Great Depression in the 1930s, this is a story of continued economic vitality in the manufacturing sector, accompanied by modest (and often complex) decline in many other lines of activity. It was a time of fierce competition in retailing, a period in which the coming of the automobile disrupted central city life utterly, a time of expanding suburban housing competition against a less and less fashionable city housing stock, and a time of loss in small-scale volunteer organizations. It was, nevertheless, a time of great gain for one critical nonprofit, Yale University, which became more worldly, less local, and vastly stronger. None of this was revolutionary or catastrophic, but it did set the stage for things to come at mid-century.

INDUSTRIAL PRODUCTION AND THE DECLINE OF LOCAL ATTACHMENT

In the years following Frank Rice's death in 1917, New Haven was still a target of capitalist development. The city economy had been running at full tilt in response to World War I spending, and its workforce was stretched to capacity. Heated by the immense demands emanating from the armies of World War I, the U.S. economy yielded remarkable profit spikes for many of the industries crowded into American cities. In 1917, steel plants and rolling mills returned 59 percent on invested capital across the whole of the U.S. economy for that year. Machine tools did 35 percent, while hardware manufacturers returned 24 percent. Metal castings surpassed a 40 percent return. These were great times, especially for major firms in advantageous urban locations, such as central New Haven. Consequently, they were great times for New Haven as an economic city. The major New Haven manufacturers—Winchester, Sargent, Candee Rubber, the railroad—were at or near peaks of production and profit. So, too, were many of the roughly 750 lesser firms located in the city. Table 7.1 shows the manufacturing numbers for New Haven in the 1920 economic census.[3] The muscle clearly lay with the larger firms toward the bottom of the table. Three-quarters of all the value being created was created within the top 40 firms, with product values ranging upward from $500,000 apiece. The 129 largest firms produced more than 90 percent of total product, and slightly more of the value was added

Table 7.1. Manufacturing Activity in New Haven

Annual value of product per firm	Firms	Total wage-earners	Aggregate value of products	Total value added	Value added per wage-earner
Below $5,000	211	105	$ 528,503	$ 375,357	$ 3,574.83
$5,000–20,000	225	660	$ 2,408,853	$ 1,490,634	$ 2,258.54
$20,000–100,000	204	2,175	$ 9,317,111	$ 4,817,746	$ 2,215.06
$100,000–500,000	89	3,879	$17,954,044	$ 9,012,547	$ 2,323.42
$500,000–$1,000,000	21	3,843	$14,915,802	$ 9,484,318	$2,467.95
Above $1,000,000	19	20,212	$ 80,331,234	$44,978,140	$ 2,225.32
Totals	769	30,874	$125,455,547	$ 70,158,742	$ 2,272.42

Source: 1920 U.S. Census (1919 data).

through manufacturing. Those same 129 firms likewise employed better than nine-tenths of the nearly 31,000 manufacturing wage-earners. But the small-fry weren't wasting their time. Value added per wage-earner was actually *highest* in the smallest concerns. With 769 manufacturing firms, spread across hundreds of specialties, there was balance and competitive vigor aplenty. This is a picture of a strong urban manufacturing economy operating in what would turn out to be its high summer.

CHANGING CORPORATE CONTROL OF LOCAL PLANTS

Precisely because of their productivity, these humming engines of capitalism were a grave threat to the city in the decades after Frank Rice's death. The city was to a great extent built around its major firms, and it was adapted to their permanent presence—financially, socially, and governmentally. Dependence is not too strong a term: city government could afford its rococo structure, and its limited capacity for strategic adaptation, largely because of the economic centering these firms provided to it. Tax revenues were secure and robust both because of the imposts levied on industrial plants and because of the returns produced by taxing the thousands of homes and retail establishments supported by industrial wages. The housing stock had been expanded rapidly to accommodate the tens of thousands of working families drawn to the city by opportunities presented by Sargent, Winchester, Candee, and the others. The school system was adapted to the needs of a large and youthful population. What worked in government for Rice and his immediate successors worked to a considerable extent because of the economic juice supplied by these firms. Bank failures had been all but nonexistent for generations, until the coming of the Depression.[4] In a very real sense, the economic governance of the city had been delegated to the private sector, which had for decades acted almost as if there was a coincidence of interest between firm and city. For all these reasons, the whiplash effect of their withdrawal—not just on workers and their families but on city institutions—would be great precisely because they had performed so powerfully since the 1840s.

Beginning even before 1920, a great many local firms, including the largest and most productive, would be drawn out of the local fabric by increasingly muscular and invasive national corporations. Many were reorganized as parts of larger corporations, often headquartered far from the city, and thus escaped the control of locally rooted managers and owners.[5] Winchester became a subsidiary of the Olin Corporation; Candee Rubber became a branch of United States Rubber. Parochial ties to the city came into competition with goals set by national boards of directors and strategic planners hired to promote the overall profits of joint stock corporations. Professional management, trained to see local loyalties and obligations largely as fetters on efficiency, eagerly applied cost accounting standards to old plants and often found them wanting. To a locally grounded businessman, 91 cents in New Haven might stand up as an alternative to $1 in Houston or Atlanta. To a hired professional whose loyalties have little to do with locality, $1 earned after taxes and expenses will invariably beat 99.9 cents without respect to place. This, in itself, had a direct impact on local leadership, turning the focus away from parochial memories and local problem-solving quite dramatically. Senior managers, once grounded in New Haven, would often be supplanted by men (yes, just men) trained to see New Haven as one among a great many cities where any given phase of production and administration might, or might not, be carried out by his firm. His ruling loyalty ran not to a workforce in New Haven or to neighborhoods built around that workforce. It ran instead to top national management, a board of directors, and shareholders. None of these constituencies could be expected to care as much about local concerns as about rates of return on invested capital. This would lead directly and irresistibly to sharp-pencil evaluation of local plants that fell behind other units of the larger firm in efficiency or quality of production. Often, the impact of corporate integration was delayed by many decades: Winchester provides a fine example of both organizational absorption and delayed withdrawal from New Haven.

Winchester Repeating Arms had expanded its New Haven manufacturing plant at breakneck speed during World War I. Between 1914 and 1917 it added nearly 40 percent to the total facility, using short-term debt to pay construction costs while booking handsome returns on military sales.[6] Facing the dark shadow of peace along with its inevitable slackening demand, management turned for help to Kidder, Peabody of New York in early 1919. The result was a firm known simply as the Winchester Company, controlled jointly by these New York bankers and shareholders of the old New Haven firm. The new firm set out to replace lost military sales with a radically diversified range of products, including equipment for football, basketball, cooking, camping, fishing, ice skating, and baseball. This strategy was executed by buying control of eleven manufacturers as diverse as the Eagle Pocket Knife Company and A. B. Hendryx of New Haven, once the world's largest manufacturer of birdcages. The new Winchester moved forward into retailing, with stores of its own in Boston, Springfield, New York, and several other cities.[7] Seemingly mad with corporate ambition, the Winchester Company married up with Associated Simmons Hardware Companies, emerging as the Winchester-Simmons Company in

1922. In 1924, the new firm booked $12,758,035 in sales against $16,735,991 in expenses—hardly a happy result.[8] As Herbert Houze observes, even this was not the end of corporate overextension:

> In late 1926, the Winchester-Simmons Company decided, despite contin- ued operating losses, to acquire another firm, the George W. Dunham Cor- poration, a manufacturer of washing machines, in order to again enlarge its production and market base. Renamed the Whirldry Corporation on Jan. 25, 1927, this division was to prove a loss throughout its operating life. . . . To shore up the unstable Winchester-Simmons Company, attempts were made in early 1929 to reorganize its assets. On Feb. 5, the Winchester Re- peating Arms Company of Delaware was established, and on May 23, the Winchester-Simmons Company changed its name to the Mercantile Securi- ties Corporation. The latter company essentially was a holding company for the former.[9]

The coming of the Great Depression soon defeated this arrangement, and no new investors could be found. Receivership followed. The rival firm, Western Cartridge of Alton, Illinois, was controlled by Franklin Olin and his sons, who had acquired the assets of Winchester of Delaware in order to re-create Winches- ter Repeating Arms of Maryland. Remarkably, the firm would continue New Haven operations for many decades to come. But never again would Winchester be so well-grounded an element of the city as it had once been.

Often, the impact of corporate reorganization on working people is more im- mediate. When the L. Candee Rubber Company was bought out by the far larger United States Rubber Corporation, its New Haven plant in the Hill neighbor- hood was still making more or less the same rubber boot on which it had been founded in the previous century. It was, moreover, making that boot by almost exactly the same batch processing system which had succeeded in earlier times. Elsewhere, continuous process manufacturing had overtaken the industry, driv- ing costs below the plane on which this old plant could compete. On April 26, 1929, U.S. Rubber, therefore, closed Candee and left its nearly eight hundred workers unemployed. For firm after firm there was a growing detachment be- tween the needs of the corporate management and those of the community that happened to have grown up around the plants owned by that firm. In the course of a century, this detachment would hit New Haven hard—with the remorseless destruction of an employment base rendered obsolete by accelerating competi- tion, by the costs of doing business in a city adapted to an earlier era, by high labor costs, and by the unhappy future of energy prices in southern New England.[10]

One might suppose that the Candee story was an omen of immediate industrial collapse in New Haven. The reason so many plants found their way to central city New Haven was the dominance of fixed-path transportation available by rail and ocean shipping. Once the age of coal and steam had begun, it would have seemed folly to locate a manufacturing facility very far from the urban core. As highway transportation developed, and trucking became an integral mode of transportation nationally, we might have expected the central city's importance to decline precipitously. This expectation, like all others based on fast absorption of technology into large-scale industry, was not fulfilled by history.

We find nothing dramatic, just a slow movement involving about one-tenth of the industrial action. We have useful data on manufacturing for New Haven County for the years 1919 and 1947. The county contains several cities in addition to New Haven with long histories of manufacturing and excellent heavy transportation services—four cities in the Housatonic River Valley with a tradition in brass and related metallurgy (Waterbury, Ansonia, Derby, and Naugatuck), and one other with a long tradition of metal fabrication (Meriden). This invites us to divide the county into three sectors for historical comparison: (1) New Haven, (2) the sum of these five older manufacturing centers, and (3) everything else, to which I give the label Greenfields (table 7.2).

The years being compared both follow the close of world wars, making them "up" years bracketing the Depression. The county total of factory operatives stayed essentially flat, falling a total of 1,202 jobs on a base of nearly 100,000.[11] In three decades, about 3,100 jobs left New Haven, and about 3,100 others left the older manufacturing centers. Most of these lost positions (5,057) emerged in Greenfield locations (they were, of course, in many instances, different jobs pro-

Table 7.2. Number of Factory Operatives, New Haven County

Sector	1919	1947
City of New Haven	30,874	27,742
Other old manufacturing centers	54,215	51,088
Greenfields	8,908	13,965
County total	93,997	92,795

Source: Census of Manufacturing.

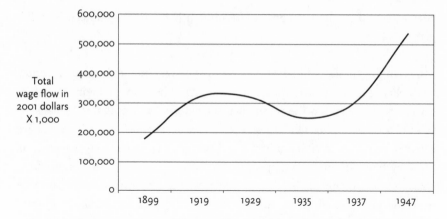

Figure 7.1. Aggregate wages paid to manufacturing operatives in New Haven plants, adjusted to 2001 dollars, 1899–1947, smoothed curve, in units of $1,000.

vided by different firms). The city's percentage of the total wage-earner jobs fell marginally, from 32.85 percent in 1919 to 29.90 percent in 1947. Meanwhile, the Greenfield share rose from 9.5 percent to just over 15 percent. This slow change probably represents the opportunity presented by truck transportation for light manufacturing in decentralized locations where land was cheap. In this era, the technical inefficiency of trucking, the mediocrity of highways, and the heavy encumbrance of Federal Transportation Commission regulations kept this shift as small as it was. With greatly improved highways in the 1960s, the trickle of movement would become a torrent.

This head-count analysis leaves out too much of the story, so I have added a long-term look at the aggregate wage flow to New Haven factory workers from 1899 to 1947, adjusted for inflation. The curve in figure 7.1 represents the number of 2002 dollars paid to New Haven city factory operatives in each of the years shown. It is a story of growth, with a swale representing the Great Depression. In 1899, blue-collar New Haven took home $179 million in wages, and this number grew to $318 million in 1919. Dipping as low as $250 million in the 1930s, the figure reached $533 million near the close of our period in 1947. So, notwithstanding a depression and many plant closings, this is a story of continued growth in the river of money delivered to city streets by the wages of factory operatives. It is a period in which many families experienced excruciating hardship, but it is also a story in which the fundamentals of the urban economy remained quite strong.

The selection of products for manufacture in a capitalist system is, of course, driven by the smell of profit and not by the needs of cities. Profitability, in turn, depends on many factors; but among those, nothing is so important as the lust of consumers for something new and something that frees them from life's tedium. Such a product burst on the scene at the height of New Haven's industrial summer.

URBAN THROMBOSIS

The American Automobile Association, founded in 1902, had established national headquarters on Fifth Avenue in New York and had developed local affiliates in several cities just one year later.[12] By 1908, the AAA had established its Connecticut Chapter in New Haven with fifty charter members. Even in 1903, some fifty New Haven families had registered cars with the state government. By 1910, hundreds of firms, most of them capitalized more with optimism and greed than with know-how and money, were manufacturing cars of every imaginable design—flourishing and collapsing in a fashion reminiscent of the dot-coms a century later. The Adams Auto Company of Hiawatha, Kansas, was turning out what it called "The Average Man's Run-About," and the Belmont Automobile Manufacturing Company of New Haven, Connecticut, was turning out its Model 30. Ford had already flopped with its high-powered Model K (48 horsepower) and settled on its modest twenty-horse Model T. Firms in other lines of business, like International Harvester, were entering the sweepstakes by 1910, and many of the historically famous firms had begun to take shape—the Stanley Steamer (Newton, Massachusetts), Peerless Motor Car (Cleveland), Hupmobile (Detroit), Oldsmobile (Detroit). Daimler (Germany) and the Fiat (Italy) were already selling cars in distant Connecticut.[13] Even so, as Frank Rice assumed office in 1910, it was still possible to think of the automobile as a privilege confined to so small a class of rich people that it would have little impact on urban life. As James Flink writes:

> Automobility remained a mass movement mainly in sentiment until after 1910 only because cars were expensive. Until well after 1910, the initial price of an automobile involved a staggering expenditure for the family of average means. And there is good evidence that prices were not lowered as rapidly as possible. The average selling price of cars produced by the Association of Licensed Automobile Manufacturers (ALAM) went from $1,170 in 1903 to an exorbitant $1,784 in 1905. As long as the early luxury market lasted, most automobile manufacturers, who were able to sell all the high-priced cars

they could produce, spurned the idea of making lower-priced cars at lower unit profits.[14]

As already recounted in Chapter 1, the Ford Model T changed that. Radically improved assembly techniques allowed management to reduce the retail price of a Model T from $850 to $360 in seven years—while at the same time increasing wages and profit margins.[15] From a 1907–8 base of about 7,000 cars, Ford thus achieved more than 110:1 expansion of sales. In the 1916–17 season, Ford rolled out 785,000 Model T's, each of which required only about 25 percent of the man-hours that had gone into the same vehicle a decade earlier. Each such car, selling for an astonishingly low price when compared with the then-recent past, became a weapon of disruptive technology for American cities—cities formed around earlier modes of transportation in which fixed-path travel was dominant. Here was the ultimate in variable-path transportation, going left or right, fast or slow, at the driver's whim. As Edith Wharton would rhapsodize, "Freeing us from the compulsions and contacts of the railway, the bondage of fixed hours and the beaten track, the approach to each town through the area of desolation and ugliness created by the railway itself, [the automobile] has given us back the wonder, the adventure, and the novelty of our posting grandparents."[16]

By the 1920s, New Haven would have more than fifty car and truck *dealerships* inside its city limits. Some appear to have been sales branches belonging to manufacturers, as with the Adams Motor Company's outlet on George Street. Others, like Superior Chevrolet of Crown Street, look to have been franchise operations. Many dealerships were devoted to brands soon to perish—Franklin, Jordan, Reo, Adams Air Cooled, Bay State, and Oakland. Others were given to products having longer futures, like Studebaker and Packard. Most notably, Ford had already developed a considerable depth of sales and service in New Haven by mid-1920s: Buell and Hines on Chapel Street sold new Fords, backed up by Mahouts Ford Repair Shop on Park Street, New Haven Ford Repair on Elm Street, and the Rent-a-Ford Company on lower Whitney Avenue.

The burgeoning market in used cars would extend the reach of the car lower and lower in the class structure of New Haven and other similar cities. In early 1929, for example, Cooley Chevrolet of George Street would offer a 1925 Ford at $100, with just $40 down as a requirement of purchase. (In twenty-first-century prices, such a Ford would cost $1,015 and the down payment would amount to just over $400.) The rival Commercial Used Car Exchange on Commerce Street would offer a 1926 Chevrolet sedan for $75 down, a 1924 Hudson Speedster for $50 down, a 1926 Overland coach for $40 down, a 1926 Essex coach for $35

Figure 7.2. Fancy roadster on Dwight Street, 1908. Photo by
T. S. Bronson. NHCHS.

down, or a 1924 Studebaker Light Six for $40 down—with the unspecified balances on "easy terms."

These tiny outposts of automobility, operating in a single city, were by the 1920s universally understood to be part of an unstoppable political, cultural, and economic juggernaut (figure 7.2). A telling article appeared in the *Register* on May 10, 1929. Titled "Motor Millionaires Pay Respects to President," the piece includes a group portrait on the White House lawn, featuring Herbert Hoover and such pals as Edsel Ford, F. A. Seibring of Seibring Rubber, A. R. Erskine of the Studebaker Corporation, Roy Chapin of Hudson Motors, C. W. Nash of Nash Motors, Alvan McCauley of Packard, F. J. Haynes of the Durant Motor Company, John Willys of Willys-Overland, and A. J. Brosseau of Mack Trucks. Only (New Haven–born) Alfred Sloan of General Motors would send junior managers to represent the firm at this occasion arranged by the National Automobile Chamber of Commerce. The great complex of suppliers and complementary producers—in steel, cement, oil, rubber, copper and chromium, plastics, glass and aluminum—could be imagined in the background, cheering on their leading consumers. And one would harbor no doubt that the real estate professions, including both land developers and speculative builders, would find no small comfort in the occasion. They would indeed have been glad to side with Henry Ford himself in saying, "We shall solve the city problem by leaving the city."[17]

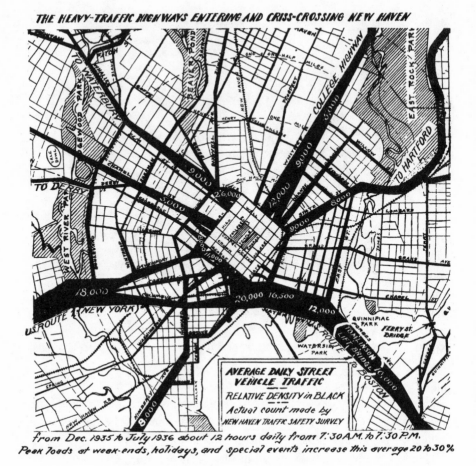

Figure 7.3. Twelve-hour daytime traffic flows around nine-square grid, averages for December 1935–July 1936. Source: Frederick Guyot Dana, 1937.

We often suppose, with justification, that the car's great impact on cities was to drain away residential populations. But its most dramatic early impact was quite the opposite. By the mid-1920s the automobile would begin the implosion on central city streets—a greater and greater crowding in of car traffic seeking access to commercial and retail space concentrated near the urban core in the era of centered urbanism (figure 7.3). In his annual message of January 1923, New Haven's mayor, David Fitzgerald, would diagnose the cause of his city's traffic clot:

> Those who, in the distant past, had charge of laying out our roadways, never for a moment imagined there would come a time when the same would be put to the use, which they are at present. They had not the faintest notion

that in the streets of New Haven, in 1923, thousands of automobiles would be in operation. They had no idea the curb lines of the streets of our city, for blocks and blocks, would be lined up with the number of motor vehicles one sees, as he travels about today. None of these conditions were ever considered by them. Hence the narrow streets of New Haven. . . . The ordinary condition is bad enough, but a very dangerous condition confronts the fire department of our city as it tries to hurry along the highways under the present traffic conditions in response to alarms of fire. The apparatus is met at every street corner by passing automobiles lined up on both sides. . . . Only a miracle has on many occasions saved life, limb and property under these conditions.[18]

Notice that the disruption here consists not in direct competition—car versus city—but in changing the way city space and services are consumed, so that good streets become bad streets very suddenly. The issue is not "car versus city" so much as it is "car versus car in city meant for neither." While the Depression slowed the national and local economies dramatically, it failed to reverse or even measurably depress the impact of cars on cities like New Haven. Depression-era Mayor John W. Murphy (1932–46), who had talked public employees into voluntary 10 percent pay cuts, tried moral suasion (of all things) to solve parking trouble in his 1937 message:

Like many other cities, New Haven has much traffic congestion caused by needless and excessive parking in and near the center of the city. Many persons residing near their place of employment or business in the center of the city, drive cars to the center and park them on the street or elsewhere. They could benefit their health by walking to and from business and relieve parking conditions by leaving their cars at home. No one has any right to park beyond the time allowed by law, and I am in favor of a strict enforcement of these laws as an air toward leaving our streets as free as possible for moving vehicles. . . . No one is entitled to special privilege or immunity from the law in these matters. No good citizen will ask for or expect special privileges. I expect the police to be vigilant in this matter.[19]

Murphy was facing an insurmountable challenge. Figure 7.3, showing traffic twelve-hour flows in 1935–36, is instructive.[20] Nearly 100,000 cars and trucks came streaming into the city center, some seeking to park there in order to shop or work. Others came because Highway 1 running up the coast between Boston and New York ran right through New Haven on perfectly ordinary city streets. By

1947, the city's last Republican mayor, William Celentano, would find it necessary to punctuate his annual message with the topic of traffic, droning on about
increasing the number of one-way streets from thirty-one to thirty-five, about
parking studies, about changing ordinances.[21] But by this point a tone of defeat
would have settled into the discourse, a sense that the automobile had irrevocably disrupted the centered city. Notice that the focus to this point has been on inward pressure, implosion toward the center, gridlock within a framework intended for an armature of sustaining technologies (most of all, trolleys) that were
all but dead.[22] Explosion toward the suburbs had of course begun in earnest and
would be further accelerated by this process of implosion.

As observed in Chapter 2, the era of centered urbanism was supported by an
immense expansion in the total horsepower output of the American economy,
with the total power of the 1850 economy being added every ninety days by the
early 1920s. In table 7.3, we see automotive horsepower in a subtotal of its own,
and as a percentage of total horsepower. In 1900, all things automotive were estimated at 100,000 horsepower in a total of nearly 64 million horsepower—an
inconsequential fraction of 1 percent. As total power increased to about 1.6 billion in 1930, the automotive portion accounted for virtually all of the increase,
reaching 1.4 billion, or 85 percent, of the whole economy. Over the remainder of
the twentieth century the automotive sector (which includes trucking, buses, and
motorcycles) would reach rough equilibrium at just under 95 percent of the total.
A single driver of a high-end General Motors car by the 1950s had, at his disposal,
more horsepower than had run the entire Du Pont chemical works on Brandy-
wine Creek or the Jerome clockworks of New Haven in a previous century.

From the triumph of Ford's Model T onward, this horsepower revolution

Table 7.3. Estimated Automotive Horsepower as a Percentage of
Total Horsepower in the U.S. Economy

Year	Total horsepower ×1,000	Automotive horsepower ×1,000	Automotive percentage of total
1950	4,754,038	4,403,617	92.63
1940	2,773,316	2,511,312	90.55
1930	1,663,944	1,426,568	85.73
1920	453,450	280,900	61.95
1910	138,810	24,686	17.78
1900	63,952	100	0.16

Source: U.S. Department of Commerce.

would drive forward a no less dramatic paving frenzy. David Goddard recounts one critical early step corresponding exactly to the Model T's birth: "As the number of motor vehicles increased six-fold from 1905 to 1910 and interchangeable spark plugs, bulbs and belts let motorists travel far afield, it quickly became apparent that macadam and gravel would not endure the wear of heavy traffic. So from 1907 to 1916, the [Office of Public Roads] built several dozen experimental roads, using materials such as oil mixtures, Portland cement, concrete, paving brick, and even a mixture of blast furnace slag with limestone, tar or asphaltic road oil."[23]

Soon enough there would be a freshly born class of highway engineers, and, with the Highway Act of 1921, a source of funding for revolutionary expansion in the national network. The paving of older roads, and construction of wholly new highways, would continue throughout the century, doubling again between 1950 and 2000. But I concentrate here on the ever-increasing pressure exerted on the road system by the operation of more and more motor vehicles. With the exception of the Depression years, 1930–35, vehicles increased relentlessly through the fifty-year period covered in table 7.4. More cars demand more roads, more roads permit more cars, more cars demand more roads.[24] The great leap on the demand side occurs between 1915 and 1930 with a tenfold increase in vehicle registrations. And the roadways are almost infinitely expandable in every terrain save one—namely, the centered industrial city, of which New Haven is an example. You can, of course, expand highways even in the middle of a city, but only at great cost to the urban fabric (a fact amply demonstrated in New Haven during the 1950s and 1960s).

In Le Corbusier's febrile passage about Paris in the 1920s, we hear of auto

Table 7.4. Highway Expansion Statistics, 1900–50

Year	Miles of paved road	Registered vehicles	Vehicles per paved mile
1915	276,000	2,490,000	9.0
1920	399,000	9,239,000	23.2
1925	521,000	20,068,000	38.5
1930	694,000	26,749,000	38.5
1935	1,080,000	26,546,000	24.6
1940	1,367,000	32,453,000	23.7
1945	1,721,000	31,035,000	18.0
1950	1,936,000	49,161,000	25.4

Source: U.S. Department of Commerce.

traffic whose "power is like a torrent swollen by storms."[25] This hyperbole captures something readily imagined, something near the heart of our lust for cars, but something unrealizable in core locations of the American city as it existed in the same period. The contrast between the individual power of cars and the collective incapacity of street systems was the poison which this implosive phase of automotive development would inject into central city retailing. It was in most places, including New Haven, lethal. Once the automobile set the standard for personal mobility, mass retailing could no longer be conducted in central city locations with what seemed adequate speed of movement, ease and cheapness of parking, and liberty from the interference of traffic cops. The development of strip centers and enclosed malls located on cheaper land outside the city center was irresistible to the mass retailers, and it became part of an enormous movement that would provide consumers with a measure of choice and "real freedom" that was previously impossible to envision.[26]

SUBURBAN DEVELOPMENT BEFORE MID-CENTURY

Aggressive optimism has forever ruled real estate development, and the New Haven suburbs are no exception. Long before the car, and without electrified trolley service, the first long-shot bet on distant suburban land took place. In 1872, two investors had bought up about 175 acres of farmland and woodlot from a Lewis Bradley in the town of Orange, about ten miles out of New Haven. With fervid imagination and no little greed, the pair laid out a grid of city blocks to form what they elected to call Tyler City, although it was never dignified as a municipality by any government.[27] Newspaper ads touted "2,000 Lots in Tyler City," and the maps showed a grid of "Avenues" crossing one another city-style. A central green straddled a railway, and this was the sales angle. The Derby & New Haven Railroad, founded seven years before, ran through the middle of the property. New Haven attorney Morris Tyler, later founder of the electric utility serving the area, was president of this little railroad: Might he not favor a town bearing his name? The Tyler City advertising contained the following forecast of his railroad's future: "Do not forget that the little Derby is destined to be one of the most important railroads out of New Haven. It is the beginning of the parallel railroad to New York City, and also the grand highway to the great West. Those taking up their residence at TYLER CITY will be on the main road for New York City and the West, and cannot help realizing largely in the future by buying now." The developers went so far as to build a two-story rail station at the center of their imaginary metropolis, which Mr. Tyler's railroad graciously accepted as a gift. Alas,

Table 7.5. Population Change in New Haven and Its Closest Suburbs, 1870–1910

Town	1870	1890	1900	1910
New Haven	50,840	86,045	108,027	133,605
Hamden	3,028	3,882	4,662	5,850
North Haven	1,771	1,862	2,164	2,254
Orange	2,634	4,537	6,995	11,272
East Haven	2,714	955	1,167	1,795
Branford	2,488	4,460	5,706	6,043
Woodbridge	830	926	852	878
Suburban subtotal	13,465	16,622	21,546	28,092
Eight-town total	64,305	102,667	129,573	161,697
Percentage in New Haven	79.1	83.8	83.4	82.6

the little Derby remained little, and the eponymous Tyler never saw fit to schedule regular stops at his town. The place never took off, although many of its avenues remain in use, and suburban ranch houses of twentieth-century origin are to be found along them.

More effective attempts at subdivision development in the years before the car were generally supported by trolleys and by fairly close proximity to the central city (table 7.5). Upscale Hotchkiss Grove on the Branford shore set out two hundred building lots in 1909, and they were rapidly developed, in considerable part as summer places for people living as far away as New York.[28] The coming of electric trolleys in 1892 spurred a good many large, near-in developments like Whitney Park (1898) in Hamden, Oaknuts Park (1902) in East Haven, and Campbell Terrace (1896) in West Haven.[29]

By the beginning of 1910, when Frank Rice became mayor of New Haven, 8,319 building lots had been created and made legal in the towns immediately surrounding the city since 1870. Population in these towns showed substantial growth over the four decades preceding 1910, more than doubling from 13,465 to 28,092. Three things are important about these numbers. First, the growth in population (14,627) is much too small to suggest full absorption of the 8,319 building lots, given a household size averaging in this period at least 4.8 persons. Doubtless, many of the building lots went unsold and unbuilt, leaving a fair degree of slack in the supply of approved suburban land for the future. Second, we are seeing no decentralization of overall population. The central city grew by 162 percent over these forty years, and the suburbs, taken together, expanded by only 108 percent. In fact, all but one of the outlying towns were growing at rates slower than New Haven's. One, East Haven, was losing population, due in part to the annexation of some territory from it to the central city in 1897. North Haven grew by just 27 percent, Woodbridge by less than 6 percent in these four decades. The big surge lay in what was at this time called Orange, but which included West Haven until the towns split in 1921. This area expanded by 326 percent, from less than 3,000 to more than 11,000. This is the third observation: namely, that an industrial working-class suburb was growing up just west of the city, a fact which would lead to the founding of West Haven in 1921.

Behind population, and no less vital to cities, is taxable property—the so-called "grand list" of homes, offices, stores, factories, warehouses, and other objects—from which municipalities derive most of their living. In 1870, the city's grand list totaled $41.3 million, compared with $6.9 million for the surrounding towns (86 percent of the regional total). By 1910, the numbers were bigger but in almost exactly the same ratio: $131.3 million to $23.4 million (85 percent). The process of suburban decentralization had doubtless begun, but its fiscal and demographic impact was masked entirely by the continued power of central city development in these years. Shortly, the mask would fall away. In the years preceding 1910, New Haven was the hub of a fast-growing region, with growth at both center and periphery. After about 1920, virtually all growth would shift to the periphery, and the region would grow at slower and slower overall rates.

Charles Guyot Dana lived through New Haven's halcyon days, having graduated from Yale College in 1883 and settled in for a career in town. More than fifty years later Dana published his dyspeptic cry for help at private expense under the title *New Haven's Problems: Whither the City? All Cities?*[30] Here is one passage on the matter of city population dynamics: "Thoughtful New Haven residents were shocked to learn from the 1930 Census that after the almost phenomenal increase in population for the better part of a century their population had stopped growing. . . . This halt in growth of population is the more remarkable because each year over a period of many years the births among New Haven residents have exceeded the deaths, and during the 1920–30 decade this excess reached a total of 14,487. . . . Manifestly a centrifugal force is acting powerfully to carry away our population from the business and industrial centers and the territory adjacent thereto to the city limits and across."[31]

Dana was right, and the city of New Haven grew very little indeed after Frank Rice's time. In the thirty years from 1920 to 1950, the city added fewer than 2,000 people to its Census-certified population, a change of less than 2 percent. Moreover, there are good reasons to doubt that the actual population increased at all (in 1950, for the first time, college students were counted as living in their col-

Table 7.6. Populations in New Haven Region, 1920–50

Town	1920	1930	1940	1950
New Haven	162,567	162,655	160,605	164,443
West Haven	NA	25,808	30,021	32,010
Hamden	8,611	19,020	23,373	29,715
North Haven	1,968	3,730	5,326	9,444
Orange	16,614	1,530	2,009	3,032
East Haven	3,520	7,815	9,094	12,212
Branford	6,627	7,022	8,060	10,944
Woodbridge	1,170	1,630	2,262	2,822
Suburban subtotal	38,510	66,555	80,145	100,179
Eight-town total	201,077	229,210	240,750	264,622
Percentage in New Haven	80.8	71.0	66.7	62.1

lege towns). In the same years, its seven close suburbs added 61,669 people—and grew by 160 percent. Three towns—Hamden, North Haven, and East Haven—would more than treble their populations in this interval. Looked at in more global terms, the eight-town region grew by 63,545, of which less than 3 percent accrued to the city of New Haven. For practical purposes, all the region's residential growth in this thirty-year period occurred at the periphery (table 7.6). Since it was relatively modest growth, as would be expected with the Depression

Figure 7.4. Suburban house, Santa Fe Street, Hamden, built in the 1920s. Author photo.

Figure 7.5. Suburban house, Harbor Street,
Branford, built in the 1880s. Author photo.

to consider, the impact on regional dynamics was important without being revolutionary. It was, however, a strong signal, as the city's population share fell from about 80 percent to just over 60 percent. More ominously, the city's share of the regional grand list dropped from almost 85 percent to just over 61 percent.

The suburban architecture of the late nineteenth and early twentieth centuries is quite often handsome, and the best of it has strong appeal to this day (figures 7.4 and 7.5). At least superficially, it often seems to define the housing ideal of the New Urbanism.[32] The numbing sameness of later tract development is often avoided, and the appeal to essentially urban sensibilities is very strong.

GROCERY RETAILING, 1913–50

The retail grocery of Frank Rice's day was remarkable for three reasons: its being grounded in a specific urban neighborhood market, its role as an element of social organization in even the smallest neighborhoods, and its economic survival in so localized and competitive a setting. With more than six hundred stores in a city comprising perhaps forty thousand households, the average store would command a clientele of only sixty or seventy households. In Chapter 3, I guessed the likely flow of profit and concluded that such a store might generate a net income of about $60 per month—in return for 300 hours or more of monthly operation. Adjusted to twenty-first-century dollars, this comes to $1,077 per month, or just under $13,000 yearly.[33] Broken down to net proceeds per hour of store operation, that comes to about 18 cents then or a trifle over $3 now, about half the minimum wage today. The return is modest, although it was probably attractive to many when compared with any but the best of industrial work—besides, family members unable to command factory jobs (or unwilling to endure them) might have been able to do all or most of the work. Often, these families combined a storekeeper and a factory operative under one roof. But, for all that, such stores faced obvious peril due mainly to the continual threat of new entry into their little territories of operation. In figure 7.6 we see two closely spaced houses left over from the Rice era in the Fair Haven neighborhood (183 Saltonstall on the left, 185 and 187 Saltonstall on the right). In 1913, both structures housed groceries—perhaps dividing the tiny territory along the ethnic lines suggested by the owners' names, Giuseppe Pappiano and Samuel Adams. By 1923, both men were out of the grocery business, replaced by a Mr. Cuomo, who ran only Pappiano's store. In 1935, the ecumenically titled Paququale Warner was operating out of 187 Saltonstall, and the other two addresses were just places to live again.

Figure 7.6. These buildings in Fair Haven, 183–187 Saltonstall Avenue, housed competing groceries in 1913. Author photo.

While competition at ten feet is far from typical of the period, it captures the spirit of a thing ripe for change.

Store death was a way of life: 329 of the 608 stores operating in 1913 were gone by 1923.[34] This is 54.1 percent of the initial total. Amortized over ten years, and taking compounding into account, this suggests a yearly attrition of about 7.8 percent.[35] I began thinking about this by supposing that the stores located away from increasing automotive traffic would die in greater numbers than those being fed customers by these arterial streets. Just the opposite turns out to be true. In 1913, about 44 percent of all groceries were on major arterial streets—those served by trolleys and soon becoming automotive thoroughfares. The remaining 56 percent were located on (generally working-class) residential streets without direct trolley service, and without much potential for high-volume car traffic. Of the stores located on these major streets in 1913, just 40.2 percent would survive until 1923; among the back-street stores, 50.4 percent would survive the period. And there is an obvious reason why shops located away from increasing competitive pressure, in low-rent buildings that often did double duty as owner housing, survived at higher rates: the lower costs of operation. But their success also had something to do with increasing competition from new stores, and stores of a new kind. There was, in other words, a certain advantage in occupying a location unpromising enough to repel competition from chain stores.

Despite all the extinctions reported, the total number of groceries alive and operating within the city *increased* substantially by 1923. To understand what happened, we need to consider the stream of new entrants who would arrive, and in particular the changing scale and locational strategies of those newcomers. Between 1913 and 1923, no fewer than 555 new grocery locations would come into play. With 330 extinctions and 555 new entrants, the total number of groceries increases from 608 to 833. The net increase of 225 stores adds well over one-third to the old total. To be sure, population is increasing at the same time, perhaps sharply enough to keep the families-to-stores ratio somewhere around 60:1. But, especially in areas close to certain of the new establishments, that ratio was actually far smaller. Of the new entrants, a majority were on arterial streets; and many were very different from most of the old enterprises. The old, utterly local, firms could be content with modest economic returns. With as little as 300 square feet of sales space, owners couldn't dream of ramping up to serve crowds. Yet, capitalist market competition can be counted upon to "think outside the box," and in so doing to upset the status quo over and over again. The coming of chain groceries is just such a story.

The first New Haven A&P store had shown up in 1905, and two more were operating by 1913 (all, significantly, on arterial streets). By 1923 these new creatures had multiplied to two dozen stores spread across New Haven. Two of these were carry-overs from the earlier vintage of A&P's. Three were conversions of privately held stores from 1913. The other nineteen A&P stores were new entries, fourteen of them located on arterial streets. Over the same years, twenty-six locations emerged for something called the Economy Grocers Company—all save one at new locations on arterial streets. This chain was developed by the Rabinovitz family of Somerville, Massachusetts, and would spawn First National stores, and eventually Stop & Shop as we know it today. These were small stores by later chain-store standards, most having perhaps 1,000 square feet of sales area, but they were numerous, held serious pricing advantages over mom-and-pops, and were designed to eat up market shares far greater than these small competitors could begin to match.

A&P and Economy Groceries were, on average, able to command far larger market shares than ordinary shops, and their multiplication must have had a devastating impact on nearby mom-and-pops. Suppose they were able to attract and hold the patronage of at least 250 households each: the 50 chain-store units would absorb at least 12,500 of roughly 40,000 families. This is almost certainly an understatement, but it is sufficient to make the point. There were perhaps another 25 nonchain stores that commanded similar markets, which would take 5,000 more households off the table for mom-and-pop establishments. It is likely that 40 percent or more of the retail grocery trade poured into these 75 or so largest outlets. Yet, in 1923, there were well over 700 small firms trying to survive.[36] One need make no great leap of imagination to suppose that extinction rates would be substantial in the years to come—and this without reckoning on the coming depression in 1929.

These developments were driven nationally by the emergence of new and more aggressive strategies for food distribution. The Great Atlantic and Pacific Tea Company—A&P—was begun in 1859 when its entrepreneurial founders bypassed tea wholesalers, going directly to ocean shippers in purchasing tea, then selling it at prices below everyone else's in the business. Having cut out the middleman for tea, A&P edged into the more general grocery trade in the late nineteenth century and developed a string of upscale outlets providing personal service, charge accounts, and home delivery. The earliest New Haven outlets were of this high-end genre. For our purposes, the firm's most significant single move would destroy these very stores. This was the decision by A&P's John Hartford in 1912 to roll out a low-end version: "In 1912 [he persuaded the firm's other owners] to try a new cash and carry 'economy' store, as opposed to the deliveries and charge accounts that were popular at the time. Competing against one of the company's most profitable stores nearby, the tiny store drove the larger one out of business in just six months! Within two years, 1,600 of the new economy stores opened, an average of almost three per day. By 1916, sales had more than doubled."37

These stores, typically just 40 by 30 feet, proliferated along the arterials of New Haven and almost every other city in the region. Each carried a predetermined array of 300 standard items, many of them manufactured privately as store label brands for A&P (8 O'Clock Coffee being the most famous surviving instance). The store interiors were standardized, making it possible to find the coffee or the baking soda in just the same place whether you were in New Haven, Perth Amboy, or Boston. Relentless price competition, reliable supply chains, and strategic location made these stores formidable machines of creative destruction. This interval, ending in 1923, was the last period in which the density of retail grocery stores would increase in three generations. A major reason for future decline in store density is suggested by the increasing discontinuity between the number of establishments and the total capacity of those establishments. In the 1913–23 period, both numbers of stores and the total capacity of stores were increasing—inevitably outdistancing the town's total appetite for groceries. As the number of chain outlets grew and corporate management learned more about their potential as factories of consumption, it became apparent that the total capacity of a single store could grow dramatically and would come to be seen as a problem of *inventory velocity* (that is, the speed at which stock turns over) to maximize earnings. As marketing historian James Mayo writes of the A&P economy store: "The economy store was designed as a factory assembly line for consumption. Each store was physically planned, stocked, equipped, and furnished with fixtures to be an economy store. . . . A&P was able to reduce construction costs by repeatedly building the same items rather than creating higher costs of designing and constructing fixtures for unique circumstances. . . . It was, in principle, a factory design that was similar to the Ford car factories. . . . Each store was issued a cash register and a small icebox. In stocking the stores, three hundred standard grocery items were predetermined and placed in preplanned positions."38 This weapon thus allowed both for rapid expansion in the number of such stores and for great growth in the velocity with which canned soup and coffee could be swept from the shelves of any single location. As velocity climbed in these chain stores, it doubtless declined in smaller establishments, shrinking profits and provoking owners to give up the grocery trade one after another.

If the chain stores defined a lethal challenge to neighborhood retailing even during the best of times, then the Great Crash of October 1929 and the decade-long Depression that followed presented quite another.[39] Many major firms would fail or greatly contract operations. By June 1931 about 10,000 New Haven-ers were out of work, not counting young people just entering the market for the first time. Many other wage-earners were placed on short hours and reduced hourly rates so that, as Margaret Hogg reports, "about 3,400 families had all their earners idle, and these contained about 10,900 persons of whom 3,100 were children under fourteen years of age. In addition, about 17,850 families had some work shortage."[40] These partly idled homes contained 56,000 adults and 19,000 youth. The basic issue of the Depression was overcapacity for production and falling demand for consumption in general. The problem of New Haven re-tailing was at least superficially similar, turning on an excess capacity of selling facilities and all too limited demand from customers.

The overall density of local retail establishments of all varieties in the early De-pression years had been amazingly high. Groceries, numerous as they may have been, constituted less than one-fifth of all establishments in this city of shop-keepers. We are fortunate to be able to draw on Thelma Dries' excellent statistical study of the city, published in 1936.[41] A survey conducted under Dries' direction, using telephone company data from 1931, yields a grand total of 4,670 active re-tail establishments within a city comprising 39,554 families. Dries correctly notes that this yields a ratio of one store to eight or nine families, and she goes on to explain this remarkable fact by attributing it to the "metropolitan character of New Haven, since these stores obviously served a greater population than that within the city limits."[42] And that was doubtless true for the centrally located de-partment stores and for strong specialty houses, which attracted regional follow-ings for everything from birdcages and recorded music to sporting goods and living-room furniture. But, given that grocery retailing and related lines of busi-ness were growing apace in every suburban location in this era, the regionalism argument has limited range: we cannot fail to see that a thinning in the fabric of enterprise was on its way for many lines of selling. Even without the Depression, retail capacity in the grocery business was growing beyond the limits of the city's willingness to consume. With the Depression, it is surprising that the carnage among retail groceries wasn't even greater than it was. Three generalizations stand out most sharply in this period:

1. *A high overall rate of extinction.* In the twelve years leading up to 1935, nearly two-thirds of the stores open in 1923 went out of the grocery trade (533 extinc-tions out of 833 stores). Of the stores operating in 1913, just 162 remained

twenty-two years later. Spread over the twelve years, and calculated to take account of compounding, the 63.91 percent extinction rate corresponds to an annual death rate of 8.5 percent. In 1930–32, the rate was doubtless above 10 percent per year. This rate of attrition would not be approached until the later decade of urban renewal, 1960–70.

2. *Fewer new entrants*. Destruction was gathering speed while creation was losing it. Whereas 555 new grocery sites appeared between 1913 and 1923, this period (1923–35) produced only 260. The number of new places fell from 55 per year to fewer than 22 per year. Between the growing capacity of chain groceries and the ravages of the Depression, people thought twice, or even three times, before entering the business of selling food. Moreover, the pressure of zoning regulations, now in full force, would discourage many new entrants in or near residential populations.

3. *A peak period for central city chain stores*. The number of chain stores increased from 58 at the beginning of this period to 106 in 1930, then fell off to 87 by 1935. This was, doubtless, the high-water mark for New Haven chain grocery retailing, with forty-nine A&P stores, thirty-six First Nationals, and twenty-one Logan Brothers outlets in 1930. New Haven was in no way exceptional. A&P, for instance, was a dominant feature of the nation's popular culture, sponsoring *Women's Day* magazine and the A&P Red Circle Orchestra on network radio. By the early 1930s, nevertheless, local numbers had begun to decline, with the closing of nearly two dozen chain outlets, some from each of the companies. These closings no doubt reflected the harsh conditions of Depression-era retailing, but they also foreshadowed a strategic change in the food distribution business. Companies began to recognize that large economies of scale were achievable not just in the production and warehousing of foodstuffs but also in the point of sale. A trend toward fewer, larger stores was the result. During the 1930s, A&P abandoned its economy store model in favor of a larger-scale layout. The result was that the company began closing stores at the rate of six to one as their superstores opened.[43]

These three developments are intertwined. The coming of chain retailing was driven to mass scale less by very large stores (of the kind we all know today) than by many stores just large enough to outdo the existing private shops in urban neighborhoods. The sheer numbers of chain deployments were equivalent to a systematic assault on mom-and-pop fauna. Almost all the chain outlets were placed on arterial streets to take advantage of the automobile and the trolley system—often both at once on thoroughfares like Dixwell, Whalley, and Congress

Avenues, and State Street. Here, for instance, are the addresses of 1930 chain stores on Dixwell Avenue: A&P (101), Logan Brothers (203), A&P (241), A&P (505), A&P (643), A&P (738). Whalley Avenue was similarly littered with chain stores spaced about three blocks apart. The densely working-class Hill neighborhood (south of the nine squares, cleaved by Congress Avenue) was riddled with chain outlets. These stores offered standardized products in uniform packaging at comparatively low prices, and they were visible wherever brisk traffic could be found. The erosive impact of chain stores on neighborhood retailing must have been very great indeed. The 8.5 percent yearly extinction rate was doubtless driven partly by the competition of chain stores, and the declining rate of new entry probably reflects a sensible intimidation at the sight of A&P stores on all the busiest corners in the city. Soon enough, however, the chain outlets themselves would become vulnerable, often to cannibalistic competition from their own teammates in the national brands.

In nearly any kind of retail business, today's killer eventually becomes tomorrow's corpse: the suburban eight-screen movie outlet inflicted deadly harm on the downtown stand-alone theater, but if that worked in 1990, why not move on to the next level in 2000?[44] Hence, the eight-screen cineplex constructed in 1985 is driven from the field of play by the sixteen-screen location built a decade later. Similar instances can be rolled out for hardware, sporting goods, funeral parlors, computers, television sets, CD players, hand calculators, dry goods, and sailboats. If a thing is worth doing, it is often, in the heat of capitalist turmoil, worth overdoing. This is especially true in fields of activity—like the grocery business in this period—where barriers to entry are relatively low. The case of urban chain groceries is such a story in the years between 1935 and 1950. Figure 7.7 shows the field of battle among New Haven chain stores in 1950. The open disks represent corpses of chain stores open in 1935, which left behind vacant sites in 1950.[45] There are fifty-four of these, accounting for 62 percent of the chain stores operating in 1935. The solid markers show new entrants during this period that were still operating in 1950—eleven of them in all. This is, in the main, a story about the chains, since 1935–50 was a period of relative overall stability. The overall annual death rate for retail groceries fell just short of 5 percent, a century low. So what became of the chains?

The first, and largest, part of the story is certainly the increasing integration of chain-store outlets into national management. Each store was hooked up by hub-and-spoke supply chains to vast national corporations, among which A&P was an overwhelming leader by 1950—at which time this retail organization ranked second in total sales among all U.S. corporations, topped only by General Mo-

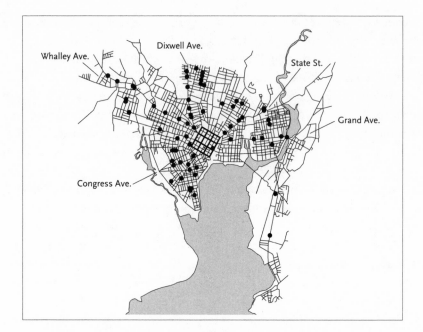

Figure 7.7. Chain grocery stores deployed along arterial streets, 1935.

tors. These companies were integrated across space and across multiple steps of food production. They thus constituted a classic example of vertical integration in a capitalist economy.[46] From the viewpoint of a New Haven neighborhood, an A&P store constituted a large facility, providing a substantial stream of supply to families electing to use it. This was true even of the smaller A&P stores, often 30 by 40 feet, sometimes as little as 20 by 30. From the viewpoint of corporate management, such an establishment would look very small indeed—one of 15,737 tentacles into the national market as early as 1930, for example.[47] For such corporate managers, the two key questions would involve strategic location and efficient scale. By the era depicted in our map of closed chain stores (figure 7.8), both of these considerations would be working against central city locations. As population, and particularly affluent population, moved away from central locations, stores would follow. Increasingly reliant on automotive traffic, stores would gravitate to heavily traveled arteries linking the central city to suburban locations. Central corporate management would, moreover, determine that large economies of scale could be won by shutting down smaller, older outlets in favor of superstores. And in direct consequence, the total number of chain stores would plummet. Where eighty-seven outlets had shared the city in 1935, just twenty-four chain groceries carved up its territory in 1950 (among them fourteen

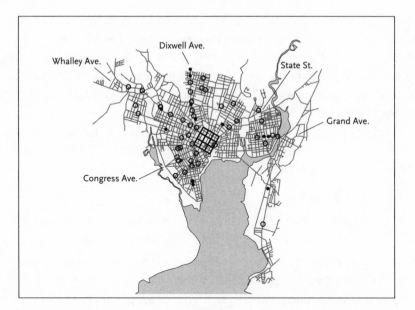

Figure 7.8. Chain groceries from 1935 no longer operating in 1950 (open circles) and chain stores entering business after 1935 (solid circles).

First Nationals, nine A&Ps, and one People's)—a number that would continue in free-fall for another half century.

CIVIC STABILITY, EROSION, AND GROWTH

The urbanist age in New Haven had been populated by a rich fauna of voluntary organizations—fraternal and sororal clubs, ethnic and athletic associates, churches and temples. These organizations were great tools for bridging differences and for practicing skills of leadership. Moreover, the empirical evidence examined in Chapter 5 suggests a wide sharing of these opportunities. Not just the boss at work would serve as potentate in civic life; so, too, would a shop foreman, a machinist, a secretary, or a retail clerk. And civic leadership came from all the city's neighborhoods. This was never a static population of organizations. As time passed, organizations died off, others were born, and a new "ecology" of organizations emerged. In later chapters, where change is more dramatic, I will return to this subject, but here it may be useful to briefly illustrate a few of the strongest patterns for the period leading up to 1950.

Many of the strongest, steadiest, most rooted organizations in any city are religious congregations, and among these, Catholic parishes are among the most steadfast. As Gerald Gamm writes, "Catholics live in another world. For them, it is the parish that names the neighborhood, and the church that names the street. . . . The Catholic Church is a permanent structure; and the parish, rooted in the specific geographical area, is permanently identified with its locality. . . . Parishes are places on maps. They are geographical areas, neighborhoods with names like St. Peter's, St. Mark's, and St. Matthew's."[48]

Parishes were very like political wards in having precise and more or less enduring boundaries. Thus, for example, would the bishop of Hartford write to a New Haven priest in March 1913:

Dear Father Russell:

The territory of St. Patrick's Parish in New Haven on and after April 13th will include all that section of the city within the following bounds:

Beginning at the junction of State St. and Olive St., thence running southwesterly along State St., but excluding both sides of State St., to the foot of State St., thence running easterly in the line of the present boundary to the present boundary of St. Rose's Parish, thence northerly to the . . .

All Catholics living in the above section after the above date will be subject to the jurisdiction of the Rector of St. Patrick's Parish.

Yours Sincerely,

Bishop of Hartford

This entirely routine missive follows the form letter written to the priests in parish after parish, and parishes remained in place like geological fixtures during this period: St. Rose, St. Anthony, St. Boniface, St. Brendan, St. John, St. Joseph, St. Louis, St. Mary, St. Michael, and all the others from 1917 that were still in place in 1950. Others were added, sometimes carving out territory from existing parishes, as with St. Aedan's subtraction from St. Mary's catchment. Others spread toward suburban development, as with Our Lady of Pompeii in East Haven and St. Barnabas in North Haven.

Judging by the Congregationalists, the Protestants were fairly stable but a little less so than the Catholics. Thus, the great old Center Church, the Church of the Redeemer, the Dixwell Congregational, Pilgrim Congregational, and many others stood their ground while others vanished—Plymouth, Howard Avenue, and the Italian Congregationalists from Greene Street. The Jewish temples were similarly stable, as Mishkan Israel, B'nai Jacob, Sheveth Achim, and a few other older synagogues stayed put while a few smaller congregations vanished or were absorbed into larger communities of Jews. Later in the century, both Protestants and Jews would begin to show more inclination to abandon old neighborhoods; but in this period, little changed.

Fraternal and sororal organizations reveal some deep gullies carved by social erosion in the years from 1917 to 1950 (table 7.7). One grouping, the Masons, actually expanded, more or less doubling its number of chapters during these decades while building their massive temple on Whitney Avenue near the Yale campus (completed in 1926). The Odd Fellows and Daughters of Rebekah, and the Improved Order of Red Men, also held their own. The Knights of Columbus, with world headquarters in New Haven, showed fewer local branches but not less total strength. For good actuarial cause, the Grand Army of the Republic petered out. By reason of stunning success with Prohibition, the Women's Chris-

Table 7.7. Chapter Counts for Fraternal and Sororal Organizations in New Haven, 1913–50

Organization	1913	1920	1930	1940	1950
Masons, Colored Masons, and Scottish Rite	23	25	48	52	51
Independent Odd Fellows and Daughters of Rebekah	17	18	21	16	14
Improved Order of Red Men	3	4	6	4	10
Knights of Columbus	10	8	7	7	6
Knights of Pythias	11	9	10	9	5
New England Order of Protection	12	10	11	3	2
Ancient Order of United Workmen	10	8	6	2	2
Foresters of America	9	6	7	3	1
Grand Army of the Republic	7		6	2	1
Royal Arcanum	6	3	3	2	1
Eagles	4	3	1	1	1
Fraternal Benefit League	8	0	0	0	0
Order of United American Mechanics	7	5	0	0	0
Ancient Order of Hibernians	6	5	3	1	0
Eastern Star	6	6	0	0	0
Women's Christian Temperance Union	5	3	0	0	0
Improved Order of Heptasophs	4	0	0	0	0
Woodmen of the World	4	4	2	2	0
Catholic Temperance Societies	3	3	0	0	0
Encampment	3	3	0	0	0
Patriarchs militant	3	0	0	0	0
Patriotic Order Sons of America	3	3	2	0	0
Totals	164	132	133	104	94
Totals less Masonics	141	107	85	52	43

tian Temperance Union died out in the 1920s, as did the parallel Catholic women's organization. After the repeal of Prohibition, they never regained their former vigor, at least not in the northeastern United States. Putting the Masons to one side, about 70 percent of the local branches for these organizations died out during this period without being replaced in kind. According to Peter Dobkin Hall, "The decline of fraternal/sororal bodies, most of them chapters of national associations, was due in large part to the creation of government-run social insurance, since most of these organizations provided a variety of sickness, funeral, and life insurance benefits for their members. Assimilation and the erosion of ethnic identities through intermarriage undoubtedly helped to undermine the basis for these organizations."[49] Hall is doubtless right in these conjectures, though other forces were beginning to appear by 1950 and would lead to a larger discontinuity in decades to come.

Hall's study contains one remarkable finding that will require continued attention in upcoming chapters: the total number of nonproprietary organizations alive in New Haven was remarkably stable throughout the century. Hall counts a total of 605 such outfits in 1910. In no period does the number drop by more than 22, to 583 in 1980, and never does it exceed 676 in 1930.[50] The roiling process of organizational birth and extinction is doubtless complex, but a major feature demands special attention. Hall directs our attention to a "massive die-off of traditional voluntary and membership associations. They were replaced by charitable tax-exempt non-profit service entities operated by credentialed professionals of one sort or another. Entities of almost every type disappeared—fraternal/sororal, patriotic, veterans', labor, PTAs, and religious.[51]

This change was profoundly important in the years after 1950, and it is correlated with a shifting geography of service: civic authority and responsibility increasingly gravitated to credentialed professionals, many of whom were not living at all close to the people they served. Peer civics as expressed in the clubs of 1913 became less important, and clinical civics, if I may use so odd a term, became more so. Social work implicitly replaced social life, as professional replaced potentate. This is a story that became more important, and more obvious, after mid-century.

YALE BECOMES A UNIVERSITY

In 1920, when Arthur Hadley retired from Yale's presidency, it was widely supposed that Anson Phelps Stokes would succeed him. A member of New Haven's 1907–10 Civic Improvement Committee (with Sylvester Poli and the others), and secretary of the university, Stokes was deeply rooted both in Yale's past and in its connection to the city of New Haven.[52] He was perhaps an elitist, but an elitist with local roots. Stokes, alas, had accumulated his share of detractors and was eventually turned away in favor of a total outsider, only the second person ever made president without benefit of a Yale degree. He was James Rowland Angell, a distinguished psychological researcher, a dean at the University of Chicago, and the son of the man who had made the University of Michigan into a world university as its president a generation earlier. Naming a midwesterner—a man with little concern for the local and provincial lore of Yale, a man with no Eli pedigree—was a jolt. As one faculty member put it, many Blues felt "exactly as a Catholic would feel if a Mohammedan were elected Pope."[53]

Angell had no interest in running a local college, or even one that held sway over a whole region. Neither did he suppose that the success of a university could exceed the distinction of its faculty. As he said in his 1921 inaugural, "It will always be true that where the great investigators and scholars are gathered, thither will come the intellectual elite from all the world."[54] Under his leadership, which stretched deep into the Depression era, Yale began its climb from local institution toward the status of a world university. Its faculty grew stronger intellectually, and its range of recruitment broader. The undergraduate college remained central, but the graduate and professional schools grew stronger than ever and began to set increasingly rigorous intellectual standards for the faculty. Law and medicine, in particular, achieved world stature.

The university's physical plant remained that of a college in 1921; but by happy circumstance, lawyer John W. Sterling had given Yale $15 million to do something about it. Angell jumped at this opportunity, and in "the years from 1922 to 1932 so many buildings were constructed and named after Sterling—Sterling Chemistry Laboratory, Sterling Hall of Medicine, Sterling Power House, Sterling Memorial Library, Sterling Law Building, Sterling Divinity Quadrangle, Sterling Tower, Sterling Quadrangle, and (by some strange oversight not called Sterling) the Hall of Graduate Studies—that some observers thought Yale should change its name to Sterling University."[55]

A total of twenty-seven new buildings had been built and eight were under construction by 1931. The university budget had increased dramatically, the endowment had nearly quadrupled, and the faculty reached nearly a thousand members in that decade.[56] Yale would never be the same clubby place it had once been, although a great deal remained to be accomplished, most notably under the later leadership of such long-serving figures as A. Whitney Griswold, Kingman Brewster, A. Bartlett Giamatti, and Richard C. Levin.

The enduring consequences of Angell's period for the city's future were three: that New Haven would, like it or not, be married to a world-famous research university; that Yale would increasingly identify itself with ideas, fields of research, and goals of education, and not with its local surroundings; and that an immense investment would be sunk into New Haven dirt, anchoring Yale to the city even when it would rather not acknowledge its local ties. This last would become overwhelmingly important by the late twentieth century. But in the 1930s it meant mainly that the locals tried assiduously to tax Yale. They would resent its tax-free status bitterly for decades to come.[57]

EMERGENCE OF MORE LOCAL HIGHER EDUCATION

As Yale became more cosmopolitan, a variety of other colleges began to fill greater New Haven's needs for higher education. In 1893, New Haven State Teacher's College had been founded as a two-year program. It expanded to four-year instruction in 1937 and eventually became a large state university campus offering comprehensive curricula in a wide range of subjects. Later renamed Southern Connecticut State University, the institution boasts a student body of more than 12,000 in more than one hundred fields of study. In 1920, Springfield College founded the New Haven YMCA Junior College as a branch campus. Its focus was primarily vocational subjects aimed at first-generation Americans and World War I veterans. By 1926, with some help from Yale in the form of borrowed classrooms and faculty, the Junior College was chartered as New Haven College. It would eventually become the University of New Haven, located just over the line in West Haven.[58] In 1926, the Connecticut College of Commerce was founded in New Haven on a proprietary basis. By 1951 it would become Quinnipiac College, which would in turn take over Larson College, which had served women only, in 1952. By 1966 the college had expanded and moved its main campus to the Sleeping Giant area of suburban Hamden. In 1995, Quinnipiac added a law school, and by 2000 it had become a university, serving students from across the New York–New Jersey–Connecticut region. Thanks to a series of brilliant marketing stratagems, such as the influential Quinnipiac Poll, growing visibility and prestige would make this institution a major influence in the region. The Dominican Sisters of St. Mary of the Springs formed Albertus Magnus College in 1925 on Prospect Street in the East Rock neighborhood of New Haven. This small liberal arts college for Catholic women continues at its original site to this day (and now accepts male students). Taken together with Yale, these institutions would eventually make New Haven an important center for higher education and provide an important share of the region's economic energy.

THE LABOR MOVEMENT'S SUCCESS AGAINST ADVERSITY

The New Haven labor movement, well established by the 1880s, contained an element of revolutionary zeal at the dawn of the twentieth century. In 1899, a respected publication of the New Haven Trades Council contained the following lines of bombast by one George McNeil: "The thunder of denunciation of wage slavery startles the possessor of wealth, opportunity, and position into fear for the structure of society. The lightning of the awakening hate of the unpossessed, and the terror of the earthquake of despair, are the lords of industry, commerce, and finance as unexplainable as natural phenomena is to the savages of the plains and jungles."[59]

Of such idealogical zeal the New Haven labor movement was not made. Its aims ran toward reforms such as the eight-hour day, increased wages, better health benefits, and the organization of new plants and facilities wherever possible. The union movement was fairly strong throughout the first half of the twentieth century, probably reaching its peak in the 1950s and 1960s. As would be expected in the American context, the movement worked its politics through the major parties, over time increasingly with the Democrats, and never formed an enduring political identity apart from those parties.[60] To be sure, in 1947, Socialist candidate Alfred Tong garnered 11,377 (nearly 20 percent) of the total votes cast for mayor. But this was entirely exceptional and has yet to be repeated. More typical would be the case of John W. Murphy, a member and official of the cigarmakers local, who was elected mayor in 1931 as a Democrat. Murphy was a labor loyalist of great energy and ingenuity but with a preference for pragmatic detail over fighting the slogan. Here is an example. When the makers of cheap machine-produced cigars began invading local markets, at the expense of New Haven's hand wrapped stogies, Alderman Murphy was ready with a political remedy:

Murphy discovered that the national company had "buttered nearly every cigar retailer in town with ornate cigar-cutters that ensured retailers' good will and emblazoned the sponsor's product in big red letters." The local retailers informed the local companies that they would "gladly turn back to home industry" if home industry would provide them with cigar-cutters, too. One day, Alderman John Murphy appeared in the City Hall Health Department, demanding that action be taken against the disease menace of cigar cutters. He told City Health Officer Frank Wright that smokers spit on their cigars before putting them in the cutters and thus furthered the spread of every kind of germ. Dr. Wright was shocked and promised to write an ordinance. Murphy whipped one, already written, from his pocket. "But you take credit, doctor," he said. Within a few weeks the Board of Aldermen, on the recommendation of the Health Department, passed Section 559 of the city ordinance, which stated: "No person, corporation, company, or partnership shall provide or allow to be used a common or public cigar cutter in or upon the premises of any public building, hotel, restaurant, theater, hall or store within the city." The cigar industry depression was over.[61]

After his election as mayor, Honest John Murphy became just about as strictly a fiscal conservative as any mayor during the course of the twentieth century (figure 7.9). In his 1934 message to the public, Murphy proudly announced a fiscal surplus of $113,268.36, then said, "I trust that this result will be appreciated by the taxpayers . . . because a deficit would compel the levy of a special tax for its liquidation and would require further borrowing to secure money necessary to carry on. The accomplishment of finishing the year with a surplus required a daily struggle throughout the year to collect taxes and to resist pleas frequently made for additional spending. Contrary to popular but uninformed opinion, the surplus referred to cannot be distributed at this time to taxpayers, employees, or others."[62]

Mayor Murphy was fully capable of angry rhetoric addressed to the mighty—notably Yale, whose policy of purchasing property and removing it from the tax roll of the city was "eating into the vitals of the city and adding to our tax burden by reducing the amount of taxable property in the city."[63] This argument was, of course, aimed at business constituencies and homeowners, but surely not at proletarians at war with the holders of property.

Labor historian David Montgomery recounts another cherished New Haven success story from the Depression era:

In 1932, the Amalgamated Clothing Workers opened an organizing drive in the shirt factories under the direction of Aldo Cursi. Months of house-by-house discussion, followed by city-wide meetings, prepared the workers for a strike that began with a walk-out by cutters in contracting shops and reached its climax when Jenny Alfano and other women at the large Lesnow

Figure 7.9. Mayor John Murphy with Duke Ellington at City Hall, 1939. NHCHS.

Brothers factory of 500 production workers walked out for a month and put that company under contract, opening the way for unionization of every shop in town. In August, the International Ladies Garment Workers, led by Bea Bonefacio and four other women, who had dared to attend its first meeting, called a general strike of dress makers, which also brought every employer to terms. Through local negotiations, combined with intense lobbying to shape the industry codes under the National Industry Recovery Act, New Haven's clothing workers won an average wage increase of 10 percent, together with the 35-hour week for dressmaking; and by 1935, 36 hours for shirt makers. For the first time, women who were not unemployed had part of the afternoon for themselves. Moreover, through their unions, they created singing and theatre groups, educational classes, child-care centers, and, in time, a health-care plan for their families.[64]

Alas, in 1938, Lesnow Brothers moved out of New Haven in pursuit of lower labor costs. Montgomery goes on to suggest what may well have been the most consequential result of labor organizing and politicking in this period, at least insofar as we concern ourselves with the future of the city itself: "The most visible outcome of [labor's] campaign was that New Haven became a pioneer city in the development of federally funded public housing. [New Haven Central Labor Council President] Feinmark joined people from various walks of life in establishing the City-Wide Conference for Slum Clearance and Better Housing in 1937, and after an intense campaign, secured the funds to build the [Elm Haven] project at Dixwell and Webster. The struggle for decent, low-cost housing continued to bring more projects during and after the war. It demonstrated that those who need jobs can build houses [for those] who need homes, if the government makes jobs and homes a priority."[65] This victory would produce much-needed industrial housing in the 1940s and would go to public housing of a different kind and function in later decades.

As elsewhere, the early success of labor organizing lay in the private sector; but during this period, the movement began to make headway in nonprofit and governmental employment. In 1928, a Labor College was set up by Yale faculty, and the American Federation of Teachers Local 204 was formed. In 1941, Yale's service and maintenance workers staged a one-day strike and created Local 142 of the United Construction Workers Organizing Committee within the United Mine Workers of the CIO—an odd link indeed for ivied Yale.[66] By 1946, Local 933 of the American Federation of Teachers was in place for the public school system and would become stronger in coming decades. By 1950, the city was host to roughly sixty local unions, and polite middle-class opinion strongly favored the needs of working New Haveners.

Over the years between the tenures of mayors Frank Rice and Richard C. Lee (1917–50), New Haven remained economically vital, with a net increase of manufacturing wages reaching its neighborhoods annually. This was, of course, rudely interrupted by the Depression decade, and it masks many important alterations in the texture of urban life. Moreover, the rate of expansion was slowing perceptibly—a fact paralleled in the slowing growth of population, amounting at most to two thousand people in three decades leading up to 1950. The automobile took command of local infrastructure with increasing vigor over these decades; it was wholly dominant by the 1940s. Suburbanization had begun early, even before Rice became mayor, and trolley-based suburbs were important from 1900 forward. The real burst of suburban housing construction came later, in the 1920s. The legal development of building sites throughout the suburbs would create a large degree of slack, ready to accommodate more radical increases of suburban population after 1950. All the same, the 1920s, 1930s, and 1940s saw the city's share of population in its immediate region recede for the first time since the Civil War. Retailing, studied here through the case of groceries, went from a thick fabric of small enterprises to a far thinner fabric of larger enterprises—a history mediated by the evolution of chain-store marketing. Civic life would change perceptibly during this era, although much remained from the past. Most stable of all were the Roman Catholic parishes, changed only by addition from 1913 to 1950. Voluntary organizations would decline importantly in the period and would begin to be displaced by professional service organizations. Yale would expand and mature, moving away from its past as a somewhat parochial elite college and toward its future as a world university. This would make it an increasingly uncomfortable mate for New Haven. Finally, over these years, New Haven's labor movement flourished and began to establish representation in governmental and nonprofit markets.

CHAPTER 8

RACE, PLACE, AND THE EMERGENCE
OF SPATIAL HIERARCHY

Until early 1943, a muddy canal near Pike Road, just outside a hamlet called Pantego, had traced the northern rim of Arwildie Windsley's experience. Never had the name of Frank Rice, or any of the white mayors who came after him, occupied even the smallest place in the young woman's imagination. The suburban lawns of Racebrook Estates would never be part of her life. Nor would Joe Perfetto and his downtown store matter a whit to this child of the agricultural South. Unknown, cold, and distant, New Haven nevertheless loomed before her as a child's bad dream. There had been weeks of talk about a distant city where family friends earned better wages than white people were accustomed to earning in Beaufort County.[1] Her mother and aunt had gone ahead of her and found work already; now it was her turn to follow, and savings from the new place arrived in the form of a train ticket and pocket money for Arwildie's dreaded trip. On the warm evening of Monday, April 5, she was sent north by train, beyond Beaufort County and even North Carolina itself. The nine-year-old's train ride started in the unfamiliar town of Wilson, on the trunk line running up from Florida to Boston and beyond. The Atlantic Coast Line's Train 76—known to the road's scheduler as the Havana Special—all but forbade her the venture: "When we got on the train, it was like 'Never enter!' . . . 'Restricted!' . . . It was like you was sitting there and not knowing where you're going and it was really awful. [Uncle] was there and he had never been that way either so he was all excited. . . .

But then he was a minister and he was looking forward to it. I just wasn't. I was unhappy the whole trip."[2]

Train 76 carried Ardie and her reverend uncle out of Carolina about dusk, and ran on through the darkened silence of Virginia. Richmond, Washington, Baltimore, and a score of lesser towns rushed by in darkness before dawn came near 30th Street Station, Philadelphia. As she tells her story, it is easy to imagine Ardie glued in fascination to the metallic gloom of Trenton, Elizabeth, and Newark, to say nothing of the rush beneath the Hudson and into the catacombs of Manhattan. By late Tuesday morning, Ardie's train ran out of Connecticut marshlands and delivered her to a gray city of 160,000 strangers.

ARRIVING IN TIME FOR THE END OF URBANISM

The Windsleys' carefully orchestrated trip carried the family across many boundaries—from South to North, from farm to city, from familiar customs to a world of strange ways, from ear-friendly dialect to the stilted sound of urban voices. The Windsleys traveled in the vanguard of a great migration, which brought roughly 150,000 southern blacks north annually from World War II's industrial boom until the mid-1970s. The destination was chosen by Ardie's mother, Mary, and her aunt Sue partly because they had heard about high-paying Winchester Repeating Arms jobs, made available to newcomers by the war effort, and partly to escape the paternalism of Beaufort County, a place where being black in 1943 scripted one's place and prospects in some detail, with no apparent chance for editorial revision.[3] They might have chosen any of perhaps fifty northern cities—Detroit, Chicago, Cleveland, New York, Indianapolis, Pittsburgh, Philadelphia, Newark—for similar reasons and with roughly equivalent prospects of success. And, having selected New Haven, the Windsleys could have picked any of perhaps a hundred city blocks on which to establish a home.[4]

While the long trip carried this family across many boundaries in a single night, there remained other lines that fifty years of trying would not breach. Perhaps a thousand other city blocks in New Haven were closed to them, or to anyone else with no bank account, no documented history of steady employment, no ready cash, no property-owning friends, no access to Social Security, and no white skin.[5] Many jobs, including the very best factory jobs, were for all practical purposes beyond the reach of black women and men. It was within these constraints that her mother and aunt had signed the family on as subtenants in an upstairs flat in the heart of a low-rent neighborhood. Ardie recalls the shock of her arrival: "It was at 30 Gregory Street. At the end away from Dixwell Avenue.

And I looked at it and I said 'No!' I didn't want to see anyone else but my baby brother and sister. And it wasn't pretty to me and I didn't want it. When I came in my mother was working. My brother was there, and my sister and my aunt. I knew all of them, but it wasn't my cup of tea."

The flat on Gregory Street stood at the corner of Ashmun Street, which led north toward the Winchester plant, where 20,000 well-paid hands turned out the weapons of World War II, and south to Majestic Laundry, where Mary Windsley had already found work in the pressing room. Just beyond the industrial laundry, visible across the Grove Street cemetery, was the campus of Yale University. By 1943, that cemetery had come to span the full height of the American class structure. On the burial ground's southern edge, Yale stood ready to admit, educate, and credential four presidents—Bush, Ford, Clinton, and Bush—during the Windsleys' fifty-year stay in New Haven. Yale's faculty and administrative staff—virtually all white, nearly all male—lived primarily in a nearby corridor stretching north from Grove Street along Whitney Avenue, in the shadow of the cliff-face known as East Rock.

Dixwell was in some respects a quite ordinary working-class neighborhood in 1943, with perhaps three thousand frame houses—ranging from tiny bungalows to double-deckers—owned quite often by Winchester workers, who rented out the upstairs to help cover the mortgage. This housing stock—and nearly everything else in the neighborhood, including the retailers, the clubs, the churches, and the collective sense of identity—depended on the massive demand for labor generated by Winchester and its suppliers. Its people came from southern Italy, from the American South, from Germany and Russia. And yet it was the heart of a racially defined community within the larger city. As Robert Warner wrote in 1940:

> The physical Negro-town within the city of New Haven is not distinct and clear-cut, as is the social structure. . . . There is no section, perhaps no street block, where white people do not also dwell; and every ward of the city has at least one Negro resident. Yet there is a town of color with a main street, churches, halls, hotel, and movie theater. On lower Dixwell Avenue . . . the most casual pedestrian would notice that he was in Negro-town. It is "Main Street" and at its central crossing at Webster are the hotel, a hall, a hairdressing "salon" for Negro ladies, a Greek ice-cream parlor, a market, and a drugstore, both operated by whites, a gambling den, and a district police station. . . . In the adjacent blocks are barbershops, restaurants, poolrooms, sa-

loons, and gambling dives purveying almost exclusively to Negroes. Stores of all kinds, mostly white-owned, cater to their trade. Dentists and doctors serve them at residence-offices and local undertakers bury them.[6]

By the time Ardie arrived in 1943, the Dixwell neighborhood harbored two well-disguised disasters. Roughly one-third of the Dixwell neighborhood had recently been razed to create a massive public housing project—Elm Haven, as it was called. This project's northern edge was right across the street from the first flat the family occupied on Gregory Street. Winning architectural prizes, and filling up with black and white families by a checkerboard alternation of white and black buildings, Elm Haven was a great initial success in meeting the needs of a very tight housing market. It would, in time, turn into an extreme specimen of HUD low-income housing, filled entirely with blacks, and largely with single-parent families in need of services hardly imagined at the time of its construction.[7] By the late twentieth century Elm Haven would be understood by common consent to be a civic and economic disaster.[8]

The other hidden disaster was the Winchester plant itself. The retail and service economy depicted by Warner was nourished by many sources, only one of which was absolutely essential—the thousands upon thousands of manufacturing jobs in this massive industrial campus. The main Winchester plant would decline, recover during the Korean conflict, and eventually close after having been absorbed by the Olin Corporation. Those with jobs and savings would leave, and Elm Haven public housing—next to the Windsleys' original flat—would be transformed from a temporary residence for working families into the familiar role of public housing today: a long-term stay for people of color living beneath the lower edge of the mainstream economy. The service and retail economy of Dixwell would shrink and decline over the same years. A large fraction of the more successful families—and nearly all of the white ones, successful or not—would leave the neighborhood as soon as resources allowed.

People of color arrived in large numbers just in time to experience the end of urbanism full blast. Blacks had been part of the New Haven scene continuously from the early 1640s, never constituting so much as 5 percent of the total city population in the course of three centuries. As their numbers grew gradually from 1880 onward, their percentage of the city's population actually fell as they were overwhelmed by Europeans arriving in the early twentieth century. This was not just a statistical fact but also a social one, leading to white capture of many economic roles formerly dominated by blacks, such as barbering and waiting tables.[9] In 1880, 2,234 blacks amounted to nearly 4 percent of the city; in 1910, 3,561 blacks counted for just 2.7 percent. By 1940, black New Haven had grown to 6,235 people and just under 5 percent of the total. But at just that time, the white population had gone static: 157,816 whites in 1920, 154,262 in 1940. Between 1950 and 1980, the white population would more or less cut itself in half, from 154,616 to 78,326. Over the same years, black New Haven would climb fourfold, from 9,605 to 40,235. From the 1960s onward, Hispanics likewise began to become an extremely important part of the city's demography, climbing from 4,916 in 1970 to 10,042 in 1980. By the year 2000, Hispanics would reach 26,443, blacks would increase slightly to 46,181, and whites would decline to 53,723.

The end of urbanism is not, in the main, a racial story. The central dynamic of urbanism evolved long before racial minorities became a major part of city life— the centered capitalist development, the thick fabric of enterprise, the habit of living in central city neighborhoods, the rich fauna of civic organizations, the powerful layers of political and civic leadership grounded in the city. The learned capacities to deal with urban life—the social capital, if you will—had evolved in an era when racial differences were very real but fairly marginal to the overall life of New Haven. The long trends that eroded urbanism were all in progress before blacks became centrally important to the city. Centered capitalism was much more sensitive to changing energy costs and shifting market opportunities than it was to racial breakdowns in urban neighborhoods (although, as we will see shortly, race came to be a major concern among mortgage bankers). The decline of urban retailing had a logic that required little attention to race. White flight and decentralized living were sometimes accelerated by racial tension in the central city, but their dynamic was in motion decades before people of color arrived in large numbers. As late as 1961, Robert Dahl would write *Who Governs?* about New Haven and its politics with only very minor notice of what was then its "Negro" population.[10]

One historical fact about race asserts itself in every aspect of New Haven's history after about 1950. The timing of the black migration to New Haven was an economic horror: if the goal was to capture high-wage manufacturing jobs in and near central-city neighborhoods—jobs that could be performed without advanced education—the timing couldn't have been worse (figure 8.1). Just as blacks began arriving in numbers—from about 1950 forward—those factory wage dollars were disappearing from central city New Haven, and from scores of similar cities across the country. Figure 8.2 tells the story.[11] In 1954, the city of New Haven reached its peak in inflation-adjusted wages for factory operatives at

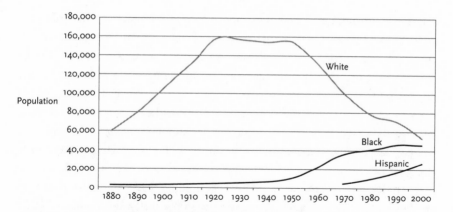

Figure 8.1. Black and Hispanic population growth, late twentieth-century New Haven. White population shown for comparison.

$580.6 million (all figures here are adjusted to 2001 prices). The curve trending downward to the right and the present represents the percentage of the peak total wage flow that remained for blue-collar New Haven. The wage flow falls to 14.7 percent of its 1954 peak, at only $84.5 million in 1997. Over these same years, the racial minority percentage of the city shifts steadily upward, from 9.6 percent in 1954 to 56.5 percent in 2000. In other words, minority concentration has moved in the opposite direction of total factory wage flow for New Haven more or less continuously for half a century. While we will explore the underly-

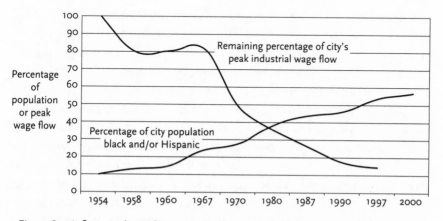

Figure 8.2. Inflation-adjusted percentage of city's (1954) peak aggregate wage flow to factory operatives declining as black and Hispanic population increases, 1950–2000 for populations, 1954–97 for wage flow.

ing facts in greater detail later, it is important here to emphasize this brute fact: as industrial opportunity has narrowed, racial minorities have expanded in the course of half a century. Nor are these small movements: a fivefold decline in wage flow coincides with a fivefold increase in the minority percentage of the city's population.

Arwildie Howard (her married name) is now in her early sixties and living with her daughter in the Atlanta suburb of Decatur. Having spent half a century in New Haven—living mostly in the increasingly ghettoized Dixwell area, working mostly in dead-end jobs while caring for her family (which later included several grandchildren), Ardie says she "just got tired." She had arrived very near the crest of New Haven's population wave in 1943 but well after the most vibrant years of economic expansion, and just before the era of population decline. With each passing decade of Ardie's life, opportunity grew thinner for people living in the Dixwell neighborhood, for her children and grandchildren. Her youngest son went to college, got an engineering job, and moved away from the city. The eldest daughter also achieved a good education and now lives in an affluent suburb of New Haven. The daughter with whom Ardie lives is a police officer in Atlanta. Her other children are still living in and around Dixwell, and all are living outside the mainstream economy. One is an occasional laborer, and another works in a fast-food restaurant or not at all. A grandson is a long-serving prison inmate. Ardie's adult life was spent struggling against the swift tide of creative destruction, at its point of convergence with racial segregation, at increasing spatial separation from an increasingly decentralized industrial system.[12] She had, by the time she left town, lived through the end of urbanism.

When people buy houses, they are also "buying" the surrounding houses and their occupants, the schools, the parks, the access to transportation, even the social fabric that knits these things together. High prices, by and large, buy surroundings people want; low prices generally don't. Consequently, spatial hierarchies are invariably present in cities, in their suburbs, and in the regions they jointly define. But as issues of race become increasingly salient over the decades, we find increasingly important acts of systematization and certification for neighborhood inequality. I review three of these actions—municipal zoning, the neighborhood security studies generated by the federal government during the New Deal, and the initial phases of public housing. All three had at least one consequence in common: to single out what were once thriving working-class neighborhoods and to stigmatize them as inferior to the rest of the city and its region. It is in these certifiably inferior neighborhoods that racial minorities would be concentrated, and on these neighborhoods that urban renewal would act most aggressively after its authorization in the Housing Act of 1949. Since zoning is more familiar to nearly all of us, I will treat it only briefly, reserving space for the very interesting and remarkably bigoted work done by the feds during the mid-1930s, and for the early development of public housing.

MUNICIPAL ZONING

Until the coming of the automotive city, zoning was rarely attempted by American cities, perhaps because transportation limitations greatly constrained the possible locations available to industrial plants.[13] By 1909, a well-developed zoning scheme had been adopted by Los Angeles, that most automotive of places. The following year Baltimore enacted a racially explicit zoning ordinance quickly imitated by cities like Atlanta, St. Louis, Louisville, Oklahoma City, Indianapolis, and New Orleans.[14] These vulgar attempts to use zoning regulation as a direct instrument of apartheid were quickly turned back by the U.S. Supreme Court in 1917.[15] Subtler uses would in the fullness of decades serve some of the same unsavory purposes. An early judicial definition of zoning in its broader use will get us moving forward with the subject: "In its original and primary sense, zoning is simply the division of a city into districts and the prescription and application of different regulations in each district, which regulations are divided into two classes: (1) those which . . . have to do with the structural and architectural designs of the buildings; and (2) those which prescribe the use to which buildings within certain designated districts may be put."[16]

Zoning of this broader type arose initially out of reaction against the negative environmental and health effects of industrial production in the major cities, and also as a device for promoting the interests of central business districts. The single most influential early application was authorized by New York state legislation in 1916, and adopted as an ordinance of New York City almost at once. This powerful instrument of urban policy spread like fire in dry grass: by 1932, 766 municipalities had comprehensive zoning ordinances, and this number included virtually all cities over 100,000.[17] Among the smaller municipalities was the village of Euclid, just outside Cleveland—a place with fewer than 4,000 inhabitants when it adopted zoning in 1922. The ordinance applied to Ambler Realty, which became the object of the suit that resulted in *Village of Euclid v. Ambler Realty Co.*[18] This Supreme Court case still stands as constitutional justification for general purpose zoning across the land.

New Haven adopted its first zoning ordinance in 1926, the very year *Euclid* was decided. One study of the New Haven case suggests, interestingly, that the ordinance was unnecessary or redundant, since the city already had arranged land use more or less as zoning would have it. As Andrew Cappel writes, "A cursory glance at maps of pre-zoning New Haven reveals an unmistakable pattern: most industrial and commercial uses were segregated from residential property. In 1912, over sixty percent of manufacturing concerns, including virtually all heavy industry in the city, were located in a relatively small number of locations. . . . Within these areas, industrial concerns tended to group themselves together in discrete units, separated from neighboring housing. The resulting concentration left other portions of the city completely non-industrial. Thus, in 1923, the northeast residential section of the city contained no manufacturing concerns."[19]

While Cappel overlooks the vital intermingling of small retailing with residential neighborhoods across the city, his major point is well taken. Differential access to heavy fixed-path transport had riveted industrial plants to a relatively small number of places, near the harbor and along rail lines. One suspects that zoning became more salient to city politics in New Haven and across America as autos and trucks began to break down these historical barriers.

I have no interest in judging the overall effect, or necessity, of zoning for New Haven or for any other city. It is obviously possible, by selecting the right stories, to build a favorable case for comprehensive zoning. And a look at Houston, where zoning still does not exist, may tend to confirm the case. It also is obviously possible to build a strong case against zoning using casuistry of the opposite kind. But for the story of urbanism and its relation to the lives of people like Arwildie Howard, we need only to concentrate on two particular effects of zoning. First, residential zoning was an act of government, making official judgments about allowable land use and unmistakable certifications of neighborhood quality. The initial New Haven classification singled out lower-density, single-family detached housing as the template for Residential A zoning, with Residential AA permitting certain upscale apartment buildings to be added to the single-family dwellings. Residential B zoning was more permissive of multi-family dwellings, while Residential C allowed just about any sort of dwelling. Many working-class areas were, moreover, classified as Industrial and Business zones. *Every* place accessible to families like the Windsleys in 1943 would bear a classification below Residential B. Moreover, the very presence of such families would tend to downgrade a neighborhood's classification.

The other major effect of zoning was to shift urban spaces away from heterogeneity of uses. No longer would it be as easy to turn a corner house into a corner store. No longer would mixed-use neighborhoods be seen as an urban norm: the very fact of mixing would consign an area to one of the lower zoning categories and signal a diminution of quality. Often, as suggested by Jane Jacobs, among others, the loss of mixed uses would reduce security, confidence, and real human value in many neighborhoods.[20] The evolution toward regional hierarchy would be nudged forward by these developments. Zoning was a relatively arid version of the spatial hierarchy, and we may turn to another governmental program that was less so.

HOLC AND ITS NEW DEAL NEIGHBORHOOD EVALUATIONS

The Home Owners' Loan Corporation (HOLC) was proposed by President Franklin Roosevelt on April 13, 1933, as part of the New Deal's response to rising chaos in the home mortgage market the previous year. Cascading defaults on mortgages were drowning families and washing away life savings that had been invested in homes. Municipalities were consequently failing to collect taxes just as social welfare costs spiked, and the building and construction trades were in near-total collapse. As economist C. Lowell Harriss writes, "The tremendous social costs imposed by these conditions of deep depression are vividly and movingly revealed in the files of the Home Owners' Loan Corporation. Demands for direct action by the government were insistent and nearly unanimous. On April 13, 1933, President Roosevelt sent each house of Congress a short message urging passage of legislation that would (1) protect the small home owner from foreclosure; (2) relieve him of part 'of the burden of excessive interest and principal payments incurred during the period of higher values and higher earning power'; (3) declare that it was a national policy to protect home ownership."[21]

Given the severity of the collapse and FDR's immense popularity, it is hardly surprising that Congress voted out the Home Owners' Loan Act just two months later, on June 13. Within a few months, the government established a HOLC presence in each state, set up 208 branch offices, and had appraisers available to work in each of the nation's 3,000-plus counties. In that first summer, HOLC received over 400,000 applications for help from homeowners, a total that would reach 1,884,356 by the close of initial applications in June 1935. Something like twenty thousand staff members were hired to address this Sisyphean task under exceedingly difficult economic conditions. Some of these were doubtless ill-equipped for the work: "Political pressure was at times effective in getting appointments for men with slight competence and insufficient objectivity."[22] In total, HOLC refinanced 1,017,821 homes at an average amount of over $3,000 apiece—more than $3 billion in total.

As the agency matured it began to produce regional studies of housing markets for city after city across much of the country, and these were classic exercises in "redlining" of neighborhoods deemed too risky to justify private mortgage credit secured by residential property. In October 1937, a team of HOLC appraisers fanned out across New Haven and its immediate suburbs, evaluating close to fifty neighborhoods as credit risks for home mortgages. Section I of the New Haven study explains the purpose and nomenclature of the work, and in so doing reveals some embedded prejudices:

The purpose of the Residential Security Map is to graphically reflect the trend of desirability in neighborhoods from a residential viewpoint. Four classifications are used by the legend, namely: First, Second, Third, and Fourth. The code letters are A, B, C, and D, and Green, Blue, Yellow, and Red respectively. In establishing the grade of an area, such factors as these are considered: intensity of sale and rental demand; percentage of home ownership; age and type of building; economic stability of area; social status of the population; sufficiency of public utilities, accessibility of schools, churches, and business centers; transportation methods, topography of the area, and the restrictions set up to protect the neighborhood. The price level of the homes is not the guiding factor. . . .

The First grade or A areas are "hot spots," they are not yet fully built up. In nearly all instances they are the *new* well planned sections of the city. . . . They are homogeneous; in demand as residential locations in "good times" or "bad"; hence, on the up grade. . . .

The Second grade or B areas, as a rule, are completely developed. They are like a 1935 automobile [in 1937]—still good, but not what the people are buying today who can afford a new one. . . .

The Third or C areas are characterized by age, obsolescence, and change of style; expiring restrictions or lack of them; infiltration of a lower grade population; the presence of influences which increase sales resistance such as inadequate transportation, insufficient utilities, perhaps heavy tax burdens, poor maintenance of homes, etc. "Jerry" built areas are included, as well as neighborhoods lacking homogeneity. Generally, these areas have reached the transition period. . . .

The Fourth grade or D areas represent those neighborhoods in which the things that are now taking place in the C neighborhoods have already happened. They are characterized by detrimental influences in pronounced degree, undesirable population or an infiltration of it. Low percentage of home ownership, very poor maintenance and often vandalism prevail.[23]

This evaluation scheme has embedded within it a whole courtroom mob of "hanging judges" for the urban neighborhoods, which still, in 1937, defined the heart and soul of the city, particularly its working districts. To be sure, several criteria are beyond controversy: good maintenance, high quality construction, access to amenities. In each of the following polarities, however, any old city neighborhood is at a disadvantage, usually a crippling one, often an unjustifiable one:

1. *New construction* yields a high grade, and is all but necessary to an A classification: old construction, even very good old construction, is by definition a weakness.
2. *Incomplete development*, virtually impossible in urban settings, is preferred to finished neighborhoods without unused building lots.
3. *Home ownership* is preferred to renting, which is to say that multifamily dwellings are by their very nature inferior to single-family detached houses.[24]
4. *Higher social status beats "lower grade population"*: white is better than black, native is better than foreign-born, WASP is better than Jew, Italian, or Pole.
5. *Homogeneity* and likeness of population is preferred to difference and heterogeneity: one may almost as well say that urbanity itself is a flaw.
6. *Single-purpose residential development*, near but not commingled with shopping, schools, or work, is preferred to mixed use of the kind that was common to older city neighborhoods.
7. *Restrictive covenants* and physical barriers that protect high-grade homogeneity are valuable: openness to difference is detrimental.

Not far below the surface here was an abhorrence of historical urbanism, embedded in a folk theory of residential succession that placed traditional city neighborhoods at the end of a long cycle which begins with the good and the new and ends with the bad and the old. A (then) two-year-old 1935 car is used to define Second (or B or blue) areas as "not what the people are buying who can afford a new one." By extension, Thirds (C, yellow) might be five-year-old cars with dented fenders and rattling mufflers, and Fourths (D, red) would be jalopies ten years off the showroom floor with gearboxes smoking at the slightest acceleration. A areas will eventually become Bs, Bs will decay into Cs, and these gradually become "transitional" toward D areas, where the "things that are now taking place in the C neighborhoods have already happened." What are these things?

They are, to begin with, wear and tear on the housing stock—sticking windows, broken shingles, chalking paint—and Frank Rice's sidewalks losing their eternal battle against tree roots and frost heaves. These deficiencies can, of course, be counteracted through attentive maintenance and an occasional infusion of capital, financed perhaps by a second mortgage—unless, on HOLC advice, money is withheld where it is most needed. Where needed interventions fail to happen, and the stock decays, neighborhood decline begins to gather momentum, and the HOLC evaluation of risk in lending is validated. This is of course the value of new construction: maintenance needs rise with the passage of time. Similarly, having incomplete development—space for newcomers—may be a virtue. Homeownership is widely thought to help neighborhood stability, and there seems no reason to cavil with that HOLC criterion.

But the remaining four considerations—social status, homogeneity, single-use development, restrictive covenants—point to a different dynamic of neighborhood succession, and a less legitimate evaluation. Here, as neighborhoods decline, covenants fall away, allowing in Jews, Italians, perhaps even blacks. Status is lost, homogeneity lies in ashes, stores appear on the corner selling all manner of low-grade comestibles, and there goes the neighborhood. The very idea of an immigrant city, and the resulting cross-currents of urban life, the richness of differences—all these are rejected by the HOLC evaluation scheme. Neighborhoods displaying these features—harboring Italians, Poles, Jews, or even blacks—are to be certified by the highest applicable government authority as inferior to neighborhoods inhabited only by descendents of early-arriving Europeans. Similarly, neighborhoods having mixed uses—with jobs close by, with stores on every corner—are to be rejected as well. It is not as if some George Babbitt of a real estate broker expressed his opinion to a seller, or to his golfing buddies: the bigoted voice here belongs to Uncle Sam himself.

In HOLC's evaluation of residential security, the United States of America is advising lenders against investing in traditional city neighborhoods and is advising against investing even in newer neighborhoods if they are "infiltrated" by the wrong people. It is evident that the attitudes leading to and supporting HOLC's approach were widely held in the civilian population of the period, and to no small extent drove markets for housing. For that reason, one must concede a measure of legitimacy to the work within its historical context. But the *signaling effect* of a governmental study embracing bigoted, anti-urban beliefs contributed to the end of urbanism by certifying the undesirable quality of city neighborhoods and flagging the dangers of social diversity within them. Who took the signals? Those who might otherwise have invested in the city might have bought houses in traditional neighborhoods, might have financed those houses with bank mortgages, and might have located jobs within reach of those who therefore lived in traditional urban settings. The certification of spatial inferiority by HOLC is therefore an important event contributing to the end of urbanism. Let's look at its details, considering examples from the Green top to the Red bottom of the security scale as it applied to New Haven and its region. Let's begin by looking at the areas HOLC found worthy of A (green) and B (blue) status.

THE GREENS AND THE BLUES

In figure 8.3 I show HOLC's top-tier areas and the second-tier neighborhoods with contrasting diagonal lines. The old working-class neighborhoods are in light gray, and the upscale areas from Frank Rice's time are in medium gray. A first observation is obvious: not one inch of working-class territory in 1913 won high praise from HOLC in 1937. Moreover, no area adjacent to working people's New Haven won A or B status from HOLC. Moreover, most of what had been up-

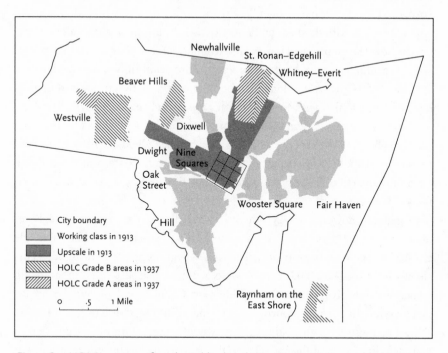

Figure 8.3. HOLC's 1937 preferred neighborhoods (grades A and B) projected over 1913 upscale and working-class neighborhoods. Source: Home Owners' Loan Corporation Mortgage Security Survey, 1937.

scale neighborhoods in 1913 failed to win upscale classification from HOLC in 1937 (the exceptions are St. Ronan–Edgehill, which won an A, and Whitney-Everit, which won a B). The HOLC team is clearly placing great weight on newness and on isolation from difference. With one notable exception, these neighborhoods were reported to be unsullied by heterogeneity of any sort—no foreign influences, no blacks, no relief families. That exception was B-rated Beaver Hills. The summary report concludes as follows: "This is a newer development of which the architecture is varied and pleasing. The houses are not built too closely together and are well cared for. Were it not for the fact that this area is entirely Jewish, it would command a higher rating." The word "entirely" is oddly chosen, given that the same page of the same report estimates that Jews constitute just 70 percent of the residents in Beaver Hills. While anti-Semitism is doubtless part of HOLC's baggage, we will soon see that Jews share a negative image with just about everyone except WASPs of native birth.

Homogeneity and spatial isolation are the common virtues ascribed to all the remaining neighborhoods—from Westville to Raynham on the east shore of New Haven harbor. Usually, this means having been largely undeveloped in 1910–17. Only St. Ronan–Edgehill, already built up by 1900, bowled over the 1937 appraisers with its sheer opulence: "This is by far the finest residential section in New Haven proper. Homes are extremely large and modern. In many instances, grounds approach estates in size and are beautifully landscaped. Extensive back yards and undeveloped land offer a barrier between this and the less desirable area to the west. Smaller homes are entirely owner occupied and the few large ones appearing in the rental market can only be rented at far less than carrying charges."[25] This elite neighborhood had been held off the development market until about 1890 as part of the Whitney family estate, and it was developed into an area of large homes occupied by the wealthy, a status which it retains today.

In general, however, HOLC was a harsh judge of New Haven's neighborhoods. In all, just 0.45 square miles made A, and 1.1 square miles made B inside city limits. The vast majority of New Haven's neighborhoods were adjudged decidedly inferior. The HOLC criteria were of course biased against urban living and toward suburban patterns of development. Of eight grade-A neighborhoods, just two were in the city—four were in Hamden, and two were in North Haven. Typical of these top suburban locations would be a section of Spring Glen in Hamden, just north of the city. The HOLC report certifies the entire absence of Negroes, foreign-born, and relief families in this neighborhood of "business and professional" residents. Of Spring Glen's architecture, HOLC's spotter writes:

"This is a very desirable, residential section . . . the majority of homes are modest and modern. Plots are in proportion to dwellings, and well landscaped and cared for."[26] Six other areas in the suburbs rate B, of which East Haven's Thompson Avenue section would perhaps be typical. This area of "school teachers and white collar" workers is also certified free of foreign or dark-skinned persons, and to entirely lack welfare clients. Of the built environment, HOLC reports an area "ranging from bungalows and one and one half story dwellings to homes of fair size. Plots are not extensive and pride of ownership is generally in evidence."[27] The importance of racial and ethnic homogeneity to these evaluators is apparent across the board. Of eighteen A and B areas, sixteen are reportedly altogether free of ethnic or racial diversity, and all are certified free of the poor. The two exceptions are made for the Jews in Beaver Hills and for a 5 percent "infiltration" of mixed-nationality foreign-born families in one grade-B Hamden neighborhood.

THE YELLOWS AND THE REDS

The HOLC report pushed forward a wholesale certification of New Haven's neighborhood inferiority. Every neighborhood with a working-class history in 1910–17 was classified as grade C or D (hence, in figure 8.4 those earlier neighborhoods are no longer visible, being entirely represented by their yellow and red colors in 1937). In 1937, New Haven remained a working-class city, and that meant a city full of people whose ethnic identities would have worried the HOLC appraisal team. Here are some observations recorded under the heading "inhabitants" in 1937:

- Newhallville's people were "mostly employed in [the] adjacent Winchester plant," none of them "Negro," none on relief, but about 50 percent were "mixed foreign."
- The Orange-State corridor had as its outstanding feature a 50 percent "infiltration" of Polish-Americans, working as operatives in nearby factories at an average income estimated at $2,000. A few families are reported to be on relief. In conclusion, the HOLC reporter writes: "Area rates a low 'Yellow.' Loans are difficult to procure."
- Fair Haven East is said to be mostly a neighborhood of factory workers, 70 percent of whom are reported as Polish or Italian, many of them on relief. No blacks are reported.

These C-level neighborhoods included the bulk of the city's housing stock, and over five square miles of area, dwarfing the A and B areas designated by HOLC.

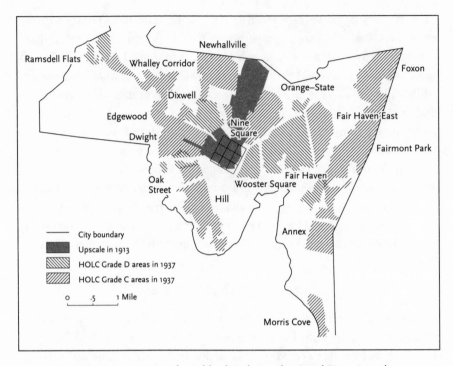

Figure 8.4. HOLC's 1937 rejected neighborhoods (grades C and D) projected over 1913 upscale and working-class neighborhoods. Source: Home Owners' Loan Corporation Mortgage Security Survey, 1937.

One inclusion in the C grade is the lower Livingston Street neighborhood, then as now an important residential area for Yale staff, including myself at this writing. The report describes an area of "white collar and college professor" types, all of them reportedly whites of the better sorts, none of them drawing relief payments. The overview is more favorable than for other C areas: "This is an older section of the city containing a mixture of singles, doubles, and apartment houses, with no type predominating. A number of the singles have been altered into two-family houses and apartments. Plots are of fair size and generally well kept. The area rates a high 'Yellow.'"

Like most other C-level areas, this was a mixed-use affair, with groceries and small retailing close to hand, and factory jobs within walking distance at Marlin Firearms and Raybestos. Interestingly, HOLC reports absolutely no black families living in any of the eleven C-grade neighborhoods. While independent evidence flatly contradicts this finding, it is easily interpreted: for these appraisers, any acknowledgment of blacks in a neighborhood almost automatically placed it in category D, which put the "red" in "redline."

The Dixwell neighborhood, where Arwildie Windsley began her life in New Haven, lies just northwest of the nine squares, directly abutting the Winchester Repeating Arms plant, within shouting distance of the Yale campus. Dixwell was HOLC's idea of a redline neighborhood in extremis. Here is a neighborhood where a 30 percent contingent of mixed foreign nationals constitutes the *upside* of the equation for HOLC; a 70 percent concentration of blacks is the downside. The report summary reads: "This is an older section of the city now given over largely to Negros [sic] employed as domestics. Dwellings vary from small singles to multi-family. Section is quite congested and gives the appearance of a slum area. Absence of market has resulted in some demolition. Section is subject to vandalism."[28] The assertion that the black population consists entirely of do-mestic servants is, of course, mistaken: many were employed by Winchester, and others ran small businesses of their own. The report's author finds it unneces-sary to declare that housing in Dixwell is unworthy of mortgage credit, the point being obvious on demographic grounds alone.

A visible black presence was sufficient to earn a neighborhood a red-zone classification, but other social dangers could also provoke the same harsh judg-ment. In figure 8.4, the "red" patch at the far west side of the city represents Ramsdell Flats, on the Woodbridge border. The HOLC team reports a 100 per-cent concentration of Italians, some of whom were thought to be on relief. Fam-ily incomes were very low, estimated at $1,000, and home values were also very modest, with a predominant value of $2,500. As the report reads: "This is a sparsely settled section containing almost nothing but small houses and shacks, surrounded by truck gardens and vineyards. Its only value is to those who want to go in for small sized farming." The adjacent section of Woodbridge, also heavy on Italian-Americans, got an identical D rating.

The Oak Street neighborhood—soon to become famous as a target of urban renewal in the 1950s—also won a D rating. Here was a neighborhood consisting mostly of frame tenements and multifamily homes in poor repair, inhabited in the main (80 percent) by mixed nationality foreign stock, with a 20 percent "infiltration" of blacks. Incomes averaged $1,200, according to the report, and the "area is given over to the laboring classes and is rapidly filling up with Negros [sic]. Vandalism may be expected."[29] Once again, this was a neighborhood that bankers should avoid like a case of syphilis.

HOLC's area D-5 is unusually extensive and historically important, being a combination of three working-class neighborhoods from the Frank Rice era. It contains all of Wooster Square (including the fine homes surrounding the square itself), the western half of Fair Haven (as far east as Ferry Street), and the smaller Cedar Hill area, tucked between State Street and East Rock Park. Here was the heartland of Sargent Hardware's Italian workforce, and here were the homes of roughly thirty thousand New Haveners, easily the densest part of the city and one of the densest parts of Connecticut.[30] Here too, true to stereotype, were hundreds of foreign-stock marriages producing large numbers of children.[31] This was a largely proletarian neighborhood—without people listed in the social register or *Who's Who*, with just a few doctors and lawyers, and with somewhat fewer schoolteachers than would be expected for so large a population. There were also more juvenile delinquents in this area than in other parts of New Haven, even though the *rate* of delinquency per 1,000 children was not much higher than in the rest of town.[32] According to the HOLC panel, this was "an area given over to the working classes. Dwellings include everything from singles to multi-family. There is a scattering of manufacturing plants. Homes are built very closely together and a large portion of the area is highly congested. Pride of ownership is entirely lacking. Absence of market plus vandalism has resulted in some demolition."[33] Here again, we have the government issuing a decisive signal to banks and their loan officers: this is beyond the range of acceptable risk. No more important certification of inferiority could have been written.

The last D-grade area identified within the city stands south and east of Fair Haven, across the Quinnipiac River on the Forbes Avenue bridge. Like Ramsdell Flats, this unnamed patch is described as 100 percent Italian-American and comes in for even harsher architectural judgment, as a "sparsely settled section of small shacks. Lots include gardens and vineyards. The neighborhood has no value except to those desiring to raise crops."[34] The authors were wrong about the eventual value of this area, which has since become a center for shipping, light industry, and warehousing. They placed the value of homes in this sad area at $1,200 apiece, lowest in the city.

CERTIFYING AND AMPLIFYING A SPATIAL HIERARCHY

As with so many other issues in urban history, the HOLC investigation of New Haven's neighborhoods was intended to accomplish one thing but actually accomplished another. The rate of home mortgage failure in 1937 was down from its 1933 crest, but it was still disturbingly high. HOLC's stated intention in conducting the residential security studies was to steer mortgage money toward economically safe neighborhoods and away from economically dangerous ones. In many respects, the HOLC evaluations achieved that goal through accurate appraisal, given the historical prejudices abroad in the real estate markets of that period. Many of the features that steered HOLC toward high or low valuations were legitimate aspects of real estate appraisal, free of bigotry. Seen in distant retrospect, the demographic bigotry that HOLC embedded in its criteria—toward blacks, Jews, Poles, Italians—is hard to stomach. It is, however, important to recognize that the existence of these prejudices in buyers and sellers, borrowers and loan officers, made them real elements in any effective evaluation. Moreover, the New Deal era was far from enlightened in matters of race. As Arnold Hirsch writes, "Beginning in the 1930s, and continuing thereafter, the operation of national agencies such as Home Owners' Loan Corporation (HOLC) and the Federal Housing Administration (FHA) reflected prevailing segregationist attitudes. Indirectly at least, they furthered the racial segmentation of metropolitan America and inner-city decay by supporting the flight of the white, middle-class population to the suburbs (which, despite government support, remained closed to blacks)."[35]

This larger drama of racial hierarchy is important in its own right as a strand in the ending of urbanism, but my immediate focus here is on the parallel development of a spatial hierarchy, laid out with a governmental stamp of approval. The effect on central cities was not to *create* spatial hierarchy, for urban history had done that already. Working-class streets were already seen as different from the tree-lined avenues of the best neighborhoods: St. John Street was not to be mistaken for St. Ronan, Lombard Street was no Loomis Place, and Mechanic Street would never rival McKinley Avenue as a prestige address. The effect of HOLC's work was instead to *certify* and by certification to *amplify* the distances between the tiers of such a hierarchy.

By certification I have in mind the official, governmental nature of the work, carried out in the public's name, with a view to stabilizing credit markets for the benefit of American families. The HOLC team for New Haven consisted of actual players in local banking and real estate. The bankers were second-tier executives (assistant treasurer, assistant secretary) and the real estate representatives were heads of brokerage firms in the city (the Kauffman and Kelly agencies). These people were doubtless knowledgeable in matters of price and stability locally, and they almost certainly acted in what they took to be ethical fashion. Be that as it may, they acted in the capacity of a government agency, and they acted in such a way as to certify the riskiness, even inferiority, of most New Haven neighborhoods.

The HOLC survey covered only areas with substantial residential populations, and it excluded the central business district altogether. It evaluated about 8.5 square miles accounting for roughly 150,000 of the city's people (of roughly 162,000). Of these 8.5 square miles, 5.3 percent got an A rating, 13 percent a B, 60.4 percent a C, and 21.3 percent a D. Given differences in housing density, this translates to 1.2 percent of the population in A areas, 4.1 percent in B, 70.1 percent in C, and 24.6 percent in D. In effect, 94.7 percent of the people living in evaluated areas were being signaled that they lived in dubious or substandard neighborhoods, and their bankers were getting the same signal. This doubtless made it more difficult, and more expensive, to borrow money for repairs or renovations: a loan at 4 percent in an A neighborhood might cost 7 percent in a C or 9 percent in a D area, if it could be obtained at all. Often, it was downright impossible to obtain money at any price for homes in D-level neighborhoods. As repairs went unmade, and paint cracked without being scraped and replaced, the downdraft would increase. Risk differences would widen as a result—the distance between D and C, C and B, even B and A would grow. These same families—most of them rooted in HOLC's yellow and red neighborhoods—were confronted increasingly with the choice of staying in their homes, or in the homes left them by parents, or moving on to the suburbs. HOLC's certification of neighborhood inferiority doubtless encouraged hundreds of families to move on, and in so doing it further depressed markets in the negatively evaluated portions of the city.

PUBLIC HOUSING BEGINS

Public housing as a national policy got its start the same year HOLC was evaluating the New Haven market. Allen Hays summarizes the early politics:

> The public housing program, enacted by Congress as the Housing Act of 1937, emerged relatively late in the New Deal period. Though there was organized opposition to it from the beginning (led by the National Association of Real Estate Boards), they were unable to block it, due to the wide congressional support engendered by the dual crisis in housing and in construction trades employment which still afflicted the country. However, the program was unable to fully capitalize on its initial support because it had barely begun to produce units when World War II began. War needs diverted materials from housing construction, and the public housing that was built was mainly utilized for war industry workers, rather than the poor.[36]

New Haven was an early adopter of public housing, partly because local labor had lobbied hard for the city to take full advantage of the opportunity presented by federal funding for a construction program.[37] By summer 1938, labor's City-Wide Council for Slum Clearance, Mayor Murphy, and the Board of Aldermen had acted to create the Housing Authority of New Haven (HANH), and its board met for the first time on August 18 of that year.[38] The new authority was independent of city government, although its board was appointed entirely by the mayor—a model followed in most cities that adopted the program. Almost at once, the U.S. Public Housing Administration granted HANH $5.5 million, which was to be devoted to the city's first public housing projects.

The Elm Haven Project No great healer can be recognized for what she is without a great pestilence to cure, and no great warrior can be known in his full greatness without a formidable enemy to defeat. Similarly, no great public improvement can be understood for what it is without a dramatic mess to fix. If New Haven had several HOLC-certified slums in the summer of 1938, its D-level Dixwell neighborhood was the most conspicuous. Soon, HANH photographers were producing horror shots like figure 8.5, showing the dilapidation of existing housing stock, and documenting the racial identity of the tenants with the photo-inside-photo at the lower right. This was doubtless among the worst interiors HANH could find, but the effect was to reinforce the previous year's HOLC condemnation of the neighborhood. Thus did New Haven embark on its long program of federally funded public housing. Constructed at a gross cost of $2,513,162 (or $5,160 per unit, $67,300 in 2002), Elm Haven won early praise for its international style design.[39] *Harper's* magazine awarded architect Douglas Orr a $2,500 prize for the layout, which, the editors wrote, broke with the U.S. Housing Administration penchant for the "stupid, over-regulated, and impersonal."[40]

Yale's dean of fine arts, Everitt Meeks, praised Elm Haven's design for its "eloquent manner," while no less prominent a national figure than Robert M. Hutchins, then president of the University of Chicago, wrote a note of congratulation, saying (oddly) that "I'm sure the Indians would take it back now. Please accept my congratulations."[41] One supposes it must have been said that Dixwell was such a mess that the Indians wouldn't take it back. The design, replicated hundreds of times nationally in years to come, would soon enough grow tired and would become an unmistakable talisman of public ownership in one American city after another. The 487 units were spread across thirty-six buildings, mostly two-story, flat-roofed affairs (five with three stories). Each apartment had an outdoor view, and buildings were set irregularly to give interest and angular-

Figure 8.5. Interior of flat scheduled for demolition to
prepare for the construction of Elm Haven public
housing, c. 1939. NHCHS.

ity to shared space. By 1942, a HANH publication would declare victory over the
Dixwell slum: "Daily since the first tenants moved into Elm Haven on September
19, 1940, . . . the Housing Authority and the public at large have witnessed an accumulation of evidence to prove the economy, practicality and wisdom of what
some realists once considered only a dream—the complete elimination of all
areas of bad housing. Slums continue to be extravagant, unnecessary and un-
healthy."[42]

A panoramic photo taken from the roof of Yale's Payne Whitney Gymnasium
in 1941 shows Elm Haven as a gleaming spectacle of health and prosperity,
ringed by what were then seen as dull streets of duplex housing—just barely
good enough to be worth saving. A portion of the Winchester Repeating Arms
plant is visible upper right, standing ready to welcome Elm Haven's new residents to its workforce (figure 8.6). And work they did. The initial tenants included 169 white households and 318 black ones, racially integrated after the
fashion of the time, each of the thirty-six buildings all black or all white and scat-

Figure 8.6. Newly completed Elm Haven public housing, as seen from roof of Yale's Payne Whitney Gymnasium, c. 1941. Winchester plant is visible at upper right. NHCHS.

tered across the seventeen-acre site.[43] Largely on the strength of jobs in the Winchester plant, the families did quite well: Elm Haven blacks averaged $1,254 in 1942, Elm Haven whites $1,330. Arwildie Windsley's family would arrive the next year, 1943, to occupy decidedly inferior space on the northeast corner of Elm Haven in market-rate housing.

Other Early Housing Projects in New Haven New Haven got a fast start in the pre–World War II public housing business. In addition to Elm Haven, HANH had two further projects in the ground by the end of 1941—Farnam Court and Quinnipiac Terrace. The latter is located on the west bank of the river for which it is named and enjoys one of the most attractive views among the city's projects. Completed in November 1941, this project bears the same architectural stamp as Elm Haven, being also a Douglas Orr international-style structure—flat roof, brick exterior, and poured concrete structure. Its 248 units on 9.5 acres cost $1,224,132, again about $5,000 per unit. Its first tenants were all white, and its relative isolation kept it out of public debate until a long generation after its construction.[44] Alone among the early projects, Quinnipiac Terrace was built in a neighborhood HOLC gave a better-than-D rating (HANH itself rated 54 percent of the homes razed for its construction as of good quality).

Farnam Court was located in HOLC's D-5 area, north of Wooster Square on Grand Avenue, between Hamilton and Franklin Streets. It was therefore located in the midst of working-class New Haven. This relatively dense project put three hundred units on 7.7 acres of land at a cost of $1,565,318. Opening for tenancy in

Figure 8.7. Family breakfast, Elm Haven, probably during
World War II. NHCHS.

February 1942, its early residents were in the main working-class white families
(267 white families, 33 "colored" ones).[45] Even in the mid-1960s the project remained home to more white than black households.[46]

Farnam Court brought the prewar HANH stock to 1,035 apartments at three
sites on a total of about thirty-five acres. All were produced by the same designer,
and all stood in sharp contrast to the architecture of adjacent neighborhoods.
Each project would in time become emblematic of the "project look" that any urban teenager could spot in an instant. Initially, as is suggested by the HANH
wartime photo in figure 8.7, there were plenty of white residents in all three
projects, with whites preponderant in two of the three. Overall, white families
amounted to 66 percent of all tenancies. Moreover, outside Chamber of Commerce halls, little or no stigma attached itself to public housing in these early
years—years when reliance on public housing was understood universally as a
brief phase in a family's history, followed with any luck by ownership of a private
home.

Public Housing and the Emerging Spatial Hierarchy Public housing in the next
generation would take on a far less positive valence for most Americans. As indicated by the figures in figure 8.2, the coming of African-Americans to the city in
unprecedented numbers corresponded historically with an unprecedented decline in the city's industrial wage flow. Not only did this restrict opportunity in
manufacturing itself; it also restricted the opportunities open to small operators

who might start retail stores, restaurants, or custodial service firms. Similarly, HOLC's stentorian judgment of the few neighborhoods open to blacks tended to dry up the credit necessary for maintenance and rehabilitation of existing homes. Gradually at first, and then by leaps, low-income public housing became in fact and fable a black institution, with overwhelming numbers of African-American tenants. This was certainly true for Elm Haven, Farnam Court, Quinnipiac Terrace, and many other New Haven projects by the closing decades of the century. By the time the 1990 reapportionment census was conducted, the most spectacular concentrations of black population at the city-block level were *all in low-income public housing projects*. In addition to the three prewar projects showing up as nodes of segregation in 1990 were McConaughy Terrace (1948), Rockview Circle (1951), Brookside (1951), Eastview (1960), and Westville Manor (1986). A short-lived high-rise development known as Elm Haven Extension had from 1955 until its demolition in 1988 been yet another point of concentration. With tenancy confined largely to blacks, and to very low income blacks, the presence of a large public housing project would come to define the lowest tier in the regional hierarchy of neighborhoods. By about 1980, New Haven would have very nearly the highest concentration of public housing units per capita in the nation, and it would thus have one more way in which many of its neighborhoods were linked to the perception of marginality.

This unhappy result would be brought about largely by HANH's well-intentioned desire to provide decent housing for the largest possible number of families, which does little to alter the real impact of marginalization on the city's future. The difficulty is practical as well as symbolic. On the practical side, public housing often anchors people to places where attainable employment is scarce, tending to preserve the spatial mismatch from which lower-end urban economies suffer so severely.[47] Other policies, having no direct relation to public housing, have exacerbated the mismatch—the decision to go for high-tech development in Science Park, next to Elm Haven, in the 1980s being an example. When major public housing projects dominate a neighborhood they tend to accelerate racial tipping and class tipping at the same time, so that most whites and many blacks decamp, leaving a more homogeneously impoverished population than before.[48] From an economic viewpoint, this "adverse selection" process threatens to induce a death spiral, leaving projects and city blocks where having at least one adult family member with a regular job has become the exception and not the rule.[49] Concentrating large numbers of low-income minority children in the neighborhood schools adjacent to major housing projects has in many instances helped to foment educational disaster. Thus, the Isadore Wexler

School, serving Elm Haven public housing (now rebuilt in New Urbanist style and christened Monterey Place) and its surrounding streets had a school lunch eligibility rate of 91.3 percent, indicating nearly uniform impoverishment, and had a racial mix of 265 black children, 12 Hispanic children, 5 white children, and a lone Asian child. In the school year 2000–2001, 8 percent of its students met state reading standards, 23 percent the writing standard, 10 percent the math standard, and just 5 percent parlayed all three achievements together.[50] These numbers are startling but not at all out of line with comparable New Haven neighborhoods, and neighborhoods like them in other cities. Over the decades, many of Arwildie Windsley Howard's children and grandchildren faced these daunting odds at school. A few, by determination, talent, and good fortune, escaped the expected outcome. Others did not, and at least one was destroyed in the process.

SPATIAL HIERARCHY AS ENDURING INSTITUTION

I began by describing the arrival of one black family in 1943, and I looked briefly at the spatial constraints that that family's decision-makers faced upon arrival: they could live in only a few of New Haven's neighborhoods, and they could select only relatively marginal housing in those places. Within a decade the Windsleys faced the unhappy coincidence of black arrival and manufacturing decline. European immigrant groups in earlier decades had faced far better economic prospects, far fewer spatial constraints, and far less virulent discrimination than these African-Americans encountered. As Douglas Massey and Nancy Denton write, "For our purposes, a ghetto is a set of neighborhoods that are exclusively inhabited by members of one group, within which virtually all members of that group live. By this definition, no ethnic or racial group in the history of the United States, except one, has ever experienced ghettoization, even briefly. For urban blacks, the ghetto has been the paradigmatic residential configuration for at least eighty years."[51]

The intense marginalization of black ghettos is an inescapable element in the end-of-urbanism story. It is a symbolic fact of great significance, causing some suburban drivers to lock their car doors while in or even near such dreaded places. It is a fact of the greatest economic significance, devaluing many central-place locations in commercial and residential credit markets. And it is a moral fact, not easily pushed aside in a nation that purports to cherish the heritage of Lincoln and the hope of opportunity for every child.

Blacks, for all that, were not alone in the evolution of regional hierarchy. Before blacks were a numerically important element in New Haven, people had be-gun to establish the habit of minting certified inequalities between neighbor-hoods. The habit of seeing neighborhoods on a vertical scale, from worst to mid-dling to best, goes back a long way and has perhaps always been part of urban life. Hierarchy is a fact even for WASPs, and certainly for everyone else—for the Irish, the Poles, the Hispanics, the Jews, and scores of other groupings. Even within groups, vital differences remained, such as northern versus southern among Italo-Americans and German versus Eastern European among Jews. All this informal elbowing is a fact of life from early on, but we have seen something different in this chapter. For the evolution of the city, the 1920s and 1930s were pivotal in fostering publicly certified spatial hierarchies. The adoption of munic-ipal zoning in 1926 was the first instance, and one of lasting importance. The New Deal HOLC residential security survey conducted in fall 1937 was another, establishing a meretriciously exact hierarchy of letter grades and corresponding colors, based as much on bigotry as on land or buildings. It is impossible to trace the long-run influence of HOLC's judgments on mortgage markets and residen-tial decisions over the decades, but it is also very difficult to suppose that they did not inflict great harm on the C and D neighborhoods, the yellows and the reds, as would-be homeowners sought mortgages and were either turned down or charged a premium interest rate to reflect the government-certified riskiness of their chosen abodes. Finally, the emergence of project-based public housing af-ter the 1937 Housing Act became a third signal source for the low end of spatial hierarchy—and one that affected New Haven more heavily than most other cities across the nation.

The certification of hierarchy, particularly at the low end, would become a po-litical habit in decades to come. In 1941–44, the housing authority would pro-duce its annual reports in then-and-now, bad-and-good rhetoric, with many horror shots from bad neighborhoods juxtaposed with flattering pictures of con-ditions in public housing projects. To go along with these the authority included a map showing just two residential neighborhood types: "poor housing" and "worse housing." Poor occupied much, but not all, of HOLC's C grade. Worse covered the HOLC D-level areas in Dixwell, Oak Street, and a great swatch of the State Street corridor.[52] In 1944 the Chamber of Commerce would commission a consultant's study of New Haven housing. The report it received the following February provided a highly detailed parsing of the city and its nearby suburbs. Going HOLC two better, Roy Wenzlick & Company of St. Louis provided *six* grades of "relative economic status" in 1945.[53] Interestingly, large patches of the suburbs—inland Branford, southern Orange, much of West Haven, and lowland North Haven received ratings of third class. Most of New Haven (save East Rock and Westville) was graded from third to sixth class. Most of the Hill, Fair Haven, Dixwell, Newhallville, and Wooster Square fell to fourth or fifth class. Patches of these areas were adjudged sixth class.

In the 1950s, New Haven's energetic Urban Renewal program would be based on project maps, laying out the streets and homes, stores and factories to be bull-dozed and replaced. The Oak Street Project Area would be defined almost exactly along the contours of HOLC's D-3 zone. The Wooster Square Project Area would consume most of HOLC's D-5 zone. The Dixwell Project Area would subsume HOLC's D-4 zone. Was there a direct causal link between HOLC judgments and renewal targeting? Things were assuredly more complex than that, but there can be little doubt that HOLC's damnation of D-level areas would have greatly re-stricted the flow of investment capital, even for routine repair. It is also likely that the HOLC classification would (perhaps having lost its formal title) have re-mained in the mental models that experts and politicians alike brought to the tasks of renewal. Whatever the link, the new mappings in the renewal era were important. The effect was on the one hand a legal maneuver, opening the federal spigot to finance the work. It was also, nevertheless, the certification of a slum—one more signal that unsubsidized investment was risky, and that all roads to personal security ran away from such places. Even in the opening years of the twenty-first century, the federal Empowerment Zone would encompass the same neighborhoods that HOLC rated as D and C areas, and which came to be the sites of low-income public housing.

DICK LEE AND OLD-TIME URBANISM

The political genius who would drive urban renewal forward in New Haven was living in the old 17th Ward as a twenty-one-year-old in his mother's three-decker when HOLC determined its status as a C neighborhood, perilously close to the neighboring Dixwell neighborhood and its D status. Whatever HOLC may have thought about life in such a place as the 17th Ward—pride of ownership was "decidedly spotty," and too many families were of "mixed foreign" national-ity—a rich life in the tradition of urbanism was to be found if one knocked on the right doors.[54]

Richard C. Lee (1916–2003) was the eldest son of Mary and Frederick Lee. While his progenitors had come from all over the British Isles, and he would eventually consort with New Haveners of *every* faith and nationality, Lee was first and last an Irish Catholic boy. This was a remarkable kid—smart, energetic, embedded in working-class New Haven's life from birth, gifted with a memory for people, and radiating a natural warmth that would carry him a long way in city politics. His father died while Lee was still in high school, and he found himself scrambling to help his remarkable mother make ends meet at an early age. "Richie," as he was often called in the early years, was an altar boy, a grocery clerk, and ten other things before he became an alderman, representing the 17th Ward, in 1939. In these early years, everything about Lee suggested a New Haven politician with all the talents and connectedness of Frank Rice. If Rice had been a crystal of civic density, Lee was just that too. In the story, penned by Lee himself, that follows we get a look into late Depression-era New Haven and the routines of grounded urbanism expressed through Democratic politics in the 17th Ward. We see the context that equipped Richard C. Lee to become the extraordinary figure who would emerge as mayor just fourteen winters later.

SNOW TICKETS IN THE WINTER OF 1940 FOR THE 17TH WARD

By the Honorable Richard C. Lee

When I was first elected an alderman in 1939, the old-fashioned political machine was very much in existence. The WPA was a vehicle by which the poor and unemployed got jobs and were able to bring home a week's paycheck—and it rarely hurt if they were deserving Democrats as well. I had grown up during the New Deal. When FDR was elected, I was 16 years old and during the next few years I saw all those alphabet agencies flourish all over the place: the WPA, PWA, SEC, CCC, and on and on and on.

Our Mayor, the late John W. Murphy, was able to procure for New Haven funds which he used without much outside interference for jobs the Mayor or his staff might assign. Though times were tough, I learned within a month and a half after I had been sworn in that there were at least part-time ways to get people some cash.

It began to snow early one morning. It snowed all day and continued into the evening. I was then employed at the Chamber of Commerce, and before I left for home, the late John M. Golden, who later became my patron in public life, called and told me to stop over at the Hall of Records and pick up my alderman's allotment of snow tickets. Even though I had been around City Hall, I had never heard the term "snow tickets" before. When I asked what they were, he explained to me that each time there was a snow storm, each Democratic alderman got 40 tickets to pass out to people in his ward. A man could take the tickets downtown to the Public Works, turn them in and be given a shovel. The ticket entitled each holder to eight hours of work at forty cents an hour. As I quickly found out there was never a scarcity of applicants. We were living on the third floor of a three decker at the time, and no sooner had I finished supper than the door bell began to ring. My brother went down the two flights of stairs. Then he called out to me to come down. What I saw at the bottom of the stairs were at least fifty people already in line, and more coming up the block to join them.

When I stepped out the first man in line, whom I knew from my grammar school days, said, "Richie, I want a snow ticket." I looked out at the crowd and said to all of them, "Are you here for snow tickets?" Almost in one voice, they bellowed back, "yes."

Followed by my brother, I went upstairs, put on my overcoat, put my gloves in my pocket, and with snow tickets in hand, started to go downstairs. My mother called to me and when I turned around she said: "Richard, where are you going?" I told her there were people at the front door who wanted to work all night shoveling snow. She had seen the tickets when I came home, and with her practical sense she had counted them. She asked me how many there were downstairs. When I told her there were perhaps fifty and the line was growing, she threw a sweater over her shoulders and followed my brother and me down the stairs.

It was a mess. There were over 100 people in line, and here I was, with only 40 tickets. I did the only thing I could do, gave out the tickets on a first-come, first-served basis. When I was hardly half-way through the line, I ran out of tickets, threw my hands up in the air and said, "I am sorry fellows, but I don't have any more tickets." Even though they understood they were grumbling, milling around angry and a little upset, for $3.20 in those days "on the side," so to speak, was a lot of money.

My mother stepped out on the porch, moving almost in front of me, and said in a very calm voice, "Why don't all of you come upstairs. I'll make some coffee and I'll get some doughnuts across the street." (We lived directly opposite a corner "mama and papa" grocery store owned by a Mr. Siskin, who stayed open all hours of the day and night.) She then turned coolly but urgently to me. "Go downtown, Richard, and tell Mr. Golden your mother has 50 people in her flat on Dixwell Avenue and they are not leaving until they get snow tickets." Then, with just a little higher pitch in her voice, she called upstairs to my sister and said, "Josephine, put your coat on and bring me down my purse. I want you to go across the street to Mr. Siskin. Buy some coffee and all the doughnuts he has left."

Then, like the field marshal she was in our family, she directed me to the car with my brother and led the somewhat abashed ticket seekers upstairs to our third floor flat. My sister rushed down the stairs, went across the street to the store, and I stood there, looking at my brother and feeling like an idiot. So, we got into my 1934 Ford Phaeton and drove down to see John Golden. There were a lot of people milling around his City Hall office as well. When I could finally catch John's eye, I told him simply, "Mr. Golden, I need more snow tickets." His answer was sharp and definite. "You have your 40 tickets. That is all you are going to get."

I flinched, but I decided I would rather incur his wrath than my mother's so I said to him simply, "Mr. Golden, I can't leave until I get at least 60 more tickets. My mother has half the neighborhood in our third floor flat, serving coffee and doughnuts, and waiting for snow tickets. I can't go home empty-handed. I just can't." Golden pushed his hat back on his head and said, "What the hell do you mean your mother has 60 people in her flat and she is feeding them all?" When I told him the whole story, he started to smile. Then he grinned. Shaking with genuine laughter, he said, "This I have got to see for myself." He put a batch of tickets in his pocket, climbed into the back seat of my car and I drove my brother and him back to Dixwell Avenue, where we lived.

The front door, naturally, was unlocked. Nobody ever locked a front door in those days. As we went up to the second floor landing, we could hear voices and snips of conversation which grew louder and louder as we climbed the final flight of stairs. I opened the door which led directly into our dining room. In the dining room and in the kitchen beyond were men sitting, standing, all drinking coffee, munching doughnuts, chatting and waiting for me. My mother had not enough cups and saucers, so she borrowed some additional ones from the tenant on the second floor and the owner of the three-decker, who lived on the first floor.

Everyone, of course, knew who I was. But as John Golden's form filled the doorway, there was silence, almost awe. Here quite literally was "the boss." He stood there for a moment with his hands on his hips, enjoying his own performance. Then he said in a loud voice, "What the hell are you all waiting for, snow tickets?" Almost in a chorus, they shouted back, "yes."

Without another word he stepped over those sitting on the floor, brushed past those standing against the well, and went out into the kitchen, looking for my mother, whom he had never met. My mother's presence dominated the kitchen. There were people standing and sitting also. Some had even opened the back door and were sitting out on the third floor landing, drinking coffee and munching on crullers. Before I could introduce John to my mother, she turned around, looked at him and said quietly, "If you are Mr. Golden, I hope you have those snow tickets with you." She was like steel.

John Golden looked at her—speechless, probably, for the first time in his life. He turned around and said to me—and this is the first time anyone had ever mentioned higher political office to me—"Dick, with this kind of mother behind you, making certain that you take care of your neighbors, you are going to be Mayor some day." Then he handed me the tickets and said, simply, "It's your ward. These are your people. You pass them out." And that I did.

When I finished with those in the kitchen and with those on the back stairs and the third floor landing, I went into the dining room, went from one person to another, giving them each a ticket, and finally wound up in the parlor. Some of them had tears in their eyes; some of them grinned and said, "Thank you, Richie." Finally, someone stood up and said, "Bring Mrs. Lee in here. We all want to thank her." John Golden himself brought her into the middle of the dining room and as she stood there, wiping her hands on her apron, they cheered her until tears came to her eyes and she began to weep. John stood there looking on silently and she finally raised her hands and said, "I thank you all, but be off with you now and get to work. And just remember as long as I live in this house with my son, and as long as he is in public life, no one will ever be turned away from this door." Then, turning to me, she said, "Isn't that right, Richard?" I looked at her, grinned, kissed her and said, "Well, as long as John Golden cooperates, that will be true." Then everyone cheered me, cheered Golden and filed down the stairs, leaving behind a clutter of dirty dishes and a messy flat.

Fifteen years later, this young alderman would become the most important figure in New Haven's twentieth-century story.

CHAPTER 9

INVENTING DICK LEE

Richard C. Lee—arguably the greatest mayor of New Haven's twentieth century—inherited a great deal from the urban past, including a political style as personal as Democratic Town Chairman John Golden's thick right hand and as local as his mother's upstairs parlor. Like Golden, Lee is a product of the Irish ascendance in New Haven's Democratic Town Committee (DTC). In 1922, when Lee was six years of age, one person served his party as "registrar's assistant" in each of New Haven's thirty-three wards. These folks were entrusted with the legal alchemy required to "make voters" every day of the year. Within a cadre of fewer than three dozen on the Democratic side, we find the following twenty names:[1] James Fitzgerald, William Keeley, Vincent Sullivan, John Cahill, George Conroy, John Morrissey, Tom Kelly, Lawrence Mooney, Ed Walsh, Peter Corcoran, Patrick O'Neil, Patrick Farrington, William McGarry, John O'Donell, William Keegan, Eugene Harrigan, Hugh McDonald, William Ryan, Frank McNeil, Charles Daley. Given the vagaries of Celtic surnames, perhaps only seventeen or eighteen were really Irish: that is still a wide majority in this critical line of politicking. Neither was Irish democracy an idle pastime, as Raymond Wolfinger reminds us: "The Irish were not reluctant to take the spoils of victory. In the early 1930s first- and second-generation Irishmen constituted 13 percent of a sample of 1,600 family heads in New Haven, but they accounted for 49 percent of all governmental jobs. The Italians suffered most of all from Irish chauvinism: there were no governmental employees among the 27 percent who were Italian."[2]

DICK LEE AND THE IRISH ASCENDANCY

By the time Lee was elected an alderman in 1939, New Haven was already a long generation into the realization of Irish democracy. The earliest Gaelic aldermen emerged in the Civil War era, and Irish-born attorney Cornelius Driscoll became mayor in 1899. Once elected in 1953, Lee would carry the mayoring of the green forward to 1970.[3] Mayors in this era stood atop a steep-sided pyramid. As long as two-party competition lasted, there were two ward committees in each of fifteen to thirty-three neighborhoods,[4] one GOP and one Democratic, each with a ward chairman and chairlady, and a band of foot-soldiers to get out the vote, each with a registrar's assistant entitled to enroll voters, each with an alderman. Throughout, the thing was very much driven by the details of space and place, not by big-picture issues of public policy. Each ward was a tiny fiefdom, each party a league of fiefdoms. Each party fielded a total of perhaps five hundred or a thousand players who worked for candidates, received public jobs and contracts, or were merely dignified by personal acknowledgment in the presence of a mayor. When players died while a mayor like Dick Lee was in office, their families could expect His Honor to send a note of condolence and to appear at the wake.

The political pyramid is of a piece with the civic fauna of the city, and it cross-connects wherever there are voters to be found—in the Catholic parishes, most of them led by Irish clergy, in the Knights of Columbus, in the social life of Congregation Mishkan Israel, in the Masonic halls, at the lunch counters which come alive each business day as urban switchboards. One could not imagine doing Republican politics in the old 10th and 11th Wards without working St. Michael's parish; neither could one expect to master the WASPish 9th Ward without taking the Congregationalist Church of the Redeemer into account. Similarly, one would have had little traction in the working-class wards of Fair Haven without the cooperation of Joe Reilly at the Trades Council. It is in these places and hundreds more like them that registrar's assistants like Bill Keeley, Patrick O'Neil, Eddie Walsh, Frank McNeil, and Archie McCullough were building a future for Dick Lee, even if none yet knew who he one day might be.

POLITICS OF ETHNIC IDENTITY

Yale political scientist Robert Dahl describes a tri-part cycle of urban ethnic succession in his 1961 *Who Governs?*[5] Each group—German, Irish, Italian, black, Hispanic—arrived in the city at the first of three stages. In this initial period, nearly all the members identify strongly with the group, but most are eco-

nomically weak and politically marginal. They are eager to gain economic and social status, and highly appreciative of political favor, even when it is largely symbolic, and is bestowed on other members of the group. A few members may be
recruited for minor political roles, but neither elective office nor important patronage is available to them. When government jobs do come, they are at the bottom of a ditch or the end of a mop. The real action comes in the two remaining
stages, as group solidarity declines while opportunity increases. At a second
stage, the moment for the group's realization of power in city politics begins:

> The group has become more heterogeneous. It is no longer predominantly
> proletarian. An increasing and by now significant proportion of the group
> have white-collar jobs and other social characteristics of the middling strata.
> Higher status, income, and self-confidence allow some to gain considerable
> political influence. They begin to challenge and overthrow the incumbent
> leaders on whom they hitherto have been dependent; amid charges of be-
> trayal and ingratitude they now move into positions of leadership. Depend-
> ing on the size of his ethnic group and local attitudes, an ethnic leader may
> even receive a major party nomination for a leading citywide office, such as
> a mayoralty, that cannot be won simply by the votes of his own ethnic group.
> Although the political homogeneity of the group declines in this stage be-
> cause of increasing differentiation of the middling segments from the
> working-class strata, even the middling segments retain a high sensitivity to
> their ethnic origins. Consequently, an ethnic candidate who can avoid divi-
> sive socioeconomic issues is still able to activate strong sentiments of ethnic
> solidarity in all strata of his ethnic group.[6]

Dahl sees this second period as beginning in about 1890 and ending in about
1930 for New Haven's Irish (and running from 1930 to 1950 for New Haven's
Italians). Ethnic solidarity grows thinner in Dahl's third stage:

> The group is now highly heterogeneous. Large segments are assimilated
> into middling and upper strata; they have middle-class jobs, accept middle-
> class ideas, adopt a middle-class style of life, live in middle-class neighbor-
> hoods, and look to others in the middling strata for friends, associates, and
> marriage partners. To these people, ethnic politics is often embarrassing or
> meaningless. Political attitudes and loyalties have become a function of so-
> cioeconomic characteristics. Members . . . display little political homogene-
> ity. Although sentimental and traditional attachments to a particular party
> may persist, they are easily ruptured. The political effectiveness of a purely

ethnic appeal is now negligible among the middling and upper strata. A middle-class or upper-class candidate who happens to be drawn from an ethnic group may use this tie to awaken sentiments of pride; he may win votes, but to do so he must emphasize socioeconomic issues, even though stressing such issues may split his ethnic group wide open.[7]

Very much a child of stage two, Lee began practicing ward politics by early adolescence in the late 1920s, and he was elected to the Board of Aldermen representing the 17th Ward in 1939 at age twenty-three—when, not altogether incidentally, a fellow by the name of Murphy was mayor. He would achieve middle-class identity, even with a high school education, as a reporter for the *New Haven Journal Courier* and as a functionary for the local Chamber of Commerce. Beginning in 1944, Lee would develop considerable sophistication as director of the Yale News Bureau. In this job he became something of a protégé of Carl Lohmann, who was secretary of the university (a more exalted job than it sounds). As Allan Talbot writes,

> "Caesar" Lohmann was a remarkable man, a connoisseur of music and art, a proficient editor, a master of heraldry, a talented gardener, a keeper of tradition at Yale, a man of immense good taste and sophistication. He became Lee's mentor, and Lee was so attentive a student that his friends noticed subtle changes in the young man's appearance and manner. Familiar French idioms such as *entre nous* and *en famille* popped up in his conversation; he became compulsively aware of carelessly phrased letters and talk; his dress was distinctively Ivy League. He also had the greenest lawn on Shelton Avenue, and was doubtless the only alderman at the time who knew that a minister should be addressed as "the Reverend Mr."[8]

Here, then, was a personal history that ran right through Dahl's second and third stages, retaining scars and skills from each for the rest of Lee's life. Dick Lee was deeply grounded in ward politics and chose, for obvious reasons, to stress his Irish blood at the expense of the Scottish and English plasmas with which his was in fact diluted. He never, even for an instant, imagined himself giving up his lace-curtain Irish identity or his place in the city's street-corner urbanism. It is true that he would dress in J. Press suits and wear neckties only a Yale man could love. A less secure and less urbane person than Dick Lee might have let these new symbols and skills displace the humbler ones he had grown up with. But for Lee, these were simply embellishments of a 17th Ward identity, emblems of a world that would provoke him to define and pursue goals not commonly taken up by New Haven ward politicians, even after their election as mayor. In an interview conducted at his elegant retirement-home apartment, Lee recalled his recruitment to become alderman:

> I gave the mayor [John Murphy] $25 when he was running in 1937. I drove a car for a state senator from my district but that was a contribution on my part. In one sense it didn't really mean much, but on the other hand it did mean a lot because I was demonstrating my own interest in the party and my own interest in becoming involved. So the mayor said to me there is a vacancy in your ward—Jim Beatty is not going to run for re-election because of the Hatch Act. Do you want to try and run for it? So I thanked him and didn't do anything about it and about a week later the mayor must have called my boss at the newspaper and said to him that he ought to do something with Dick Lee—he is a bright, bright young man and he would make a real addition to the political system. So the *Journal Courier* gives me a shove toward running for office [by reassigning Lee to a City Hall beat]. I was working all kinds of crazy hours six days a week. The only day I had off was Saturday. The ward committee called my mother, and I was in bed because I had worked until three in the morning, and they said they wanted to come visit me. So she arranged a visit without talking to me. When she awakened me, I got up and took a shower quickly—I didn't have any idea what they had on their minds. They walked in—the chairman and the chairlady, the registrar, and the state senator. There were about seven or eight people who wanted me to run for alderman. Just like that. So I ran for alderman. I won and ran ahead of the ticket. My mother and father were very nice people, and they were very much loved in that neighborhood.[9]

This short passage says a lot about Lee, about his rootedness in neighborhood, about his political skill, about his simple likeability. It also says something about the Democratic Town Committee's recruitment of young talent.[10] The New Haven DTC had identified a young star, quite probably its greatest talent of the century, and seated him at its table early on.

The Irish ascendancy had begun in earnest right after the death of Frank Rice in January 1917.[11] Less than a year after Rice died, his friend, Samuel Campner, was thrashed by Democratic Alderman David Fitzgerald in the November mayoral race. Three Irish mayors—Fitzgerald, Thomas Tully, and John Murphy—would dominate the next generation of New Haven politics. Fitzgerald would serve four terms, Tully (the lone Republican) one term, Murphy seven terms. Thus did Irish mayors serve for twenty-four of the twenty-eight years between

1917 and 1945, through the turbulence of the 1920s, the Great Depression, and World War II. All three of these men served on the Board of Aldermen before making a run at the top job, as would Dick Lee (he served four terms there, from 1939 to 1947). Counting Lee, we have Irish-American victors capturing twenty-of twenty-six general elections, and serving forty of fifty-two years between 1917 and 1969.[12]

IRISH-ITALIAN RIVALRY

The Irish were not alone in New Haven. The great wave of Italian immigration between 1885 and 1920 had been recognized by Republican leadership as an antidote to Irish Democratic voting power. Isaac and Louis Ullman, the same German Jewish business leaders who had backed Frank Rice in 1909, saw the emerging DTC majority, carried on the backs of Irish voters, and also saw a counter-strategy. As Raymond Wolfinger writes, "The Ullman brothers realized that the large and hitherto passive Italian population was an untapped source of potential Republicans, and they set out to capture them. Using familiar techniques of ethnic politics, they helped the Italian immigrants take out citizenship papers, registered them as voters, found them jobs, used their considerable political influence to smooth over administrative and legal difficulties, subsidized Italian-American fraternal and political clubs, and so on. It is not too much to say that the Ullman brothers' foresight and political skill kept the Republican party competitive in New Haven."[13]

Wolfinger is doubtless correct in this judgment, at least insofar as it pertains to the first half of the twentieth century. One useful indicator of ethnic penetration of the city's political system is the number of seats held on the Board of Aldermen, not because that body is terribly powerful but because it represents the major pool of electable political talent available at any given moment in the city. In figure 9.1, each bar represents the division of seats by ethnicity and party for the two-year term beginning with the stated year. The chart suggests three useful facts. First, the Irish Democrats are dominant, accounting for 63 percent of the "two Is" seats analyzed here, and over 30 percent of the 504 total seat-terms in the chamber as a whole.[14] Second, while the Italian GOP is far less important than the Irish Democracy over the 1920s and 1930s, it grew rapidly after 1939—the year when Italian funeral director William Celentano captured the first major-party mayoral nomination for his countrymen. Celentano would finally win a mayoral election in 1945.

In 1947, the DTC would counter by nominating a fairly obscure Italian dentist,

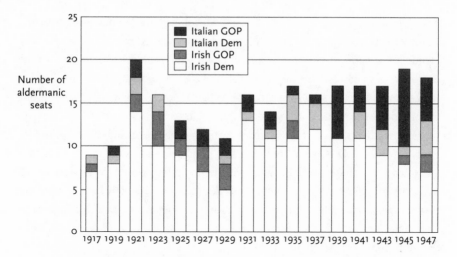

Figure 9.1. Irish and Italian division of New Haven aldermanic seats, 1917–47.

whom Celentano destroyed. Celentano would defeat Lee in 1949 and 1951 (in the second instance by a margin of just two votes). Celentano may not have been remarkable as a mayor, but, quoting Wolfinger, his "candidacy brought thousands of Italians into the Republican party, as the voting history of the heavily Italian tenth ward [the south end of Wooster Square] illustrates. In 1937 Murphy received 52 percent of the ward's vote. Two years later, running against Celentano, he got 22 percent and fared almost as badly in other Italian neighborhoods."[15]

The third fact, whispered in this evidence and shouted in later experience, is that the early Italian attachment to New Haven's GOP was fragile, being largely a tactical means to symbolic ends. As opportunity for political mobility rose during the Dick Lee years, Italian politicians and their voters would seize it. Lee and his political tacticians (most notably Democratic Town Chairman Arthur Barbieri) recognized that the Italian vote would follow Italian workers as they took over city jobs, Italian aldermen as they displaced the dwindling Irish, and ultimately, after Lee, Italian mayors elected as Democrats. Four years into the Lee era, in 1957, Italian Democrats (ten seats) would outnumber Italian Republicans (one seat), Irish Democrats (eight seats), and Irish Republicans (no seats) combined. Soon enough, a standing joke developed about the ethnicity of top officials around Lee, men with names like Logue, Katzenbach, Cogen, Paquin, Rotival, Sviridoff, Hallman, Holt, Wexler, Appleby, and Grabino. "Where," an Italian Democratic alderman is supposed to have asked the mayor, "are all the Italians?" Lee is purported to have replied, "What about Grabino?" Everyone understood that Grabino—general consul of the Redevelopment Agency—was Jewish. Another set of maneuvers, involving not policy-level officials but DTC politics, would allow Lee and his allies to all but destroy the remaining link between the New Haven Italian community and the local GOP. Working with Arthur Barbieri and John Golden in a delicate balance of control over patronage and symbolic recognition, Lee would bring Italian and Irish, Jewish and WASP players together in a disorderly but devastating partisan coalition. Soon enough, the Italians were to the DTC what the Irish had once been—dominant partners in a broad coalition, based both on symbolic identity politics and utterly practical access to jobs. Democratic mayors of later decades would mostly have names like Guida, DiLieto, and DeStefano. Thanks to these developments, Bill Celentano would turn out to be both the first of many Italian mayors and the last in a line of Republican mayors stretching back to Frank Rice.

FRANK RICE'S ITALIAN-AMERICAN GHOST

Mayor William Celentano (1945–53) grew up in Italian New Haven, the son of a fruit stand operator, who "quit school after ninth grade to help his brother through medical school and eventually earned his high school diploma at night. He became an undertaker, opened his own funeral parlor, and quickly attained prominence in his profession."[16] Like Lee, Celentano was a ward activist at an early age, and he was elected to the Board of Aldermen while still in his twenties. He ran a strong but unsuccessful mayoral race against Murphy in 1939, then took an understandably low profile in politics while the United States was at war with Italy. In 1945 he returned to challenge an increasingly vulnerable Murphy (now finishing his seventh two-year term). Celentano ran a conventional campaign, hammering away at good service themes, working the wards, asking for better schools, reminding Italians who he was and where he came from. In Wooster Square's 10th Ward, Celentano pounded Murphy 1,179 to 234, running slightly ahead of veteran alderman Mike DePalma. In the 11th Ward, covering the northern part of Wooster Square, he ran up a 1,368 to 407 plurality against the incumbent mayor, running about a dozen votes ahead of alderman Louis Ragozzino. Murphy, in contrast, scarcely held the Irish 17th Ward, 929 to 855, and he lost outright in 24 of 33 wards citywide. This was a campaign of carefully presented identities, a cautious and conservative Italian against a cautious and conservative Irishman. The Italian won, without establishing anything much in the way of a programmatic mandate, save a promise to spend more on the school system. He won, that is to say, more by being what he was than by promising what he would do.

Such politics provides little space for brilliance, and this new mayor found none of it. Celentano would prove himself a perfectly decent, ethical, and presentable mayor. In his first annual report, which bore the title "Your City's Progress in Black and White," he forwarded the theme of governmental service:

> There are approximately 2,500 municipal employees and department heads in the many branches of our city government and inasmuch as they are the faithful and loyal servants of the people, and are those who operate the machinery of city government so that the general public may benefit, it is to them that the Municipal Year Book of New Haven for 1946 is dedicated. The quality of services rendered by a city government to its people is the *full measure of the city government* itself. It has been and will continue to be my goal that the services rendered to the people of New Haven by its municipal servants be of the highest type. Our aim is to serve our citizenry well and give all the service we can within the limits of the ability of the city to pay.[17]

Urban services are very important—regular garbage pickup, good cops, efficient recordkeeping, clean parks, parking meters that give honest time for every nickel inserted. But Celentano's claim that services constitute the full measure of city government itself would seem a remarkable abdication of responsibility in an era when so much was changing so quickly in and around the city. In the buoyant urbanist environment that so favored a mayor like Rice, a fellow might pretty nearly get by on the proposition that good services altogether constitute good government. In such a period other institutions performed so many functions of governance that city government could succeed despite its passivity. But, as chronicled in Chapters 7 and 8, that happy state of affairs was rapidly decaying everywhere around Mayor Celentano.

The Great Depression was over, and incomes were increasing—a mixed blessing for New Haven as suburban developers sought paying customers in the city. Certain of New Haven's industrial plants were still running hot from what remained of the demand stimulus of World War II. But the largest plant of all, Winchester Repeating Arms, was desperately searching for customers and was now merely part of a corporate network within which Alton, Illinois, was every bit as important as New Haven. Manufacturing firms were not considering central New Haven as a site for new facilities. A sophisticated 1945 economic analysis commissioned by the New Haven Chamber of Commerce had shown that the rate of change in New Haven's manufacturing employment base had slipped markedly below national rates during 1943 and 1944.[18] It had even slipped behind many comparable cities, including Buffalo, Trenton, and nearby Bridgeport. The report, written by Roy Wenzleck of St. Louis, made unflattering comparisons between New Haven's economy and those of boomtowns like San Diego, Fort Worth, and Houston. Population growth in the city had been far below the national average for fifteen years, and scarcely two thousand new citizens had appeared since 1930 (which itself ended a decade of slowing growth). The region's overall growth rate had been below national norms throughout the twentieth century, even when the city proper was expanding rapidly, according to Wenzlick's report.

The city's central streets were crammed with automobiles, many of their drivers merely trying to get from New York to Boston or vice versa, struggling through the glacier of glass and steel along Route 1 as it crossed the center of New Haven. Average driving speeds in the immediate vicinity of the New Haven Green were on the order of five miles per hour, and a 2.7-mile trip thence to the East Haven line required twenty-two minutes.[19] About 12,000 cars jammed the "College Highway" (a.k.a. Whitney Avenue), running north from downtown each business day.[20] Parking, more exactly the lack of it, was strangling the central business district. City taxes on downtown properties were predicated on assessments running as much as 59.5 percent above actual market prices.[21] The trolley system, which had been the downtown's arterial support, was slowing in speed and losing badly in competition with the automobile. The early suburban malls were just beginning to appear across America, and they would appear near New Haven in just a few years' time.[22] Suburban housing developments were looming up from raw land in the towns around New Haven in ever-greater numbers. Wenzlick's map, showing newly developed housing in the New Haven area, looks like a pincushion, with development after development ringing the city in the years 1940–44 (figure 9.2).[23] Neighborhood retailing had been in decline since the 1930s, and the chain stores had begun to cannibalize their own outlets on New Haven streets. Commercial vacancy rates as high as 30 percent were to be found on some stretches of Legion Avenue. The New Haven public schools were losing an increased fraction of middle-class children to parochial and independent schools. Many Protestant churches closed their doors as parishioners moved to the suburbs, as did a few Jewish temples, even as the Catholic parishes stood pat in old neighborhoods. Many civic organizations were in rapid decline, with scores of the fraternal chapters, which had stitched city neighborhoods together, facing extinction. There were real and acute problems with some older

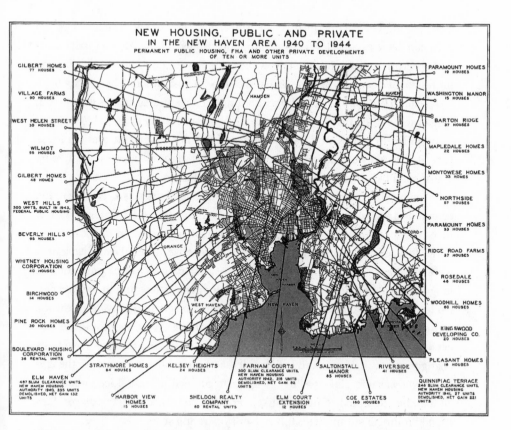

Figure 9.2. Suburban housing developments as charted by Wenzlick Associates' study of New Haven region, 1945.

working-class neighborhoods, such as Oak Street. As Allan Talbot wrote of the early 1950s, "ugliness and obsolescence were spreading over New Haven like weeds in an unkempt garden, and not just in poor neighborhoods but in the downtown retail section and in industrial areas."[24] The federal government, through its HOLC survey, complicated matters by certifying the majority of New Haven neighborhoods as problematic mortgage targets under the headings class C and class D. Downtown banks developed a standard preference for suburban mortgages over all but the safest New Haven neighborhoods. Racial heterogeneity was becoming important for the first time, and savvy observers began to sense the evolution of a regional hierarchy with major parts of New Haven defining its bottom tier. Its geography closely approximated the old HOLC studies, but with an increased preference for suburban areas.

As Jeanne Lowe wrote in 1967, "For decades, capable and ambitious young men had been leaving New Haven for opportunities in New York or giant industrial enterprises in the Midwest. Now the city's growing middle white-collar and professional class followed the Yankees out to the nearby suburbs."[25] The business leadership that remained was no longer concentrated inside the city but spread across the hills of Woodbridge, the plains of Hamden, the ridge running through North Haven, and the shorelines of Branford, Guilford, and Madison. City Hall could no longer count on a grounded class of business leadership whose members understood themselves as New Haveners.

Taken together, these changes announced the end of urbanism. No longer did centered capitalism provide city government with great economic leverage over firms that need opportunities for land use. No longer was a central location superior to a peripheral one for a new factory, warehouse, or retail store. No longer were middle-class workers compelled to live near their places of work, and no longer were nearly all those places of employment located within the central city. No longer did civic institutions and neighborhood retailing provide so thick a web of social connectedness within city neighborhoods. No longer could city government afford to remain passive, rigid, unobservant, and unresponsive to its changing environment—and still, for all that, succeed in governance of the city. No longer was it feasible for Bill Celentano to succeed as Frank Rice's ghost. For all that, he attempted something like a Frank Rice reenactment as mayor. Raymond Wolfinger summarizes this mayor's operating style:

> He had wanted to be mayor for a long time and very much enjoyed the job, but apparently his ambitions for higher office were mild. His political strategy seemed to be cautious and unenterprising, based on "recognition," jobs for supporters, compliance with those interest group demands that did not arouse significant opposition or require major political effort, and staying on the good side of the newspaper. The mayor was seldom given to bold ventures; he did not seem to feel that the returns from innovation would outweigh the risks of opposition from some affected interest or from the Register. . . . Celentano spent only a few hours a day at city hall and devoted the rest of his time to his business interests. The calculus of rewards favored sitting tight except when popular demands for action were strong enough to suggest that inaction would be politically costly. . . . Such demands were unlikely. In the absence of ideological preferences, public pressure, or an ambition which he [might have] tried to serve by spectacular achievement, Celentano had no real reason to interfere in the activities of many city agencies

except to control spending and be sure that no serious violence was done to his popularity. Celentano's response to the city's economic decline was consistent with his performance in other fields.[26]

Nothing is said here to impugn Celentano's integrity, decency, urban patriotism, skills as a politician, or considerable intelligence. Like Rice, he apparently made a good assessment of what the role of mayor would comfortably support in the way of an agenda, confined his goals to those limitations, and went about the business of being mayor accordingly. Unlike Rice, notorious for his intense work as mayor, Celentano found ample time to continue burying the dead and comforting the bereaved. In this he had an advantage over Lee, who attended ten or more wakes each week, because Lee had to attend on his own time.

LEARNING BY LOSING

During the mayoral campaigns of 1949 and 1951, Dick Lee took leaves of absence from the Yale News Bureau to run as a full-time candidate, hoping to become a full-throttle mayor of the city. He ran with energy, political skill, and media savvy. But he ran within the framework of New Haven politics as he had learned it representing the 17th Ward on the Board of Aldermen. He therefore attacked Celentano within the local conventions, which prescribed that "issue" attention focus on the efficiency and integrity with which the inherited tasks of government were being performed. As Yale Law School Dean Eugene Rostow recalled, "Very few of us at the university took any great interest in Dick's first two attempts to become mayor. He was part of Yale, so we followed his campaigns, but they were really ordinary affairs with Dick hitting conventional themes of efficiency and honesty."[27] In Dahl's terminology, Lee's 1949 and 1951 campaigns were "stage two" affairs, wherein "an ethnic candidate who can avoid divisive socioeconomic issues is still able to activate strong sentiments of ethnic solidarity in all strata of his ethnic group."[28] Lee ran almost as if he wanted to become Bill Celentano, only in a more energetic way, and with a different ethnic and rhetorical style.

Within that framework, the mobilization of friendly voters was the essential tactic, and those voters were distributed quite unevenly across the thirty-three-ward geography of the city.[29] Wards where a candidate's potential voters are most densely clustered offer greatest potential payoff for such mobilization. Such places, known as the candidate's base, become the foundation of a conventional strategy. Typically, only a modest effort is made to "convert" voters belong-

Table 9.1. Celentano's Base Wards Seen from Lee's Perspective

Ward	Lee 1949	Celentano 1949	Lee net result 1949	Lee 1951	Celentano 1951	Lee net result 1951
7	947	1,377	−430	952	1,432	−480
10	397	1,401	−1,004	423	1,326	−903
11	556	1,271	−715	508	1,346	−838
25	1,065	1,756	−691	1,037	1,715	−678
32	1,019	1,416	−397	822	1,540	−718
33	670	887	−217	677	910	−233
Subtotal	4,654	8,108	−3,454	4,419	8,269	−3,850

ing to the opponent's base; most of a candidate's work consists of mobilizing voters belonging to his or her own base. In table 9.1 we look at Celentano's base from Lee's point of view, hence the columns toting up the net outcomes for Lee in 1949 and 1951. Italians recruited to Sargent Hardware in 1910 had massed together in three of these: Wards 10, 11, and 25 (in 1910 these were Wards 5,6, and 11) remained predominantly Italian-American at mid-century. Moreover, these Wooster Square and Fair Haven wards represented a way of life very much like Dahl's second stage ethnic politics. Ethnic appeal turns these voters out and renders them relatively impervious to rival appeals, especially from a candidate whose name ends in a vowel without a trace of Italian identity. Ward 7, just south of the nine squares, was also heavily Italian and working class. Wards 32 and 33, both on the eastern shore of the New Haven harbor, were special cases. They were just beginning to be developed as substantially Italian residential neighborhoods, and they were still part of a special district exempt from the full burden of city taxes. During these elections they behaved very much like the rest of Celentano's base, for reasons I have been unable to fully discover. In both 1949 and 1951, Celentano could count on a net plurality running well over three thousand coming out of his six-ward base.

Celentano could appeal to a stage-two Italian base while Lee had to work with what remained of a stage-three Irish base. Ethnicity was, therefore, stronger magic on one side than on the other. The Irish were, by and large, further along in their economic advancement, and further along in their "Americanization." If we attempt, in retrospect, to find a cluster of Lee wards approximating Celentano's base, table 9.2 is the result.

Three of these wards were still broadly Irish in the late 1940s—16 and 17

Table 9.2. Lee's Base Wards Seen from Lee's Perspective

Ward	Lee 1949	Celentano 1949	Lee net result 1949	Lee 1951	Celentano 1951	Lee net result 1951
14	1,194	711	483	1,131	746	385
16	1,438	1,093	345	1,494	1,001	493
17	1,446	905	541	1,388	914	474
19	1,203	916	287	1,058	874	184
23	1,482	1,213	269	1,609	1,100	509
26	1,074	742	332	1,059	756	303
Subtotal	7,837	5,580	2,257	7,739	5,391	2,348

(Newhallville, Lee's home ward), and 14 (the Orange-State corridor). The 26th Ward, in Fair Haven, was a mixed industrial working-class area in which Italians were present but far from dominant. The 19th Ward, Dixwell Avenue, was increasingly African-American in this period and had been voting Democratic only in recent years (the 19th Ward returned GOP aldermen in virtually every election prior to 1947). This base, taken as a whole, is similar to Celentano's base only in the total vote count. It is more mixed than Celentano's, smaller than Celentano's, and less productive of electoral advantage than Celentano's. With Lee gaining only a small margin in the wards belonging to neither base, he was beaten by about seven hundred votes in 1949 and by fifteen votes on the first count in 1951, narrowed to two votes by judicial inquiry (Lee later joked that if his Republican neighbor and his wife had only switched sides out of neighborly sentiment, he would have won outright in 1951). He was, in short, able to produce a near tie, without winning. A front-page *Register* editorial the day before the 1951 election had this to say of Lee's effort: "The Democratic candidate began his campaign by launching a sharp attack on alleged waste in handling the City's affairs, which attack has continued to the very end, without announcing what his own program would be, if elected, except in the vaguest details with no specific facts and figures presented in those proposals."[30]

The anonymous editorialist, doubtless publisher John Day Jackson, went on to excoriate Lee as a tax-and-spend Democrat, concluding that "there is nothing to be gained and a great deal to be lost" in electing Lee to replace Celentano. Lee had in fact provided too little in the way of a program, which might have provided the hope of something gained to the broad electorate. Talbot nicely sums up this phase of Lee's development:

Like his townsmen, Lee was aware of his city's decline. Yet until 1953 he, like so many others, had accepted New Haven's unhappy condition. The problems were not new and they did not scream for action. They were, instead, old problems that had merely worsened with age, and the townspeople had adjusted accordingly. The reformer within Lee manifested itself hardly at all in 1949 and 1951. His promises were routine: to deal with isolated and superficial symptoms of the city's over-all physical and economic decline, such as the need to provide a better street-paving program, a new playground in one neighborhood or a better school in another. The approach was not different from that used by the man whom Lee had tried to unseat.[31]

Dick Lee would run a different kind of campaign two years later and would become a very different sort of mayor in January 1954. That new campaign required him to escape the blinders of normal politics, and that escape lay in New Haven's most troubled neighborhood.

THE SLUM AS MASTER TROPE

In the earlier elections, both Lee and Celentano had conducted themselves as if city government were still working, still succeeding in the governance of the city and its neighborhoods. Sometime between 1951 and 1953, Lee decided otherwise and elected to run an entirely different kind of campaign. It is perhaps not too much to say that Dick Lee elected to become a different sort of public man. He told Dahl about a decade later that one incident in the 1951 election was of special importance:

I went into the homes on Oak Street and they set up neighborhood meetings for me. I went into block meetings . . . three and four in one night. And I came out of those homes on Oak Street, and I sat on the curb and I was just as sick as a puppy. Why the smell of this building; it had no electricity, it had no gas, it had kerosene lamps, light had never seen those corridors in generations. The smells . . . It was just awful and I got sick. And there, there I really began . . . right there was when I began to tie in all these ideas we'd been practicing in city planning for years in terms of the human benefits that a program like [urban renewal] could reap for a city. In the two-year period [before the next election] I began to put it together with the practical application. . . . And I began to realize that while we had lots of people interested in doing something for the city they were all working at cross purposes. There was no unity of approach.[32]

This established a deep trope in Lee's thinking, in his political rhetoric, and a lasting theme in his attempted transformation of New Haven. Nearly half a century later, in 2002, I asked him about the experience and its literary echoes, with this result:

DOUGLAS RAE: In one of the books about that period, actually in two of them, there is a paragraph where the author talks about your 1951 campaign and going to meetings in homes on Oak Street—and being totally disgusted by the physical conditions you saw in the tenements in that neighborhood, and that somehow being a moment at which ideas about the city's future jelled for you. Would you say that is true, or is that just kind of a figure of speech?

DICK LEE: Well, that happened. That is true. I am not sure whether it was before I was mayor or after I became mayor. It happened either time. It doesn't make any difference because it had the same effect on me—just a question of the calendar. I went down there one morning at 7 o'clock and my driver was with me and he parked the car and I was just wandering around getting the feel and I saw an old man, a black man, who was missing one leg. He had a crutch for that one leg in one hand and a pail in that same hand. With the other hand he held on to his granddaughter, went over to the gas station to fill the pail with water, probably a couple of gallons. He started back and I went over to him and I approached him and he became very upset. He said, "It's all right, I have permission to take the water." I said that I was not interested in that. I would just like to say hello, my name is Dick Lee and I am your mayor and I am looking around in neighborhoods like Oak Street and Wooster Square because the housing conditions, to put it mildly, are not very good. So he brought me back to his house, and I can see him right now. It was terrible. The house had no central heating, it had no water, it had nothing, nothing, nothing. It was alive with cockroaches and rats. That man was trying to raise his son's family. His son was in prison. That old man and his wife, the grandmother, had four children they were trying to raise and they were getting them ready to go to school, cleaning them up, washing them, brushing their teeth, making coffee. It was a terrible experience. I went outside and threw up. I couldn't help it.[33]

Historical exactitude is beyond redemption here, but exactitude isn't required. Lee was operating in a city and an era within which the phenomenon of the slum was a certified reality. Dick Lee, both as a human being and as a politician, discovered the slum as a master trope around which to organize a new way of running for mayor.[34] It worked for him, and it worked for a large segment of his electorate, including one of the most influential segments of that electorate. As Eugene Rostow would say:

> When he campaigned to rebuild the city, in 1953, he struck a responsive chord. He was attacking fundamental ills of our time, the moral, economic, and social injustice of the slum. Dick is no ordinary politician. He has successfully developed the skills of that trade, but he has to use them to help others. I believe the reason he finally won in 1953 is that he abandoned the stock clichés of electioneering and allowed his morality to come through. Voters sense this in a candidate. From 1953 until now [c. 1967], the people have understood that Dick means it when he says that the slums are evil and the city must be rebuilt. They sense his commitment and that's more important to them than any mistakes he might have made.[35]

Slum clearance and redevelopment quickly became Lee's passion, and he became a national figure almost overnight by doing it with unmatched energy and ingenuity. Of greatest practical importance was the existence of federal funding, authorized several years earlier by Congress and, in 1953, not yet effectively exploited by cities and developers across the country. Section 2 of the 1949 Housing Act declared a vast and expensive national objective: "The Congress hereby declares that the general welfare and security of the Nation and the health and living standards of its people require housing production and related community development sufficient to remedy the serious housing shortage, the elimination of substandard and other inadequate housing through clearance of slums and blighted areas, and the realization as soon as feasible of the goal of a decent home and a suitable living environment for every American family."[36]

By 1953, the local Chamber of Commerce had spotted the potential in a law that backed its aspirations with $1 billion in loans and $500 million in capital grants. By early 1954, Lee would be mayor, and he would soon fashion himself a "beggar with a bushel basket" in his pursuit of these funds. The slum-clearance ideal was of course problematic. It entailed a premise that government should intervene to do things *for* city neighborhoods, even *to* city neighborhoods, not *with* city neighborhoods. Renewal also invited extravagant environmental determinism. In its simplest form, such a doctrine looked at healthy neighborhoods—sustained by good economics, strong civic institutions, deeply felt social trust—and supposed that their one most visible feature (a good built environment) was the cause of all the rest. It seemed to follow, if one remained careful not to think too far into the problem, that bad neighborhoods that were given good built environments would function like good neighborhoods.[37] Often this confused cause and effect: "Good buildings make good neighborhoods" is not true if the other key features of urbanism are absent. One could better say that "Good neighborhoods make good buildings," if that meant that people make the necessary effort and investment in buildings because of other values attached to the place and relationships within it. The process of renewal was also often exceedingly disruptive to the civic and business fabric of neighborhoods, a point made forcefully in Herbert Gans' 1966 critique: "Because the policy has been to clear a district of all slums at once in order to assemble large sites to attract private developers, entire neighborhoods have frequently been destroyed, uprooting people who have lived there for decades, closing down their institutions, ruining small businesses by the hundreds, and scattering families and friends all over the city. By removing the structure of social and emotional support provided by the neighborhood, and by forcing people to rebuild their lives separately and amid strangers elsewhere, slum clearance has often come at a serious psychological as well as financial cost to its supposed beneficiaries."[38]

Lee would soon execute both the best and the worst of urban renewal policies, at a level of intensity and competence matched nowhere else in the country. First, of course, there was the matter of getting elected in 1953.

LEE IS ELECTED MAYOR

On Monday, November 2, 1953, the Republican Town Committee ran a full-page ad in the *New Haven Register* that read as if a campaign committee had solved its differences by saying yes to everything, so long as it was obvious and shopworn:

- Vote for a Better City
- Vote for Sound and Solid Business Management (with a reasonable tax rate!)
- Vote for Steady Improvement of Our School System (High quality education!)
- Good Municipal Labor Relations!
- Completion of East Shore Sewerage Disposal Project!
- Improved Municipal Recreational Facilities and Playgrounds!
- No Bumps—No Ruts in City Streets!
- High Quality Protective Services in the Police, Fire and Health Departments!
- Sensible Planning to Provide Needed Housing!
- The Constructive Efforts of the Parking Authority, Urban Redevelopment Agency and Civilian Defense!

- Continued Municipal Refuse Collection Service!
- Vote for Experienced Leadership: Humane, Honest, Sincere, Able, Experienced.

These tepid words risk nothing and gain less. On the same level, the Celentano administration held a press conference the previous Friday to announce the completion of seventy-four street-paving and repaving projects. It is the sort of approach Bill Celentano had used in 1945, 1947, 1949, and 1951; if it had worked then, perhaps it would work now. The same issue of the same newspaper offered a photo of Celentano cutting the ribbon on the first parking lot opened by the city's recently established Parking Authority. A front-page editorial, flat in tone, called itself "A Final Word" and read in full as follows: "It appears necessary to repeat again that New Haven, under the administration of Mayor William C. Celentano, is in first class financial condition. It has an AAA bond rating which is the highest accorded. Because of this present financial condition the City is well prepared to meet any necessary expenditures without incurring increased taxation at a time when Federal and State tax burdens are at their peak. In view of certain recent claims to the contrary, these facts should be restated at this time for the guidance of those who tomorrow will go to the polls on Election Day." All within the envelope of New Haven convention. Against this background, Lee seemed almost fair-minded in calling Celentano's a "plodding maintenance administration."

There is, however, another layer to the Celentano story in 1953. The administration had actually made several of the moves Lee advocated for New Haven, but made them without energy or conviction. It had (reluctantly) set up a parking authority, pressed into doing so by the Chamber of Commerce. It had retained Yale's Maurice Rotival as a planning consultant, simply carrying forward a 1941 contract issued by the Murphy administration. By 1953, the Chamber of Commerce had taken over much of Rotival's 1942 master plan for the city as its own "Ten Point Program." Celentano had maintained a fairly strong city plan department, headed by Norris Andrews, but had given it very little to do. Pressured by the Democratic majority leadership in the Board of Aldermen, Celentano had agreed to the establishment of a redevelopment agency, provided only that the ordinance be sponsored by someone in the Republican minority. The resulting Urban Redevelopment Agency had already designated the Oak Street neighborhood as a target, and the mayor had endorsed the idea of seeking federal funding. But, as Raymond Wolfinger reports, "A federal survey and planning grant was obtained for Oak Street, but then nothing much happened. There is no indication that Celentano impeded the Redevelopment Agency's progress, but he did not press for action, either. For one thing, doing so would have required a level of active direction and advocacy that very likely would have exceeded his allocation of time for mayoral duties."[39]

Beyond his modest commitment of time and energy to city work, Celentano was a cautious man, and he seems to have *correctly evaluated the capacity of city government to conduct the kind of work that urban renewal involved*. Under the existing City Charter, with the actual boards and commissions in place, with the time-burning habits of the Board of Aldermen rutted a century deep, with the entropy of ward politics (in twice as many wards as Philadelphia!), with the hostility of the local press to government spending, Celentano figured that it just couldn't be done. Lee entirely agreed with Celentano's assessment, thinking that the existing apparatus of government could not bring it off.[40] So without entirely knowing *how* it might be done, Lee rested his 1953 campaign on the proposition that regular city government could no longer cope with the city's problems. Something different, which he could provide and the incumbent could not, was required by the increasingly dramatic challenges faced by New Haven.

The hinge of the 1953 election was Lee's *believable commitment* to actually go forward with the transformation of New Haven. Everyone, at some level of abstraction, bought into the broad policy goal, even Bill Celentano. Lee's campaign strategy was to convince voters that he could and would succeed in attaining goals which had seemed well beyond the capacity of city governments heretofore. The challenger used a political device, known as Independents for Lee, to hammer away at the incumbent while Lee himself concentrated on making his urban renewal vision plausible to voters. Rostow, speaking for the putative Independents, pounded away on Celentano, who rightly (if lamely) pointed out that many of the so-called Independents were registered Democrats (a fact that Lee readily conceded the night he was elected). The appeal of Lee's 1953 campaign did only a little to improve his result in the base wards: his net gain from 1951 to 1953 in his own base came to 863 votes, and the change in Celentano's wards added up to 299 more votes for the incumbent. Between the two modest and offsetting shifts, Lee gained a grand total of 564 votes. But this must be seen against a net loss of 1,502 in the base-versus-base contest in 1951, leaving Lee still 938 in the hole in these wards. Given a loss by only two votes in 1951, ceteris paribus, 564 added base-versus-base might have seemed enough for Lee to win with. But Lee wasn't satisfied to merely hold his own in the non-base neighborhoods (table 9.3).

Table 9.3. 1953 Results in Base Wards and in Other Wards

Area	Celentano	Lee	Net for Lee
Celentano base wards	9,044	4,895	−4,149
Lee base wards	5,512	8,723	3,211
Subtotal for base wards	14,556	13,618	−938
Other wards	21,438	25,911	4,473
Totals	35,994	39,529	3,535

Lee's trump cards lay in the wards that had no obvious bias for or against him on ethnic identity grounds. In the 1953 counts, just as in the previous elections, the ethnic mobilization contest ran Celentano's way, saddling Lee with a 938-vote deficit for all such wards combined (down, to be sure, from 1,502). In the other twenty-one wards having no special identity attachment to either candidate, Dick Lee cleaned house in 1953, willing a decisive 4,473-vote plurality (54.7 percent). Subtracting Celentano's plurality in the base wards, we arrive at an overall plurality of 3,535 for Lee (52.3 percent). In Dahl's terms, one might say that Lee lost the stage-two election and won the stage-three contest—and he would win seven more such contests in years to come. New Haven had a new mayor, and a new kind of mayor—one who would leave office voluntarily sixteen years later after having orchestrated a not-so-quiet revolution in city government and in the city itself. I place great stress on the unusual in Dick Lee's administration, but it would be a grave error to omit his talent for the routine play at second base in local baseball.

ORDINARY POLITICIAN EXTRAORDINAIRE

When Eugene Rostow said, "Dick Lee is no ordinary politician," he surely meant that Lee was not *merely* an ordinary politician—that he was also something much rarer. But Dick Lee was at every stage, among other things, an ordinary politician of the highest quality. He was master craftsman of the conventional means by which the business of the DTC, and of Irish job-seekers, and shortly of Italian job-seekers, and of contract mongers who supported his campaigns was accomplished. He knew how regular politics worked, and how to make it work for his own goals. Take the ancient matter of political loyalty. The following letter from one Ralph "Rocky" Bello to Lee, about sixteen months into his first term, is suggestive of the mayor's political skill and his reputation for distributing both pleasure and pain to players in New Haven politics.[41]

926 Howard Avenue
New Haven, Connecticut
May 2, 1955

Honorable Richard C. Lee
Mayor
City Hall
New Haven, Connecticut
Dear Mayor Lee:

I know that you are aware of the fact that for many months I have been grumbling a great deal and probably had no right to do so. I want you to know that I had been made promises, which I felt were not being kept.

I am writing you this letter to clear up this situation, and let you know that I am very appreciative and thankful for the fact that you have seen fit to show your confidence in me by having the Police Department entrust me with towing work for it. This has been a great help to me, and I want to assure you that I am not only grateful but shall do everything in my power to show my appreciation by my continued support of you and your administration.

Respectfully yours,
Ralph Bello

Rocky Bello, quite possibly a 7th Ward adherent of Bill Celentano's in 1953, is "kissing the ring" in gratitude for a notoriously profitable towing contract. He is doing so because someone has pointed out to him that he enjoys no firm right to its continuation without the mayor's indulgence. This is classic Lee—generosity constrained by a quietly signaled willingness to punish those few fools who fail to properly reciprocate a favor—with loyalty, political contributions, and recognition of the mayor's great service to the public good.

Lee was also an adroit manager of the DTC. Here, as mayor, he dealt with John Golden and Arthur Barbieri, whom Golden had recently made New Haven's first Italian-American Democratic Town Chairman. As Allan Talbot relates, Lee formed the following treaty with these two operatives:

Lee indicated the following: that he would clear his appointments with Golden; that Golden would handle political arrangements with the state machine; that steps would be taken to assure that Golden's insurance business would be given favorable consideration whenever the city required such services; that Golden's candidates would be given serious consideration for available city jobs and patronage; and that Golden would be the senior partner as far as the party was concerned. Lee wanted full control over redevel-

opment decisions and jobs, although he would clear major decisions affect-
ing the party with the other two. Barbieri the Town Chairman was made
Barbieri the Public Works Director. This gift was perfectly consistent with
previous practices during most of this century, for Public Works had always
been turned over to the politicians. . . . [Barbieri] cut fifty-two "unnecessary
jobs" from the department ("all of 'em held by Republicans" he later
boasted). . . . Sometimes by having patronage meetings held in his [Lee's]
office, other times by making personal calls to notify those who were to get
city jobs, Lee showed the party that he was the supplier and not the delivery
boy.[42]

Lee was a world-champion on the "recognition" side of city politics. For New
Haven's Italians, he established a Columbus Day parade to parallel the long-run-
ning march on St. Patrick's Day. He had the existing statue of Columbus in Italian 10th Ward handsomely refurbished. But his great flair for recognition politics ran to smaller and sadder occasions. As Wolfinger writes, the mayor "read
the obituary columns faithfully, wrote letters of condolence whenever he had the
slightest connection with any of the principals, and attended two or three wakes
a day on his way home from work. He made sure that his frequent drives through
the city would not go unnoticed by using an enormous late-model Cadillac as his
official limousine, and then carefully showed how he had a heart despite the
cares of office by making a habit of giving children a ride home from school."[43]
Lee arranged for his driver to drop him at the front door of each wake, and drive
around to the back door, so that in one pass through the hall he would be visible
to all the assembled mourners.

The mayor was likewise good at highlighting the small victories that create
confidence in constituents. Thus, for instance, his 1956 State of the City message
made much of a refurbished Jocelyn Square, which he depicted as a "wonderland
replete with a Swedish slide, shower spray, swings, chutes, story book cut-outs, a
giant concrete turtle, miracle whirl, a Little League baseball field; and even basketball, bocci, and shuffleboard courts." In public works, Lee found much to
praise in the purchase of new "snow-fighting" gear, street sweepers, street flush-
ers, and a new municipal garage. Like Celentano, he continued to pave streets and
take credit for the job—in 1955, thirty-two miles of new pavement. Similarly, he
proudly took credit for 587 new streetlights installed during the same year. Larger
accomplishments, such as centralized purchasing and the elimination of obvious
managerial waste, added substance to these quotidian accomplishments.

Lee was also attuned to the intelligence-gathering requirements of city politics. Who is working for us and who is working against us? Who is badmouthing the administration behind its back? An incident involving one of the working-class Catholic parishes makes the point nicely. Young Bill Donohue came home from Providence College in 1959, looking for a job. After surviving Ed Logue's penetrating evaluation he found himself working on redevelopment and shuttling between that work and the local political scene. He may have worked with Ed Logue, but he worked *for* Dick Lee. A 1962 memo from Donohue to Lee demonstrates the young man's devotion to duty even on Sunday morning, and suggests Lee's keen interest in political intelligence gathering:

> Per our conversation of Monday, April 2, 1962, please be advised that on Sunday, April 1, 1962, Fr. Sanders of St. Patrick's Roman Catholic Church on Grand Avenue severely criticized and questioned the handling of the acquisition of property from St. Patrick's. His remarks came from the pulpit and his justification was that he felt he owed it to his parishioners to let them know the "lack of consideration the City administration" had for them. . . . The parishioners were told that if they came from a more wealthy neighborhood, or had people with political prestige, or if he himself had been here for many years with a large parish that such procedures would never have taken place. . . . On another occasion Fr. Sanders used the comparison of "the Russians have their way of doing things and Dick Lee has his—I think Dick Lee gets what he wants done even quicker."[44]

This too is evidence of an effective politics within the ordinary tool kit. According to Donohue, Lee later revealed that he had actually cut a deal with the regional archdiocese for acquiring the St. Patrick's parcels, of which Father Sanders was obviously and embarrassingly unaware.[45]

Lee was thus a conventional politician and a regular mayor. For a great part of city government business, Dick Lee belonged to a lineage stretching from Cornelius Driscoll and Frank Rice to Honest John Murphy and Bill Celentano. He allowed many of the government's agencies to function in the way they had been functioning for decades past. He adroitly asserted his authority over boards and commissions, and reinforced it by rewarding loyal members with relevant favors, punishing knaves with banishment. He made thousands of alliances at little cost to himself or to the city. He is said to have helped roughly half the families in New Haven to convince themselves that His Honor was a close family friend. All this conventionality, and the high quality of his conventionality, was a necessary part of Dick Lee's performance in politics of a far less conventional variety.

CHAPTER 10

EXTRAORDINARY POLITICS: DICK LEE, URBAN RENEWAL, AND THE END OF URBANISM

By the time he settled into the mayor's office in the first week of January 1954, Richard Charles Lee knew he was very good at politics. In this, he was a lot like Frank Rice—skilled at cultivating relationships, bringing people together in agreement and leaving them to their own devices when agreement could not be expected. He was, if anything, even better than Rice at regular politics. But there was an important difference: Rice had figured, more or less correctly, that ordinary politics of high quality would get him through his years as mayor. In contrast, Lee knew with certainty that ordinary politics alone wouldn't do the job he had promised his constituents in the 1953 campaign. Lee knew the city had big problems, but he did not know (and in some cases could not have known) just what they were or how hard they would be to fix. Dick Lee doubtless knew things about politics which you and I, good reader, do not know. We, on the other hand, know things about the history of the city that he could not have known in 1954. Hindsight is easy; leadership is hard. But hindsight is the business of this book, and with it comes a responsibility for forthright judgment. Here, in all its brutal simplicity, is my two-part conclusion about this mayor:

Government. Richard C. Lee was the greatest mayor of New Haven's twentieth century and was among the most remarkable mayors who served anywhere in the United States during that century.

Governance. Lee and his administration failed to achieve the overall goal of renewing the city of New Haven.

The seeming contradiction formed by greatness and failure is apparent and not real. In his management of government—of the Redevelopment Agency, of the federal grants process, of state regulations and grants—Lee had no peer. Yet in the goals of governance, of revitalizing the city, he was in the main unsuccessful. This is because the underlying problems faced by Lee's New Haven were so deeply rooted in its history, so powerful, and so complex that no mayor and no mayoral administration lasting a mere sixteen years could have overcome them. His principal resources—delivered through the Federal Housing Acts of 1949 and 1954—were, moreover, poorly suited to many of the tasks that needed to be performed.

ACCIDENTS OF URBAN DESTRUCTION

By "renewing" the city, as I use the term here, please understand that I refer to the restoration of urbanism—making central-city land an object of competition between would-be investors, restoring the vital fabric of enterprise downtown and in the neighborhoods, making the central-city housing stock desirable again (both to potential residents and to mortgage underwriters), enlivening the civic life of neighborhoods and the city at large, and restoring a class of grounded leadership linking citizenship based on residence with citizenship based on ownership and investment. These features of urbanism were created in a long, complex historical sequence, running back at least to the 1840s. The same features of urbanism were dismantled by a similarly long, complex sequence running from the 1920s into the 1980s. The tectonic forces that pressed themselves against the city, and against the major features of urbanism within it, were so powerful as to dwarf even the remarkable resources that Dick Lee had amassed during his eight terms of office. What had been a convergence of accidents favoring urbanism had turned into a convergence of accidents working against it. These changes of underlying structure ran far beyond Lee's reach—even when he had the benefit of large federal funding and the gifts of superb talent—his own and that of his lieutenants. Here are a few important forces pressing against urbanism, and against its renewal in mid-century:

- The near-total obsolescence of steam-driven manufacturing, and of the plants built to take advantage of it.

- The decline and partial obsolescence of freight rail services, which had once made central-city New Haven a privileged location for manufacturing.
- The maturation of an AC electrical grid making virtually every location in the region accessible for commerce, production, housing, and civic life.
- The seemingly limitless development of the automobile as the hegemonic technology of daily life, and with it the success of suburban housing for city workers.
- The emergence of trucking as a rival to rail, and with it the development of Greenfield manufacturing.
- The declining advantage of northeastern cities as sites of production and commerce, as contrasted with sunbelt and overseas locations.
- Declining rates of immigration, and continuation of restrictions upon it.
- The rigidity, and uneven quality, of the housing stock developed between 1870 and 1920 to accommodate industrial workers.
- The iron girdle of New England towns that grasped New Haven, and which had by 1954 become bastions of resistance to control (much less taxation) from the central city.
- The surge of African-American migration from the agricultural South, which had begun in the 1940s and continued into the 1970s, in pursuit of jobs that disappeared just as the newcomers arrived.
- The decline of the civic fauna, particularly of peer-led organizations existing by and for the city's citizens.
- The signaling effect of zoning, HOLC's mortgage study, and other events tending to stigmatize working-class neighborhoods in the city.

Forces like these are largely beyond the reach of City Hall, even with a titan in the mayor's office. Lee would succeed at many specific tasks: he would clear fetid tenements and bulldoze decrepit stores; he would assemble land for new uses; he would actually market some of that land to new users; he would mastermind and finance the restoration of older neighborhoods such as Wooster Square; he would immensely improve the circulation of auto traffic in the city and through it; he would upgrade the staffing of city government. But, for all that, he would in the main fail in his resolve to renew the city. His failures would, in the very long run, be productive, for they would unveil the end of urbanism, and, a generation later, allow new blood to steer a different course—one which restores what is restorable in the urban past, and which has the wisdom of accumulated hindsight to let go of the rest.

Lee's situation in 1954 differed from Rice's in 1910 in two fundamentals:

Sharp decline of grounded leadership. Rice came to office with an active, grounded civic and business leadership. Indeed, that leadership had pressed forward a plan for "civic improvement" that was delivered without help or encouragement from Rice in 1910.¹ Rice rejected most of its recommendations, focused on such matters as uniform sidewalks, and still found a supportive business constituency. Lee, in contrast, came to power when business leadership was weaker, thinner, less grounded in the city. He would be compelled, in effect, to invent a business leadership and ask it to support his program under the heading of a Citizens Action Commission.

End of urbanism: While Rice saw no reason for pessimism about the city, Lee was elected on what amounted to an end-of-urbanism campaign. He was committed in advance by his 1953 campaign to the proposition that the city was in trouble, that politics and policy as usual were not enough, and that something extraordinary was required by way of response.

Lee had built his winning campaign on a shrewd denial of the first, and frank acceptance of the second. His promise to create a Citizens Action Commission was a way of flattering what remained of a business elite, and of mobilizing it to his purposes (figure 10.1). His whole campaign had been built around the end of

Figure 10.1. Citizens Action Commission leadership "muscles" pose for planning session with Mayor Lee, 1955. NHCHS.

urbanism, around the need for radical intervention in the fate of the central business district (CBD), and of the decaying neighborhoods around it. Lee's vision was remarkable but less than clairvoyant: he failed to anticipate the changing economic functions of urban space, failed to anticipate the future of retail markets, sometimes failed to fully understand that the centered city of old could not be restored by bricks and mortar. The great positive factor in Lee's situation was the availability of large-scale help from the federal government, and he would zero in on that opportunity from the beginning. At first called "urban redevelopment," the federal program was renamed "urban renewal" in 1954, just as Lee came to power.[2] He would respond by hiring a technocratic elite (I will call them the tigers), creating a virtual alternative government for them to operate (I will call it the Kremlin), obtaining a stream of financial resources from outside the city to nurture their programs (the federal aorta, discussed below), and assaulting the problems of the city and its neighborhoods with urban renewal and social renewal programs on a massive scale. Together, these constitute the extraordinary politics of the Lee era and urban renewal.

A TIGER IN THE CELLAR

Lee set out to recruit the smartest and most arrogant people who had ever served in the management of so modest an American city as New Haven. In Ed Logue he hit that target dead center. Logue would be Lee's most essential partner (and sometime rival) in running New Haven. A World War II combat veteran and 1948 graduate of the Yale Law School, Logue had most recently served Chester Bowles, who was then ambassador to India, as an executive assistant. Ivy-educated and testosterone-powered, Logue would earn a reputation second only to Robert Moses' as a practitioner of urban transformation in New Haven, Boston, and New York. A stocky man of 5 feet 8, Logue seethed with energy. He seemed to think faster, move farther, dominate more of his environment than anyone else around town—even, on occasion, than Dick Lee. The mayor later recalled having fired Logue for his arrogance and stubbornness as often as several times a week. His place in the early days of the Lee administration is nicely captured by Allan Talbot:

> Keeping a man like Logue under wraps is something like hiding a tiger in the cellar. By the end of the first year of the Lee administration Logue was running the city's Redevelopment Agency. By the beginning of the second year, he became the redevelopment czar through his appointment as Devel-

opment Administrator, a new city post which put him in charge of all city agencies which had anything to do with redevelopment. His only boss on an organization chart or in reality was the Mayor. Thus the conflict between the two men stemmed from the natural problem of how such strong-minded people could coexist in a milieu of action and power. Yet the full character of their relationship is best indicated by the fact that twelve years later, and separated by a hundred and twenty miles, both men used exactly the same language in summing up their quarrels: "We fought like brothers."[3]

Logue was the administration's four-hundred-pound Bengal tiger, capable of finding and clawing apart the shoddy staff-work in which city government abounded. He often communicated with subordinates by humiliating them. He took over formerly independent boards and commissions, such as the Board of Zoning Appeals, subordinating their decisions to the objectives he and the mayor had set for renewal. He was capable of immense work and willing to demand the same of all members of the minority whose efforts he thought worth having. Writing and managing the city's capital budgets, he was quickly able to gain leverage over the line departments, and, on occasion, he won grudging respect in the Board of Aldermen. Logue made enemies often, but only rarely were these enemies strong enough or smart enough to pay him back.

The case of Samuel Spielvogel, holdover head of the Redevelopment Agency from Celentano's years, is perhaps a fair illustration. Spielvogel was well suited to a relaxed schedule of action under the former mayor: "He responded to pressure for action by dwelling on obstacles and depicting arcane mysteries which had to be mastered before success could be assured."[4] Lee sent Logue in to deal with Spielvogel and to get him to work cooperatively with Norris Andrews, who was heading the City Plan Department in a more action-inducing fashion. Logue immediately crossed Spielvogel, who erred by publicly challenging Logue's right to interfere in Redevelopment business (Logue was then merely Lee's executive secretary). Logue, confident of the mayor's allegiance, asked for Spielvogel's immediate ouster. The Redevelopment Agency, Republican majority and all, was shortly induced by the mayor to demand Spielvogel's resignation, followed quickly by Logue's appointment to his job. Lee would soon create a super-departmental position, Development Administrator, from which Logue would be able to control Redevelopment and a cluster of related agencies.

Logue needed a staff able and willing to spearhead the difficult work of urban renewal, and he recruited *all* of its six top members from outside the reach of New Haven politics. Harvard-educated Ralph Taylor became the number two official. Thomas Appleby became the number three. Harold Grabino became the agency's inside attorney. Charles Shannon and Robert Hazen completed the team. As Raymond Wolfinger points out: "These six had a good deal in common: none was from New Haven; all were in their twenties or thirties; all had attended elite colleges or universities; all had postgraduate degrees . . . ; all had cosmopolitan, nationally oriented career expectations."[5] Another equally valid description focused on the hiring criteria that generated this group: "The screening process was long and personal. . . . The criteria for selection were simple and straightforward: intelligence, readiness to work seven days a week, ability to withstand pressure and abuse, willingness to learn, and a high metabolic rate."[6] Logue's Irish name notwithstanding (he was in point of fact a Protestant), these people had nothing to do with New Haven's Irish ascendancy, and they mixed poorly with the Democratic Town Committee. Neither could most regular city employees be expected to readily accept such a staff, most of whose members would leave the city during Lee's mayoralty without having adjusted to the folkways of New Haven politics.

THE KREMLIN

Urban redevelopment, as laid out in the Housing Act of 1949, was aimed at decaying residential areas—neighborhoods full of voters and children, whose homes and businesses would be bought out (if need be, taken by eminent domain), bulldozed, and combined into parcels large enough to attract developers who would create facilities for other, and presumably more upscale, inhabitants. Thus did Lee suffer Ed Logue and his staff to tear down blocks and blocks of the city, and to build highways through certified slums, which incidentally also had political identities such as the 2nd, 3rd, 4th, and 10th Wards. It was clear from day one that work of this kind could not possibly be accomplished within the rococo structure of city government as it stood. City Hall was still as fragile, and as rigid, as the one over which Frank Rice had presided.[7] The Board of Aldermen was, moreover, given to a degree of compassion for neighborhood interests that would have stopped urban renewal cold (some projects more or less destroyed entire aldermanic constituencies). Lee therefore worked toward charter revision as a means to making the city's formal system of government less fragmented and more friendly to concerted policy. In this effort he failed entirely. The DTC and hundreds of office-holders at every level derived advantages from the complexity and infirmity of city government, and they sabotaged all serious proposals for change. Lee would need to find solutions that allowed authority to flow to him and Logue through arteries of power not contemplated by the city charter. He found them beyond the conventionally understood body politic of New Haven, and he used them to extraordinary effect over the course of his years in office.

The Lee administration was thus founded upon a partnership between two gifted young men, only one of whom had been elected mayor. The two shared unusual drive, unusual talent, and the good timing to which Machiavelli conceded the irreducible element of *fortuna* in politics. Lee was a regular politician of high accomplishment; Logue assuredly was not. Lee had deep roots in the city; Logue was a Yale-blue cosmopolitan. Lee had begun his professional career in journalism and public relations, working for a local paper, the local Chamber of Commerce, and the world-class university that happened to be located in New Haven. Logue was a lawyer with world experience in government stretching from state politics to international diplomacy. Lee would do the regular politics; Logue would stay out of it whenever possible.[8] Lee would protect the boundaries of Logue's realm against invading office-seekers, and he would deliver the permissive consensus required to legitimate urban renewal and the considerable coercion it would require. Logue would deliver first-class staff work, master the federal regulations required to get at the money, and keep his operation free of corrupting influences. When necessary, Logue would take the heat for disappointing outcomes, jobs denied, and feathers ruffled.

Lee wisely elected to separate Logue and his people from politics and routine administration by housing them in a facility of their own. City Hall stood as now on the east side of the New Haven Green, and just to its north stood 177 Church Street—a nondescript office structure in which Lee located the Redevelopment Agency, with City Plan above it, and Maurice Rotival's planning consultancy above that. Redevelopment was the controlling institution, and Logue was, by 1955, its undisputed sovereign. When planning help was needed, Logue called upstairs—sometimes skipping over the city planning staff and bringing Rotival's people directly to the table. Redevelopment field offices, each situated out in a project area, formed tentacles of the Kremlin, and they were the places where political appointees who survived Logue's scrutiny were apt to find themselves. Four decades later, an elderly Lee would smile at the ironic simile to the shadowed command center of the Soviet empire. Throughout its history, the Kremlin exhibited two key features: top-down technical superiority in management, divorced insofar as possible from regular government and regular politics, and externalization of funding sources so that taxpayers and foundation coffers elsewhere paid for as much of Lee's program as was lawfully feasible. Clearly, the outside funding made possible the inside independence from ordinary local politics.

TOP-DOWN TECHNOCRATIC SUPERIORITY

As already observed, Lee went for top managerial and planning talent, and allowed that talent to recruit in kind: Logue, Taylor, Appleby, Grabino, Hazen, and Shannon were ranking officers early. Younger people such as Katherine Feidelson, Joel Cogen, Harry Wexler, Philetus Holt, Byrn Stoddard, and a score of other smart professionals would follow. Rotival's urban planning office became a second column of Logue's army, and Commissar Logue ran a very tight operation. As one keen observer of the period observes, the top people in Redevelopment "regarded themselves as something of an elite group, much in the same style as paratroopers or law professors."[9] In another formulation, there was a tendency to think of New Haven as "the West Point of Urban Renewal."[10] The group as a whole focused on achieving something like an urban revolution, and the small doings of regular politics were impediments to be overcome, or to be ignored if possible. In a sense, therefore, the effective element of city government itself became detached from local issues and local potentates—a fact noticed early and often by Lee's detractors.

The Kremlin was not a consensus-seeking affair, and it was not given to the sufferance of fools. In most cases, Kremlin-dwellers were better paid than the rest of the city's staff, and for good reason. They sometimes thought of themselves as "paying rent" for the opportunity to be part of Lee's effort, since each could command a higher salary elsewhere. How, one may wonder, could such a crowd get along with their colleagues in the old-line city departments, many of whom shared no sense of mission with these high-handed newcomers? There were two answers to this question: (1) to leave alone most of the activity in city government that didn't affect redevelopment, and (2) to simply do (or, even worse, outsource) the work of old-line departments when it was essential to redevelopment. As Wolfinger reports:

> Redevelopment officials were somewhat reluctant to rely on the staff support of politically appointed city departments, whose members they considered inferior in ability, dedication, and energy. . . . Rather than using the Corporation Counsel's office, the Agency had in Grabino its own very competent legal officer. When the Church Street Project was threatened by liti-

gation, the Agency retained one of the city's two prominent law firms. Many party regulars resented Lee's giving this plum, which resulted in fees of more than $100,000 to a Republican firm instead of spreading it around among more "deserving" lawyers. To a considerable extent the Redevelopment Agency was bureaucratically self-sufficient. Instead of working through other city agencies it performed their functions itself insofar as they pertained to urban renewal, or contracted out for the work. This freed the Agency from inertia and bureaucratic self-interest and made it easier to avoid the party organization's claims in regard to patronage. It also, of course, made the Agency itself a bureaucratic empire; in the late 1960s it had grown to 250 employees.[11]

Lee had taken care to issue an executive order stating that department heads answered to Logue in relation to redevelopment activities, but this greatly understated the matter. Logue was free to ignore department heads whenever he found a more expeditious way of accomplishing his goals. Often, being ignored was preferable to being accosted by Logue. As one department chieftain reported, "There's a difference between telling a man he's done something wrong and humiliating him in front of his colleagues for doing it. Humiliation was a standard Logue device, and by using it he unnecessarily offended and hurt people."[12]

It is widely believed that public bureaucracies are incapable of sustaining high levels of quality and productivity, and there are good reasons to agree.[13] Process and procedure, once ingrained deeply enough, overwhelm results: a middling result attained by standard procedure trumps a far better result that violates conventional practice. The shadow of failure falls on public managers; the glow of success falls on elected officials. The burden of conventional mediocrity, even failure, is not a career-breaker; the burden of innovative failure is often catastrophic. The best way of doing something demands far greater courage and skill than the best defended way of doing it. All of these canards are commonplace generalizations about public management, and are quite often sustained by the evidence in local government. But Lee's Kremlin was a startling exception: its project plans, its budgetary ingenuity, its shrewd organizational workings, its capacity to compete for federal funding, all of these and more of its aspects were of the very highest quality. This quality, and the availability of federal funding, created a self-expanding cycle of growth: technically and conceptually superb grant proposals generated funding; that funding allowed the hiring of more and more very able staff people in Redevelopment, which in turn increased the agency's ability to attract new money. After a time, Logue and his colleagues managed to influence the terms and requirements included in the federal requests for proposals—drawing the bull's-eye for whatever arrow New Haven was ready to shoot. [14] Most important of all, perhaps, very few members of the Kremlin gang needed to protect a long-term future in New Haven city government—each was satisfied with establishing an external reputation based more on results than on congeniality or popularity.

THE FEDERAL AORTA

It will be remembered that the industrial economy of New Haven had for many decades generated a river of cash flowing into town. Early in Chapter 1, I wrote of industrial exporters who "fed cash to thousands of wage-earners and to a multitude of smaller specialty manufacturers and machine tool shops that in turn furnished them with supplies and expert services." This great river spread economic energy across ten thousand households and more, creating diverse demand for whatever might be desired. The flood was, by Dick Lee's time, beginning to dry up, and the federal government's Urban Renewal Administration would for a time partially replace it—without ever beginning to replace its function in the city's economy. A great aorta, pumping economic energy into the Lee-Logue Kremlin, ran north along the coast from Washington, as if following the course of soon-to-be-built Interstate 95. It carried not hemoglobin but dollars. The IRS collected cash from taxpayers across America, Congress placed it at the disposal of the Housing and Home Finance Agency (HHFA), and later the Urban Renewal Administration, and the Redevelopment Agency of New Haven competed with remarkable success for the resulting swag.

The money came to that "local agency" under federal law, and not to the general fund of city government, which is to say it came to Logue and his Redevelopment colleagues. Their projects and plans required approval from the Board of Aldermen, and some cooperation from any number of city agencies, but the Redevelopment budgets were virtually autonomous from city politics. The Kremlin was financed largely by people who were not entitled to vote in New Haven, mostly on a funding formula which granted two-thirds of net project costs in federal dollars and then allowed the local agency to count many in-kind items toward the local third. Due to the audacity and ingenuity of Logue and his staff, Lee managed in one instance to count $7,827,600 of Yale's spending on its elegant Eero Saarinen–designed residential colleges (Morse and Stiles) as part of the local match for urban renewal. [15] Let's get into the spirit of the thing by hearing from the mayor's testimony to the Board of Aldermen's Committee on Streets and Squares in October 1959, just before an election, as he defended his urban renewal program. The immediate issue was the wholesale reconfiguration of the commercial downtown, the so-called Church Street project, which had been delayed by lawsuits and unsteady business decisions. It was a difficult moment in redevelopment politics, and Logue sent his mayor into battle well prepared with facts, and with astonishing amounts of money from elsewhere:

My name is Richard C. Lee. I reside at 350 Shelton Avenue. I am mayor of the City of New Haven. I appear before your Honorable Committee tonight to testify in support of the disposition agreement between the City of New Haven, the Redevelopment Agency and the Stevens New Haven Development Co., Inc.

You have heard testimony by Mssrs. Logue and Appleby, who have set forth the detailed information concerning this agreement and the changes it proposes from the previous agreement. I hope you will find their testimony persuasive. Tonight I am here to give you some additional information which I have collected specially for this meeting because, as you have all noticed, there has been considerable politically motivated criticism of the delays which have taken place in this project. . . .

The redevelopment process is divided as you all know into two basic steps. The first is what might be called the "red tape" stage. This begins with the filing of a survey and planning application, goes through the compliance with all Federal regulations, the execution of a loan and grant contract—right down to the relocation of the first family and the demolition of the first building. During all of this period there is no physical evidence of any kind that the redevelopment process is even at work. During this period if there are delays, there are of course many doubting Thomases who are willing to state that demolition will never happen—not to mention construction. We have been through that period and we know what it means.

By any standard of comparison, the performance of this administration in getting projects into and through the "red tape" stage is beyond challenge the outstanding one in the United States. We now have four projects in the execution stage:

Oak Street,

Church Street,

Wooster Square, and

Long Wharf

. . . All four projects are now in the action stage. The total Federal grants for the four are $27,424,108. The total Federal loans are $42,099,674. The total State contribution is $3,609,058.

On the basis of the latest information available, New Haven ranks fifth among the first ten cities in the United States in its program under execution. Here is a list of the first ten in order of total federal capital grants:

1. New York, $89,951,699
2. Chicago, $73,462,006
3. Washington, D.C., $50,277,824
4. Philadelphia, $36,249,061
5. NEW HAVEN, $27,424,108
6. Norfolk, $25,799,865
7. St. Louis, $25,563,731
8. Detroit, $15,069,063
9. Pittsburgh, $12,472,767
10. San Francisco, $9,327,260

An even more interesting comparison is the rank on a per capita basis. On this basis we are far and away out in front.[16]

When the figures for leading cities were tabulated on a per capita basis six years later, New Haven was indeed "far and away out in front." Indeed, the city was so well financed by the Urban Renewal program as to create an embarrassing imbalance. Listed is per capita spending by city:

New Haven, $745.38
Newark, $277.33
Boston, $218.16
Pittsburgh, $160.29
Cincinnati, $154.81
San Francisco, $123.68
Philadelphia, $104.66
Washington, D.C., $94.09
Baltimore, $76.06
Detroit, $68.37
Chicago, $47.42
New York, $36.77[17]

Lee was, moreover, able to keep the city's own out-of-taxpayers'-pocket expenditures extremely low. The basic ratio required by the federal government was 2:1, federal share to local share. But there were countless accounting adjustments available to skilled staff, and endless opportunities to include "non-cash" expenditures on the local side. Most of the local share was offset by noncash items, including donated land, street and utility improvements, and the like.[18] The Kremlin's sale of land assembled in the project to developers left a net cash surplus in Lee's coffers. Some hard-to-calculate sum had been spent on streets and utilities using city money which would not otherwise have been necessary. The accounting and regulatory processes are intricate beyond ordinary understanding, but the big story is that Lee and Logue could export nearly all the net costs of renewal work. At the same time, the state of Connecticut had, with some urging from Lee, passed Public Act 24 (1958), Public Act 8 (1958), and Public Act 594 (1961) offering state funding for the local share of specified aspects of urban renewal.[19] The net effect of these machinations is that the local percentage of total urban renewal costs was very low indeed. City urban renewal cash spending from locally generated revenues appears to have amounted to as little as 5 percent of total urban renewal costs during the Lee era as a whole.

Not only was the funding largely beyond the pockets of New Haven voters, it was largely beyond the control of city government at large. Funds came directly into the accounts of the Redevelopment Agency and provided Logue and his successors with considerable leverage in dealing with budgets. Often, indeed, the Kremlin could provide the city's general fund with a net operating surplus at year's end. Most important, politically, the Lee administration had, in effect, created an alternative city government that could carry out transformative change, even when it was painful in the extreme, so long as Lee could perform the political magic required to keep the public willing to accept this arrangement.[20] One critical feature of his strategy, first mooted in the 1953 campaign, was his Citizens Action Commission.

THE CITIZENS ACTION COMMISSION

Lee began, in his 1953 campaign, by proposing an extragovernmental body, the Citizens Action Commission (CAC), to be composed of leading business and civic personalities in the city (and, often, its suburbs). Such a body would legitimate policy and help Lee mobilize the momentum needed to overwhelm established political resistance. It would include all the "brains" and "muscles" Lee could find to support, refine, and advocate his policies. It would provide Lee with an alternative political organ not within the purview of the Democratic Town Committee or its chairman. The CAC's table of organization would look for all the world like an alternative government, with the mayor on top, the CAC execu-

tive committee of top guns just below, then six topic-related committees of the
CAC, and then, at the very bottom, the "cooperating city agencies" (a.k.a. the departments of local government), such as public works, engineering, parks, welfare, the Board of Education, and the Redevelopment Agency. Nowhere visible
on the chart are the Board of Aldermen, the Board of Finance, the city controller,
or any of a hundred established commissions governing the line departments of
city government. The topical committees focused on industrial and harbor development, on the CBD and its traffic problems, on housing and slum clearance,
on welfare and human relations, on education, and on metropolitan cooperation. This looked like an alternative government, but it was actually anything but
an alternative government—a role taken by the Kremlin.

The Citizens Action Commission was a simulacrum for the supportive force
of a local business elite. The old, grounded business class was thinning and
spreading by now: the CAC would focus and greatly amplify its influence in support of the mayor's agenda. It would stress generally shared benefits as interest
groups came forward complaining about harms done to them in the process
of urban renewal. In the 1953 debate, Celentano had countered by calling the
CAC "ridiculous" and unrealistic. Lee had answered that New York, Baltimore,
Philadelphia, and Detroit had put similar bodies in place, so if Celentano were
right, "hundreds of thousands of persons have joined in a ridiculous crusade—
that of acting in concert to bring about better living conditions and community
health."[21] Lee would, as we have already seen, create an alternative to city government, but the CAC would support rather than constitute that alternative.

It took Lee most of 1954 to round up a plausible top-echelon for his Citizens
Action Commission, and when he did, the local Chamber gladly took credit for
the organization and its agenda: "The formation of the Citizens Action Commission by the Mayor marks an important milestone in the efforts of the Chamber of
Commerce to revitalize our city by a planned program of redevelopment, and the
exercise of vigorous initiative to fully further our city's many advantages. The
appointment of Carl G. Freese, a Chamber President from 1947–49, as chairman of the CAC, brings to this important post a man of vision and faith in the future of New Haven. . . . Mr. Freese will be ably served by the two vice-chairmen:
A. Whitney Griswold, president of Yale University, and Merritt D. Vanderbilt,
president of Greast Manufacturing."[22]

The Chamber of Commerce (where Lee had been a staff member fifteen years
earlier) actually was already engaged with the redevelopment agenda, as were
Chambers in many parts of the country, and as was the national organization itself.[23] One may fairly wonder whether Lee was the ventriloquist (manipulating the

Chamber) or its dummy in this transaction, and the answer is quite probably both. That is, Lee shaped his agenda partly by keeping in tune with the Chamber and other such organizations, and also used them as voices for his own intentions.

In creating the CAC, the mayor was creating a voice that he, in consort with others, could use to speak up on behalf of the redevelopment process. It was in some key ways very like a speaking dummy—a representation of a business elite that had ceased to be. As Allan Talbot writes:

> By the time Lee became mayor, New Haven no longer had a strong, unified business community. What it did have was certainly not running the town as in earlier years. The business leadership was a heterogeneous mixture of new ethnics, imports who ran the family businesses which had been acquired by national firms, a handful of firms still run by old-line families, and other established Yankees who quietly served on bank boards, as partners in law firms, or stayed home clipping coupons.... Gone were the hard-working, strong-minded Yankee leaders who as a unified group had built the town and given it a university and economic growth. Only the weakest of their legacy was apparent: the rigid conservatism of their ideology and the caution born of their failures. The only true voice of New Haven business was the city's Chamber of Commerce: it neither led nor dragged. It was just there. Lee's goals, therefore, were not to overcome strong business opposition; they were centered on mobilization—to give the business community the appearance of unity and power, a group whose members were from top to bottom solidly for Lee. The vehicle for this effort was the Citizens Action Commission (CAC).[24]

Lee shamelessly lionized the senior leadership of his creation. These men (no women were to be found among the top CAC figures) were for Lee the "big muscles" of the city, who controlled the banks, the industries, the money in town. The costs of urban renewal were readily apparent in ward politics, and grumbling became a way of life for many street-corner chatterers. The benefits of urban renewal were less visible to ward politicians than they were to Lee's CAC. The benefits of renewal were conversely far more visible to the top CAC leadership than they were to citizens on the ground. Whereas a mayor like Frank Rice was beholden to a grounded business elite, Lee needed very nearly to invent such an elite in order to give weight to his long-term vision for New Haven.

In his notable study of Atlanta politics, Clarence Stone elaborates a theory of "regime politics," which sheds light on what Dick Lee was up to in forming the CAC:

Even though the institutions of local government bear most of the formal responsibility for governing, they lack the resources and the scope of authority to govern without active support and cooperation of significant private interests. An urban regime may thus be defined as the informal arrangements by which public bodies and private interests function together in order to be able to make and carry out governing decisions. . . . The mix of participants varies by community, but that mix is itself constrained by two basic institutional principles of the American political economy: (1) popular control of the formal machinery of government, and (2) private ownership of business enterprise."[25]

Lee was all but inventing a business regime for New Haven, at the very least exaggerating the power, groundedness, and solidarity of business leadership in a city where that feature of urbanism had begun to fade from existence.

The spatial decentralization of top-leadership may be suggested by comparing figure 10.2 and figure 10.3, both drawn to the same scale. The former shows the home addresses of the leaders composing the Civic Improvement Committee, which served from 1907 to 1910 and produced the Gilbert and Olmsted City Beautiful plan for New Haven. These people were all living close to the city center, grounded more or less around the clock to urban life. One individual lived on Whitney Avenue in Hamden, north of the city, another lived right on the city line (Frederick Brewster's estate is now Edgerton Park). Most of the 1910 people were living in the compact upscale areas—of East Rock, and, to a lesser extent, Dwight. All but two were within easy walking distance of the nine squares on a sunny morning. Figure 10.3 shows the top tier of Lee's CAC leadership (the executive committee, plus the chairs of each topical taskforce). The one major point of continuity between these two spatial distributions is the East Rock neighborhood, above the nine squares in each map: it remains (even to this twenty-first-century day) a bastion of upper-tier leadership. The geography of leadership has, however, shifted in three major ways over the intervening four decades from Rice to Lee. First, within city limits, the Westville neighborhood (far left of the nine squares) has become an important leadership community (Lee himself would move there during his incumbency as mayor). Second, the old Dwight neighborhood (just left of the nine squares) is no longer a leadership node by 1955. Once people like Sylvester Poli, John Studley, and Rollin Woodruff were living there. By Lee's day, people of that rank and prominence were no longer living in the Dwight area. Third, and by far most important, the 1955 CAC leadership was dispersed well beyond city limits. Only ten of twenty-one lived in

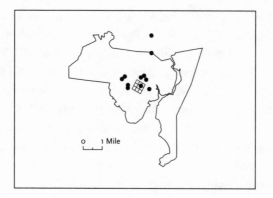

Figure 10.2. Homes of Civic Improvement
Committee members, 1907–10.

New Haven. Of the remaining eleven, five were housed in Hamden, one each in
Bethany, Branford, Trumbull, West Haven, Woodbridge, and Staten Island (New
York). In 1910, eleven of thirteen putative leaders were New Haven citizens (85
percent). Even putting aside the outlier living on Staten Island, the mean distance between homes and the CBD increased something like fivefold.

A closer look at who lived where in Lee's CAC sharpens the contrast further.

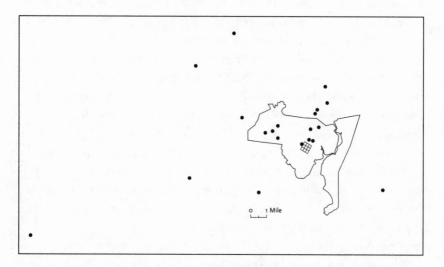

Figure 10.3. Homes of committee heads and executive committee members, Citizens
Action Commission, 1955.

Of the eleven CAC members living outside New Haven, ten would be described as top business leaders—figures like Patrick McGinnis, president of the New York, New Haven & Hartford Railroad, and James Walsh, CEO of Armstrong Tire and Rubber. Of the ten living inside the city, just two could be described as business leaders of any sort, while the vast majority were working for city government, for Yale, or for the labor movement. What remained of business leadership, in other words, was no longer grounded in city life. Indeed, to use the phrase "Citizens Action Commission" greatly stretched the ordinary meaning of municipal citizenship.

Whatever sociological deficiencies the CAC may have had, and there were many, it provided a convincing surrogate for a supportive business elite, forming a regime structure that gave Lee leverage he would otherwise have been without. It provided a forum which focused on broad goals for urban renewal. It provided the mayor with a counterweight to the Democratic Town Committee and the Board of Aldermen in local debate. It became a fund-raising mechanism for Lee's campaigns, which asked little in patronage. It articulated a justification for a program of change that hit many neighborhoods, particularly the old working-class areas, pretty hard.

THE IMPACT OF URBAN RENEWAL

Urban renewal, inextricably intertwined with a program of highway construction, did more to change the built city than had any single intervention in New Haven's three centuries of history. As would be expected under the federal legislation, the impact fell largely on residential areas, and almost entirely on the old working-class sections. In Figure 10.4, the working-class streets from 1910–17 are shown in black. The gray tone constitutes the urban redevelopment and renewal "project areas" from 1954 to 1967. The heavy lines indicate highways completed during the Lee years: I-95 was planned as the Connecticut Turnpike before Lee's time, and opened in 1958, while the Oak Street Connector (1959) and I-91 (1966) were plotted and built on Lee's watch. Highway building was in this period wildly popular with people living away from the cities they traversed. Intellectuals were harshly critical, as, for instance, Lewis Mumford's jeremiad: "This is pyramid building with a vengeance: a tomb of concrete roads and ramps covering the dead corpse of a city."[26] Mumford was thinking of New York; his rhetoric would have fit New Haven with equal force. Highways removed everything in their paths, while urban renewal was in most cases somewhat more selective. Highways are plotted by engineers and seem (to the very casual observer)

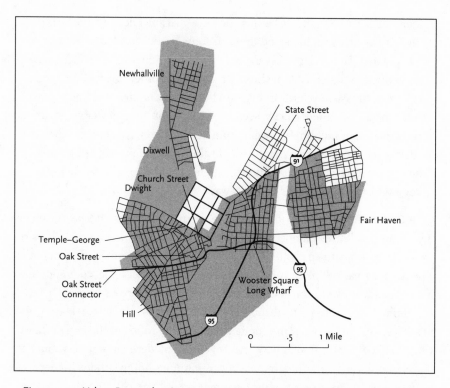

Figure 10.4. Urban Renewal 1967 project areas (in gray) projected over working-class neighborhoods, 1913. Nine-square grid shown for reference.

apolitical; urban renewal projects are carried out with sociological, architectural, and economic targets, often reflecting political ideas and ideologies. Of course, highway routing is political as well in an urban setting: the Oak Street Connector helped clear out a dense working-class neighborhood, even as it served the purpose of increasing east-west circulation in New Haven's CBD (its gratuitously ample 500-foot width says a great deal about its implicit purpose).

The overall impact of urban renewal may conveniently be parsed into three streams of change: in the built environment, in residential life, and in the fabric of business enterprise. We could, of course, chop the impact into smaller pieces, but these headings will, I believe, serve us well enough.

MODERNISM AND THE BUILT ENVIRONMENT

Redevelopment brought a wave of modernism to New Haven, and with it, the linear rationalism of its most terrifying proponent:

Man walks in a straight line because he has a goal and knows where he is going; he has made up his mind to reach some particular place and he goes
straight to it. The pack-donkey meanders along, meditates a little in his scat-
ter-brained and distracted fashion, he zigzags in order to avoid the larger
stones, or to ease the climb, or to gain a little shade; he takes the line of least
resistance. . . . A modern city lives by the straight line, inevitably; for the
construction of buildings, sewers, tunnels, highways, pavements. The circulation of traffic demands the straight line; it is the proper thing for the
heart of a city. The curve is ruinous. . . . The winding road is the Pack-Donkey's Way, the straight road is man's way.[27]

Le Corbusier was profoundly hostile to urbanism—to its endless meander-
ings, to its small lives planned around small places and modest goals, to its reliance on the unplanned civilities of everyday life, to the woeful inefficiency of its
streets, to the pack-donkey ways of untutored citizens. Dick Lee would not have
had time to study Le Corbusier's doctrine, and, if he had done so, would have rejected much of it. But, partly through Maurice Rotival's role in New Haven, and
his offices within the Kremlin, modernism infused much of the early renewal
work that Logue and Lee endorsed. And of course modernism was very much in
the air at mid-century, as nearby Yale began commissioning famous modernists
to expand its facilities. Many of the designers brought in to do specific buildings
connected (or merely confused with) to urban renewal—Paul Rudolph, Marcel
Breuer, Eero Saarinen, John Johansen, Louis Kahn, and Philip Johnson—were
deeply engaged with modernism and its internecine variants.

At a deeper level, the grandiose requirements of modernism found a remarkable fit with the practices of urban renewal. Small land parcels were, under law,
to be condemned and combined into large parcels. Small structures were, under
the same law, to be bulldozed in the preparation of the resulting spaces for fresh
development. These large parcels invited large development—commonly the
rectilinear, high-rise "tower in the park" of Corbusier's rationalism. Moreover,
the then-irrevocable dominance of the automobile placed highway development
in close parallel with the erection of towering architecture. Yale architectural historian Vincent Scully, Jr.—a New Havener by birth, and son of Alderman Vincent Scully, Sr.—would use three "fallacies" to excoriate both the national
process in general and the specific way it was unfolding in New Haven:

> The architectural and planning concepts of a generation ago, upon which
> the first phases of urban redevelopment were generally based, have now
> clearly shown themselves to be obsolete. Hence, the threat of redevelop-

ment in New Haven, as elsewhere, derives from the possibility that it might continue to act upon those discredited principles and, by so doing, destroy the town. . . . Most planning of the past fifteen years has been based upon three destructive fallacies: the cataclysmic, the automotive, and the suburban. These fallacies may be characterized in a few words: the cataclysmic insists upon tearing everything down in order to design from an absolutely clean slate; the automotive would plan for the free passage of the automobile at the expense of all other values; the suburban dislikes the city anyway and would just as soon destroy its density and strew it across the countryside.[28]

The Oak Street Connector (figure 10.5) quickly became Exhibit A for all of these charges. To this day the endless parked cars occupy ground that was once in major part a working-class neighborhood. It was also, as Lee said, a slum neighborhood; after redevelopment it was not so much a neighborhood as it was a

Figure 10.5. Mayor Richard C. Lee and manufacturer Merritt Vanderbilt, vice president of the Citizens Action Commission, pose at newly poured Oak Street Connector.

wasteland of automotive infrastructure. The cataclysm of land clearance remains. Beyond Dwight Street, stretching west from downtown, a still undeveloped parcel—more than half a mile long—stands idle after four decades. Nearby are two famous modernist (some would say "brutalist") structures from the period, Paul Rudolph's Crawford Manor and Philip Johnson's Yale Laboratory for Epidemiology and Public Health.

In figure 10.6 we see Rudolph's public housing for the elderly, springing up on Park Street near the connector. This structure dominates its urban setting, as does the Laboratory for Epidemiology and Public Health, completed the same year, and showing very much the same relationship to its now-vanished urban context. Scully and others made themselves clear in evaluating these transformations, and on more than one occasion they stirred Lee to defend what was being done. One letter, from Lee to Scully, captures some of the difference in perspective:

Figure 10.6. Crawford Manor public housing for
the elderly. Paul Rudolph design, completed in
1965. Author photo.

You know, I have given my life to my city, and, indeed, much of my health. New Haven was a mess when I became Mayor on January 1, 1954—a rotten, stinking, decaying mess. When I think of the gin mills, the pool parlors and flop houses which dotted our main avenues—Church Street, Temple Street and such important side streets as Crown Street—I cannot help but feel a deep sense of pride in the transformation from what New Haven was like to what it is today. I recognize we all have our differences of opinion on what is beautiful and what is lovely and what is art and what is not. I respect very much your position as an authority on architecture and on beauty; but, Vince, for the life of me—and I say this in the kindest way I can—I cannot understand your constant posturing as a critic of New Haven, as a critic of redevelopment, and as a critic of Dick Lee (and I say this very sorrowfully). You talk about the city beautiful, but you talk in terms of nostalgia for the old days. The old days, which I remember very well, were the stinking, rotten slums of Oak Street; the decaying, dilapidated, abandoned structures which disgraced our central city; and the old days when everyone simply turned his eyes away as he drove through Oak Street, and ignored the plight of hundreds—if not thousands—of people who were confined there because of our community's carelessness or ignorance or complete indifference.[29]

Much of what Lee says is true. Many of the bulldozed houses and stores were hopelessly dilapidated, and a few had been abandoned. Some stank and many were ill-maintained. Credit to buy or refurbish these homes—or any other nearby structures—had been hard to come by for a generation, first due to the Depression, then due to the uniformly negative evaluation given these areas by the federal government's HOLC study in 1937. Beyond that, the end of urbanism had indeed begun to drain away people, to erode customs and institutions, to thin the civic fauna, and to make life little by little more difficult in these old streets. It is surely, therefore, a mistake to imagine that the "old days" were entirely benign and the costs of renewal a gratuitous waste. And yet Scully and other critics were really arguing not for a literal return to the previous condition, but instead for a set of more disciplined transformations that would respect the past and preserve the complex particularity of the urban experience. As Scully wrote in another essay of the same time, "Perhaps we need most of all to develop our sense of the particular, of an infinity of particular images of particular places, loved and specific."[30]

Architectural form was, on both sides of this debate, functioning as a place-holder for other hopes and fears. For Scully and others, large projects, inevitably

Figure 10.7. Knights of Columbus world headquarters tower under construction, c. 1965.

controlled by large organizations, were displacing smaller undertakings, controlled by people and households, or by small firms, rooted to place. The outer pretensions of grand projects expressed a loss of urban particularity, groundedness, and humanity. For Lee, quite understandably, new, well-capitalized, innovative-looking construction meant success, meant the regeneration of the city (figure 10.7). In the beginning, he and others allowed themselves to believe that these newer structures would reshape old lives for the better: that whatever looked like a good neighborhood would ipso facto become a good neighborhood. This hope was by and large dashed by experience. In the cases where a neighborhood was transformed socially after being transformed physically, it was usually accompanied by a wholesale displacement of the original residents. When Oak Street was leveled, "luxury apartments" took the place of squalid tenements: physicians replaced rag dealers, merchants replaced peddlers, capacity replaced need. Among the poor, only the elderly were housed in large numbers by the new structures. In such cases—to which we apply the odd name "gentrification"—the transformation of place says little about the transformation of lives. In other instances, such as the vast emptiness left by the clear zone that accompanied the Oak Street Connector, open space replaced a neighborhood.

In the earliest and largest urban redevelopment projects—Oak Street and Church Street—the process was often devastating to what remained of urbanism (figure 10.8). Small holdings were taken by eminent domain and combined into large parcels. The large parcels either remained undeveloped or were developed in ways that offered no consolation to ordinary residents or businessmen.[31] When redevelopment actually occurred, many original residents were displaced to other neighborhoods, where familiar conditions prevailed and rents were still affordable. Larger families, especially large families of color, were concentrated in public housing, notably in Elm Haven Extension, a high-rise cluster opened in 1955 and demolished in the late 1980s as a civic disaster. In his polemical critique, Herbert Gans summed up this story by comparing old houses to jalopies: "Suppose that the government decided that jalopies were a menace to public

Figure 10.8. Downtown New Haven during urban renewal, c. 1960. Oak Street Connector is at bottom, New Haven Green at center, Church Street demolition between the two. NHCHS.

337

safety and a blight on the beauty of our highways, and therefore took them away from their drivers. Suppose, then, that to replenish the supply of automobiles, it gave these drivers a hundred dollars each to buy a good used car and also made special grants to General Motors, Ford, and Chrysler to lower the cost—although not necessarily the price—of Cadillacs, Lincolns, and Imperials by a few hundred dollars. Absurd as this may sound, change the jalopies to slum housing, and I have described, with only slight poetic license, the first fifteen years of a federal program called urban renewal."[32]

While the sensitivity of urban renewal architecture improved as Lee moved into other areas, notably Wooster Square, the administrative harshness of the equation remained—a great many lower-income working families were kicked out of their jalopies and sent elsewhere to occupy other jalopies while their former neighborhood was put at the disposal of new populations, or perhaps left to lie fallow over the decades that followed. These shortcomings were embedded in the federal program and were felt everywhere across the country, although perhaps more acutely in New Haven because such an intense program was developed there. Lee did as good a job with urban renewal as was done anywhere in the nation, but the social costs were almost inescapable, given the federal mandates which local government had to embrace.

RESIDENTIAL AND RACIAL IMPACT OF URBAN RENEWAL

The problem of relocating people displaced by urban renewal would become a real one by summer 1956, when the first director of New Haven's Family Relocation Office resigned, telling his successor that "this job is impossible. There is more prejudice up North than there is in the South—only here it is often more subtle. When you answer an ad in the newspaper, all you hear is 'no children, no pets, and whites only'—so how is it possible to find a place for Negro families too large for public housing and unwanted by private landlords?"[33] His replacement was Alvin Mermin, a white who served with decency and ingenuity, attempting to mitigate the trauma of relocation, from 1956 to 1966. The displacement of families created a legally mandated obligation for the Redevelopment Agency to make reasonable attempts to find housing satisfactory to each household.[34]

The overall scale of displacement can be estimated from Mermin's tallies, and from a secondary analysis provided by Fainstein et al.[35] Table 10.1 breaks down the number of households (including households as small as a single individual) by renewal project areas, then provides a 2.92-for-1 guess about the number of individuals involved.[36] Mermin estimates that 22,000 individuals were relo-

Table 10.1. Estimated Residential Relocations Due to
Urban Renewal, 1954–68

Neighborhood	Households displaced	Persons @ 2.92 per household
Wooster Square	2,710	7,913
Dixwell	1,127	3,291
Hill	1,049	3,063
Oak Street	886	2,587
Church Street	707	2,064
Dwight	485	1,416
Newhallville	363	1,060
State Street	270	788
Fair Haven	107	312
Temple-George	0	0
Long Wharf	0	0
Totals	7,704	22,496

cated during his eleven-year watch. The grand total for dislocation of residences, counting the impact of highways, and counting moves before and after Mermin's watch, is probably close to 30,000 individuals and about 10,000 households. Taking the 1960 population of 152,045 as a base, with about 49,000 households, we may suppose that a little over 20 percent of the city's households and individuals were compelled to move during the Lee era.[37] This suggests a monumental impact on the civic life of any municipality, and if the calculations could be made, it almost certainly would rank among the most severe impacts anywhere in the country.

In order to see what this meant in practice, let's look at the destinations of people living on Oak Street and its immediate vicinity who were in the first wave of relocations during early 1957 (figure 10.9).[38] Their original addresses, indicated by the black markers, are concentrated in and around Oak Street. Their addresses in 1960, after their moves, are indicated by the circles. The "Oak Street Diaspora," sent people into adjacent West Haven, into the Dixwell neighborhood (often to Elm Haven), further south into the Hill neighborhood, and to a scattering of other places.[39] Most disruptive of all, it separated neighbor from neighbor, presumably undercutting many ties of loyalty and familiarity. To this day, nevertheless, an annual celebration is conducted by "Oak Street Alumni" and their descendents. Smaller groups, totaling about thirty individuals, meet at weekly

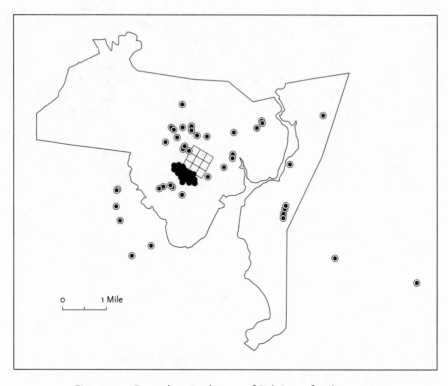

Figure 10.9. Post-relocation homes of Oak Street families, 1957.

lunches, and certain individuals have developed substantial followings for their recollections of the old life on Oak Street.[40]

WHITE REMOVAL?

It quickly became fashionable to call urban renewal "Negro removal," and it is worth examining the truth of this barb as it applied to New Haven. In its bald version, the Negro-removal thesis is simply false, since the best available data suggest that about 56 percent of the people relocated as a result of urban renewal were white, 44 percent not white—perhaps 42 percent black.[41] That being said, it is well to note that 85 percent of the city was white, so that nonwhites constituted only 15 percent. This suggests that any one family of color had a far greater chance of being relocated than any single white family. The ratio is roughly 4.5:1, a very real difference. On the other hand, blacks were more apt to live in the target neighborhoods than whites, partly due to their exclusion elsewhere, partly

Table 10.2. Residential Destinations of Displaced Families

	Percentage of white families	Percentage of nonwhite families
Public housing in the city	8.1	29.5
Private rental in the city	38.5	57.2
Homeownership in the city	26.9	7.7
Out of the city altogether	26.5	5.6

due to their typically lower incomes. Thousands of blacks were in fact displaced, often to their disadvantage, but this is not the main residential dynamic that needs to be understood. The critical question concerns the residential destinations of displaced families. In table 10.2, using partial data provided by Mermin, I chart the destinations of white and nonwhite families, revealing three significant differences.[42] First, families of color were being placed in public housing well over three times as frequently as white ones (29.5 percent to 8.1 percent). Second, whites were moving to in-town home purchases more than three times as frequently as nonwhites (26.9 percent to 7.7 percent). Many of these whites owned homes in the condemned neighborhoods and would have received market-rate compensation, allowing them to buy elsewhere. Finally, whites were leaving the city at far greater rates than other groups (26.5 percent to 5.6 percent). These figures apply only to people moved by urban renewal, and the differences noted here are part of a larger pattern. That larger pattern led toward the near-total Africanization of public housing, and to racial tipping in neighborhood after neighborhood.

At the center of that story is something closer to "white removal." The city experienced a precipitous loss of white population between 1950 and 1970, much of which was not directly related to urban renewal's pattern of relocation. In 1950, 154,618 whites were living in New Haven. Twenty years later, their number had declined to 99,986. In figure 10.10, we have tracts that added white population at the left, tracts that lost it at the right.[43] Only five tracts added white population, all of them "in-town suburbs." Three are on the east shore, beyond the Quinnipiac River and the harbor. Two are in Westville, beyond the West River. All are neighborhoods that feature single-family detached homes, with the accoutrements of postwar suburbia everywhere in evidence. None were within sight or an easy walk of any urban redevelopment or renewal project. None had a visible minority population in 1950, and none were attracting one during these decades.

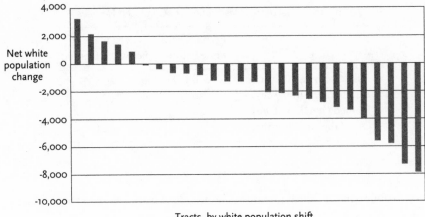

Figure 10.10. Gains and losses of white population, 1950–70, by census tract.

Of the tracts that lost whites in greatest numbers, all but two were wholly or sub-stantially included within the boundaries of urban renewal project areas. Of the twelve that lost 2,000 or more whites apiece over these years, all included urban renewal projects, and some of the hardest hit were decimated by highway con-struction.

The impacts were tectonic in some places, notably Wooster Square. Take tracts 21 and 22 (later 1421 and 1422), which encompass the Wooster Square area, and the old 10th and 11th Wards in which Bill Celentano had once found so much support. In 1950, their combined population was 17,364, including 16,163 whites. By 1970, total population would fall to 4,372, of whom about 3,000 were whites. The Wooster Square neighborhood had been hit hard by highways: all the new roads meet on turf once belonging to working-class families in this one place (see figure 10.4). Densities plummeted, sensitive renewal of remaining properties partly gentrified Wooster Square, and I-91 cut off the public housing located near Grand Avenue to the north from the rest of the area. But, most of all, a large number of mainly Italian-American whites were lost to the neighborhood in a very short period of time.[44]

A major residential story in late twentieth-century New Haven is the decen-tralization of white households and their replacement by people of color—but on a rough two-for-three basis, two new families of color for three departed white families basis—so that total population in the central city diminished pretty steadily over the decades. Did urban renewal and highway construction cause these shifts? I do not think so, at least not in any simple way. These changes were under way long before Lee came to power in 1954, and they have continued since. The earliest instances of "white flight" trace to the 1920s, long before blacks arrived in numbers and long before urban renewal began.[45] One could say that the visibility of urban renewal, reinforcing the certification of working-class neighborhoods as slums, may have sent a signal that encouraged departure. And, certainly, the highways made it easier to move into relatively distant suburbs and still hold on to a city job. These are credible guesses. What can be said with complete confidence is that urban renewal failed to reverse the growing trend toward the suburbanization of whites, most notably middle-class whites.

BUSINESS IMPACT OF URBAN RENEWAL AND REDEVELOPMENT

The impact of urban renewal on business was often lethal. As can be seen in table 10.3, the wrecking ball fell hardest and most often upon the CBD (a.k.a. Church Street), followed by the nearby working-class neighborhoods—Oak Street, Wooster Square, State Street, and Dixwell. Downtown accounted for more than a third of all firms dislocated, and well over two-thirds of the total dollar cost in lost sales. In September 1953, just before Lee's electoral victory, the Gamble-Desmond department store downtown closed its doors for good. Urban renewal would take out the premises of rivals Malley's and Shartenberg's, as well as hundreds of smaller, more specialized retailers. It would also remove nearly

Table 10.3. Total Business Displacement
by Project Areas

Neighborhood	Businesses displaced
Church Street	785
Wooster Square	450
State Street	385
Oak Street	250
Dixwell	193
Hill	81
Dwight	54
Newhallville	10
Fair Haven	8
Temple-George	0
Long Wharf	0
Totals	2,216

Figure 10.11. Mayor Richard C. Lee, in front of completed
Church Street buildings, c. 1964. NHCHS.

all of the single-room occupancy hotels in the downtown area, and it would destroy one of the most intensive small retailing stretches in the city when Gregson's Alley was razed. Perhaps forty clothing stores, catering to different budgets
and sensibilities, were lost. Little restaurants and delis perished in large numbers. Joe Perfetto's store moved locations within the CBD but withstood the on-
slaught of change, at considerable cost in lost business. The construction and destruction of central space discouraged CBD shopping, as did the loss of all the
major department stores, at least temporarily. While much of the lost business
fabric was tired and often frankly second-rate, the nuance and variegation of urban shopping that went out with the bathwater was a genuine loss. Indeed, the
historical value of retailing to neighborhood life has never depended on the newness or even the spiffiness of storefronts.

Something like a full decade of continuous disruption took its toll on business
and civic morale. Luke Hart, supreme knight of the Knights of Columbus, wrote
Lee in April 1959 calling "attention to the great injustice that is being done to the
Knights . . . by the closing of Meadow Street" and renewing his "protest against
this unwarranted, arbitrary, and unjust treatment of our organization, and disre-
gard for its rights."[46] Similarly, David Fishman, owner of the Commercial Hotel

on George Street, complained to Lee of Kremlin staffers who were "unreasonable, arbitrary, drunk with a little delegated power."[47] Robert Savitt, among others, brought suit to protect his (jewelry) store from being taken by the government, leading to a protracted and expensive negotiation that further delayed the completion of a new downtown plan.

The strategy of redevelopment created in cooperation with the Stevens Development Corporation for downtown appears, at least in retrospect, to have been unfortunate. Stevens undertook a unified development project for three contiguous city blocks south of the New Haven Green, what had for decades been the commercial and business administration core of the city.[48] A massive parking structure was built to flank the project, and was its most famous piece of architecture. Traffic entered that behemoth on a ramp, allowing shoppers to drive up and into an encapsulated suburban mall, very few of whose establishments opened out to the surrounding streets. In most malls, the "anchor" stores are placed at opposite ends, with small retailers in between, so that foot traffic between the major stores must pass by the little guys. In what came to be Chapel Square Mall, the smaller retailers were isolated at the northern end of the project, nearest the Green. The two department stores, Macy's and Malley's, were together at the southern end and directly accessible from the parking garage. Shoppers could walk car-to-anchor-to-car without seeing either the smaller mall stores or any other element of the CBD. Despite some good years, the mall never approached expectations, and it competed uphill against such places as the so-called Miracle Mile in nearby Hamden, and against the strip retailing on the Boston Post Road in the towns of West Haven, Orange, and Milford (figure 10.12). The attempt to replace or resuscitate the downtown mall remains near the top of the city's public discourse even in the twenty-first century.

The loss of small retail outlets in the mixed-use neighborhoods is less visible, less easily related to urban renewal politics, but no less important to the historical legacy of this period than was the downtown's wholesale transformation. These streets were dotted with historically given stores, adapted to very local purchasing habits, often already in economic trouble by the 1950s as cars made larger, cheaper merchants accessible to neighborhood families. But urban renewal took out roughly 1,400 neighborhood retailers, and in so doing accelerated the thinning out of urban connections within the city. In the majority of cases, moving meant death to the business, so local were its roots.

It should not be imagined that every business closing, even every closing that came down to a condemnation decision by government, killed a healthy firm. A late 2002 interview with Lawrence Schaffer, a leading New Haven businessman,

Figure 10.12. Dale clothing store, Boston Post Road, Orange, Connecticut, c. 1950.

made the point for me. Schaeffer's father had brought a needle trades firm, May Manufacturing, to New Haven long before urban renewal, and had located its plant in what turned out to be the path of the highways in Lee's era. Schaeffer reports that labor costs and other considerations had made the plant uncompetitive by the time Lee took the property. Management was perfectly content to move the capital into more profitable pursuits. The same would have been true for other manufacturers and was doubtless true for many small retailers suffering scorching competition from chain outlets.

COMMUNITY PROGRESS INCORPORATED

By about 1962, it had become clear that: (1) the built environment could not be transformed in its entirety with any realistic amount of urban renewal money, and (2) not even the most complete transformation of the built environment would convincingly renew the city. Think about it in dollars: Could $725 per capita reverse history? Could ten times that reverse history? Could micro-policy changes reverse macro-historical movements? Did the Lee administration have the capacity, notoriously lacking in redevelopment efforts worldwide, to allocate money so that it would produce the greatest available market response?[49] Were it so, how would things work out for the residents, many of them now living in unfamiliar places? Most obvious and least discussed, urban renewal could improve housing and might spruce up the downtown business district, but it offered no plausible remedy for the course of decline in manufacturing that was the basis for so much of New Haven's economic life. As these realities forced themselves upon the city's sense of its realistic future, and with a bead drawn on the Ford Foundation's "gray areas" initiative,[50] the mayor would write:

> We in New Haven believe that the goal of a democratic society is the fullest possible development of the individual potentialities of its people. In urban America, despite great material wealth, there are many obstacles to the achievement of this goal. Most visible are the blight and obsolescence of the environment of a large portion of all but the newest cities. Equally present are social, economic, and cultural obstructions which prevent people from attaining a full measure of personal fulfillment.
>
> We believe that planning and action to renew the central city can remove some of these obstructions. Able and imaginative urban renewal programs are under way in many communities. In this respect, New Haven to date [April 1962] has outstripped other cities in the breadth of its program, the speed of execution, and the quality of accomplishment.
>
> As a result of physical renewal, a decent physical environment is being created for the first time in a century. New Haven is being renewed to promote social goals. Along with the rebuilding process, basic human needs are being tackled through relocation, homemaking, education, and housing programs. The time is now at hand to expand these efforts to put into effect a comprehensive program which goes to the root of the city's social problems. Such a program demands vision, dedication, and courage. Its implementation will mean that the people of our city will have a chance for much greater personal achievement. The great strength of the program is its focus on self-improvement. Services are but means to ends, and the ends are the ones people select for themselves. . . . I call upon my fellow citizens to dedicate themselves to a great new task which will bring our total renewal program even closer to the great goal we have set before us: a slumless city with greater opportunity for all.[51]

Lee here acknowledges that many of the substantial changes being wrought in the built environment were not doing poor people a lot of good. He was edging up to the unhappy prospect that a city could have sociological "slums"—or something as bad—in places where it did not have bad buildings, only lives lived in isolation from work and civility. As one journalist writing in the period put it: "New Haven has more to show for renewal than shiny new buildings. In tearing down old slum walls, New Haven found it did not relieve the real problems of the poor; it merely revealed them."[52]

Community Progress, Inc. (CPI), was the mayor's answer—a sociological version of Logue's Kremlin, run by no less formidable a figure. CPI's first (and historically dominant) chief executive was Mitchell (Mike) Sviridoff. Unlike other top officials brought in by the Lee administration, Sviridoff had been born in New Haven, lived in the city until he was nine, and finished high school in New York City. Unable to afford college, this flinty dynamo was a sheet metal worker at Sikorsky Aircraft, fabricating helicopters in nearby Stratford by the time he was twenty. With uncanny political skill Sviridoff became head of the United Auto Workers local at Sikorsky almost immediately, and was Connecticut state president of the AFL-CIO by the time he was twenty-five. Sviridoff was neither Ivy-educated nor technically sophisticated, but he was among the very smartest and shrewdest of Lee's top brass. After New Haven, he went on to become a senior vice-president at the Ford Foundation and a leading public intellectual on America's urban problems.

Like the Kremlin, CPI was organized as a relatively closed structure, responsive to the mayor's office but not to others—including city politicians and the poor it was intended to serve. Its nine-seat board included three people appointed by the mayor, one by the Redevelopment Agency, one by the Citizens Action Commission, one by the Board of Education, and three others by the likes of Yale University and the United Way.[53] Lee could and did pack the board with his loyalists—people of quality and integrity, but loyalists all the same. With Sviridoff at the helm, CPI was both an offshoot and twin of the Kremlin as a branch of alternative city government in Lee's New Haven.

CPI was a material and pecuniary success from day one. Its staff peaked at about three hundred full-time employees, and its budget reached $7,700 for each lower-income family it served by 1965—more than twice the annual income of most such families.[54] Perhaps its most important initiative was a job-training and placement program that involved a substantial client base. By May 1965, 4,124 workers, nearly half of them young adults, had entered the program. A majority (2,481) were black, 1,509 white, 134 were listed as Puerto Rican. About 1,400 were actually placed in jobs.[55] Such a program presupposed the existence of appropriate jobs, not enough of which existed. CPI was predictably unable to overcome the economic trends working against less skilled workers (see figure

8.2) and the awkward trend toward increasing concentrations of lower-income blacks in certified slums. Segregation, northern style, was an increasingly awkward and visible fact about New Haven in the 1960s. Indeed, Lee's school board attempted a plan of school integration during the same period and was turned back by vociferous white resistance.[56] Moreover, CPI was making enemies among its clients, and among rivals who sought to accomplish black goals through black power, and, more to the point, black payrolls.

Like Logue and the Kremlin elite, Sviridoff was given to top-down management, and the agency eventually accumulated a great deal of bad will among the poor it was intended to serve, among leaders of organizations unable to compete effectively with CPI for funding or volunteers, and among Yale intellectuals.[57] The organization had, from the outset, hired as its own staff many of the people living among the poor who might have become critics of its programs. But there remained many "independents" operating out of their own organizations, working with budgets small enough to be overlooked as rounding errors in CPI's bankroll. At the same time, rumblings of discontent were emerging in New Haven, as in many other cities. It was becoming obvious to everyone that the industrial jobs that had attracted generations of New Haven newcomers were drying up fast, and that people of color were by and large going to get the lowest-paid, least rewarding of the jobs that remained, or no jobs at all. And the newest, densest public housing, at Elm Haven Extension high rise, just west of the Yale campus, became a point of concentration for displaced black families who seemed permanently marginal to the economy. As "dispossessed families poured into the new red-brick structures [b]ack came the echoes through the schools, the Police Department, the Welfare Bureau, little in the misery-ridden lives of these families had really changed."[58] Lee would discover, and the CPI staff would know first-hand, that even the best built public housing sometimes created "nothing but transplanted ghettos where the poor are lost among the poor, the alienated among the alienated, unmotivated school children consigned to schools full of their own."[59]

The most talented spokesman against CPI and its white leadership turned out to be Fred Harris, president of an outfit called the Hill Parents Association (HPA). The 1964 Economic Opportunity Act had put forward the criterion of "maximum feasible participation" by low-income clients for its community action programs, which ran smack into the top-down professionalism of CPI under Sviridoff and his colleagues. Although Sviridoff and many others in the organization supported the idea of participation, CPI never did reach the point of effective client participation,[60] and, by 1967, Harris was angling for pass-through funding from CPI directly to his own organization. After protracted confrontation, his Hill Parents Association achieved that end.

Congressman Robert Giaimo, whose district included New Haven, investigated the matter several months later and read the following (hearsay) into the *Congressional Record:* "According to another official of CPI, representatives of HPA appeared at CPI on June 13, 1967, and "demanded" funds to support summer programs of HPA. This official said CPI declined to fund the HPA program and coincidentally in the early morning hours of June 14, four neighborhood offices of CPI were struck with fire-bombs, inflicting minor damage. He said that on June 15, 1967, HPA representatives met with the Mayor of New Haven following which CPI personnel were told that the HPA summer program would be funded with OEO (Office of Economic Opportunity) funds."[61]

At about the same time, a federal Commission on Urban Problems arrived in New Haven to hold hearings at the newly completed modernist Conte School. Its chief of staff, Howard Shuman, would later report, "In New Haven, HUD's showcase for urban renewal, we sensed great local hostility to the program. Over $800 per capita had been spent—the highest in the country—but the community was seething. . . . Unknown to us until the end of our day of hearings there, the New Haven police had been stationed inside and outside the hall in case our hearings got out of hand. We prevented that by welcoming the views of unscheduled as well as scheduled witnesses. In fact, the 'walk-in' witnesses talked with a fire and an eloquence which the others had not matched."[62] We are talking about the febrile 1960s, and a national pattern of protest politics was very much in evidence. At the same time, in New Haven, conventional politics offered limited opportunities to those who would criticize CPI or other major elements of the Lee program. It is therefore far from surprising that people would take opportunities like this one to express their criticisms—even of so famous a mayoral regime, perhaps especially of so famous a mayor as Dick Lee.

Would a more democratic approach to New Haven's programs of physical and social renewal have generated better results? On the physical side, perhaps. On the social side served by CPI, almost certainly. Indeed, the manipulative conduct of "spokesmen" for the poor would have been undercut by a more effective politics to which ordinary people had access. The trouble with democracy in the CPI era, so far as I can tell, was twofold. First, the ordinary aldermanic ward politics had been marginalized by the Kremlin and CPI. Access to an alderman had close to zero net value in influencing CPI outcomes. Second, these alternative government structures were by their very design intended to perform by standards for which the "democracy" occurred in congressional elections, or in the boardroom of the Ford Foundation. They just were not themselves democratic institutions.

MODEL TO A NATION

Over the first decade of his mayoralty, Dick Lee had become a national celebrity. His urban renewal, photographed as fresh pavement and tall buildings, was generally considered the best such effort in the country. Labor Secretary Willard Wirtz would tell a reporter that Lee's New Haven was the "greatest success story in the history of the world."[63] HUD's Robert Weaver would reportedly speculate that "New Haven is coming closest to our dream of a slumless city."[64] Much of Lee's fame came from the relentless pace of urban renewal in the years before 1962; thereafter, CPI became increasingly visible as a focus of national attention. That organization became a national leader in urban poverty policy development, with such programs as Head Start, Job Corps, and neighborhood employment centers that were funded nationally and implemented across the country in later years. Seen against the background of urban renewal, CPI's existence and accomplishments made New Haven an unbeatable candidate for Model City designation when the 1966 Demonstration Cities and Metropolitan Development Act passed Congress. President Johnson had said of that program, "to build not just housing units, but neighborhoods, not just construct schools, but to educate children, not just to raise income, but to create beauty and end the poisoning of our environment."[65] These were the very things CPI was doing or trying to do, and the designation came promptly. The timing could hardly have been worse: I have never quite understood what Hegel meant in saying that "the Owl of Minerva flies only at dusk," but dusk came for New Haven's status as an unblemished national model not long after it became such a model under law.

RIOTING IN AUGUST 1967

On Saturday, August 19, 1967, four young men entered Tony's Snack Bar on Congress Avenue in the Hill neighborhood, whereupon one of them "spit on the floor and then threatened a customer with a knife."[66] The white restaurateur, Ed Thomas, pulled a pistol and demanded that the group leave his place, which they did, although one threatened to return with a gun of his own. He came back just before 6 P.M., and, according to the police, "threw a rock through the window of the restaurant and then reached under his shirt and started to pull out a gun." Thomas fired his pistol at the floor, perhaps as a warning, and when another man barged into the restaurant carrying a knife, Thomas shot him in the chest. Julio Diaz, age thirty-five, suffered only a superficial chest wound, and he was released to police custody by hospital officials that evening. But New Haven's "civil disturbance" would begin less than three hours later as rumors of the shooting spread through the streets.

The city's four-night riot took place almost entirely on business streets in low-income neighborhoods, most notably Congress Avenue in the Hill, Dixwell Avenue in its own neighborhood, and Grand Avenue in Fair Haven. Partly due to impressive police discipline, no fatalities or grave injuries were inflicted on civilians, although several firefighters were seriously hurt. Perhaps the worst single incident occurred at the headquarters of the Housing Authority, on Ashmun Street, just off Dixwell. The building was set ablaze, and, when the fire trucks arrived, miscreants standing on nearby rooftops attacked the firefighters by throwing down heavy objects. About one hundred fire alarms were turned in, and something on the order of forty serious structural blazes occurred. Many places of business were destroyed by fire, and still more were taken apart by looters. About forty liquor stores were looted, at a loss of between $20,000 and $50,000 apiece. Several large groceries were looted and then gutted by fire, as were perhaps two dozen smaller shops, whose lines of trade ran from bicycles to women's clothing. Altogether, about 225 arrests occurred, as city, state, and National Guard forces overwhelmed the streets. Armored personnel carriers rolled down streets, giving the impression of military occupation. Three hundred Hill residents, black and white, fled to a suburban Congregational church for shelter from the firestorm.

New Haven's riot did irreparable harm to the business climate in the affected neighborhoods. A central reason for the Lee revolution in city government had of course been the commercial decline of the central city, both in the CBD and in the neighborhoods. Competition from suburban retailing was rising sharply, bank credit for business investment in increasingly black neighborhoods was scarce, and then the much-publicized trashing of existing stores seemed one problem too many. At the same time, urban renewal itself had placed great stress on many small enterprises, causing hundreds to go out of business. Most of the affected streets—Congress, Dixwell, Grand—never fully recovered from the era, and from the four-night crisis that seemed to rub in its harshest lessons. Levels of confidence and trust—social capital, if you will—were falling long before these August nights, but they were doubtless pushed down faster in that long weekend than in most years of the previous generation.

New Haven's August riot was altogether unoriginal. As early as May 16, violence had surfaced in Houston, followed by Atlanta, Cincinnati, and Dayton in mid-June. The three weeks following Tampa's uprising on July 11 brought fresh trouble to nearby New Jersey more or less every day: Plainfield on July 14, Paterson the next day, Elizabeth on the 17th, along with Newark, New Brunswick, and Jersey City. Lesser eruptions followed on the 20th and 21st in two smaller New Jersey towns, and the big bomb exploded in Detroit on the 23rd. Other incidents occurred in places as varied as Tucson, Grand Rapids, and Cambridge, Maryland, before the end of July. Even sleepy Rockford, Illinois, had a riot going by the end of July. By July 28, President Johnson had already appointed the Kerner Commission to investigate the causes and cures for urban violence.[67] On August 19, New Haven was very much a follower, and it seems very probable that nothing like a riot would have occurred in New Haven absent news of repeated trouble across the country that summer.

In its duration and intensity of violence, New Haven's disturbance occupied a middling tier of the national story. The Kerner Commission invented a sort of grading scale for the intensity of disturbances, running A1, A2, A3, A4, A5, B1, B2, and so forth down to E5. New Haven's worst day rated a B4, well below the A1 riots of Detroit, Newark, and Plainfield. Below New Haven were places like Paterson (C3), Houston (D4), and Tucson (E1). While the economic and social consequences of these days in August are hard to measure, their political impact was out of all proportion to the actual violence.

What made New Haven special was that it had already begun doing many of the things that experts and politicians recommended as preventive medicine for future violence. As *Time* magazine wrote in its September 1, 1967, issue:

> In the past decade, New Haven has pioneered nearly every program in the Great Society's lexicon. Months and years before the Federal Government showed any interest in the cities, it had its own poverty and manpower-training projects, a rent-supplement demonstration, and a promising Head Start program. Washington had rewarded the city's imaginative urban-renewal administration with a greatly disproportionate share of federal renewal money—$852 per capita (given or pledged) or six times as much as Philadelphia, in terms of population, 17 times as much as Chicago, 20 times as much as New York. . . . Yet last week the model city was racked with the same virus of ghetto discontent that has plagued scores of other U.S. cities this summer.

Clearly, New Haven's riot did not represent a rational, or even explicit, critique of urban renewal, CPI, or Dick Lee. Yet it provoked a dialogue that undermined the morale and conviction with which Lee and his associates could go forward in their efforts. African-American minister Bishop C. H. Brewer used the local press to advise Lee as follows: "Talk to the Negro youth and find out what's bothering them. There are legitimate reasons for their 'don't give a damn' attitude. You can't promise the Negro anymore, you've got to deliver."[68] Urban renewal, where most of the new construction was for business, the well-to-do, or the elderly did not count as "delivering" to black youth. What was worse, even Lee's super-funded, high-powered version of city government was obviously unable to "deliver" all or even most of the things in question. These were the children of families which had come to New Haven in search of industrial jobs—with good wages, steady work, and demands for education within the reach of ordinary folks. Generations of Irish and Italian kids had had these things in New Haven, and this generation of blacks in the main did not have any such opportunity. City Hall had raised expectations and had been over-grand in advertising its accomplishments. In early 1964, Lee's annual report to the aldermen included a sweeping claim of victory: "In 1954, we set out to transform the face of New Haven—to build on the foundations of a proud and historic New England city the structures and the facilities of a modern American city. As I look at the accomplishments of 1963, I can report to you with both pride and humility that the success of this transformation is now assured . . . and it is clear that what we have struggled and sacrificed for has been or soon will be attained."[69] These words, spoken in the midst of what might today seem the last gasp of urbanism, have been hard to live down. The statement may well have been the sort of hopeful gesture one is tempted to make as the shadow of doubt gathers itself around a program—but it and all the national adulation combined to set up Lee and his people for harsh criticism after the events of 1967.

The fundamental issue behind the city's incapacity to "deliver" was the drying up of plant-gate opportunity for people without advanced education. Such opportunity had, historically, stood at the very core of New Haven's urbanism, and it had been a matter for private-sector governance, not city government, to sustain. Lee had, in a sense, been mousetrapped by history: nobody living in 1915 could have imagined the possibility that Frank Rice could deliver large numbers of manufacturing jobs, much less that he should be criticized for failing to do so. Perhaps a little patronage here and there to deserving citizens, but the big supplies of good jobs were understood to come from private hands. Yet, abetted by federal legislation, a little hubris of his own, and Ford Foundation munificence, Lee in his capacity as a government official was now being called to account for creative destruction over which he had no control whatever. Government and governance had fallen out with one another, and Dick Lee was there to take the fall.

EXCLUSION, INDIGNATION, AND THE DEMISE OF CPI

Nobody could resolve or ignore the vexed issue of participation, raised so vehemently against CPI in the months preceding the riots. From the viewpoint of poor people of color, the regular and ordinary politics of New Haven offered limited opportunities to influence policy. In a thirty-member Board of Aldermen, blacks elected six members for the first time in 1967, all of them Democrats in a chamber shared by eighteen white Democrats and six white Republicans. Being a minority of six in a majority party that would remain in control without the minority's support was not a great source of leverage. No black alderman wielded any real influence over Lee, and most blacks could aspire at most to becoming second-tier players in the DTC. A great many blacks would sharply contest Dahl's 1961 generalization that "Negroes are not discriminated against in city employment; they have only to meet the qualifications required of white applicants to become policemen, firemen, school teachers, clerks, stenographers."[70] Bitter claims of job discrimination, notably in the fire department, remained part of city life in 2003.

But, in the Lee years, even substantial influence over ordinary politics would yield little control over extraordinary politics in the spheres of urban and social renewal. The whole design of Lee's alternative government was to insulate these activities from regular politics, and certainly from non-elite groups, most of whose members stood outside ordinary politics. As early as 1959, Lee had assigned Sviridoff the task of scouting New Haven's black leadership. The young operative observed that the "natural identification of the Negro with the Democratic party" left him nowhere to go in New Haven politics, and greatly weakened the black community's bargaining power in ordinary politics. Sviridoff saw the "immoderate" or "radical" black leadership as critically important—and that is what it had become by 1967.[71] These blacks, speaking on behalf of the very poor, would be joined by white radicals in criticizing Lee and his programs loudly and publicly for the remaining months and years of the administration. They had been boxed out of New Haven politics and New Haven super-politics, but national attention brought by the August riot slotted them into a national agenda over which Lee had no control. By December 1967, a violent racial confrontation at Hillhouse High School would add visibility to these issues.

The Kerner Commission put New Haven in the bad company of Detroit in its record of listening to citizen-clients: "Ghetto residents increasingly believe that they are excluded from the decision-making process which affects their lives and community. The feeling of exclusion, intensified by the bitter legacy of racial discrimination, has engendered a deep seated hostility toward the institutions of government. It has severely compromised the effectiveness of programs intended to provide improved services to ghetto residents. In part this is the lesson of Detroit and New Haven where well intentioned programs designed to respond to the needs of ghetto residents were not worked out and implemented sufficiently in cooperation with the intended beneficiaries."[72]

This criticism was heard in important places, including Congress and the Ford Foundation. The latter, in fact, was on the same negative course toward CPI before the Kerner Commission was formed at the end of July 1967. By this time, Sviridoff had left CPI to become a senior program officer at Ford, and an evaluation of CPI had been commissioned during the summer of 1967. In August, the very month of the riot, Ford's nominally confidential report was completed. Much of the document is couched in the apparently neutral gray tones for which consultants are famed, but its central conclusion is downright harsh: "CPI seems to be cast in the mold of doing for rather than with people, and it is having a most difficult time breaking out of this mold. . . . Within a developing climate of open urban democracy, no city can successfully keep a control strategy of social development programming. The more CPI attempts to deliver without indigenous participation in planning and execution the more it is likely to fail. No amount of technical expertise and public relations can make the control approach work."[73]

Within weeks, Congressman Robert Giaimo initiated his own investigation of CPI's operations, and by January 18, 1968, he had issued a scathing denunciation of the agency. Here is the most salient conclusion from Giaimo's printed testimony to his peers in the House of Representatives:

It is clear that CPI is an overly centralized, paternalistic, big brother institution, manned by "planner-administrators" who believe that they know what is best for everyone. We have had these people in our midst for a long time in New Haven, but at long last their ineffectiveness is beginning to show through. They serve themselves rather than the poor whom they are supposed to help. The investigation proves conclusively that they know how to take care of themselves. At the same time, it is quite clear to me that they have accomplished little if anything at all in bettering conditions among the poor in our cities. Salaries are extremely high, especially when one considers the 35-hour workweek and liberal fringe benefits.[74]

The report flagged high spending rates on the leasing of 60,000 square feet of office space, travel, telephone, cars, public relations, and, most of all, administrative staffing (117 full-time administrative staff in 1965, according to the report). Salaries for top administrators struck Giaimo as high: Executive Director Lawrence Spitz at $30,000 ($160,600 in 2002 dollars), Frank Logue, younger brother of Ed Logue, at $17,674 ($94,614 today), and fifteen others identified by name. But, for Giaimo, failure to listen to the poor, and failure to change real social conditions in low-income neighborhoods, was the big problem with CPI: "The real losers will not only be the taxpayers but the very poor whom these programs were designed to help."[75] After Giaimo's report, CPI was on the defensive for the rest of its short life and never recovered. Judged by its extraordinary aspirations, CPI was a failure. Judged against the standards of initiatives in New Haven and other American cities in the succeeding thirty-five years, CPI looks a little more ambitious and a good deal more top-down than average, but no less effective than what followed.

HOW MUCH WAS NOT ENOUGH

For all that, I remain convinced that Richard C. Lee was a remarkable mayor. Compared with his regional peers—Fred Palomba in Waterbury, Hugh Curran in Bridgeport, Paul Manafort in New Britain—there is nothing to talk about. On the larger stage more appropriate to a figure of Lee's talent, he was among the most brilliant, boldest, and most effective mayors at mid-century anywhere in America. He dared to break the mold of ordinary mayoral politics, to create a powerful alternative to ordinary city government, and to reach for goals that would have been (literally) inconceivable to mayors like Frank Rice, David Fitzgerald, John Murphy, or Bill Celentano. No twentieth-century mayor of New Haven—and few in America—came close to Lee in personal vision, in quality of appointed staff, or in ability to articulate issues for just about any imaginable audience. Few if any dared to dream of attempting as much as Lee actually accomplished. And he achieved some very tangible successes, such as greatly alleviating traffic on arterial streets, sensitively refitting the best residential areas in Wooster Square, expanding and improving low-income housing for the elderly, and setting a new standard for technical proficiency in city government. Some of his other efforts—such as the Dixwell Plaza, the downtown mall, the Veteran's Memorial Coliseum, the still-vacant scar over what had once been the Oak Street neighborhood—are more difficult to see as success stories.

Many New Haveners old enough to qualify as witnesses are inclined these days to think that Lee did the city grave harm. Many let themselves say that "Dick Lee ruined New Haven." Pressed for details, most mention the Oak Street Connector, a couple of ugly downtown buildings, and then fall silent. A few go on to say that they and their parents were better off in their shoddy apartments before renewal, even in their slums, and go on to talk the language of old-time urbanism.[76] Moreover, academic and intellectual commentators have come to a largely negative consensus on the efficacy and value of urban renewal nationally. One respected analysis of American urban life expresses that consensus thus: "Overall, urban renewal did little to stem the movement of people and businesses to the suburbs or to improve the economic and living conditions of inner-city neighborhoods. To the contrary, it destabilized many of them, promoting unmanaged racial transition and white flight."[77]

The difficulty one faces in evaluating Lee, and which he faced in governing the city, is an extreme case of shifting expectations. A more passive mayor, like Rice, Murphy, or Celentano, would have won great praise on Lee's administrative performance, precisely because nobody would have expected those mayors to solve problems beyond the routine ken of local government. Lee placed himself in a different frame of reference, which invited people to hold him accountable for things mayors usually don't have to worry about. A letter, written in May 1955 to Lee by a North Haven housewife, probably could not have been written to any previous mayor. It read in part:

> What has New Haven to offer? What would it be without Yale? No, my husband wasn't a Yale man. Being a young mother, the stores are my biggest interest. I don't drive, so I have to depend on ordering. New Haven stores will not deliver unless they have a three dollar order. Fox's [in Hartford] will deliver any amount to your door within 24 hours.
>
> Malley's is famous for not having things right this minute, but they have ordered it and it should be in next week. You go in and it hasn't come in yet, it should be in next week and so it goes. Their clerks are so snotty that it isn't much fun to do business with them.
>
> In filling orders I have had so much trouble with them being filled right. I ordered six undershirts for my daughter, three came in one size and three

in another. . . . In my opinion they should have called me and said they would send the other three as soon as they came in. . . .

I was given a pair of fur lined gloves by my husband from Hamilton's last Christmas. At the time he bought them he was told they could be exchanged if they weren't right. They were too big and when I took them back they had no fur gloves, they were all sold from Christmas. I tried to get my money back to buy them somewhere else and the fuss and fan-fair they made was terrific. I finally got my money and there wasn't a pair of fur lined gloves in New Haven my size. I called Fox's [in Hartford] at 4:30 PM and they were delivered to my home the next noon.[78]

Mrs. Russell Bacon, as she signs herself, finishes by absolving Lee of personal blame for the specific failings of New Haven retailers. But the letter's rhetoric flows from Dick Lee's presumed status as an agent for nearly *everything* within city limits. It is as if the responsibilities of government had expanded to occupy the entire function of governance—right down to delivering Mrs. Bacon's gloves to her suburban home.

By radically expanding the apparent agenda of local government, Lee had set himself up to be held accountable for events and decisions in the private sector, in civil society, and in the lives of newcomers having neither jobs nor established roles in civil society. In the case of Mrs. Bacon, who had moved from the city to one of its suburbs before complaining to the mayor about limited delivery services from downtown retailers, Lee was the lightning rod for a problem he surely did not create and certainly could not correct. He might as well have been asked to tutor Mrs. Bacon's daughter in math and to mow her neighbor's unkempt lawn.

The whole roiling torrent of creative destruction that we have been charting produced an immense historical accumulation of "problems" that would overwhelm the best and strongest government imaginable within the American urban context. Lee was facing the countless burdens sketched in Chapters 7 and 8, including the downward trend in industrial production at New Haven factories, the integration of New Haven firms into national corporations, the emergence of the automobile to choke city streets, the waning of small-scale retailing in New Haven neighborhoods, the decay of housing quality in some areas of the city, the destruction even of many chain-store outlets by competition from their own firms, the decline of civic density, the emergence of wholly novel racial tensions in New Haven, the federal government's intervention in mortgage markets for

New Haven's housing stock, the decision, taken nearly a generation earlier, to develop large-scale public housing in New Haven, the emergence of colossal housing supply in nearby suburbs, and the appearance of a regional hierarchy with much of New Haven at its lowest level of prestige. Set against these burdens, the task of promptly delivering to Mrs. Russell Bacon one set of well-fitting fur-lined gloves would seem child's play.

By setting out to re-create a region in which firms and families pressed inward on the central city, seeking out opportunities to produce, sell, and live in the middle of New Haven, Dick Lee had set himself against history. By setting CPI the task of expertly repairing a tattered social fabric, Lee had addressed a project of social engineering that no government on any scale has to my knowledge managed to fulfill. In his last years as mayor Dick Lee would often say, "If New Haven is a model city, God help America's cities." He had, in so saying, come to acknowledge the end of urbanism.

CHAPTER 11

THE END OF URBANISM

The Lee administration had struggled, often valiantly, to retain New Haven's manufacturing jobs. Some supposed that having the new interstate highways I-95 (which was originally called the Connecticut Turnpike) and I-91 meet in the center of New Haven would encourage manufacturers to locate in the city much as the convergence of rail lines had done a century before. They were mistaken: the highways decentralized everything they touched (figure 11.1). New facilities totaling roughly 500,000 square feet were created for Sargent hardware and Gant manufacturing along the Long Wharf landfill in the harbor, snug against I-95.[1] Subsidies were gathered and disbursed. Some projects worked out well enough to keep factories from closing or moving out of the city for years (Gant) and even decades (Sargent). But the eventual impact of these policies on New Haven's manufacturing job base was, at best, to slightly diminish its rate of decline. In Lee's first year as mayor, five hundred firms (mostly very small, many utterly marginal) conducted manufacturing operations in the city. By 1972, two years after he left office, that number was 244. The large plants folded at disproportionate rates, so the number of wage-earners fell even faster than the number of firms: from 26,180 in 1954 to 9,300 in 1972—roughly a 60 percent decline during the redevelopment era (table 11.1).

New Haven's abrupt loss of manufacturing jobs follows from the convergence of two potent historical trends. First, the larger region of which New Haven is a

Figure 11.1. Limited-access highways crossing New Haven, 1965. Interstate 95 crosses from lower right along the shore, crosses the bridge, and exits upper right. Interstate 91 is shown left center. The Oak Street Connector is bottom, center.

Table 11.1. Factory Jobs, 1947–97

Year	Number of establishments	Factory wage-earners in New Haven plants	Factory wage-earners in suburban areas
1947	444	27,742	35,055
1954	500	26,180	34,711
1958	459	18,948	32,844
1967	343	16,100	47,300
1972	244	9,300	37,500
1987	186	5,700	31,500
1992	145	3,500	27,700
1997	106	2,804	27,415

part has been in absolute decline since the 1960s (it has been in relative decline, against national benchmarks, since the 1920s).[2] Defining the region for this purpose as New Haven County minus the large outlying manufacturing centers of Waterbury and Meriden,[3] we start in 1954 with about 61,000 operatives in total, move up to a peak of 63,400 in 1967, and then fall steadily in succeeding years to a reported total of 30,218 in 1997. This decline, notorious for the northern United States as a whole, represents competition from places with equal or better transport facilities, often based primarily on trucking, places with lower labor costs, places with lower energy costs, places with lower tax rates, places with fewer burdens from obsolete plants and equipment. Some such places are in the American South, others in the global south and in Asia. In the era of global markets and free trade, this trend seems irreversible.

The second trend concerns competition within the region. As the interstates opened new territory to manufacturing—abetted by lesser roads and underwritten by the AC grid—it became feasible to build low-cost horizontal plants on cheap land without losing competitive advantage. If taxes were lower, and capital costs were kept down by open-space construction sites, what was the point of enduring the strain of life in the central city? If crime was a further concern, driving up security costs and making the recruitment of skilled personnel more difficult, why not flee to Greenfield locations near highway ramps? If trucking, and truck-oriented warehousing, was now superior to available rail service (and it was), wasn't the decision a no-brainer? New Haven factories went from about 43 percent of the region's wage-earner jobs in 1954 to less than 20 percent of the total in 1972. The impact was immense—fewer good jobs, especially fewer good working-class jobs, fewer opportunities for high school graduates without academic pretensions, fewer households in the city, fewer taxable properties, fewer dollars flowing from wage-earners to neighborhood merchants, decreasing leverage for city government in regulating central-place land use.[4]

A RAPID DISASTER WRAPPED IN SLOW CATASTROPHE

By 1975, Winchester Repeating Arms, the sole remaining mass manufacturer still operating in New Haven, was wallowing in economic trouble. It had already spent two decades as a minor division of a corporate conglomerate with plants in more than sixty cities, carrying out all manner of manufacturing operations producing everything from chemicals to firearms, from films and emulsions to brass castings. During periods of high military demand—wars in Korea and Vietnam—Winchester was a handsome little asset for Olin. At other times, especially after the dark shadow of peace crossed the Connecticut landscape in 1973, Winchester was a losing proposition for the parent company. Indeed, losses became a standard expectation in the late 1970s.[5] The division reported a loss of $6.07 million in 1977, and $7.22 million the next year. These numbers could scarcely have been tolerated by a management team grounded in New Haven and concerned for its communal welfare. For a management team held accountable by a national firm, such losses could not be allowed to continue.

The company had long withheld capital investment from its antiquated New Haven plant and had begun substituting cheap castings for machined parts in 1964, making that a watershed date among gun collectors, who value "Winchester before 1964" at a premium over later models.[6] One report, written by a former employee, gives a sense of what the work was like: "Milling was done on Lincoln machines so old that no one could recall when they were introduced. Springs were hand-wound, hand treated and hand-tested. These processes were incapable of producing dimensions within the tolerances required to manufacture interchangeable components. Units were built and rebuilt many times, creating a constant parade of firearms between test ranges and the assembly area."[7]

The Winchester machinists had organized themselves as Local 609 in 1955 and had achieved a series of strong contracts in the decades that followed. A divisive strike in 1969 had provoked management to cut the total size of the local workforce substantially, and Olin's corporate headquarters had come to think of New Haven as a costly location even before serious losses began to mount in the post-Vietnam period. They focused on problems of labor productivity, while the machinists' union focused on inadequacies of machinery and technical sophistication on the company's part. A pivotal component of the 1969 settlement was something called Article 4, which protected workers against the imposition of production quotas. From labor's side throughout the story: production quotas were unfair if the machinery wasn't reliable. From management's side in 1979: the New Haven plant would have to meet national standards of productivity per labor hour if it was to continue operation.

On July 16, 1979, one day after Local 609's contract expired, 1,356 hourly wage-workers went on strike.[8] As William Doyle, who represented Olin in the end-stage litigation, would write:

There was trouble from the beginning. On July 17, two days after the strike began, Olin's labor lawyers were in Superior Court seeking injunctive relief, claiming unlawful mass picketing, the blocking of ingress and egress to the plant and harassment of non-striking employees and vendors seeking to enter the plant. On July 20, the union and 15 of its members [agreed to] a temporary injunction preventing them, under pain of $1,000 a day, from blocking people and damaging vehicles. . . . On July 30, Olin's lawyers were back in court claiming the defendants had violated the injunction on that day when over 150 strikers at the north and south gates damaged vehicles, harassed people and prevented ingress and egress to the plant. Olin later amended its papers to allege similar unlawful conduct on August 1, 8, and 9. After reviewing evidence and viewing video tapes, Judge Dorsey found the defendants had violated the injunction and were in contempt [and raised the fine to $5,000 per day].[9]

Olin management, looking at a bad situation getting worse, elected to accelerate the trend:

On September 20, Olin raised the stakes and set the stage for real trouble. On that day, Olin sent the strikers a letter inviting them to return to work at the higher wages and benefits it had offered during the negotiations but, more importantly, in that letter Olin warned the strikers that it would immediately begin to advertise for replacements to begin work on October 1 if the strike did not settle by then. Although not stated in the letter, Olin let it be known that these replacement workers would be guaranteed permanent jobs and would have seniority over any strikers who returned to work. There was no dispute that Olin had the right to do this. Whether it was wise was another matter.[10]

Mayor Frank Logue had trouble of his own. The younger brother of Ed Logue, czar of Dick Lee's Kremlin, Frank Logue had served two terms on the Board of Aldermen and then run a winning reform primary campaign against fellow Democrat Bart Guida (mayor, 1970–76). Challenged by the DTC's preferred candidate in a 1977 primary, Logue had barely survived (to complicate matters, the challenger was his own police chief). In September 1979, another primary was won by DTC favorite Biagio DiLieto, while the reform vote was split between Logue and African-American insurgent Henry Parker. By October 1979, at the moment of crisis, Logue was therefore a lame duck mayor with limited political leverage. After Logue intervened to restart negotiations, the union conceded that Olin could unilaterally set production quotas but insisted that it could not actually fire workers who failed to meet them without a probationary period lasting until an arbitrator settled the individual case. Olin would agree only that such an employee should stay on the payroll for fifteen workdays. Negotiations broke down, Olin reasserted its position on replacement workers, and the early morning of Monday, October 1, became the moment of truth at which the first of these new workers would enter the plant. As Doyle recalls,

> By 6:30 A.M. an estimated 600–700 strikers and their supporters clogged the streets at seven intersections near the plant and refused to allow anyone to pass. . . . The police made tentative efforts to clear the way but the strikers formed human walls and would not budge. The police then ceased their efforts. There was no violence and there were no arrests. . . . Mayor Logue had been out there since 5:30. At about 7:30 he directed [Police] Chief Morrone to secure the Olin plant and prevent persons from entering the plant between that time and 7:00 A.M. the next day, October 2. Tuesday morning, October 2, was a repeat of Monday, except this time there were 800 people blocking the streets. . . . When the Mayor announced that he'd decided to close the plant for a second day in order "to avoid bloodshed" the strikers and their supporters cheered him.[11]

Next day, Logue ordered the plant closed for a third day and shared the street with DiLieto, who had defeated him in the Democratic primary weeks earlier and who was on the streets offering good will, coffee, and doughnuts to the strikers. At this point, Olin engaged Doyle and his firm (Wiggin and Dana) to seek an injunction against the mayor's order to close the plant. In Doyle's able hands, the law took Olin's side, and the plant gates were open by October 9. Replacement workers were hired, and, under court injunction, the city's police force protected their entry to the plant. The strike wore on for half a year, as "Olin was forced to halt 80 percent of its production in New Haven, resulting in $25 million–$30 million in losses, and began to make detailed plans to close the brass mill and other production facilities."[12]

Mayor Logue's attempt to close down the Winchester plant symbolized the limited power of city government as clearly as any event in New Haven's long history. The tidal wave of creative destruction that would wash away the last of the city's industrial base could be held back neither by Local 609 nor by City Hall. On December 12, 1980, Olin formally gave up plans to continue the operation of Winchester Repeating Arms. Subsequently, some former managers of Winchester obtained financing to buy the remaining assets and to found a far smaller enterprise, U.S. Repeating Arms Company, which was itself eventually acquired by a European multinational. A workforce of several hundred still produces firearms in a new, horizontal design plant awkwardly settled in a tiny fraction of what had for so many decades been the home of Winchester Repeating Arms.

The Winchester strike was a rapid disaster wrapped in a slow catastrophe: the city's 9,300 factory wage-earners of 1972 would dwindle to 5,700 in 1987, 3,500 in 1992, 2,804 in 1997, and an estimated 2,500 today. The tidal wave had swept away the principal basis of the New Haven economy—90 percent of the factory jobs in 1954 would be gone by 1997—in the four decades that followed Richard Lee's first election as mayor. The tsunami was not of Lee's making, but its impact was far greater than the sum total of redevelopment efforts—for city neighborhoods, for city retailing, for the civic fauna, for the city's tax base, and for the community's sense of itself. The impact was, of course, magnified and deepened by the community's longstanding dependence on manufacturing jobs and the cash they pumped into the local economy. If centered industrial development had never happened, a far smaller city would have had far less to lose.

RENDING THE FABRIC OF ENTERPRISE

During the Lee decades, 1950 to 1970, the city's fabric of enterprise was torn to pieces. I will concentrate here, as elsewhere, on groceries and the central business district, but a similar set of results would reward an analysis of hardware stores, confectioners, or barbershops. In 1950, 494 groceries were open inside city limits: more than half of them (259) would close by 1960, replaced by just over 50 start-ups. By 1970, only 153 stores would be active in the city—a total decline since 1950 of nearly 70 percent. This is a collapse by any test: no longer would a grocery be within shouting distance of virtually every home in most neighborhoods. No longer would the identification between proprietor and place be visible wherever one went in the city's streets. The dramatic decline of grocery outlets of course says nothing bad about the flow of food goods into city kitchens and pantries. Indeed, it is quite probable that the efficiency of distribution was actually improved by the substitution of larger outlets for smaller ones, standardized marketing for ad hoc mom-and-pop selling.[13] The old way had been a case of useful inefficiency: its demise was both a gain to the consumer economy and a loss to the urban community.

Grocery Die-Off Can the Lee administration be blamed for this change? The easy argument for the prosecution is the simple observation that 2,200 or more business properties were moved or extinguished by highway takings and takings aimed at creating land parcels for redevelopment.[14] Hundreds of these were groceries, others dealt in dry goods, still others were candy stores or bars. Many, as one official from the period suggested to me, were dives and holes, and not a few

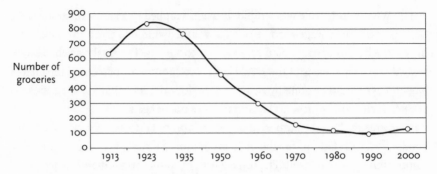

Figure 11.2. Approximate number of grocery stores operating in New Haven, 1913–
2000, smoothed curve.

were so weak economically that governmental seizure was akin to mercy killing. This line of reasoning—emphasizing that the stores taken by government might have died on their own—is probably correct as far as it goes, but it is not the main story. Another official from the period confessed that Lee's so-called business relocation program was "a mess" or "a joke." But the grocery die-off began before urban renewal and continued after it, so Lee is not our prime suspect.

In figure 11.2, we see the approximate number of groceries operating in the city over the course of the twentieth century.[15] The trend is downward, steeply so from 1935 through 1980. From a high of well over 800 in 1923, the total falls to 766 in 1935, 494 in 1950, 290 in 1960, 153 in 1970, 117 in 1980. In the decade after 1990, there is a modest resurgence from 91 to 125 stores—an interesting fraction of which are micro-enterprises operated by Hispanic and Asian immigrants, primarily in Fair Haven, the Hill, and other working-class neighborhoods. One important lesson to be learned here is that the Lee era is merely part of a long, seemingly irresistible trend that diminished the fineness of the fabric provided by grocery retailing to city neighborhoods.

But didn't urban renewal accelerate that trend? Many stores of every type were, after all, subjected to the wrecking ball in Oak Street, the CBD, and the Dixwell area. The annualized rate of closings for groceries would advance from under 5 percent in the 1935–50 period to 7.1 percent in the 1960s and to 9.7 percent in the 1970s. This last is as high a rate of retail grocery extinction as was encountered during the twentieth century in New Haven. Over the twenty-year span, 431 groceries would go blank,[16] which is a considerable number, especially if you keep in mind that the initial number of open stores is much lower in this period than in earlier ones.[17] But two other nearby cities, each with far less extensive urban renewal and redevelopment programs than New Haven's, had similarly stag-gering die-offs in this period. Hartford went from 516 groceries in 1950 to 137 of them in 1970; Bridgeport went from 572 to 256.[18]

The controlling feature lies on the other side of the ledger—new entries into the grocery business, or the lack of them (figure 11.3). Across the whole span of twenty years, 1950–70, just 93 freshly sited groceries seem to have emerged.[19] This compares with 223 in the shorter 1935–50 interval. It seems plausible to suggest that the turmoil and uncertainty associated with urban renewal and highway construction exerted a chilling effect on would-be entrepreneurs, caus-ing them to put their energies (and money) elsewhere. But we are dealing here with a very long trend—from very high entry rates to very low ones. Every inter-val from 1913–23 through 1980–90 shows a lower rate of new site entry than its predecessor. Remember, moreover, that two long-developing trends were reach-ing full force at the same time: (1) the emergence of chain-store groceries and the subsequent trend toward massive superstores, and (2) the growing move-ment of population, and particularly affluent population, toward the suburbs. For every period after the 1920s, one should add a third factor: after 1926, zoning regulations would have worked against close intermingling of residential space with new commercial activities, such as grocery stores, making it more difficult to establish new outlets. Even more broadly, the substitution of the automobile for pedestrian shopping would energize all three of these factors and would es-pecially encourage a shift toward giantism in grocery retailing—with the emer-gence of five-acre asphalt parking lots and stores ranging into the neighborhood

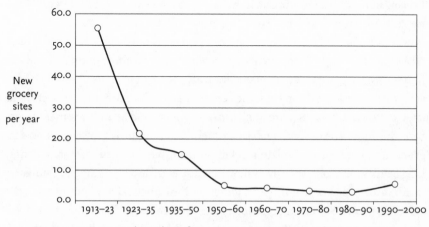

Figure 11.3. Estimated number of new grocery store sites established per year, 1913–2000.

of 60,000 square feet apiece. Cars pouring into asphalted acres of surface parking allowed giant-scale establishments in this era much as trolley-fed downtown hubs had allowed the flourishing of big-time department stores in a previous era.[20] All of this would become easier and easier to accomplish, especially in suburban locations, after World War II. With the increasing integration of food distribution, and the economies of scale made possible by it, price differences between large, established stores and would-be startups were dramatic. It therefore seems improbable that Lee and his program played a preponderant causal role in the low rate of new grocery sites in the 1950s and 1960s. A more informative conclusion would perhaps suggest that redevelopment and renewal did little or nothing to reverse a trend which had been in progress since young Richie Lee was a stock boy shelving canned vegetables for the A&P near his mother's house in the 1930s.

What eventually emerged, and prevails today, was utterly different from the fabric of enterprise described in Chapter 3. If we leap forward to the present, we see that the city itself retains about 125 stores, nearly all of which are small operations. Some are parts of larger chains, such as the convenience outlets linked to gasoline stations such as Shell. Most are independents operating on a relatively small scale. But the great volume of business goes to large chain operations, among which Stop & Shop and Shaw's are dominant. Most of these are sited in suburban locations, relatively close to the city. Only one large chain store is located near low-income neighborhoods, and that store was subsidized heavily. In the map (figure 11.4) for groceries in 2002, we see a smattering of small operations, primarily in working-class neighborhoods, such as the Hill and Fair Haven, along with a few upscale mom-and-pops in fashionable East Rock. What we do not see is the thick layer of little stores from the urban past.

Downtown Retailing The opera of downtown retailing is more dramatic, and the fingerprints of governmental intervention are everywhere on its libretto. The development that loomed up from the center of Lee's Church Street Project Area, later known as Chapel Square Mall, must be understood as an investment in urban education. The design, modeled crudely after a suburban mall, surrendered every urban advantage, isolating retailing from outdoor pedestrians, creating long blank walls along once lively downtown streets, dwarfing surviving stores in nearby areas, including our friend Perfetto's New England Stationery and Typewriter on Crown Street, barely a stone's throw from the mall. Inside, the mall located its two anchors together, at one extreme, denying the smaller shops the advantage of foot traffic between the anchor stores.[21] The Oak Street Connector,

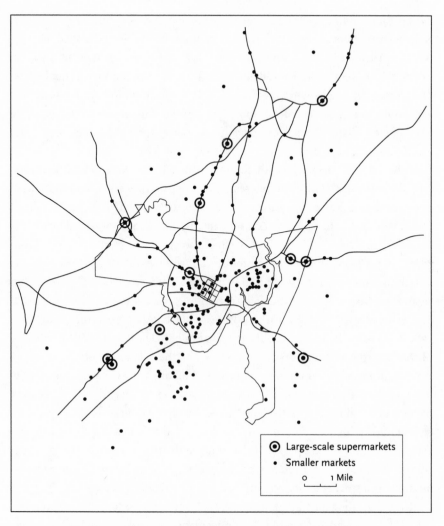

Figure 11.4. Groceries operating in and near New Haven, 2002.

ultimately renamed the Richard C. Lee Highway, ran just south of the mall, cutting the downtown district almost irrevocably in two. Alexander Garvin writes that "from the start, redeveloping downtown New Haven was a mistake. The market survey on which the project was based had incorrectly predicted that the city's population would remain stable for thirty years. By 1980 it had shrunk to 126,000. Although the shrinkage meant fewer customers, the suburban market, which in 1980 had grown to 635,000, should have been more than enough to fill the gap. Instead, this suburban population had chosen to shop elsewhere. Between 1960 and 1973, seven major shopping complexes containing 3,342,000 square feet of floor area opened in surrounding suburbs. They attracted the market New Haven lost."[22] In another context, Garvin is even blunter in his judgment: "What went wrong? The diagnosis was faulty. New Haven was not in trouble because of an obsolete physical plant. It was in trouble because suburban competitors were doing a better job supplying the same market. Restructuring the business district to accommodate unnecessary new retail structures could never be much help."[23]

Only in a much later era, defined intellectually by the New Urbanist cherishing of small-scale retailing on interestingly variegated streets, would something more desirable find its way to New Haven.[24] Even before the New Urbanist movement began to gain ground at the nearby Yale School of Architecture, developer Joel Schiavone's work on Chapel Street just west of the New Haven Green was a pioneering effort to produce a downtown retail ambiance that was utterly urban, and that could within select niches compete effectively even against the best of mall culture. It is a continuing success, although it passed into the ownership of Yale in the early 1990s. Critical to its success is the intimate relationship to such cultural facilities as the Shubert Theater, the Yale Center for British Art, the Yale University Art Gallery, and the Yale Repertory Theater. Despite centralized university ownership of the buildings, the Chapel Street district is dominated by small shops and restaurants, mostly owned by independent firms with local ties. Moreover, the Chapel Square Mall itself is slated to be reconfigured at this writing, "turned outside in" so that stores face the streets and welcome pedestrian shoppers. The downtown district will not return to its preautomotive role as a dominant retailing center, but it may very well continue to improve as a smaller entertainment and specialty retailing area.

Remember the asphalt parking lot across from Joe Perfetto's store, the one under which I unearthed ten live properties dating to 1913? In table 11.2, I have looked up the uses of those properties from 1930 to 1980. The properties begin to change hands and go blank in 1930: Emil Scheuerman's Saloon has fallen victim to Prohibition and is replaced by Schemitz Electric Supply, and Berg the barber has been replaced by an optician. The pattern is one of decline on the upper end of the block but of relative stability elsewhere. Even in 1950, nine live addresses have survived the ten we found in 1913. The street doubtless became a little shabbier over these decades, but it remained a vital street, and close by, just across the street, Joe Perfetto made a living into the late 1990s. This suggests that the claim, sometimes pronounced in the Lee years, of the downtown business

Table 11.2. Uses of Properties on Crown Street, 1913–80

Year	Crown Street Addresses

Year	101	103	105	107	109	111	113	115	117	119	121
1913	Residence	Saloon	Deli	Hotel & Residence		Caged Bird Store	Barber	Restaurant	Residence	Club & Residence	Saloon & Office
1930	Rooming House	Electric Supply	Restaurant	Hotel & Residence	Banking	Caged Bird Store	Optician		Hotel & Residence		Wall Paper Store
1940		Coal Dealer	Sporting Goods	Hotel & Residence	Typewriters	Coal Dealer	Optician	Banking			
1950	Rooming House	Electric Supply	Sporting Goods	Hotel & Residence	Typewriters	Coal Dealer	News and Candy	Appliance Stores	Rooming House		
1960		Electric Supply	Sporting Goods		Dental Lab	Coal Dealer	News and Candy				
1970											
1980	Entire Space is a Parking Lot for Cars by 1980										

district's death by the 1950s was open to dispute so far as Crown Street was concerned.

DISPERSION OF THE GRAND LIST

Lee and his staff had repeatedly maintained that the renewal effort would, in the end, lead to increasing property values and thereby to an expansion of the city's tax base. On very casual inspection, the historical evidence lends some support to this prophecy. Between 1950 and 1960, despite all the razed properties, New Haven's grand list increased from $376.8 million to $560.7 million—a 49 percent gain (it boils down to a 21 percent gain after inflation is taken into account). A longer time horizon is less encouraging. Between 1960 and 1970, the list reached $629 million—a 12 percent nominal gain (a loss of 14 percent after inflation). On the thirty-year period, 1950–80, New Haven's grand list went up from $376.8 million to $1.15 billion—a nominal increase of about $777 million, or 206 percent. Yet the "stagflation" of the 1970s destroyed this gain, leaving the city's grand list 10 percent less valuable in 1980 than it had been in 1950. There are many reasons not to place too much emphasis on small fluctuations in grand lists, which are notoriously inexact measures of actual values. And inflation is a tricky notion for city budgets, consisting substantially of union-contract wage

Table 11.3. Grand Lists for New Haven and Ten Suburbs, 1959–80

Town	1950	1960	1970	1980	1980 in 1950 dollars	Real % change, 1950–80
New Haven	$376,797,137	$560,720,405	$628,960,119	$1,116,534,605	$338,286,372	−10.2
Orange	$10,019,945	$54,572,410	$136,040,122	$391,091,716	$114,394,327	1,041.7
Madison	$11,442,223	$23,927,306	$98,038,225	$370,072,371	$108,246,169	846.0
North Branford	$5,653,160	$24,546,241	$63,278,538	$175,226,964	$51,253,887	806.6
Branford	$20,532,255	$58,694,400	$171,046,560	$571,542,670	$167,176,231	714.2
Guilford	$15,844,879	$41,608,264	$90,664,965	$272,472,991	$79,698,350	403.0
North Haven	$25,934,630	$92,993,056	$167,836,090	$308,782,467	$90,318,872	248.3
Hamden	$76,192,311	$167,179,039	$315,307,161	$848,412,175	$248,160,561	225.7
West Haven	$68,923,198	$136,466,071	$346,287,164	$635,241,970	$185,808,276	169.6
Woodbridge	$9,706,218	$27,794,163	$49,177,059	$89,087,128	$26,057,985	168.5
East Haven	$25,607,150	$61,250,795	$82,249,662	$150,916,333	$44,143,027	72.4
Total of 11 towns	$646,653,106	$1,249,752,150	$2,148,885,665	$4,969,381,390	$1,453,544,057	125
Ten suburb subtotals	$269,855,969	$689,031,745	$1,519,925,546	$3,812,846,785	$1,115,257,685	313
% in New Haven	58.3	44.9	29.3	23.3	23.3	−60.1

agreements. But these numbers do suggest that the city's grand list was either not increased at all or was increased at a very modest pace over these decades.

The big action took place outside New Haven over the same years. Table 11.3 gives nominal dollar grand list totals for each town from 1950 to 1980, then converts the 1980 figures to 1950 dollars, and in the far-right column indicates percentage changes adjusted for inflation across the thirty-year period. Considered as a group, the ten suburban towns experienced an inflation-adjusted growth of 313 percent. Some of them did far better: Orange (1,041 percent), Madison (846 percent), North Branford (806 percent), Branford (714 percent), and Guilford (403 percent) stand out. Even the older suburbs had real growth in their grand lists, ranging from 72 percent in East Haven to 248 percent in North Haven. The unmistakable bottom line is that New Haven's percentage of the total grand list for the region fell by 60 percent—from well over half in 1950 to less than a quarter in 1980. Even allowing for the vagaries of grand lists, the effective decentering of the regional tax base during these decades is dramatic.

This thirty-year analysis is of course just a piece in the far longer history of property values for New Haven and its suburbs. In figure 11.5, I show New Haven's share of the eleven-town total grand list (and population) from 1890 to 2000.[25] Here we see the magisterial arc of urban centering as the city reaches 88

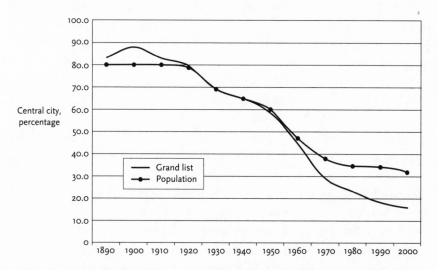

Figure 11.5. Decentering of population and grand list real estate values, 1890–2000. Curves show New Haven as percentage of eleven-town region (with Branford, Guilford, North Branford, Madison, Orange, West Haven, East Haven, Hamden, North Haven, and Woodbridge).

percent of the regional grand list in 1900, and we see the long downward progression as investments in property move from center toward periphery in every decade from 1910 to 2000.[26] Up through 1950, population and investment as recorded in grand lists track one another very closely—diverging by fractions of 1 percent. Then, from 1950 onward, the central city begins to lose its share of taxable property faster than it loses population.

DECLINE OF AMATEUR-LED ORGANIZATIONS

By the time Dick Lee became mayor, the "civic die-off," that had begun about the time of Frank Rice's death was well advanced. Bracketing Masonic organizations for the moment, 70 percent of the city's fraternal and sororal chapters from my 1913 count were gone by 1950, and very few had been replaced in kind.[27] A handful of sporting associations were still operating even in 1980: Campania Athletic, Bummy Moore's Barbell Club, and Carl Grande's imaginative attempt to make slow-pitch softball a spectator sport. A larger array of organizations were operating on the basis of national origin—a Colombian social club, an Antillean center, several Puerto Rican clubs, and a few enduring Italian and Polish societies. Informal organizations emerged from Jamaican and Central American communities. A Sunday league of adult soccer teams was active, with teams typically organized around national origin, even regional origin within Italy. The Jewish Community Center remained strong, although its main facility would soon be moved to a suburban location in Woodbridge. Little League and Pop Warner football were active, and the "New Haven Italians" youth soccer club would form the nucleus for a much larger citywide New Haven club and league by 1981. But the great trend of the period was the erosion of volunteer-based civic organizations, which fell to century lows in about 1980.

In part, these organizations were crowded out by alternative uses of leisure time, particularly with the rise of television. In 1950, according to the U.S. Census, just under 9,000 New Haven households had TV sets (about 20 percent of the total). But TV ran through American neighborhoods at epidemic speed in the 1950s, penetrating 90 percent of homes nationally in time for the 1960 Census.[28] By 1980, everyone in New Haven save the very poorest or visually impaired (and a puritan fringe of the professorate) had succumbed to this newly dominant medium. In part, the fraternals were stretched to death by the suburbanization of their membership rosters. And, critically, their mutual insurance functions were displaced by government and market programs offering cheaper alternatives.[29] Whatever the causes, the effect was to greatly reduce the civic education for city-dwellers, an education that had been provided by the civic fauna of an earlier era. Arthur Schlesinger, Jr.'s 1944 assertion that these peer-run voluntary organizations had "provided the people with their greatest school for self-government" was true in 1913 and even to a degree in 1950, but it was far less true by 1980.[30] At the very heart of the matter was the rapid privatization of leisure and entertainment, a tale summed up with force and elegance by Robert Putnam:

When the history of the twentieth century is written with greater perspective than we now enjoy, the impact of technology on communications and leisure will almost surely be a major theme. At the beginning of the century the communications and entertainment industries hardly existed outside small publishing houses and music halls. The first quarter of the century had nearly passed before the term "mass media" was invented. At the end of the century, by contrast, the gradual merger of the massive telecommunications and entertainment industries had become the very foundation for a new economic era.

Among the effects of this century-long transformation, two are especially relevant here. First, news and entertainment have become increasingly individualized. No longer must we coordinate our tastes and timing with others in order to enjoy the rarest culture or the most esoteric information. In 1900 music lovers needed to sit with scores of other people at fixed times listening to fixed programs, and if they lived in small towns as most Americans did, the music was likely to be supplied by enthusiastic local amateurs. In 2000, with my hi-fi Walkman CD player, wherever I live I can listen to precisely what I want when I want and where I want. As late as 1975 Americans nationwide chose among a handful of television programs. Barely a quarter century later, cable, satellite, video, and the Internet provide an exploding array of individual choice.

Second, electronic technology allows us to consume this hand-tailored entertainment in private, even utterly alone. As late as the middle of the twentieth century, low-cost entertainment was available primarily in public settings, like the baseball park, the dance hall, the movie theater, and the amusement park, although by the 1930s radio was rapidly becoming an important alternative, the first of a series of electronic inventions that would transform American leisure. In the last half of the century television and its offspring moved leisure into the privacy of our homes. As the poet T. S. Eliot observed early in the television age, "It is a medium of entertainment which permits millions of people to listen to the same joke at the same time, and yet remain lonesome."[31]

The volunteer organizations had, to a great extent, withered away. They had, moreover, withered from bottom toward top, reducing the democratic patterns of recruitment and leadership celebrated in Chapter 5. By the late twentieth century, organizational participation had become economically selective. Across America, people with higher incomes were far more apt to be involved with those organizations which continued to operate.[32] Unsystematic evidence suggests that this was true of New Haven too. Most residents of low-income public housing had few if any organizational ties, even to associations created to express their shared interests in housing authority policy.[33] The poor were notoriously difficult to mobilize politically, and they showed limited enthusiasm for the meetings staged by community development corporations throughout the city. The one spectacular exception concerns religious life.

FRATERNAL DIE-OFF

The classic fraternal and sororal organizations of the late nineteenth and early twentieth centuries were subjected to withering competition with the coming of broadcast media, automotive travel, and the dispersion of population into the suburbs. Let's concentrate on those organizations that were well established in New Haven in 1913, with three or more chapters apiece. As with many other features of urban life, *differential rates of survival* are critical to understanding what happened to these outfits over time. A large class of the 1913 organizations were readily winkled out. Some were linked to earlier historical generations (Grand Army of the Republic), others were ruined by the success of their causes as early as the 1920s (WCTU, Catholic Temperance), still others were effectively insurance schemes defeated by better market instruments and New Deal social legislation (Fraternal Benefit League). Yet others, such as the Hibernians and Heptasophs, seem to have withered as members found other ways to express their identities. As indicated by the lower curve in figure 11.6, these low-endurance organizations suffered an 80 percent die-off between 1913 and 1940. Another grouping, consisting of higher endurance fraternals, persisted longer and in greater numbers. The Masonic orders—including Scottish Rite and the "Colored Masons"—lived on in numbers, increasing in chapters from 1913 into the 1940s, and remaining in 1980 more numerous than in 1913. Also robust were the Knights of Columbus (with world headquarters in the city) and the Knights

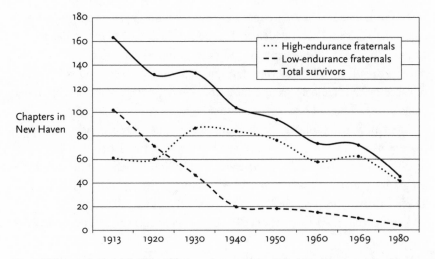

Figure 11.6. Survivorship of fraternal organizations in New Haven, 1913–80.

of Pythias. The middle curve, which moves up over the first few decades of the century in figure 11.6, represents these groups. The top curve indicates the overall pattern of decline, from a total of 164 to a total of 45 New Haven chapters over these decades.

Now the reader may reasonably object to this limited analysis. If we start with the trees that defined a forest in 1913, we may record their many deaths and be surprised to discover that the forest nevertheless remains as dense and alive at the end as it was at the beginning—the old trees have been replaced by greener wood.[34] This is true of New Haven if we confine ourselves to the overall number of nonbusiness, nongovernment organizations active at any time during the twentieth century. Peter Dobkin Hall has made a systematic survey of nonprofit organizations, and he reports an *increase* in their number from 458 in 1900 to 630 in 1989.[35]

PROFESSIONALIZATION OF THE CIVIC FAUNA

These older organizations were important for their flat structures—activity both *by and for* citizens of the city. My analysis demonstrated that their potentates came from all economic strata save the very lowest, from myriad lines of employment within any such stratum, and lived in every one of the city's neighborhoods. Schlesinger's conjecture that they represented a schoolhouse for democracy in that period thus seemed at least circumstantially to be confirmed in the

New Haven data.[36] They were replaced, but were not replaced in kind. Hall reports, on the basis of solid evidence, that the civic fauna was transformed in kind: "Though the overall organizational population remained stable . . . there was a massive die-off of traditional voluntary and membership associations. They were replaced by charitable tax-exempt nonprofit service entities operated by credentialed professionals of one sort or another."[37]

These newer organizations generally shifted the role of mass participants from *member* and its variants to *client* and its variants. In the traditional voluntary organization, members elected members to positions of leadership, and shaped programs of activity, albeit with a little guidance from national organizations.[38] The individual who was a clerk or factory operative during the day was a member, a potential leader, a performer of actions on behalf of others, and not just a client or customer.

Many of the professionally staffed organizations were and are superb, especially when inspired by great locally grounded leadership. The Yale Child Study Center, for example, under the leadership of Albert Solnit (and later Donald Cohen) provided a generation of brilliant service to the children and families of New Haven and its region. The Long Wharf Theatre, with board leadership from the likes of Newton Schenck and later Barbara Pearce, became one of the finest regional stages in the nation. Much the same can be said for the Hill Health Center, Farnam Neighborhood House, Community Mediation, Inc., the Community Foundation of Greater New Haven, Leeway, Inc., and Cold Spring School, to name a handful among hundreds. On average, one imagines, these organizations are more efficient and decidedly more expert than were their more democratic predecessors.

Hall notes two further differences between these organizations and those they have tended to displace. First, their geography is very different. They tend to cluster in planned neighborhoods, which Hall sees as "products of the city's zeal for urban renewal, the result of intentional efforts by urban planners to create centers of community activity." As a result, Hall continues, "by the 1990s the city's nonprofits were unlikely to be located in or near communities of need." Hall indeed documents a broadly "inverse relationship between the neighborhoods in which nonprofits were located and the areas in which their clients were likely to reside."[39] Very often, both the place where services are delivered and the home and life experience of the staff will be entirely alien to the client, especially the lower-income client of color. A second important difference analyzed by Hall concerns the funding base of these organizations. Such organizations are typically funded by charitable giving, government grants, and grants from large foundations. This arrangement tends to make the client less central to decision-making than if her or his dues provided the organization's budget.

Taken together, these changes in the civic fauna make it less *civic* because it is less a fabric of mutual engagement among the city's citizens. One may impute countless benefits to a high-competence service organization, but providing a schoolhouse for democracy is not among them. Neither, in candor, is it easy to suppose that most of these organizations help to foment a sense of neighborhood solidarity or mutual engagement among otherwise different households. Rather like the neighborhood grocery, the old fraternal associations were inefficient, but usefully so. Services to clients are doubtless delivered faster and better, if not more cheaply, by the new generation of nonprofit organizations. That is a gain, but it is not a gain without a compensating loss in the civic fauna of urbanism.

DECLINE AND REGENERATION AMONG RELIGIOUS CONGREGATIONS

The number of religious congregations was increasing in New Haven between 1950 and 1980, even as many other civic organizations died off. What had been 118 churches and temples in 1950 became 190 by 1980.[40] But where were the newcomers? Most of the old standbys were static or declining. Most Catholic parishes had endured, with the one important loss being St. Patrick's of Grand Avenue, taken with the consent of the church hierarchy during urban renewal. Two leading Jewish congregations were now suburban: B'nai Jacob in Woodbridge and Mishkan Israel in Hamden. Five smaller and less affluent congregations remained in the city as of 1980. The old-line Protestants were in retreat, as were the Congregationalists who may serve as a main illustration. The older neighborhood churches on Grand Avenue, Orange Street, Humphrey Street, and in the Hill were gone by 1980. The upscale Church of the Redeemer in East Rock and the venerable Dixwell United Church of Christ endured along with the ancient houses of worship on the Green (Center Church and United Church). Among both Catholic and mainline Protestant churches remaining in the city, congregations were getting smaller, older, and often less able to pay the costs of their organizations. So where was all the growth?

The growth occurred entirely among evangelical congregations serving recently arrived groups , mainly in very low income neighborhoods. Star of Jacob is a major example, arising in the Hill neighborhood as Puerto Rican families began to gather there during the 1970s. This grew into a major congregation, later splitting into two branches serving each of the city's large Spanish-speaking neighborhoods (the Hill, Fair Haven). It provided a dense civic structure, including a broad array of social and athletic activities, for its hundreds and hundreds of congregants. Along with certain Pentecostal churches, Star of Jacob posed a major competitive challenge to Catholicism in Hispanic New Haven. Perhaps even more important were the small, sometimes storefront churches that grew up mostly in black neighborhoods. Sometimes led by clergy who might have been refused ordination by more conservative denominations for want of sufficiently formal training, these became enormously important in filling an organizational niche that had largely been abandoned. I remember attending the funeral for Ardie Windsley's mother in Pitt Chapel and thinking to myself that the fervor of commitment, and strength of congregational identity, were very impressive indeed. Among the scores of other examples would be Beulah Heights, Faith Deliverance, Glad Tidings Tabernacle, Applied Faith, Bethlehem Missionary Church, and Mount Ararat High Ground Pentecostal. These organizations taken singly would seem quite minor. As a group, they were by the 1980s dominant civic influences in many working-class and ghetto neighborhoods of the city.

CRATERS AT THE CENTER

The relationship between reputation and reality in urban places runs in both directions: not only do bad conditions lead to negative opinions, but negative opinions lead to the development of bad conditions.[41] The old working-class neighborhoods, especially those which had been supplemented with large-scale public housing projects, became for many people in the region (including real estate brokers) definitive instances of bad housing and bad environments, often in contrast with the lovely structures that remained in good condition along their streets.[42] One element in this evolution was the layering up of project-based public housing in the central city, a pattern that would place New Haven near the top of the national standings in subsidized units as a percentage of total housing stock across the closing decades of the twentieth century.

Public Housing Projects in Operation by the Early 1980s The city had, as seen in Chapter 8, been an early leader in public housing construction, with Elm Haven, Farnam Court, and Quinnipiac Terrace all accepting tenants by early 1943. In 1949, McConaughy Terrace would present three hundred additional units of low-income housing. By 1951, a thirty-three-acre site in the city's northwest corner would become the Rockview project, and another three hundred units would open nearby as Brookside the same year. The year 1955 would produce the city's first and last low-income public housing high-rise complex in Elm Haven Extension—six towers varying from eight to ten stories in height, located just west of Yale's campus (the complex was an almost immediate disaster). A small low-income project would go in at the corner of Front and Lombard in Fair Haven in 1967. More units would appear as the Waverly Street Townhouses (1973) and the Valley Townhouses (1974). A whole tier of moderate-income projects—Fairway Gardens (1960), Florence Virtue (1965), Columbus Mall (1964)—would appear in the 1960s. Church Street South, across from the train station, would be funded independently of the housing authority but would serve a similar function in the local housing market, concentrating the very poor in large numbers. So too would a thick layer of public housing for low- and moderate-income elderly appear over these decades, much of it high-rise in design.

The housing provided real benefits to families in need, but it also had less favorable effects. All of these units tended to compete against nearby market-rate housing for tenants, very probably accelerating blight and abandonment in some of the latter. This was true especially for the generally very successful elderly projects. As the decades passed, New Haven's low-income family housing became harder and harder to defend in four important respects:

1. It anchored a large population of unemployed people in places where (attainable) jobs were scarce.[43]
2. It overwhelmed nearby elementary schools with very poor children, in many instances children with limited family support for bookish learning.
3. After about 1975 the larger projects became massive instruments of de facto racial segregation.
4. Certain projects became public symbols of social pathology that diffused itself across adjacent neighborhoods in the beliefs of fleeing residents and in the febrile imaginations of suburban householders unwilling even to drive by the places.

Together, these unintended consequences of project housing helped to peg several of the city's old working-class neighborhoods as the absolute bottom of a regionwide hierarchy. If public housing were a minor element of the remaining urban fabric, perhaps these shortcomings would seem justifiable costs of providing needed shelter to the poor. But, due to New Haven's unusually high density of public housing, these considerations would present the post-urban city with many of its greatest challenges. By 1992, for example, Elm Haven listed 449 official household heads as tenants, just 45 of whom had jobs.[44] At Farnam

Court, 16 of 143 were working. At Rockview, 23 out of 191 had jobs. Quinnipiac Terrace's 193 tenants yielded 31 jobs. Together, Brookside and McConaughy had 567 tenants, of whom 137 were working. These depressing numbers reflect many forces, including the perverse incentives set up by HUD and the Brooke Amendment of 1969.[45] But they also sum up a central fact about the city: it is retaining a large population of working-age households, most of whose adult heads do not participate in its market economy except as consumers—not necessarily through their own decisions, and not without performing many other arduous tasks, such as childcare. Absent the incentive to live in places with few attainable jobs, many more might be working in market-rate jobs within reach of their (admittedly low-end) market-rate homes. By about 1980, this state of affairs had become one of the most important facts about New Haven, and it would impact virtually everything else about the city—schools, civil organization, crime rates, and real estate markets. Residents of public housing would often be victimized by crime at rates almost unimaginable to outsiders. Beyond that, public housing would help to place New Haven near the top of the national charts for official rates of impoverishment.

Concentrated Poverty My own decidedly amateur career in New Haven's political life began in February 1981 when Ben Amorotti and I cofounded New Haven Youth Soccer. With the help of scores of volunteers from every neighborhood, and some funding from a local bank, that program grew in just a few years to about 1,000 players from across the city—with every race, income level, and nationality represented in abundance among our girls and boys. A problematic feature of the exercise was the abundance of wonderful children and the paucity of playing fields in the old working-class neighborhoods. The "soccer mom" solution was beyond reach for most of these city kids, a fact that was dramatically demonstrated when our kids played against suburban teams, borne forth in an endless parade of Volvo station wagons driven by moms and dads. For many of our parents, neither the car nor the leisure thus deployed was available. Getting fields established and maintained, and transport made feasible, required help from City Hall, in the person of then-mayor Biagio (Ben) DiLieto and his chief administrative officer, David Warren. Especially as the number of players (spanning almost all the aldermanic wards) became evident, city government came through handsomely with flood control money for two new fields, and the renovation of several old ones for youth soccer.

Shortly thereafter, in early 1983, the income analysis from the 1980 Census came to the attention of the press. Headlines fell quickly on urban poverty, and cities were ranked by the percent of their populations living below the "poverty line" established by the federal government.[46] Here are the "top ten" as reported to the public (percentage of city residents living below the poverty line in parentheses):

1. Newark (32.8 percent)
2. Atlanta (27.5 percent)
3. New Orleans (26.4 percent)
4. Hartford (25.2 percent)
5. Paterson, New Jersey (25.2 percent)
6. Miami (24.5 percent)
7. **New Haven (23.2 percent)**
8. Baltimore (22.9 percent)
9. Macon, Georgia (22.4 percent)
10. Savannah, Georgia (22.3 percent)

When Warren invited me to breakfast a few days later, his pitch was that I should chair a "Special Commission on Poverty" that the mayor would be appointing in response to this distressing news (New Haven had come on fast, from thirty-eighth place and a 17.5 percent poverty rate in 1970, at the end of Lee's era). With something less than outright enthusiasm, I agreed to the task, which consumed about half my time for several months. The twenty-person group included Warren and his consultant Harry Wexler, State Senator John Daniels (later the city's first black mayor), activists Anne Boyd and Betsy Henley-Cohn, Community Action head Marcial Cuevas, "Puerto Rican Godfather" Gumercino Del Rio, Housing Authority Director Linda Evans, the Reverend Charles King, and congressional staffer Jean Sanderson. This group reported its findings in July 1983, beginning thus:

> Poverty is a tangible reality in New Haven. It is experienced daily by thousands, even tens of thousands of our citizens. On Arch Street in the Hill, on the streets between Winchester and Dixwell Avenues in Newhallville, in the streets and alleys above River Street in Fair Haven, in the Elm Haven high rises, in Farnam Court, the poor are massed together in great numbers. Smaller but significant numbers of poor people are scattered through other neighborhoods, commonly hidden from view by the relative affluence of their surroundings. Though Blacks and Hispanics are greatly over-represented among the poor, nearly half of the poor are White and English-speaking.

And continuing: "The 'flight' of middle-class families from the central city to a nearby ring of suburbs further accentuates the concentration of poor in the cities of the Northeast. In other regions, impoverished cities have annexed their suburbs, and thus spread the burdens of poverty. Chattanooga, for instance, had a poverty rate of 24.9 percent in 1969 (3rd nationally), and a rate of 17.9 percent in 1979 (48th nationally)—because of annexation. New Haven has not been able to thus recapture its exurbanites, and its high concentration of poverty therefore remains in place."[47]

The "poverty areas" identified by that commission report followed well-worn historical contours—all but one had been working-class areas in 1913, all were classified as third or fourth (yellow or red) tier by the 1937 HOLC survey, all were urban renewal "project areas," and all had been heavily involved in the work of Community Progress, Inc. In most cases, low-income public housing projects formed dense clusters of impoverishment, sometimes exceeding 50 percent of total population, routinely reaching beyond 40 percent of population in a given neighborhood. Nearly 75 percent of the poor families turned out to be female-headed, aligning New Haven with a well-documented national pattern.[48]

None of the remedies proposed by the Special Commission on Poverty made an iota of difference to the city's poor. The Comprehensive Youth Program was enacted by the Board of Aldermen, funded poorly, and crushed by bureaupathic defense mechanisms. Public transportation was dreadful and remained dreadful. Reindustrialization did not happen. The quality of public housing continued to sink for more than a decade, although modest changes for the better were evident by the late 1990s. The Center for the City of New Haven, meant to apply technical knowledge to urban problems, smacking of Dick Lee's CPI, fell dead early on. The exercise was widely reported in the local press, serving mainly to further confirm the public image of unlivable working-class neighborhoods in the city. Otherwise, it is difficult to see what we accomplished.

Rising Crime Rates In May 1969, Alex Rackley was assaulted in an Orchard Street apartment, just a few blocks west of Yale in the Dixwell neighborhood, his body later found in a marsh. The killing won national attention because both Rackley and the two men imprisoned for killing him were active members of the Black Panthers. It eventually came to light that national Panther chairman Bobby Seale had been in the Orchard Street apartment on the day of the killing, and it was alleged that he had ordered the others to carry it out on the grounds that Rackley was an FBI informer. Seale (and Ericka Huggins) were later tried in New Haven, producing mass demonstrations and great disruption on the downtown

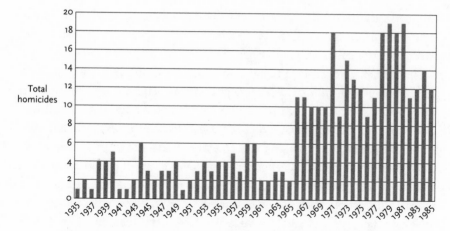

Figure 11.7. Numbers of homicides each year in New Haven, 1935–85.

Green and at Yale.[49] Speaking to a packed house at the new Richard C. Lee High School, Huey Newton would intone, "We may not see the fruits of our revolution in our lifetime, but we will go on struggling while the tanks roll up to our doors. We only have two alternatives—reactionary suicide and revolutionary suicide. We prefer the latter."[50] This irresponsible and florid language, unusual even for the period, soon burned itself out, but it would more or less permanently mark the end of urbanism as seen from City Hall.

The Rackley killing would have been a local story of very modest notoriety absent its racial politics. It would also have been a bigger story if it had occurred a decade or more earlier. In figure 11.7, I show the number of homicides in New Haven from 1935 to 1985.[51] Since 1935 (and earlier), homicide had been rare in the city: between 1935 and 1965, 95 cases were reported, an average just under 3.1 per year.[52] Between 1966 and 1985, 262 cases were recorded, implying an average of a little over 13 annually. The shift is somewhat more dramatic than these

Table 11.4. Violent Crimes per 100,000

City	Violent crimes per 100,000						
	1940	1950	1960	1970	1980	1990	1999
U.S.	55.7	104.7	136.0	360.0	580.1	731.8	524.7
U.S. cities 100–250K	118.2	129.2	154.0	424.6	798.2	992.1	*
U.S. cities over 250K	142.5	219.6	230.8	609.9	1,287.1	1,460.1	*
New Haven	43.0	45.6	64.5	404.5	1,519.6	3,058.8	1,552.3

Note: * Not reported.

numbers make it seem, because the city's population had been larger in the earlier period. Homicides per 100,000 rose from about two to more than ten between the two periods—roughly a fivefold increase.

This unhappy story is not unique to New Haven. In table 11.4, I place the total
rate of violent crime (homicide, non-negligent manslaughter, rape, robbery) per
100,000 for New Haven in comparison with national rates, rates for all U.S.
cities of specified size classes, and for twenty eastern cities, including New
Haven. Note, first, that through 1960, New Haven was safer than the nation as a
whole, and safer than the general run of other cities. Whereas cities in its
125,000–250,000 class have (on average) more violent crime than the nation as
a whole in this period, New Haven has far less. In 1970, we see cities moving past
national rates, with big cities moving at a faster pace than small ones. New
Haven is in the middle of its small-city pack at this point. In 1980, we see New
Haven looking more like a big city in its rate of violent crime, indeed greatly exceeding national rates for cities of any size. Even in this it is far from unique, running well behind places like Boston, Hartford, Camden (New Jersey), Atlantic
City, Washington, D.C., and Philadelphia.

In the years around 1980 the New Haven Police Department was at an all-time
high in budget and number of sworn officers—491 of them in fiscal 1980, with
a total payroll of 564 employees. That comes to about 3.8 sworn officers per
1,000 in population (as against about 2.7 in the calmer 1950s). Aside from rare
emergencies, you would seldom expect to see more than 30 percent of the officers on duty at any one time, and of these not more than 80 percent would be
"out there" performing police work. One hundred and twenty officers might, at
the outside, be found in cruisers or walking beats at any given moment. A more
likely number is well under one hundred. If the city had 50,000 residential
units, along with perhaps 10,000 buildings devoted to commerce, production,
and services, spread across 1,200 city blocks, then each officer would be poten-
tially accountable for goings-on at something like six hundred locations. Even
with the quasi-military approach of the period—radio-dispatched cruisers—this
is thin coverage. Moreover, such police work was largely reactive, the standard
measure of coverage being response time—the minutes elapsed between a call
for help and the arrival of the first cop. For most purposes, five to ten minutes
was considered desirable.

This reactive police coverage, while utterly essential, was not and had never
been the principal mechanism for crime prevention. The work of preventing
crime is largely that of civil society—the connectedness of neighborhoods, the

teachings of countless unheralded leaders at street level, the casual surveillance of street-corner shopkeepers, and the sense of trust and obligation we associate with high levels of social capital. A major part of what I mean by urbanism is the effectiveness of these extragovernmental mechanisms for the most fundamental task of governance—preventing criminal aggression in the city's streets and homes. These informal mechanisms had become ineffective, at great cost to the livability of the city. Let me be very specific, using the FBI records for 1980 in New Haven: 2,252 thefts of autos or their contents, 8,756 cases of larceny, 4,910 burglaries, 300 aggravated assaults (beatings, muggings), 1,500 robberies, 98 reported rapes, 18 homicides. This totals to well over one criminal event for every ten residents of the city in a single year. It also comes to about three dozen crimes per sworn officer. To be sure, 1980 was a very bad year, but there would be several worse years in the decade ahead, with homicides becoming nearly twice as numerous as they were in 1980. No red flag for the end of urbanism could be more obvious—redder, if you will—than a crime rate like that.

While crime against property is quite democratic in its attitude toward neighborhoods, violent crime has a definite affinity for the poor. I have used 1990 Census data to show the percentage of households with very low incomes and have projected the exact sites of assaults occurring in the first quarter of 1992 across those areas. In the fifth of Census tracts with the fewest poor households—all in Westville or the East Shore—only 4.9 percent of the assaults occurred. In the next quintile, 10.9 percent occurred. In the middle quintile, 19.8 percent occurred. The poorest 40 percent of the city's households were exposed to two-thirds of the assaults in this period. The Dixwell neighborhood represented about 5 percent of the city's population and endured nearly 15 percent of the assaults in this period. Some blocks, often near large public housing projects, endured far greater disproportions—often ten or even fifteen times their pro rata shares of the incidents. In these crime-prone areas, the end of urbanism—the end of trust, the end of tightly woven connections—was evident beyond question.

From about 1970 forward, state and federal prisons became increasingly important instruments of urban government in New Haven and across America. Partly for reasons already set forth here, the mainstream prospects for many inner-city youths were increasingly bleak in the 1960s, 1970s, and 1980s. The U.S. prohibition on recreational and hallucinogenic drugs, little more effective than prohibition of alcohol had been, created illicit opportunities for city kids, who found ready markets in more affluent strata of society as well as among their economic peers.[53] New Haven was no exception, and the familiar neighborhoods dating to the HOLC survey became depressingly crime ridden, and (slightly less) depressingly full of empty beds belonging to young men now sleeping in the state pen at Somers or at a youth facility elsewhere.[54] A recent set of rigorous estimates suggest that a black male born in the late 1960s who failed to complete high school had a 58.9 percent chance of spending time in prison before reaching his early thirties.[55] That figure may actually be low in the case of New Haven.

WEEDING OUT USEFUL INEFFICIENCY

The city of late urbanism was a massive collection of useful inefficiencies— things that were below par from a market point of view, or from the modernist ethic of linear rationality, but that nevertheless produced value of other important kinds. Le Corbusier would have looked with horror at the higgledy-piggledy scattering of small groceries, oddly shaped hardware stores, and streets on which a seller of caged birds competed for space and attention with a saloon, all housed in buildings meant for some earlier use now long forgotten.[56] The housing stock, built at ten discernable levels of expense and elegance, designed in a dozen or more very different architectural vocabularies, would for this cardinal of modernism have seemed nothing more than a dog's breakfast of mistakes. So, too, from an accountant's perspective would it seem a waste of resources to provide hundreds of tiny groceries across the city, and to operate civic organizations whose salable work could in good measure be replaced by television sets emitting *Monday Night Football* or *Saturday Night Live*.

The manufacturing core of the city was itself less and less efficient in competition with alternative locations for the production of identical products in the years after 1950. During fevered bursts of demand, usually occasioned by warfare, industrial capacity elsewhere was absorbed so fully that New Haven's aged plants could hold their own for orders not yet accommodated. The Vietnam War, over in 1975, was the last such spike capable of stimulating massive contracts for New Haven manufacturers. Between 1954 and the present, at least 90 percent of the blue-collar industrial jobs that had been so important earlier were lost. The world and national economies were, quite arguably, benefited by the redistribution of contracts and investments that accounted for this fact—largely because these jobs were less productive per hour or per dollar of wages than others in places where women and men were willing and able to produce more widgets for less pay, and where those widgets were easier to transport to their buyers than they might have been if made in New Haven. High energy costs, union trouble, rising security expenses, and other factors pushed managerial decision-makers in the same direction. As the plants closed, as shifts were pared away, as workers were furloughed and fired, inefficiencies that had helped to sustain an urban community were removed from the national economy.

The old fabric of enterprise was similarly a mare's nest of useful inefficiencies. Chain retailing, sophisticated systems of distribution, and economies of scale were noisy facts of life by the 1950s that had been whispering threats to small shopkeepers since the 1920s. By the redevelopment era it had become obvious that most mom-and-pop firms were doomed to extinction—and they did indeed for the most part die away in the face of Stop & Shop, Home Depot, Barnes and Noble, and McDonald's. Goods were in most cases sold better, more efficiently, and more cheaply. The villains here are certainly not the small-timers, who couldn't be expected to raise the capital or engineer the scale of operation required for survival. Neither, in truth, were the managerial officials of the big-time businesses: they were simply making (or trying to make) profitable decisions about the deployment of capital belonging to their investors. The acid test of these investments, of course, stood with people who elected to spend their money at Stop & Shop instead of Rascatti's, at Borders instead of at Book Haven, at Home Depot instead of Roland T. Warner Hardware. Are these disloyal shoppers villains? Of course not. They are just trying to make ends meet for themselves and their families. Like so many painful changes in a capitalist society, this is a story with neither heroes nor villains—just useful things for which people decided not to pay the necessary cost of upkeep.

The decline of the amateur-led civic organization is of a piece with the retail story, although the exact mechanisms are less direct. Before suburban sprawl, and before mass media broadcasting, evenings spent in the company of others in pursuit of shared goals or symbolic ideals, or even plain mischief, had many attractions. An Odd Fellows' lodge meeting on Tuesday night was at once social, identity-affirming, and (I am led to believe) fun. On a Saturday morning, the Washington Glees football team could draw a crowd before far better and more glamorous sport became available in every nearby living room. Here again, the choice was our own: people *could* have kept joining the clubs, attending the games, sending in their monthly dues.

Even peace on city streets was partly lost in this era, although it will not be lost to the future. If Jane Jacobs is right, and I believe she is broadly correct, then the tiny texture of retailing, of mixed-use neighborhoods, and of civic engagement played powerful and intertwined roles in signaling norms of conduct—norms covering topics as minor as properly disposing of a candy wrapper or as large as redirecting the anger that might lead to assault or even homicide. In this matter, criminals are assuredly villains, but the changes that seemed to increase their numbers are not the product of villainy. They came along in the bargain with the end of urbanism.

CHAPTER 12

A CITY AFTER URBANISM

The future once happened here, and it will again, although it will be a smaller, less imposing future in an information age economy that disperses and decentralizes everything from capital markets to car manufacturing. . . . Whether industrial or postindustrial, cities nurture the face-to-face contact within creative communities that drives the advanced sectors of the economy.—FRED SIEGEL, 1997

In the years immediately after Dick Lee's reign, it became apparent that New Haven would not become the slumless city once advertised, that its fabric of enterprise was in tatters, that its industrial might was all but gone, that the vitality of its civic fauna was being supplanted by professionally staffed service organizations, that crime was a growing problem, especially in lower-income neighborhoods, and that the inner city would continue to house the neediest households in the region in wildly disproportionate numbers. The central city had, moreover, become a zone of specialization in services to the poor, to the recently incarcerated, to the substance addicted, and to the homeless. A large cadre of professional service providers, many living in the suburbs, had become de facto spokespersons for the concentration of clinical facilities in the city.

As these observations sank in, the balance between political and market responses to urban problems shifted sharply toward markets. When a problem presents itself, the political (or "voice") response is to seek a change in its causes or to diminish its magnitude—in brief, to join with others in an effort to fix it.[1] If schools are failing, one would help to make them better, form a parent-teacher organization, and lobby for better teachers' salaries, smaller class sizes, higher budgets for computer-aided learning. If taxes are too high, one might join the Republican Party, organize his neighbors to fight for budget cuts at each year's aldermanic hearings, and work to limit the impact of union work-rules on overtime spending. If these efforts seem ineffective, or become too burdensome (or both), the market (or "exit") solution beckons: Leave the problem for others to solve, and get out of its way. This, for increasing numbers of families, meant leaving a city home and buying one in the suburbs.[2] This move, encouraged by all manner of commercial ventures, tended to undermine healthy tension in city politics by removing many critical voices from the scene—leaving a lesser politics to confront an increasing body of urban problems. It also tended to drain economic capacity from the city's neighborhoods and to create a regional hierarchy of municipalities based on economic and racial differences, with the central city at its bottom—with more problems and fewer resources than any other government in the region. These two closely related phenomena—central-city political decline and regional hierarchy—represent the triumph of exit over voice and market over polity, which characterized the city after urbanism. I will start with the suburban market and finish with city politics.

JOE AND HOPE PERFETTO OF RIDGE ROAD FARMS

Between his move to suburbia in the summer of 1950 and the final closing of his downtown store in 1999, Joe Perfetto must have crossed New Haven's city limit close to thirty thousand times—over and back each morning and evening, six days a week, fifty weeks a year, five decades running. For Perfetto, as for millions of other 1950s Americans, life was newly orchestrated by the sun's diurnal cycle. Morning was for the city—its noise, its traffic, its strangers, its cash. Evening was for home and hearth in his little colonial Cape, away from the hated and beloved downtown. Six mornings a week found Perfetto on Crown Street, rambling about New England Stationery & Typewriter, sharing coffee next door at Jimmy's, berating the landlord for the noisome bums upstairs in the so-called National Hotel. But now, after the store's closing, the city has become a distant place, more often remembered than visited. Consequently, a chat with Joe Perfetto requires automotive pursuit beyond city limits.

I drive along Davis Street, in suburban Hamden and just north of New Haven, looking for the home he shares with his wife, Hope. Davis Street crosses Lake Whitney on a low concrete bridge, then rises sharply into wooded parkland, with fine homes discreetly tucked into the hillsides (many were built as part of a high-end subdivision created in the early 1920s). Each occupies an acre or so, and no two houses appear to have been built from the same set of blueprints. As the land begins sloping down into the next valley, details of the built environment begin to hint at a dividing line between upper-middle-class and flatly middle-class sub-urbia. The houses grow a little smaller and sit closer to the street; differences between properties are less striking. Farther along, the land slopes toward indus-trial State Street and the heavy rail line running north from the city. Crossing under a stoplight, I find myself in a tract development different from Levittown mainly in scale—more exactly in constituting something like a 1 percent model of the famed Long Island development.[3] A place whose 1944 birth name was Ridge Road Farms consists of about a hundred small homes, all well kept, all about fifty years of age, all of the same general Cape colonial design—each with a centrally placed front door, each offering an unceremoniously straight cement walk running about twenty feet to the street.[4] Perhaps half a dozen of these neat little properties would fit on the acre occupied by one house a few blocks to the west.

It occurs to me, ever so slowly, that the drive I have just made passes forward through historical time and downward through the class structure. The larger houses, and the more affluent form of suburbia, came ahead of the later, smaller houses for which I am looking. First came upper-middle-class housing, then later came middle-middle-class housing. This is certainly no general law of ur-ban history, but it is suggestive of a historical fact about many American suburbs and about this patch of Hamden, Connecticut. Here, suburban development began on a relatively small scale and was aimed at affluent business and pro-fessional buyers. Later—with help from FHA loans and tax advantages on mortgage payments—suburban tract developments arose to democratize the process, immensely increasing the market possibilities by reaching the great middle band of the income structure. The development where the Perfettos bought in at mid-century was just such a case.

One tidy house, with a 1985 Cadillac Coupe de Ville in the driveway, seems to be the right place. It is a Cape, more or less like all its neighbors, but with an ex-tra dormer on top and a handsome sun-room to one side. A mountain of neatly raked leaves at curbside pretty much confirms the address (Joe Perfetto would, so far as I can tell, rather work than eat or drink). Perfetto, who began school in New Haven while Frank Rice was still mayor, greets me wearing a sweatshirt that reads "World's Greatest Grandpa." That, he says without evident self-consciousness, is "what the kids think of me." When I congratulate him on the leaf mountain, the ninety-year-old offers a good-natured boast: "No Hoover, just a rake." He introduces Hope Carpentieri Perfetto, who is seated with assertive dignity on a richly upholstered sofa in the living room. When she sees me glance at the mural over the fireplace I learn that it shows the Hotel Luna, on Italy's Amalfi coast, a place whose history stretches back to and far beyond the ministry of St. Francis—and which happens to be the place from which her family set out for America nearly a century ago. The Hotel Luna is in a gorgeous natural setting, situated in a village community Americans would think of as more nearly suburban (or pre-urban) than urban. After an initial stay in greater Boston, the Carpentieris came to New Haven in 1920 when Hope's father landed a well-paid job as a "brace-maker" with New Haven Hospital. Polio being the scourge it was, she says, braces were a big deal in a city hospital, and Mr. Constantino Carpentieri became an important man (figure 12.1). Naturally, the family found a place to live downtown, not far from the hospital, on Davenport Avenue in the Hill neighborhood. Hope was five in 1920.

The Perfettos speak with nostalgia about the city of New Haven as it was before "Dick Lee and Redevelopment," a period of which they are quite critical. Their shared memories of residential New Haven wander through Vernon Street, Congress Avenue, Oak Street, and Washington Avenue—working-class neighborhoods mingling homes with grocery stores, theaters, meat markets, and trolley stops where one would see the same people every morning. St. Anthony's parish, to which both had belonged, was an ever-present source of trust and solidarity within the neighborhood. Hope is proud of her New Haven generation, about how one could "work with the door wide open" and fear nothing. Joe keeps circling back to his New England Typewriter & Stationery. The store is a sort of time machine, carrying forward all the old virtues of city life into the decades rolling on in the After Lee era. The shop had been closed for well over a year as we spoke in November 2000, yet the business, and the network of relationships that enveloped it, remained nearly as important as family in defining this man's sense of himself. "Down there, in my store, I was somebody."

Joe's identity-defining downtown life went on for nearly five decades after the day when he and Hope used savings from the business to make a down payment on their house and its 60-by-110-foot parcel of land, also known as 314 Davis Street. The couple finalized the purchase on June 30, 1949, with a mortgage for

Figure 12.1. Constantino Carpentieri (father of
Hope Carpentieri Perfetto) crafting a brace for
a polio victim at New Haven Hospital, c. 1920.
Photo courtesy Mr. and Mrs. Joseph Perfetto.

$7,000, monthly payments of $52.50 stretching into the then distant future.
Joseph and Hope would move in during July 1950, before the development was
really finished. The acres of land behind the house were still an open field, and
Joe jokes about being able to hunt rabbits in his back yard. Many other couples
soon enough settled in their vanishing "back yard," and the Perfettos settled in to
raise their children with the benefits of homeownership on a suburban street.
The new neighborhood was cleaner, quieter, more homogeneous than the old
Hill area of New Haven—less apt to produce a surprise, at once more relaxed,
and on occasion a trifle boring. The couple likely agreed with an opinion piece in
the *New Haven Register* two springs later that "bringing up children on city streets
cannot be compared with rearing a family in a small town or country environment. No matter how poor a home owning family may consider itself, it is getting more out of life than tenancy."[5] Their kids now grown and married, the Perfettos have been in the same trim little house for 2,500 Sundays since.

CULTURAL SUPPORT FOR ESCAPING THE CITY

The Perfettos, like millions of other Americans of their generation, made their residential choice within a field of cultural forces that made them apt to choose a place like 314 Davis Street. A whole library of ideas, many of them so powerful as to move people without conscious articulation, lay slumbering in the hearts of city dwellers throughout the decades. One large volume in that library was the city's preindustrial memory of itself. Before the centered industrial city took shape, New Haven's boosters portrayed a place interweaving town life with country amenity. As Timothy Dwight wrote of New Haven in 1822: "A considerable proportion of the houses have courtyards in front and gardens in the rear. The former are ornamented with trees and shrubs; the latter are luxuriantly filled with fruit trees, flowers, and culinary vegetables. The beauty and healthfulness of this arrangement need no explanation." The heaping up of industrial capital, interlarded with tenements for freshly recruited labor, had violently distanced the city from these genteel images. By the time Perfetto had reached the age of reason in the late 1920s, a Vernon Street home might have a grape arbor in the back yard, but it was visibly embedded in industrial society. To use a phrase common to New Haven streets, the grape arbor would have seemed to some like an earring on a pig. Noise, soot, and the acrid odor of burned coal gave the lie to any rustic delusion on the working-class streets of New Haven. Only the most upscale neighborhoods in the city—Westville, East Rock—could pretend to reenact Dwight's naturalism, and even there one could sense the city's engines running not far away.

Many people living in the mature industrial city remembered its earlier contours in idealized form. A charming instance is recorded in Jane Bushnell Shepherd's memoir, written in her ninth decade of life during the early 1930s:

> As in these hectic years I stand apprehensively at the street crossings, watching for the red light to appear, and when it does hurrying faster than a woman of my age should, lest a motor car swing around the corner and lay me low (eyes on the back of one's head being a necessity of modern life, are perhaps slowly evolving), I recall with mournful pleasure that distant time when we stepped into our phaeton in front of No. 17 College street, and drove leisurely down Chapel street to do a few errands ... and never dreamed of fastening Dick [the horse] when we went into Fenn's shoe store, or Monson's and Carpenter's, or any other of the nice stores that lined either side of that delightful thoroughfare in the days of our youth.[6]

The striking feature of Shepherd's recollection, and others like it, is that the re-membered city is in tone and aspiration more suggestive of a twentieth-century *suburb* than of a twentieth-century city. The *present* city of 1932 is a crowded buzz of danger and apprehension. The *remembered* city is without crowding, without congestion, filled with outdoor pleasures. It is also remembered from the per-spective of an affluent family, so that need and necessity take a back seat to plea-sure and discretion. The city past, before the crescendo of centered urbanism took hold, is not quite so rustic as Dwight's, but it is far more so than any reality available in central places. And the coming of the car—disruptive technology ex-traordinaire for New Haven—becomes part of the implied critique of urban life by the early 1930s.

The Perfettos' suburban home, built after many decades of centered urbanism, can be understood in part as an attempt to recapture these same features from the collective memory, with all their "healthfulness" and openness. Even the modest Cape-style homes in the new development were metaphorically consistent with Dwight's preindustrial observation: "The style of building is neat and tidy. Fences and outhouses are also in the same style; and, being almost universally painted white, make a delightful appearance by the great multitude of shade trees, a species of ornament in which the town is unrivaled." Dwight goes on to observe that the "views in and around this town are delightful. Scenery does not often strike the eye with more pleasure. A great number of charming rides in its envi-rons add not a little to the pleasure of a residence in New Haven."[7] What the Per-fettos have elected to do goes Dwight one better, for they have managed to *move into the view* without giving up their urban source of income. For good measure, they have established themselves in a tidy house, painted white, with scarcely a leaf out of place in the yard. In so doing, they join a vast movement toward the for-mation of a suburban region—and, in the case of 314 Davis Street, the disappear-ance of the view itself into a relatively dense maze of streets and housing.

There was also, as Robert Fishman has shown, a long-established idea of what a suburb was and how it was related to a central city. While the early modern city in Europe had treated its suburban fringe as inferior space, the view of suburbia that shaped American beliefs in the nineteenth and twentieth centuries was one of upscale privilege. In his telling, the upper-income merchant class of eighteenth-century London invented suburban development and suburban life by a sort of trial and error, transforming rural villages—Clapham, Hampstead, Highgate, Walworth—and the surrounding farmlands into a specialized, class-restricted form having a distinctive set of identifying traits:

Though physically separated from the urban core, the suburb nevertheless depends on it economically for the jobs that support its residents. It is also culturally dependent on core for the major institutions of urban life: professional offices, department stores and other specialized shops, hospitals, theaters, and the like. The true suburb, moreover, is more than a collection of dense city streets that have reached the edge of the built-up area. The suburb must be large enough and homogeneous enough to form a distinctive low density environment defined by the primacy of the single-family house set in the greenery of an open, parklike setting. . . . Suburbia can thus be defined by what it includes—middle-class residences—and second (perhaps more importantly) by what it excludes: all industry, most commerce except for enterprises that specifically serve a residential area, and all lower-class residents (except for servants).[8]

With a more singular emphasis on the United States, Kenneth Jackson's *Crabgrass Frontier* identifies suburbs with a single sentence: "Affluent and middle-class Americans live in suburban areas that are far from their work places, in homes that they own, and in the center of yards that by urban standards elsewhere are enormous."[9]

Recall the view expressed in 1904 by Adna Weber: "We have learned that the packing of human beings into tenement barracks devoid of light and air is not due to the necessity of any natural law, but to the greed of man. The city, even the largest city, can now be made as healthful as the country, because cheap rapid transit enables city workers to live many miles away from their work-places."[10] Here was an idea that could wed doing good for humanity with greed, a marriage that sold like hotcakes in mid-century America. What began as a narrow, highly exclusionary idea became less so in the course of the twentieth century. As Fishman observes, "If there is a single theme that differentiates the history of twentieth century suburbia from its nineteenth century antecedents, it is the attempt to secure for the whole middle class (and even for the working class as well) the benefits of suburbia, which in the classic nineteenth century suburb had been restricted to the bourgeois elite alone."[11]

Here was a thought that appealed both ideologically and economically to the most influential segments of a capitalist democracy. Barring the difference between cars to reach suburban plots and homes to occupy those plots, this was the same idea as Henry Ford's: "I will build a motor car for the great multitude. . . . It will be so low in price that no man making a good salary will be unable to own one—and enjoy with his family the blessing of hours of pleasure in God's great open spaces."[12] Why, indeed, should the white-collar and even blue-collar denizens of the city be denied the balm of suburban escape? And is it not the case with suburban land and construction—as with every other product line in a capitalist market system—that the greatest money is to be made in serving the tastes of the less-than-great masses? Is it not probable that suburban housing in the thousands and hundreds of thousands and eventually millions of units offers an unprecedented opportunity to investors and managers? Indeed, the real estate profession would turn this idea into an *ethical* precept. Here, speaking in 1952, is John Lund, president of the National Association of Real Estate Boards: "Placing of property ownership within the reach of the average citizen has been the highest goal of professional people in real estate work since realtors adopted their code of ethics 40 years ago. This is one expression of the American tradition, and it is supported by the wishes and actions of the American people."[13] Here, as often in real estate, professional ethics, patriotic ideals, and the surest road to profit coincide with surgical precision. Here, too, was an idea that might very well enlist the full support of government at every level, save perhaps that of centrally located municipalities.

SUBDIVISION OF SUBURBAN TOWNS

Inflamed by the ethical imperatives of this supportive ideology, and propelled by automotive technology, an opportunity for mutual gain quickly emerged among three groups. First, of course, came the growing ranks of developers and real estate brokers looking for fresh opportunities beyond the bounds of exhausted cities, many of them desecrated by the judgments of HOLC surveys in the 1930s. Second came the owners of undeveloped land in towns like Hamden, Branford, North Haven, West Haven, East Haven, and Woodbridge. Third, and critically, came officials of the town in question, for whom tax revenue on undeveloped land was painfully low, especially since most serious agricultural uses for pasture and field had disappeared with the invasion of cheap products grown in softer and flatter parts of North America under the spur of railroad transportation. The triangular alchemy amounted to the transfer of land from owner to developer, made profitable by town government approval of a plan for the land's subdivision into lots for individual houses. Land valued at $500 per acre before the alchemy of subdivision might command $5,000 per acre just after the approved plan was officially filed in the town vault. Developer, land seller, and property tax collector could share in mutual gain from deal after deal—and they did.

I have examined hundreds of such plans in the fireproof vaults found in every one of Connecticut's 169 town halls. The vault in working-class West Haven, for example, contains old planning maps for places like Campbell Terrace, authorizing 529 building lots in 1897, and New Haven Investment Company's 1909 Colonial Park, offering 796 lots.[14] A score of other early West Haven developments—Blythdale, Sea Bluffs, Home Gardens, Minor Park, Hoffman Park, Allingtown Park, and Graham Manor, for instance—promise large numbers of small building lots, many constituting less than 5,000 square feet of land. Thanks to electric trolley service, initiated in 1892, these became working people's homes. Modest though they were for buyers, such projects gave their developers the hope of exceedingly handsome returns per acre of land.[15] Later West Haven subdivisions included Burwell Park in 1933, offering 414 lots from Ideal Homes of New Haven, Paradise Gardens (1945, 455 lots), and scores of smaller developments, with a strong emphasis on condominium projects by about 1980—Savin Harbor, Oronoque Forest, Orange Landing, and Waddington Foundry.

The much smaller vault in picturesque Woodbridge, west and north of the city, begins with two similar subdivisions—the 1910 Warren division, with 231 small lots, and the 1925 Woodbridge Heights (200 slightly larger lots), promoted by Tri-State Realty of downtown New Haven as "New Haven's Finest Residential Suburb." After the 1920s, Woodbridge devoted itself to developments based on small numbers of large lots, such as Pease Road (21 lots) in 1926, Dogwood Circle (10 lots) in 1940, the Rimmon Road Association (13 lots) in 1948, Old Barnabas Road (20 lots) in 1953, and Warren Gardens (9 lots) in 1978. These developments, and a score like them, reflect high-end development, regulated by two-acre zoning. This was a shrewd maneuver, reducing taxes for existing homes, limiting the burden of children requiring schools and teachers, and homogenizing the adult population. It would be repeated often in other places.[16]

REGIONAL HIERARCHY

The contrasting development histories of West Haven and Woodbridge led over the decades to the evolution of very different housing inventories, and, more critically, very different economic class distributions in the burgeoning suburbs. West Haven emerged from the 1920s as a decidedly working-class industrial suburb of New Haven. Woodbridge, much of which has remained undeveloped altogether, seemed a rural village into the 1940s, except for the "flats" adjacent to New Haven (much vilified by the 1937 HOLC survey). But it emerged as

the most exclusive suburb in the region during the 1950s and was by 1980 a preserve of the doctor-lawyer-merchant-chief crowd, most of whose members relied
on upscale service-sector jobs related to Yale University and the city's two major
medical centers. Woodbridge and West Haven stand in polar contrast among
New Haven's suburbs in nearly every way, most of all in the economics of their
housing stocks. Woodbridge, with just over 2,000 single-family houses in 1980,
had 16.1 percent of the eleven-town region's upscale inventory ($100,000 and
up). West Haven, with 8,970 units, provided just 1 percent of the upscale inventory. Put another way, two-thirds of Woodbridge's homes were priced above
$100,000, while just 1 percent of West Haven's were that expensive. Equally sit-
uated in Connecticut law, the two places are equal in no other respect—having
different resources, different class structures.

With a wider angle of vision, a regional hierarchy emerges, its basic shape suggested by table 12.1. These 1980 single-family housing values, as estimated from
Census data, show that Woodbridge, Orange, Madison, and Guilford led the region at its high end. These four towns had two-thirds of all the region's houses
valued above $100,000 (roughly equivalent to $220,000 in 2002). Adding
Hamden and Branford to the tally brings us to 91.8 percent of the high-end
stock. New Haven accounts for under 5 percent of that tier in the housing market, despite its large size. Switching attention to inexpensive houses, those under
$50,000 in table 12.2, we find 83 percent of the regional total lodged in New
Haven, East Haven, West Haven, and Hamden (where most of affordable hous-

Table 12.1. Regional Hierarchy of High-Cost Housing, 1980

Town	Percentage of town's houses over $100,000	Percentage of region's houses over $100,000
Woodbridge	65.9	16.1
Orange	48.1	20.8
Madison	41.3	16.4
Guilford	27.1	13.3
Branford	17.6	9.1
North Haven	11.5	8.1
Hamden	6.2	8.0
North Branford	5.7	1.9
New Haven	4.4	4.6
West Haven	1	1.0
East Haven	1	0.6

Table 12.2. Regional Hierarchy of Low-Cost Housing, 1980

Town	Percentage of town's houses under $50,000	Percentage of region's houses under $50,000
New Haven	54.2	28.5
East Haven	48.8	15.8
West Haven	42.6	22.3
Hamden	25.9	16.6
Branford	18.8	4.8
North Haven	14.6	5.1
North Branford	12.7	2.1
Guilford	9.5	2.3
Madison	6.0	1.2
Woodbridge	4.7	0.6
Orange	3.4	0.7

ing is in the African-American area adjacent to the Dixwell-Newhallville ghetto of New Haven). Almost no such housing is available in Woodbridge, Orange, Madison, or Guilford. If low-income rental housing is included in the calculation, New Haven itself becomes the singular leader.

In order to see how such a hierarchy might bear on the city's government, it is useful to examine the taxable property, or grand list, of each town, and to calculate its value per capita in any given year. Table 12.3 tells this tale for each town across the decades from 1970 to 2000. Due to the timing of revaluations, and the accounting tricks associated with them, there are odd fluctuations in the details here (for example, Woodbridge is greatly undervalued in 1970 and 1980), but the broad picture is unmistakable. Orange, Woodbridge, Madison, North Haven (helped by industrial properties), and Guilford occupy commanding heights in the region's political economy. New Haven is at a great disadvantage, even in comparison to its blue-collar suburbs, such as East Haven and West Haven. The gaps, moreover, increase across the years. New Haven's per capita grand list in 1970 is 76.8 percent of the region's average, and 45.4 percent of the top suburb (Orange). By the year 2000, New Haven's per capita valuation is less than half the regional average (49.3 percent), and less than a quarter of the top suburb (24.6 percent). State policies, such as PILOT[17] and the educational funding formula, compensate for part of these inequalities, but they are among the most fundamental inequalities visible in this or any other region today.[18]

Table 12.3. Grand List Value Per Capita, 1970–2000

Town	1970	1980	1990	2000
Orange	$44,562	$61,750	$51,864	$141,409
Woodbridge	$28,392	$23,991	$59,227	$141,071
Madison	$44,462	$55,124	$42,583	$139,124
North Haven	$33,501	$29,228	$55,480	$125,944
Guilford	$33,379	$32,775	$59,967	$122,288
Branford	$37,064	$51,129	$39,892	$103,936
North Branford	$26,009	$31,697	$26,369	$78,758
Hamden	$28,300	$34,720	$27,894	$63,824
East Haven	$14,505	$12,602	$23,440	$55,912
West Haven	$29,026	$24,963	$19,853	$50,759
New Haven	$20,233	$19,167	$15,091	$34,758
Top suburb	$44,562	$61,750	$59,967	$141,409
Region as a whole	$26,337	$28,471	$28,217	$70,535
New Haven as percentage of region	76.8	67.3	53.5	49.3
New Haven as percentage of top suburb	45.4	31.0	25.2	24.6

New Haven also became and remained the principal residential site for very low income black households. Using 1970 Census data, figure 12.2 shows the tracts within which black families below $2,000 per year (about $9,500 in 2003) lived. Only the gray-shaded tracts contain *any* of these families: the vast majority of tracts or neighborhoods throughout the region are wholly without poor black households. Only four tracts outside New Haven—sections of West Haven, Hamden, East Haven, and Guilford—are involved, and none has a large representation. New Haven's old working-class neighborhoods all are home to some low-income blacks, and those with major public housing projects are home to disproportionate numbers of them. This is one more feature of the regional hierarchy, with important implications for school management, for real estate integration, for neighborhood stability. Very low income whites, in contrast, were relatively widely dispersed across the region in 1970 and in succeeding decades. The concentration of low-income blacks remained highly skewed toward the central city even in the year 2000. The overall cross-racial distribution of low-income families remained heavily skewed toward the city in the 2000 Census.[19]

POPULATION CENTERING AND DISPERSION, 1800–1990

The whole history of New Haven and its region, complex as it may have been, has one absolutely central feature. Population begins in rural dispersion, presses toward the center in the era of urbanism, and then disperses again after the urbanist era. This process, covering two centuries, is recorded by the curve in figure 12.3. The diagram shows the percentage of population concentrated in New Haven, using it and ten nearby town populations as a basis of comparison, starting in 1800. The towns are selected because they—Woodbridge, Hamden, Orange, Madison, Guilford, Branford, North Branford, North Haven, East Haven, and West Haven—become the city's principal suburbs at the end of the story.[20] In 1800, when the whole region had just 16,751 people, New Haven's 5,157 was 30.8 percent of the total. In 1840, as capital development of New Haven began, the region grew by about 11,000, with almost all of the growth in New Haven: the city's share climbed to 51.9 percent. During the era of industrial take-off, 1840–70, the region added 41,978 people, of which 36,450 were New Haveners, bringing the ratio up to about 73 percent. In the key period of rail-before-highways development, 1870–1920, the region grew by 137,117, and the city increased by 111,727, reaching about 80 percent of the total. This era of very rapid growth, concentrated largely within the city of New Haven, is at the heart of

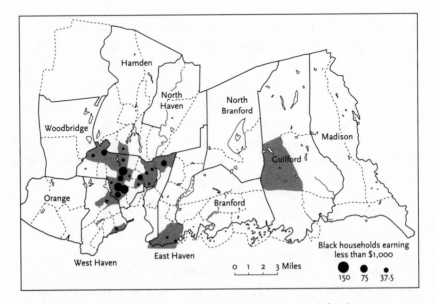

Figure 12.2. Residential locations of very low income black families, 1970.

urbanism historically. After 1920, New Haven's population remained more or less flat until 1950, then began to fall, reaching 126,109 by 1980 and 123,626 by 2000. The entire region grew slowly over these years, from about 207,000 in 1920 to 275,000 in 1950 and roughly 365,000 in 1980. New Haven's percentage of the total fell steadily, from 78.6 percent in 1920 to 59.8 percent in 1950, and to just 34.6 percent by 1980. By 2000, New Haven's percentage had dipped to 31.8 percent. In other words, in two centuries, the region had grown from a small, thinly settled area with decentralized living arrangements to a larger, more densely populated region with nearly the same degree of decentralization. Indeed, the city's share of regional population is slightly less today than it was in 1810, and far less than it had been in 1910.

POLITICS AFTER URBANISM

In 1969, with Dick Lee's decision to quit running for mayor, Democratic Town Committee Chairman Arthur Barbieri inherited something pretty close to monopoly control over New Haven politics. As the *New York Times* reported, "When the Democratic Mayor called a news conference last Monday to announce that he would not seek a ninth consecutive term, the chairman of the city Democratic party, Arthur T. Barbieri, had to get the word from a reporter. 'Like the husband whose wife is cheating on him, I was the last guy in town to know,' Mr. Barbieri later remarked in an interview. But for most of the week following the Mayor's disclosure, Mr. Barbieri neither looked like an outraged husband nor the head of a political organization that had just lost its most attractive candidate. He beamed, he chuckled, he roared with laughter."[21]

Barbieri, unhorsed by Lee some years earlier as director of public works, would return to control the DTC, and in so doing would anticipate the perquisites of a political monopolist. In the 1969 election, five candidates would come forward, and Barbieri's chosen man, Bartholomew Guida, would win the party nomination in a hotly contested primary, then serve three terms as mayor (figure 12.4). A half-serious joke from the period held that Barbieri had bragged of his own power to make *anyone* mayor, and set out to prove the point with Guida's candidacy.

By the end of Guida's third term, in 1975, it was obvious to everyone that the city had shifted from fairly competitive two-party politics to a one-party system—or, in a great GOP year, a one-and-a-half-party system. In 1951, Republican incumbent Bill Celentano had nipped Lee by two votes. Four years later, in his first election as incumbent mayor, Lee would defeat his GOP challenger by more than

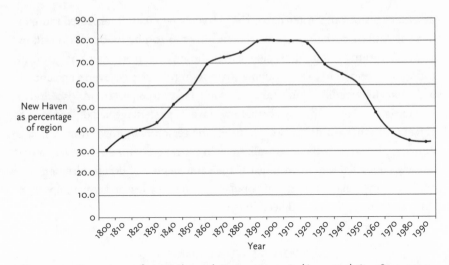

Figure 12.3. Percentage of regional population concentrated in central city, 1800–1990. (Eleven-town region made up of New Haven, Branford, Guilford, North Branford, Madison, Orange, West Haven, East Haven, Hamden, North Haven, and Woodbridge.)

Figure 12.4. Honorable Bartholomew Guida, mayor 1970–76. NHCHS.

20,000 votes and 30 percentage points—43,847 to 23,239. In twenty-three general elections held since the 1955 landslide, only the years 1961, 1969, 1975, and 1991 produced anything that could be mistaken for competitive elections between the parties.[22] In the other nineteen elections, the GOP has fluctuated between 11 percent and 39 percent of the total vote, with a decidedly negative trend line in recent years (table 12.4). The GOP party organization atrophied over the 1960s and 1970s, and has been unable to elect aldermanic candidates in any number since it reached a high of nine seats (one-third of the twenty-seven-seat chamber) in 1975. Currently, the Green Party more or less equals the GOP in stature within New Haven's city politics. Neither is by any test an effective opposition to the DTC.

It is perhaps fair to say that the Lee era of New Haven history killed the local Republican party twice over, once by its brilliance in government, and again by its failure in governance. Lee and his operatives—Barbieri and John Golden, most notably—made the DTC overwhelmingly important to New Haveners who wanted to run for office or to become city employees or to receive discretionary contracts from City Hall for paving, towing, maintenance services, and the like. Going around the DTC was, by 1960, considered suicidal. Moreover, as seen earlier, the ethnic and nationality loyalties once bonding Italians and some Jews to the GOP were dissolved in the first few electoral cycles under Lee's leadership. Hence, the first extinction story. The second extinction story had to do with the disproportionate loss of potential Republicans to suburban life. As the post-urban era of sprawl matured, higher-income white families of every nationality took themselves out of play in central city politics, much as Hope and Joe Perfetto had done in 1950.

As the DTC monopoly became more mature and more confident, its opponents became dispirited or, in some instances, delusional. As GOP effort declined, the DTC allowed its own operatives to go slack in the traces. Many potential Republicans of course left town for the suburbs, many of which had GOP majorities. Many who stayed in the city retreated from politics, at least from local politics. Many others became Democrats on a can't-beat-'em-then-join-'em basis. Let's put this into historical perspective. The data in figure 12.5 suggest a great arc of urban politics. Participation is relatively low in the early twentieth century, partly because many immigrants are not yet voters, and partly because women are ineligible. With women's suffrage under the Nineteenth Amendment (1920) came a surge from 21,523 in 1919 to 36,154, in 1921, both in contests won by the same Democratic incumbent, David Fitzgerald. Voting climbed gradually into and through the Depression, spiking with John Murphy's 1939 defeat

Table 12.4. Mayoral Pluralities, 1899–2001

Year	GOP mayoral	Dem mayoral	Democratic plurality
1899	F. B. Farnsworth	Cornelius Driscoll	1,525
1901	J. P. Studley	Driscoll	−946
1903	Studley	Thomas Kinney	−1,773
1905	Studley	Pardee	−2,988
1907	Chatfield	J. B. Martin	1,567
1909	Frank Rice	Martin	−406
1911	Rice	Martin	−2,029
1913	Rice	Lane	−1,201
1915	Rice	Matoon	−2,013
1917	S. C. Campner	D. E. Fitzgerald	2,735
1919	Haggarty	Fitzgerald	2,830
1921	Ford	Fitzgerald	1,409
1923	Walker	Fitzgerald	1,245
1925	J. B. Tower	Lane	−4,709
1927	Tower	Philip Troup	−2,116
1929	Thomas Tully	Troup	−4,244
1931	Hall	John W. Murphy	9,338
1933	Major Edward White	Murphy	7,924
1935	T. A. Tully	Murphy	5,138
1937	George F. Barnes	Murphy	14,729
1939	William Celentano	Murphy	3,719
1941	Thomas FitzSimmons	Murphy	10,822
1943	Angus Fraser	Murphy	2,727
1945	William Celentano	Richard C. Lee	6,156
1947	Celentano	Dr. Frank Anastasio	−4,253
1949	Celentano	Lee	−712
1951	Celentano	Lee	−16
1953	Celentano	Lee	3,535
1955	P. Mancini, Jr.	Lee	20,608
1957	Cook	Lee	23,330
1959	Valenti	Lee	13,984
1961	Henry Townshend	Lee	4,000
1963	Townshend	Lee	11,534
1965	Jonathan Einhorn, Sr.	Lee	16,293
1967	Whitney	Lee	9,502
1969	Paul Capra	Bart Guida	1,687
1971	Capra	Guida	5,815
1973	John Esposito	Guida	7,533
1975	Frank Mongillo	Frank Logue	2,002
1977	Mongillo	Logue	6,874

Table 12.4. Continued

Year	GOP mayoral	Dem mayoral	Democratic plurality
1979	George Longyear	Biagio DiLieto	10,939
1981	Elaine Noe	DiLieto	12,199
1983	Ed White	DiLieto	17,401
1985	Car. Dinegar	DiLieto	14,614
1987	Dinegar	DiLieto	15,479
1989	Robie Pooley	John Daniels	12,268
1991	Jonathan Einhorn, Jr.	Daniels	3,783
1993	Kevin Skiest	John DeStefano	12,647
1995	Ann Piscitattano	DeStefano	10,789
1997	Piscitattano	DeStefano	11,832
1999	none	DeStefano	12,328
2001	Joel Schiavone	DeStefano	9,642

of Bill Celentano in a race producing a then-record 63,372 votes. Lee's early years represented the top of the long arc. Lee *was* different from his GOP challengers: general elections which meant so much drew massive turnout, as with the all-time record of 76,055 votes in Lee's 1953 win over Celentano. In seven subsequent elections, Lee rolled up 60–40 wins or even more lopsided results

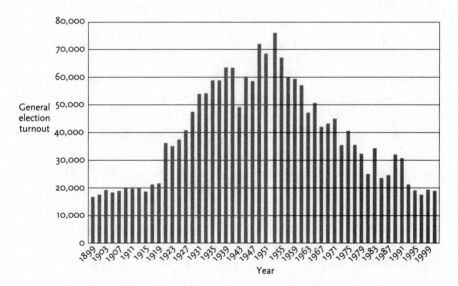

Figure 12.5. Total votes cast in general elections for mayor, 1899–2001.

in all cases except his close run with GOP stalwart Henry Townshend in 1963 (53 – 47). Beginning when Lee's last (and rather uninspired) win in 1967 produced just 42,118 votes, total participation declined steadily for the rest of the century.[23] Partly, of course, this reflected population loss, although simple ratios of votes to population have fallen by about half between 1967 and 2001. One may also look at shifts in age, income, education, and other predictors of voting to find explanations for decline. It is difficult to resist two other explanations.

MARGINALIZATION OF CITY POLITICS

First, city government had come to be marginal in importance for most people. Few great decisions are taken by mayors and aldermen, as had been the case for most of the city's history. Except for the increasingly important Hispanic and African-American populations, political ties based on personal identity have become weak for most of the city's remaining citizens. The DTC is a monopoly institution, and a fairly unappealing, oligarchic, and private one for many potential voters. Perhaps more decisive: even with nearly four thousand full-time positions, job-seeking is now a weak motive for political activism. Opportunities for *new* employment in city government are extremely limited. The combination of civil service protection and the accumulated seniority rights of workers covered by eleven municipal union contracts gives even a freshly elected mayor far fewer than one hundred jobs to dispose, and many of these require advanced professional education. Most of the jobs are not just out of reach for political climbers and insurgents, they are very commonly held by comfortable suburbanites. A block of nearly four thousand people holds more or less permanent city jobs, from which it is very difficult to dislodge them.[24] Dismissal for cause is all but impossible without proof of criminal conduct. Abolishing positions is legal and feasible, but leads to a cascade of union-driven displacements. If one is "organized out of a job," he or she is entitled to "bump" less senior people whose jobs have been spared. Of these four thousand people, a very large percentage lives *outside the city* and therefore votes in a suburb, if at all. In 1991, 1,823 full-time city employees lived outside the city, while 2,166 lived within its boundaries.[25] Those living outside town hold most of the best-paid, most senior positions in City Hall.[26]

BEYOND PLURALISM

In the words of political scientist Douglas Yates, the situation in the 1970s and 1980s was beginning to resemble "street-fighting pluralism."[27] New Haven had developed a "political and governmental free-for-all that makes urban policy making chaotic and unstable . . . a pattern of unstructured, multilateral conflict in which the many different combatants fight one another in an almost infinite number of permutations and combinations."[28] The service providers and the federal Community Development Corporations (CDCs), once having fed from Dick Lee's federal aorta and from its Ford Foundation tributary, were again and again pitted against one another in quest of Community Development Block Grant (CDBG) funding from the Board of Aldermen, and other streams of support stemming from state government.[29] Neighborhood rivaled neighborhood, potentate rivaled potentate, and the mayors who followed Lee found themselves ensnared by intractable distributive conflicts.[30] Race and ethnicity became bases of deep division between political elites, even as the mass public ignored these considerations and bigotry against white ethnics became common on the local scene.[31] Urbanism's sense of commonality and trust was deeply eroded by protracted conflict—and conflict now less and less disciplined by the work of political parties.[32] It became impossible to identify a business elite that might unite the city behind shared economic goals, or that could counterbalance the provincialism of neighborhood potentates. More and more of the city's most able workers and managers and intellectuals were no longer staying in town at night, as the "exit option" seemed preferable to slugging it out in an increasingly unproductive urban arena.

REGULARS AND REFORMERS IN THE AGE OF THE PRIMARY

Over the thirty years that have elapsed since Lee left office, political competition has shifted to the internecine workings of the DTC and to primary elections held whenever the DTC fails to rally a consensus around a single candidate. In every election year, the DTC stages a convention in July, at which members of the Town Committee vote on the endorsement of a mayoral candidate. Seldom, if ever, is the outcome of convention voting in doubt. If a loser at the convention elects to petition for a primary, and gathers the required number of qualified signatures, a September primary follows. Every one of the five mayors (table 12.5) has engaged in a primary, even when he was a regular of the DTC. Guida fought off four rivals in 1969 and was taken out in 1975 as an incumbent by a primary challenge from Frank Logue. Ed Logue's younger brother was a "best-practices" reformer who implemented an effective and ingenious anti-arson program, and who worked with Yale's Sam Chauncey and David Warren to create a state PILOT program that compensated cities for part of the revenue lost through the tax-exempt status of universities and hospitals.[33] Logue was challenged in 1977 by DiLieto (his own police chief at the time) and fought him off narrowly, but lost to him in 1979, when a third Democratic candidate (Henry Parker) siphoned off a goodly fraction of the reform vote. DiLieto thereafter held serve steadily, until retiring in 1989, at which point Daniels had assembled a coalition of African-Americans and white liberals. The DTC turned to DiLieto's key aide, John De-Stefano, who was defeated in the 1989 primary by John Daniels. The first African-American mayor had great difficulty dealing with the DTC, and with the rival factions within his own administration. I, as chief administrative officer, and Comptroller Ralph Peter Halsey, both of us whites affiliated with Yale play-ing top budgetary roles in the administration, were (to say the least) less than effective in welding the expectations of African-American supporters to the pol-icy options and employment opportunities available from the administration. Neither were we able to win compromise or concession from the (largely white) leadership of city unions. DeStefano won the job in 1993 and has served since. He has been a strong administrator, as might be expected from his experience under DiLieto, and has addressed some of the city's most pressing needs in com-mercial development, in handling vacant and abandoned residential properties, and in working hand-in-hand with the arts community, with such initiatives as New Haven's International Festival of Arts and Ideas.

LIMITS OF PLURALIST DEMOCRACY AFTER URBANISM

In his magisterial *Who Governs?* Robert Dahl offers one major conclusion that must be taken into account as we conclude our inquiry into the end of urban-ism.[34] Dahl interprets mid-century New Haven as a democratic success story: the resources of political power and control over government were widely dis-persed among different groups of citizens. Nobody, save the mayor, wins consis-tently in contested policy decisions at City Hall. There are clear political inequal-ities, but they tend either to offset one another or to arise legitimately from the "unending competition between political parties."[35] Some outcomes, such as the taking of a business property for redevelopment, or the routing of a highway across a neighborhood, may be decidedly coercive, even if taken in the pursuit of

Table 12.5. Mayoral Administrations After Dick Lee

Mayor	Political type	Policy highlights	Identity and political base	Term
Bartholomew (Bart) Guida	Regular Democrat, backed by the DTC	Fought Yale expansion, otherwise a very weak policy maker	Italian, long history of family engagement with DTC, wife linked to Irish community	1970–76
Frank Logue	Reform Democrat, unworkable relations with the DTC	PILOT, arson control plan, faced constant conflict with DTC	Weak ethnic ties, an Irish Protestant, many links to Yale community	1976–80
Biagio (Ben) DiLieto	Regular Democrat, backed by the DTC	Downtown development, neighborhood development, strong administration	Strong Italian identity, strong ties to municipal unions, former police chief	1980–90
John C. Daniels	Reform Democrat, uneasy relations with the DTC	Community policing, airport development, based on unstable coalition	First African-American mayor, strong ties in state government, attractive to much of the Yale community	1990–94
John DeStefano	Regular Democrat, backed by the DTC	Livable City Initiative, downtown redevelopment, strong administration	Strong Italian identity, strong ties to municipal unions, chief administrative officer under DiLieto	1994–present

a public goal vetted by democratic process. But ever has that been so in the acts of government, democratic or not. In short, New Haven is a pluralist democracy. The findings of the present book complicate and in some respects amend Dahl's thesis.

Mayor Lee, by winning election after election (in which thousands of citizens had their say about *Who Governs?*), and by making skillful use of his powers as mayor, was able to create what Dahl terms an "executive-centered coalition." In this coalition, different groups, and individual leaders, would join on the mayor's (generally winning) side of issue after issue: Lee would recruit first one set of coalition partners and then another, so that over the years most groups would in some fashion have their say. As Dahl writes, "The preferences of any group that could swing its weight at election time—teachers, citizens of the Hill, Negroes on Dixwell Avenue, or Notables—would weigh heavily in the calculations of the Mayor, for the executive-centered coalition was not the *only* important pattern of influence in New Haven. The unending competition between political parties constituted another pattern of influence; thanks to the system of periodic elections, the Mayor and his political opponents were constantly engaged in a battle for votes at the next election, which was always just around the corner."[36]

The broad pattern of which such electoral competition is an illuminating feature contrasts sharply for Dahl with the pre-democratic past, dominated by a patrician oligarchy: "In the political system of the patrician oligarchy, political resources were marked by cumulative inequality: when one individual was much better off than another in one resource, such as wealth, he was usually better off in almost every other resource—social standing, legitimacy, control over religious and educational institutions, knowledge, office."[37] In contrast, Dahl concludes of mid-twentieth-century New Haven: "In the political system of today, inequalities in political resources remain, but they tend to be *noncumulative*. The political system of New Haven, then, is one of *dispersed inequalities.* . . . Within a century a political system dominated by one cohesive set of leaders had given way to a system dominated by many different sets of leaders, each having access to a different combination of resources. It was, in short, a pluralist system."[38]

Dahl of course accepts that New Haven politics was a messy pot of ethnic and racial and class differences. There were inequalities within and between these groups. But these inequalities generally offset one another, with shifting coalitions and partnerships through time. The overall arrangement was kept more or less democratic by the force of "unending competition between political parties." Dahl could find no business elite capable of manipulating the overall working of the city's political system. This, boiled down to one word, is pluralism. This idea, linked for the generations to New Haven, and amplified by sophisticated criticism and elaboration in seminar rooms across the land, can be given fresh interpretation in light of what has been shown here.[39]

Dahl's critics—however various in matters of detail—were more or less united in the underlying suspicion that democratic pluralism was an illusion. It was, for most, an illusion created by a business elite whose members controlled important city government decisions, presumably from behind a smokescreen through which neither the common man nor the press nor Robert Dahl could see. The most insistent, even dogmatic, of these critics would seem to have been G. William Domhoff, whose 1978 tract purported to discover *Who Really Rules?* in New Haven.[40] Domhoff began with the proposition that members of leading social clubs in New Haven (the Lawn Club, the Quinnipiac Club, the New Haven Country Club) and board members of leading banks and business corporations formed a cohesive web of interlocking directorates. Domhoff identified 416 people, of whom (as might be expected from the current study) 97 lived in "Hartford, Boston, New York, Los Angeles, and other cities outside the greater New Haven area."[41] Domhoff counted the number of interlocking board members and asserted that he was thus able to "pinpoint the central institutions of this network."[42] These included six banks, three utilities, and one law firm. People turning up on these boards, especially those turning up more than once, became for Domhoff members of a "ruling class."

Seen against the long dispersion and near-disappearance of business leadership witnessed in this book, such evidence is decidedly unpersuasive. Not only are business leaders less and less grounded in the city itself, but their local operations are more and more often controlled by corporations having no important connection to New Haven or its region. All save one of the banks Domhoff thinks of as defining the central web of a local ruling class would, within the following decade, be absorbed as holdings of corporations with headquarters in places like New York, Boston, and Charlotte, North Carolina. One utility would be absorbed by a Texas corporation, another would become something of a disadvantage to the region due to its restricted size and higher-than-market rates.

Any collection of boards might very well yield Domhoff's modestly overlapping memberships, and the existence of shared members suggests exactly nothing about interest in or control over city government. Moreover, business strategists would be aware of the legal weakness of city governments in the face of state government authority.[43] Very likely, such strategists would focus heavily on state and national politics, perhaps even on opportunities outside the United States. And, after the era of locally grounded business leadership had faded, they would also find it more efficient to *choose between* municipalities, rather than run them. Domhoff pretty nearly ignores these considerations, and he resorts to anecdotal speculation, anchored in (of all things) the records of a U.S. Chamber of Commerce confab held in 1950 in Washington, D.C., on the theme of "building better cities." At that meeting it was repeatedly asserted that urban redevelopment, typically leading to commercial land uses, should take precedence over the construction of public housing. Creating a separate redevelopment agency was touted as a way of achieving that end. Sure enough, with support from the New Haven Chamber, such an agency was created (before Lee, by Celentano), and, sure enough, it does redevelopment work (under Lee). As the author writes, "Leaders of the local Chamber of Commerce, who were overwhelmingly members of the ruling class . . . , were also involved in the origins of the agency, which is hardly surprising given the aforementioned evidence that the Urban Land Institute and the U.S. Chamber of Commerce had been working with local businessmen and planners to create such agencies."[44]

Domhoff is correct if he wants to assert that business interests at the national level, working through lobbyists, influenced the Housing Acts of 1949 and 1954, which formed the legislative basis of urban redevelopment and renewal across the country. He is wrong if he supposes that this shows the existence of a cohesive business elite in New Haven controlling the specifics of city government policy. He shows nothing of the sort, and this is because the business elite that remained in Lee's time was neither cohesive nor well grounded in the city, nor much engaged in city politics. Lee's Citizens Action Commission was a simulacrum for such a class of politically interested business leaders. Moreover, Domhoff's major specific claim about how the rulers shifted New Haven policy outcomes—redevelopment taking precedence over public housing in New Haven—achieves very little support from the facts. The Housing Authority had been in business a decade before redevelopment began, and by about 1980, New Haven ranked in the top five cities nationally for the density of low-income public housing projects in relation to total housing stock or total population (it still ranks very high).[45]

There of course *were* business people who took an active interest in New Haven politics. Hundreds, even thousands, of retailers had their life's savings tied up in their stores, and many did their best through politics and other means to protect themselves and their families. Perhaps a few hundred vendors, large and small, competed for opportunities to perform contract services for city government—people like Rocky Bello, who used politics to earn a towing contract from the police department under Dick Lee in 1955 (see Chapter 9). Larger fish sought larger prizes: developers sought land at favorable prices (or with tax abatements), construction firms sought city contracts to rend and build, insurers sought contracts from city agencies, law firms sought chances to provide litigation services to the city, firms specializing in the issuance of debt sought to provide their services to City Hall. Often a major fund-raiser for a mayoral campaign might turn out to be an officer or owner of a firm offering construction services, and a few firms such as the Fusco Corporation often won contracts for city work.

Fund-raising parties for a New Haven mayor seeking reelection might be held in New York by a Manhattan firm interested in the city's bond business. Democratic Town Chairman Barbieri's real estate and insurance businesses doubtless prospered on account of his political connections. In a later period, developer-architect Wendell Harp might use a web of political connections to seek work from the city school system or the housing authority.

Many of the results from these practices were odious, and a few doubtless used taxpayer money with less than perfect efficiency. But these firms by and large sought competing, not convergent, interests. They sought to capture the spoils of city politics, and in that endeavor found themselves in competition with one another, not in shared conspiracy. Moreover, their fingerprints were in most cases readily detected. In fact, the basic power regime of business had less and less to do with control over the particulars of city governments and more and more to do with the choice of cities or municipalities in which to locate facilities and the jobs they generate. Sometimes, by threatening to go elsewhere, a firm might win concessions from the city. More often, it would just go—as did Winchester after the 1979 strike.

The pluralism that *Who Governs?* identified in the process of government during the Lee years surely did exist, and Dahl was right to conclude that no shadowy business elite was pulling its strings from secluded positions in the locker room at the Lawn Club or the boardroom of Winchester Repeating Arms. With Lee, his Kremlin, and the federal aorta in control, it could also be seen that government was purposively seeking to make a difference within the city. Slums were cleared, highways constructed, homes renovated, old downtown stores replaced by a big mall, parks made better. Whatever one thought of the particulars, government was indeed active and purposeful. But, if my earlier analysis is broadly correct, most of the goals that were hoped for—most of the governance—failed in important degree. After Lee, government would become less brisk, less assertive, less active. And governance would—witness the evidence in Chapter 11—deteriorate. The older urbanist pattern, with business elites more engaged in city life, may in that measure have been an instrument to promote the effectiveness of governance, and to give effect to the working of urban democracy.[46] Surely anyone interested in promoting the interests of ordinary working people in New Haven at mid-century might have wished for a more enduring bond between the city and its major business firms. In the event, those bonds were dissolved in the course of economic change, and it is not clear that any alternative existed. One must wonder about the extent to which government-defined pluralism was the product of a historical epoch in which the old pattern of political integration between business leadership and government had more or less vanished. In the years just after Lee, the end of business leadership became painfully apparent.

If the ultimate purpose of pluralist democracy in a city is to generate outcomes which fit the wants and needs of majorities among the people, it can be argued that a *greater* business role would have been desirable even on democratic grounds. Take the case of the neighborhoods—Dixwell, Newhallville—which grew to rely on jobs at Winchester Repeating Arms. Surely, if those jobs could have been saved by granting the managers of that firm more influence at City Hall, it would have been a worthwhile bargain for the thousands of households living in that area, even for families lacking a Winchester worker. Put another way, pluralist government may not in certain critical instances lead to pluralist governance.[47]

The "unending competition between political parties" which was for Dahl a hallmark of New Haven's pluralist democracy is gone, replaced by street-fighting pluralism within the formal structure of the DTC.[48] Turnout in primaries is often *very* modest, as in the 1999 race between DeStefano and challenger James Newton, where the two *combined* for fewer than 10,000 votes. Many voters are unable (or unwilling, or both) to discern the programs, allegiances, and affinities of the candidates in DTC primaries. Incumbents are often pleased to leave it that way, and accountability is frequently blurred. This is *not* at all the work of a powerful and manipulative elite within the DTC, or anywhere else. It is the result of one-party rule in a city where the incentive to control city politics has been diminished for many residents, where business has almost entirely vanished from the field of political combat, and where a different kind of regime has long since begun to replace the grounded politics of historical urbanism.[49]

Finally, in connection with pluralist democracy, the larger regional story is less supportive of the view that inequalities have come to offset rather than reinforce one another. While Dahl was right in his major conclusion about New Haven politics, a politics wrapped around city government, there are reasons to doubt or even reject his generalizations as the subject of inquiry switches to the region as a whole. The spur of party competition has dwindled within the central city (though not in the region as a whole), and the machinations of the DTC cannot count as a replacement for interparty competition. But that is not my central concern. Imagine the following thought experiment. While Frank Rice is still mayor, the city is broken into ten or a dozen neighborhoods, some rich in the main, others poor in the main. A few would fall toward the middle. Overall, adjusted for inflation and scaled down in total numbers, the resulting "towns" would look a lot like the ones I have been analyzing here. The Hill or Wooster Square in 1913 might be analogous to New Haven in 2002. East Rock 1913 might be analogous to Madison or Guilford in 2002. Fair Haven might be analogous to East Haven, and Westville might correspond to Woodbridge. Now suppose we had turned each of these micro-cities into a municipality, asked it to raise its own tax revenues, all this most emphatically *without recourse to the resources of other micro-cities.* The resulting arrangement would not be what Dahl has in mind by pluralist democracy, and its inequalities might very well be *cumulative rather than offsetting.*

Yet this, in rough-and-ready terms, is what we have in the region today. Resources are most available in towns like Madison, Guilford, and Woodbridge. Needs are fewest in those same places. Resources are fewest on a per capita basis in New Haven, and needs greatest. To a very considerable extent, inequalities reinforce one another: access to the best schools goes with lower taxes, access to good municipal services corresponds to insulation from the risks associated with crime, and vice versa. To a considerable extent, government policy has helped to exaggerate the impact of these inequalities by implicitly competing to keep poor people anchored where they are—as residents of public housing, as clients of social service clinics funded on the basis of head counts, as members of the "base" for inner-city elected officials. Being able to choose *where* is a more powerful instrument for deciding *what* and *how* one's family will live than anything else. In the familiar language of Albert Hirschman, *exit* has become even more vital than *voice,* and in certain contexts, the capacity to threaten exit has become a powerful tool for the amplification of one's voice.[50] Differential ability to move where and when one chooses is in this context a trump card of no small importance.[51]

ANOTHER URBANISM?

Most of the material forces that encouraged urbanism a century ago—steam-powered manufacturing, a strategic position in the national rail network, the absence of trucking and automobiles, the immaturity of distance-shortening technologies in the early twentieth century—are gone from the northeastern United States and will not come back. Moreover, competition from manufacturers across the globe, and the very high cost of energy in New Haven's region at this time, more or less rule out a resurgence of heavy manufacturing in decades to come. Even if such production were to return to the region, it would not center itself within the city, as manufacturing did in 1900. In addition, distance-compressing technologies are in 2003 more powerful than ever before, and in the view of many pose new threats to urbanity not heretofore seen.[52] One urbanism-enabling force is resurgent in the early twenty-first century, namely immigration: waves of new Americans are arriving today much as they were in 1910, and some sections of New Haven are alive with the energies they bring.[53] Another of the old forces, the agricultural surplus, never went away and retains its impact worldwide. Everywhere, cities and urban agglomerations of increasing size are being created, many of them now booming far more dramatically than New Haven did a century past.

There is little chance that the hard-edged features of urbanism will be restored. Heavy industry will not soon crowd its way into the center of New Haven or any strategically similar city. City government will not gain great leverage by controlling land use for manufacturing facilities in the foreseeable future. If a denser fabric of neighborhood retailing asserts itself, it will not be because large retailing organizations are unable or unwilling to compete against it. If weekday evenings are again given over to lodge meetings and amateur sport by throngs of New Haveners, it will not be because Comcast and Direct TV have lost interest in competing for the time and dollars of households living in New Haven or any other North American city. If regional population is ever again centered in the city as it was in 1910, it will not be because automobiles or close substitutes for them have disappeared from America's material culture.

It is nevertheless entirely possible to seek an urban future—in New Haven and other such places—that recaptures much which was desirable on the "soft" side of urbanism. Important parts of the city have preserved the ambiance of an earlier urban age, and have done so without much help from government. Adaptive reuse of old facilities, based on needs people express in daily life, is a key. Consider figure 12.6, depicting one of the many small stores operating on Orange Street. This was an A&P in the 1920s and 1930s, and has been combined with upstairs housing from the beginning. Today it is operated as a high-end food market, Romeo & Giuseppi's, one of several serving the East Rock neighborhood. A more robust fauna of amateur-led civic organizations can also be rebuilt, not with large grants, but with the work and enthusiasm of volunteers. Building organizations that cross class and racial lines, and do so without condescension, is not only possible, it is entirely practical. In greater New Haven at this time, several such efforts are in progress, and they give promise of success. Seeking to understand our neighborhoods—without signaling their inferiority of one to another or to suburban rivals—should be a top priority.[54] People living in city neighborhoods can make the effort to become more urbane again, to reach out across social distances to those walking on the same sidewalks or sharing the

Figure 12.6. Adaptive reuse of home and store. Author photo.

same streets. People can become "public characters" of the sort Jane Jacobs has been and has written about, helping to provide the modicum of social glue that makes so great a difference on city streets.[55] Where one can afford the premium, why not patronize neighborhood stores, paying the extra quarter for a half-gallon of milk, making it a point to interact with other customers? These small efforts at becoming a thread in the city's civic fabric may seem trivial, but they are not. God, as one great man said, is in the details.

There are larger possibilities, of which I will mention just three. One is the attempt at what Gerald Frug calls "community building" across the maze of municipal boundaries that fragment urban regions.[56] As regional hierarchies isolate their citizens from difference, and as households focus on the narrow range of contacts provided by their (typically very homogeneous) neighborhoods, the impulse to reach out toward difference can be liberating for the individual and civilizing for the region. The development of both organized and individualistic relationships across strata in the regional hierarchy is an important objective. Many local government services—emergency response, fire, police, libraries, recreation, and waste management—can and should be shared on a regional basis. While sharp resistance from unions and bureaucratic potentates is all but inevitable, the potential gains in efficiency, and in community building, are im-

mense. Second, there are specific policies from our twentieth-century urban inheritance that need rethinking and in some cases political action to alter what by
now seem deeply pernicious (if unintended) consequences. One of these is the
drive toward homogeneity of land use and social typing within neighborhoods.
Zoning in particular has driven out mixed uses from urban neighborhoods,
compelled urban retailers to put in suburban infrastructure, reduced contact
with difference, and thereby undermined urbanism. The effect on street civility
of the sort Jacobs reveres, and on the urban sophistication about contact with difference eulogized by Richard Sennett, has been dreadful.[57] I do not recommend
that cement plants be encouraged to move in next to Mrs. Jones, or that tanneries
be juxtaposed to schools. But I do think smaller differences—mixing housing
types, encouraging the redevelopment of small retailing near people's homes,
wherever the market will bear it—is worthwhile.

Another policy that demands sharp revision is the massive low-income public
housing project. No single institution does more to isolate the poor, and to pile
up the score on de facto segregation, than these HUD-funded installations. Recent policies aimed at renovating the worst of these places ("HOPE VI" in HUD
jargon) often make for improvements, especially where New Urbanist design
opens up the texture and encourages softer boundaries with the surrounding
neighborhood.[58] But, in most cases, the nation could do more for its cities by
abandoning a policy born of the Depression and substituting less isolating ways
to improve housing conditions for the urban poor. Both zoning and public housing represent attempts to use government as a substitute for the joint working of
civil society and market economy, and neither has been a great success.

Finally, city government can get better, stronger, and more agile than it has
been in recent decades. Frank Rice's city is gone, and the present one will not
work on the basis of a sidewalk republic. Mayors can be given more authority and
held accountable for their actions. City boards and commissions can be simplified and put more firmly under the control of top elected officials. The endless
waste associated with many public-sector union contracts, and the filigree of
work rules built up over the decades, can be renegotiated. If it cannot be renegotiated, it must become an issue at the state level. The ponderous red tape of civil
service systems can be reduced considerably. If one is in the mood for a real
struggle, it may eventually be possible to reduce the Board of Aldermen to manageable size—say half its thirty seats, more or less the same scale as Philadelphia's seventeen-seat city legislature. These are, alas, issues that require help
from state government, so larger coalitions must be built across regions and between them.

The most important step of all requires no act of legislation, no renegotiated labor contracts, but it does require something even harder to achieve than these things. That is the courage to repeatedly assert civic norms in daily life. We have grown used to very low standards of civility on city streets, and we have substituted avoidance for citizenship. The more we avert our eyes, the worse it becomes. A renewed urbanism begins with very small acts of courage. I remember walking down a New Haven sidewalk with a friend when the hulking teenager walking ahead of us casually dropped the paper from a McDonald's sandwich on the sidewalk. "Excuse me, you dropped this paper. Why not put it where it belongs?" said my friend, all one hundred pounds of her. The kid took the paper from her hand and put in his pocket. This is the sort of elemental governance for which there is no substitute in public policy. That sandwich paper is merely a token for a larger and absolutely pivotal set of issues. As Fred Siegel writes of New York in its darkest period:

> What unnerved most city dwellers . . . was the sense of menace and disorder that pervaded day-to-day life. It was a gang of toughs exacting their daily tribute in the coin of humiliation. It was the "street tax" paid to drunk and drug-ridden panhandlers. It was the "squeegee men" shaking down the motorist waiting for a light. It was the threats and hostile gestures of the mentally ill making their homes in the parks. It was the provocation of pushers and prostitutes plying their trade with impunity. It was the "trash storms," the swirling masses of garbage left by peddlers and panhandlers, and the open-air drug bazaars on city streets. These were the visible signs of cities out of control; cities, regardless of their economic health, that couldn't protect either their space or their citizens.[59]

Those of us who care deeply about New Haven and cities like it should make choices that reflect their urbanist commitment. In the words of the late Bart Giamatti:

> Human beings made and make cities, and only human beings kill cities, or let them die. And human beings do both—make cities and unmake them—by the same means: by acts of choice. We enjoy deluding ourselves in this as in other things. We enjoy believing that there are forces out there completely determining our fate, natural forces—or forces so strong and overwhelming as to be like natural forces—that send cities through organic or biological phases of birth, growth, and decay. We avoid the knowledge that cities are at best works of art, at worst ungainly artifacts—but never flowers

or even weeds—and that we, not some mysterious force or cosmic biologi-cal system, control the creation and life of a city.[60]

Make no mistake, there *are* "forces" that limit the range or possibilities for any given city at any given moment. Things that happened in 1917, 1937, 1954, and 1979 will affect the range of futures open in 2003 or 2023, even perhaps 2050 or 2100. Big economic and technological events create and destroy options for cities, as they have done for New Haven. No amount of good will or determina-tion will restore the manufacturing base of New Haven. And, as citizens of one small city, we have only a certain degree of control over the national and world currents of culture and communication that affect the ability of our police to keep order, our teachers to educate, our physicians to heal.

Understanding all that, we may aim for the best realistic futures, and New Haven has many such possibilities. It is, for openers, possible to see New Haven in a far wider regional context than one that begins in Madison and ends in Woodbridge. When New York's Regional Plan Association looked at that great city's available futures, one of the questions asked concerned the availability of interesting, fairly affordable places for people to live outside the five boroughs and their immediate suburbs.[61] One of the answers given was New Haven, a place with high-quality housing stock, an array of cultural amenities, and an ap-pealing history stretching from 1637. If Metro-North commuter railroad can be induced to improve the speed and desirability of its service—some trains ran faster in 1946 than today—and if New Haven can provide the downtown ameni-ties required by commuters (to Manhattan, or to edge-city places like Stamford), then the competitiveness of New Haven's housing will make itself felt.

The urbanist city was built upon its export industries, which brought skilled workers and investors and money to New Haven because her manufacturers—Winchester, Sargent, and the rest—were able to compete in national markets against the very best in their fields. The jobs they created were a material founda-tion on which the fabric of enterprise, the civic fauna, and even Frank Rice's sidewalk republic could draw. Dollars and energy and talent flew in because com-petitive products flew out. The business management and ownership anchored to the city by these organizations, and hundreds of smaller firms, provided a grounded leadership class that made the tasks of governance more manageable than they otherwise would have been. Is there no successor in sight? There is, al-though not the sort that would have been envisioned in 1916, and not the sort that could accommodate itself easily to the political routines of post-urbanist New Haven. A small case study, dating to the transition from Lee to Bartholomew Guida in City Hall, and from A. Whitney Griswold to Kingman Brewster in the Yale presidency, suggests its identity and some of the difficulties that future leaders would need to address.

IMAGINARY COLLEGES

When philanthropist Paul Mellon approached Yale president Kingman Brewster in the late 1960s with the thought that his world-renowned collection of British art might come to Yale, Brewster arranged lunch at his Hillhouse Avenue residence for Mellon, Mayor Lee, and himself. There was, he told Lee, no desirable site north of Chapel Street, and one rather seedy commercial block south of it (between High and York) beckoned—save for Lee's standing policy to the contrary. Lee had held, from his aldermanic days forward, to the rule that Yale must stay north of Chapel Street so as to preserve the taxable core of the commercial city. Over lunch, Lee and Brewster roughed out an exception to that rule: the Yale Center for British Art would be built *south* of Chapel, preserving a Baptist church on one corner of the site (itself eventually converted to the Yale Repertory Theatre but treated as a taxable commercial space) and offering two tax concessions to the city. First, while the museum proper would be tax-free as of right, it would stand on *land* that remained taxable by the city. Second, most of the museum's extensive frontage on Chapel and High Streets would be devoted to 100 percent taxable retail uses. Between these two provisions, city government would gain considerably *more* tax revenue with Yale's purchase of the land than it would have enjoyed by keeping it in private hands—at least the private hands then in possession of it. The university would engage Louis I. Kahn to design a remarkable structure, completed in 1977, that would become one of the most appealing destinations for visitors to New Haven. Over the decades, its retail space would include a basement restaurant, a tennis shop, a wine shop, a jeweler, a bookstore-café, a souvenir shop, and an interior decorator. By common understanding, the deal served the interests of Yale and the city quite admirably. There were some problems with John McGuerty, director of New Haven's City Planning Department, who sought to assert far more regulatory authority than suited the mayor and his Yale friends. Yale made repeated modifications to satisfy McGuerty and his staff about parking, circulation, and other considerations more important to planners than to Yale. This apparently created an expectation in McGuerty, and the city planning board, for other projects like the Yale colleges a few years later. In the end the deal went through city government quite nicely. These events, and the lessons they seemed to teach Yale administrators, would bait a trap. When it

Figure 12.7. Yale President Kingman Brewster, in full academic regalia, c. 1970.
Yale Office of Public Affairs.

came time to expand Yale's residential college system, partly to accommodate newly arriving Yale College women, Brewster and his colleagues would encounter an entirely different mayor and a withering barrage of political trouble (figure 12.7).

Undergraduate Yale is organized around residential colleges, most of them built in the 1930s (two colleges were built during Lee's administration, and were, remarkably, used by the city as part of the local match for federal urban redevelopment funding). Already crowded in the 1960s, the twelve colleges were too small to house their students fully, and many members were living off-campus—missing what Brewster thought to be the core of a Yale education. Many of the existing colleges, built in ersatz Gothic style, would be difficult or impossible to expand. With the coming of women in 1969–70, Brewster, his staff, and the Yale Corporation concluded that the construction of two additional facilities made sense. The thirteenth and fourteenth colleges would need to be close to the center of campus and should not encroach on residential neighborhoods. Given these constraints, and a need to preserve the remaining open space on the main campus, Brewster and his people soon zeroed in on a commercial block just east of the campus, at the corner of Grove and Church streets. Already owned by the university, and occupied mostly by a second-rate bowling alley, the property seemed ideal. It was being taxed at modest rates by the city, partly because Yale had made no visible effort to upgrade its commercial quality.

Remembering his success negotiating the Mellon project, Brewster approached the colleges in similar fashion. Clearly this would be a delicate political issue, clearly taxation would be a bone of contention, clearly the details of design and planning would be scrutinized by McGuerty and his staff. Brewster tapped his special assistant, Jonathan Fanton, as point person on the project, and in so doing allocated a very considerable talent to the task. Fanton—later president of the New School University and then of the MacArthur Foundation—was well known for his energy, ingenuity, and determination.

As with the Mellon project, Fanton and Brewster set about to negotiate at the top of city government, which they took to mean *both* mayor Bart Guida *and* town chairman Arthur Barbieri. Guida would be treated like the CEO, Barbieri like chairman of the board. This tactical decision rested on the belief that the mayor owed his job to Barbieri, a view the latter greatly enjoyed having affirmed in a place like Yale. Sparing no effort, Yale rolled out such figures as Cyrus Vance, who represented the Lyndon Johnson administration at the Paris peace talks on Vietnam, and who soon would become President Jimmy Carter's Secretary of State. Vance spoke privately with Barbieri, as well as with Guida. According to at least one high-level participant, this was taken as a personal and official affront by Guida: Surely, he thought, Yale would have gone to Dick Lee alone, without going to the town chairman. This reinforced Guida's long-standing hostility to Yale and its patrician ways and inflamed his very real wish to greatly increase the flow of fresh funding for the city. As shown earlier, the real value of the city's tax base was falling in the 1960s and 1970s: Guida was under enormous pressure to find new funding for a city unable to sustain the spending habits of the Lee era. Guida resolved to hammer Yale hard on issues of taxation arising from the colleges.

The mayor's weapons were of course the long-standing routines of city government—the Board of Aldermen, its committees on Legislation and Urban Development, the City Plan Commission, and the legendary capacity of City Hall to delay decisions. These were, with minor modifications, the institutions that had long ago confined Mayor Frank Rice to such objectives as uniform sidewalks, and which Dick Lee had found it necessary to circumvent time and again. Now Guida would cheerfully allow governmental sclerosis to decompose Yale's imagined colleges. The mayor invoked something known as the Guida Amendment, under which any project that would remove property from the grand list for a tax-exempt institution would face special rigors as it applied to have the city designate its project as a Planned Development District (churches and the like were exempted on the theory that they served *local* congregants). The city, acting on the urging of preservationists, would also demand that Yale save the Kingsley-Havemeyer house (dating to the Civil War), which stood on Grove Street and blocked the proposed 2.5-acre construction project.

Following its experience with the Mellon project, Yale would begin jumping through the hoops, one after another. It would stress the impact of $15 million in construction spending, and the economic stimulus of more students for local re-tailers. It would agree to increase the retail space to a level at which city tax rev-enues exceeded those generated before the conversion. At one point, Yale told an aldermanic hearing that the taxable component of the new structures would have a value of $672,000, nearly doubling the then-present value for the whole package, $341,000. Confronted by the demand to preserve the Kingsley-Have-meyer house, Yale would find congenial room for it to become 33 Whitney Av-enue and be restored to its former grandeur. Unable to satisfy the city's demand for parking on site, Yale would offer an outright $200,000 grant toward the con-struction of parking at a site of the city's choosing. None of these steps seemed to placate the mayor, and Guida showed neither the capacity nor the inclination to deliver his Board of Aldermen for Yale.

Throughout late 1972, the Board of Aldermen would delay decision for the be-ginning of 1973. By the end of January 1973, the City Plan Commission would turn down the proposal. The planners demanded more street-level retail space, underground parking and loading facilities, office development comparable to then existing space, a diagonal walkway reaching out to the Audubon arts district across Whitney Avenue, a lower building profile, and other amendments to Yale's plan.[62] In his report, John McGuerty proposed that Yale be "given leave to withdraw" its plans pending improvements meeting the city's objections. Days later, Fanton and another Yale representative told the Board of Aldermen that a "withdrawal of the petition and complete redesign of the colleges to satisfy Mr. McGuerty's views is impossible because of the increased building costs and pro-gram disturbances which such a delay would cause."[63] At this point, some alder-men began encouraging Yale to press forward with the proposal, but key DTC leadership was pressing an even harder line. Aldermanic President Vinny Mauro (a Barbieri in-law, and later town chairman himself) soon went so far as to tell the press that "anything less than the entire taxing of the entire parcel—land, buildings and commercial space—will meet with my personal disfavor."[64] Yale was now backing away from the effort, having concluded that it knew not how to negotiate with the city in this new era. In a *New York Times* postmortem, Yale would take a whipping from the DTC town chairman:

> Proletarian New Haven, for the first time in memory, said no to aristocratic Yale. "They were flabbergasted—they thought they owned us," said Arthur T. Barbieri, the powerful Democratic Town Committee chairman, who runs much of the affairs of this city of 137,000 from his combination real estate, insurance, and travel agency here. "They are going to have to realize that we are not peasants, and they are not the manor on the hill. They are going to come down off their high horse and change their relationship with us. I guess there are certain people who took joy in saying no to them."[65]

By the early twenty-first century, those thirteenth and fourteenth colleges remain unbuilt. Yet Barbieri's gloat looked past the larger truth implied by the incident: as the city's manufacturing base disappeared over the course of the late twentieth century, Yale was growing larger and more important to the city—a growing fish in a shrinking pond, one might say. No longer a local or regional institution in any sense, Yale would compete for the best students from across the globe. Its research output would become as important as the city's manufacturing output had once been, and the university would lead the local economy. By the 1990s, Yale would attract more than half a million visitors annually, and a 1993 study would estimate spending on the order of $675 million from "Yale's payroll in the state, and spending by Yale students and out-of-state visitors."[66] The university would by this writing employ nearly ten thousand full-timers. Yale University and Yale–New Haven Hospital would rank one and two as New Haven's employers in the 1990s, accounting for fifteen thousand jobs between them. The next eight employers would total fewer than the university alone. By the time Richard C. Levin became its president in 1993, Yale was among the wealthiest educational institutions in the world. Levin, with skilled help from the likes of Bruce Alexander and Linda Lorimer, would almost immediately engage the challenges of urban governance. Bidding against the suburbs, Yale would initiate a Home Buyer Program that offered $24,000 subsidies to employees who would buy houses in the city, a policy later restricted to selected neighborhoods near the campus. Few major initiatives on any front—public education, neighborhood development, arts and culture, downtown commerce—would fail to attract Yale's comment or concern in the 1990s. Yale was, of course, problematic as a patron of City Hall. It would produce no miracles in public education, and most of its faculty would express little if any enthusiasm for solving urban problems.

And the university's labor relations—troubled, and visibly so in the national press—were a major irritant. The institution's wealth would invite populist attention whenever city budgets fell short of aldermanic hope. A slow learning process at Yale and in City Hall—How shall such very strange bedfellows divide their covers?—would promise to stretch into the distant future. Thus would New Haven begin a new course of change, rare among cities built by smoke and steam. New Haven's story—its urbanism, and the end of that urbanism—up through about 1980 had been broadly representative of older American cities. But what happened as Yale became the city's dominant export industry is far from representative. That new tale is, alas, the subject of another book.

NOTES

PREFACE

1. Among the notables are Peter Bachrach and Morton Baratz, "The Two Faces of Power," *American Political Science Review* 56 (1962); Steven Lukes, *Power: A Radical View* (London: Macmillan, 1974); G. William Domhoff, *Who Really Rules? New Haven and Community Power Reexamined* (New Brunswick, N.J.: Transaction, 1978); John Gaventa, *Power and Powerlessness: Quiescence and Rebellion in an Appalachian Valley* (Urbana: University of Illinois Press, 1980); Douglas W. Rae, "Knowing Power," in *Power, Inequality, and Democratic Politics: Essays in Honor of Robert Dahl,* edited by Ian Shapiro and Grant Reeher (Boulder, Colo.: Westview, 1988).

2. Others had come to terms with this fact much earlier. See Michael A. Pagano and Ann O. M. Bowman, *Cityscapes and Capital* (Baltimore: Johns Hopkins University Press, 1995); Paul E. Peterson, *City Limits* (Chicago: University of Chicago Press, 1981); Clarence N. Stone, *Regime Politics: Governing Atlanta* (Lawrence: University of Kansas Press, 1989). My own understanding was advanced substantially by these works, and especially by the more recent Gerald Frug, *City Making: Building Communities Without Building Walls* (Princeton, 1999). Even some of the early twentieth-century scholarship has the weak power position of cities clearly in view. See, for instance, Frank Goodnow, *City Government in the United States* (New York, 1904).

3. The scholarly literature now formalizes this and related observations through "regime theory," following the pioneering work of Clarence Stone. See, in particular, Stone, *Regime Politics.*

4. The theory on police visibility goes roughly like the story about Joe DiMaggio in the late years of his career as the Yankees' center fielder. His arm was greatly weakened and yet

he would go out of his way to make a hard throw all the way to home plate in warm-ups just before the game began—so that he wouldn't have to make such throws later on because runners would respect his arm.

CHAPTER 1. CREATIVE DESTRUCTION AND THE AGE OF URBANISM

1. See "New Haven Directory Including West Haven, 1913" (New Haven: Price & Lee, 1913), 894.
2. Localism is quite dead in practice: when I asked permission for a photograph recently, the local manager said he would need to consult "central" in Charlotte, N.C. A large literature has developed around the globalization of urban commerce. See, for instance, Saskia Sassen, *The Global City* (Princeton: Princeton University Press, 2001).
3. The same boyfriend, as it happens, turns up elsewhere in our story. By the 1920s he was operating the New Haven Baseball Exhibition Company, scheduling major league opponents for local teams. He eventually left the city and became general manager of the New York Yankees. See *New Haven Register,* December 24, 1999, p. D3.
4. Dollars, denominated in 2002 currency, refer to the first quarter of each named year. GDP per capita is not, of course, equivalent to income per capita, but it provides a broad indicator of total prosperity per person. Inflation from 1996 to 2002 is calculated at 15.36 percent using U.S. Bureau of Labor Statistics calculations available at www.bls.gov. Source: Raymond Fair at www.Fairmodel.econ.yale.edu. Because the distribution of personal and household incomes is very unequal, real families experienced unequal changes over very much larger or smaller starting points across these decades.
5. Conversely, cities have been engines of growth in the American economy, just as they were centers of growth and innovation in earlier Western history. One compelling analysis of the role cities played in the embryology of capitalism is provided by Fernand Braudel, *Capitalism and Material Life, 1400–1800,* trans. Miriam Kochan (New York: Harper & Row, 1973), esp. 373ff.
6. In certain respects, this is an instance of emergence from complex systems of the sort described in John H. Holland, *Emergence: From Chaos to Order* (Reading, Mass.: Addison-Wesley, 1998).
7. The dates used in illustration here are of course inexact, lagging considerably behind the invention dates of the relevant technologies. Steam, for instance, was practical on a limited scale something like sixty years before it was dominant in the eastern U.S. Similarly today, digital communication was practical half a century before it reached its current dominance. See Victor S. Clark, *History of Manufactures in the United States,* 3 vols. (New York: McGraw-Hill, 1929); David E. Nye, *Consuming Power* (Cambridge: MIT Press, 1998); Peter Temin, ed., *Engines of Enterprise* (Cambridge: Harvard University Press, 2000); Harold M. Watkins, *Coal and Men* (London: George Allen & Unwin, 1934).
8. "Water and Steam Power," *Scientific American* 4 (1849). Quoted in part and discussed in Nye, *Consuming Power.* Nye's discussion of steam and urban history, "Cities of Steam," is a superb synthesis of its subject. See 72ff.

9. *Historical Statistics of the United States* (Washington, D.C.: U.S. Government Printing Office, 1975), Series C 89–119, pp. 105ff.

10. Andrew Carnegie, *Triumphant Democracy* (New York: Charles Scribner's Sons, 1886), 1.

11. The classic history of this process is Alfred D. Chandler, *The Visible Hand* (Cambridge: Belknap Press of Harvard University Press, 1977).

12. Carnegie, *Triumphant Democracy*, 227. Carnegie is specifically referring to the manufacture of shoes but generally to the manufacturing sector of the U.S. economy.

13. Paul R. Krugman, *Development, Geography, and Economic Theory* (Cambridge: MIT Press, 1996), 46. A more technical description of the production side of this phenomenon is offered by Irwin and Kasarda: "Agglomeration economies involve local cost sharing of commonly held external resources used by individual producers. The presence of these external resources drives down unit costs of production within the firm by substituting for internal scale economies. In turn, this growth attracts larger pools of labor and capital, further reinforcing agglomeration effects for firms. The upward spiral between growth in production factors and local productivity creates greater economic specialization and diversity of production, which also creates external economies for the firms. Thus advantages within firm scale economies are attained by the aggregation of a large number of small firms in one area." See Michael Kasarda and John D. Irwin, "Trade, Transportation, and Spatial Distribution," in *The Handbook of Economic Sociology*, edited by Neil J. Smelser and Richard Swedberg (Princeton: Princeton University Press, 1994), 349.

14. Direct labor means that all activities on site are included. Indirect labor costs, as in the assembly of farm equipment, is neglected.

15. These data are from *Historical Statistics of the United States*, Series K 445–85, p. 500.

16. *Historical Statistics*, Series K 459, p. 500. I have converted hours per bale of cotton into pounds using the standard bale weight of 480 pounds, net of lint.

17. *Historical Statistics*, Series K 407, p. 498.

18. And by 2000, 238 municipalities would exceed 100,000 population—many of which hardly look like traditional cities.

19. *Historical Statistics*, Series Q 284–312, pp. 729ff.

20. *Historical Statistics*, Series Q 329, p. 732.

21. Gary Cross and Rick Szostak, *Technology and American History* (Englewood Cliffs, N.J.: Prentice Hall, 1995), 120ff.

22. William Cronon, *Nature's Metropolis* (New York: Norton, 1991).

23. It also created much of the basis for the "forward integration" of manufacturing firms so that they handled the distribution and sale of their own products on a national basis. See Chandler, *Visible Hand*, esp. chap. 7, pp. 209ff.

24. Colin Clark, "Transport: Maker and Breaker of Cities," *Town Planning Review* 28 (1957).

25. Ibid., 242.

26. No less an authority than Max Weber charts the connection between commercial transport and urban development, even in the ancient world. See Weber, *General Economic History* (New York: Greenberg, 1927). A well-nuanced account of European cities be-

fore the age of rail is to be found in Paul M. Hohenberg and Lynn Hollen Lees, *The Making of Urban Europe, 1000–1950* (Cambridge: Harvard University Press, 1985), esp. chaps. 1–5.

27. Clark, "Transport," 245. Clark's use of the deterministic formulation "inevitable consequence" is of course a trifle too strong: a nation willing to forgo a major source of wealth might have prevented the concentration of industry in railhead cities. But within the ordinary range of practical possibilities, Clark seems to be on good ground in asserting a very strong causal connection.

28. The following simple tabulation of population change from 1870 to 1920 is suggestive. Note that it fails to capture the direct surge of manufacturing investment in these cities.

City	1870	1920	Percentage change
Baltimore	267,354	733,826	174.5
Boston	250,526	748,060	198.6
Bridgeport	18,969	143,555	656.8
Buffalo	117,714	506,775	330.5
Camden, N.J.	20,045	116,309	480.2
Canton, Ohio	8,660	87,091	905.7
Cincinnati	216,239	401,247	85.6
Cleveland	92,829	796,841	758.4
Detroit	79,577	993,678	1,148.7
Hartford	37,180	138,036	271.3
Minneapolis	15,000	381,582	2,443.9
New Haven	**50,840**	**162,537**	219.7
Philadelphia, PA.	674,022	1,823,770	170.6
Pittsburgh, PA.	86,076	588,343	583.5
Rochester, NY.	62,386	295,750	374.1
Syracuse, NY.	43,051	171,717	298.9
Trenton, NJ	22,874	119,289	421.5

29. It should be added that in many cases street rail decentralized population even when industry remained centered. See, among others, Sam Bass Warner, Jr., *Streetcar Suburbs* (Cambridge: Harvard University Press, 1978). See also Kenneth T. Jackson, *Crabgrass Frontier: The Suburbanization of the United States* (New York: Oxford University Press, 1985).

30. Clark, "Transport."

31. This general thesis is so well established in the urban history literature as to require little documentation. See, among others, Clark, "Transport"; Stephen B. Goddard, *Getting There* (New York: Basic Books, 1994); Nye, *Consuming Power;* Tom F. Peters, *Building the Nineteenth Century* (Cambridge: MIT Press, 1996).

32. The analysis given in this passage can be expressed more elegantly in numerical form, as in the following table.

Year	Railroad cars	Motor vehicles
1876	340,000	
1880	557,000	
1890	1,091,000	
1900	1,400,244	8,000
1910	2,195,657	468,000
1920	2,444,526	9,239,000
1930		26,749,000
1940		32,453,000
1950		49,161,000
1960		73,868,000
1970		108,407,000

The table includes all the decades in which each mode was increasing between 1876 and 1970—e.g., rail cars failed to increase after 1920. To be precise, the all-time maximum was 1919, with 2,483,179 revenue cars in active service. See *Historical Statistics,* Series Q 301, Q 304, and Q 325, pp. 729–731.

33. A bristling polemical literature has been constructed on the collision between car and city. See, among others, Vincent Scully, "America's Nightmare," *Zodiac* 17, no. 1 (1967). And see Jane Holtz Kay, *Asphalt Nation* (New York: Crown, 1997). On the automobile-driven suburb, see James Howard Kunstler, *The Geography of Nowhere* (New York: Simon & Schuster, 1993).

34. See, for instance, Maldwyn Allen Jones, *American Immigration,* 2nd ed. (Chicago: University of Chicago Press, 1960). See also John Bodnar, *The Transplanted* (Bloomington: Indiana University Press, 1987).

35. *Historical Statistics,* Series C 89–119, pp. 106ff.

36. *7th Census of the United States* (1850) and *14th Census of the United States* (1920). The countries of origin of immigrants living in New Haven, ranked from the top for 1920, were: Italy (15,084), "Russia" (8,080), Ireland (7,219), Poland (3,009), and Germany (2,770).

37. Author's interview with Joseph Perfetto, March 20, 1998.

38. This classic story is told in several fine business histories, but GM's public positioning is told with special flair in Roland Marchand, *Creating the Corporate Soul* (Berkeley: University of California Press, 1998). See also Alfred D. Chandler, Jr., *Strategy and Structure* (Cambridge: MIT Press, 1962), and Thomas K. McCraw, *American Business, 1920–2000: How It Worked* (Wheeling, Ill.: Harlan-Davidson, 2000).

39. Sinclair Lewis, *Babbitt* (New York: Harcourt, Brace, 1922).

40. Thomas Alva Edison, "The Dangers of Electric Lighting," *North American Review,* 1892.

41. See, esp., Warren D. Devine, Jr., "From Shafts to Wires," *Journal of Economic History* 43, no. 2 (1983), and David E. Nye, *Electrifying America* (Cambridge: MIT Press, 1990).

42. *Historical Statistics,* Series S 45, p. 821.

43. See Nye, *Electrifying America*, 165ff.

44. To be specific, 20,642 accounts in United Illuminating's New Haven district were central-city addresses and just 4,579 were suburban. Of the latter, well over half were located in the working-class and highly urbanized suburb of West Haven. See John D. Fassett, *UI: History of an Electric Company* (New Haven: United Illuminating, 1990), 173.

45. Contact with strangers, handled with responses that allow civil cooperation well short of personal intimacy, is at the heart of Jane Jacobs' justly celebrated work on urbanism. See Jacobs, *The Death and Life of Great American Cities* (New York: Random House, 1961). See also Lyn H. Lofland, *A World of Strangers* (New York: Basic Books, 1973). For a more developed theoretical treatment of contact with diversity, see Richard Sennett, *The Uses of Disorder* (New York: Norton, 1970). Gerald Frug has constructed an inspiring and complex theory of urban change that hinges to a considerable degree on overcoming the sorting processes of late twentieth-century urban regions. See Frug, *City Making: Building Cities Without Building Walls* (Princeton: Princeton University Press, 1999).

46. By way of counterpoint, the explicit idea of urbanism was quite commonly used in a positive, normative vein. Thus, in 1934, Columbia University established an Institute of Urbanism. See Robert Beauregard, *Voices of Decline* (London: Routledge, 2003), 71.

47. The most influential of all such tracts was probably Lincoln Steffens, *The Shame of Our Cities* (New York, 1904).

 The evolution of adequate urban waste management and water supply is in itself a major historical episode, corresponding broadly to the urbanist era. See Martin V. Melosi, *The Sanitary City* (Baltimore: Johns Hopkins University Press, 2000).

48. Author's interview with Joseph Perfetto.

49. John R. Stilgoe, *Borderland, 1820–1939* (New Haven: Yale University Press, 1988), 7, 9.

50. In Steffens' own words, the series of magazine articles from which the book was compiled set out "to see if the shameful facts, spread out in all their shame, would burn through our civic shamelessness to set fire to American pride" (Steffens, *Shame of Our Cities*, 12). Jacob Riis, *How the Other Half Lives* (New York: Charles Scribner's Sons, 1910); Adna Weber, "The Significance of Recent City Growth," *Annals of the American Academy of Political and Social Science* 23, no. March (1904).

51. See David A. Hounshell, *From the American System to Mass Production, 1800–1932* (Baltimore: Johns Hopkins University Press, 1984), 224. The innovative assembly line is of course not the only driver in this story. To a considerable extent, economies of scale worked to Ford's advantage in lowering prices, upping sales (which in turn made possible the capitalization of further improvements), yielding still lower prices and still higher sales levels, fostering still greater economies of scale. See also Lindy Biggs, *The Rational Factory* (Baltimore: Johns Hopkins University Press, 1996). For a contrasting view of these events, see Eric H. Monkonen, *America Becomes Urban* (Berkeley: University of California Press, 1988), 162.

52. See Martin La Fever, "Workers, Machinery, and Production in the Automobile Industry," *Monthly Labor Review* 19 (October 1924). Quoted in Biggs, *Rational Factory*, 106–7.

53. Quotation from *New Haven Evening Register,* January 1, 1910, p. 1.

54. The pages of the *New Haven Register* in the year 1910 give more attention to trolley service and trolley accidents than to any other topic. This is hardly surprising in a city where virtually every adult used this means of transportation daily.

55. This to a considerable extent was accomplished for New Haven by Robert Dahl, Raymond Wolfinger, Nelson Polsby, and certain of their critics. See in particular Robert A. Dahl, *Who Governs?* (New Haven: Yale University Press, 1961); Raymond E. Wolfinger, *The Politics of Progress* (Englewood Cliffs, N.J.: Prentice-Hall, 1974); Nelson W. Polsby, *Community Power and Political Theory* (New Haven: Yale University Press, 1980). The standard works critical of these "pluralist" authors include Peter Bachrach and Morton Baratz, "The Two Faces of Power," *American Political Science Review* 56 (November 1962); John Gaventa, *Power and Powerlessness* (Urbana: University of Illinois Press, 1980); Steven Lukes, *Power* (London: Macmillan, 1974); and G. William Domhoff, *Who Really Rules?* (New Brunswick, N.J.: Transaction, 1978).

56. Many urbanists are indeed united in believing that the economic institutions of capitalism exert disproportionate control over urban outcomes. See, among others, Joe R. Feagin, "Arenas of Conflict," in *Zoning and the American Dream,* edited by Charles Haar and Jerold Kayden (Chicago: Planners Press, 1989).

57. This is a point of overarching importance to our understanding of urbanism, but it is not at all exclusive to cities, as is suggested by Robert Ellickson's fine study of informal norms among cattle ranchers in Shasta County, California. See Robert C. Ellickson, *Order Without Law* (Cambridge: Harvard University Press, 1991). A related set of studies is provided by David T. Beito, Peter Gordon, and Alexander Tabarrok, eds. *The Voluntary City: Choice, Community, and Civil Society* (Ann Arbor: University of Michigan Press, 2002).

58. Frug, *City Making,* 5. Another important strand of analysis asserts a secular trend toward the marginalization of local government and politics. See in particular, M. Gottdiener, *The Decline of Urban Politics* (Newbury Park: Sage, 1987).

59. Horace E. Deming, *The Government of American Cities* (New York: G. P. Putnam's Sons, 1909), 26–27.

60. *Hunter v. City of Pittsburgh,* 207 U.S. 161, 178–179 (1907). Cited in Frug, *City Making,* 17.

61. See David Rusk, *Cities Without Suburbs,* 2nd ed. (Washington, D.C.: Woodrow Wilson Press, 1995).

62. See, especially, Paul E. Peterson, *City Limits* (Chicago: University of Chicago Press, 1981). For a more general statement of the theoretical issues, see Albert O. Hirschman, *Exit, Voice, and Loyalty* (Cambridge: Harvard University Press, 1970).

63. Douglas Rae, "Viacratic America," *American Review of Political Science* 4 (2001): 417–38.

64. Peter Marris and Martin Rein, *Dilemmas of Social Reform* (Chicago: University of Chicago Press, 1967), 7.

65. There is a vast literature on these developments. Among the leading critical statements are Kunstler, *Geography of Nowhere;* Vincent Scully, "The Architecture of Community," in *The New Urbanism,* ed. Peter Katz (New York: McGraw-Hill, 1994); Kay, *Asphalt Na-*

tion; and Moshe Safdie and Wendy Kohn, *The City After the Automobile* (Toronto: Stod-dart, 1997).

66. For a critical revision of the usual adulation for Lee as grant-getter, see Clarence Stone and Heywood T. Sanders, "Reexamining a Classic Case of Development Politics: New Haven, Connecticut," in *The Politics of Urban Development,* ed. Clarence Stone and Heywood T. Sanders (Lawrence: University of Kansas Press, 1987), 159–81.

67. Fernand Braudel, *Afterthoughts on Material Civilization and Capitalism,* trans. Patricia M. Ranum (Baltimore: Johns Hopkins University Press, 1977), 6–7, 17.

68. Jacobs, *Death and Life,* 31–32. In a very different setting, namely California ranching, it is possible to detect the similarly central role played by informal norms and processes. See Ellickson, *Order Without Law.*

69. Nye, *Consuming Power,* 196.

70. The most influential contemporary work on social capital includes Robert Putnam, *Making Democracy Work* (Princeton: Princeton University Press, 1993), and Putnam, "The Prosperous Community," *American Prospect* (Spring 1993). The earliest use of the term in its present sense appears to be contained in a remarkable 1916 article: Lyda Judson Hanifan, "The Rural Community Center," *Annals of the American Academy of Political and Social Science* 67 (1916). A useful compilation of critical perspectives is offered by Scott McLean, David Schultz, and Manfred Steger, eds., *Robert Putnam and Social Capital* (New York: NYU Press, 2001).

71. Sennett, *Uses of Disorder.* See also Frug, *City Making,* 115–42. See also Peter Dreier, John Mollenkopf, and Todd Swanstrom, *Place Matters* (Lawrence: University of Kansas Press, 2001). Also of interest is Myron Orfield, *Metropolitics* (Washington, D.C.: Brookings Institution Press, 1996). On the internal democracy of suburban municipalities, see Eric Oliver, *Democracy in Suburbia* (Princeton: Princeton University Press, 2001).

72. See, for instance, Peter Katz, *The New Urbanism* (New York: McGraw-Hill, 1994). See also Andres Duany and Elizabeth Plater-Zyberk, "Neighborhoods and Suburbs," *Design Quarterly* 164 (Spring 1995).

CHAPTER 2. INDUSTRIAL CONVERGENCE ON A NEW ENGLAND TOWN

1. New Haven was importing small quantities of British coal before the Revolution, but its economy was virtually unaffected by it.

2. Yale President Timothy Dwight offered very nearly the same view of New Haven in the same period:

> The area occupied by New Haven is probably as large as that which usually contains a city of six times the number of inhabitants in Europe. A considerable proportion of the houses have courtyards in front and gardens in the rear. The former are ornamented with trees and shrubs; the latter are luxuriantly filled with fruit trees, flowers, and culinary vegetables. The beauty and healthfulness of this arrangement need no explanation.
>
> The houses in this city are generally decent, and many of the modern ones handsome. The style of building is neat and tidy. Fences and outhouses are also in the same style; and, being almost universally painted white, make a delightful appear-

ance by the great multitude of shade trees, a species of ornament in which the town is unrivaled.

The views in and around this town are delightful. Scenery does not often strike the eye with more pleasure. A great number of charming rides in its environs add not a little to the pleasure of a residence in New Haven. Take it all in all, I have never seen the place where I would so willingly spend my life.

See Timothy Dwight, *Travels in New England and New York (1822)*, 4 vols., edited by Barbara Solomon (Cambridge: Harvard University Press, 1969), 1: 131, 141. Quoted and discussed in William L. Philie, *Change and Tradition: New Haven, Connecticut, 1780–1830* (New York: Garland, 1989). This is the elder of the two Timothy Dwights who were Yale presidents, this one having served from 1795 to 1817.

3. Amos Doolittle, "Plan of the City of New Haven" (New Haven, 1824). An 1830 map, signed by D. W. Buckingham, supplements the Doolittle map nicely.

4. See particularly William Cronon's chapter "Dreaming the Metropolis" in Cronon, *Nature's Metropolis*, 23–54.

5. I have in mind the sorts of idealizations discussed in Robert Fishman, *Bourgeois Utopias* (New York: Basic Books, 1987), Jackson, *Crabgrass Frontier*, and Stilgoe, *Borderland*.

6. Chauncey Jerome, *History of the American Clock Business for the Past Sixty Years and Life of Chauncey Jerome* (New Haven: F. C. Dayton, 1860), 18.

7. One excellent general source here is Floyd M. Hegel and Richard Shumway, "New Haven," *Journal of the New Haven Colony Historical Society* 34, no. 2 (1988).

8. Taking the rod to be 16.5 feet, and 3 by 52 rods for each block, and 4 rods for each street's width, we have $172 \times 16.5 = 2,838$ outer dimension for each side. This is roughly consistent with the half-mile distance observed today.

9. For a fair-minded overview of this literature, see Norris C. Andrews, "Davenport-Eaton and 52 Rods," *Journal of the New Haven Colony Historical Society* 33, no. 1 (1986).

10. See, for instance, Doris B. Townshend, *The Street Names of New Haven* (New Haven: New Haven Colony Historical Society, 1984).

11. From Kevin Lynch, *The Image of the City* (Cambridge: MIT Press, 1960).

12. Amy L. Trout and Julie Ponessa Salathe, "A Brief Introduction to the Maritime History of New Haven," *Journal of the New Haven Colony Historical Society* 37, no. 1 (1990).

13. Rollin G. Osterweis, *Three Centuries of New Haven* (New Haven: Yale University Press, 1953), 201.

14. This idea of a second nature derives from Hegel and is applied admirably in Cronon's analysis of Chicago. See Cronon, *Nature's Metropolis*.

15. See, e.g., Rutherford H. Platt, *Land Use and Society: Geography, Law, and Public Policy* (Washington, D.C.: Island, 1996).

16. The size-of-place rankings used are from Campbell Gibson, "Population of the 100 Largest Cities and Other Urban Places in the United States: 1790 to 1990," *U.S. Bureau of the Census Technical Papers* (1998).

17. Jeremy Atack and Peter Passell, *A New Economic View of American History from Colonial Times to 1940* (New York: Norton, 1979), 144.

18. Fernand Braudel, *Capitalism and Material Life, 1400–1800*, trans. Miriam Kochan (New York: Harper & Row, 1973), 318.

19. George Dutton Watrous, "Travel and Transportation," in *History of the City of New Haven to the Present Time*, edited by Edward A. Atwater (New York: Munsell, 1887), 352.
20. Ibid., 355.
21. Trout and Salathe, "Introduction to the Maritime History of New Haven." The estimated length is from Osterweis, *Three Centuries of New Haven*, 244.
22. In one instance, the 350-ton ship *Neptune* returned to New Haven from Canton with so valuable a cargo that it paid $75,000 in duties—more than the tax revenue of the state of Connecticut for that year, according to Abraham Bishop, Collector of the Port of New Haven. See Thomas R. Trowbridge, Jr., "Commerce—Foreign and Domestic," in *History of the City of New Haven to the Present Time*, edited by Edward E. Atwater (New York: Munsell, 1887), 500.
23. The Quinnipiac is by far the largest of the three with a drainage basin of 169 square miles. See Marianne McElroy, "Natural Drainage Basins of Connecticut" (Hartford: Connecticut Geological and Natural History Survey, 1981).
24. This tidy bit of shorthand comes from Lewis Mumford, *Technics and Civilization* (New York: Harcourt Brace, 1934). I understand it to indicate a complex of interdependent technologies working together in a particular period. Mumford's further elaboration of such things as "otechnic" and "paleotechnic" seems unnecessary for present purposes.
25. As counterpoint, very inefficient steam engines were used much earlier to drive mining pumps at sites where fuel was abundant and cheap (e.g., at a coal mine).
26. *Hartford Courant*, March 29, 1815, quoted in Sidney Withington, "Steamboats Reach New Haven," *Papers of the New Haven Colony Historical Society* 10 (1951).
27. Nye, *Consuming Power*, 44.
28. Data are from Census of 1880. See under "Water Power in the United States, Region Tributary to Long Island Sound," 137.
29. The Census of 1880 records five plants using the Mill River to generate horsepower adding up to 490. By way of comparison, the Connecticut River was generating a total of 19,745 horsepower. Ibid., 291.
30. William P. Blake, "Sketch of the Life of Eli Whitney," *Papers of the New Haven Colony Historical Society* 5 (1894).
31. Zachariah Allen, *Practical Tourist or Sketches of the State of the Useful Arts of Society* (Boston, 1832), 153–54. Quoted by Joyce Appleby, *Inheriting the Revolution: The First Generation of Americans* (Cambridge: Harvard University Press, 2000), 78.
32. Daniel P. Tyler, "Statistics of the Condition and Production of Certain Branches of Industry of Connecticut" (Hartford: State of Connecticut, 1846), 193ff.
33. Ira Katznelson, *City Trenches* (Chicago: University of Chicago Press, 1981), 47.
34. Tyler, "Statistics."
35. See Richard Hegel, *Carriages from New Haven* (Hamden, Conn.: Archon, 1974).
36. The classic work on this point is Alfred D. Chandler, *The Visible Hand: The Managerial Revolution in American Business* (Cambridge: Belknap Press of Harvard University Press, 1977).
37. This is a special case of a far more general and speculative analysis offered by Mumford, *Technics and Civilization*.

38. Tyler, "Statistics." Here are some summary comparisons:

Town	Corn (bushels)	Rye (bushels)	Barley (bushels)	Oats (bushels)	Potatoes (bushels)	Hay (tons)	Butter (pounds)
Branford	8,623	1,695	2,729	2,331	22,032	2,429	21,775
East Haven	7,556	2,309	2,964	464	20,271	2,047	12,444
Hamden	7,053	4,550	447	2,524	15,832	2,104	38,338
North haven	5,622	3,374	147	2,152	6,733	1,735	26,760
Orange	8,183	4,600	30	6,520	11,570	1,940	55,708
Woodbridge	3,874	1,644	118	1,619	5,987	1,355	46,200
New Haven	3,558	2,398	301	654	4,346	1,097	5,233
Total	44,469	20,580	6,736	16,256	86,771	12,707	206,458
New Haven percentage	9.9	12.7	7.5	4.7	6.7	10.7	2.8

39. See Tyler, *Statistics*.

40. According to one historian, the Farmington Canal "cut deeper into the financial prosperity of the place than into its soil," inflicting high taxes in the 1820s to cover the city's investment in the project, undertaken in 1822 in the amount of $100,000. See Charles H. Levermore, *The Republic of New Haven* (Baltimore: Johns Hopkins University Press, 1886), 257.

41. All from Tyler, *Statistics*.

42. Edward E. Atwater, ed., *History of the City of New Haven to the Present Time*, 2 vols. (New York: Munsell, 1887), 513.

43. Derby, Naugatuck, Oxford, and Middlebury lie to the west of the New Haven region in the drainage of the Housatonic and Naugatuck Rivers. Meriden and Wallingford lie to the north of New Haven's immediate region.

44. *New Haven of Today* (New Haven: Clarence H. Ryden, 1892), 42.

45. *Daily Palladium*, June 5, 1864, p. 2. Quoted in Jon E. Purmont, "Sargent Comes to New Haven," *Journal of the New Haven Colony Historical Society* 24, no. 1 (1976).

46. Jerome, *History of the American Clock Business*, 139.

47. Temin, *Engines of Enterprise*, 117. The original reference seems to have been in Joseph W. Roe, *English and American Tool Builders* (New Haven: Yale University Press, 1916). See also Jerome, *History of the American Clock Business*.

48. The quote is here reproduced from John E. Sawyer, "The Social Basis of the American System of Manufacturing," *Journal of Economic History* 14 (Autumn 1954): 373.

49. *Historical Statistics of the United States*, Series Q 329, p. 732.

50. See Mary Hewitt Mitchell, *History of New Haven County, Connecticut* (Chicago: Pioneer Historical Publishing, 1930), 579. See also Osterweis, *Three Centuries of New Haven*, 247ff. A good short summary is Sidney Withington, "New Haven and Its Six Railroads," *Railway and Locomotive Historical Society Bulletin* 56 (1940).

51. Withington, "New Haven and Its Six Railroads," 513–15.

52. Here I have combined materials transport and passenger transport.

53. A very influential piece of scholarship on this important point is Clark, "Transport."

54. D. W. Meinig, *The Shaping of America*, vol. 3 (New Haven: Yale University Press, 1998), 243.

55. It is of course possible to combine electrical distribution with steam generation, in which case the centering effect of steam is undone. To be very precise, the centering force derives from the combination of high-output steam and high-friction methods of distribution, such as belts and pulleys.

56. See, for instance, Jeremy Atack et al., "The Regional Diffusion and Adoption of the Steam Engine in American Manufacturing," *Journal of Economic History* 40 (1980).

57. Kenneth Jackson observes that a whole series of intermediate technologies—omnibus, horsecar, commuter rail—emerged beginning in about 1815. And where circumstances were favorable (as with New York's outer boroughs or Boston's cross-Charles rivals), early decentering is to be observed. See Jackson, *Crabgrass Frontier.*

58. See Otto L. Bettmann, *The Good Old Days—They Were Terrible* (New York: Random House, 1974).

59. This photo is used courtesy of collector Joe Taylor of New Haven.

60. *Historical Statistics of the United States*, Series 54, 811–18. Martin V. Melosi, *The Sanitary City: Urban Infrastructure in America from Colonial Times to the Present* (Baltimore: Johns Hopkins University Press, 2000), 31.

61. Chandler, *Visible Hand.*

62. From Alfred Chandler, "The Large Industrial Corporation and the Making of the Modern American Economy," in *Institutions in Modern America: Innovation in Structure and Process*, Stephen E. Ambrose, editor (Baltimore: Johns Hopkins University Press, 1967).

63. Mitchell, *History of New Haven County*, 813–14.

64. West Haven is left out here because it was created as a municipality only in 1921.

65. Annexation is also part of this story. Fair Haven and Westville became New Haven wards in 1870–72 and were made parts of the city with special conditions in 1897 when city and town governments were merged. See Osterweis, *Three Centuries of New Haven*, 337–38. These boundary changes account for only a small fraction of the population history in question.

66. It would be mistaken to think of New Haven County as having been in any way remarkable for its population growth. Compared with other urbanized counties nationally, New Haven County was below average in its rate of growth for all decades after 1850 except 1850–60 and 1890–1900. New Haven itself, on the other hand, was a fast-growing central place for far longer periods. See, among other sources, Roy Wenzlick, "Housing and Construction in the New Haven Area" (New Haven: New Haven Chamber of Commerce, 1945).

67. U.S. Census of 1900, Manufacturing, vol. 8, table 5, Connecticut Urban Manufactures, p. 83.

68. U.S. Census of 1910, vol. 7, Manufacturing, tables 7 and 10, pp. 69ff.

69. Meinig, *Shaping of America*, 3: 242. The internal quotation is to Cronon, *Nature's Metropolist*, 374.

70. Daniel J. Tichenor, *Dividing Lines* (Princeton: Princeton University Press, 2002).

71. Most of these numbers come from the U.S. Census of 1910. The 1850 figure comes

from *Benham's New Haven Directory and Annual Advertiser* (New Haven: J. H. Benham, 1852).

72. Here and in the chapters to follow, the 1911 mapping of the city's streets, buildings, and sewer and water lines is taken as definitive for 1910–16. See Cassius W. Kelly, ed., *Atlas of New Haven* (Boston: Walker, 1911).

73. Cass Gilbert and Frederick Law Olmsted, "Report of the Civic Improvement Committee" (New Haven Civic Improvement Committee, 1910).

74. The City Beautiful Movement crested at about this time. On its high-water mark, see Daniel H. Bennett and Edward H. Burnham, *Plan of Chicago (1909)* (New York: Princeton Architectural Press, 1993). See also William H. Wilson, *The City Beautiful Movement* (Baltimore: Johns Hopkins University Press, 1989).

75. Gilbert and Olmsted, "Report of the Civic Improvement Committee," 13–14.

76. In making these estimations, I have done what I suppose the 1910 researchers to have done. This is to assume a linear rate of growth over the Census interval during which the city passed from fewer than 108,000 to more than 108,000, then to place the date at the appropriate year. With Boston, for example, the relevant decade is 1840–50. In 1840, her population stood as 93,383, leaving 14,617 needed to reach 108,000. Using the 1850 total of 136,881, we infer a yearly growth increment of 4,350 persons. It would take roughly three years at this rate to make up the required number, leaving us with a notional date of 1843. This is doubtless crude reasoning, but it isn't what made the 1910 calculations so profoundly mistaken.

77. Gilbert and Olmsted, "Report of the Civic Improvement Committee," 14.

78. The question of when New Haven reached its maximum population is actually pretty complicated. By Census counts, the date is 1950, and the peak number is 164,443. Two considerations lead me to question this conclusion. First, as will be seen below, postal estimates suggest a figure substantially higher than 164,443 for the World War I period, perhaps as high as 175,000. Second, it turns out that the U.S. Census changed a critical counting rule in 1949. Before that date, college students were counted at their parental home addresses; after that date, they were counted at their campus addresses. New Haven is almost certainly, throughout the twentieth century, a net "importer" of students. This change would, that is, inflate the 1950 number and all subsequent ones in comparison with earlier Census counts. I conclude that the city's peak population probably occurred before 1950, although I cannot say with any confidence exactly when it occurred.

CHAPTER 3. FABRIC OF ENTERPRISE

1. See Haar and Kayden, *Zoning and the American Dream.*

2. A sense of competition, contradicting a sense of inevitable success, is to be found in Isaac Ullman's 1909 Chamber speech urging a wide-ranging set of strategies to attract industry and people to the city. See Osterweis, *Three Centuries of New Haven*, 394.

3. On this and all other points about Poli's biography I rely on Kathryn Jane Oberdeck, "Labor's Vicar and the Variety Show" (Ph.D. diss., Yale University, 1991). Various obituaries from early June 1937 are also used.

4. Ibid., 139ff.

5. Ibid., 171.

6. "To Celebrate 25th Wedding Anniversary," *New Haven Evening Register,* August 25, 1910.

7. See, in particular, Wolfinger, *Politics of Progress,* 267, 286.

8. This and related information from the Parish Reports Files, Diocese of Hartford, 1913.

9. Poli would retain his Italian patriotism in later life, being named Chevalier of the Crown of Italy for his fundraising efforts during World War I. Oberdeck, "Labor's Vicar," 159.

10. There is little doubt on this point, although the nearest year for which Lawn Club membership is available is 1904.

11. Census of Manufacturing, 1910, table 1, p. 153, under Connecticut.

12. That $50 translates to about $900 in 2002 dollars, according the Bureau of Labor Statistics at www.bls.gov.

13. Census of Manufacturing, table 11.

14. The dynamics of locational decisions and the evolution of manufacturing clusters are curiously underdeveloped in contemporary economics. For an interesting diagnosis and a sketched strategy of change for economic analysis in this field, see Krugman, *Development, Geography, and Economic Theory,* and Peterson, *City Limits.*

15. Thomas K. McCraw, *Creating Modern Capitalism* (Cambridge: Harvard University Press, 1997), 321.

16. George Dudley Seymour, *New Haven* (New Haven: N.p., 1942), 16–49.

17. Ibid., 19

18. Ibid., 37.

19. "Depot Architect Is with Mr. Seymour," *New Haven Evening Register,* June 6, 1907.

20. One might propose that Poli ranks seventh (hence, in the middle) among the thirteen names and thus lands on a line of his own. But if alphabetical order is important, how do Adler, Brewster, and Day find themselves so low in the batting order?

21. Gilbert and Olmsted, "Report of the Civic Improvement Committee," 3.

22. Adler was born in Bavaria in 1841, served on the Union side of the American Civil War, served as president of the New Haven Chamber of Commerce and of Mishkan Israel. He was a leading member of New Haven society for roughly half a century before his death in 1916. See Barry E. Herman, "Max Adler, 1841–1916," *Jews in New Haven* 7 (1997).

23. Rollin Woodruff was president of both C. S. Mersick Co. and White Adding Machine; John Studley was a probate judge and later a Democratic candidate for governor of Connecticut; Farnam was part of a major railroad family, a lawyer, and president of the city's Parks Commission; Stokes was assistant rector of St. Paul's church, and a Yale official; Watrous practiced law and taught it at Yale; Harry Day practiced law with Watrous; Moran was a lawyer and vice president of Southern New England Telephone; Townshend practiced law; Poli, as we know, ran theaters and other entertainments.

24. Oberdeck, "Labor's Vicar," 386.

25. The Polis eventually built for themselves an extraordinary home at 1031 Forest Road in the Westville neighborhood. The mock Tudor design is festooned with gargoyles and beasties in unexpected places; it has a Hollywood feel which may well have infected Poli during business hours.

26. Gilbert and Olmsted, "Report of the Civic Improvement Committee," 13–15.

27. See more generally Wilson, *City Beautiful Movement*.

28. See David P. Jordan, *Transforming Paris* (New York: Free Press, 1995).

29. I do not propose to suggest that these patterns begin or end in this period. A useful analysis of such conflict and the associated politics is provided by Wolfinger, *Politics of Progress*, esp. 30–73.

30. "New Haven Road to Get Rid of Italian Help," *New Haven Register*, June 6, 1907.

31. Ibid.

32. For the classic treatment of ethnic succession, see Dahl, *Who Governs?*

33. Seymour, *New Haven*, vi, emphasis added.

34. "Mayor Rice Reviews Administration," *Saturday Chronicle*, December 31, 1910. Emphasis added.

35. Ruth Ginsberg Caplan, "Harris Ginsberg of State Street," *Jews in New Haven* 6 (1993): 127. Harris Ginsberg's store appears only as "confectionery, etc" in the 1913 city directory.

36. See particularly Jacobs, *Death and Life of Great American Cities*, chaps. 3 and 4.

37. Fred Ticotsky, "Ticotsky's Bakery and the Legion Avenue Jews," *Jews in New Haven* 3 (1981): 45. Ticotsky is referring to a somewhat later period, but the point surely held in 1913.

38. See in particular Thelma A. Dries, *A Handbook of Social Statistics of New Haven, Connecticut* (New Haven: Yale University Press, 1936).

39. See William F. Hasse, *A History of Banking in New Haven Connecticut* (New Haven: N.p., 1946), 120.

40. Dries, *Handbook of Social Statistics*, 78.

41. Ann Satterthwaite, *Going Shopping: Consumer Choices and Community Consequences* (New Haven: Yale University Press, 2001), 82–83.

42. These figures, from the Price and Lee "New Haven Directory, 1913," are doubtless misleadingly low for most of these firms but provide a simple screen for our purposes.

43. These statistics, and others in this passage, are taken from the information sheet distributed at the Sargent Company's Salesmen's Conference in June 1916. These are available from the Thomas Dodd Archive at the University of Connecticut, Storrs.

44. Chandler, *Visible Hand*.

45. Sargent information sheet, 45.

46. Ibid., 67ff.

47. From the scrapbook kept by Ziegler Sargent on J. B. Sargent's political career. "Message of the Mayor," January 1, 1891. Original in the New Haven Colony Historical Society Library.

48. Z. Sargent, scrapbook, "Monopolies Opposed."

49. Ibid., 50.

50. John L. Weller, *The New Haven Railroad* (New York: Hastings House, 1969), 51.

51. The specifics in this paragraph come from a report done in 1910 by Stone and Webster of Boston in conjunction with the prosecution of New Haven management for restraint of trade. The leading voice in the attack on monopolistic practices by this railroad was Louis Brandeis, later a Supreme Court justice. The report may be seen at Yale's Mudd Library.

52. Joseph Dobrow, "A Farewell to Arms," *Journal of the New Haven Colony Historical Society* 39, no. 2 (1992): 28.

53. These capsule summaries are in some cases adapted from A. B. Underwood, "Manufacturing Interests of New Haven," in *History of the New England States,* edited by W. T. Davis, vol. 2 (1897), 863–94 (W. D. Hurd, 1897).

54. This clustering of locally rooted firms is nicely treated under the term "civic capitalism" in John T. Cumbler, *A Social History of Economic Decline* (New Brunswick, N.J.: Rutgers University Press, 1989).

CHAPTER 4. LIVING LOCAL

1. A. Bartlett Giamatti, *Take Time for Paradise: Americans and Their Games* (New York: Summit, 1989), 51–52.

2. A pattern quite brilliantly captured by Richard Sennett. See his *Uses of Disorder.* See also, for a more empirical account, Peter Drier, John Mollenkopf, and Todd Swanstrom, *Place Matters: Metropolitics for the Twenty-First Century* (Lawrence: University of Kansas Press, 2001). See also Myron Orfield, *Metropolitics: A Regional Agenda for Community and Stability* (Washington, D.C.: Brookings Institution Press, 1996).

3. This thesis is spelled out in considerable detail and sophistication by Katznelson, *City Trenches.*

4. There appear to have been roughly two thousand Sargent jobs in all. If about a thousand new hires were made in 1910, as the ledgers suggest, this would appear to be 50 percent turnover. If we factor in day labor, the underlying rate is probably lower by 10 percent or so. Given that Sargent had notorious labor trouble and recruited actively in the old country, this is not terribly surprising.

5. The Sargent Company records are held by the Thomas Dodd Research Center at the University of Connecticut, Storrs.

6. An interesting study of a similar city, Wooster, Massachusetts, is offered by Harold F. Creveling, "Mapping Cultural Groups in an American Industrial City," *Economic Geography* 31, no. 4 (1955).

7. Twelve tenements, for example, went up on Wallace and Hamilton Streets between 1888 and 1897. See Mark Wright, "Factory, Neighborhood, and Workers" (Senior essay, Yale University, 1982).

8. In 1913, when the first reverse directory appears, 41 Silver lists only Martin Szabo— perhaps another Pole—renting rooms to newcomers. See Price and Lee's "New Haven Directory . . . , 1913," 989.

9. Kelly, *Atlas of New Haven.* The 1911 street index was constructed by the author, and is available upon request.

10. The shoreline in this and succeeding maps is inexact. It is shown coming up to Water Street, as it surely did, but details of its curvature are approximate. The present shore is up to half a mile further out in the harbor.

11. An earlier study of 272 new hires at Sargent in the year 1890 found 74 percent living in these four neighborhoods combined, with 54 percent in Wooster Square alone. See Wright, "Factory, Neighborhood, and Workers."

12. The evidentiary advantage offered by the Sargent employees is the complete independence between our information on home addresses and that of the city of New Haven. In the other data sets examined here, employees living outside New Haven and its immediate suburbs may in many cases be omitted since we rely on city directory data. Often, especially with senior figures, out-of-town and out-of-state addresses will be offered.

13. Quasi-random here means that pages from the directory were selected at random. My assistants were given an assortment of twelve templates that opened to a subset of names when placed over a page. The templates were drawn at random and applied to the random pages. This procedure has no obvious bias but does not meet the strict canon of independent probabilities for selection (for example, if Jones is selected, a close-by person—say, Jackson—has a slightly increased chance of inclusion as a result). For our purposes, this poses no obvious difficulty.

14. See Dobrow, "Farewell to Arms."

15. It also may reflect the bias in the city directory sample data away from suburban locations. The area of Hamden just north of the plant would in more complete data probably account for a number of workers at Winchester.

16. When employees are identified by employer, it is fairly safe to guess what a job status like "engineer" means. When, however, we have only job categories such as engineer (locomotive or civil?), fireman (railroad or municipal?), conductor (steam train or trolley?), a cloud of guesswork settles over the work. In the current mapping I have included 203 people who are identified explicitly as working for a railroad. I have excluded all "conductors" except the few who have a specified link to railroading. Engineers lacking explicit railroad links are omitted. Firemen are included, except where it is evident that they work for the city.

17. Of 310 addresses, 300 were successfully geocoded.

18. Data are from the 1910 U.S. Census, using the occupation by city tables. The narrow definition is the Census one, which excludes "clerks in stores" and other retail jobs having a large clerical component. The broadest definition simply adds these figures to the Census numbers. Women constitute 1,997 (41 percent) on the narrow definition, and 2,907 (39 percent) on the broader.

19. In all, 1,408 of 1,736 address points for the workers considered to this point were in these areas.

20. I am including what might be thought of as the York Square neighborhood as part of Dwight. Dwight is defined as running as far west as Orchard Street. Edgewood runs from Orchard on the east to Pendleton Street on the west. Both neighborhoods are bounded to the north by Whalley Avenue. Dwight runs south to George, while the southern edge of Edgewood is the avenue for which it is named. East Rock runs between Mansfield Street and/or Prospect Street on the west to Orange Street on the east.

21. Gilbert and Olmsted, "Report of the Civic Improvement Committee," 22.

22. The standard historical work is Chandler, *Visible Hand.*

23. A good summary of Flagler's career is offered by Edward N. Akin, *Flagler* (Gainesville: University Press of Florida, 1988).

24. The firm returned to local control and remained there into the 1930s. See Osterweis, *Three Centuries of New Haven,* 428.

25. Brooks Mather Kelley, *Yale* (New Haven: Yale University Press, 1974), 317.

26. Hadley also introduced several key practices increasing competition for faculty appointments, including the "up or out" rule, which prevented people from staying in a junior rank without attaining the distinction required for promotion to senior rank. See ibid., 327ff.

27. James Oren, *Joining the Club* (New Haven: Yale University Press, 1985).

28. One lived in Derby and the other in West Haven. Six others lived at some distance: one each in Hartford, Los Gatos (California), Cambridge and Long Meadow (Massachusetts), Washington (D.C.), and Rome.

29. Camp was unique in belonging to both groups, running Yale Athletics *and* New Haven Clock Company.

30. Richard Hegel and Floyd Shumway, "The First Century of the Greater New Haven Chamber of Commerce," *Journal of the New Haven Colony Historical Society* 40, no. 2 (1994):27.

31. These specific years are selected simply because they are the closest available dates for which we have records of meetings. The minutes of Proprietor's meetings up through 1927 are archived at the New Haven Colony Historical Society library.

32. Henry T. Blake, *Chronicles of New Haven Green from 1638 to 1862* (New Haven: Tuttle, Morehouse, & Taylor, 1898), 12.

33. See Isabel MacBeath Calder, *The New Haven Colony* (New Haven: Yale University Press, 1962), and Floyd Shumway, "New Haven and Its Leadership" (Ph.D. diss., Columbia University, 1968).

34. Blake, *Chronicles of New Haven Green*, 15.

35. Church runs along the eastern edge of the Green. Everit is a short street in the north end of the East Rock neighborhood.

36. Census of 1910.

37. Gilbert and Olmsted, "Report of the Civic Improvement Committee," 39.

38. Census of 1910.

39. This analysis is due entirely to Stephen Lassonde, "Learning to Forget: Schooling and Family Life in New Haven's Working Class, 1870–1940" (Ph.D. diss., Yale University, 1994).

40. Sennett, *Uses of Disorder*, 53–54.

41. For the Boston parallel, and an insightful interpretation, see Warner, *Streetcar Suburbs*.

42. Mitchell was also known by the pen name Ik Marvel.

43. See relevant city charter sections and Osterweis, *Three Centuries of New Haven*, 385.

44. Service began in early 1861, with separate runs from the center of the city to each of the two destinations on a one-track system. See also Mitchell, *History of New Haven County, Connecticut*, 596.

45. Census of 1910. I am equating Westville with Ward 13, Fair Haven East with Ward 15, and the Annex with Ward 15.

46. Mitchell, *History of New Haven County*, 686.

47. Arnold Guyot Dana, *New Haven's Problems: Whither the City? All Cities?* (New Haven: N.p., 1937), 97.

CHAPTER 5. CIVIC DENSITY

1. Karen R. Frankel, "Selections from the Diary of Michael Campbell," in "Work and Ethnicity in the Gilded Age," Senior Essay, Yale University, 1982.

2. In 1913, vacuum sweepers had reached just 1 percent of American homes. See Robert Putnam, *Bowling Alone* (New York: Simon & Schuster, 2000), 217.

3. Peter Dobkin Hall, "Vital Signs," in *Civic Engagement in American Democracy*, edited by Theda Skocpol and Morris P. Fiorina (Washington, D.C.: Brookings Institution Press, 1999).

4. Theda Skocpol, "How Americans Became Civic," in Skocpol and Fiorina, *Civic Engagement*, 33.

5. Ibid., 49.

6. Thomas S. Duggan, *The Catholic Church in Connecticut* (New York: States History, 1930), 4–5.

7. Osterweis, *Three Centuries of New Haven*, 212.

8. Ibid.

9. In Hall's data for 1910, and in my own for 1913, the counts are ninety and eighty-nine. This is doubtless a fairly accurate census, which perhaps omits some small congregations lacking the resources to get themselves listed in city directories.

10. Duggan, *Catholic Church in Connecticut*, 318.

11. "The Story of Seventy-Five Years in Commemoration of the Diamond Jubilee of the Grand Old Parish on the Hill, Sacred Heart Church" (New Haven: Sacred Heart Church, 1950).

12. A 1901 Yale College student publication, the *Yale Courant*, offered this piece of doggerel bemoaning the church's transfer to Italian Catholics:
The old white church in Wooster Square
Where godly people met and prayed
Dear Souls! They worship Mary there,
Italian mother, man and maid
In gaudy Southern scarfs arrayed,
The horrid candles smolder where
The godly people prayed.
Alas, the fall of Wooster Square!
See Marcia Graham Synnott, "A Social History of Admissions Politics at Harvard, Yale, and Princeton, 1900–1920" (Ph.D. diss., University of Massachusetts, 1974), 478.

13. The reports are filed with the Archdiocese of Hartford, on Farmington Avenue in that city.

14. Letter dated December 1, 1959, filed under "Parish Boundaries, New Haven," at the Archdiocese.

15. John T. McGreevy, *Parish Boundaries* (Chicago: University of Chicago Press, 1996). This sort of friction is illustrated for New Haven by Duggan's account of the founding of St. Boniface as a German national parish in the 1850s: "In the middle of the fifties there was a movement among the German Catholics of New Haven to have a church where they could assemble and hear the gospel in their own tongue. It was a sinister

movement—a movement to sow discord among them and place them in revolt against the discipline and faith of the Church. The active and avowed leaders of the rebellion were three—a Jew, a Protestant, and a publicly professed infidel." Duggan, *Catholic Church in Connecticut*, 335.

16. Charles R. Morris, *American Catholic* (New York: Random House, 1997), 50.

17. Interestingly, the Easter count for St. Michael's is probably inflated. The priest records 2,554 males and 4,150 females, then enters a total of 7,004 instead of 6,704.

18. Gerald Gamm, *Urban Exodus* (Cambridge: Harvard University Press, 1999), 22.

19. Quoted in Dan A. Oren, "A Jewish Student at Yale," in *Jews in New Haven*, edited by Jonathan D. Sarna (New Haven: Jewish Historical Society of New Haven, 1978), 57.

20. The congregation moved from buildings called "Armstrong's" to "Brewster's" to "Todd's Hall" in the 1840. See Werner S. Hirsch, "The First Minute Book of the Congregation Mishkan Israel, 1849–1860," *Jews in New Haven* 6 (1993).

21. Ibid., 3. Hirsch appears to be writing of an earlier period, but what he says seems entirely appropriate to the 1885–1910 period.

22. Jonathan D. Sarna, "Synagogue Structures of Greater New Haven," in Sarna, *Jews in New Haven*, 21–22. The dates given for B'nai Jacob, B'nai Israel, Shara Torah, and Adas B'nai Jeshurun in the text above are earlier than those given in Sarna. His dates are for temple foundings; mine are for the founding of congregations, getting started before having official temples. Myron Barger of the Greater New Haven Jewish Historical Society assisted me in establishing these dates.

23. Oren, "A Jewish Student at Yale," 59–60. The original source is Arthur Chiel, "Looking Back," *Connecticut Jewish Ledger*, November 16, 1972.

24. For a detailed review of these clubs, see Hall, "Vital Signs, Connecticut, 1850–1998."

25. These records are archived for 1902–54 at the New Haven Colony Historical Society.

26. These records are archived by the New Haven Colony Historical Society. The agreed conclusion about piecework was that it was "of no advantage to workmen as the price per piece is liable to be cut by the employer if the workman succeeds in making over what is considered a fair wage."

27. See Marcia Graham Synnott, *The Half-Open Door: Discrimination and Admissions at Yale, Harvard, and Princeton, 1900–1930* (Westport, Conn.: Greenwood, 1979), and "Social History of Admissions Politics at Harvard, Yale, and Princeton," 462–64.

28. The Harmonie or Harmony or Harmonia Club was related to a similar club in New York City. In New Haven, manufacturer Max Adler was the founding president. See Herman, "Max Adler, 1841–1916."

29. Hall, "Vital Signs," 215.

30. See Gamm and Putnam, "Growth of Voluntary Associations in America, 1840–1940." The authors track national organizations in a panel of twenty-six large, medium, and small U.S. cities. What they find is that: (1) the level of local penetration was generally high, but (2) it was not a function of immigration or industrialization, since many smaller, not-very-industrial towns with limited immigration had many fraternal and sororal chapters and lodges. In table 6.3 I rely on the Harvard Civil Engagement Project as reported in Skocpol, "How Americans Became Civic," 72–75. In the right-hand column, a "yes" means that in at least one year (1900, 1910, or

1920) the organization's national membership exceeded 1 percent of men or women or both.

31. Eight other nationals had one or two New Haven chapters: Elks 2, Knights of Honor 2, Modern Woodmen 2, YMCA 2, Christian Endeavor 1, Daughters of the American Revolution 1, German National Alliance 1, American Red Cross 1.

32. Arthur Schlesinger, Jr., "Biography of a Nation of Joiners," *American Historical Review* 50 (1944): 24.

33. Katznelson, *City Trenches,* 51.

34. No great weight should be placed on the exact numbers here. There are plenty of near-miss cases, such as Isaac Ullman, who headed both the Chamber of Commerce and the Harmonie Club and was a very senior business manager in a large corporation, but not quite head of a business. Surely he is closer to what we need to measure than is someone who heads a tiny retail firm. In evaluating the overall generalizations, one could perhaps double the number of business heads running clubs and nonprofits without changing the main conclusions reached.

35. Strictly speaking, we are counting presidencies, not persons. One case, in which one individual occupied four such slots, may in some degree distort the total. It does not make a difference exceeding 5 percent in any generalization being made here.

36. Some confirming evidence is to be found in David T. Beito, *From Mutual Aid to the Welfare State* (Chapel Hill: University of North Carolina Press, 2000).

37. For instance, Henry Menges, who was employed as music director of the Poli theater group, lived in a fine house at 78 Howard Avenue.

38. Defined for this purpose to include "Fair Haven East," on the east shore of the Quinnipiac River. Without this section, the count falls to forty-four.

39. Fifty-four leaders, roughly 16 percent, live either in transitional zones (fourteen in the State-Orange corridor) or in the city's internal suburbs. Notably, seventeen are in Westville, four others in the Annex.

40. "Report of the President" (New Haven: Yale University, 1909), 127–38.

41. See particularly Synnott, *Half-Open Door,* and Synnott, "Social History of Admissions Politics at Harvard, Yale, and Princeton," and Oren, *Joining the Club.*

42. Wolfinger, *Politics of Progress,* 177ff.

43. The header of the story reads: "Chief Executive of City in Indignant Frame of Mind Over Outbreak Last Night in Which He Was Surrounded. Urges Police Court Punishment—Dean Jones, Present at Trial Says He Will Act to Curb Such Demonstrations." "Mayor 'Roughed' by Students: Dean Jones to Take Action," *New Haven Register,* November 3, 1915.

44. Annual Report, New Haven Hospital, 1909, 38–39.

45. Annual Report, Hospital of St. Raphael, 1909, 47.

46. Frederick Kaye, "City Year Book of the City of New Haven for 1913" (New Haven: City of New Haven, 1913), 535.

47. The Normal School later became the kernel around which Southern Connecticut State University developed.

48. Kaye, "City Year Book of the City of New Haven for 1913," 534–69.

49. Without denying the sensitivity of some (and good will of many) teachers and adminis-

trators, we must bear in mind that overcrowding and strained resources compounded the social biases that such people inevitably brought to their jobs. Well into the 1930s school administrators and teachers in New Haven—themselves mostly Yankees and Irish-Americans, respectively—read decades-old ethnic prejudices into their assessments of grammar school children. Even though I.Q., aptitude, and developmental testing had been locally in vogue since the early 1920s, principals and teachers continued to rattle off ethnic stereotypes when asked about the academic strengths and weaknesses of city school children. Yankees were "shrewd and set in their ways," Poles "slow-witted" and "stubborn and phlegmatic," Jews "ambitious" but "aggressive and loud," Italians "slow learning" and "emotional and temperamental" but musically and artistically inclined, African-Americans were carefree and happy, and (like Italian children) gifted in music and art. Carl F. Butts and Joseph Young, "Education in Connecticut: A Study of Public, Parochial, and Sunday School Education in Connecticut, with Emphasis on the Ethnic Factors" (Peoples of Connecticut Ethnic Heritage Project, Works Progress Administration, Federal Writers' Project, New Haven Division, April 1939), box 37, folder 134:5a, 264–65; Manuscripts and Archives, University of Connecticut Libraries, Storrs.

50. Lassonde, "Learning to Forget."

51. Enrollments in the elementary schools ranged from 100 to a few hundred pupils, and between 1,500 and 2,000 students attended the junior high schools. The enrollment at Hillhouse was 4,261, and enrollment at Commercial High School stood at 2,036 in 1930. Moreover, since the beginning of the century Hillhouse was forced to hold "double sessions" to accommodate all of its students—half of the students attended in the mornings and half in the afternoons.

52. New Haven Board of Education, Annual Report, 1930. It is perhaps worth noting that the academic high school faculty was recruited nationally, although substantial minorities on the faculty had local education. Of ninety-two faculty in 1913, thirty had attended Yale College or one of Yale's professional schools. All but eight of the ninety-two were living in the city, although they were somewhat less tightly clustered around the school campus than was common for neighborhood school faculties.

53. These statistics, and a great many insights about the New Haven sporting scene in this period, are captured in Bob Barton's turn-of-millennium series in the *Register*, particularly those dated December 22 and 23, 1999. I have used Barton's work often in this section, although all quotations are from original sources in the period.

54. Bob Barton, "20th Century Sports, the 1900s," *New Haven Register*, December 22, 1999.

55. Ibid.

56. Hanifan, "The Rural Community Center," 130, quoted in Putnam, *Bowling Alone*, 19.

57. Putnam, *Bowling Alone*.

58. Ibid., 22–24.

CHAPTER 6. A SIDEWALK REPUBLIC

1. *New Haven Evening Register*, October 6, 1915.

2. Ibid., January 1, 1910.

3. See Dahl, *Who Governs?* 19–22.

4. This tension is interestingly resolved in Peterson, *City Limits*. Peterson ends up, in effect, giving priority to propertied interests, and argues that the "city's interest" is by nature a corporate conception, not reducible to the interests of current residents.

5. *New Haven Evening Register,* October 18, 1909, p. 1.

6. This is of course overstated and simplified in order to represent an ideological position. The voluntary content of market transactions is of course compromised by all manner of complications, including large differences of bargaining power, asymmetrical information, fraud, and the like.

7. This point is explored at length in the literature on welfare economics. See, for instance, I. M. D. Little, *A Critique of Welfare Economics* (Oxford: Clarendon, 1957).

8. Ad appearing in the *New Haven Evening Register,* October 2, 1911.

9. *New Haven Evening Register,* October 6, 1915.

10. They were J. B. Tower (1925–28), T. A. Tully (1928–31), and William Celentano (1945–53). The East Shore wards carried by Campner in 1917 remain the GOP's principal base in the early twenty-first century. See, among others, Dahl, *Who Governs?* 11ff.

11. Specifics for this paragraph are from David Montgomery et al., "160 Year of Labor's Struggle for a Better New Haven," in *Labor Almanac: New Haven' Unions in the 1990s* (New Haven: Labor History Association, 1995), and from Price and Lee, "New Haven City Directory . . . 1913."

12. Republican Town Chairman Colonel Isaac Ullman might have written part of Rice's speech and selected these references in consequence of his additional role as president of the Chamber. Or Rice himself could have made the choice in his anxiety to please Ullman.

13. *New Haven Evening Register,* October 8, 1909, p. 1.

14. Ibid., October 1, 1917, editorial page.

15. Clarence N. Stone, *Regime Politics* (Lawrence: University Press of Kansas, 1989), 3.

16. *Hunter v. City of Pittsburgh,* 207 U.S. 161, 178–179 (1907). Cited in Frug, *City Making,* 17.

17. Before continuing to describe the 1899 Charter as monument to the legislative imagination, I must acknowledge that it simplified the immediate past in three respects. First, before 1897, the whole apparatus had been defined in duplicate, for town government and city government were considered separate, even though their constituencies were mostly the same. The two were now, mercifully, made one (Section 1 of the 1899 document). This same decision placed the city's territorial limits very close to their present bounds. Second, the 1899 document had continued to treat the city's legislative branch as having two houses—a body of twenty-one aldermen and another of thirty-six councilmen—so that no affirmative act could go forward save by the consent of two bodies, elected in different elections at different seasons of the year, with leaders and procedures of their own. An amendment adopted in June 1901 had killed off the councilmen. Small mercy. The charter, finally, granted the mayor a term of two years, not one, as in previous eras.

18. See Schlesinger, "Biography of a Nation of Joiners."

19. Frank Goodnow, *City Government in the United States* (New York: Century, 1904), 63.

For a recent interpretation of the same phenomenon, see Dennis R. Judd, *The Politics of American Cities: Private Power and Public Policy* (Glenview, Ill.: Scott, Foresman, 1988), 37ff.

20. The case of New York City is actually more dramatic than New Haven's in this particular. See Seymour Mandelbaum, *Boss Tweed's New York* (New York: Wiley, 1965).

21. Maher got the contract, and he "left money on the table," nearly $700 of it, suggesting that the bidding process was not manipulated (or, if such an attempt was made, the collaborators didn't include Maher). In 1910, bids came from just five firms on twenty projects. Three firms (Maher, Whitby, and Dwyer & Mannix) won all twenty, but the gaps between first- and second-lowest bids are usually large and irregular enough to make collusion seem improbable. Only a relatively sophisticated strategy of bid-rigging is consistent with the data. It is possible that the firms divided the projects, and once A had been awarded a given project, B and C agreed to bid well out of the money. The winning firm would rotate between projects. This seems improbable but cannot be ruled out.

22. These ordinances and the others are taken from the aldermanic journals of 1910–11 and 1912.

23. For the broader policy context, see Melosi, *Sanitary City.*

24. This figure suggests something like sixty visits per day by these two men, thirty each. This seems pretty high by modern standards.

25. A total of 7,039 units were started in the years 1910–16. Data from City Yearbooks.

26. Katznelson, among others, stresses the importance of neighborhood to working-class identity, and how it softened, buffered, or even displaced class-based identification based exclusively on work settings. See Katznelson, *City Trenches.*

27. See Burnham and Bennett, *Plan of Chicago (1909), and* Wilson, *City Beautiful Movement.*

28. *Saturday Chronicle,* December 31, 1910.

29. E. H. Arnold, "Playgrounds of New Haven," *Saturday Chronicle,* January 2, 1915.

30. Seymour, *New Haven,* 593–94.

31. *New Haven Evening Register,* August 23, 1916, p. 1.

32. Ibid., January 18, 1917.

33. Ibid., August 25, 1916.

34. Ibid., September 3, 1916.

35. Stilgoe, *Borderland, 1820–1939,* 9.

CHAPTER 7. BUSINESS AND CIVIC EROSION

1. Lewis Mumford, *The City in History* (San Diego: Harcourt Brace Jovanovich, 1961), 413.

2. When I say that urbanizing technologies built cities and dimmed their hinterlands in this passage, I of course mean that they played a dominant enabling role in the trains of human decisions, embedded in capitalist institutions, to bring about these changes.

3. The New Haven manufacturing data are from the 1920 U.S. Census, vol. 9, table 9, 179. The profit estimates for national sectors are based on Ralph C. Epstein, "Industrial Profits in 1917," *Quarterly Journal of Economics* 39 (1925): 241–266.

4. Hasse, *History of Banking in New Haven, Connecticut.*

5. Chandler, *Visible Hand.* See also Thomas K. McCraw, *American Business, 1920–2000: How It Worked* (Wheeling, Ill.: Harlan-Davidson, 2000).

6. Herbert G. Houze, *Winchester Repeating Arms Company* (Iola, Wis.: Krause, 1994), esp. 208ff.

7. Ibid.

8. Ibid., 211. Houze attributes the figures to an Arthur Young Company report, dated April 27, 1925.

9. Ibid., 212.

10. According to Energy Information Administration data for 1999, the local electric utility's average price per kilowatt hour ranks sixth in the nation among utilities serving ten thousand or more accounts in the forty-eight contiguous states. The average United Illuminating price was 13.22 cents per kilowatt hour. Of roughly two thousand utilities in the comparison group, here are the priciest half-dozen:

Utility	Price/kwh	Customers
United Illuminating	13.22	282,986
Bangor Hydro-Electric [Maine]	13.76	91,726
New Hampshire Electric Coop	17.38	59,701
Public Serice Co. of New Hampshire	14.59	367,119
Long Island Power Authority	13.43	941,437
New York State Electric and Gas Co.	13.84	719,833

The overall U.S. average stood at 8.16, placing New Haven and its region 62 percent above the mean nationally—no small handicap.

11. This is, nevertheless, a period of relative decline for this region. Total U.S. manufacturing employment increased by about 50 percent over the interval from 1919 to 1947 while the New Haven area stood still.

12. Goddard, *Getting There*, 50.

13. I rely in this discussion on the archives of the Connecticut Department of Motor Vehicles, housed by the Connecticut State Library in Hartford.

14. James J. Flink, *The Car Culture* (Cambridge: MIT Press, 1975), 29.

15. See Hounshell, *From the American System to Mass Production*, 224. The innovative assembly line is, of course, not the only driver in this story. To a considerable extent, economies of scale worked to Ford's advantage in lowering prices and upping sales, which in turn made possible the capitalization of further improvements that yielded still lower prices and still higher sales levels, fostering still greater economies of scale. See also Lindy Biggs, *The Rational Factory: Architecture, Technology, and Work in America's Age of Mass Production.*

16. Quoted by Goddard, *Getting There*, 43.

17. William Dix, "The Automobile as Vacation Agent," *Independent*, June 2, 1904.

18. David E. Fitzgerald, "Sixth Annual Message of the Honorable David E. Fitzgerald,

Mayor of the City of New Haven to the Board of Aldermen" (New Haven: City of New Haven, 1923).

19. John W. Murphy, "Municipal Activities of the City of New Haven, Connecticut, for the Year Ending December 31, 1937" (New Haven: City of New Haven, 1937), 6.

20. Dana, *New Haven's Problems*, 16c.

21. William C. Celentano, "Annual Message of Hon. William Celentano, Mayor, City of New Haven, to the Board of Aldermen" (New Haven: City of New Haven, 1947).

22. The reference is to the contrast between sustaining and disruptive technologies developed in Clayton M. Christiansen, *The Innovator's Dilemma* (New York: Harper Business, 1997).

23. Goddard, *Getting There*, 54.

24. The AAA's official history tells the early story simply: "At the turn of the century, existing roads had been designed for the horse and buggy—not the auto. Traveling on those dirt paths was often risky, and AAA's earliest goal was to lead a fight for improvements in the nation's roads—ones which could better accommodate automobile traffic. By 1916, AAA had won a major battle in its campaign for better roads when the principle of federal aid to highways was initiated" (www.aaa.com).

25. Le Corbusier, *Cities of Tomorrow*.

26. The great marketing industrialists of the early twentieth century frequently portrayed their mission by reference to "real freedom," by which they meant mainly the ability to command consumer goods through buying power in the marketplace. Merchandiser Edward Filene's doctrine ran to the effect that high wages and high consumption would offer "real freedom to the masses—that economic freedom which underlies all other kinds of freedom, except perhaps the special freedom of the saint who renounces the world and takes a vow of poverty." Edward A. Filene, *The Way Out* (Garden City, N.Y.: Doubleday Page, 1924), 199. See also Henry Ford, *My Life and Work* (Garden City, N.Y: Doubleday Page 1922).

27. "History of Orange: Sesquicentennial, 1822–1972" (Orange, Conn.: Town of Orange, 1972).

28. Trolley service was close to hand.

29. The book's website, www.endofurbanism.com, contains an inventory of over eight hundred suburban developments in the towns around New Haven from 1872 to 2001.

30. Dana, *New Haven's Problems*.

31. Ibid., 17–18.

32. Peter Calthorpe, *The New American Metropolis* (New York: Princeton Architectural Press, 1986). Andres Duany, Elizabeth Plater-Zyberk, and Jeff Speck, *Suburban Nation* (New York: Farrar, Straus, Giroux, 2000); Thomas Hylton, *Save Our Land, Save Our Towns* (Harrisburg, Pa.: Seitz and Seitz, 1995); Katz, *New Urbanism;* Philip Langdon, *A Better Place to Live* (Amherst: University of Massachusetts Press, 1994).

33. The calculation is made using the Bureau of Labor Statistics inflation calculator at www.bls.gov. The exact figure is $12,924.

34. The death rate among firms may well be somewhat higher. Here, as elsewhere in this analysis, I am counting as extinctions those cases in which a store operates at a particular address in the initial period, and no store operates there in the second period.

Many cases of nonextinction entail a change of name and quite possibly a change of ownership.

35. By "compounding" here I mean that the number of stores available to become extinct declines as extinctions occur. Were this not so, we could obtain the extinction rate simply by dividing the total percentage of extinctions by the number of years in question. In the case of 1913–23, that would give us 54 percent/ten years or 5.4 percent per year. But as the number of survivors dwindles, the annual rate must advance to make up the effect of decreasing exposure. This is accomplished by taking the natural log of the percentage lost in total divided by the number of years. This corresponds to the constant death rate in actuarial modeling.

36. Deducting 50 chain stores and 25 large nonchains from 834 yields 759 small stores. This is, of course, guesswork; but it is almost certainly close enough to the truth to capture the main predicament faced by the mom-and-pop enterprises.

37. From "Great American Tradition" at www.aptea.com/history. See especially James M. Mayo, *The American Grocery Store: The Business Evolution of an Architectural Space* (Westport, Conn.: Greenwood Press, 1993). See also Morris Albert Adelman, *A&P: A Study in Price Cost Behavior and Public Policy* (Cambridge: Harvard University Press, 1959).

38. Mayo, *American Grocery*, 86–87.

39. The rest of the Roaring '20s exerted only a modest downward pressure on the number of stores, trimming the herd from 834 in 1923 to 739 in 1930.

40. Margaret Hogg and Ralph Hurlin, *The Incidence of Work Shortage in New Haven, Connecticut* (New York: Russell Sage Foundation, 1932), 23.

41. Dries, *Handbook*.

42. Dries, *Handbook*, 5.

43. See the web location, yalebooks.com/city.

44. The Loew's Company, author of the vast cineplex, filed for bankruptcy protection in 2001 because it, along with its competitors, had taken the scale of competition one level beyond the limit set by the paying public.

45. Vacant outright, or vacant of a grocery of any sort.

46. For the classic analysis, see Chandler, *Strategy and Structure*.

47. Mayo, *American Grocery*, 99.

48. Gamm, *Urban Exodus*.

49. Hall, "Vital Signs."

50. Ibid., table 6.1.

51. Ibid., 221.

52. Kelley, *Yale*. I rely heavily on Kelley here and in succeeding passages.

53. Ibid., 371.

54. Ibid.

55. Ibid., 372.

56. Ibid., 389.

57. See Dana, *New Haven's Problems*.

58. Joseph B. Chepaitis, *The University of New Haven* (South Bend, Ind.: Carlton Graphics, 1995).

59. "Illustrated History of the Trades Council of New Haven and Affiliated Unions" (New Haven: Greater New Haven Trades Council, 1899).

60. In the same general period, neighboring Bridgeport repeatedly reelected Socialist Jasper McLevy, who formed a working relationship with powerful local business leaders in managing that city. See Cecelia Bucki, *Bridgeport's Socialist New Deal, 1915–36* (Urbana: University of Illinois Press, 2001).

61. Mark J. Mininberg, *Saving New Haven* (New Haven: Fine Arts, 1988).

62. "City Year Book of the City of New Haven for 1934" (New Haven: City of New Haven, 1934).

63. Ibid., 64–65.

64. Montgomery, "160 Year of Labor's Struggle for a Better New Haven." See also Frank R. Annunziato, "Made in New Haven," *Labor Heritage* 4 (Winter 1992).

65. Montgomery, "160 Years," 23.

66. Labor Almanac, 50.

CHAPTER 8. RACE, PLACE, AND THE EMERGENCE OF SPATIAL HIERARCHY

1. In general, black wages in the north ran 20–45 percent above black southern levels, and quite commonly exceeded southern white wage levels. See, among other sources, Gunnar Myrdal, *An American Dilemma* (New York: Harper & Row, 1944). In appendix 6, Myrdal gives data for several industries, broken down by wage and region for the late 1930s. For example, in iron and steel working, we have the following average hourly wages for 1937: northern blacks $.74, southern blacks $.54, northern whites $.86, southern whites $.75. In slaughterhouses: northern blacks $.71, southern blacks $.46, northern whites $.69, southern whites $.53. See esp. p. 1124.

2. The story of Ardie's journey was first told to me in November 1988, on several extended occasions in 1989, and during a July 4 visit we made together to Beaufort County in 1993. The train's name and schedule is inferred from *Official Guide of the Railways and Steam Navigation Lines of the U.S., Puerto Rico, Canada, Mexico, and Cuba* (New York: National Railway Publications, 1943), 539.

3. Another factor in the decision of families to leave the South was the increasing mechanization of agriculture, which generally lowered wages and reduced demand for farm work. This particular family remembers none of this, and members report having been employed fairly satisfactorily as farmworkers, most notably as field workers on a large farm devoted to flowers, notably gladiolas, aimed at northern markets.

4. Myrdal reports that in a sixty-four-city study, 84.8 percent of all city blocks were occupied solely by whites. See *American Dilemma*, 619.

5. The original Social Security Act had been crafted so as to achieve support from all regions, including the South. The price for this last had included the exclusion of agricultural laborers from eligibility, which is to say virtually all the blacks who came north in the 1940s.

6. Robert Austin Warner, *New Haven Negroes* (New Haven: Yale University Press, 1940), 195.

7. It was actually necessary in the early years to relax income limits for residents so that

Winchester workers could remain at Elm Haven in the face of rising incomes. See Douglas W. Rae, "Elm Haven's Baseline Study" (Washington, D.C.: HUD, 1995).

8. In the late 1990s, Elm Haven was chosen by HUD for radical transformation under a Hope 6 grant. Renamed "Monterey Place," and rebuilt in New Urbanist style, it looks much better than before, and some indices show improvement (most notably, less crime). On the other hand, its employment rates remain very low by city, regional, and national standards.

9. Warner, *New Haven Negroes,* VIII.

10. Dahl, *Who Governs?* William Julius Wilson, *When Work Disappears* (New York: Knopf, 1996).

11. Data here are from Census sources, as well as BLS surveys. The Census of Manufacturing provides most of the jobs data. Inflation is calculated using the BLS urban wage deflator.

12. See, among others, George C. Galster, "Polarization, Place, and Race," *North Carolina Law Review* 71, no. 5 (June 1993), or John F. Cain, "The Influence of Race and Income on Racial Segregation and Housing Policy," in *Housing Desegregation and Federal Policy,* edited by John M. Goering (Chapel Hill: University of North Carolina Press, 1986). The classic study of race in New Haven predates the arrival of this family, as well as most other black households. See Warner, *New Haven Negroes.*

13. I have relied heavily here on one exceptional collection of work on the history and consequences of zoning in the United States, namely, Haar and Kayden, *Zoning and the American Dream.*

14. W. R. Pollard, "Outline of the Law of Zoning in the United States," *Annals of the American Academy of Political and Social Science* 155, no. 2 (1931); Yale Rabin, "Expulsive Zoning," in Haar and Kayden, *Zoning and the American Dream.* See also Joe R. Feagin, "Arenas of Conflict," in Haar and Kayden, *Zoning and the American Dream;* Gordon Whitnall, "History of Zoning," *Annals of the American Academy of Political and Social Science* 155, no. 2 (1931); Frank Backus Williams, *The Law of City Planning and Zoning* (New York: Macmillan, 1922).

15. *Buchanan v. Warley,* U.S. 60 (1917) 287.

16. From the opinion in *Miller v. Board of Public Works,* 195 Cal. 477, 38.

17. Feagin, "Arenas of Conflict," 82. Of ninety-three cities with 100,00 or more population, Feagin reports that eighty-two had zoning.

18. *Village of Euclid v. Ambler Realty Co.,* 272 U.S. 365 (1926).

19. Andrew J. Cappel, "A Walk Along Willow," *Yale Law Journal* 101, no. 3 (December 1991): 622.

20. Jacobs, *Death and Life of Great American Cities.*

21. C. Lowell Harriss, *History and Policies of the Home Owners' Loan Corporation* (New York: National Bureau of Economic Research, 1951), 9.

22. *Ibid.,* 43.

23. Home Owners' Loan Corporation, Residential Security Map and Explanation, New Haven, Connecticut (October 1937). This set of documents is available from the National Archives of the United States of America.

24. For an early attack on one class of rental housing common in New Haven, see Prescott F. Hill, "The Menace of the Three-Decker," *Housing Problems in America* 5 (1916).

25. HOLC, Report A-8.

26. Ibid., Report A-3.

27. Ibid., Report B-10.

28. Ibid., Report D-4.

29. Ibid., Report D-3.

30. Estimated as follows from the 1930 Census: HOLC D-5 included all of Wards 10, 11, 12, and 27, plus 30 percent of Ward 25 and 10 percent of Ward 14. The estimate works out to 29,862 and is probably conservative in assigning only 30 percent of the very large Ward 25 to HOLC D-5.

31. In one enumeration we may estimate that HOLC D-5 contained 1,835 families with six or more members apiece of foreign or mixed-stock parentage. The same area contained an estimated 47 similarly large families of native white parentage. See Dries, *Handbook*, table 34. Estimates are based on the same percentages used to estimate total population.

32. Dries, *Handbook*.

33. HOLC, Report D-5.

34. Ibid., Report D-6.

35. Arnold R. Hirsch, *Making the Second Ghetto* (Chicago: University of Chicago Press, 1983), 10.

36. R. Allen Hays, *The Federal Government and Urban Housing* (Albany: State University of New York Press, 1985), 89. I have spelled out the "National Association of Real Estate Boards" in place of "NAREB" in Hays's text.

37. Montgomery, "160 Years of Labor's Struggle for a Better New Haven."

38. The best history of public housing in New Haven is provided by Robert A. Solomon, "Building a Segregated City," *Saint Louis University Public Law Review* 16, no. 2 (1997). See esp. p. 291.

39. Here I make liberal use without further citation of my own "Elm Haven Baseline Study" from 1995.

40. Quotation taken from *New Haven Courier Journal*, January 15, 1942. Orr was a leading architect of the period. He designed, among other buildings of the time, the clubhouse of the New Haven Lawn Club.

41. *New Haven Courier Journal*, February 2, 1942.

42. *Then and Now* (Housing Authority of New Haven, 1942), 9.

43. See Solomon, "Building a Segregated City."

44. "Fourth Annual Report of the Housing Authority of New Haven" (New Haven: Housing Authority of New Haven, 1942), 9.

45. Housing Authority of New Haven.

46. Ludwig L. Geismar and Jane Krisberg, *The Forgotten Neighborhood* (Metuchen, N.J.: Scarecrow, 1967), chap. 2.

47. See, e.g., Harry J. Holzer, "The Spatial Mismatch Hypothesis," *Urban Studies* 28, no. 1 (1992); Keith Ihlanfedt, "Spatial Mismatch Between Jobs and Residential Location

Within Urban Areas," *Cityscape* 1, no. 1 (1994). Also Katherine M. O'Regan and Douglas Rae, "Segregation and Isolation," unpublished paper, Yale School of Management (1993).

48. The classic essay is Thomas C. Schelling, "Models of Segregation," *American Economic Review* 59 May 1969.

49. See, e.g., Wilson, *When Work Disappears*. Owen Fiss, "What Should Be Done for Those Who Haven Been Left Behind?" *Boston Review of Books*, July–August 2000.

50. Data are available from the Connecticut Department of Education via web at www.csde.state.ct. The statewide achievement rates were 56.9 percent for reading, 57.5 percent for writing, 60.2 percent for math, and 40.2 percent for the three-test parlay.

51. Douglas S. Massey and Nancy A. Denton, *American Apartheid: Segregation and the Making of the Underclass* (Cambridge: Harvard University Press, 1993), 18–19.

52. "Third Annual Report of the Housing Authority of the City of New Haven" (New Haven: Housing Authority of New Haven, 1941). The map is on the inside front cover and is entitled "Housing Conditions in New Haven." A great many areas are left blank, presumably being better than poor.

53. Wenzlick, "Housing and Construction in the New Haven Area."

54. The old 17th Ward was in Newhallville, and Lee's part of it, on upper Dixwell, was included in HOLC's area C-5; quotes in the text are from that report.

CHAPTER 9. INVENTING DICK LEE

1. Price and Lee New Haven City Directory (1923), 1285.

2. Raymond Wolfinger, "The Development and Persistence of Ethnic Voting," *American Political Science Review* 54, no. 4 (1965): 899. Wolfinger relies on a sample survey of New Haven reported in John W. McConnell, *The Evolution of Social Classes* (Washington, D.C.: American Council on Public Affairs, 1942), 214.

3. One more individual of Irish lineage, Frank Logue, would serve as mayor after Lee, from 1976 to 1980. As Lee once pointed out to me, however, Logue was (merely) a Protestant.

4. The major shifts in ward structure occur in 1921 and 1967. Before 1921, there were fifteen wards (and an additional six at-large seats on the Board of Aldermen). From 1921 to 1967, thirty-three wards, with no at-large aldermanic seats. In 1967, no wards were allowed as bases of election, and the Board of Aldermen was elected at-large. In recent years there have been thirty wards, with no at-large representation.

5. Dahl, *Who Governs?* chap. 4.

6. Ibid., 35.

7. Ibid., 35–36.

8. Allan R. Talbot, *The Mayor's Game* (New York: Harper & Row, 1967), 7. Raymond Wolfinger cautions that Lee's ordinary speech and manner seem *not* to have been much influenced by Yalish affectation. Wolfinger is almost uniquely qualified, having spent months as an observer in Lee's mayoral office.

9. Douglas Rae, interview with Dick Lee, 2002.

10. The story about Mayor Murphy calling the newspaper is wholly believable, since Mur-

phy's notorious fiscal conservatism was exactly what the paper's publisher liked best in public officials (Murphy, a Democrat who was conservative beyond Republican aspirations, often was invited to the newsroom to celebrate on election night).

11. This is not at all a unique story. For a look at the larger picture, see Steven P. Erie, *Rainbow's End* (Berkeley: University of California Press, 1988).

12. Protestant Frank Logue would serve from 1976 to 1980. Irish-American Martin Looney would attempt a run against incumbent John DeStefano in 2001 and lose badly in the September primary.

13. Wolfinger, *Politics of Progress*, 39.

14. Before 1921, the board had twenty-one seats, thirty-three thereafter until 1967.

15. Wolfinger, *Politics of Progress*, 40. The triggering power of Celentano's name here conforms to Wolfinger's generalization that "the most powerful and visible sign of ethnic relevance is a fellow ethnic's name at the head of the ticket, evident for everyone who enters the voting booth" (49).

16. Wolfinger, *Politics of Progress*, 158.

17. William C. Celentano, "Your City's Progress in Black and White" (New Haven: City of New Haven, 1946). Emphasis added.

18. Wenzlick, "Housing and Construction in the New Haven Area" 7.

19. Ibid., 18.

20. Dana, *New Haven's Problems*.

21. Wenzlick, "Housing and Construction in the New Haven Area," 30–31.

22. Satterthwaite, *Going Shopping*.

23. A few years later, Joe Perfetto, with whose account of the city this book begins, would move into Ridge Road Farms, shown lower right in Wenzlick's map.

24. Talbot, *Mayor's Game*, 10.

25. Jeanne R. Lowe, *Cities in a Race with Time* (New York: Random House, 1967), 412.

26. Wolfinger, *Politics of Progress*, 162–63.

27. Quoted in Talbot, *Mayor's Game*, 16.

28. Dahl, *Who Governs?* 35.

29. A fine analysis of ethnic voting in New Haven during this period is provided by Wolfinger, "The Development and Persistence of Ethnic Voting," *American Political Science Review* 59, no. 4 (1965): 896–908. I have been guided by it but doubtless have failed to capture its subtlety in this discussion of the 1949 and 1951 mayoral elections. Another source is Alan G. Lopatin, "The Rise and Fall of the New Haven Democratic Machine: A Statistical Analysis, 1951–73" (unpublished term paper, Yale College, 1975).

30. "The Real Issue in Tomorrow's Election," *New Haven Register*, November 5, 1951.

31. Talbot, *Mayor's Game*, 10–11.

32. Dahl, *Who Governs?* 120. Quoted also by Fred Powledge, *Model City* (New York: Simon and Schuster, 1970), 28–29. The same quote appears also in Bernard Asbell, "Dick Lee Discovers How Much Is Not Enough," *New York Times Magazine*, September 3, 1967.

33. Rae, interview with Dick Lee.

34. Lee adapted the trope endlessly. Thus, for instance, in a 1956 message to the Board of Aldermen, Lee would describe himself as "sick at heart to see children sitting on dilap-

idated furniture, some of it more than fifty years old. . . . Just think, if you will, what this does to their morale and attitude toward their work to say nothing of their posture."

35. Talbot, *Mayor's Game*, 16–17.

36. *Housing Act of 1949*, 171. Public Law 171.

37. This line of fallacious reasoning is famously pilloried in Jacobs, *Death and Life of Great American Cities*.

38. Herbert Gans, "The Failure of Urban Renewal," in *Urban Renewal*, edited by James Q. Wilson (Cambridge: MIT Press, 1966).

39. Wolfinger, *Politics of Progress*, 165. I have relied heavily on Wolfinger's excellent narrative of this period, and of the Lee administration's politics and policy.

40. Interview evidence, from 2002, with Lee confirms this.

41. Ralph Bello, 1955.

42. Talbot, *Mayor's Game*, 50–51.

43. Wolfinger, *Politics of Progress*, 185–86.

44. William T. Donohue, "Memo to the Mayor Re: Father Sanders," 1962.

45. Douglas Rae, interview with William T. Donohue, 2002.

CHAPTER 10. EXTRAORDINARY POLITICS

1. Gilbert, "Report of the Civic Improvement Committee."

2. The 1949 Housing Act used the term "redevelopment," and focused almost exclusively on slum housing. The 1954 act used the term "renewal," and permitted attention to commercial properties while also demanding a more rigorous land-reuse planning process. See Hays, *Federal Government and Urban Housing*, 178ff.

3. Talbot, *Mayor's Game*, 23–24.

4. Wolfinger, *Politics of Progress*, 273.

5. Ibid., 275. Wolfinger later reports having asked Logue whether there were any cities where planners had more influence than in New Haven. The response: "Not any place where they want to get anything done!"

6. Talbot, *Mayor's Game*, 41.

7. The best and most compelling treatment is provided by Frug, *City Making*.

8. This generalization applies to Logue's service in New Haven city government. He later made a failing run for mayor of Boston, and reportedly contemplated a similar run in New York City.

9. Wolfinger, *Politics of Progress*, 276.

10. William Lee Miller, *The Fifteenth Ward and the Great Society* (Boston: Houghton Mifflin, 1966), 148.

11. Wolfinger, *Politics of Progress*, 279.

12. Talbot, *Mayor's Game*, 39.

13. See, e.g., James Q. Wilson, *Bureaucracy* (New York: Basic Books, 1989), esp. chap. 7.

14. A comprehensive and complex political analysis of the bureaucratic politics, and their powerful bearing on politics in the larger sense, is offered by Phillip Allan Singerman, "Politics, Bureaucracy, and Public Policy: The Case of Urban Renewal in New Haven." Ph.D. diss., Yale, 1980. A revisionist interpretation, suggesting that Lee and Logue were

pushing on open doors, is provided by Clarence Stone and Heywood T. Sanders, "Reexamining a Classic Case of Development Politics: New Haven, Connecticut," in *The Politics of Urban Development*, edited by Clarence Stone and Heywood T. Sanders (Lawrence: University of Kansas Press, 1987), 173.

15. The total included $7 million for the two colleges and $827,600 for the adjoining Yale Co-Op bookstore. These dollars were booked in 1967 as part of the local match for the Dixwell urban renewal project.

16. Aldermanic Committee on Streets and Squares, *Statement of Mayor Richard C. Lee*, October 13, 1959.

17. Fred Powledge, *Model City. A Test of American Liberalism: One Town's Efforts to Rebuild Itself* (New York: Simon and Schuster, 1970), 160. See also Susan S. Fainstein, Norman I. Fainstein, Richard Child Hill, Dennis Judd, and Michael Peter Smith, *Restructuring the City*, 2nd ed. (New York: Longman, 1986), table 2.7.

18. Less an unspecified sum representing the opportunity cost of taxes not collected or forgiven.

19. "Blight and Urban Renewal, Technical Report 123" (Hartford: Connecticut Development Commission, 1963).

20. This point is developed nicely by Miller, who makes the further point that Lee was in some sense a "double agent," representing national government to the city and the city to the national government, often influencing federal granting procedures in ways that advantaged New Haven. At the same time, of necessity, the federal government's policy priorities were enforced locally by this back-and-forth. See esp. 198. See also Fainstein et al., *Restructuring the City*, 37–38.

21. "Lee Reviews His Policies in Campaign," *New Haven Register*, October 29, 1953.

22. "Mayor Appoints Action Commission Headed by C of C Past President Freese," *New Haven Newsletter*, September 1954.

23. "National C of C Adopts Policy Resolution on Slum Clearance," *Journal of Housing* 7, no. 6 (1950).

24. Talbot, *Mayor's Game*, 62–63.

25. Stone, *Regime Politics*, 6. A broader, more theoretical work closely related to Stone's theory is Stephen L. Elkin, *City and Regime in the American Republic* (Chicago: University of Chicago Press, 1987). See also Cynthia Horan, "Beyond Governing Coalitions," *Journal of Urban Affairs* 13, no. 1 (1991).

26. Lewis Mumford, *The Highway and the City* (New York: Harcourt, Brace & World, 1953), 238.

27. Le Corbusier, *City of Tomorrow*, 5–12.

28. This and the preceding quotations are from Vincent Scully, "The Threat and the Promise of Urban Redevelopment in New Haven," *Zodiac* 17, no. 1 (1967).

29. Richard C. Lee, July 22, 1966.

30. Scully, "America's Nightmare."

31. The parcels assembled by renewal often failed to generate markets for themselves among developers. In the New Haven case, see particularly Holt, "Downtown Renewal Land Conversion."

32. Gans, "Failure of Urban Renewal," 537.

33. Alvin A. Mermin, *Relocating Families* (Washington, D.C.: NAHRO, 1970), 4. Mermin, who served ten years as director of Family Relocation, is taken as a primary source for purposes of this discussion.

34. This mandate, and the necessary funding, applied only to victims of renewal, not to those whose homes were taken for highway construction, creating serious equity problems for the people administering the program.

35. Fainstein et al., *Restructuring the City.*

36. The 2.9:1 ratio comes from New Haven's section of the 1960 U.S. Census. Note that this is not equal to the population divided by the number of households, since some persons were attributed to nonhousehold units.

37. Not all were instances of compulsion in a substantive sense. In some cases, residents doubtless welcomed the chance to move and to have help with the costs entailed by it.

38. All these data are from Alvin Mermin, "Papers of Alvin Mermin" (1970). The daily case log kept by Mermin is in Box VII of his papers at the New Haven Colony Historical Society. The side streets included here are Lafayette, Commerce, Spruce, Hill, York, Park, and a section of Congress.

39. Names and original addresses come from Mermin's daily logs. Later addresses come from the 1960 city directory.

40. Among the leading figures in this Oak Street Alumni movement are Vincent Inglese, Warren Kimbro, Mickey Kliger, Sherman Kramer, Leonard Margolis, and Joseph Ciaburri. The New Haven Colony Historical Society distributes a film in which they and others recount life in the Oak Street neighborhood, titled *New Haven Renewed?*

41. Computed from Mermin, "Papers," 127.

42. Computed on the limited basis of 4,601 families in Mermin, "Papers," 127.

43. Two tracts, 1402 and 1403, are left aside for this analysis, since their boundaries shifted radically. It is, for this purpose, clear that both would have lost white population if the comparison could be made with any accuracy.

44. It may be supposed that Lee targeted opposition wards for urban renewal or highway bulldozers. Peter Hall, for instance, seems to suggest as much. But note that Lee's own 17th Ward lost more population than any other in the city during his administration. See Hall, "Vital Signs."

45. See, for instance, Dana, *New Haven's Problems.*

46. Luke E. Hart, letter to Richard C. Lee, April 1, 1959. Sterling Library, Yale University, Manuscripts and Archives.

47. David Fishman, letter to Richard C. Lee, February 17, 1959. Sterling Library, Yale University, Manuscripts and Archives.

48. The project ran from Chapel to George, and from Church to Temple.

49. This shrewd test is explored at length in many cities in Alexander Garvin, *The American City* (New York: McGraw-Hill, 1996). Garvin's specific judgment of Lee's New Haven, especially of its downtown renewal effort, is decidedly negative. "From the start, redeveloping downtown New Haven was a mistake" (129). Garvin is more positive in evaluating renewal in Oak Street and Wooster Square (211). See also Robert M. Fogelson, *Downtown: Its Rise and Fall, 1880–1950* (New Haven: Yale University Press, 2001).

50. Marris and Rein, *Dilemmas of Social Reform.*

51. "Opening Opportunities" (New Haven: Community Progress, Inc., 1962). Discussed by Marris and Rein, *Dilemmas*, 36ff. Discussed and quoted in Powledge, *Model City,* 51–52.

52. Asbell, "Dick Lee Discovers How Much Is Not Enough."

53. See Marris and Rein, *Dilemmas*, esp. 25–26.

54. See Wolfinger, *Politics of Progress*, 198.

55. "Community Action Policy Review" (New Haven: CPI, 1965).

56. See Miller, *Fifteenth Ward and the Great Society*, chaps. 3–6.

57. Edgar Cahn and Jean Cahn, "The War on Poverty: A Civilian Perspective," *Yale Law Journal* 73, no. 8 (1964).

58. Asbell, "Dick Lee Discovers How Much Is Not Enough."

59. Ibid.

60. In 1966, CPI staffer Peter Almond would report: "They would call meetings, at which their programs were discussed. There was never, at least at any meetings I ever attended, any opening where the citizen's word would have any kind of direct and obvious impact. . . . And that is where CPI and the city and the mayor are failing, as far as I'm concerned." Quoted in Powledge, *Model City,* 143.

61. Robert Giaimo, "Investigation into the Operation of Community Progress, Inc." (Washington, D.C.: Congressional Record, 1968).

62. Howard Shuman, "Behind the Scenes and Under the Rug," *Washington Monthly,* 1969.

63. "Old Industrial City Wages Dramatic War on Poverty," *Trenton Sunday Times Advertiser,* July 12, 1964. Quoted in Powledge, *Model City.*

64. Although this quote is often repeated in the secondary literature, I have been unable to find a primary source for it.

65. Quoted in Powledge, *Model City,* 149.

66. All quotations and facts in this section are taken from stories in the *New Haven Register* for August 20, 21, and 22, 1967.

67. *Kerner Commission Report* (New York: Pantheon, 1968).

68. *New Haven Register,* August 22, 1967.

69. "Annual Report of the City of New Haven" (1964). Quoted also in Talbot, *Mayor's Game,* 66.

70. Dahl, *Who Governs?* 294.

71. Mitchell Sviridoff, "Problems of Leadership in the Negro Community" (1959).

72. *Kerner Commission Report.* The quote appears on p. 149 of the original Government Printing Office version.

73. Ford Foundation Review Team, "Report to John R. Coleman" (New York: Ford Foundation, 1967). Discussed in Powledge, *Model City,* 134–42.

74. Giaimo, "Investigation," 167.

75. Ibid., 164.

76. I have talked with about twenty individuals, all but one men, who meet at weekly lunches (there are two groups, meeting Wednesdays and Thursdays, respectively) to remember Oak Street before renewal. In hindsight, they can tell you about no end of good features there.

77. Dreier, Mollenkopf, and Swanstrom, *Place Matters.*

78. Mrs. Russell Bacon, letter to Mayor Richard C. Lee, 1955.

CHAPTER 11. THE END OF URBANISM

1. "Annual Report of the New Haven Redevelopment Agency" (New Haven: City of New Haven, 1967), 40.
2. Data reported in this analysis come from the U.S Census of Manufacturing for the relevant years and is supplemented by Connecticut Department of Labor data for recent years. The spike of regional manufacturing shown for 1967 is difficult to reconcile with other observations.
3. The included towns are Ansonia, Beacon Falls, Bethany, Branford, Cheshire, Derby, East Haven, Guilford, Hamden, Madison, Middlebury, Milford, Naugatuck, New Haven, North Branford, North Haven, Orange, Oxford, Prospect, Seymour, Southbury, Wallingford, West Haven, Wolcott, and Woodbridge.
4. A particularly instructive case is offered by the corporate history of Seton Nameplate, which was a 1956 start-up in the city of New Haven, and whose management actively sought to stay in the city for years as the company grew and required more and better space. Eventually, Seton was bought out by a Canadian firm, and, still selling under its original name, has manufacturing facilities in suburban New Haven. Fenmore R. Seton, *A Seton Memoir: Seton Name Plate Corporation, the Early Years, 1956–81* (North Haven: N.p., 1995).
5. In this section I rely particularly on Dobrow, "Farewell to Arms." See also Houze, *Winchester Repeating Arms Company*, esp. 304–22.
6. See Bill Miller, "Winchester Before '64 and After," *American Rifleman* (1989). See also Houze, *Winchester Repeating Arms Company*, 309.
7. From Miller, "Winchester Before '64 and After." Quoted in Dobrow, "Farewell to Arms."
8. I rely heavily in the following paragraphs on William Doyle, *"Olin Corporation v. Frank Logue"* (New Haven, 1998), in New Haven Colony Historical Society Library.
9. Doyle, *"Olin Corporation v. Frank Logue,"* 4.
10. Ibid., 5.
11. Ibid., 8–11.
12. Dobrow, "Farewell to Arms," 46.
13. There are a few exceptional stories in New Haven's retail grocery business today. The most striking is perhaps Ferraro's Food Center on Grand Avenue, just across from Farnam Court public housing. This is a locally owned and managed store of about 20,000 square feet, selling both the regular goods of everyday life for a low-income clientele, and the best fancy meats in the city for those who can afford them.
14. See, among other sources, Fainstein, *Restructuring the City*. These authors estimate 2,216 business relocations, or attempted relocations. While conflicting figures both higher and lower can be generated from redevelopment documents, the exact number is unimportant to the broad conclusion being sought here.
15. I say "approximate" because the curve is based on only the years indicated on the time scale, and is smoothed arbitrarily for intervening years. Thus, for instance, a great dip in 1942–45, followed by a compensating surge in 1945–47, would be missed altogether.
16. The apposite twenty years were 1950–70. Note that the number of stores going out of

business will always be larger than the net decline in store count. As shown below, however, the gap declines sharply in this period, as entry grows rarer and rarer.

17. For instance, 533 store sites were extinguished between 1923 and 1935, but the starting total of 834 is quite different from the 1950 start at 492.

18. Estimates based on city directory data for relevant years in the two cities.

19. To be exact here, a new site at a given point (say 1960) is one not housing a grocery in the immediately previous period (1950). Some sites thus count as new even if they were occupied at a still earlier time (1923). Others may fail to be counted if their birth and death are between our observation years—for example, a store founded in 1924 and dead in 1934 would be missed. This imperfection aside, I am confident that the broad story being told here is sound.

20. See, among others, William Leach, *Land of Desire* (New York: Vintage, 1993), and Satterthwaite, *Going Shopping.*

21. Jeff Hardwick, "A Downtown Utopia?" *Planning History Studies* 10 (1996): 41–54.

22. Garvin, *American City*, 129. The planners clearly ignored one market study of New Haven, written a decade earlier, that correctly predicted slackening of demand for housing and, by implication, retail. See Wenzlick, "Housing and Construction in the New Haven Area."

23. Garvin, *American City*, 12.

24. See, for instance, Duany, Plater-Zyberk, and Speck, *Suburban Nation*. See also Katz, *New Urbanism.*

25. The number of towns starts out at ten, before West Haven is chartered in 1921. The total envelope of places nevertheless remains constant, since West Haven was carved out of Orange.

26. The grand list data shown as 2000 actually represent the equalized net grand lists for fiscal year 1999, as compiled by the Connecticut Office of Policy and Management. Earlier data are derived from a variety of state publications for each year shown.

27. See Chapter 7.

28. A fine interpretive discussion is offered by Putnam, *Bowling Alone*, esp. chap. 13.

29. See, in particular, Hall, "Vital Signs." See also Beito, *From Mutual Aid to the Welfare State.*

30. Schlesinger, "Biography of a Nation of Joiners."

31. Putnam, *Bowling Alone*, 216–17.

32. Kay Lehman Schlozman, Sidney Verba, and Henry E. Brady, "Civic Participation and the Equality Problem," in *Civic Engagement in American Democracy*, edited by Theda Skocpol and Morris Fiorina (Washington, D.C.: Brookings Institution Press, 1999).

33. Rae, "Elm Haven's Baseline Study."

34. Moreover, the analysis given here does include new births within the fraternal brands represented.

35. Hall, "Vital Signs," table 6.

36. See Schlesinger, "Biography of a Nation of Joiners."

37. Hall, "Vital Signs," 221.

38. See, e.g., Skocpol, "How Americans Became Civic."

39. Hall, "Vital Signs," 203.

40. Ibid., table 6.1.

41. A classic statement of this point from the period is offered by Rolf Goetz, *Understanding Neighborhood Change* (Cambridge: Ballinger, 1979). See also Richard P. Taylor, D. Garth Taub, and Jan D. Dunham, *Paths of Neighborhood Change* (Chicago: University of Chicago Press, 1984). A policy overview from the period in question is offered by Harry J. Wexler and Richard Peck, *Housing and Local Government* (Lexington, Mass: Lexington Books, 1975).

42. Some leading examples would include Howard Avenue in the Hill district and East Pearl Street in Fair Haven.

43. Especially in the early years, many tenants were working full time, and to this day a certain percentage are doing so. Often, alas, the figure is around 20 percent.

44. Housing Authority of the City of New Haven, "Tenant Income Analysis," February 20, 1992.

45. See Hays, *Federal Government and Urban Housing*, esp. chaps. 5 and 6. It is worth noting that two other housing programs—federal Section 8 and Connecticut Rental Assistance Program (RAP)—between them add about 5,000 low-income family units to New Haven's inventory.

46. At that time, $7,500 for a family of four was the line of demarcation, with various adjustments for households of different types and sizes.

47. "The Extent, Distribution, and Causes of Poverty in New Haven" (New Haven: City of New Haven, 1983). David Rusk would soon generalize the point about annexation into the notion of regional elasticity in his influential *Cities Without Suburbs* (Washington, D.C.: Woodrow Wilson Center Press, 1993).

48. The leading figure in this analysis is of course William Julius Wilson. See his *The Declining Significance of Race* (Chicago: University of Chicago Press, 1978), *The Truly Disadvantaged* (Chicago: University of Chicago Press, 1987), and *When Work Disappears*.

49. Seale's trial ended in a hung jury. One useful summary of the incident is provided by Robert J. Leeney, *Elms, Arms, and Ivy* (Montgomery, Ala.: Community Communications, 2000), 75ff.

50. *New Haven Register*, January 31, 1971.

51. Source: Uniform Crime Reports from the FBI.

52. Four years were exceptional: 1905, 1906, 1917, and 1918, all exceeding ten homicides.

53. See Steven B. Gross and Albert C. Duke, *America's Longest War* (New York: G. P. Putnam and Sons, 1993), David B. Kopel, "Prison Blues," *Policy Analysis* (Cato Institute) (1994). In a more popular vein, see Eric Schlosser, "Reefer Madness," *Atlantic Monthly*, August 1994.

54. In New Haven, a fine piece of journalism made the story national. See William Finnegan, "A Reporter at Large: Out There," *New Yorker*, September 10, 1990, and September 17, 1990.

55. Becky Pettit and Bruce Western, "Inequality in Lifetime Risks of Imprisonment" (forthcoming). This is one in a series of papers, with Western as an author, sponsored by the Russell Sage Foundation exploring these remarkable rates of imprisonment.

56. See, for instance, Le Corbusier, *City of Tomorrow and Its Planning*.

CHAPTER 12. A CITY AFTER URBANISM

1. The vocabulary here is derived from Albert O. Hirschman, *Exit, Voice, and Loyalty: Responses to Decline in Firms, Organizations, and States* (Cambridge: Harvard University Press, 1970).

2. This is essentially the same impulse as John Stilgoe's American come-outer trope discussed in Chapter 1. See Stilgoe, *Borderland*.

3. This remarkable project created 17,500 homes on what had been agricultural land between 1947 and 1951. The reference here is to architecture and landscaping, not sociology. This tract development, unlike Levittown, is small in scale. The classic work on Levittown is of course Herbert Gans, *The Levittowners* (New York: Columbia University Press, 1967, 1982). A useful work, giving more stress to the creation of the project, is John Thomas Leill, "Levittown" (Ph.D. diss., Yale University, 1952). See also Rosalyn Baxandall and Elizabeth Ewen, *Picture Window* (New York: Basic Books, 2000).

4. The Perfetto home, and its neighbors, closely resemble what Dolores Hayden describes as the "dream home" of the 1950s. See Dolores Hayden, *Redesigning the American Dream* (New York: Norton, 1984).

5. *New Haven Register*, February 25, 1952. Cited in Leill, "Levittown."

6. Jane Bushnell Shepherd, *My Old New Haven and Other Memories Briefly Told* (New Haven: Tuttle, Morehouse & Taylor, 1932), 1.

7. Dwight, *Travels in New England and New York (1822)*, 4 vols., 1: 131, 141.

8. Fishman, *Bourgeois Utopias*, 5–6.

9. Jackson, *Crabgrass Frontier*, 6.

10. Weber, "Significance of Recent City Growth."

11. Fishman, *Bourgeois Utopias*, 15.

12. Ford, *My Life and Work*, 73. Ford is quoting his own early announcement of the Model T here.

13. *New Haven Register*, February 24, 1952. Discussed in Leill, "*Levittown*," 72, and Baxandall and Ewen, *Picture Window*.

14. Until 1921, West Haven was a borough within the town of Orange. Largely because of its increasing density and its industrial tenor, West Haven was created as a Connecticut town by the General Assembly in 1921. The records to which I refer are thus, strictly speaking, developments within Orange at the time.

15. I use the word "hope" here advisedly. Few developers managed anything like 100 percent sales on these projects.

16. See Haar and Kayden, *Zoning and the American Dream*, and especially Rabin, "Expulsive Zoning." See also Anthony Downs, *Opening Up the Suburbs* (New Haven: Yale University Press, 1973). In connection with declining central cities, see Witold Rybcynski, "Downsizing Cities," Wharton Real Estate Center Research Impact Paper #5 (Wharton School of the University of Pennsylvania, 1994). A useful institutional overview is offered by Anne B. Shlay, "Shaping Place," *Journal of Urban Affairs* 15 (1993).

17. PILOT, "payment in lieu of taxes," compensates municipalities for the tax impact of university and hospital facilities. It was instituted in the late 1970s with a major lobby-

ing effort from Yale University and its Office of the Secretary during the term of Henry ("Sam") Chauncey, Jr.

18. This phenomenon is put in national perspective by Dreier, Mollenkopf, and Swanstrom, *Place Matters*. See also Orfield, *Metropolitics*.

19. Here are the data by household from the 2000 Census:

Town	Less than $10,000	Percentage of pro rata share	$10,000–$15,000	Percentage of pro rata share	$15,000–$25,000	Percentage of pro rata share
Woodbridge	88	28.0	47	24.8	95	28.4
Orange	115	24.0	171	59.2	248	48.5
Madison	150	22.8	176	44.4	339	48.2
North Branford	151	29.1	169	54.0	310	55.9
Guilford	225	27.4	183	36.9	452	51.5
North Haven	363	41.8	217	41.4	503	54.2
Branford	543	42.9	627	82.1	1,075	79.5
East Haven	840	74.3	579	84.9	1,177	97.4
Hamden	1,538	68.2	1,276	93.8	2,305	95.7
West Haven	1,736	81.6	1,384	107.9	2,683	118.1
New Haven	9,447	198.6	4,335	151.1	7,041	138.6

20. Some of these towns did not exist in 1800, but the comparisons remain more or less valid, since the new towns were carved out of older ones. The sole exception is Orange, which captured a piece of Milford when it was carved from New Haven and Milford in 1822. The effect is not major (Milford had fewer than 3,000 citizens before losing a piece). Madison was carved from Guilford in 1826. North Branford was carved from Branford in 1831. The latest to emerge was West Haven, in 1921.

21. Jon Nordheimer, "Lee's Bowing Out Pleases New Haven Democratic Chief," *New York Times*, July 13, 1969, p. 48.

22. An early analysis of the GOP crash is provided by Philip Allan Singerman, "Politics, Bureaucracy, and Public Policy" (Ph.D. diss., Yale University, 1980), esp. chap. 6. Singerman's sophisticated analysis attributes much of the GOP's decline to the impact of Lee's alternative government structures, such as the Kremlin and CPI, along with the principal patterns noted here.

23. In 1967, 30 percent of the total population voted for mayor. In 2001, just over 15 percent did so.

24. Long ago, thoughtful observers of public administration concluded that civil service protection might create a quite unresponsive and perhaps excessively independent government workforce. See, for instance, Woodrow Wilson, "The Study of Administration," *Political Science Quarterly* 2, no. 2 (1887): 197–222.

25. Source: Payroll files, City of New Haven, February 1991.

26. Data for the city payroll as of the first quarter of 1991 reveal the following illustrative

distributions. Among 69 employees earning over $70,000, 50 (72 percent) lived in the suburbs. Of 732 earning $50,000 to $60,000, 68 percent were living in the suburbs. Of 1,458 earning less than $30,000, 77 percent were living in the city.

27. See Douglas Yates, *The Ungovernable City: The Politics of Urban Problems and Policy Making* (Cambridge: MIT Press, 1977), and Yates, "Urban Government as a Policy-Making System," in *The New Urban Politics*, edited by Louis H. Masotti and Robert L. Lineberry (Cambridge: Ballinger, 1976).

28. Yates, *Ungovernable City*, 244.

29. On these and related policy problems, see Avis C. Vidal, "Rebuilding Communities" (Community Development Research Center, Graduate School of Management and Urban Policy, New School for Social Research, 1992).

30. For an analysis specific to New Haven in this period, using Yates's notion of street-fighting pluralism, see Fainstein, *Restructuring the City*.

31. Michael Lerner, "Respectable Bigotry," in *Overcoming Middle-Class Rage*, edited by Murray Friedman (Philadelphia: Westminster, 1971).

32. The GOP had, for all practical purposes, disappeared. One interesting analysis of its disappearance is offered by Singerman, "Politics, Bureaucracy and Public Policy," 273ff.

33. Under Chauncey's direction, the Yale Office of the Secretary became an effective and proactive lobbying organization during the 1970s.

34. Dahl, *Who Governs?*

35. Ibid., 214.

36. Ibid.

37. Ibid., 85–86.

38. Dahl, *Who Governs?*

39. The best and most nuanced account of the events leading Dahl to his conclusions remains Wolfinger, *Politics of Progress*. A more popular account, covering many of the same events, is offered by Talbot, *Mayor's Game*.

40. Domhoff, *Who Really Rules?*

41. Ibid., 20.

42. Ibid.

43. Frug, *City Making*.

44. Domhoff, *Who Really Rules?* 76.

45. The current ranking turns out to be fourth nationally.

46. A common fact in many cities. See especially Stone, *Regime Politics*.

47. A complex literature seeks to deal with these issues in the political science literature. Of special interest would be John Gaventa, *Power and Powerlessness: Quiescence and Rebellion in an Appalachian Valley* (Urbana: University of Illinois Press, 1980). See also Steven Lukes, *Power: A Radical View* (London: Macmillan, 1974); Jeffrey C. Isaac, *Power and Marxist Theory: A Realist View* (Ithaca, N.Y.: Cornell University Press, 1987). A decidedly original slant is offered by Clarissa Rile Hayward, *De-Facing Power* (Cambridge: Cambridge University Press, 2000).

48. Dahl, *Who Governs?* 85–86.

49. Dahl observed in the Lee era that political resources were used with a great deal of

"slack"—people could have applied more resources to controlling outcomes than they in fact did apply to that purpose. In later decades, slack is greatly increased, and very few people are applying their maximum effort to managing the DTC or the city at large. See Dahl, *Who Governs?* 270ff. Dahl writes, for example, that "most citizens use their political resources scarcely at all" (270). See also Singerman, "Politics, Bureaucracy, and Public Policy."

50. Hirschman, *Exit, Voice, and Loyalty.*
51. My own speculations on this point are offered in Rae, "Viacratic America."
52. See, among others, Joel Kotkin, *The New Geography* (New York: Random House, 2000).
53. The resurgence of small-scale retailing evident on Grand Avenue in Fair Haven is energized in considerable degree by Hispanic newcomers.
54. It is easy to err on this point. For example, I personally regret some of my earlier work on the geography of crime, which further tended to stigmatize certain parts of New Haven.
55. Jacobs, *Death and Life of Great American Cities*, chap. 3.
56. Frug, *City Making*, esp. chap. 6.
57. Sennett, *Uses of Disorder.*
58. As with New Haven's Homes at Monterey, the new version of the old Elm Haven project.
59. Fred Siegel, *The Future Once Happened Here: New York, D.C., L.A., and the Fate of America's Big Cities* (New York: Free Press, 1997), 197. See also Robert Ellickson, "Controlling Chronic Misconduct in City Spaces: Of Panhandlers, Skid Rows, and Public-Space Zoning," *Yale Law Journal* 105, no. 1165 (1996).
60. Giamatti, *Take Time for Paradise*, 49.
61. Robert D. Yaro and Tony Hiss, *A Region at Risk* (Washington, D.C.: Island, 1996).
62. *New Haven Register,* January 29, 1973.
63. Ibid., February 1, 1973.
64. Ibid., March 7, 1973.
65. *New York Times*, November 30, 1973.
66. "Economic Impact" (New Haven: Yale Office of the Secretary, 1993), 9.

BIBLIOGRAPHY

Adelman, Morris Albert. *A&P: A Study in Price Cost Behavior and Public Policy.* Cambridge: Harvard University Press, 1959.

Akin, Edward N. *Flagler: Rockefeller Partner and Florida Baron.* Gainesville: University Press of Florida, 1988.

Aldermanic Committee on Streets and Squares. *Statement of Mayor Richard C. Lee,* October 13, 1959.

Allen, Zachariah. *Practical Tourist or Sketches of the State of the Useful Arts of Society.* Boston, 1832.

Andrews, Norris C. "Davenport-Eaton and 52 Rods." *Journal of the New Haven Colony Historical Society* 33, no. 1 (1986): 3–14.

"Annual Report." New Haven: Redevelopment Agency of New Haven, 1967.

"Annual Report of the New Haven Redevelopment Agency." New Haven: City of New Haven, 1967.

Annunziato, Frank R. "Made in New Haven: Unionization and the Shaping of a Clothing Workers' Community." *Labor Heritage* 4 (Winter 1992): 20–33.

Appleby, Joyce. *Inheriting the Revolution: The First Generation of Americans.* Cambridge: Harvard University Press, 2000.

Arnold, E. H. "Playgrounds of New Haven." *Saturday Chronicle,* January 2, 1915, 1.

Asbell, Bernard. "Dick Lee Discovers How Much Is Not Enough." *New York Times Magazine,* September 3, 1967.

Atack, Jeremy, et al. "The Regional Diffusion and Adoption of the Steam Engine in American Manufacturing." *Journal of Economic History* 40 (1980): 281–308.

Atack, Jeremy, and Peter Passell. *A New Economic View of American History from Colonial Times to 1940.* New York: Norton, 1979.

Atwater, Edward E., ed. *History of the City of New Haven to the Present Time*. 2 vols. New York: Munsell, 1887.

Bachrach, Peter, and Morton Baratz. "The Two Faces of Power." *American Political Science Review* 56 (November 1962): 947–52.

Bacon, Mrs. Russell. "Letter to Mayor Lee." Yale Manuscripts and Archives, Richard C. Lee Papers, 1955.

Banfield, Edward C. *The Unheavenly City: The Nature of Our Urban Crisis*. Boston: Little, Brown, 1970.

Barton, Bob. "Twentieth-Century Sports: The 1900s." *New Haven Register*, December 22, 1999, C3.

Bass, Paul. "Mayor Campaigns for History's Vote." *New Haven Independent*, June 11, 1987.

———. "Developer Lynn Fusco Doesn't Pull Punches." *New Haven Independent*, February 12, 1987.

Baxandall, Rosalyn, and Elizabeth Ewen. *Picture Window: How the Suburbs Happened*. New York: Basic Books, 2000.

Beach, Randall. "Longyear Hurt by Rejection." *New Haven Register*, 1979, p. 47.

Beauregard, Robert A. *Voices of Decline: The Postwar Fate of U.S. Cities*. 2nd ed. New York: Routledge, 2003.

Bechard, Gorman. *Ninth Square*. New York: Tom Doherty, 2002.

Beito, David T. *From Mutual Aid to the Welfare State: Fraternal Societies and Social Services, 1890–1967*. Chapel Hill: University of North Carolina Press, 2000.

Beito, David T. "To Advance the 'Practical Thrift & Economy': Fraternal Societies and Social Capital, 1890–1920." *Journal of Interdisciplinary History* 29 (Spring 1999): 585–612.

Beito, David T., Peter Gordon, and Alexander Tabarrok, eds. *The Voluntary City: Choice, Community, and Civil Society*. Ann Arbor: University of Michigan Press, 2002.

Bello, Ralph. "Letter to Mayor Lee." Yale Manuscripts and Archives, Richard C. Lee Papers, 1955.

Benham's New Haven Directory and Annual Advertiser. New Haven: J. H. Benham, 1852.

Bettmann, Otto L. *The Good Old Days—They Were Terrible*. New York: Random House, 1974.

Biggs, Lindy. *The Rational Factory: Architecture, Technology, and Work in America's Age of Mass Production*. Baltimore: Johns Hopkins University Press, 1996.

Birch, David, et al. *Patterns of Urban Change: The New Haven Experience*. New York: D.C. Heath, 1974.

Bishop, J. Leander. *A History of American Manufactures from 1608 to 1860*. Vol. 3. Philadelphia: Edward Young, 1868.

Bissinger, Buzz. *A Prayer for the City*. New York: Random House, 1997.

Blake, Henry T. *Chronicles of New Haven Green from 1638 to 1862*. New Haven: Tuttle, Morehouse & Taylor, 1898.

Blake, William P. "Sketch of the Life of Eli Whitney." *Papers of the New Haven Colony Historical Society* 5 (1894), 109–31.

Blakely, Edward J., and Mary Gail Snyder. *Fortress America: Gated Communities in the United States*. Washington, D.C.: Brookings Institution Press, 1997.

"Blight and Urban Renewal: Connecticut Interregional Planning Program, Technical Report 123." Hartford: Connecticut Development Commission, 1963.

Bloom, Nicholas D. *Suburban Alchemy: 1960 New Towns and the Transformation of the American Dream.* Columbus: Ohio State University Press, 2001.

Bodnar, John. *The Transplanted: A History of Immigrants in Urban America.* Bloomington: Indiana University Press, 1987.

Braudel, Fernand. *Afterthoughts on Material Civilization and Capitalism.* Translated by Patricia M. Ranum. Baltimore: Johns Hopkins University Press, 1977.

———. *Capitalism and Material Life, 1400–1800.* Translated by Miriam Kochan. New York: Harper & Row, 1973.

Brown, Elizabeth Mills. *New Haven: A Guide to Architecture and Urban Design.* New Haven: Yale University Press, 1976.

Bucki, Cecelia. *Bridgeport's Socialist New Deal, 1915–36.* Urbana: University of Illinois Press, 2001.

Burnham, Daniel H., and Edward H. Bennett. *Plan of Chicago (1909).* New York: Princeton Architectural Press, 1993.

Cahn, Edgar, and Jean Cahn. "The War on Poverty: A Civilian Perspective." *Yale Law Journal* 73, no. 8 (1964).

Cain, John F. "The Influence of Race and Income on Racial Segregation and Housing Policy." In *Housing Desegregation and Federal Policy,* edited by John M. Goering, 99–118. Chapel Hill: University of North Carolina Press, 1986.

Calder, Isabel MacBeath. *The New Haven Colony.* New Haven: Yale University Press, 1962.

Calthorpe, Peter. *The New American Metropolis: Ecology, Community, and the American Dream.* New York: Princeton Architectural Press, 1986.

Caplan, Ruth Ginsberg. "Harris Ginsberg of State Street." *Jews in New Haven* 6 (1993): 123–35.

Cappel, Andrew J. "A Walk Along Willow: Patterns of Land Use Coordination in Pre-Zoning New Haven (1870–1926)." *Yale Law Journal* 101, no. 3 (1991): 617–42.

Carnegie, Andrew. *Triumphant Democracy.* New York: Charles Scribner's Sons, 1886.

Caskey, John. *Fringe Banking: Check-Cashing Outlets, Pawnshops, and the Poor.* New York: Russell Sage Foundation, 1992.

Celentano, William C. "Annual Message of Hon. William Celentano, Mayor, City of New Haven, to the Board of Aldermen." New Haven: City of New Haven, 1947.

———. "Your City's Progress in Black and White." New Haven: City of New Haven, 1946.

Chandler, Alfred D. "The Large Industrial Corporation and the Making of the Modern American Economy." In *The Essential Alfred Chandler: Essays Toward a Historical Theory of Big Business,* ed. Thomas K. McCraw. Boston: Harvard Business School Press, 1988.

———. *Strategy and Structure: Chapters in the History of the Industrial Enterprise.* Cambridge: MIT Press, 1962.

———. *The Visible Hand: The Managerial Revolution in American Business.* Cambridge: Belknap Press of Harvard University Press, 1977.

Chepaitis, Joseph B. *The University of New Haven: A Celebration of Learning.* South Bend, Ind.: Carlton, 1995.

Chiel, Arthur. "Looking Back." *Connecticut Jewish Ledger,* November 16, 1972.

Christiansen, Clayton M. *The Innovator's Dilemma.* New York: Harper Business, 1997.

City Directory of New Haven. New Haven: Price & Lee, 1913, 1923.

"City of New Haven Teacher's Manual." New Haven: City of New Haven, 1925–48.

"City Year Book of the City of New Haven." New Haven: City of New Haven, 1913–57.

Clark, Collin. "Transport: Maker and Breaker of Cities." *Town Planning Review* 28 (1957): 237–50.

Clark, Victor S. *History of Manufactures in the United States.* 3 vols. New York: McGraw-Hill, 1929.

Coleman, James S. "Social Capital and the Creation of Human Capital." *American Journal of Sociology* 94 (1989): 95–120.

"Community Action Policy Review." New Haven: CPI, 1965.

Le Corbusier. *The City of Tomorrow and Its Planning.* Translated by Frederick Etchells. New York: Dover, 1987.

Creveling, Harold F. "Mapping Cultural Groups in an American Industrial City." *Economic Geography* 31, no. 4 (1955): 364–71.

Cronon, William. *Nature's Metropolis: Chicago and the Great West.* New York: Norton, 1991.

Cross, Gary, and Rick Szostak. *Technology and American History: A History.* Englewood Cliffs, N.J.: Prentice Hall, 1995.

Cumbler, John T. *A Social History of Economic Decline.* New Brunswick, N.J.: Rutgers University Press, 1989.

Cupelli, Alberto. *The Italians of Old New Haven.* Branford, Conn.: Branford Printing, 1972.

Dahl, Robert A. *Who Governs? Democracy and Power in an American City.* New Haven: Yale University Press, 1961.

Dana, Arnold Guyot. *New Haven's Problems: Whither the City? All Cities?* New Haven: N.p., 1937.

Danielson, Michael. *The Politics of Exclusion.* New York: Columbia University Press, 1976.

David, Paul A. "The Hero and the Herd in Technological History: Reflections on Thomas Edison and the Battle of Systems." In *Favorites of Fortune: Technology, Growth, and Economic Development in the Industrial Revolution,* edited by Patrice Higonett, 72–119. Cambridge: Harvard University Press, 1991.

Davis, Mike. *Magical Urbanism: Latinos Reinvent the U.S. City.* London: Verso, 2000.

Deming, Horace E. *The Government of American Cities.* New York: G. P. Putnam's Sons, 1909.

"Depot Architect Is with Mr. Seymour." *New Haven Evening Register,* June 6, 1907.

Devine, Warren D. Jr. "From Shafts to Wires: Historical Perspectives on Electrification." *Journal of Economic History* 43, no. 2 (1983): 347–72.

Dix, William. "The Automobile as Vacation Agent." *Independent,* June 2, 1904.

Dobrow, Joseph. "A Farewell to Arms: The Mutual Rise and Fall of the Winchester Repeating Arms Company and New Haven, Connecticut." *Journal of the New Haven Colony Historical Society* 39, no. 2 (1992): 20–65.

Domhoff, G. William. *Who Really Rules? New Haven and Community Power Reexamined.* New Brunswick, N.J.: Transaction, 1978.

Donohue, William T. "Memo to the Mayor Re Father Sanders." 1962.

Doolittle, Amos. "Plan of the City of New Haven." New Haven, 1824.

Downs, Anthony. *Opening up the Suburbs: An Urban Strategy for America.* New Haven: Yale University Press, 1973.

Doyle, William. "*Olin Corporation v. Frank Logue:* The Limits of Police Power." In New Haven Colony Historical Society Library. New Haven, 1998.

Dreier, Peter, John Mollenkopf, and Todd Swanstrom. *Place Matters: Metropolitics for the Twenty-First Century.* Lawrence: University of Kansas Press, 2001.

Dries, Thelma A. *A Handbook of Social Statistics of New Haven, Connecticut.* New Haven: Yale University Press, 1936.

Duany, Andres, and Elizabeth Plater-Zyberk. "Neighborhoods and Suburbs." *Design Quarterly* 164 (Spring 1995): 10–23.

Duany, Andres, Elizabeth Plater-Zyberk, and Jeff Speck. *Suburban Nation: The Rise of Sprawl and the Decline of the American Dream.* New York: Farrar, Straus, Giroux, 2000.

Duggan, Thomas S. *The Catholic Church in Connecticut.* New York: States History Co., 1930.

Duke, Steven B., and Albert C. Gross. *America's Longest War.* New York: G. P. Putnam and Sons, 1993.

Dwight, Timothy. *Travels in New England and New York (1822).* 4 vols., edited by Barbara Solomon. Cambridge: Harvard University Press, 1969.

"Economic Impact: Yale and New Haven." New Haven: Yale Office of the Secretary, 1993.

Edison, Thomas Alva. "The Dangers of Electric Lighting." *North American Review* (1892): 625–34.

Ehrenhalt, Alan. *The Lost City: Discovering the Forgotten Virtues of Community in the Chicago of the 1950s.* New York: Basic Books, 1995.

Eisinger, Peter. *The Rise of the Entrepreneurial State.* Madison: University of Wisconsin Press, 1989.

Elias, Keith H. *Rites of Manhood: Walter Camp, College Football, and the Revitalization of Upper-Class Masculinity.* Senior essay, Princeton University, 1994.

Elkin, Stephen L. *City and Regime in the American Republic.* Chicago: University of Chicago Press, 1987.

Ellickson, Robert C. "Controlling Chronic Misconduct in City Spaces: Of Panhandlers, Skid Rows, and Public-Space Zoning." *Yale Law Journal* 105, no. 1165 (1996).

———. *Order Without Law: How Neighbors Settle Disputes.* Cambridge: Harvard University Press, 1991.

Elliott, Cecil D. *Technics and Architecture: The Development of Materials and Systems for Building.* Cambridge: MIT Press, 1992.

Erie, Steven P. *Rainbow's End: Irish-Americans and the Dilemmas of Urban Machine Politics, 1840–1985.* Berkeley: University of California Press, 1988.

"The Extent, Distribution, and Causes of Poverty in New Haven." City of New Haven, 1983.

Fahey, Joseph, et al. "The New Haven Farmer's Market and Kitchen Incubator." Unpublished paper, Yale School of Management, 1996.

Fainstein, Susan S., Norman I. Fainstein, Richard Child Hill, Dennis Judd, and Michael Peter Smith. *Restructuring the City: The Political Economy of Urban Redevelopment.* 2nd ed. New York: Longman, 1986.

Fairfield, John D. *The Mysteries of the Great City: The Politics of Urban Design, 1877–1937.* Columbus: Ohio State University Press, 1993.

Fassett, John D. *UI. History of an Electric Company: Problems, Personalities, and Power Politics.* New Haven: United Illuminating, 1990.

Feagin, Joe R. "Arenas of Conflict: Zoning and Land Use Reform in Critical Political-Eco-
nomic Perspective." In *Zoning and the American Dream: Promises Still to Keep,* edited by
Charles M. Haar and Jerold S. Kayden, 73–100. Chicago: Planners Press, 1989.

Filene, Edward A. *The Way Out: A Forecast of Coming Changes in American Business and Industry.* Garden City, N.Y.: Doubleday, Page, 1924.

Finnegan, William. "A Reporter at Large: Out There." Two parts. *New Yorker,* September 10,
1990, 51–86, and September 17, 1990, 60–90.

Fishman, Robert. *Bourgeois Utopias: The Rise and Fall of Suburbia.* New York: Basic Books,
1987.

Fiss, Owen. *A Way Out: America's Ghettos and the Legacy of Racism.* Princeton: Princeton
University Press, 2003.

———. "What Should Be Done for Those Who Haven Been Left Behind?" *Boston Review of
Books,* July–August 2000.

Fitzgerald, David E. "Sixth Annual Message of the Honorable David E. Fitzgerald, Mayor
of the City of New Haven to the Board of Aldermen." New Haven: City of New Haven, 1923.

Flink, James J. *The Car Culture.* Cambridge: MIT Press, 1975.

Fogelson, Robert M. *Downtown: Its Rise and Fall, 1880–1950.* New Haven: Yale University
Press, 2001.

Ford Foundation Review Team. "Report to John R. Coleman." New York: Ford Foundation,
1967.

Ford, Henry. *My Life and Work.* Garden City, N.Y.: Doubleday, Page, 1922.

"Fourth Annual Report of the Housing Authority of New Haven." New Haven: Housing
Authority of New Haven, 1942.

Frank, Robert H. *Choosing the Right Pond: Human Behavior and the Quest for Status.* Oxford:
Oxford University Press, 1985.

Frankel, Karen. "Work and Ethnicity in the Gilded Age: The Diary of Michael Campbell."
Senior essay, Yale University, 1982.

Freedman, Samuel G. *Jew versus Jew: The Struggle for the Soul of American Jewry.* New York:
Simon & Schuster, 2000.

Frieden, Bernard J. *The Future of Old Neighborhoods.* Cambridge: MIT Press, 1964.

Frieden, Bernard J., and Lynne B. Sagalyn. *Downtown, Inc.: How America Rebuilds Cities.*
Cambridge: MIT Press, 1990.

Frug, Gerald. *City Making: Building Communities Without Building Walls.* Princeton: Princeton University Press, 1999.

Galster, George C. "Polarization, Place, and Race." *North Carolina Law Review* 71, no. 5
(June 1993): 1421–61.

———. "White Flight from Racially Integrated Neighborhoods in the 1970s: The Cleveland Experience." *Urban Studies* 27, no. 3 (1990): 385–99.

Gamm, Gerald. *Urban Exodus: Why the Jews Left Boston and the Catholics Stayed.* Cambridge: Harvard University Press, 1999.

Gamm, Gerald, and Robert Putnam. "The Growth of Voluntary Associations in America,
1840–1940." *Journal of Interdisciplinary History* 24 (Spring 1999): 511–57.

Gans, Herbert. *The Levittowners: Ways of Life and Politics in a New Suburban Community.*
New York: Columbia University Press, 1967, 1982.

———. "The Failure of Urban Renewal." In *Urban Renewal: The Record and the Controversy*, edited by James Q. Wilson, 537–57. Cambridge: MIT Press, 1966.

———. "The Negro Family: Reflections on the Moynihan Report." *Commonweal*, October 15, 1965.

Garreau, Joel. *Edge City: Life on the New Frontier*. New York: Doubleday, 1988.

Garvin, Alexander. *The American City: What Works, What Doesn't*. New York: McGraw-Hill, 1996.

Gates, Henry Louis Jr. "Two Nations, Both Black." *Forbes* 150 (1992): 132–35.

Gaventa, John. *Power and Powerlessness: Quiescence and Rebellion in an Appalachian Valley*. Urbana: University of Illinois Press, 1980.

Geismar, Ludwig L., and Jane Krisberg. *The Forgotten Neighborhood: Site of an Early Skirmish in the War on Poverty*. Metuchen, N.J.: Scarecrow, 1967.

Giaimo, Robert. "Investigation into the Operation of Community Progress, Inc." *Congressional Record* (1968): 164–67.

Giamatti, A. Bartlett. *Take Time for Paradise: Americans and Their Games*. New York: Summit, 1990.

Gibson, Campbell. "Population of the 100 Largest Cities and Other Urban Places in the United States, 1790 to 1990." *U.S. Bureau of the Census Technical Papers* (1998).

Gibson, Robert A. "A Deferred Dream: The Proposal for a Negro College in New Haven, 1831." *Journal of the New Haven Colony Historical Society* 37, no. 1 (1991): 23–29.

Gilbert, Cass, and Frederick Law Olmsted. "Report of the Civic Improvement Committee." New Haven Civic Improvement Committee, 1910.

Gillette, Jonathan. "Inside Contracting at Sargent Hardware Company: A Case Study of a Factory in Transition at the Turn of the Century." *Theory and Society* 17 (1988): 159–77.

Gilpin, Tony, et al. *On Strike for Respect: The Clerical and Technical Workers' Strike at Yale University, 1984–5*. Chicago: Charles Kerr, 1988.

Glaeser, Edward. "Why Economists Still Like Cities." *City Journal* (Spring 1996): 70–77.

Glaeser, Edward, and Jesse M. Shapiro. "City Growth: Which Places Grew and Why." In *Redefining Urban and Suburban America: Evidence from Census 2000*, edited by Bruce Katz and Robert E. Lang, 13–32. Washington, D.C.: Brookings Institution Press, 2003.

Goddard, Stephen B. *Getting There: The Epic Struggle Between Roads and Rail in the American Century*. New York: Basic Books, 1994.

Goetz, Rolf. *Understanding Neighborhood Change: The Role of Expectations in Urban Revitalization*. Cambridge: Ballinger, 1979.

Gold, Michael. *Jews Without Money*. Carol & Graf, 1930.

Goldstein, Brandt J. "Panhandlers at Yale: A Case Study in the Limits of Law." *Indiana Law Review* 27, no. 2 (1993): 295–359.

Goodnow, Frank. *City Government in the United States*. New York: Century, 1904.

Gosnell, Harold F. *Machine Politics: Chicago Model*. Chicago: University of Chicago Press, 1937.

Gottdiener, Mark. *The Decline of Political Culture: Political Theory and the Crisis of the Local State*. Newbury Park: Sage, 1987.

Gottmann, Jean. *Megalopolis: The Urbanization of the Northeastern Seaboard of the United States*. Cambridge: Twentieth-Century Fund, 1961.

Green, James R. *The World of the Worker: Labor in Twentieth-Century America.* New York: Hill and Wang, 1980.

Gronovetter, Mark, and Roland Soong. "Threshold Models of Diversity: Chinese Restaurants, Residential Segregation, and the Spiral of Silence." *Sociological Methodology* 18 (1988): 69–104.

Grossman, James R. *Land of Hope: Chicago, Black Southerners, and the Great Migration.* Chicago: University of Chicago Press, 1989.

Gurwitt, Rob. "Rooted in Suburbia: How Generations of a Hamden, Conn., Family Turned a Postwar Neighborhood into a Satisfying Place to Live." *Preservation,* May–June 2000, 42–47.

Gyourko, Joseph, and Richard Voith. "Does the U.S. Tax Treatment of Housing Promote Suburbanization and Central City Decline?" Wharton Real Estate Working Paper. Wharton School of the University of Pennsylvania, 1998.

Haar, Charles M., and Jerold S. Kayden, eds. *Zoning and the American Dream: Promises Still to Keep.* Chicago: Planners Press, 1989.

Hall, Peter. *Great Planning Disasters.* Berkeley: University of California Press, 1982.

Hall, Peter Dobkin. "Is Tax Exemption Intrinsic or Contingent? Tax Treatment of Voluntary Associations, Nonprofit Organizations, and Religious Bodies in New Haven, Connecticut, 1750–2000." In *Property-Tax Exemption for Charities: Mapping the Battlefield,* edited by Evelyn Brody. Washington, D.C.: Urban Institute Press, 2002.

———. "Vital Signs: Organizational Population Trends and Civic Engagement in New Haven, Connecticut, 1850–1998." In *Civic Engagement in American Democracy,* edited by Theda Skocpol and Morris Fiorina. Washington, D.C.: Brookings Institution Press, 1999.

———. "Images of Innovation: The New Haven Water Company, 1894–1906." *Journal of the New Haven Colony Historical Society* 35 (1988): 23–40.

Halpern, Robert. *Rebuilding the Inner City.* New York: Columbia University Press, 1995.

Handlin, Oscar. *Boston's Immigrants: A Study in Acculturation.* 3rd ed. Cambridge: Harvard University Press, 1979.

Hanifan, Lyda Judson. "The Rural Community Center." *Annals of the American Academy of Political and Social Science* 67 (1916): 130–38.

Hardenbergh, Margot B. "The Telephone Connection." *Journal of the New Haven Colony Historical Society* 33, no. 2 (1987): 56–72.

Hardwick, Jeff. "A Downtown Utopia: Suburbanization, Urban Renewal, and Consumption in New Haven." *Planning History Studies* 10 (1996): 41–54.

Harriss, C. Lowell. *History and Policies of the Home Owners' Loan Corporation.* New York: National Bureau of Economic Research, 1951.

Harvey, David. *The Urban Experience.* Baltimore: Johns Hopkins University Press, 1989.

———. *Social Justice and the City.* Baltimore: Johns Hopkins University Press, 1973.

Hasse, William F. *A History of Banking in New Haven, Connecticut.* New Haven: N.p., 1946.

Haverland, Michael, and Alan Plattus. "Upper Albany Neighborhood: Economic Development Plan." Yale Urban Design Workshop, 1994.

Hayden, Dolores. *Redesigning the American Dream: The Future of Housing, Work, and Family Life.* New York: Norton, 1984.

Hays, R. Allen. *The Federal Government and Urban Housing: Ideology and Change in Public Policy*. Albany: State University of New York Press, 1985.

Hayward, Clarissa Ryle. *De-Facing Power*. Cambridge: Cambridge University Press, 2000

Hegel, Richard. *Carriages from New Haven: New Haven's Nineteenth-Century Carriage Industry*. Hamden, Conn.: Archon, 1974.

Helper, Rose. "Success and Resistance Factors in the Maintenance of Racially Mixed Neighborhoods." In *Housing Desegregation and Federal Policy*, edited by John M. Goering, 170–94. Chapel Hill: University of North Carolina Press, 1986.

Herman, Barry E. "Max Adler, 1841–1916." *Jews in New Haven* 7 (1997): 315–16.

Hill, Everett G. *A Modern History of New Haven and Eastern New Haven County*. New York: S. J. Clarke, 1918.

Hill, Prescott F. "The Menace of the Three-Decker." *Housing Problems in America* 5 (1916): 133–52.

Hillier, Amy. "Redlining in Philadelphia." In *Past Time, Past Place: GIS for History*, edited by Anne Kelly Knowles, 79–92. Redlands, Calif.: ESRI, 2002.

Hirsch, Arnold R. *Making the Second Ghetto: Race and Housing in Chicago, 1940–1960*. Chicago: University of Chicago Press, 1983.

Hirsch, Werner S. "The First Minute Book of the Congregation Mishkan Israel, 1849–1860." *Jews in New Haven* 6 (1993): 1–34.

Hirschman, Albert O. *Exit, Voice, and Loyalty: Responses to Decline in Firms, Organizations, and States*. Cambridge: Harvard University Press, 1970.

Historical Statistics of the United States. Washington, D.C.: U.S. Government Printing Office, 1975.

"History of Orange: Sesquicentennial, 1822–1972." Orange, Conn.: Town of Orange, 1972.

Hochschild, Jennifer L. *Facing up to the American Dream: Race, Class, and the Soul of the Nation*. Princeton: Princeton University Press, 1995.

———. *The New American Dilemma: Liberal Democracy and School Desegregation*. New Haven: Yale University Press, 1984.

Holland, John H. *Emergence: From Chaos to Order*. Reading, Mass.: Addison-Wesley, 1998.

Holt, Philetus H. "Downtown Renewal Land Conversion: An Examination of the New Haven Experience." *Journal of Housing* 9 (1973): 449–51.

Holzer, Harry J. "The Spatial Mismatch Hypothesis: What Has the Evidence Shown." *Urban Studies* 28, no. 1 (1992): 105–22.

Horan, Cynthia. "Beyond Governing Coalitions: Analyzing Urban Regimes in the 1990s." *Journal of Urban Affairs* 13, no. 1 (1991): 119–35.

Hounshell, David A. *From the American System to Mass Production, 1800–1932*. Baltimore: Johns Hopkins University Press, 1984.

Housing Act of 1949. 171.

Housing Authority of New Haven. "Annual Report," issues from 1942 to 2002.

Houze, Herbert G. *Winchester Repeating Arms Company: Its History and Development from 1865 to 1981*. Iola, Wis.: Krause, 1994.

Hudson, Hellen. *Dinner at Six: Voices from the Soup Kitchen*. New Havens: Wildfire Press, 2002.

Hunter, Floyd. *Community Power Structure.* Chapel Hill: University of North Carolina Press, 1953.

Hylton, Thomas. *Save Our Land, Save Our Towns: A Plan for Pennsylvania.* Harrisburg, Pa.: Seitz and Seitz, 1995.

Ihlanfedt, Keith. "Spatial Mismatch between Jobs and Residential Location Within Urban Areas." *Cityscape* 1, no. 1 (1994): 219–44.

"Illustrated History of the Trades Council of New Haven and Affiliated Unions." New Haven: Greater New Haven Trades Council, 1899.

Irwin, Michael, and John D. Kasarda. "Trade, Transportation, and Spatial Distribution." In *The Handbook of Economic Sociology,* edited by Neil J. Smelser and Richard Swedberg, 342–67. Princeton: Princeton University Press, 1994.

Isaac, Jeffrey C. *Power and Marxist Theory: A Realist View.* Ithaca, N.Y.: Cornell University Press, 1987.

Jackson, Kenneth T. *Crabgrass Frontier: The Suburbanization of the United States.* New York: Oxford University Press, 1987.

Jacobs, Jane. *The Economy of Cities.* New York: Vintage, 1969.

———. *The Death and Life of Great American Cities.* New York: Random House, 1961.

Jaffe, Harry S., and Tom Sherwood. *Dream City: Race, Power, and the Decline of Washington, D.C.* New York: Simon & Schuster, 1994.

Janick, Herbert. "Yale Blue: Unionization at Yale University, 1931–1985." *Labor History* 28, no. 3 (1987): 349–69.

Jargowsky, Paul A. "Ghetto Poverty Among Blacks in the 1980s." *Journal of Policy Analysis and Management* 13, no. 2 (1994): 288–309.

Jaynes, Gerald David, and Robin Williams, Jr. *A Common Destiny: Blacks and American Society.* Washington, D.C.: National Academy Press, 1989.

Jencks, Christopher. *Rethinking Social Policy: Race, Poverty, and the Underclass.* Cambridge: Harvard University Press, 1992.

Jerome, Chauncey. *History of the American Clock Business for the Past Sixty Years and Life of Chauncey Jerome.* New Haven: F. C. Dayton, 1860.

Johnson, Steven. *Emergence: The Connected Lives of Ants, Brains, Cities, and Software.* New York: Scribner, 2001.

Johnston, William Michael. *On the Outside Looking In: Irish, Italian, and Black Ethnic Politics in an American City.* Ann Arbor: UMI Dissertation Services, 1977.

Jones, Maldwyn Allen. *American Immigration.* 2nd ed. Chicago: University of Chicago Press, 1960.

Jordan, David P. *Transforming Paris: The Life and Labors of Baron Haussmann.* New York: Free Press, 1995.

"Journal of the Board of Aldermen of the City of New Haven 1910." New Haven: City of New Haven, 1910.

Judd, Dennis R. *The Politics of American Cities: Private Power and Public Policy.* Glenview, Ill.: Scott, Foresman, 1988.

Katz, Michael B. *In the Shadow of the Poorhouse: A Social History of Welfare in America.* New York: Basic Books, 1986.

Katz, Bruce, and Jennifer Bradley. "Divided We Sprawl." *Atlantic Monthly,* December 1999.

Katz, Peter. *The New Urbanism: Toward an Architecture of Community.* New York: McGraw-Hill, 1994.

Katznelson, Ira. *Marxism and the City.* Oxford: Oxford University Press, 1992.

———. *City Trenches.* Chicago: University of Chicago Press, 1981.

Kay, Jane Holtz. *Asphalt Nation: How the Automobile Took Over America and How We Can Take It Back.* New York: Crown, 1997.

Kaye, Frederick. "City Year Book of the City of New Haven for 1913." New Haven: City of New Haven, 1913.

Kelley, Brooks Mather. *Yale: A History.* New Haven: Yale University Press, 1974.

Kelling, George L., and Catherine M. Coles. *Fixing Broken Windows: Restoring Order and Reducing Crime in Our Communities.* New York: Free Press, 1996.

Kelly, Cassius W., ed. *Atlas of New Haven.* Boston: Walker, 1911.

Kerner Commission Report. New York: Pantheon, 1968.

Kopel, David B. "Prison Blues: America's Foolish Sentencing Policies Endanger Public Safety." *Policy Analysis* (Cato Institute), 1994, 380–439.

Kotkin, Joel. *The New Geography: How the Digital Revolution Is Reshaping the American Landscape.* New York: Random House, 2000.

Kreas, Saul. *My Life and Struggle for a Better World.* N.p., 1983.

Krugman, Paul R. *Development, Geography, and Economic Theory.* Cambridge: MIT Press, 1996.

———. *The Age of Diminished Expectations.* Cambridge: MIT Press, 1995.

Kunstler, James Howard. *The Geography of Nowhere: The Rise and Decline of America's Man-Made Landscape.* New York: Simon & Schuster, 1993.

La Fever, Martin. "Workers, Machinery, and Production in the Automobile Industry." *Monthly Labor Review* 19 (October 1924).

Labor Almanac: New Haven's Unions in the 1950s. New Haven: Labor History Association, 1995.

Langdon, Philip. *A Better Place to Live: Reshaping the American Suburb.* Amherst: University of Massachusetts Press, 1994.

Lasch, Christopher. *The Revolt of the Elites and the Betrayal of Democracy.* New York: Norton, 1995.

Lassonde, Stephen. "Learning to Forget: Schooling and Family Life in New Haven's Working Class, 1870–1940." Ph.D. diss., Yale University, 1994.

Lattanzi, Robert M. *Oyster Village to Melting Pot: The Hill Section of New Haven.* Chester, Conn.: Pattaconk-Brooks, 1994.

Leach, William. *Land of Desire: Merchants, Power, and the Rise of a New American Culture.* New York: Vintage, 1993.

Le Corbusier. *The City of the Future and Its Planning.* Translated by Frederick Etchells. New York, 1987.

"Lee Reviews His Policies in Campaign." *New Haven Register,* October 29, 1953, 3.

Leeney, Robert J. *Elms, Arms, and Ivy: New Haven in the Twentieth Century.* Montgomery, Ala.: Community Communications, 2000.

Leill, John Thomas. "Levittown: A Study in Community Building and Planning." Ph.D. diss., Yale University, 1952.

Lemann, Nicholas. *The Promised Land: The Great Black Migration and How It Changed America.* New York: Knopf, 1991.

Lerner, Michael. "Respectable Bigotry." In *Overcoming Middle-Class Rage,* edited by Murray Friedman, 145–59. Philadelphia: Westminster, 1971.

Leven, Charles. *The Mature Metropolis.* Lexington, Mass.: Lexington Books, 1978.

Levermore, Charles H. *The Republic of New Haven.* Baltimore: Johns Hopkins University Press, 1886.

Lewis, Sinclair. *Babbitt.* New York: Harcourt, Brace, 1922.

———. "Young Man Axelbrod." In *Selected Short Stories of Sinclair Lewis,* 281–91. Garden City, N.Y.: Doubleday, Doran, 1935.

Little, I. M. D. *A Critique of Welfare Economics.* Oxford: Clarendon, 1957.

Lofland, Lyn H. *A World of Strangers: Order and Action in Urban Public Space.* New York: Basic Books, 1973.

Lopatin, Alan G. "The Rise and Fall of the New Haven Democratic Machine: A Statistical Analysis, 1951–73." In unpublished term paper, Yale College, 1975.

Lowe, Jeanne R. *Cities in a Race with Time: Progress and Poverty in America's Renewing Cities.* New York: Random House, 1967.

Lukes, Steven. *Power: A Radical View.* London: Macmillan, 1974.

Lynch, Kevin. *The Image of the City.* Cambridge: MIT Press, 1960.

McCluskey, Dorothy S., and Claire C. Bennitt. *Who Wants to Buy a Water Company? From Private to Public Control in New Haven.* Bethel, Conn.: Rutledge, 1996.

McConnell, John W. *The Evolution of Social Classes.* Washington, D.C.: American Council on Public Affairs, 1942.

McCraw, Thomas K. *American Business, 1920–2000: How It Worked.* Wheeling, Ill.: Harlan-Davidson, 2000.

———. *Creating Modern Capitalism: How Entrepreneurs, Companies, and Countries Triumphed in Three Industrial Revolutions.* Cambridge: Harvard University Press, 1997.

McElroy, Marianne. "Natural Drainage Basins of Connecticut." Hartford: Connecticut Geological and Natural History Survey, 1981.

McGreevy, John T. *Parish Boundaries: The Catholic Encounter with Race in the Twentieth-Century Urban North.* Chicago: University of Chicago Press, 1996.

McLean, Scott, David Schultz, and Manfred Steger, eds. *Robert Putnam and Social Capital: Critical Perspectives on American Democracy and Social Engagement.* New York: NYU Press, 2001.

Malaspina, Mark. "Demanding the Best: How to Restructure the Section 8 Household-Based Rental Assistance Program." Unpublished paper, Yale Law School, 1995.

Mandelbaum, Seymour. *Boss Tweed's New York.* New York: Wiley, 1965.

Marchand, Roland. *Creating the Corporate Soul: The Rise of Public Relations and Corporate Imagery in American Big Business.* Berkeley: University of California Press, 1998.

Marris, Peter, and Martin Rein. *Dilemmas of Social Reform: Poverty and Community Action in the United States.* Chicago: University of Chicago Press, 1967.

Marshall, Harvey, and John Stahura. "White Movement to the Suburbs: A Comparison of Explanations." *American Journal of Sociology* 44 (1979): 975–94.

Marx, Karl, and Friedrich Engels. *Communist Manifesto*. 1848.

Massey, Douglas S., and Nancy A. Denton. *American Apartheid: Segregation and the Making of the Underclass*. Cambridge: Harvard University Press, 1993.

Mayo, James M. *The American Grocery Store: The Business Evolution of an Architectural Space*. Westport, Conn.: Greenwood, 1993.

Mayo, Reginald. "Comprehensive District Plan for New Haven Public Schools, 1993–1996." New Haven: New Haven Board of Education, 1993.

"Mayor Appoints Action Commission Headed by C of C Past President Freese." *New Haven Newsletter*, September 1954, 1.

"Mayor Rice Reviews Administration." *Saturday Chronicle*, December 31, 1910, 3, 12.

"Mayor Roughed by Students; Dean Jones to Take Action." *New Haven Register*, November 3, 1915, 1.

Meinig, D. W. *The Shaping of America: A Geographical Perspective on 500 Years of History*. Vol. 3. New Haven: Yale University Press, 1998.

Melosi, Martin V. *The Sanitary City: Urban Infrastructure in America from Colonial Times to the Present*. Baltimore: Johns Hopkins University Press, 2000.

Mermin, Alvin. "Papers of Alvin Mermin." 1970.

———. *Relocating Families: The New Haven Experience, 1956–1966*. Washington, D.C.: NAHRO, 1970.

Messner, Steven F. "Poverty, Inequality, and the Urban Homicide Rate." *Criminology* 20, no. 1 (1982): 103–14.

Miller, Bill. "Winchester Before '64 and After." *American Rifleman*, 1989.

Miller, William Lee. *The Fifteenth Ward and the Great Society: An Encounter with a Modern City*. Boston: Houghton Mifflin, 1966.

Mininberg, Mark J. *Saving New Haven: John W. Murphy Faces the Crisis of the Great Depression*. New Haven: Fine Arts Publications, 1988.

Mitchell, Mary Hewitt. *History of New Haven County, Connecticut*. Chicago: Pioneer Historical Publishing, 1930.

Mollenkopf, John H. *The Contested City*. Princeton, N.J.: Princeton University Press, 1983.

Molotch, Harvey. "The City as a Growth Machine." *American Journal of Sociology* 82 (Fall 1976): 309–32.

Monkkonen, Eric H. *America Becomes Urban: The Development of U.S. Cities and Towns, 1780–1980*. Berkeley: University of California Press, 1988.

Montgomery, David, et al. "160 Year of Labor's Struggle for a Better New Haven." In *Labor Almanac: New Haven's Unions in the 1990s*, 17–26. New Haven: Labor History Association, 1995.

Morris, Charles R. *American Catholic: The Saints and Sinners Who Built America's Most Powerful Church*. New York: Random House, 1997.

Moynihan, Daniel Patrick. "Employment, Income, and the Ordeal of the Negro Family." *Daedalus: Journal of the American Academy of Arts and Sciences* 94 (Fall 1965): 745–70.

Mumford, Lewis. *The City in History: Its Origins, Its Transformations, and Its Prospects*. San Diego: Harcourt Brace Jovanovich, 1961.

———. *The Highway and the City*. New York: Harcourt, Brace & World, 1953.

―――. *Technics and Civilization*. New York: Harcourt, Brace, 1934.

Murphy, John W. "Municipal Activities of the City of New Haven, Connecticut, for the Year Ending December 31, 1937." New Haven: City of New Haven, 1937.

Myrdal, Gunnar. *An American Dilemma: The Negro Problem and Modern Democracy*. New York: Harper & Row, 1944.

"National C of C Adopts Policy Resolution on Slum Clearance." *Journal of Housing* 7, no. 6 (1950): 250.

"New Haven Directory Including West Haven, 1913." New Haven: Price & Lee, 1913.

Nathan, Richard P. "The 'Devolution Revolution.'" *Rockefeller Institute Bulletin*, no. 1996 (1996): 5–13.

―――. *A New Agenda for Cities*. Washington, D.C.: National League of Cities, 1992.

Nelson, Richard R. *The Moon and the Ghetto*. New York: Norton, 1977.

New Haven Colony Historical Society, Photographic Archive.

New Haven of Today: Its Commerce, Trade and Industries. New Haven: Clarence H. Ryden, 1892.

"New Haven Road to Get Rid of Italian Help." *New Haven Register*, June 6, 1907, 5.

Nivola, Pietro S. *Tense Commandments: Federal Prescriptions and City Problems*. Washington, D.C.: Brookings Institution Press, 2002.

Norquist, John O. *The Wealth of Cities: Revitalizing the Centers of American Life*. Reading, Mass.: Addison-Wesley, 1998.

Nye, David E. *Consuming Power: A Social History of American Energies*. Cambridge: MIT Press, 1998.

―――. *Electrifying America: Social Meanings of a New Technology*. Cambridge: MIT Press, 1990.

Oberdeck, Kathryn Jane. "Labor's Vicar and the Variety Show: Popular Theatre, Popular Religion, and Cultural Class Conflict in Turn-of-the Century America." Ph.D. diss., Yale University, 1991.

"Old Industrial City Wages Dramatic War on Poverty." *Trenton Sunday Times Advertiser*, July 12, 1964.

Oliver, J. Eric. *Democracy in Suburbia*. Princeton: Princeton University Press, 2001.

Olson, Susan. *Tax Delinquency in the Inner City: The Problem and Its Possible Solutions*. Lexington, Mass.: Lexington Books, 1976.

"Opening Opportunities: New Haven's Comprehensive Program for Community Progress." New Haven: Community Progress, 1962.

O'Regan, Katherine M., and Douglas Rae. "Segregation and Isolation: A Case Study of New Haven." Unpublished paper, Yale School of Management, 1993.

Oren, Dan A. *Joining the Club*. New Haven: Yale University Press, 1985.

―――. "A Jewish Student at Yale: A Preliminary Examination." In *Jews in New Haven*, edited by Jonathan D. Sarna, 56–69. New Haven: Jewish Historical Society of New Haven, 1978.

Orfield, Gary, and Carole Ashkinaze. *The Closing Door: Conservative Policy and Black Opportunity*. Chicago: University of Chicago Press, 1991.

Orfield, Myron. *Metropolitics: A Regional Agenda for Community and Stability*. Washington, D.C.: Brookings Institution Press, 1996.

Orfield, Myron, and Thomas Luce. *Connecticut Metropatterns: A Regional Agenda for Community and Prosperity in Connecticut*. Minneapolis: Metropolitan Research Corporation, 2003.

Osterweis, Rollin G. *Three Centuries of New Haven, 1638–1938*. New Haven: Yale University Press, 1953.

Pagano, Michael A., and Ann O'M. Bowman. *Cityscapes and Capital: The Politics of Development*. Baltimore: Johns Hopkins University Press, 1995.

Page, Max. *The Creative Destruction of Manhattan, 1900–1940*. Chicago: University of Chicago Press, 1999.

Pardee, W. S. *The Relation of New Haven and Yale University*. New Haven: Tuttle, Morehouse & Taylor, 1911.

Park, R. E., E. W. Burgess, and R. D. McKenzie. *The City*. Chicago: University of Chicago Press, 1925.

Patton, Phil. *Open Road*. New York: Simon & Schuster, 1986.

Pease, John C., and John M. Niles. *A Gazetteer of the States of Connecticut and Rhode Island*. Hartford: William S. Marsh, 1819.

Peters, Tom F. *Building the Nineteenth Century*. Cambridge: MIT Press, 1996.

Peterson, Paul E. *City Limits*. Chicago: University of Chicago Press, 1981.

Pettigrew, Thomas F. "Complexity and Change in American Racial Patterns: A Social Psychological View." *Daedalus: Journal of the American Academy of Arts and Sciences* 94 (Fall 1965): 974–1007.

Pettit, Becky, and Bruce Western. "Inequality in Lifetime Risks of Imprisonment." Princeton, N.J., 2002.

Philie, William L. *Change and Tradition: New Haven, Connecticut, 1780–1830*. New York: Garland, 1989.

Pivin, Francis Fox, and Richard Cloward. *Regulating the Poor: The Functions of Public Welfare*. 2nd ed. New York: Random House, 1993.

Platt, Rutherford H. *Land Use and Society: Geography, Law, and Public Policy*. Washington, D.C.: Island, 1996.

Plattus, Alan. "The American Vitruvius and the American Tradition of Civic Art." In *The American Vitruvius: An Architect's Handbook of Civic Art*, edited by Werner Hegemann and Elbert Peets. Princeton: Princeton Architectural Press, 1988.

Pollard, W. R. "Outline of the Law of Zoning in the United States." *Annals of the American Academy of Political and Social Science* 155, no. 2 (1931): 15–33.

Polsby, Nelson W. *Community Power and Political Theory: A Further Look at Problems of Evidence and Inference*. New Haven: Yale University Press, 1980.

Powledge, Fred. *Model City. A Test of American Liberalism: One Town's Efforts to Rebuild Itself*. New York: Simon & Schuster, 1970.

Purmont, Jon E. "Sargent Comes to New Haven." *Journal of the New Haven Colony Historical Society* 24, no. 1 (1976): 17–30.

Putnam, Robert. *Bowling Alone: The Collapse and Revival of American Community*. New York: Simon & Schuster, 2000.

———. *Making Democracy Work: Civil Traditions in Modern Italy*. Princeton: Princeton University Press, 1993.

———. "The Prosperous Community: Social Capital and Public Life." *American Prospect* (Spring 1993): 35–42.

Rabin, Yale. "Expulsive Zoning: The Inequitable Legacy of *Euclid*." Edited by Charles M. Haar and Jerold S. Kayden, 101–21. Chicago: Planners Press, 1989.

Rae, Douglas. "Viacratic America: *Plessy* on Foot v. *Brown* on Wheels." *American Review of Political Science* 4 (2001): 417–38.

———. "Elm Haven's Baseline Study." HUD, 1995.

———. "Knowing Power." In *Power, Inequality, and Democratic Politics: Essays in Honor of Robert Dahl*, edited by Ian Shapiro and Grant Reeher, 17–49. Boulder, Colo.: Westview, 1988.

Rapkin, Chester. "The Economic Feasibility of Urban Renewal in the Dixwell Area." New Haven: New Haven Redevelopment Agency, 1960.

Reed, Adolph. "Pimping Poverty, Then and Now." *Progressive*, August 1994, 24–26.

"Report of the President." New Haven: Yale University, 1909.

Rieder, Jonathan. *Canarsie: The Jews and Italians of Brooklyn Against Liberalism*. Cambridge: Harvard University Press, 1985.

Riis, Jacob. *How the Other Half Lives*. New York: Charles Scribner's Sons, 1910.

Roe, Joseph W. *English and American Tool Builders*. New Haven: Yale University Press, 1916.

Rosenman, Dorothy. *A Million Homes a Year*. New York: Harcourt, Brace, 1945.

Rothenberg, Jerome. *Economic Evaluation of Urban Renewal*. Washington, D.C.: Brookings Institution Press, 1967.

Rusk, David. *Cities Without Suburbs*. Washington, D.C.: Woodrow Wilson Center Press, 1993, 1995.

Rybczynski, Witold. "Downsizing Cities." Wharton Real Estate Center Research Impact Paper #5. Wharton School of the University of Pennsylvania, 1994.

Rybczynski, Witold. *Home: A Short History of an Idea*. New York: Penguin, 1986.

Saegert, Susan, and Erik K. Glunt. "Community Development Corporations and Community Behavior: Implications from Environmental Psychology." Community Development Research Center, 1990.

Safdie, Moshe, and Wendy Kohn. *The City After the Automobile: An Architect's Vision*. Toronto: Stoddart, 1997.

Sargent, David C. *Joseph Bradford Sargent, 1822–1907: Captain of Industry*. West Hartford, Conn.: N.p., 1973.

Sarna, Jonathan D. "Synagogue Structures of Greater New Haven." In *Jews in New Haven*, edited by Jonathan D. Sarna, 21–28. New Haven: Jewish Historical Society of New Haven, 1978.

Sassen, Saskia. "The Informal Economy: Between New Developments and Old Regulations." *Yale Law Journal* 103 (1994): 2289–304.

———. *The Global City: New York, London, Tokyo*. Princeton: Princeton University Press, 1991.

Satterthwaite, Ann. *Going Shopping: Consumer Choices and Community Consequences*. New Haven: Yale University Press, 2001.

Sawyer, John E. "The Social Basis of the American System of Manufacturing." *Journal of Economic History* 14 (Autumn 1954): 361–79.

Schelling, Thomas C. "Models of Segregation." *American Economic Review* 59 (May 1969): 488–93.

Schiff, Judith A. "Colonel Isaac Ullman: Philanthropist, Politician, and Patriot." *Jews in New Haven* 2 (1992): 32–40.

Schlesinger, Arthur Jr. "Biography of a Nation of Joiners." *American Historical Review* 50 (1944).

———. *The Rise of the City, 1878–1898.* Columbus: Ohio State University Press, 1933, 1999.

Schlosser, Eric. "Reefer Madness." *Atlantic Monthly,* August 1994, 45–63.

Schlozman, Kay Lehman, Sidney Verba, and Henry E. Brady. "Civic Participation and the Equality Problem." In *Civic Engagement in American Democracy,* edited by Theda Skocpol and Morris Fiorina. Washington, D.C.: Brookings Institution Press, 1999.

Schumpeter, Joseph. *Capitalism, Socialism, and Democracy.* New York: Harper, 1946.

Schwirian, Kent, Martin Hankins, and Carol Ventresca. "The Residential Decentralization of Social Status Groups in American Metropolitan Communities, 1950–80." *Social Forces* 68, no. 4 (1990): 1143–63.

Scully, Vincent. "The Architecture of Community." In *The New Urbanism,* edited by Peter Katz, 221–30. New York: McGraw-Hill, 1994.

———. "America's Nightmare: The Automotive Megalopolis." *Zodiac* 17, no. 1 (1967): 11–17.

———. "The Threat and the Promise of Urban Redevelopment in New Haven." *Zodiac* 17, no. 1 (1967): 2–7.

Sellers, Jefferey M. *Governing from Below: Urban Regions and the Global Economy.* Cambridge: Cambridge University Press, 2002.

Sennett, Richard. *The Uses of Disorder: Personal Identity and City Life.* New York: Norton, 1970.

Seton, Fenmore R. *A Seton Memoir: Seton Name Plate Corporation, the Early Years, 1956–81.* North Haven: N.p., 1995.

Seymour, George Dudley. *New Haven.* New Haven: N.p., 1942.

Shapiro, Bruce. "How the War on Crime Imprisons Americans." *Nation,* April 22, 1996.

Sheehy, Gail. *Panthermania: The Clash of Black Against Black in One American City.* New York: Harper & Row, 1971.

Shepherd, Jane Bushnell. *My Old New Haven and Other Memories Briefly Told.* New Haven: Tuttle, Morehouse & Taylor, 1932.

Shlay, Anne B. "Shaping Place: Institutions and Metropolitan Development Patterns." *Journal of Urban Affairs* 15 (1993): 387–404.

Shuman, Howard. "Behind the Scenes and Under the Rug." *Washington Monthly,* 1969, 13–22.

Shumway, E. J., Floyd Shumway, and Richard Hegel. *The New Haven Lawn Club Association: A History of the First One Hundred Years.* New Haven: New Haven Lawn Club Association, 1991.

Shumway, Floyd. "New Haven and Its Leadership." Ph.D. diss., Columbia, 1968.

Shumway, Floyd, and Richard Hegel. "The First Century of the Greater New Haven Chamber of Commerce." *Journal of the New Haven Colony Historical Society* 40, no. 2 (1994).

———. "New Haven: A Topographical History." *Journal of the New Haven Colony Historical Society* 34, no. 2 (1988): 3–64.

———. "New Haven in 1884." *Journal of the New Haven Colony Historical Society* 30, no. 2 (1984): 3–59.

Siegel, Fred. *The Future Once Happened Here: New York, D.C., L.A. and the Fate of America's Big Cities.* New York: Free Press, 1997.

Singerman, Philip Allan. "Politics, Bureaucracy and Public Policy: The Case of Urban Renewal in New Haven." Ph.D. diss., Yale University, 1980.

Skocpol, Theda. "How Americans Became Civic." In *Civil Engagement in American Democracy,* edited by Theda Skocpol and Morris P. Fiorina, 27–80. Washington, D.C.: Brookings Institution Press, 1999.

Sleeper, Jim. *The Closest of Strangers: Liberalism and the Politics of Race in New York.* New York: Norton, 1990.

Solomon, Robert A. "Building a Segregated City: How We All Worked Together." *Saint Louis University Public Law Review* 16, no. 2 (1997): 265–320.

Steffens, Lincoln. *The Shame of Our Cities.* New York, 1904.

Stegman, Michael A. *Housing Investment in the Inner City: The Dynamics of Decline, a Study of Baltimore, Maryland, 1968–70.* Cambridge: MIT Press, 1972.

Stilgoe, John R. *Borderland: Origin of the American Suburb, 1820–1939.* New Haven: Yale University Press, 1988.

Stone, Clarence N. *Regime Politics: Governing Atlanta.* Lawrence: University Press of Kansas, 1989.

Stone, Clarence, and Heywood T. Sanders. "Reexamining a Classic Case of Development Politics: New Haven, Connecticut." In *The Politics of Urban Development,* edited by Clarence Stone and Heywood T. Sanders, 159–81. Lawrence, University of Kansas Press, 1987.

"The Story of Seventy-Five Years in Commemoration of the Diamond Jubilee of the Grand Old Parish on the Hill, Sacred Heart Church." New Haven: Sacred Heart Church, 1950.

Summers, Mary, and Philip A. Klinkner. "The Daniels Election in New Haven and the Failure of the Deracialization Hypothesis." *Urban Affairs Quarterly* 27, no. 2 (December 1991): 202–15.

Sviridoff, Mitchell. "Problems of Leadership in the Negro Community." Unpublished memorandum, 1959.

Synnott, Marcia Graham. *The Half-Open Door: Discrimination and Admissions at Yale, Harvard, and Princeton, 1900–1930.* Westport, Conn.: Greenwood, 1979.

———. "A Social History of Admissions Politics at Harvard, Yale, and Princeton, 1900–1920." Ph.D. diss., University of Massachusetts, 1974.

Talbot, Allan R. *The Mayor's Game: Richard Lee of New Haven and the Politics of Change.* New York: Harper & Row, 1967.

Taub, Richard P., and D. Taylor, D. Garth, and Jan D. Dunham. *Paths of Neighborhood Change.* Chicago: University of Chicago Press, 1984.

Teaford, Jon. *The Twentieth-Century American City.* Baltimore: Johns Hopkins University Press, 1993.

Temin, Peter, ed. *Engines of Enterprise: An Economic History of New England.* Cambridge: Harvard University Press, 2000.

Thernstrom, Stephan. *Poverty and Progress*. Cambridge: Harvard University Press, 1964.

"Third Annual Report of the Housing Authority of the City of New Haven." New Haven: Housing Authority of New Haven, 1941.

Thomas, Hugo F. "Natural Drainage Basins of Connecticut." Hartford: Connecticut Geological and Natural History Survey, 1981.

Thornberry, Terrence P., and R. L. Christianson. "Unemployment and Criminal Involvement: An Investigation of Reciprocal Causal Structures." *American Sociological Review* 49, no. 3 (1984): 90–98.

Thurow, Lester C. *Poverty and Discrimination*. Washington, D.C.: Brookings Institution Press, 1969.

Tichenor, Daniel J. *Dividing Lines: The Politics of Immigration Control in America*. Princeton: Princeton University Press, 2002.

Ticotsky, Fred. "Ticotsky's Bakery and the Legion Avenue Jews." *Jews in New Haven* 3 (1981): 37–49.

"To Celebrate 25th Wedding Anniversary: Elaborate Plans for Function at the Home of Mr. and Mrs. Sylvester Poli This Evening." *New Haven Evening Register*, August 25, 1910.

Tobin, James. "On Improving the Economic Status of the Negro." *Daedalus: Journal of the American Academy of Arts and Sciences* 94 (Fall 1965): 878–98.

Townshend, Doris B. *The Street Names of New Haven*. New Haven: New Haven Colony Historical Society, 1984.

———. *Fair Haven: A Journey Through Time*. New Haven: New Haven Colony Historical Society, 1976.

Trachtenberg, Alan. *The Incorporation of America: Culture and Society in the Guilded Age*. New York: Hill and Wang, 1982.

Trout, Amy L., and Julie Ponessa Salathe. "A Brief Introduction to the Maritime History of New Haven." *Journal of the New Haven Colony Historical Society* 37, no. 1 (1990): 3–12.

Trowbridge, Thomas R. Jr. "Commerce—Foreign and Domestic." In *History of the City of New Haven to the Present Time*, edited by Edward E. Atwater, 489–510. New York: Munsell, 1887.

Tyler, Daniel P. "Statistics of the Condition and Production of Certain Branches of Industry of Connecticut." Hartford: State of Connecticut, 1846.

Underwood, A. B. "Manufacturing Interests of New Haven." In *History of the New England States*, edited by W. T. Davis, vol. 2 (1897), 863–894. Hurd, 1897.

Vidal, Avis C. "Rebuilding Communities: A National Study of Urban Community Development Corporations." Community Development Research Center, Graduate School of Management and Urban Policy, New School for Social Research, 1992.

Warner, Robert Austin. *New Haven Negroes: A Social History*. New Haven: Yale University Press, 1940.

Warner, Sam Bass Jr. *Streetcar Suburbs: The Process of Growth in Boston, 1870–1900*. Cambridge: Harvard University Press, 1978.

"Water and Steam Power." *Scientific American* 4 (1849): 269.

Watkins, Harold M. *Coal and Men: An Economic and Social Study of the British and American Coalfields*. London: George Allen & Unwin, 1934.

Watrous, George Dutton. "Travel and Transportation." In *History of the City of New Haven to the Present Time,* edited by Edward A. Atwater, 351–72. New York: Munsell, 1887.

Weber, Adna. "The Significance of Recent City Growth." *Annals of the American Academy of Political and Social Science* 23, no. March (1904): 234–35.

Weber, Max. *General Economic History.* New York: Greenberg, 1927.

Wehner, Harrison G. Jr. *Sections 235 and 236: An Economic Evaluation of HUD's Principal Housing Subsidy Programs.* Washington, D.C.: American Enterprise Institute, 1973.

Weir, Margaret. "Central Cities' Loss of Power in State Politics." *Brookings Review,* Spring 1995.

Weller, John L. *The New Haven Railroad: Its Rise and Fall.* New York: Hastings House, 1969.

Wells, H. G. "The Probable Diffusion of Great Cities." *In Works of H. G. Wells,* 4: 32ff. New York: Scribner's Sons, 1924.

Wenzlick, Roy. "Housing and Construction in the New Haven Area." New Haven: New Haven Chamber of Commerce, 1945.

West, Cornel. *Race Matters.* Boston: Beacon, 1993.

Wexler, Harry J., and Richard Peck. *Housing and Local Government: A Research Guide for Policy Makers and Planners.* Lexington, Mass: Lexington Books, 1975.

Whiting, John D. "New Haven in the 1890s." Unpublished paper, 1972.

Whitnall, Gordon. "History of Zoning." *Annals of the American Academy of Political and Social Science* 155, no. 2 (1931): 1–14.

Whyte, William H. *The Social Life of Small Urban Spaces.* Washington, D.C.: Conservation Foundation, 1980.

Wilhelm, John. "A Short History of Unionization at Yale." *Social Text* 49 (1996): 13–19.

Williams, Frank Backus. *The Law of City Planning and Zoning.* New York: Macmillan, 1922.

Wilson, David, et al. "Spatial Aspects of Housing Abandonment: The Cleveland Experience." *Housing Studies* 9, no. 4 (1994): 493–510.

Wilson, James Q. *Bureaucracy: What Government Agencies Do and Why They Do It.* New York: Basic Books, 1989.

Wilson, William H. *The City Beautiful Movement.* Baltimore: Johns Hopkins University Press, 1989.

Wilson, William Julius. *When Work Disappears: The World of the New Urban Poor.* New York: Knopf, 1996.

———. *The Truly Disadvantaged: The Inner City, the Underclass, and Public Policy.* Chicago: University of Chicago Press, 1987.

———. *The Declining Significance of Race: Blacks and Changing American Institutions.* Chicago: University of Chicago Press, 1978.

Wilson, Woodrow. "The Study of Administration." *Political Science Quarterly* 2, no. 2 (1887): 197–222.

Withington, Sidney. "Steamboats Reach New Haven." *Papers of the New Haven Colony Historical Society* 10 (1951): 147–87.

———. "New Haven and Its Six Railroads." *Railway and Locomotive Historical Society Bulletin* 56 (1940): 1–20.

Wolfinger, Raymond. *The Politics of Progress.* Englewood Cliffs, N.J.: Prentice Hall, 1974.

———. "The Development and Persistence of Ethnic Voting." *American Political Science Review* 59, no. 4 (1965): 896–908.

Wood, Robert C. "People Versus Place: The Dream Will Never Die." *Economic Development Quarterly* 5, no. 2 (1991): 99–103.

Wright, Frank Lloyd. *The Disappearing City*. New York: Payson, 1932.

Wright, Mark. "Factory, Neighborhood and Workers: Sargent & Company, Wooster Square, and Italian Immigrants in 1890." Yale University, 1982.

Yaro, Robert D., and Tony Hiss. *A Region at Risk: The Third Regional Plan for the New York–New Jersey–Connecticut Metropolitan Area*. Washington, D.C.: Island, 1996.

Yates, Douglas. "Urban Government as a Policy-Making System." In *The New Urban Politics*, edited by Louis H. Masotti and Robert L. Lineberry, 235–64. Cambridge: Ballinger, 1976.

———. *The Ungovernable City: The Politics of Urban Problems and Policy Making*. Cambridge: MIT Press, 1977.

Yinger, John. "On the Possibility of Achieving Racial Integration Through Subsidized Housing." In *Housing Desegregation and Federal Policy*, edited by John M. Goering, 290–312. Chapel Hill: University of North Carolina Press, 1986.

Zigler, Edward, and Susan Muenchow. *Head Start: The Inside Story of America's Most Successful Educational Experiment*. New York: Basic Books, 1992.

ACKNOWLEDGMENTS

City: Urbanism and Its End is a many-sided collaboration. Foremost among the book's collaborators are some stalwart friends—Rick Antle, Cynthia Farrar, Stan Garstka, Joseph LaPalombara, Mimi Liu, Sharon, Oster, Alan Plattus, Ian Shapiro, and Harry Wexler—who encouraged and sometimes shaped my drafts. Two others are, literally, co-authors—the late Dick Lee, who wrote the section included as "Snow Tickets," and Stephen Lassonde, who wrote most of the section on public education in Chapter 5. A number of local authors (whether at Yale or not, whether writing about *this* city or not) have likewise influenced the work, among whom are Robert Dahl, Robert Ellickson, Alex Garvin, Jay Gitlin, Philip Langdon, Vincent Scully, and Carter Wiseman. Barbara Campbell and her husband, Hank, were valuable guides in the effort to manage Yale's Neighborhood Partnership Network and HUD's Community Renaissance Fellowship. Amanda Lehrer Nash and Dena Wallerson, who staffed these programs brilliantly, were sources of light and hope for my research. Other Yale-in-New-Haven influences include Nancy Alderman, Arjun Appadurai, Bill Brown, Joseph Dobrow, Ray Fair, Will Goetzmann, Richard Hegel, Ed Kaplan, Paul Kennedy, Peter Marris, the late Rollin Osterweis, Max Page, Patricia Pierce, the late Floyd Shumway, and Amy Trout. A generation of independent journalists in the region pushed me to look at old questions in new ways; they include Carole Bass, Paul Bass, Randall Beach, Robert Leeney, and Khalid Lum.

Peter Lamothe, executive director of the New Haven Colony Historical Society, has led a minor revolution in bringing the recent past into public consciousness and has been an invaluable ally in my own work on twentieth-century New Haven.

Leading scholars on urban history and its variants have of course influenced this work. Centrally important were the authors of two remarkable pieces of urban scholarship in (and on) my chosen city: Robert Dahl and Raymond Wolfinger. Both were exceedingly generous in their counsel, and neither is to be blamed for my errors. I have followed and been greatly influenced by the Harvard-based civil engagement project, including people like Gerald Gamm, Peter Dobkin Hall, Robert Putman, and Theda Skocpol. Some other notables—Robert Fishman, Kenneth Jackson, Jane Jacobs, Lewis Mumford, David Nye, Richard Sennett, and John Stilgoe—were engaged in the project simply by my plucking their works from the shelf and poring over them again and again during the writing of *City*. Others—Gerald Frug, Campbell Gibson, Fred Siegel, Clarence Stone, Allan Talbot, and Bob Yaro come quickly to mind—had slightly more targeted influences upon the work, without assuming the risk of error.

Several senior players in New Haven political, economic, and intellectual circles have been immensely generous with their wisdom and their time. Mayor Lee, even in his waning months of life, was certainly a stalwart interpreter of his own voyages in urban renewal. John Daniels, whom I served during part of his 1990–94 term as mayor, has always been a kind and informative friend and advisor. Joel Cogan, who heads the Connecticut Conference of Municipalities, provided cogent and detailed criticism of my drafts. Less scholarly wisdom came from the late Newton Schenck and the still very lively Cheever Tyler. Gerald Clark, Larry DeNardis, Walt Esdaile, Anne Marie Foltz, Lynn Fusco, Karyn Gilvarg, Will Ginsberg, Dr. Marshall Holley, Phil Holt, Warren Kimbro, Frank Logue, Nick Pastore, Rebecca Royston, Larry, Ted, Debbie, and Michael Schaffer, Joel Schiavone, Judy Sklarz, Robert Solomon, and Steven Yandle have all been valuable sources of wisdom and information over the years. Yale administrators past and present have over the years been generous as well, especially Bruce Alexander, Sam Chauncey, Jonathan Fanton, Peter Halsey, Richard Levin, Linda Koch Lorimer, Michael Morand, Barbara Stevens, and David Warren. Several "alumni" of the Oak Street neighborhood have been more than generous with their memories and interpretations, including Jimmy Deangelis, Vinny Inglese, Kimbro, Micky Kliger, Sherm Kramer, and Lenny Margolis.

The privilege which is a teaching appointment at Yale consists in good measure of the chance to learn from students. A virtual generation of Yale students, many of them undergraduates, have served as able research assistants or have written papers that changed my thinking. Among these I would especially include Brooks Allen, Annie Barrett, Sari Bashi, Gabrielle Brainard, Difei Cheng, Josh Civin, Anna Dolinsky, Patrick Hazelton, Clarissa Hayward, Jessica He, Chloe Holtzman (of Brown), Alethia Jones, Claire Jean Kim, Jody LaPorte, Jeremy Licht, Jennifer Nou, Alexandra Reeve, Lucy Romeo, Kira Ryakina, Xu Hui Shen, Robynn Sturm, Natalya Sukonos, Morgan Swing, Chi Tschang, Jorge Vargas, Devon Williamson, Christina Wooldridge, and Emily Yuhas. Dolinsky, in particular, helped me rub away some of the less inspiring bureaucratic passages in Chapter 6 and replace them with interesting politics.

Several administrative assistants (including Eva D'Agistino, Ava Artaiz, Karen Donnegan, Jessica Gernatt, and Geri Spadacenta) have steadfastly pushed the project along—and sometimes saved the book from my misplaced enthusiasms.

Uniquely valuable was the collection of visual documents assembled by Joe Taylor, most notably the 1911 street atlas that he sold to me and that became the matrix for my spatial analysis of the city in that era. Taylor is, in the spirit of Jane Jacobs, a "public character" who does much to spread civility, and historical memory, through the streets of New Haven. Another public character who has been helpful is Bill Donohue, ever vigilant to protect the memory of Richard C. Lee against the overblown theories of a Yale academic. New Haven trial lawyer Bill Doyle has also been immensely helpful to my work.

Able professionals in research and publishing have also been very important. Here I especially thank Heidi Downey, John Kulka, Nancy Ovedovitz, and Tina Weiner (all of Yale University Press), James Campbell, Judith Carnes, Diane Kaplan, William Massa, Fred Musto, Abraham Parrish, Sandra Peterson, Judith Schiff, Francis Skelton, and Amy Trout (librarians and archivists all), and John Covell of MIT Press.

Institutional support has been important. Yale's Institution for Social and Policy Studies, and its director, Don Green, deserve special appreciation. The Yale School of Management has munificently sponsored half a dozen summers of research. The Russell Sage Foundation sponsored an earlier project, which illuminates the portions of this book having to do with race and racial isolation. A small grant from the Community Foundation of Greater New Haven, awarded long ago, is also indirectly reflected in these pages. The Jewish Historical Society of Greater New Haven has given me access to its rich archive. The New Haven Colony Historical Society has granted extensive use of its archival and photographic collections, and generous access to its able staff. The Greater New Haven Labor History Association has also provided useful guidance. The Caliper Corporation of Massachusetts has been generous with data and GIS software.

INDEX